BETTER
HOME MAKING

BETTER HOME MAKING

EDITED BY

Beryl Conway Cross

GEORGE NEWNES LIMITED

CARLTON HOUSE, 66–69 GREAT QUEEN STREET

LONDON, W.C.2

PRINTED AND BOUND IN ENGLAND BY
HAZELL WATSON AND VINEY LTD
AYLESBURY AND LONDON

FOREWORD

ALL of us lead different lives. Some of us live in the country, perhaps far from neighbours; others settle in a new suburb where it may be difficult to make friends. Yet again there are people who are surrounded by friends and acquaintances all the time.

However, there is one thing we have in common. We can all welcome a new friend. *Let this book be that friend in your home.* There are times when we need advice, and we feel that to discuss a subject exhaustively would be to impose on any of the people we know. What career is the child best fitted for? Browse over the information given in this book. Should petunia curtains be put with a lime-green carpet? Read what *Better Home Making* has to say about colour. There are ideas for definite schemes, and many photographs of arrangements by experts to give you fresh inspiration on old problems.

Whether a house becomes a home depends always on the individual. That is why there are not only easy-to-follow instructions for making loose covers or on how to cook an appetising meal, but other suggestions for extending the horizons of your life. The complete and happy person is the one with the most interests—if one fails, there are others to fill the void! If you lead a dull life, don't *let* it be dull. If you lack confidence, learn to do one thing very, very well—whether it is cooking, embroidery, painting pictures, decorating or becoming the most beautiful person possible! All lives are pleasanter if surrounded by beauty, whether of flowers, colours or of form and face . . . so this book deals with each kind of beauty, as well as the more practical 'chores,' such as laundry.

Life has to be well-rounded, not all earnest, not all gay. But it *can* always be interesting.

Beryl Conway Cross

CONTENTS

A COMPLETE CLASSIFIED KEY WILL BE FOUND ON PAGES 555–559
AT THE END OF THIS BOOK

ILLUSTRATIONS IN COLOUR

FURNISHING

CREATING A LOVELY HOME

*H*OME! There has never been a lovelier word, since it conjures up pictures of a refuge from day-by-day cares, a place that we can call our own. To start a home book for the modern woman with the old song-title 'There's no place like home' might seem a mixture of times and manners, but it is perhaps almost truer today than before.

There have always been periods in history when the style of furnishing and interior decoration pervaded the epoch. Everyone had to own a *chaise-longue*, a spinet or an aspi-distra. Today, however, there is the stamp of individuality on our homes. We make use of the most beautiful of the period styles and happily own a Regency dining-room, a Jacobean lounge and a Louis XIV bedroom. More conventional souls, of course, cling to one period throughout the whole flat or house. Who is to issue a command as to right or wrong? To the mistress of the home it is 'MY home,' and a home is nothing, however gracious and carefully planned, if it lacks the stamp of the personality of its owner.

THE OLD AND
THE NEW

This lovely old 14th-century house is Valley Farm, restored by the Society for the Protection of Ancient Buildings

Council of Industrial Design

Here we take a leap into the modern age. This building, with severe and beautiful lines, was designed by Wells Coates, O.B.E., F.R.I.B.A., R.D.I. It is planned to catch all the light and air possible, and is not overshadowed by the surrounding trees

Council of Industrial Design

Space-making

Again, accommodation being scarce and hardly on lavish lines when found, the one-room-and-bath flatlet issues a challenge to the woman who wishes to build around herself an atmosphere of serenity and happiness. It should be hardly necessary to say that even a small boxroom should be as pleasant as it can be made; it is a challenge. Yet many people do feel that space is necessary before they can use their imagination in decoration and furnishing.

There are many women—and some men—who are the natural home makers of the world. They have only to occupy a rather dreary, small flat for it suddenly to become a place of warmth and charm. Their own natures, a desire for the comfort not only of themselves but of their friends, make them automatically arrange a table where an ashtray is at hand; a settee and a chair or chairs from which they can talk to one another in their usual tones, without either having to shout across an expanse of space or be hidden one from another by a table, to place each piece of furniture so that it appears to be in its right place as far as the design of the whole is concerned, yet for comfort to be paramount.

'An Englishman's home is his castle' has often been quoted, yet one is led to wonder why an Englishman has been singled out. Yet it is true that there is no exact word for 'home' in other European languages. It is probably because the insistence in England has been on comfort. Other countries led in design, another Continent in plumbing and labour-saving devices, but today all that is altered. In the English design for living with grace and comfort there is beauty and simplicity in modern furniture; labour-saving advances forge ahead. The woman who longs to express herself in her surroundings has everything she needs to hand.

Comfort is allied to practicality. Gone are the myriads of little what-nots, unsteady bamboo tables, overmantels with many shelves needing continual dusting. Long gone are the days when the best parlour was shut up for use only on Sundays.

Greaves & Thomas, Ltd.

This does not usually look like this! Here it is ready to form a divan bed for the bachelor flat, or the occasional guest, with the wooden sides extended and the arm-rests dropped down. When being used in the daytime, a locking device holds the arms in position.

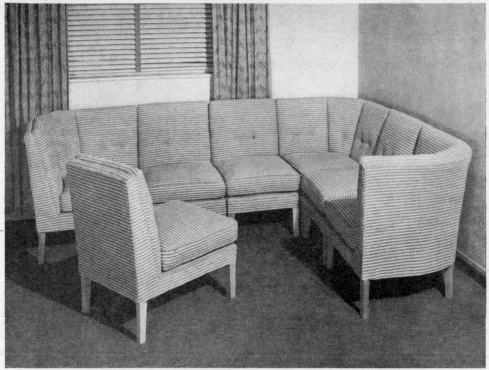

R. S. Stevens, Ltd.

A sectional settee such as this is practically all that is needed to furnish the seating arrangement of a quite large room, and allow scope for varied groupings. It is upholstered in rubberised hair

The Right Chairs

Perhaps the most important article of furniture in a home is a chair, or maybe, one should say 'the chairs.' Comfortable beds are naturally very desirable, although some people can sleep almost anywhere, anyhow. While not decrying the value of the right bed for the right person (some folk liking mattresses into which they can sink, and others preferring a firmer one), a chair that is 'nice to come home to' sets the keynote of ease. 'This is my *home*, this is where I belong.'

What so many householders do not realise is just how many kinds of chair there are on the market. They will try one or two when buying them and think they are comfortable. But a chair that is comfortable after a few hours of walking about through large stores is not always just the right one for all times. Measurements and special features should be taken into account.

An investigation undertaken by a well-known furniture firm showed that men are inclined to sit lower than a woman and prefer a chair with a sloping back. Women prefer a smaller seat and more upright back. In a long seat they perch on the edge and wear down the spring. Then again, a *flat* upright back does not curve to the body, and every woman who runs a house knows just what grateful ease she experiences in finding a curve in the chair where it fits into the tired part of her back. Some people prefer latex foam upholstery, others like tension springing.

Plenty of folk prefer an upright chair, and however extraordinary this may appear to the comfort-loving sybarite, there is no reason why they should not be catered for . . . not by being given a kitchen chair or one of the dining-room chairs, but a specially chosen modern one with arms the right height, or none at all, head-rest catered for, upholstered with about $1\frac{1}{2}$ in. foam rubber, and a charming covering.

Everyone likes to have *their own* chair !

Buying Separate Pieces

Although three-piece suites are always popular and no doubt will continue to be so, there is a trend for buying settee and chairs

11

SO NICE TO COME HOME TO

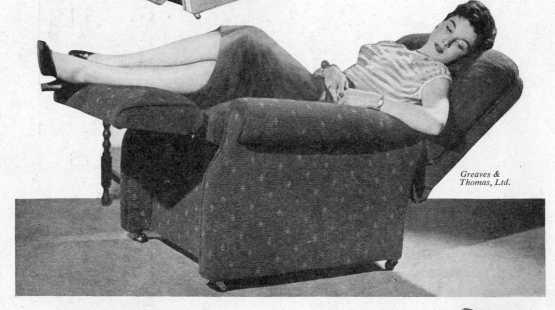

It tilts according to the degree at which the sitter leans back

This chair provides 'scientific relaxation,' based on the assumption that the human body finds its ideal resting position when floating in water. No muscles need to work, and the spine is not required to support the head

Greaves & Thomas, Ltd.

A needlework chair with box underneath to keep all sewing necessities

A fireside chair, the right height to catch all the warmth. Two or more form a semi-circular settee

Heal & Son Ltd.

It is ideal for everyone to have their own chair. If the man of the family wants to lounge with his legs over one arm, the back of the chair on the right is wide enough still to support his head

Minty of Oxford

Rocking soothes taut nerves and this is a modern version of an old favourite, made of light or dark waxed elm and beech

Furniture Industries, Ltd.

This chair comes from Switzerland and is angled for comfort

Council of Industrial Design

An ultra-modern design by Hille with steel-rod legs, latex-foam upholstery and wide wooden arms. It curves into the back and has a welcome head rest

Measure the space available for the new chair before going shopping, or you may find that it prevents a door from opening widely, or will not fit in by the fireplace or window

separately, in different sizes, to suit varying needs and tastes. After all, for those with an eye for uniformity they can all be covered with the same fabric to match. At the same time, the modern idea is to choose different coverings for effect, so long as they blend or contrast happily with one another. Stripes are used, say, on a settee, and plain colours for the chairs. A settee covered in a light tweed or coarsely woven fabric in cream can be allied with much effect with another piece of furniture covered in vivid scarlet. A close small check in one covering can be a foil for another in a deep plain shade. Patterned cretonnes with plain shades have often been used, of course, but it is very rarely a happy combination to have two kinds of pattern together—a different, strongly-patterned curtain and carpet, for example, 'cancel each other out.'

One of the first articles of furniture to arise from the influence of television was the television chair. While usually our leisure time is often taken up by jumping up and down to fetch and carry, even on the quietest evening, television brings sessions of marathon sitting which, unless really comfortable, can be even more tiring than a long walk. Some chairs adaptable for television have no arms, but one specially made for this purpose has low arms so that the viewer can relax and knit if she wants to (but preferably *behind* the other viewers, whose eyes will not be distracted by the darting of needles!). It also has a low back up to average neck height so that it does not obscure anyone else's

Greaves & Thomas, Ltd

Ideal for the bed-sitting-room is this 'Bedinet' which, with a vase of flowers and a photograph on top, appears to be just a cabinet. Actually it holds a single bed, a dressing-table and a drawer

Here is the bed extended ready for use; the eiderdown is kept in the capacious drawer underneath. The top holds dressing-mirror, jewellery, trinkets and beauty aids. The bed has a spring mattress

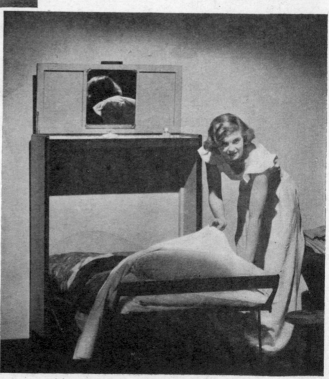

Council of Industrial Design

The polka-dotted wallpaper makes a good background for the occasional tables in beech
and the flower-prints arranged in a grouping of four. There are several lamps to provide
light in the right place when needed. Note the modernistic magazine and paper rack

vision. It is mobile and can be wheeled about
to suit the length of vision of its various
occupants, or to place in another room.

Suiting Everyone

There are special needlework chairs. One
has very low arms and a fairly firm seat, as
otherwise needlework is apt to get crumpled,
and it is an effort to drag out of the depths of
a too low chair every time the door bell
rings or a reel of cotton may have to be
chased across the floor. Others have no arms
at all, so that the work can flow over the lap
unimpeded; the seat of these is fairly low.
Yet another, with low arms, has a box seat
with a drawer in which can be held every
necessity for the home needlewoman.

A well-sprung armchair, mainly for men
since they are more apt to 'sprawl' at ease,
has an extra-wide top. This means that
whichever way the occupant of the chair is
sitting, even if right to one side, with legs
draped over one arm, there is somewhere to
rest the head. An ultra-modern chair is designed with the top of the chair coming forward so that it supports the head. This is

comfortable when reading, since then there
is no reason to drop the head right back and
hold the newspaper almost horizontally so
that it blocks out the light! Another modern
design, called a 'reclining chair'—which
description, after all, would fit most easy
chairs—has widish wooden arms, a 'tilt' that
just receives the body cosily, and a headrest
pillow suspended from the top of the back.

Sit by the Fire

Then there is a low fireside chair with tension springing and loose-stuffed seat cushion,
just the right height for catching all the warmth
from the fire. Two or more form a semi-circular settee, which also makes them ideal for
television viewing.

There are many kinds of sectional seating.
A three-seater settee can make an ideal 'cosy
corner' arrangement, with one chair at one
side of a corner table or fitment, and the other
two the other side as a small settee. It is an
arrangement that commends itself for small
parties, since if some of the guests are playing card games, three or even four other
guests can seat themselves right away in the

Council of Industrial Design

The two-way light fitting can cast light either down or upon the ceiling. The settee, having no arm at the end, is ideal for a friend staying overnight. The coverings are varied but linked by being several tones of one colour

corner for a low-toned gossip. A cocktail party, too, always has some guests who hate to stand for very long, and this little corner gives the ideal amount of seating room for such a small space. There are, of course, sectional seating arrangements up to any number, and for the hospitable family who like to have a television party these are especially useful. Besides, once they are broken into their separate portions again, being the main seating furnishing of a quite large room, they can be made into settees and a couple of chairs, or several chairs and one small settee . . . the combinations are endless and intriguing, allowing for attractive groupings.

Antique chairs are mostly for show. Excellent copies can of course be bought that are very utilitarian. For the very small flat the copy of a 17th-century monk's seat provides not only an attractive piece of hall furniture, but storage space in the lidded top for rugs and so on, and a pull-over top forming a table, on which occasional meals can be taken, to avoid cluttering up the lounge or dining-room.

Relaxation is Important

Since relaxation is more needed in our everyday, hectically rushed life than in more spacious, slowly-moving times, the acme of comfort is the easy chair that gradually tilts back until its user is at the exact level that is comfortable. Its design is based on the theory held by physiologists that the body achieves the ideal resting position when floating in water. The idea is that because the body displaces its own weight in water, it thus achieves a perfect equality; no muscles need to work, the spine does not need to strain to support the head and carry the weight of the torso, and the legs are idle. The ideal body profile is alleged to be 'Upper body reclined at 45 degrees; thighs at 20 degrees; feet elevated at 90 degrees.' The chair tilts flexibly according to the amount the sitter leans back, thus finding its own correct level. If nerves are in-

With kind co-operation of Minty of Oxf

TELEVISION PARTY

The folding television table swivels round.
The occasional chair is for the friend who
prefers to sit upright, and the armchair
has a separate pouffe which will serve as
an extra seat. The youngest one of the
family can perch on the stool, which has
a detachable loose cover. Little palette
tables fit around the arms of the chairs
to hold refreshments

The needlework lamp is low enough to cast a light without interfering
with the vision. The lamps of the ceiling fitment can be turned up to
cast a reflected glow, or they can be moved in any direction needed.
The curtain is a popular rust-red, Whitehead design

BACHELOR FLAT

Many couples start married life in one room these days, and a bachelor (girl or man!) can live alone in the utmost comfort in a well-planned flatlet of this type. The fact that it is about three rooms in one does not have to be obvious. The secret is to have 'a place for everything, and everything in its place'

First of all, choose your colour-scheme. Does the room face north or south? What are your favourite colours? The basic colours of this room are green and red, with other tones of these two as accessory shades. There should not be too many chairs in one room, but seating-space is still ample

A ONE-ROOM HOME

The built-in furniture, which you can make yourself (directions are given on pages 284–287) is planned to be of many uses. The divan is a bed, of course; the wall seat has a loose top and can be used for storage. The desk is a dressing-table, when opened, and there is a shelf for linen, with castors, that slides under the divan

So these are the items to be made: A. Bedside cupboard. B. Tray to slide under the divan. C. Bookshelves and cupboards to fit around divan bed. D. Wall seat with loose top, to enable things to be stored away. E. Low table. F. Cooking-unit with space for saucepans, etc. G. Dressing-table-desk

CONVERSATION PIECE

Our rooms are not cluttered these days with photographs on overmantel and whatnot. Nevertheless, we still have a streak of sentiment and there are photographs and souvenirs we wish to keep. Any old screen can be re-covered with a strong light-coloured plastic, and upon this, snapshots, photographs, pictures of scenes we love, can all be glued, not haphazardly, but to some sort of rough design. They form a constant subject for discussion, too, when the conversation runs low

There is nothing so romantic and happy as lazing in a garden on a summer's afternoon reading a book and with your back against a tree. Make this picturesque seat by building a circular wall of bricks or breeze blocks about 18 to 24 in. from the trunk. Make it wide enough to lounge on comfortably when doing a little sun-bathing

Dye some old curtains a deep, rich shade of midnight blue and sprinkle them with copper-coloured sequins, sewn from top to hem

Gold, silver or multi-coloured sequins can be sewn on any plain-coloured curtains to give them new life. A fringe in silver or gold to blend can be sewn along the pelmet. Standard lamp and contrasting chair make a happy grouping

clined to get ragged, it is very rarely that the young mother thinks of buying a rocking-chair. Why, they went out with the bustle! Quite apart from the fact that rocking is a soothing motion, and babies appreciate it when it is gentle and not a violent jogging, there are not only old rocking-chairs sometimes to be picked up in antique shops or auctions, but there are newly-designed ones of beech and elm with gay pallet cushions at a moderate price. Then wing-back chairs are more in favour than for some time and they do keep off draughts. We have many combinations of bed and chair, and these can be copied quite easily. For instance, a settee formed of three separate sections can be placed against a wall and at right angles to it, a double divan forms an 'L' with the headpiece into the room, with cushions against the wall at the foot. This forms a roomy arrangement of furniture that is ideal for a small room which must serve for bedroom and sitting-room, since it gives an illusion of spaciousness.

From chairs to settees is but a step, and here is where so many young couples make a mistake when buying. They may want to put up a friend for the night, but they have bought a settee that is too small for this purpose, so the friend has a pain in the neck, cramp and painful ankles from trying to balance them on the arm of the temporary bed. It is so simple to buy with a view to putting up a friend if there is no spare room.

The Settee for a Bed

There are long settees with only one end which fit admirably into a one-roomed flat, or in a larger domain can be used for the odd guest. There is the settee with arm-rests which extend and drop down, making a full-length bed. Also a settee of normal length, fitting easily into a small room, which has bolts to be unscrewed, when it can be laid flat to form a flat, fully-sprung sleeping surface.

A useful folding bed for either bachelor, girl-living-alone or for the guest is one that is folded into a cabinet. The bedclothes are kept in a drawer underneath the cupboard which houses the actual sprung bed (which lets down), and the top opens up with a mirror in the lid to form a small dressing-table. Shut, it is just a nice cabinet with apparently no other purpose. This is a help, for no one wants a bed-sitting-room to look too much *like* a bed-sitting-room! In fact, we want to eat our cake and have it, and owing to the ingenuity

Vono, Ltd.

This settee is constructed with a metal frame, and takes to pieces to provide a completely flat, fully sprung sleeping surface large enough for a double bed. When buying a settee it is useful to bear in mind the possible future need of increased sleeping accommodation

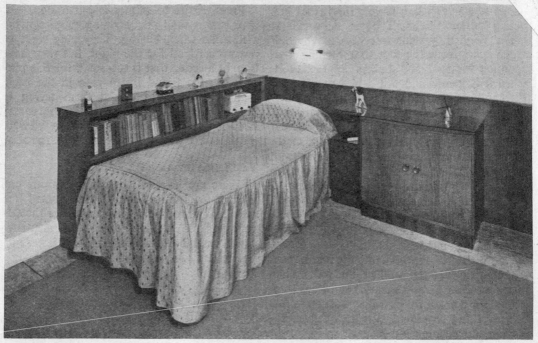

A divan fitment in Australian walnut tailored to use every inch of space whether it is in a one-room flat or small bedroom, with room for books, radio, personal odds and ends and bedside table. Enclosed washbowls can also be fitted in this way

of manufacturers these days that is just what we succeed in doing.

It is important, especially in the small flat, not to have pieces of furniture which are too cumbersome, since it means a good deal of heavy shifting when cleaning the rooms. Most modern furniture is designed with a kind of lightweight mobility even to the larger pieces. Big, heavy settees are apt to become fixtures, and it is nice to be able to alter the arrangement of a room sometimes. Most women appear to be divided into two very definite types—the ones who move the furniture every week: one week everything is across corners, the next straight against the walls, or in little groups; then there is the other type of housewife who takes a good deal of trouble to find out the exact and ideal position for all her chairs and tables and, feeling that she cannot improve upon the scheme, everything 'stays put' for the next twenty years!

Put Your Feet Up

A footstool or little stool is useful to put up the feet rather than to use the settee, and a detachable cover should be made for this

which can be taken off and washed. It can have one or two in varying shades or designs, which makes for variety. Some armchairs have a detachable extension to the seat which can be used either for an extra seat, especially for a child, as it resembles a square pouffe, or to recline with the feet up when it is in position against the chair seat.

If you are looking at a catalogue and you like a chair or a suite, cut out in newspaper its exact measurements and see if it really blends in well with your room. You may find it will come too near a doorway, or won't fit under the window or at the side of the fireplace. By taking precautions you will not buy a 'white elephant.' Also, when purchasing, it is usually best to choose separate cushions, since they can be turned to share all the wear evenly.

Choosing Chair-coverings

When deciding on a chair- or settee-covering, it is best, if possible, to have the store send round some lengths so that they can be tried in the actual room, when you will have a much better idea of how they will look. However, if this is not practicable, then

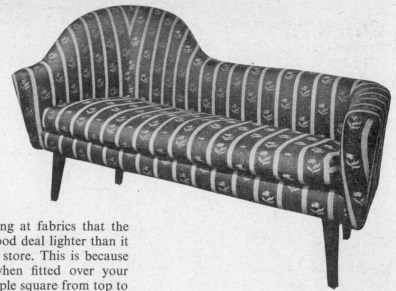

remember when looking at fabrics that the material will look a good deal lighter than it appears to you in the store. This is because it stretches slightly when fitted over your furniture. Pull the sample square from top to bottom to see if the weave opens to reveal the backing. If it does, reject it, or after a short time your chairs will begin to look shabby. Pull the two opposite corners diagonally, both ways. If it stretches too much it will soon 'bag.' If it has too little elasticity it will not 'give' as the chair settles and will soon become a bad fit.

To test its density, hold the sample up to

An attractive and gay arrangement of divan and settee which comes from an experimental department in Norway. Hard-wearing woven fabrics and rugs can still be both gay and practical. Scandinavians pay special attention to the distribution of adequate lighting

An example of how different coverings can be combined with excellent effect. The settee on the right has an off-white rough-surfaced tweed; the small chair is in a vivid scarlet, the same note caught up in the curtains. The dining recess has a light immediately over the table

The dining-table in this grey, green and beige room has all the daylight and a view. The writing-desk on the right is an unused dressing-table with its mirror removed

A bedroom of a very feminine type, blending pastel shades and darker tones, with a contemporary sycamore suite, yet borrowing from the past with its candlewick bedspread and 'buttoned' bedhead. The chair, with its back-rest, is more comfortable for a leisured half-hour than a stool. The design of the carpet is brought out in a raised pile

Council of Industrial Design

the light. The less light shining through the better, for then the cloth is closely woven, has substance and should wear well. A stiff material may contain too much dressing.

Even the most charming design may be of inferior quality. You need both, your choice in design and value. Then, as to fabrics, there are advantages and disadvantages for both cottons and wools. Close-weave cottons, for instance, wear well, are not susceptible to moths and are tougher than wool. On the other hand, although wool cloths do not show the grease and dirt so readily, they clean well, look warmer and wear excellently.

If you like hardwearing uncut moquettes, and today new moquettes are available in colours and designs to suit all tastes, bear in mind that a wool-pile moquette is better than one with a cotton pile. However, if you have a pet in the house, beware uncut moquettes and tufted wool fabrics, for the loops and tufts are apt to pull out under animals' claws.

YOUR BEDROOM

Bedrooms are usually places that are used only to sleep in. Some may have a desultory armchair of the type that isn't of any use any-

where else, that will do to drape clothes on, or for a visitor if one is ill, but actually, the bedroom can be made into another living-room. So many people like to 'escape' from the family sometimes, that a comfortable bedroom, where some sewing or writing a few letters in quiet is possible, is something that adds to one's home life.

If there is an elegant bed, then, of course, it is always obviously a bedroom, but it can still represent a 'boudoir' or a refuge to relax from the cares of the day. It does not have to be in any sense a bed-sitting-room, with a divan, if there are already other living-rooms, but it can have a small writing-table, a little window seat with a small table to take books or a sewing-basket, an armchair with a footstool. If the bed is one with a satin-quilted top, then a satin-quilted chair to match can look very charming.

Feminine or Severe?

A wash-bowl in the bedroom should be enclosed in a cupboard, or at least be hidden behind an attractive screen, since it gives rather a bathroom air to the room. If you haven't the money to buy a screen, then an ordinary clothes-horse covered with cretonne

Courtesy of Heal & Son, Ltd.

The kind of room that serves as a haven for writing letters, reading or studying as well as sleeping. Teak furniture, and walls in two shades. The window-wall and wall behind divan is papered in white on grey-blue wallpaper. Curtains of 'Ticker-tape' fabric

or silk to match the curtains will serve quite delightfully! Glazed chintz is dust-resisting, and can be tacked on with a braid edging secured by brass-headed nails. Your bedroom should be a place you are happy in, not just to dash in and snatch enough sleep to get you through the next day. Have your favourite flowers in it, so that when you go in you have a feeling of welcome and pleasure.

Then the picture you have in a bedroom should blend with the room. If it is a very feminine room, a reprint of a Marie Laurencin, or other similar painters, in a light frame will go beautifully with the style. If it is a severe room, with tailored, dark covers, vivid but plain curtains, then one or two good reprints of the Impressionists (if you like them) or a landscape by a modern painter. Nothing is lovelier than to sit and look straight into a beautiful scene so that you might be there, as long as you don't follow the example of Alice and find yourself the other side—in Wonderland! If you know

something about pictures, you may be able to pick up some originals by someone who will be famous in twenty years' time! A bedroom does not want many pictures, but one or two, selected with care—flowers are a happy choice—lend interest and depth to the room.

Your Own Taste

As to what kind of furniture to choose for your room, before planning just where the pieces will go, make up your mind as to the general 'theme' of the room. Is it to be fussy and frilly or severe and plain? Pastel-shaded or brightly-coloured? Ordinary modern furniture of the bedroom-suite type, or something unusual?

It is of no use mixing a severe divan with some frilly curtains, with an old mahogany tallboy, and a cubist table thrown in for good measure. It will miss all the way round. But it must express *you*. If you like frills, and have always yearned for a four-poster bed, have

A four-poster is charming in a room in which the furniture is Regency or Early Victorian in style. In this room, the wallpaper is blue patterned in white, and the fabric for curtains and four-poster hangings is white patterned with blue. The room also had a blue-draperied dressing-table, with ruffles of white

one. The film-star who had a bed shaped like a swan was criticised . . . but why? If that was what she wanted, at least the first essential was taken care of!

With your four-poster, of course, you would have period furniture. Lovely gleaming mahogany (not last century's yellow shiny oak); and you will be amazed if you haunt a few auction sales just how cheaply such pieces can be picked up. You could have a frilled bed-cover, candlewick, or even plaid taffeta; a plain-colour rayon, with frilled edging, would look right in such a room, too.

It is best when you decide just what 'character' bedroom you are going to have, to make a list of what pieces you have in hand to use. Either you can renovate them to go with the room, or they will fit in anyway.

People with very definite tastes in furnishing usually have pieces that will unite happily in almost any room they put them in, because the same style is part of them all. Then if they are antique or modern, it is likely that they will combine without any discord.

A more conventional bedroom on popular modern lines. It is carpeted in a rich plum colour; the walls a pale green and white stripe. The chair is upholstered in the same material as the bedspread —lime green with a metal thread. Curtains are a Whitehead design in grey, pink and yellow

Designed by F. M. Gross, M.S.I.A., F.R.S.A., Dip. Ing. Arch.

A beautifully streamlined writing-desk and dressing-table in pale green Japanese lacquer. The carpet is silver-grey, and the upholstery in rust-coloured, woven material

The Dressing-Table

Lighting is extremely important in a bedroom. The dressing-table must have its back to the light: if the sun falls directly on the glass you will not get a good impression of just how you look. If you see yourself in the most revealing light there may be days when it is a trifle depressing, but you will know the worst and be able to cope with it! An overhead light just above the mirror is the clearest at night.

Dressing-tables with flounced skirts go with many schemes, both modern and an-tique, except the plain and tailored. A very pretty dressing-table can be made of a small wall-table (plain or coloured glass or of wrought iron) with an exceptionally charming mirror on the wall above it. A small waste-paper basket painted to match is a necessity for pieces of cotton-wool used during make-up, or for torn-up letters. A hand-mirror of charm, bought in some art shop or store that specialises in such things, together with a brush and comb and a powder-bowl, is all that is needed on the glass table top. If the brush and comb are strictly utilitarian, then

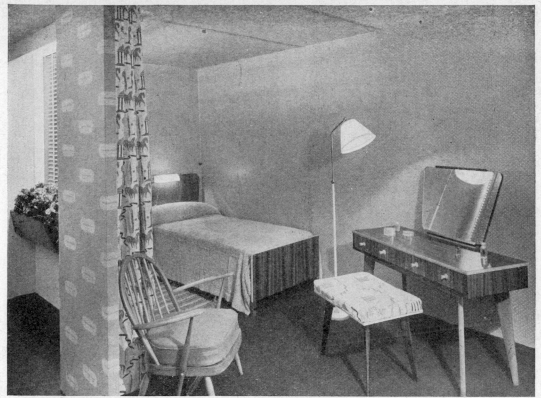

The gay little bedroom is in yellow, blue and pink. Notice the white plastic Venetian blind and unusual window-box of flowers. Curtains are yellow and blue on a white ground, bedspread in yellow and the tub chair has a coral-pink seat. Wallpaper is blue with a white polka-dot

the table will possess a drawer or two drawers side by side and they can be popped in there with a few odd pots—skin food, foundation and so on. The skirted type of dressing-table can cover several drawers (but see that there is a gap for your knees when sitting to brush your hair), or even shoe-rails can be fixed behind its camouflage.

Charming furnishing is never so much a matter of money as of ideas. One woman might say she had only a wooden kitchen chair to put in the bedroom. Another would pad the seat and back and give it a 'frock' of cretonne. Two old rugs can be stitched together and the joins hidden by braid to give a most modern effect. Two very ordinary candlesticks with cream shades and yellow candles on an old wooden table enamelled pale blue with a narrow yellow line running around can appear very expensive.

If you do not like straightly hanging net curtains, then—if it is that type of room—tie them in the middle with a flat bow of ribbon so that they are 'X' shaped. Always try something a little different.

Man's Room

A man's room naturally needs to be fairly severe, although brocade curtains and period pieces are usually liked by the male sex. Little Sheraton tables that can be found in antique shops make excellent bedside tables (although originally being 'sofa-tables'). If there is not a fitted cupboard, then an old one that goes with the furnishings can be fitted up inside, although most manufacturers sell fitted 'robes of several woods and designs. A very plain painted cupboard, however, is more suitable in a period room than some highly varnished contemporary oak.

Then pale walls—pale green, lemon, grey-blue, peach—are lovely foils for dark furniture, but light modern beech or pine, often hailing from Scandinavia, can be placed with effect against darker walls . . . burgundy or an almost midnight blue, very deep yellow.

Designed by Ian Henderson

Furniture very suitable for a masculine room in satinwood with surrounds of Nigerian pearwood. To have wardrobe doors fitted flush with the wall as they are here would need some co-operation with the architect. The gold-leaf, hand-carved Italian mirror (these often can be found at quite reasonable prices) gives a simplicity of decoration

Make sure that the furniture in a man's room is solid. A fitted or big carpet is best, too, for though rugs on a polished floor look effective, if he catches his foot in one or slips there is likely to be a stormy atmosphere for a short while! Actually all rugs should have weighted or rubbered corners to stop their sliding about, for this can be not only irritating but quite dangerous.

Silhouettes, hunting prints or old maps are decorative for the walls.

Towel-rail Bookcase

All sorts of useful etceteras can be picked up in second-hand shops for very little money and make expensive-looking furnishings. The Georgian mahogany towel-rail illustrated takes more than eighty books, and a similar item would be ideal in the young student's room. Grandparents may have an Edwardian mahogany towel-rail they do not want, which can be used in a similar way, or even a cheap, old white-painted one can be repainted in a gay shade. It is important that a very sturdy stand should be chosen.

This old mahogany Georgian towel-rail makes an excellent bookcase

This is the principal bedroom of one of two experimental, space-saving houses built for the Department of Health for Scotland. It has pale green figured wallpaper, and a leaf-green carpet. Both curtains and bedspread provide a sunny note of golden-yellow ribbed silk

Council of Industrial Design (Scottish Committee)

Designed by Jacques Groag

A wall recess has been used to build up a shelf at the back of the bed to hold library book, telephone, favourite photograph and lamps. The two side-tables are on wheels so that they can be moved to make the bed. The Cole wallpaper is in white with gold stars

These four attractive, mahogany units house cocktail cabinet, gramophone and books with storage for records underneath. These are hung between brass supports and can be built up higher when needed. The two shelves are on a double bracket made of brass

The shelf curving under the window, for plants, is of beige-colour marble, easy to wipe clean. Walls are cream, carpet beige, curtains in rust and off-white

HOW COMFORTABLE IS YOUR HOME?

DOES the front gate open easily, shut automatically and latch firmly?

An inefficient gate can admit destructive animals, let children stray into the road or upset the milkman. A good type of catch is spring-loaded; firm pressure on the gate causes the catch to spring back and it latches automatically when closed. It can be used with a pair of gravity self-closing hinges.

Can the name or number of the house be read from across the road in the dark?

The best place for a name or number is on a fanlight over the front door, where it shows up in the dark when the hall light is burning. Alternatively it can be painted on an external light fitting or, in luminous paint, on the door or gate. Very attractive numbers in stainless steel can be bought quite cheaply.

Is the front path in good order?

Paths overgrown with foliage, or with a muddy or slippery surface, create a bad impression and make it difficult to keep the hall clean. Crazy paving or concrete paving is a labour-saving investment.

Is the approach to the house accident-proof?

If there are unexpected steps, bends or slopes outside the front or back doors, illuminate them or use white paint to make them conspicuous, and so avoid an accident on your own doorstep.

Have you cut back trees or shrubs which rob your house of winter daylight?

A house cannot be bright or cheerful if overshadowed by dark branches. White-washing the walls opposite basement windows is another lightening idea.

Are the walls in good condition?

Ivy and other creepers, if not controlled, force their way into cracks in the wall, widen them as they grow and eventually have the wall down. See that the pointing of brick walls is intact, and repair cracked or damaged stucco.

Are gutters and down pipes clear?

Half an hour spent in clearing out leaves may save pounds in redecoration later on. Copper or galvanised wire globes fitted into the tops of down pipes and vent pipes prevent birds from nesting in them.

Is the roof weatherproof?

If you cannot answer 'yes' to this question, your house is not comfortable, however luxuriously it is equipped. Damp-marks on a ceiling may be a symptom of internal trouble in the roof timbers. If the surface of the roof is porous, there are specialist firms who will treat it with a waterproofing compound and guarantee the result.

Have the chimneys been swept since last winter?

They should be done regularly. See also that chimney-pots are free from birds' nests, and that cowls are in working order.

Are the windows in good repair?

Sliding sash windows need attention at least once a year. Pulleys need oiling, cords and catches checking. Wooden casement windows are apt to shrink, and may need to be fitted with draught excluders. Metal windows appreciate an occasional drop of oil on catches, hinges and stays.

Is the fuel store big enough?

For additional storage capacity, pre-cast concrete bunkers are economical and efficient. A ten-hundred-weight-capacity bunker is only 4 ft. by 3 ft. by about 3 ft. high.

Is there a bootscraper by the door?

If you live in the country, a scraper (or brusher) is essential. Why not get the village blacksmith to make a wrought-iron one for the front porch? For the back door, drill a hole in the handle of an old stainless-steel knife and hang it up near the door.

Is the bell reliable, and can it be heard all over the house?

There are several first-rate mechanical and electrical bells now on the market. One electric bell goes 'ping-pong' when the front-door button is pressed, and just 'ping' for the back door.

Is the bell-push easy to find?

Many man-hours are wasted annually by people playing 'hunt-the-bell-push' on strange front doorsteps. Some luminous paint round the bell-push will make it more visible by night or day.

Is there a light outside the front door?

Whether your nocturnal visitor is welcome

Schweizerischer Werkbund

This well-arranged room comes from Zürich. The furniture is in light ash, upholstered in a warm red, hand-woven fabric. The table is in glass and walnut. The dining-table has an unusual extra occasional leaf. Carpet is of beige with a red design, on a parquet floor

The most has been made of an awkwardly shaped lounge-hall. A high cupboard shuts away outer clothing from view, and with its top cupboards provides extra storage space in the small house. The built-in fitment on the wall has a cupboard for telephone directories and a built-in fire. The mirror above the fire is strip-lighted, increasing the hall's apparent size

or not, a light is useful. To give the front door distinction, fix a pair of old carriage lamps, wired for electricity, on either side of it.

Is the letter-box big enough?

It is most annoying to have to get out of bed on a cold morning merely because a small parcel will not go through the letter-box. Get a bigger one, but avoid the type with a spring like a mouse trap, for this damages letters—and the postman's temper.

Do letters land in a cage or a box?

If not, they are liable to get trodden on, and chewed by the dog. Some receptable is essential.

Does the door open and shut easily?

A drop of oil on every hinge, lock, bolt, catch, latch and castor in the home is an important item in an autumn overhaul.

Does it clear the doormat?

The mat should be in a recess in the floor. This prevents it from sliding about, allows the door to open over it, and keeps dust and dirt in a confined space from which it can be removed by a vacuum cleaner.

Are there hooks in the hall for visitors' coats and hats, as well as your own?

A coat cupboard is much tidier than the old-fashioned hall-stand. Extra hooks can be fixed unobtrusively on the inside of cupboard doors, with spare coat hangers.

Is there anywhere to dry damp coats, etc.?

It is not always convenient to spread them over a chair in front of the fire. There is a tiny electric heater of novel design which will transform a wardrobe or coat cupboard into an airing cupboard.

Is there a mirror in the hall?

One can sometimes buy a large second-hand mirror cheaply and have it cut down to fit a picture frame. A mirror makes the hall seem bigger.

Is there a place in the hall for parcels, messages, a clothes brush and the dog's lead?

If the hall is small, a shelf beneath the

mirror is enough, with hooks for dogs' leads, keys, etc., and a receptacle in which to stand wet umbrellas.

Is the hall warm and cosy?

If the hall is a cold and draughty passage, the whole house will be cold and draughty too. Money spent on making the front door draught-proof—and the metal strip method is about the best for this purpose—will be repaid by reduced fuel bills. A portable radiator in the hall raises the temperature of the rest of the house.

Is the hall floor easy to clean and non-skid?

Carpet is out of place in a hall, especially in the country and where dogs are kept. Tiles and linoleum are more practical. There is a special powder which prevents loose rugs from slipping, or weights can be fixed at each corner.

Do you keep a torch in the hall?

Small pocket-torches have a limited life, and when an emergency arises the battery is often flat; but a powerful torch has innumerable uses indoors and out.

Is the hall lighting satisfactory?

Indirect lighting is ideal for halls where intense direct lighting would dazzle people coming in from the dark. Stronger light is needed near the mirror and by the telephone.

Is there a comfortable chair by the telephone?

There should be—but not too comfortable, or the telephone bills may go up.

Is there a pad with a pencil attached within reach of the 'phone?

The flash pad, from which writing can be erased by pressing a lever, is suitable; another has a magnetic pencil which stays put on the plastic case.

Can telephone numbers be found quickly?

There should be a rack or decorative holder for directories, and an indexed list of commonly used numbers. The most convenient variety flicks open at the right place when a button is pressed.

Is the sitting-room well lit by day?

Lace or net curtains should be washed frequently to admit maximum light—or dispensed with. Summer curtains should be

This small room has a white-painted fitment differently arranged, a 'shortboy' giving both drawer space and dressing-table at one end. Striped material in deep blue and red is used for both curtains and divan-spread, with a dark blue, polka-dotted chair-covering for balance

Courtesy of Chippendale's Workshops, Ltd.

The hallway sets the stamp on a house, since it attracts or repels at the moment of entry. This is, in reality, a quite small hall, yet the comfortable chair, the attractively designed fitment providing both cupboards and decoration, achieve a warmly welcoming note

replaced by heavy, draught-excluding, full-length winter ones, and light-obstructing plants removed.

And is it well lit by night?

It is not well lit if there is only a central light, unless it is fluorescent and casts no shadows. Lighting should be flexible, capable of being concentrated for specific activities. For safety's sake eliminate long lengths of flex, and install an extra plug or two.

Are lampshades and bulbs free of dust?

A bulb and shade can collect enough dust in a summer to reduce its efficiency more than 25 per cent.

Is the sitting-room well ventilated without being draughty?

Draughts are caused by cold air being drawn into the room to replace the hot air which rises up the chimney. One cannot eliminate them, for a supply of fresh air is necessary for health and comfort, but one can prevent them from causing discomfort by controlling them with screens.

Is it adequately heated?

If the family huddles round the fire on cold days, getting toasted on one side and chilled on the other, the room is not properly heated. Background heating by means of radiators or convection heaters is recommended.

Is your fire up-to-date?

If it will not stay alight overnight, and does not possess a large enclosed ash-pan, a gas poker and an easily cleaned finish, it is a labour-creating antique.

Is there enough indoor fuel-storage capacity?

Cold and wet trips to the fuel store are avoided by having a second coal-scuttle, an extra large log basket, or by adapting the bottom of a cupboard or an old chest for fuel storage.

Can the fire be left alight and unattended safely?

Unless the fire is of totally-enclosed type, a spark-proof guard is essential. Additional precautions must, of course, be taken where there are children.

Courtesy of Vantona Textiles, Ltd

Soft Colours *for the* Bedroom

A bedroom can have a colour-scheme built up from walls or the bed. It is better to make the bed-cover the focal point, for you will wish to choose one that you like; paint can always be obtained in a shade to blend. Here the spread has a simple design based on the classical Greek honeysuckle convention in soft blue and white. The window and door curtains are provided by three other single bedspreads to match

The carpet is a very dark brown, and the little recess above the bed is papered in a similar dark brown. Too much of a heavy shade in a room is depressing, but this small area acts as a balance for the pale petunia and blue. It also provides an effective foil for flowers, ornaments and photographs. This idea of a square, black or brown wall-paper panel with a shelf beneath can be utilised in any room. The furniture is of polished beech in dark brown and beige. A recess for the bed is formed by the built-out cupboard fitment, painted to match the wall

1. Paper the area of wall immediately behind the most important piece of furniture; here, it is the settee. Choose a fairly deeply coloured pattern that will not show marks. Finish the panel with an edging of painted picture moulding either side

2. This flower-container was an ordinary bicycle-basket distempered white. Such a container could, of course, be painted any colour to blend with a room's decoration. It needs a vase, tin or bowl inside to hold the water, and can hang or stand against a wall

3. A plain whitewood chest is covered with the gay pictures from seed packets! The name is cut away, leaving a squarish flower or vegetable picture. The finished decoration is coated with clear varnish to make the pictures fast to cleaning with a damp cloth

4. This practical and elegant table was only a cheap wooden stool, painted white. A picture frame, enclosing a piece of glass over a traycloth, was screwed to the top. A clear piece of glass could be used over any piece of tapestry or a picture

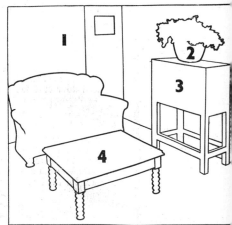

The book-lover with a new home can start his collection in a single unit for the mantelpiece. This can grow, unit by unit, until it houses a young library

The bookcase can comprise a combination of 8-in. sections, 30 in. long (with polished top board). Corner shelves can be linked with side units

Minty of Oxford

Have you an efficient set of fire-implements?

Good tools are a joy to use and a pleasure to look at, but many modern sets do not deserve a place by the fire. A good pair of bellows is a great asset. They can also be an ornament.

Is the sitting-room designed for hard wear?

Unlike the old-fashioned parlour, which was a show-piece with 'Do not touch' metaphorically written all over it, the sitting-room of today is meant to be used. Furnishings must stand up to normal wear, and be easily cleaned. Breakable valuables should not be in vulnerable positions.

And is it flexibly furnished?

In winter the modern sitting-room may be a drawing-room, library, study, nursery, schoolroom, card-room, smoking-room, boudoir, games-room or music-room. Therefore it needs light, versatile furniture.

Is there a corner for letter-writing?

The pleasures of letter-writing are increased and its trials diminished if envelopes, stamps, addresses, ink, calendar and waste-paper basket are all at hand, in an attractive desk placed, if possible, with light coming over the left shoulder.

This comfortable 'den' has an adjustable light fitting, casting a glow over both the radio and reading-chair. The dark green settee blends in with the green-striped chair. The spotted carpet is an unusual design

Council o
Industrial Design

Is the dining-area adequately heated?

A dining-recess in a well-heated living-room often needs no other heating, but the heating of a separate dining-room is too often ignored. Gas, electric or hot-water radiators, oil heaters, portable radiant fires and convectors can all solve the problem.

And satisfactorily lit?

A dining-table is often used for other activities, so dual-purpose lighting is an advantage. There are many electric light fittings which can be moved to cast concentrated light for homework or sewing.

Is the table top protected from hot dishes?

The ideal top for a domestic dining-table would resist staining, heat and moisture, and have a warm and pleasant surface. If such a material exists, it is very rare. Rubber, cork, linoleum, hardboard and felt are all suitable for place-mats, which can be big enough to accommodate knives and forks as well as plates.

Are there enough electric plugs in the dining-area?

Plugs are needed here more than anywhere else, for toaster, coffee-pot, hot-plate and possibly electric iron and sewing-machine. For real comfort they should be placed at table-top height.

Can you clear the table in one journey?

Some people may enjoy the exercise involved in unnecessary journeys between kitchen and dining-table; others do it without thinking; but it is usually possible to clear a table in one go with a little thought and the help of a hatch or a trolley.

Do you keep marmalade, sugar, pepper, salt, jam, pickles, table-mats and cloths in the dining-room?

It is waste of energy carrying articles which do not need washing and are not perishable to and from the kitchen.

Can you open the kitchen door when your hands are full?

It can be opened with an arm or an elbow if it has a lever handle, while a check-action door-spring makes a catch redundant.

Is the kitchen door fitted with a stop to prevent it banging against walls or furniture?

Rubber stops cost a few pence but may safe pounds' worth of damage. They should be fitted to every door in the house.

Is there a stop to hold it open?

One cannot risk the door blowing shut when one is passing through it with a tray of crockery and glass. A lump of stone or artistic door-stop will hold it open, but a special rubber-tipped pedal fixed to the door is more convenient.

Is the kitchen lighting good?

Again the central light is unsatisfactory. Separate lights over sink, work-table and stove are ideal.

A desk is a most useful article of furniture, since correspondence, even if not over-whelming, can be filed away together with writing necessities

This very modern desk is waxed mahogany with small drawer and deep file drawer, 3 ft. wide. The chair is upholstered in blue-green linen

Heal & Son, Ltd.

Council of Industrial Design

A long, narrow room arranged to the very best advantage. The colour scheme is brown, heliotrope, mustard yellow and blue

Are the light switches safe?

Cord-operated switches are best, especially where there are children.

Is the kitchen well ventilated?

In the summer one can cook with all windows open, but in winter special steps must be taken to get rid of cooking-smells—either a hood over the cooker with a flue to the open air, or an electric extract fan.

Is there a radio in the kitchen?

If not, an extension loud-speaker is easily installed and enables programmes to be heard without turning the sitting-room radio on full strength and possibly annoying neighbours.

Are the cupboard door catches easily operated?

Some cupboard doors are difficult to open with wet or greasy fingers, but there is a latch which works by simply pressing the door to open or shut. A magnetic catch is another new idea.

Are the working surfaces the correct height?

This must be determined by experiment, and cannot be standardised. A sink, table or stove that is a few inches too high or too low may cause real physical injury, and even the expense of raising or lowering the sink is justified if it corrects the trouble. Remember that too high is much better and more unusual than too low.

Do you use a grease-solvent when washing up?

In the winter there are more greasy dishes to wash, and an efficient grease-solvent helps, especially in a hard-water district.

Is there a mat to stand on when washing up?

The average housewife and some husbands spend a lot of time standing at the kitchen sink. A resilient mat of rubber, cork or fibre insulates them from the cold hard floor and reduces the strain on the feet.

Is there an adjustable stool in the kitchen?

A stool which is adjustable in height and has a back-rest can take the cook's weight off her feet while she is preparing vegetables, etc.

Do your tea-cloths dry quickly?

An excellent device for this purpose is a set of towel rails fixed to, and radiating from, a flue pipe, taking advantage of its warmth.

Can washing be dried indoors?

An airing cupboard, which can be improvised by hanging a low-power portable electric heater in an existing cupboard, supersedes the

This is a bachelor's very self-contained room with an individual assembling of furniture. Note the unusual, hand-carved sideboard, the adjustable settee-divan with a swivel back, and the movable reading-table at the back of the room. There is also a shower-unit on the left

familiar pulley-airer, and protects clothes from dust and kitchen smells.

Is there always plenty of hot water at the sink?

Even if there is a tap connected to the hot-water supply, a gas or electric water-heater is a valuable standby.

Is there a light in the larder?

It is surprising how often this simple aid to convenience is forgotten.

Are there enough shelves in the larder?

Shelf area can usually be increased by careful spacing. A rack on the back of the larder door for spices, flavourings, matches and other small packets will release shelves for bulkier objects.

Is there a shopping-and-message pad?

Paint a rectangular patch of wall with special blackboard paint, surround the patch with an empty picture frame, and you have a permanent notice-board for memoranda or messages, which can be rubbed off.

Can you see who is at the back door before opening it?

A safety device is a small porthole which can be fitted into any door and enables one to see out without being observed.

Is there a safe place for tradespeople to leave parcels when everyone is out?

A weather-proof box with a hinged door, fixed to the wall by the back door, is one solution to this problem.

Have you any way of leaving messages for baker and milkman?

Scraps of paper blow away, but there is a novel device which is screwed to the back door and acts as a permanent adjustable message, with milk and bread lettered thereon and an indication for amounts.

Are the stairs well lit?

Badly arranged lighting casts shadows in awkward corners and may be more dangerous than no lights at all. Lights should be double-switched at top and bottom of the stairs.

Are the banisters easy to dust?

Ornate dust-collecting banisters can be boxed in on both sides with sheets of plywood or hardboard, and small lights fitted into the hollow space so formed to improve staircase lighting.

Is the stair carpet firmly held?

There are special clips (some made of rubber) to hold the carpet firmly at the edges without damaging it, but rods hold the full width of the carpet and prevent sagging.

Are the bedrooms heated?

If there is no general heating by radiators or convectors, an electric or gas radiant heater should be provided in every room. Warmth and comfort improve tempers.

Can bedroom ventilation be controlled?

For good ventilation bedroom windows should open at top and bottom. Casement windows need 'hit-and-miss' glass ventilators fitted in them, or top-hung night ventilators above them.

Is there a lamp for every bed?

The most convenient type is fixed above the bed, leaving the bedside table free and enabling one to read in comfort. A double bed needs two lights, independently switched.

Are the bedside tables big enough?

The larger the bedside table, the less often you need to jump out of bed to fetch things. It should consist at least of bookshelf, table-top and drawer.

Can the main light be switched from both bed and door?

The cost of installing double switching is worth-while if it saves getting out of bed on a freezing night.

Is the dressing-table lighting as it should be?

Pendent lights with parchment shades are apt to cast shadows on the face. Two low sidelights are best, but fluorescent lights are also popular with people who want to make up in the type of light now used in restaurants, etc. Bad lighting can result in too bright make-up being applied.

Is there a full-length mirror in every bedroom?

One can see oneself full length in a mirror just over half one's height, if it is correctly hung. If fixed to a cupboard door, it can be moved to reflect in various directions. Do not put it above a divan or table which prevents half the body being reflected.

There are many labour-saving features in this kitchen. There are two revolving cupboards, one on floor level, and one on the wall, making articles easier to see and to reach

Under the stainless-steel double-drainer sink unit is a pull-out cutting board, and beneath that, a large cupboard. On the right is the cutlery drawer, and three drawers for vegetables, concealed by a sliding door

A small plate rack is fitted conveniently low just over the sink

Kitchen planned by Froy

Council of Industrial Design

A little imagination can create a comfortable and homely corner that is up
to date and charming as well. The trolley has a useful detachable tray

Are the cupboards illuminated?

All dark cupboards should be fitted with automatic switches so that a light comes on when the door opens.

Have wardrobes, etc., been cleared of unseasonable clothes?

Summer dresses, bathing suits, sunhats, etc., should be packed away during winter, and heavy clothes cleaned, moth-proofed and put between sheets of newspaper in the summer.

Is there enough wardrobe space?

One way to increase hanging space is for the pelmet and window curtains to be extended to form two corner cupboards, with shelves above the hanging-rails. When the curtains are drawn, the effect is that of a wide bay-window.

Can the beds be moved easily?

Big French castors enables beds to be moved about and pulled away from the wall for making up and cleaning.

Is the dressing-table easy to dust?

Before dusting some dressing-tables one has to pick up twenty or thirty bottles, lipsticks, brushes, combs, puffs, etc., but if they are kept on trays they can all be moved more easily. A plate-glass top is also an advantage.

Can you walk barefoot from bed to bathroom without stepping on a cold surface?

In a really comfortable house, bedroom slippers are hardly necessary. There should be at least a nice warm rug beside the bed.

Have you slept in the spare room recently, and is it properly equipped?

Only by spending a night in the spare room can one be sure it is comfortable and welcoming with spare blankets, wastepaper basket, magazines, ash-tray, matches, books, writing-paper and biro pen.

Are there washing facilities in the spare room?

A wash-basin with hot and cold water benefits the family as well as the guest. An instantaneous water-heater over the basin avoids expensive extensions to the hot-water system if the water-heating does not already extend throughout the house.

Is there enough cabinet space in the bathroom?

Bathroom cabinets are often cluttered with

boxes of anonymous pills, unlabelled medicine bottles, old razor blades and other rubbish, which can be dangerous and should be discarded. Most medicines lose their efficacy after three months.

Are all taps in perfect order?

A defective hot tap can waste gallons of hot water and so increase the fuel bills, while a dripping cold tap may cause the waste pipe to freeze up.

Is the hot water really hot?

A common cause of an inefficient system is loss of heat through lack of insulation. A specially made jacket of glass fibre or mineral wool covering the cylinder keeps the heat in.

Is the bathroom heated?

Unless the bathroom derives enough warmth from the hot-water system, heating is necessary. An electric fire fixed high up on the wall also helps to prevent frost damage.

Is roof space accessible and well lit?

If there is space in the roof for luggage, it is worth installing a folding ladder and an electric light which switches off automatically when the trap-door is shut.

Is plumbing protected from frost?

A few shillings spent on lagging pipes and protecting the cold-water tank may save as many pounds. When this is impossible, a frost-preventing pressure valve can be fitted.

Is the roof insulated?

It costs only £5 to £10 to lay a warm blanket of mineral wool, glass fibre or aluminium foil over the ceiling joists in the roof space, thus preventing heat being lost through the roof, and raising the temperature of the whole house appreciably.

A dual personality may not always be a bad thing. Here we have a two-seater chair

And now, on the right, the chair has a fool-proof action which turns it into a comfortable single bed

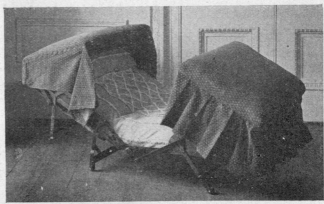

One of the benefits of the couchette is that it can be made up before closing again. It obviates getting out bedclothes to make up a bed when one is tired

Bruce Bros. (Bedding), Ltd.

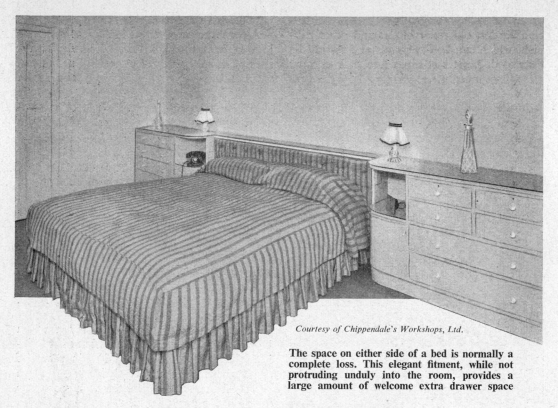

Courtesy of Chippendale's Workshops, Ltd.

The space on either side of a bed is normally a complete loss. This elegant fitment, while not protruding unduly into the room, provides a large amount of welcome extra drawer space

BUILT-IN FURNITURE

BUILT-IN furniture, not so very long ago, was a term used to describe only such things as a cupboard built into a recess or bookshelves each side of a fireplace. Nowadays, with so much less space at our disposal, the entire furniture of a room (including bed and table, but not chairs) can be built-in. Thus every available inch of space is utilised. To achieve a similar amount of wardrobe or drawer-space by the use of separate pieces of furniture would give a room a crowded, in-artistic appearance, whereas the lines of built-in wardrobes, dressing-tables, extra drawers and bookshelves can all flow into one another to form an harmonious whole. In fact, using up every available inch of room has become an exact science. It also avoids a good deal of heavy dusting.

Built-in cupboards and shelves were usually cream-painted or, a little further back in time, varnished a hideous and depressing chocolate-brown. These days, cream is still used a great deal, because it not only is light and easily cleaned, but affords the best background for many other colour schemes, allow-ing these to be varied without changing the colour of walls and paintwork. Cream-painted furniture, however, can be varied by the decorative mouldings being picked out in gold, silver or pale blue, or indeed any shade that will blend with the colour scheme chosen.

Both Old and New

The first Elizabethan age may have been more spacious, but an effect of ample room combined with furnishing reflecting the Tudor period can be obtained by the style of the Tudor being used for built-in panelling. Those who like period effects and rebel against built-in furniture as looking too modern can eat their cake and have it by having the furniture tailored not only to the room, but to the period desired.

Cupboards go right to the ceiling, instead of stopping short and leaving a space that is wasted, or that is often used for storing cases or boxes that show and spoil the look of a room, even if it is one that is not used very often. By taking the cupboard right up to the ceiling there is all that additional storage

46

This room began by being a drab Victorian one. The ugly fireplace was removed and created a recess in which to put the bedhead. The recess is made still deeper by the wardrobes being built-out, and gaily covered with the wallpaper. Note the little bracket wall-tables on each side of the bed

Tailored-to-fit furniture need not only be in cream-painted wood. The whole style of the house, whether Tudor or ultra-modern, can be reflected in the fitments

Here you have agreeable built-in furniture of oak with linenfold carvings, specially designed for an old country house. The window treatment is unusual

Courtesy of Chippendale's Workshops, Ltd.

A wall-to-wall scheme, in which there are two large wardrobes with dressing-table between. The latter has lighting especially arranged, rather than depending on chandelier or other lamps. The carved mouldings are picked out in silver

space for suitcases, linen or out-of-season clothes—even unused wedding gifts! The space under a man's short-hanging suits is usually wasted and would yield another drawer.

Dressing-tables can be built across corners, or in some hitherto wasted alcove, or fitted into a bay-window with cupboards (level with the dressing-table top) of drawers at either side. Ugly wash-bowls in corners can be hidden by a long panel mirror set in a door.

One apparently very modern room seen recently had been an unattractive bedroom with an ugly iron-barred firegrate. Now, the bedhead covered the grate and hid it from view, and whereas built-in cupboards are usually thought of as using recesses already existing, in this case—and many others—cupboards were built out to form a recess for the bed and then papered to match the rest of the room which gave a uniform effect.

The Nursery

Children's rooms lend themselves especially to such planned space-providing furniture, for tidiness can be taught only when there are plenty of drawers and cupboards to aid the young in their 'clearing-up' efforts. Each child can have its own set of drawers and little cupboard, and as each unit is built on to the next this not only avoids knocked knees, elbows and even eyes, but leaves the centre of a room free for a little romping. Also, the drawers can be planned to be of the same use as the children grow older. The fairy stories on the bookshelves will give place to adventure tales, to novels, schoolbooks, and biographies. The top recess of a cupboard which has been used for toilet requisites to make sure that they are high out of the toddler's hands can be used for a different purpose, and talcum, hair-lotion, brilliantine brought down to eye-level.

The bachelor-room is often very much in

This was another ordinary room until it was 'taken in hand.' In one corner there was a wash-bowl. Now two mirrored doors have been built across it, so that it is still of use, but disguised attractively in a way that also provides a necessary full-length mirror

There is also a small cupboard above the mirror, carrying on the line of the very spacious wardrobe arrangement

Courtesy of Chippendale's Workshops, Ltd.

It is 'better-looking' to follow on a built-in fitment with others, so that they flow unnoticeably into one another, rather than to have one single jutting-out piece

Here the window-seat, ever useful for odd rugs, golf-clubs, and all sorts of things that need to be stored out of sight, blends in stream-lined fashion into the telephone-book holder, book-shelves, and, on the left, an additional cupboard, which could be used for china

Courtesy of Chippendale's Workshops, Ltd.

Chippendale's Workshops, Ltd.

This sturdy and interesting fitment was made especially for twin boys. Here they can study side by side, keep their books, have an identical set of drawers for clothes, with storage space for sports equipment and various oddments above

need of a tailored furnishing fitment, for even so small a living-space as a boxroom of 8 ft. 6 in. by 7 ft. may as well be made ideally comfortable instead of a cramped makeshift, with a garment or magazine having to be moved before something else can be laid down. Such a fitted room had a divan, a wardrobe, with a built-in console table between divan and wardrobe. The dressing-table and chest of drawers are combined, with the top drawer setting up a mirror when opened. The stool before the dressing-table—which also could be used for a guest, or to put a magazine or tea-tray on—contained a cosmetic drawer. A bookshelf and make-up cabinet were placed on the wall over the divan to save space.

Idea for Shoes

Built-in wardrobes should always have shoe-rails. Or a piece of strong material can be nailed to the inside of the door and strong bands of webbing sewn across, each piece wide enough to take the heels of one pair of shoes. This should have a loose covering top of material which can be drawn back or left over the shoes so that they do not come into contact with the dresses.

A Welcoming Hall

Hallways lend themselves to intelligent treatment with built-in fitments, which not only add a luxury touch to what might be just a passage, but give space to keep golf-clubs, spare umbrellas, rugs and so on; the tops of drawer fitments provide a 'table' for colourful flower-arrangements, setting a note of charm and welcome the moment the front door is opened. If a small hall is square and not draughty (which it need not be), even a dining-flap can be attached to the wall and used for impromptu meals.

In fact, the hall can be made to serve as an extra room.

THE CHILDREN'S ROOM

NURSERIES never vary greatly, although the trend is always towards the hygienic, with clear attractive colours. Patterned wallpapers (varnished so that they can be wiped clean from the marks of sticky fingers) are quite a happy choice if the pattern is amusing or unobtrusive. But some designs are irritating to the eyes, and should be avoided. A lamp of a globe of the world is useful for the children to absorb a geographical idea of their own planet, even though place-names may have been radically altered by the time they are grown-up!

The introduction of bunks in these past few years saves space, especially if they are arranged with one under the other. A small step-ladder adds to the sense of fun and adventure such an arrangement gives, but it should be firmly fixed.

As the Twig is Bent

Plenty of planned cupboards may teach the young one to be orderly, especially if it is taken for granted from the earliest age that he should put away his toys every night. It then becomes ingrained habit and is not a chore to be begged off. Left a little too late, however, and mother will usually finish up by tidying the nursery. A blackboard fixed on the wall and coloured chalks *may* keep them from drawing on the surrounding walls. In any case, they can have no sense of grievance at not being allowed to if they have a space where colour can run riot.

In place of the old-fashioned nightlight, an electric-light cord fixed so that he can pull on the light quite easily will give him a sense of security. A shelf above the bed can hold favourite toys, a book or two. Once children have learnt to tell the time, it is a good idea to let them have a clock, either a grown-up one or a real one that is amusing in some way, such as one with nursery figures painted on its surrounds, or one of the painted peasant-type

Council of Industrial Design

Another boys' room. Double bunks are always appealing to the adventurous spirit. A small ladder may be provided, or even a rope-ladder fixed to make 'going to bed' a romantic rather than a boring idea. The pale-blue cotton bedspreads, easily washed, tone in with the deeper blue, durable carpet

Courtesy of Chippendale's Workshops, Ltd.

A delightful idea for a nursery for two little girls, with the sprigged rosebud coverlets and wallpaper to match. A recess has been created by building out two cupboards and an overhead piece papered to match the walls

derived from Austria or Switzerland.

A large waste-paper basket should be part of every nursery. One of the little brightly coloured 'binettes' for rubbish, with a foot pedal to lift the lid, makes it enticing for the youngster to use. Keeping a few pot-plants or a window-box teaches them to water the flowers and take off dead leaves, also to inculcate a slight idea of seasons for plants. The child usually loves something of his own to take care of.

Nursery furniture is delightful with its small wardrobes, coloured clothes-hangers—sometimes adorned with individual names, little beds with side-arms at the top to prevent bumps in the night, and dressing-tables upon which one or two toilet accessories can be put 'just like Mummy.'

Other Features

Lights should be placed to shed light *down* on any work the child is doing, whether it is needlework or painting. Little dressers for the children's own china (a trifle more solid than used downstairs) are another feature of modern nursery furnishing, or a dining-table with loose leaves—later on the child can take charge of inviting someone to a meal and at least having the illusion of 'doing it all myself.'

There are chests of drawers with letters of the alphabet on; counterpanes, with the alphabet and fairy-story characters, that can also be used for curtains. Everything that can be kept washable in the nursery should be: washable rugs, lino or rubber-tiled floors. Cretonnes and cottons or ginghams make pretty curtains, but plastic that can be wiped over, too, is another hygienic choice, although not suitable unless there is a blind, since too much light may be let in at night, causing wakefulness and too early playing about in the morning.

Opposite: This built-in furniture was planned to last the children through the early days, adolescence, and, with a few minor adjustments, into adulthood

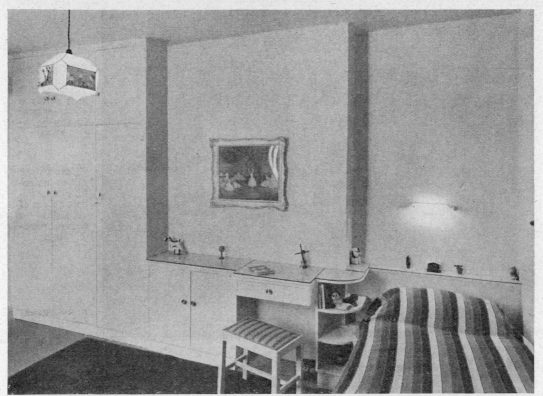

Courtesy of Chippendale's Workshops, Ltd.

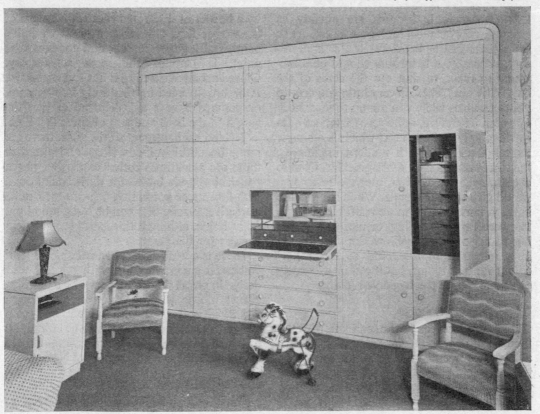

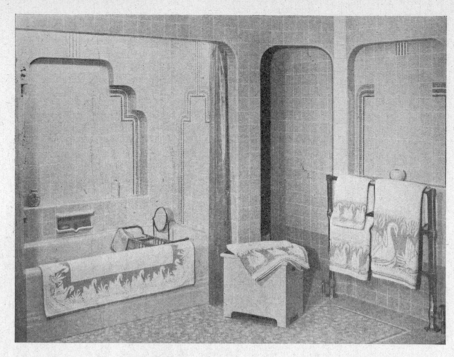

Matched hand towels, bath-sheets and bath mat unify a colour-scheme in the bath-room

These swans sailing peace-fully along im-part an air of serenity to their surround-ings

Barlow & Jones, Ltd.

YOUR BATHROOM

SO many people, unless they live in luxury flats where bathrooms are already as elegant as they can be, look on a bathroom as somewhere just to bath! While this is necessary, naturally, a bathroom should be somewhere to relax, to shut out the cares of the day. Why not? There is very little you can do about troubles while you are up to your neck in water. Therefore, quite apart from an adequate supply of hot water, which is a simple matter these days with modern appliances, the surroundings should be agreeable. Choose a colour-scheme with as much care as you would give to your lounge. While lying in the bath, you may find it more restful to gaze up at a cerulean-blue ceiling, or more invigorating to regard a sun-yellow one. White has long remained in the mind as the 'right' colour for bathrooms, but it can be extremely cold, and a little too hygienic-looking.

Tiles are most Suitable

It is not everyone who can afford tiles, though, of course, they are always most suitable for floor and walls in a steamy atmosphere. Even a half-tiled bathroom is a help to the housewife who does all her own cleaning. There are plain tiles in many lovely pastel shades, which can be broken at dado height by a border of decorated tiles with designs of flowers or fish. Otherwise a good washable paint, hard gloss, or an anti-condensation paint, is perhaps the most satisfactory. Glazed asbestos sheeting is not too expensive. A bathroom need be tiled only half-way up, or perhaps have a splash panel of tiles the length of the bath and two or three feet high.

To lend enchantment to the view, there are many beautiful wall-coverings, and although these are sometimes rather expensive, just a panel above the bath of a dark background with flowers or swimming fish can look quite attractive. Plastic tiles can be bought and put on at home, although this is not too simple a process for the amateur.

There is a wide variety of washable papers: embossed papers in white with raised flower design in pastel shades; papers with a marbled effect; plastic papers with raised patterns; varnished wallpapers with a linen finish, or a design in several tones of the same colour, all of which have artistic attractiveness, and are far from ordinary, without being bizarre.

Old-fashioned into Modern

Those who have rather old-fashioned or

IDEAS
for
BRIGHTNESS

Carry a gaily striped pelmet as a frieze right around the walls of your bathroom. Fix mirrors to the linen-cupboard doors. Paper the area around the bath with a varnished paper in midnight blue. Hang plastic shower-curtains beside the bath

Right: The hall is the first impression we have of anyone's home. Make it welcoming. The tops of the stair-treads have been painted blue; the balusters in a harmonising shade

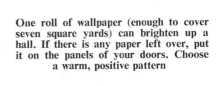

One roll of wallpaper (enough to cover seven square yards) can brighten up a hall. If there is any paper left over, put it on the panels of your doors. Choose a warm, positive pattern

The chimney-breast in this room has been papered with a deep golden-yellow wallpaper, which enlivens the whole room and costs under £1. The pale blue ceiling is softer than a hard white. Paste coloured prints directly on to the wall, and paint simple frames around them. Give the prints two coats of clear varnish

TRANSFORMATION SCENE

This delightful and happy bedroom was once a cold and dreary attic. Anyone can modernise a similar room in the same way. A false wall of cheap plaster-board was built about 4 ft. out from the sloping roof and two small whitewood chests built into this wall. Two more cupboards were built *out* from the sides of the window. A strong, warm coral was chosen for coverings to offset any coldness of the blue carpet and walls

Other notes to observe: the two-in-one bedheads were bought quite cheaply and matched up with the chair. The attractive valance on the bed was made for hygiene's sake from white plastic material. A gathered valance softens the line of the alcove

Curtains would have darkened the room, so a plastic Venetian blind was installed, with another valance along the top of the window recess. Finger-plates, enamelled sky-blue were used to break up the white areas of the cupboards. The dressing-table came from a second-hand shop, and was rejuvenated with white paint; the stool is a cut-down kitchen chair. The twin lights are old oil lamps adapted for electricity and painted blue. White flowers were stencilled with lino paint between strips of carpet. An easy-to-do and very pretty idea!

By Courtesy of Froy

The chromium-plated towel ring, rather like a door-knocker, is ideal to keep each person's towel completely separate. They are simply screwed to the wall. Children especially can be persuaded to use their own ring

inadequate bathrooms can use a little ingenuity to bring them up to date and modern taste. An old-fashioned bath can be fenced in with a panel of wood, painted to match the colour-scheme, or a panel of laminated plastic. Marbled compositions can be used but are a little more expensive. Gay plastic curtains can be hung beside the bath. Bathmats are an important part of the bathroom equipment. There are cotton-twist rugs which are both gay and washable, soft to the feet. It is also a happy idea to have bath-towels, mat and face-flannels to match.

While large baths look luxurious, there is no doubt that a smaller bath for the not-so-tall is more comfortable, when the feet can be braced against the bottom while reclining. It is an accepted rule, but unnecessary myth, that the bigger the bath, the better. Rubber mats, of course, can be used in the bottom of the bath to prevent slipping, but they are not always very satisfactory. Chromium-plated handgrips to pull oneself out of the bath are

also a guard against slipping, which can be quite dangerous to the elderly or unwell.

Perhaps the first essential for comfort is a warm bathroom. There are those who would prefer a lukewarm bath in a warm bathroom, and others who would choose a very hot bath in a chilly room, but assuming the hot-water supply is adequate, let us discuss heating. There have been too many accidents with electric fires. An electric heater placed very high on the wall is satisfactory, so of course, are various types of radiator, whether heated by water or oil. Even a heated two-bar towel rail takes the chill from the air. There are also heated floors for the luxury-loving.

Heating the Water

There are many types of water-heater from the electric thermostatic immersion heater, which, when the water reaches a certain degree of heat, automatically shuts off the current, and switches on again without attention when the water becomes less warm, to the modern-

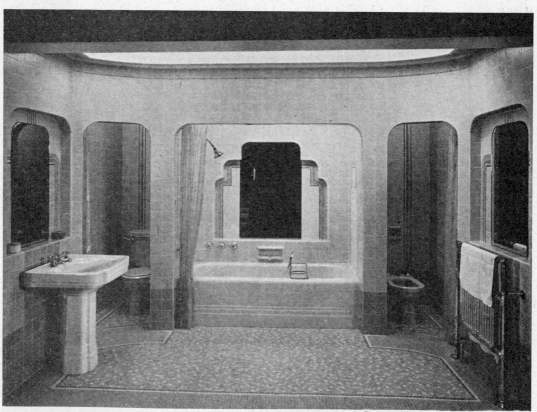

Courtesy of Ideal Boilers & Radiators, Ltd.

A dream bathroom which has everything, including a heated floor. More ordinary bathrooms can be modelled on this, with its lovely pastel colours—hyacinth-mauve and pale yellow—practical appliances, tiled floor and a pretty plastic curtain

More improvements invade the modern bath. No more slipping and sliding with the convenient hand-grip at the side. The built-in thermometer in the inlet nozzle ensures a comfortable temperature being obtained at a glance; this is especially useful where there are children

By courtesy of Froy

ised form of the kitchen boiler. The electric thermostatic heater needs lagging to conserve the heat and reduce bills. There are gas-heaters which, when the pilot-light is left on (using practically no gas), give very hot water within fifteen seconds of turning on the tap. There are other geysers, also immersion heaters, many combinations of types, which can be run in conjunction with coal fires or on their own. The best thing is to make all enquiries of suppliers of electricity, gas appliances and boiler companies before choosing what seems to meet the individual case most happily. It is usually much more convenient to link up all water used in the house, but there are exceptions to every rule and, luckily, modern appliances can be found to suit both rules and exceptions.

Cheerful Touch

Flooring contributes to the general comfort, cork or cork tiles or rubber being warmer to the touch than linoleum. There are thermoplastic tiles, which come in many varieties of colour, and should last the life of a house. They should be laid by an expert, whether an expert in the home or a professional. It is not a job for a real amateur. These tiles are usually 9 in. by 9 in. by $\frac{1}{8}$ in. thick. Linoleum provides, with the varied marbled or large check designs available, some attractive floor-coverings.

Materials such as chintz, cretonne, gingham can be used with great effect in the bathroom, but they do tend to become limp-looking with the steamy heat, and, undoubtedly, plastic curtains are much more suitable. The plastic materials are made in a variety of the most charming designs, birds, fish, flowers, stars or plain pastel and vivid colours, so there should be no difficulty in finding one to suit almost any taste. Turkish towelling in a gay colour with contrasting edges can be used, too, and is easily laundered. There are baths with toe-space at the bottom; with built-in thermometer which saves testing with the elbow for children, and misjudging the heat with the hand for adults.

Such accessories as a tray for resting across the bath, and a cork-seated stool (or small dirty-linen container with cork-seated top) are a 'must.' The tray is not only for holding soap, face-flannel, nail-brush and loofah, but will also be there to take a magazine or a cup of tea for those who really enjoy their bath-time. Also cosmetics for the beauty-conscious.

Cupboards are more useful than shelves for holding toilet requisites, as otherwise it means an extra job of dusting each article every day. The cupboard, however, should always be placed where its corners will not give nasty knocks to shoulders or head. A mirror is an essential in a bathroom. It should be placed in a good light and at a height to suit each member of the family. If their heights are very varied, then a long mirror may do, or if not, more than one mirror will make for everyone's comfort. Monogrammed towels are liked by some people and are certainly very smart.

Courtesy of English Electric Co.

An ordinary kitchen which has been converted into an ideal room. The old-fashioned sink was replaced with one of more modern design; wall spaces, both ugly and wasteful, were filled with cupboards, giving extra table room as well. A new electric cooker with bottom storage drawer; refrigerator instead of a larder, a food mixer to help save work—all these can be added very gradually to a home in which economy has to be practised

Let it be a Happy Workroom

YOUR KITCHEN

IT is usual to look upon a kitchen either as a workroom to do a rather boring job in (bending over a hot stove and, ugh! washing-up) or else as a kitchen-dining-room where meals are eaten as hastily as possible, so that it can all be 'got out of the way.'

But the newest fitments for kitchens make them almost into games-rooms. They are exciting, labour-saving, interesting. The only trouble at present is that most of them are a drain on the pocket. However, many women who look on domestic life as a job to be performed with as much intelligence as any other job save to buy one thing at a time.

The main thing is one's attitude to the kitchen. If it is made to look gay to begin with, that is half the battle. Sitting down to have a mid-morning cup of coffee in a room with primrose walls, fresh green plastic curtains, pale yellow ceiling and touches of cardinal red here and there, is quite different from snatching a hasty cup of tea in a cluttered, unattractive room with no curtains (because it's only the kitchen), a dreary-looking stove, and a pile of washing-up to be done.

Colour Brings Cheer

An old-fashioned kitchen that has no very modern gleaming fitments can have brightly coloured pots and pans, perhaps a floor of large red and white tiles (modern plastic) or a similarly patterned linoleum. A dresser can be picked up very cheaply in an old market, and painted jade-green and white, with some scarlet-patterned peasant pottery to make a brave show placed on it. And why shouldn't there be a window-box (with some useful herbs, perhaps) outside the kitchen window as well as in the bright, front lounge? After all, if it is a workroom, it may as well be a pleasure to be there.

There are so many movements in getting a meal that everything should be placed to be at hand with the minimum of movement. There are some wonderful ideas for dividing kitchens by various means from a little dining-corner or portion of the room. Even just a couple of screens can shut off the working part of the room. Or a kind of trellis can be built quite cheaply with the cheapest wood and ivy trained over it. Two or three chests of drawers can be put side by side, and a frame-like structure fixed over them with a Venetian blind fitted to it. This can be pulled down to shut off the kitchen, or left up when the tops of the chests of drawers

Astral Equipment, Ltd.

This all-silent gas refrigerator will hold the average family needs for storing perishable foods. It can be installed handily on the wall, or mounted on a stand

Thomas de la Rue & Co., Ltd.

All the working surfaces are practically and hygienically covered with Scarlet Softglow laminated plastic. This can be bought to size and fixed by the handyman at home

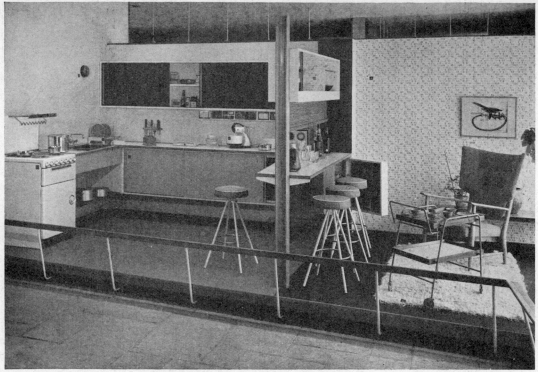

Council of Industrial Design

The breakfast-bar kitchen is growing in popularity, and has become 'smart' rather than just convenient. In America, dining recesses are mostly in view of the kitchen equipment. Here it is a separate compartment, which makes for more relaxation

(covered in laminated plastic) are needed as a shelf for dishes being passed from the kitchen side. The blinds can be white, green or painted in different shades.

'A place for everything and everything in its place' may have been a copybook maxim that we never thought about, because familiarity dulled its sense, but the new fitments do conserve energy, because everything is to hand. There is no wild hunt around at the last moment, while something boils over, for a mislaid article.

Kitchen walls should be treated in much the same way as bathroom walls, by the use of tiles to dado height, or at least a gloss paint or enamel that can be wiped over quite easily. Plastic sheeting can also be used. Nevertheless, good ventilation is the best preventive against condensation. An electric fan is a help towards cooling and dispersing smells. Lights must be well placed to allow the utmost illumination for the job in hand.

Choosing Kitchen Units

If there is room, a bunk can be installed in one corner of the kitchen where the tired housewife can recharge herself by relaxing full length for a few minutes, or even reclining with the evening paper while her husband (if he likes cooking, and many men are better cooks than their wives) decides to be chef for a change!

When choosing kitchen units, it is a good idea to consult one of the manufacturers (who may have a kitchen-planning expert) on the best and most economical way to lay out money for installing or modernising individual kitchen equipment. You can gradually convert your own by replacing your sink unit with a more modern design; filling in wall spaces with cupboards, which give extra table room as well.

Then add labour-saving 'gadgets' as and when it is possible. A refrigerator is a 'must' if it can be afforded—and prices are dropping, not soaring! There are many different types on the market. A wall refrigerator that is easy to reach for the small family. Very large refrigerators that can store enough for a large household. Here are some notes that will help you in its use.

Refrigerators aid home economy in preventing waste, and are a source of pleasure in providing dishes that are 'different,' drinks that are icy cold, and salads really crisp.

If all foods, especially those with a pronounced odour, such as cheese, fish, bacon, etc., are wrapped and stored in their indicated place, they will keep longer in good condition, and taste better when consumed, than if just pushed in where they will fit. Perspex or glass boxes, plastic bags, transparent wrappings, greaseproof paper are all useful for enclosing foodstuffs.

Using Your Refrigerator

If you have a large modern refrigerator you will have indicated compartments for storage of meat, salads and fish. Otherwise, wrap your foodstuffs as advised above. The newest refrigerators have transparent fish-, meat- or poultry-keepers; humidrawers to keep fruit and vegetables; extra-high bottle storage, a lack with the old ones; new

defrosting methods and ice-cubes loosened by a patent snap release.

Milk and other liquids have a place near the super-freezer either at one side or on both sides, which means you can also chill your soft drinks or beer.

Meat, bought frozen, will keep a week or longer if kept in the super-freezer, or at one side for a little less time. Minced meat and offal will not keep much longer than 24 hours without deteriorating.

The plate-rack, with a door to prevent dust settling, is handy to the sink. There is a removable tray underneath to catch excess water

The drop-down ironing board is concealed in the door of the broom cupboard. One cupboard on right contains three wire containers for vegetables. Red and white rubber floor covering

Froy Planned Kitchens

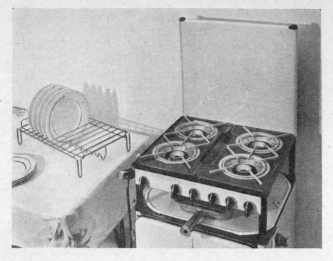

Left: A special feature of this gas cooker is the plate rack, which has a handle each side, enabling it to be removed from the top of the cooker to the table and used as a plate-rack for drying

Below: No more backaches with this visual grill; the meal that is cooking can be viewed from any part of the kitchen. The oven is also raised, preventing undue stooping. The drop door of the oven forms a convenient rest when removing dishes

Master Gas Cookers, Ltd.

Put ordinary joints and poultry on floor of refrigerator.

Poultry, if freshly dressed, will keep, properly wrapped and clean, two to four days, though it is preferable to cook it after two days, depending on the known time that has elapsed since the bird was killed.

Bacon, if kept longer than a week, is apt to get hard and develop mould unless first wrapped in vinegar-moistened muslin before covering as advised.

All left-over cooked food should be kept in a covered dish, or wrapping, bearing in mind that food thus stored has a time-limit of 48 hours or so for good keeping. Deterioration will set in if the food is left out of the refrigerator for an unnecessary space of time. (This applies to both raw and cooked food after it has been thawed out.)

Fish.—For best enjoyment, cook fresh fish within 24 hours of purchase, though it will keep fresh, if well stored, another 24 hours.

Eggs.—Fresh eggs will keep well for several weeks in your refrigerator. For boiling, put into cold water, otherwise, they'll crack if used straight from the refrigerator.

Cheese.—A wedge of cheese is apt to get dry if stored for any length of time in a refrigerator, but will keep better if wrapped first in muslin wrung out in vinegar and water, then in double greaseproof paper.

It is better not to refrigerate cream cheese unless necessary, but to buy in small quantities and consume.

Frozen Vegetables and Fruit.—These store excellently for several days if put into the super-freezer as soon as possible after purchase. Vegetables deteriorate first.

Fresh Fruit and Vegetables.—It is sometimes an advantage to prepare these a day or so

Courtesy of the Gas Council

before required. Wipe and wrap carefully as advised, or put into covered dish. Time limit for keeping is 48 hours.

A dish-washing machine is a great help, too, although less necessary for the small family. Dishes can be accumulated in the machine instead of cluttering up a sink, and an ordinary size can hold a dinner service complete with cutlery and glass for six people. It occupies two minutes' washing time, a minute rinse and then dry, and works out at about one penny a day to run. The initial cost is still high, and its purchase depends on how badly a dish-washing machine is wanted!

There is also a compact unit to be obtained which takes all kitchen waste, such as bones, rinds, scraps, etc., shreds them to tiny pieces and flushes them down the drain.

English Electric Co.

A washing-machine is useful in the modern kitchen. The wringer is power-driven and can be used so that soapy water drains back into the tub to be used again

Metal or Wood

One has to decide whether kitchen units are to be in wood or metal, as both materials have their advantages and disadvantages.

WOOD is, of course, more adaptable, especially when the modernisation of an existing kitchen takes place in an older type house, when it may be found that the floor is uneven or the walls are out of true. It is in such cases that wood, as a material, has a far greater flexibility; also, when it is necessary to design a special unit to suit individual requirements, wood is the most obvious choice and most suitable material. Noise is practically eliminated when opening and closing the doors of wooden fitments. Repainting units made from wood is also easier.

*   *   *

The use of METAL for kitchen equipment is a comparatively new development, but today there is a wide selection from which to choose. The incorporation of steel in the construction of the metal kitchen makes more attractive and original design possible, also metal takes a higher gloss than wood and results in a more decorative finish.

Although metal units have a tendency to make a slight metallic sound when doors are closed, on the best makes this has been eliminated by careful damping and the use of rubber lining. The range of metal units is wider than that of wood, with each manufacturer introducing their own labour-saving ideas. One particular firm even make special-size metal units to suit individual requirements and measurements.

Shoe Rack

It is useful to have a shoe rack in the kitchen, as there are all the shoes ready to clean and put on in the morning. (Although, remember that shoes wear longer if pairs are worn alternately.) The man who makes a hobby of woodwork will not need telling how to make one. Even the amateur, however, can make an adequate shoe rack by taking two pieces of wood, one for each end, 30 in. by 8 in., and six pieces of $\frac{1}{2}$-in. dowelling 18 in. long. Cut the base of each side piece of wood in an arc, so that it stands more firmly. Glue and screw the dowelling into position . . . one piece near the front and higher, another piece of dowelling towards the back, so that it forms a rest for toes and heels of the shoes. The six pieces in position allow for three rows of shoes.

Keeping the Door Open

This is a useful gadget: when going to and fro setting a meal, or if listening for a sleeping child, you may need to keep a door ajar without its banging in every breeze. A good way of doing this is to make a sausage buffer. Cut a strip of woollen material measuring 12 by 8 in. Join into a tube, gather up one end tightly, and stuff loosely with bran or tightly with cut-up rags. Close the other end by gathering, and to each end sew loops of cord or ribbon which will slip over the handles, one on each side of the door, thus holding it ajar but stopping any swinging or banging.

COMBINING OLD *and* NEW

IF a husband and wife have differing tastes, with one loving antiques and the other having a passion for everything that is up-to-date, there is no need for one to give in completely to the other. With a little care, old and new furniture can be combined with charm and grace. Keep the best of the old and incorporate it with the new. The points to bear in mind when mixing different periods of furniture are few, but they *are* most important.

First and foremost, there should be a natural 'affinity' between the pieces used. In other words, they should go together pleasantly.

For instance, you may see an attractive old carved Jacobean chair. This looks perfect teamed with a modern Swedish dresser; they spring from the same roots—whether those roots grew in 1660 or 1954. They have the same woody, country look. On the other hand, you would *not* use a fine, highly-polished Regency table with early Tudor oak chairs, or a delicate chest in satinwood with certain types of contemporary furniture in spindly metal with canvas seats. This sort of mixing is best left to professional decorators who thrive on unusual experiments and can change a room when the whim has passed.

Secondly, study the contours of the furniture. You can contrast these or harmonise them. This is a perfect matching of shapes and there is a strong affinity between the things chosen.

Thirdly, study the colour values of the wood. Old oak is invariably dark through

Room arranged by Minty of Oxford

Harmony is the keynote of this room, combining both old and modern furniture. The settee, chair, mahogany sofa table, and mahogany bookcases are modern. Yet they have an affinity with the Sheraton (late-18th-century) mahogany sideboard, having the long, straight legs reminiscent of contemporary sideboards. There is the old grospoint needlework firescreen, an Indian carpet, and the curtains are of cotton damask. The colour scheme is deep blue, autumn red and nutria, with touches of gold

Council of Industrial Design

Another nteresting arrangement. The 18th-century mahogany tallboy is a surprisingly good neighbour to the modernistic beech and mahogany trolley, contemporary easy-chair and bookcase. The wallpaper is blue and chair-covering gold, the curtains combining both colours

centuries of usage and handling. Use this mellow darkness to throw up the light fresh effect of contemporary furniture—the pale woods such as birch, sycamore, from which it is made. Keep together the finer woods, which have acquired a rich, lovely patina from years of polishing.

They Must Tune in to Each Other

This point really re-emphasises the importance of the feeling of 'affinity' which should exist between the old and the new.

The Elizabethan 'Age of Oak' was the first recognised era of English furniture. Much of it was clumsy, but it has a simple, sturdy charm. There is plenty of this period to be had, and because it has never been in great demand, the prices are reasonable.

Jacobean furniture was more ornate—and their handsome carved chairs are a good buy. They look very fine in light modern settings with richly-coloured contemporary fabrics, which often derive their inspiration from a bygone period.

William and Mary furniture is expensive and rare, and the Queen Anne era which ushered in the 'Age of Walnut' is considered to be the finest England has ever made.

Use contemporary wing armchairs with this period. These have the same graceful curved lines of the wing armchair of the Queen Anne period, and the same comfort.

Georgian and Regency furniture, though not usually cheap, can be picked up with diligent hunting. A modern setting can—and does—improve even on its elegance.

Remember, this furniture was new and daring in its day, and its *good* design is the reason why we treasure it now, and why we team it successfully and very decoratively with furniture produced today. But the contemporary setting must be chosen with care, taste and imagination.

Courtesy of Chippendale's Workshops, Ltd.

Roughcast walls always look well with dark furniture. This was a narrow hallway without character, except for the two attractive windows. The two dark cabinets either side of the fireplace, following the line of the wall, and the well-placed mirror give a spacious and impressive effect

BACKGROUND *for* FURNITURE

Plain walls or one of the beautiful new wallpapers?

On Choosing Wallpapers

ALTHOUGH there has been a period when a great number of home makers adopted plain walls as a standard 'uniform' for their rooms, wallpapers have subtly changed their character, and make an appeal to the artistic sense that cannot be denied. Also, the vogue of putting just a panel of wallpaper as a background for some particularly attractive furnishing feature, or to vary the layout of the room, lends itself to the use of a bolder-patterned paper than one would care to have covering all four walls.

Naturally, care has to be taken for, if patterned curtains or carpets are used, you may have them 'quarrelling' with one another, and losing all the charming effect which they would have when contrasted with plain or striped materials.

Soothing Effects

The character of the room naturally has to be taken into consideration. A very pale, satin-striped paper makes an excellent foil for brocades and heavy silken materials. A medium-size flower motif, especially as a panel, provides a good background for old, dark, rather heavy pieces of furniture. Light dots, delicate formal sprigged patterns, are happy with almost any kind of furniture except the aggressively modern. New Tudor patterns stemming from old designs mate attractively with period furniture. Some Regency wallpapers go excellently with contemporary furniture of a light, graceful type.

Your sitting-room, being the room in which you spend most of your time, needs great care in the choice of a paper. If it is too heavily 'spotty' in its design, it may be found extremely irritating, and when seeing only small samples of a paper, this should be taken into account.

Dark or Light

When choosing paper for the hall, its size must of course be considered, for a dark paper in a dark hall, or a large pattern in a small space, is going to emphasise the negative aspects. If the ceiling is extremely high, a wallpaper with a pattern running horizontally will tend to lower the effect, so also will a picture rail set fairly low down from the ceiling. The white or colour of the ceiling will then be carried down to the rail. In fact, any-

thing that cuts the line will shorten the apparent height. With a low ceiling, of course, the reverse holds good. A paper with vertical stripes or pattern will give a more lofty effect, and there should be no picture-rail.

Contrast of Tone

A modern geometrical paper is not very suitable for a hall, since it confuses the eye. Effect is the thing to aim at. A bowl of flowers against a cream wall; an antique chair or colourful modern one set against a panel of plain wall with the rest papered in design; or a panel of wallpaper with the rest of the walls plain, and a carefully chosen picture or two.

There are so many extremely beautiful patterns these days that, however prejudiced you may be in the matter of plain walls, it is as well to look at some samples before deciding which you will have, and just how to utilise them in the most attractive manner.

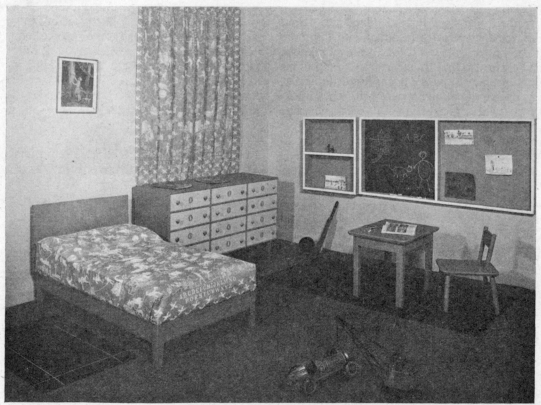

Vantona, Ltd.

It is never too early to learn. The kindergarten counterpane is used also for curtains, and the many-drawered chest repeats the same ABC motif. Putting up a blackboard to draw and scribble on should ensure that the young artist does not decorate the walls, since he has no need to. Floor coverings should be washable for hygiene

Brass decoration on the library door of a house designed by the Adam brothers about 1775. The two lions' masks are linked to the handle by festoons of husks, and the keyhole is protected by a drop escutcheon (centre) on which is embossed a double profile

HOW TO CHOOSE

ANTIQUE FURNITURE

THE study of antique furniture is a subject that grows in fascination. It is exciting gradually to learn how to 'place' the period of various pieces of furniture, and the more one knows, the more one wants to know. There is also the attractive idea that a genuine antique may be picked up for very little money, as does quite often happen. A Regency bookcase which, mended and polished, became worth five times as much as the £20 paid for it in a little seaside antique shop. Six Cromwellian chairs which fetched only 10s. each at an auction sale. A Queen Anne dressing-table made of yew wood, with its original handles, bought for 50s. in a London street and now in a museum. A fine piece of Stuart embroidery, nailed to the top of an ottoman, which went for 5s.; a William and Mary bureau, disguised under a thick coating of black varnish, which cost only £7 10s., and is now worth at least £50. The embroidery is now in a private collection.

Experience Plus Flair

Naturally, it takes a lifetime of experience —although some people undoubtedly have a

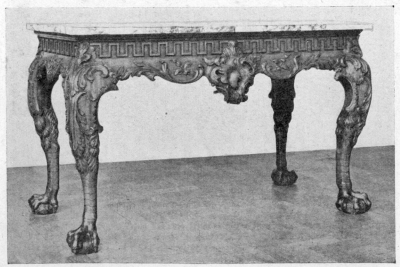

This sturdy but elegant side-table is of elaborately carved walnut, with a marble top, date about 1740. The ball-and-claw legs were much used by artist-craftsmen of this period

flair as well—to recognise the genuine article from a good reproduction, but nevertheless, for those with knowledge and a keen eye (and a sense of adventure), Regency and early Victorian pieces especially can still be found at prices that, a few years hence, will seem ridiculously low.

The basic knowledge which enables the style of a typical period piece to be identified can be acquired quite easily. Most of this basic knowledge is set out in visible form on the chart on pages 74 and 75. It is not exact, for changes in fashions are never sudden or complete, as one period slightly overlaps the next. When referring to the chart, it must be remembered that many genuine old examples have been altered, or had their handles changed, more than once during their history, to make them more fashionable. In antique furniture, as in everything else, there are exceptions to every rule.

Elizabethan and Stuart Periods

In the time of Queen Elizabeth I furniture was made of oak, by carpenters. It was rough and heavy, with thick panels, fat turned legs and iron locks, hinges and handles. The panels were often decorated with carving, such as linenfold, which was cut out of the solid structural parts but never added afterwards. Sometimes the panels were inlaid with holly, black bog oak, box, yew and other woods in geometrical or formalised floral patterns. Rails between the panels were enriched with simple repetitive carvings composed of flutes, or interlocking circles or semi-circles. Columns, such as bedposts, were ornamented with great bulbous turnings, deeply carved.

During the Stuart period furniture was still mostly of oak, but it was more accurately made, by joiners, and put together with proper mortises and tenons. Turning was popular, and the spiral twist was introduced. Panels were emphasised by applied mouldings arranged in geometrical patterns, and decorated with half-turnings and other shapes, which were glued on. A form of flat surface carving known as strapwork was much used. Handles were still of iron.

Refugees Bring New Fashions

At the Restoration of the monarchy in 1660 the Court, returning from exile in France and Holland, brought with them many continental ideas. These were put into practice by refugee French Huguenot craftsmen, many of whom were specialists in veneering. It was found that English walnut, which up to this time had been little used for furniture, was excellent for veneering, since its grain showed up attractively when sliced at an angle to the direction of growth. The thin slices were glued on to a carcase of oak or some other reliable wood. This innovation altered the whole character of furniture. Cupboard doors and drawer fronts were made flush, instead of with recessed panels, since this suited the veneering process better and showed off the high polish possible with walnut. Sometimes veneers were cut from burrs or from small branches of certain trees and grouped together to form a sur-

Council of Industrial Design

This early-17th-century oak chair is known as the Yorkshire type, since it is particular to that part of England. The decoration is different from chairs of the South, having a rather Scandinavian feeling. The chair is recessed to take a squab cushion

face pattern; or different woods were pieced together to make decorative panels, a process known as marquetry, which had for some time been popular in Holland. A little later lacquer was all the rage.

Among other introductions in this period were woven cane, for chair backs and seats, screws instead of wooden dowels, and brass for handles and hinges. A favourite decorative motif, used in carving and metal work, was a crown, often supported by a pair of cupids, an expression of the people's loyalty to the restored monarchy.

When William of Orange became King in 1689 he brought with him more Dutch ideas and craftsmen. Furniture became extremely ornate and richly carved. The splat-backed chair and the cabriole leg made their first appearance.

More Severity

During the reign of Queen Anne there was a reaction against excessive ornament. Chair splats, brass handles, escutcheons and the frames of mirrors all had decorative silhouettes but perfectly plain unpierced surfaces. There was little turning or carving, but the shell motif began to appear on the knee of cabriole chair legs.

Victoria and Albert Museum. Crown Copyright

Above: Oaken spinning-wheels are known to all of us, but it is a more effective ornament to manage to find one so completely different as this. It is in mahogany banded with satinwood, by John Plants, c. 1790

Left: This massive and beautifully carved chest dates about 1653. Such furniture was, happily, built to endure, so that it comes down to us without much deterioration. It is of oak, chestnut and ebony, inlaid with ivory and mother of pearl

Victoria and Albert Museum. Crown Copyright

Modern furniture with its clean lines is reminiscent of the simplicity of ancient Greece, and has a chaste beauty of its own. Several tones of one colour are sometimes favoured instead of bright contrasts, and can be used sometimes with more effect than a decided contrast

A Jacobean room usually has an atmosphere of warmth, comfort and durability. It is as well to choose the lightest room you have for this style, as panelling is apt to darken the room. However, light roughcast walls also provide a good background for the heavy oak furniture

ANTIQUE FURNITURE

PERIODS	TUDOR	STUART		RESTORATION	
STYLE	ELIZABETHAN 1558–1603	JACOBEAN 1603–1649	CROMWELLIAN 1649–1660	CAROLEAN 1660–1689	WILLIAM & MARY 1689–1702
WOODS	O A K			W A L N U T	
	1570 1580 1590	1600 1610 1620	1630 1640 1650	1660 1670 1680	1690 1700

CHAIR LEGS

CHAIR BACKS

CARVING & ORNAMENT

METAL-WORK

RECOGNITION CHART

Q. ANNE	GEORGIAN						VICTORIAN	
QUEEN ANNE	EARLY GEORGIAN	CHIPPEN-DALE	ADAM	HEPPLE-WHITE	SHERATON	FRENCH EMPIRE	REGENCY	EARLY VICTORIAN
1702–1714	1714–1745	1745–1780	1758–1792	1760–1790	1790–1810	1793–1830	1810–1837	1837–1850

WALNUT   MAHOGANY   (SATINWOOD)

1700 1710 1720 1730 1740 1750 1760 1770 1780 1790 1800 1810 1820 1830 1840 1850

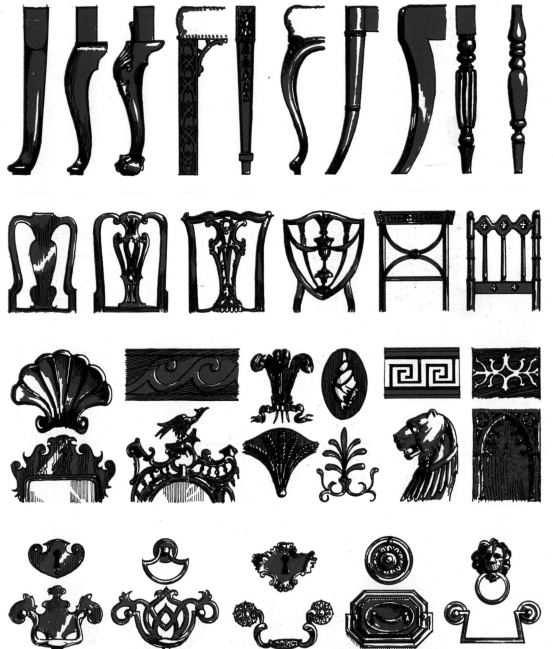

H. DALTON CLIFFORD

This beautiful Regency room has striped chair fabrics and draped curtains which are entirely in keeping with its own period

The next important influence was the introduction of mahogany from the West Indies (known as Spanish mahogany). This strong, easily worked wood, obtainable in huge planks and capable of taking a high polish, soon surpassed walnut in popularity. At first the new furniture was massive, with large undecorated panels and architectural cornices enriched with carved mouldings borrowed from classical architecture, and with friezes of Greek key pattern or scroll. Chair backs were pierced and heavily carved and the cabriole legs often terminated in claw feet. William Kent, 1684 to 1748, an architect, was a leader of this fashion.

Gradually, as a result of French influence, furniture became lighter and more delicately carved, and then in 1754 Thomas Chippendale published the first of his books of designs. He popularised the straight leg, moulded along its length and supported by stretchers, and adapted Chinese motifs, then popular, to furniture design, his asymmetrical Chinese-rococo mirror frames being the final expression of this phase. He also borrowed from Holland and France, and even used Gothic decoration on some of his pieces.

Enter Adam and Hepplewhite

Then Robert Adam, returning from travels in Italy in 1758, set up as an architect and furniture designer and evolved the style with which his name is associated. It was applied not only to furniture and fireplaces, but to architecture, metalwork and pottery, and characterised by great delicacy and refinement. He used decorations of Graeco-Roman motifs—urns, swags, pendent husks, lyres and skulls.

Although Hepplewhite's guide, published in 1788, claims really only to be a record of the latest fashions in furniture, most of the pieces illustrated in it, particularly the shield-back chairs, are now labelled with his name. His pieces are slender and graceful, with carved decorations, of which the Prince of Wales' Feathers and the wheat-ear are the most typical. There is no hard and fast rule by which Hepplewhite designs can be recognised, but whereas in all Chippendale chairs the back splat was housed into the back-rail of the seat, in Hepplewhite chairs the back is usually (but not always) held by the two side pieces and does not connect into the back-rail. Most Hepplewhite furniture is in mahogany.

Strength and Apparent Fragility

Thomas Sheraton, who published his Drawing Book in 1791, used many of Hepplewhite's shapes but made them still lighter, strength being sacrificed for daintiness. Most of his chairs were intended not for everyday wear and tear, but for occasional use in bedroom and drawing-room; yet so carefully were they constructed that many have lasted intact until today. There is no sure way of distinguishing Sheraton from Hepplewhite, but he often used satinwood, sometimes painted, or inlaid with marquetry shell and fan motifs.

The Sheraton style merged into the Regency which, although historically dating from 1810 to 1820, is usually applied to the period 1800 to 1830, corresponding roughly to the French Empire period. Archaeological discoveries in Greece, Rome and Egypt had their effect on the decoration of this time.

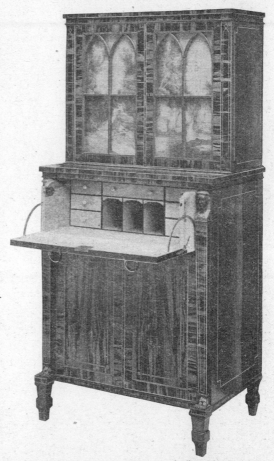

Victoria and Albert Museum.
Crown Copyright

A secretaire both elegant and beautiful, veneered with zebra wood and mounted in ormolu, c. 1810

A WORD ON CARPETS

IF we consider the most comfortable homes we know and then subtract the carpets, it becomes quite clear that the warmth, the welcome, the very essence of that characteristic we describe as 'homelike,' lies a good deal in the right choice of floor covering.

Wilton and Axminster wear equally well if of comparable quality and price. Have which you prefer. The difference is, of course, in the weave, each tuft in an Axminster being individually knotted; while in a Wilton the pile is looped over wires and then mounted on a strong fabric composed of jute, cotton and linen, the wires having been withdrawn, cutting the pile in the process. With these carpets, the more tufts or points to the square inch the longer their lives.

Then there are the Oriental carpets: Persian, with their floral designs; the geometrically figured Turkish carpets; and the fanciful Chinese rugs, patterned with flowers and dragons, and other mythical creatures. They are all hard wearing and the colours are very fast. Indian carpets are good and moderately priced, and purchasers can protect themselves if they buy from those which carry the label of the Associated Indian Carpet Traders.

Carpets of this type are more usually combined with antique furniture, but when no particular attention is being paid to 'period,' but only to charm, a plain and fairly light carpet does act as an effective foil for dark and gleaming old oak or mahogany.

The pros and cons of tailored carpets and squares are sometimes more difficult to weigh up. A room with its floor-covering fitted looks more restful and roomy; there are no fussy borders to complicate the picture, no edges to curl up, no border to polish. But a square can be moved round to distribute wear and tear. The deciding factor is the one applied to the patterned-or-plain problem; if the room gets rough treatment, choose a square, and patterned; if there are no children they can be fitted and plain where you will! Otherwise plain, fitted ones should be confined to guest-rooms and bedrooms. A rug to fit a room can be made of several lengths of carpet stitched together with a fringe on each end.

The atmosphere of your room is often dependent upon the colour of your carpet. The reds, from the pigment of earth to dark, dark burgundy, convey the sensation of warmth and are admirable where sun never looks in through the windows. In this kind of shaded room the yellows look well, too, since they are a hint of the sun itself. Green is always a good choice, for it is the colour of grass and a good background. Blues and mauves are even cooler and are delightful where the rest of the decoration is brilliant.

Draw the Curtains

No carpet can be guaranteed absolutely 'fadeless,' but many are fade-resisting. Curtains should always be drawn against powerful sun to protect carpets and upholstery.

The moth is no longer a menace, since carpets can be bought mothproof; this resistance will survive washing or dry-cleaning.

To prolong the life of the carpets you choose, always buy an underfelt for them, and keep them free from dirt and grit with your reliable vacuum cleaner. Clean stains away the moment they occur.

Two tablespoonsful of turpentine to a pint of hot water will clean rugs of spots.

Also many detergents are excellent for the same purpose, as they do not need rinsing. Great care must be taken not to wash a ' clean patch ' that shows in the middle of the surrounding gloom. A small spot can sometimes be cleared up by dropping a little petrol or lighter fluid directly on to it.

A ' cute ' little dumb-waiter that will serve to take amusing ornaments of any period

VICTORIANA

Enhanced by a modern setting, the graceful furnishings of another young Queen's reign have a thousand uses in our homes today.

This arrangement lends a small window importance. The grouping of china balances the draped curtain, which is frilled with broderie anglaise

EARLY Victorian furniture occasionally comes back into fashion, but more as a 'quaint conceit' than a very serious furnishing scheme. It is amusing to have a top hall-way with ruffled curtains and wax flowers under a glass case; or china dogs sitting on a mantelpiece that is covered with a cloth edged with a bobble-fringe. So long as the heavily crowded rooms are not copied, some of the more graceful pieces of this period make for original and picturesque groupings.

Naturally, one must be selective and must buy with an eye to one's own particular room. Then your piece of Victoriana will mix beautifully with your existing furniture. To many people, the word 'Victorian' means heavy, over-ornamented mahogany sideboards, fussy 'what-nots,' overmantels, and a welter of knick-knacks. This, however, came in the latter part of the last century. Today, when we speak of 'Victoriana,' we mean the small, graceful buttoned settees, the balloon-back dining chairs, the delicate embroidery—all the lovely things which were born right at the beginning of a long and rich reign.

One of the nicest things about acquiring Victoriana is that a clear, uncluttered modern setting does so very much more for it than the era to which it belonged, since it has a frame in which to show to advantage.

Look at any photograph of a room in the middle nineteenth century. With appalling thoroughness, everything possible has been put into the room—Aunt Lucy's embroidery, aspidistras, stuffed birds, antimacassars and masses of furniture; endless photographs.

The way we use it today gives it a new life and a new elegance. This is because our modern idea of planning a room is (for most people) based on a minimum of space, so that we do not have too much furniture.

The Right Setting

The secret of success with Victorian furniture is to give it the right setting.

Colour is a great asset here, and a pastel shade on the walls helps to throw up the good lines of Victorian furniture, apart from giving a lift to the whole room.

Or you might like to try wallpaper. There are some delightful Victorian styles to choose from, and this would give your room a charming period air.

Picking up small objects is one of the cheapest ways of acquiring Victoriana—you can use a collection of this most decoratively and successfully by making a 'Victorian corner.'

Have a dumb-waiter or a what-not in a corner which gets a fair amount of light, and arrange your little collection of old *bric-à-brac* or Victorian Wedgwood on it. Make an attractive grouping of black and white 'silhouettes' on the walls around it, or perhaps small paintings on glass.

You can use a dumb-waiter, or a what-not, for very modern pottery as well or for small pieces of sculpture. What you *should not do* is mix them with the old Victorian pieces.

Highly decorated Victorian furniture, such as *papier mâché* sewing-tables, needs to be seen in a clear setting. Use them against a coloured wall, or in a bow window, with flowers. And at the end of the fireside settee, they can be useful for holding a lamp. Since they are such a decoration in themselves, they should be given full value as pieces.

Victorian dining chairs have many uses. They provide extra seats in a living room.

The modern aim is often to use an ornament for the very opposite of the use for which it was intended. This candle lustre makes a delightful and unusual vase

They are sometimes charming when teamed with a modern writing-desk. And you can find endless jobs for them in a bedroom, hall or dining-room.

In looking for pieces to buy, take your time in choosing. Potter around for a little in the second-hand shops and get to know the owners. You will find this a great asset in your search, as once you have established yourself as an enthusiast, they will go to endless trouble to look out for any good bargains at the sales which they attend. They will also be happy to let you wander around their shops to your heart's content. Thus you get the benefit of their greater experience and judgment.

Here are some of the things to look out for when buying Victoriana.

Iron-frame Chairs

You have probably seen these many times —they are small and comfortable, with rounded, buttoned backs. They have a pretty shape and look enchanting when re-covered in striped fabric, velvet or a sprigged chintz.

Love-seats

These are generally circular in shape—or prettily curved, with low backs. Cover them in velvet or *plain* glazed chintz and have a long cotton fringe running round the bottom. They look unbelievably decorative, and make a useful and graceful contribution to the seating in a large room, or alone in a hall.

Chaise-longue

A very useful buy for a bedroom. They make an excellent contrast to contemporary chairs, and if the shape is elegant don't hide it under a patterned fabric and frills. Choose a brilliant colour in a plain fabric to throw up the good lines, but if it is not particularly elegant, you can hide any discrepancies with a softening frill.

Buttoned Settees

Small versions of these settees are charming, and a pair standing each side of the fireplace, with perhaps two small *papier mâché* tables to balance them, will make the room look attractive—(the fireplace being such a focal point). Two oil lamps modernised with attractive shades would give a nice touch to the scene.

This Victorian frame was bought for a few shillings and first of all given a good wash in soapy water

When it was dry, it was given two coats of white distemper, put on very thickly, like paint. Such frames look charming touched up with flecks of gold or silver paint

Mahogany Ditty Boxes

In the Crimean War, officers used these for their personal possessions. Today, however, we can use them as chests of drawers, either together or separately, and you could find many uses for them. They are not so easy to come by as other things, but are well worth looking for.

Dumb-waiters

These make splendid little sideboards for small dining-rooms, and are ideal for holding plants. Or if you like to collect small things— a dumb-waiter makes a good background for them.

Papier Mâché

Look out for trays which can be made into low coffee tables (by the simple addition of a stand), letter racks, blotters and sewing-tables (often inlaid with mother-of-pearl). You can still use these attractive little tables for sewing, as when the top is lifted the inside compartment is beautifully fitted. Small chairs in *papier mâché* are also greatly to be prized.

China

This is a wide field for those who do not want to buy furniture, but like to pick up now and then something small, old and useful as well as pretty.

Old Victorian soap dishes with covers make excellent boxes for cigarettes as well as mother-of-pearl trinket boxes.

Candlesticks are another idea if you want to pick up something which costs little.

One of the best buys of all is the large Victorian meat dish.

These dishes usually have the ends scooped out (to hold the juices while papa was carving the family roast), and the thing to do is to fill the hollows in the dish with moss and add flowers. Florists' wire will keep them firm. With sandwiches, cocktail savouries, or slices of cold meats arranged in the centre, it will be the showpiece of your party table.

Some of these old dishes have lovely designs, and when not in party use you could put fruit in them and have an arrangement of leaves or berries at the ends.

Even Victorian slop pails have risen to undreamt-of social heights. They now appear in smart flats as waste-paper baskets, or filled with tall flowers by a fireplace.

Try and pick up, when you can, blue jasper ware by Wedgwood—it is now a collector's piece as well as being the perfect complement to Victorian furniture. The classic 'urns' can be made into really beautiful lamps, the bowls filled with flowers or used for growing spring bulbs. You could start a collection of this ware by looking out for scent bottles, plaques, cameos and so forth.

Collecting Victoriana—in either furniture or small objects—can be not only a fascinating hobby, but very soon you will find that your time and money have been well invested, as many of these pieces (especially the furniture) will continually be joining the ranks of valuable antiques.

ACHIEVE A LITTLE GAIETY!

WHILE the main feature in a home is comfort, colour comes a very close second. Many people say that they are not responsive to colour, but it is just that they do not recognise the influence varying shades can have. If colour therapy is now so prevalent in treating disease, it stands to reason that it will influence the healthy folk as well, whether they know it or not; therefore, it is very important to take note of the colours with which we surround ourselves. It has to relate to our characters as well as to our tastes. The colours that are soothing, invigorating or depressing will be so in the home just as much as in the clinic. An apoplectic, high-geared person would do well not to have too much red around, and the easily depressed should shy away from quantities of cold blue. If a colour irritates you for no known reason, then there must be a hidden one, and that shade should be eliminated from your decorating chart.

North or South?

Then, of course, north rooms need colours that give a warm effect, to take the place of the sun. But even south rooms, since sun is not all that prevalent in our isles, should have some sunshiny note in their furnishing. Schemes for rooms can be built up around a bowl of fruit, a vase of flowers or a favourite picture. It is fortunate that, nowadays, colour can be used so much more lavishly, with one wall in a different shade of paper or paint from the other three; ceilings coloured softly; different colours for different chairs. Such effects, however, must be achieved by the use of discrimination. A colour palette run wild in a room simply gives no sense of form or balance.

If you keep the chart illustrated in mind, and know your three primary colours (blue, red and yellow), you will realise that all the rest are made from combinations of these three with black, white, and sub-tones such as beige and grey as background. The modern taste is for varying tones of one colour—deep blue, medium blue, ice-blue—and some very lovely schemes can be evolved in this way, with a note of contrast to show up the whole.

Complementary (or contrasting) colours

A guest-room that is inexpensively fitted up, with attention paid to cheerfulness and comfort. The dark blue, spotted with white, panel of wallpaper at the bedhead shows up the lagoon-blue bedspread. The other three walls have a very faint silver-blue striped paper. The mirror slides back, leaving the room as a sitting-room, which would also be ideal for a young daughter

Courtesy of Vantona, Ltd.

If you can find a real old-fashioned cruet, or vinegar and oil stand, put in a little glass bowl and use it for flowers on a small table

are those opposite o one another in the wheel. While they go well together, the contrast is rather violent, and it is the off-tones of each colour blended together that provide the most artistic effects. Analogous colour schemes are those side by side in the chart.

How to Blend Colours

If you cannot match a piece of material or your walls, it is better, rather than to have a discord in a bad match, to go right away from the original and choose a contrast, or perhaps you may find a good harmonising shade.

Warm tones are those with red and yellow in them. Blue is the cold colour. If you add yellow to red, it becomes warmer; add blue and it cools down. Purple is a difficult colour to live with, especially the very dark shade; it is apt to be depressing. But as you gradually add red it becomes violet, then petunia, with warmer shades of maroon all stemming from the same root, but having more warmth. A single note of a 'difficult' colour in a room is quite different, for its influence is offset by the larger quantities of other colours by which it is surrounded.

Those folk with an eye for colour can often mix shades that would cause an average person to shudder at the idea, yet the result is successful. However, those without the artistic flair would do well to keep to basic schemes

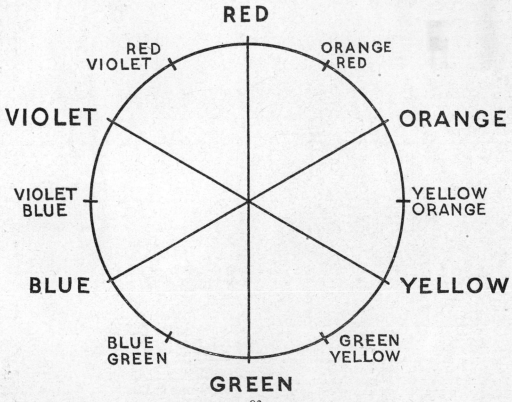

that, while being gay, are safe! If you have a warm, a cool and a neutral shade in a room, at least the balance of colour is right.

Sometimes it is easier to choose a carpet and build the scheme around it. If it is neutral or white, it is simpler. Though white gives a luxurious effect to almost any room, the constant tread causes it to be almost continually at the cleaners. It is best to put a white carpet in a room that does not have much traffic— the bedroom, perhaps, or one's own den; even a dining-room, if it is separate. It is the lounge usually that has all the wear and tear. Neutral shades 'wear clean' and do not show the dirt as much as might be expected. Dark plain shades are apt to show dust or mud-marks, especially if they have a fleck or slight line running through. A patterned carpet is excellent, so long as you can evolve a happy scheme to go with it. Make up a colour chart for yourself, working out the shades of curtains, walls, carpets, furniture.

Plain or Patterned Walls?

Small rooms are apt to look even smaller

This old coffee-grinder was painted with scarlet lacquer and given a gay spotted shade. The light is adjustable

with large-patterned wallpaper or dark walls. The lighter the walls are, the more is the apparent size of the room. Striped wallpaper in a light shade (of the Regency type) gives a room height, more especially if there are no picture-rails. If you like a gay, floral paper, you can always have one panel on the chimney-breast, or in an alcove, with the rest of walls in a plain shade to contrast or blend.

The advantage of plain walls and carpets is that the basic colour scheme can be so easily changed when fresh covers are needed, or new curtains. However, if you have a panel of bright paper, a portion of the wall can always be repapered, and at very little cost, if done by yourself!

For a dark room, choose some acid yellow; see that the curtains are hung at the *sides* (covering the wall) of a window, not across any of the window itself, and that they are drawn well back. Place a mirror where it will catch and reflect the light. If it is a basement or semi-basement room, paint the wall outside that the window looks on to, cream or white. A dark ceiling can bring down the height of an old Victorian room, but is not advisable for a low-ceilinged room . . . it would have the effect of being on top of one's head. The insides of china cabinets can be painted in colour, midnight blue, deep buttercup yellow, jade green, to give brightness and gaiety. And why not be gay? It doesn't cost any more than sombre, dark-brown rooms with no vivid note of relief.

Arthur Sanderson & Sons, Ltd.

A grouping which proves the value of harmony between walls and furniture. The cerise-striped Regency fabric on the chair shows up beautifully against the hand-printed paper, which has a grey distemper background

Do You Like These Schemes?

If you have a house that is decorated already, you can always warm up cold shades

COLOUR COUNTS

The corner of a room that could be ordinary becomes friendly and gay when autumn tints . . . golden yellow, vibrant red, orange, brown and some green . . . are used. Wallpaper and rug are the same colour

Foliage and berries from the woods will give you your colours

A bowl of fruit can suggest more than one decorative scheme. The furnishing is simple here, with no bits and pieces to distract the eye. Emphasis is on colour . . violet carpet and curtains against lemon walls; deep-rose cushions on the apple-green settee

A white rug often ' wears clean,' and provides a luxurious note. Do not choose too blue a violet, for it can be depressing. Lighten the windows with the palest, acid-lemon ninon or net

ACHIEVE A
LITTLE
GAIETY!

The plain bed-cover is made with a zip fastener so that it fits in tailored fashion. It is piped in a deeper shade. Unit furniture is used so that, as more drawers are needed, they can be added without breaking the design-continuity of the room

Right:
There are many pretty antique frames to be found in old junk-shops. Buy one, paint it cream, give it a sunshine-yellow board background and fix three glass shelves across. Your favourite ornaments will look still more attractive in such a setting

Kitchen chairs, when dressed up with a frill, become 'Old Colonial Style' and therefore something quite different! The frill can be tacked directly on to the chair or sewn to the cushions

Small prints which may not be very imposing on their own can be given bright frames and grouped with painted plates against striped paper

A very ordinary plain wooden chest becomes a most expensive-looking piece when painted and decorated with gay floral transfers, which are simple to apply to clean woodwork

NATURE'S PALETTE

Nature paints glowing harmonies and to her we can turn for fresh inspiration for our colour-schemes. This is Nature in a gentle mood . . . earth-brown, solid and enduring; potato-brown; mushroom pink deepening to the warm pink of a full-blown rose

Green pimentos and the mauve-red heart of a pickling cabbage supply the tones for a background to highly polished antiques. The magenta carpet and the pimento-green chair-coverings are silhouetted against the pale-mauve walls

The five flower-pictures are in pale, wide maple frames; the candelabra and wall-troughs form a delightful setting for dinner for two

Courtesy of Heal & Son, Ltd.

Even the toddler will like his gay Picasso-ish cane rocking-horse. The Unit Nursery furniture is in flame birch and ramin-wood. The dresser-top has sliding glass doors

that may be there. For example, if the walls are pale green (against which mahogany looks wonderful), a rust-coloured carpet and curtains with some peach in them will take away any cold effect. Peach and rust sound as if they would not go well, but the right shades of each harmonise excellently. The covers can then be patterned, with notes of green and rust in the design. Pale green and petunia are lovely together, with a darker green carpet. Or buff walls, green-painted furniture and petunia carpet. Try pale blue with plum and reddish brown; or golden yellow, tobacco brown and green combined.

A vivid shade such as scarlet is best used in small quantities, for a chair, or pipings to neutral covers with cushions in plain scarlet. It can be used with great effect with navy blue, or with white or beige. Chairs covered in a bright navy blue, with primrose curtains, and very pale yellow walls is a smart scheme. Though white curtains are rather out of date,

This bright orange rubber-proofed fabric pool with inflatable rim holds about 5 to 6 in. depth of water. To be able to paddle on the lawn and not have to wait to go to the seaside will account for hours of fun

Li-Lo Pool

Heal & Son, Ltd.

A variation on a popular theme, that of conserving space without sacrificing looks and charm. Here we have to hand practically the whole furniture of a lounge-bedroom with table, closed-in bed, drawers, clothes cupboards and bookshelves

used with navy coverings they become completely modern.

For those who revel in colour, many different shades can be blended happily with a little imagination. Take a room with a deep grey carpet and primrose walls. The settee can be covered in primrose with petunia-mauve cushions and chair covering. The curtains may be a deep blue-rose that picks up the red in the petunia. A sapphire blue can be used in another part of the room to provide both contrast and harmony. Or the carpet may be blue, with primrose walls, chairs covered in petunia, and here and there small notes of coral. One should not be afraid of using several colours, but they must have an affinity with each other.

The Brightening-up Process

If rooms seem to have become stale and dull, use a little initiative to brighten them up. A front door can be painted scarlet. It does not have to be all one colour; its panels can be white. Geraniums or a small tree in a jade, green or yellow tub can be placed outside by the step to cheer up the dingiest aspect. A flower-box can be placed at each side of the front door (vertically), too; all window-boxes do not have to be on balconies. To brighten a hall, the stair-treads can be painted a clear bright shade to match, perhaps, a lampshade, but they must blend with the stair carpet. The

Buy a gaily-painted small wheel-barrow at a toyshop and use it for plants on your window-sill. Plain unpainted wood also makes a good background for vivid flowers. They can look pretty standing on the hearth

banisters can be painted, too. A panel or two of wallpaper can enliven one corner of the hall, but if the hall is small, then the pattern on the paper must be small, too. The frame of a mirror can be painted to tone; or a modern wooden chest. Stair carpet can be dyed, if neutral, and moved to one side of the stairs. This gives an effect of width and brings the tread in a different place.

Kitchens need clean shades such as fresh spring-green and yellow or cream; red and white is conventional, but always cheerful. Blue is clean-looking again, and a few notes of yellow will form a contrast.

A paint-brush skilfully wielded (but try it on things that do not matter, first) can bring some colourful notes. Cocoa or other tins can be painted for use as containers on both kitchen and bathroom shelves. You can also cut out a flower illustration from a magazine, stick it on with thin glue size and, when dry, varnish the whole. Punch a hole in the lid and screw to this a small plastic knob. For a cotton-wool container, punch a larger hole and, instead of fastening a knob, draw a piece of the cotton-wool through so that you can draw on it as you will.

Use oil-cloth in a gay colour for covering seats and backs of kitchen chairs. Tack it in position with upholsterer's braid and covered

Make your own verandah by using a sun awning in gay canvas supported on two jointed poles at the front, with eyelets on the back edge. A decorative tub with a shrub or flowers each side of the door completes the picture

nails, or large brass-head tacks. If the seats are not padded, use cotton-wool or upholsterer's hair.

Pleasing the Children

Have a little snack-bar for the children by having a shelf fixed to the kitchen wall and giving them tall stools to sit on. Cover plain wooden cabinets with the pictures from seed-packets stuck on and varnished over. Flower motifs can also be traced and painted on to cupboards, nursery furniture or the plain white backs of kitchen chairs. Put a vivid pink, polka-dotted paper at the back of a shelf of utilitarian

This makes a cosy corner arrangement for tea and conversation, or for a party; or it can be used together as a settee

The seat and back cushions are of foam rubber covered in clear vivid blue and white tapestry. The frames are of hardwood in natural colour

Courtesy of Goodearl Bros., Ltd.

91

tins, so that the colours of the tins show up vividly against it. It's more interesting to remember 'The right blue tin is sugar, scarlet holds tea, jade green is sago,' and so on!

Pastel, restful shades are better in a bedroom than strong colours, and one acid note of colour will take off too much 'sweetness' in a pastel colour scheme, and draw the whole thing together.

Bedroom colours can often be taken from a garden or the country. 'Nature knows best' may be a phrase worth remembering, and if you disagree with Nature you can always have your own way. For instance, if you love bluebell mauve, you have only to remember the setting in which you saw bluebells to have your colour-scheme: the bluebells; the palest pink of a wild apple tree close at hand; the jade carpet of long green grass; the brown of the earth; the pale blue of the sky (or even pale grey!). The yellow of the sun. The silvery birch with its bark gleaming. It can suggest endless combinations of tones and harmonies.

Colours in Small Quantities

The superstition that green is unlucky arose from the age-old belief that it was 'the fairies' colour,' and that they did not care for mortals to use it! It is difficult to imagine that a lovely shade of pale or leaf green could ever bring anyone bad luck! In fact, if you want to remember the effect too much of a colour can have on your mental attitude, you have only to call to mind various phrases such as 'an attack of the blues' (too much blue is depressing); 'red with rage' (too much red is not for the apoplectic); 'everything seems black' (black used with discretion is smart, but a great quantity of any shade so sombre is bound to react drearily). 'The cool green of the grass' (it needs a little warmth from touches of another colour, primrose or pink, or splashes of scarlet). 'A sunny nature. . . .' Well, the yellow that is like the golden rays of the sun, buttercups or primroses *is* joyous. But there is a bilious shade approaching green that is not so happy a choice!

Unit Furniture

To buy furniture in units is quite an adventure. It does mean that a portion of sitting-room or bedroom need not be bare until the wherewithal to buy the right piece of furniture is available. A small drawer on legs can be purchased; this is followed by two more drawers, and you have a shortboy. Another two drawers, and there is your tallboy!

The two chairs added to, become a settee by being put together. A dressing-chest side by side with a bookcase saves the space between two separate pieces because they look as if they are one single piece. The single-unit drawer on legs needs only a mirror added to become a dressing-table. Six or seven pieces not only makes comprehensive

The interiors of houses to order can be as colourful and lavish as any mansion. This study has cream walls, with a panel of green figured wallpaper on the end wall. Note the unusual position of the shelves to one side. The writing desk is of mahogany, and the sideboard in mansonia and abura. Although of the utmost simplicity, there is an atmosphere of glowing warmth about the room.

Colt Timber Houses.
Furnished by
Heal & Son, Ltd.

Courtesy of Hunt Unit Furniture

The shortboy above which can be bought on a plinth base or legs, can be added to, drawer by drawer, until it is a tallboy. The man's wardrobe has hanging space, drawers and a flap-up mirror

furnishing for a room, but it can be changed about for variety, and as needs change, perhaps, with a growing family or growing house-room.

Some unit furniture is made in laminated woods which allows not only for lightness in moving pieces about, but for strength in wear. Many originally designed and attractive pieces are made to fit into corners, which does allow of every inch of space being used.

The useful little bureau was designed to use with the bookcase unit. Another can be placed at the other side or diagonally across a corner. The shelves need not be the same height, which forms a pleasing irregularity

A single section can be fitted on top of the bureau for books being read. A variety of groupings is possible

Courtesy of Minty of Oxford

Courtesy of Minty of Oxford

Mother and Father Chairs. The one on the left, for the man, has a long seat and more sloping back; that on the right a shallower seat and straighter back

Courtesy of Hunt Unit Furniture

The top of the dumb-waiter is formed by a tray which can be lifted off to reveal a cloth recess. The swivel castors allow for easy movement

This three-bedroomed house has a Colonial-style verandah

HOUSES *to* ORDER

WE have waited a long time for the day when a home can be delivered in neat parcels, opened and set up with great ease and minimum fuss.

These 'pre-fabs' are all architect-designed, beautifully fitted and skilfully planned which any woman would be delighted to own.

They can be erected in a very few days once the site has been prepared by your builder, and provided you have had the blessing of your local Council, to whom the plans of the house must be submitted.

Designed originally for shipment abroad to Australia, New Zealand and Canada, these 'packaged' houses are a great success.

Their exterior design is, of necessity, plain. The fact that they can be built so quickly and securely calls for simplicity of construction and appearance, but rooms can be added, and eventually a charming, well-planned home will grow up.

For a moderate price by today's standards you can have a spaciously designed two-bedroomed home, with a large living-room, dining-annexe, and fitted kitchen and bathroom units. The smaller-type home is equally well served with capacious built-in wardrobes, cupboards, and maximum storing space.

The cost of the house includes the equipment, such as modern sink with cupboards, and cooker. Space is planned for a washing machine and refrigerator.

Nice and Warm

All these houses are very well insulated, as the walls are packed with fibre-glass. (The windows are draught-proof.)

Attractive contemporary fireplaces in brick are in most houses, but others are heated by means of hot air which will be blown through the rooms from an oil-fired boiler.

This will ensure an even, warm temperature on the coldest day, but for those who miss the cheery atmosphere of a fire in winter, a fireplace can be built.

One house looks rather like a Swiss chalet. The whole front wall of the living-room consists of windows, and the interior design is as modern as tomorrow. A small dining-room is at one end of the L-shaped room, leading to the kitchen.

Plenty of Cupboards

A small room just off the kitchen could be used as a laundry or a children's play-room. Cupboard space is enormous.

Other houses retain their Colonial style by keeping the wide verandah in front of the house. A mortgage on good terms can be arranged on most of the houses—which in itself is a guarantee that they are well built and altogether a good investment.

This attractive modern fireplace incorporates a two-shelf bookcase on either side. The tiles have Regency-style motifs and decoration, and the hearth tiles match. The shelves, surround and mantel are in un-polished hardwood so that they can be painted to match any colour scheme

Courtesy of Froy'

FIREPLACES *and* HEATING

A FIREPLACE is usually the very centre of the room, and on the Continent, where there are many buildings centrally heated with no fireplace at all, some friendly aspect of life seems sadly missing. There are many very beautiful fireplaces made, some on chaste modern lines, others real or excellent copies of Elizabethan, Adam and other Georgian fireplaces. There are surrounds of patterned tiles, two contrasting-colour tiles, or of marble. Sometimes they are combined with a mantel (modern or antique); at other times there is none.

For the wide open fireplace there are wrought-iron or polished steel basket grates in many lovely designs, or severely plain for those who prefer them. These serve for the use of coal or logs.

Much progress has been made with fires. No longer does a chilled person set light to a fire that refuses to burn and smokes badly. There are smokeless-fuel grates, with a built-in gas-burner to make sure the fire does light. With this you can have an intermittent fire, or with another model the fire will burn all night. There is a combination grate that will

This chaste and elegant contemporary design can be used with a dog-grate or any make of all-night burning fire. The wrought-iron fire-irons are designed to hang conveniently to hand from the tile face. The stone-grey tiles provide a striking contrast with the black egg-shell tiles of the hearth, and blend with the current vogue for lightly patterned wallpapers

Courtesy of Froy's

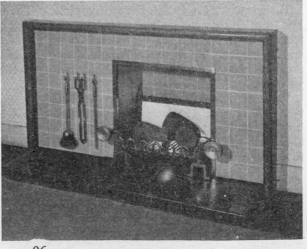

Radiation, Ltd.

burn all solid fuels for ten hours without attention, and combines, as well as an ordinary fireplace, a boiler, oven and hotplate!

Warm Landings

There are gas convector heaters which are much in use now, especially for landings, hall-ways, which send out warm air to the sur-rounding rooms. They can be obtained run either by gas or electricity. These heaters can be used in bedrooms, too, where they have to be kept at an even temperature, though for occasional use an ordinary wall gas or electric fitment is perhaps better.

Then for heating a room, in place of the kind of old-fashioned fireplace where most of the heat went up the chimney and you were roasted in front and frozen with draught at the back, there is the Adaptor. It burns only $\frac{1}{2}$ lb. to $\frac{3}{4}$ lb. of fuel an hour; ventilation can be controlled by opening or closing the damper in the flue-pipe; it can be moved or stored away in summer.

Above: The Luma gas convector radiator gives a pleasant warmth to halls and landings and is quietly unobtrusive in shape. No fluing is needed with this type of radiator, given normal ventilation

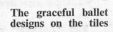

The graceful ballet designs on the tiles

Courtesy of Bratt, Colbrans, Ltd.

A wood overmantel with 'Ballet' decorated tiles inset in tile surround, and new 'heaped' continuous-burning fire

While it looks a little like something from Mars, it is cosy-looking, too. It shuts off the chimney so that heat cannot be swallowed, reducing its area to a small oval hole to take the Adapta flue pipe, cuts out draughts and is extremely reasonable in cost.

A fireplace of such beauty can set the key-note of a room. This is a Queen Anne fireplace, with carved moulding surround, and a Queen Anne dog-grate, to hold either coal or logs. The furnishing needs to blend with this centre-piece of the room

Courtesy of
Bratt, Colbrans, Ltd.

Tailored Heat

Where there is not sufficient heat in a room, electric radiators can be put under a window or along the wooden surround of a dining-alcove. There is a back-boiler conversion unit to be placed in a grate against a back boiler to solve the hot-water question in the summer, when there is no fire. It is portable, weighs about 8 lb. and is not intended for a continuous supply of hot water, but for periodical use for baths or laundry work.

A gas-fired space-heater that gives exactly the same temperature from floor to ceiling is another useful warmth-providing piece of 'furniture.' A special electric fan 'boosts' the warm air into the rooms. Such totally enclosed units are perhaps safer where there are children. All modern gas fires are supplied with a 'dress-guard,' which should be absolutely imperative. There have been too many accidents of dresses being caught alight.

They can be operated either by hot water, electricity, gas or paraffin, and 'tailored' to the room or portion of a room they are designed to heat.

Fireplaces in Summer

A fireplace in summer is rather sad-looking without the cheerful glow it has in winter. Even a decorative firescreen isn't the complete answer to the problem. Decorate your fireplace so that it is brought into the bright, sunny atmosphere of summer living.

In all cases the opening in the fireplace is blocked by plywood or stiff cardboard which has been cut to fit the opening very firmly. It holds there by itself without nails or screws and can be removed at a moment's notice.

If you have a pretty garden or a nice view, re-arrange your furniture to face *away* from the fireplace. This gives the room a feeling of space and airiness instead of the cosy, enclosed look it has in the winter.

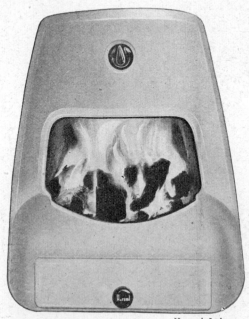

Hurseal, Ltd.

The 'Adaptor' cuts down coal consumption, stops draughts, warms the whole room thoroughly, and burns all night

The first things that come to mind are indoor plants.

An idea is to have gay Chinese ginger jars in bright blue and white with plants or flowers in them, standing 'all in a row' before the fireplace.

You can choose what plants you like—but those which give the most summery look are trailing plants—miniature ivy (Hedera Helix), Cissus Antarctica, Sansoveria.

A wooden trellis could be used with this type of plant. It gives a lovely effect, which can be made doubly attractive if a large mirror is placed on the wall opposite the fireplace to reflect the vine-and-trellis decoration.

Do not give such plants too much water— once a week is enough. The leaves can be lightly sprayed with water in a fine atomiser to clean them, but those plants which have big leaves should be wiped over with cotton-wool and a little milk.

Colourful Camouflage

If you have a fireplace with a raised tile hearth, you can turn it into a veritable garden of colour by having tubs of hydrangeas in different colours massed around it.

The Gas Council

This convector radiant gas fire gives an output of radiant heat and convected warm air, thus enabling warmth to be radiated over a large area. There is a constant stream of warm air circulated through the convector louvres at the top of the appliance. This ensures that one does not have to be seated close to the fire to feel the heat

Gimson & Slater, Ltd.

This fireplace is frankly 'bogus,' deriving from farmhouse chimneys of the 14th century, but even though the logs are unreal, too, it gives a comfortable and picturesque effect. The two-seater settees are still the favourite of most small flat or house dwellers, as they take up little space

If you have an original painting or print of a picture you particularly like, this can be used before the fireplace, if it *looks* suitable. Stand well back to get a bird's-eye view of the whole. Many ideas sound bad, and look well; or sound as if they are exactly what is needed, and somehow do not appear right when carried out. A little experimenting is always healthy. A piece of needlework or a piece of tapestry can also be framed and used in the same way.

Built-in Fitments

Where a new fireplace has to be built into an old house, this can be done with weathered bricks that keep to the 'atmosphere' of the period, and yet still discreetly make use of all modern improvements. In one old house a very old oak beam was used as a mantel-shelf to lend a genuinely antique appearance.

If your fireplace is modern it is a quite charming idea to have the tops of built-in shelves of the same tiles as the fireplace.

Hurseal, Ltd.

A domestic boiler that needs ash emptying only once a fortnight has a space for casserole cooking on the lid, burns any fuel, including peat, and has a refuelling hopper so that there is no spill-over

Another idea is to put bookshelves immediately in front of the 'blocked' fireplace. Or, fit the mantel, if it is not an expensive one, with a pelmet and skirt of striped, glazed chintz.

*   *   *

The continuous-burning stove is the greatest problem to deal with when it comes to making it decorative. It juts into the room just enough to be difficult to hide successfully.

It can be fitted with a trimly tailored linen cover piped with white cord over a plywood case.

It is better to keep the material to a plain colour so that the stove becomes just as unobtrusive as possible.

On each side of the stove, place a low table with books, flowers, magazines, etc., and so bring the whole group into the room as a complete 'unit.'

Samuel Smith & Sons, Ltd.

This all-purpose cooker heats the water, cooks a meal, and warms the room. Control is maintained by adjustment of the damper and spin wheel

Timber houses differ from 'pre-fabs,' as they became commonly known, in that they are individual in style. This shows the entrance front of a revised Kent cottage. There are also bungalows, two-storey detached houses, and semi-detached cottages. All are easily assembled, although the cost for this is naturally additional

W. H. Colt, Son & Co., Ltd.

Save Money
When Building a House

THESE days it is essential for builders to use every permitted square foot of floor area to maximum advantage, to adopt new building techniques, to use substitute materials and to eliminate luxurious or showy finishes. There is no need, with a little thought, to waste space or materials by careless planning.

The biggest savings can be worked out on the drawing-board. An efficient plan can cut out unnecessary passages and landings and so save perhaps 100 square feet of floor area —and that amounts to at least £150 nowadays. Ask oneself, 'Is it necessary to be able to walk from the kitchen to the front door without going through the living-room?' or, 'Is direct access from the entrance-hall to a cloakroom of real importance?' It may be found that the answer is, 'Well, not really,' and another few square feet are saved. Most house-plans are still dominated by planning conventions which were evolved a hundred years ago, when life was much more formal. In the small modern home privacy is needed only in bedrooms and bathrooms, and there is no valid objection to using certain rooms as corridors.

If the dining-room can be dispensed with, or combined with the kitchen, the living-room or even the entrance-hall, another 100 square feet of floor space can be saved, as well as the cost of a door, a window, a light point, a length of partition and maybe a fireplace. The separate dining-room is not a necessity, but a luxury which costs a lot to maintain and makes extra work for the housewife.

The staircase takes up a minimum of 100 square feet (50 square feet on each floor). This can be saved by adopting a bungalow plan, or greatly reduced if the stairs are planned to rise out of the living-room. At the same time the apparent size of the living-room is increased, and the whole house receives benefit from the warmth of the sitting-room fire.

One cannot afford to waste the space under the stairs. A clever planner will put a cloakroom or larder beneath them, increasing the headroom, if necessary, by lowering the floor a step or two.

Do You Need a Spare Room?

The spare room should be kept small, or left out. It is very nice to be able to impress friends with a large room, but can one afford it? One hundred and twenty square feet is ample for a double bedroom, and 80 for a single. Remember that building costs not much less than £2 a square foot, and then ask yourself if you can spare £150 to £250 for a room that will probably be empty 70 per cent of the time. An economical plan is to have double doors which cut off a portion of the living-room, turning it into a spare room, dining-room or study when required. A desk, and a divan with a severe, unbedroomlike wardrobe fitment will be endlessly useful.

Incidentally, by planning the spare room on the ground floor it will be far more useful, as it can serve as a sick-room if necessary, and will save carrying trays upstairs.

Practical Planning

Efficient practical planning also saves money. For instance, an experienced planner will take advantage of a sloping site, and perhaps produce a house on three levels—ground floor, first floor and an in-between floor—with the hall and sitting-room up the slope on the intermediate floor, and so equally accessible from upstairs and down; while the amateur might ignore the slope, and so incur the expense of excavation and retaining walls.

A house should be placed near the front of the site for economy, to keep to a minimum the length of pathway and drive, as well as drains, and gas, water and electricity mains. If possible, it should be rectangular in shape. Angles, corners and bits jutting out mean extra labour and lead to expensive complications at roof level, extra 'hips' and 'valleys,' extra bends and junctions in the gutters, extra rain-water pipes and drains. A square house, though it may not be so attractive to look at, is more economical than a long, narrow house, because it has a shorter length of outside wall for the same floor area. It is also warmer because heat losses through the walls are reduced.

Bay windows, projecting porches, verandahs, loggias and covered ways should be planned for, but not built till later. It is better

Courtesy of 'Country Life'

This is a small Yorkshire manor-house of the early 17th century. You can check up the features of the furniture in the antique furniture chart. Old houses need the interiors to be in sympathy with the outside, even though some contemporary pieces will not jar if chosen with discretion

Chippendale's Workshops, Ltd.

This was a very awkward room, in which it was difficult to fit separate pieces of furniture. The problem was solved by building the wardrobe exactly between the two windows, and the dressing-table curved into the window-corner. A small cupboard fitted in neatly between dressing-table and fireplace

to spend whatever sum is permitted to be spent on the real essentials of a house than to fritter it away on frills.

If the roof is steep, 45° or more, it should be kept low so that the underside of it shows at the junction of the ceiling and wall in the upstairs rooms. It is possible in this way to reduce the over-all height of a house by 2 ft. 6 in. or more, a saving of perhaps 1,750 cubic feet at between 2s. 6d. and 3s. 6d. a cubic foot.

Roof Materials

Many builders consider, however, that a greater economy results from using interlocking tiles on a roof of much flatter pitch because of the consequent reduction in the length of the roof timbers. Other materials which can be used on a flatter-pitched roof are cedar shingles, corrugated asbestos sheeting, aluminium or copper. Shingles give an additional saving because they are so light that the roof timbers can be reduced in section or spaced farther apart; but unfortunately some local authorities still consider them a fire-risk, and will not allow their use except under certain conditions. Corrugated asbestos, being in large sheets, needs no battens to support it. Though not particularly attractive to look at, it can be used at such a flat pitch that on a two-storey house it is scarcely visible; or it can be hidden completely behind a low parapet.

Flat roofs of reinforced concrete can be economical if the builder has the necessary equipment and experience. There need be no fear of a flat-roofed house being too hot in summer, because modern insulating materials can be applied to the ceiling at very reasonable cost. A small expenditure on insulation will not only save fuel—it may save the cost of additional fireplaces or a central-heating system.

How Many Windows?

The number of windows should be reduced to a minimum. One large window, provided it is not so wide as to need a steel beam or a specially reinforced concrete lintel over it, is cheaper than two small windows of equivalent size.

Tall, narrow window-openings from ceiling to floor are cheaper than wide windows of the

Heal & Son, Ltd.

A room for the growing son or daughter with a reasonably priced suite in French walnut and beech. Young people dislike fussiness; they need light and colourful environment with practicability

same area, and leave more wall space for furniture and pictures. They also enable any-one sitting in a chair to get a better view of the garden.

Saving on Plumbing

The plumbing represents a surprisingly high proportion of the cost of a new house, and money can be saved if the plumbing installa-tion is compact, with short runs of pipe between the boiler and tank, and tank and taps. This will reduce heat losses and make for economical running as well. When the plumbing is compact, the drainage is compact too, and this means a saving of excavation and drain pipe, and possibly of one or more inspection chambers.

By placing the bathroom on the ground floor next door to the kitchen there may be an appreciable saving, especially if this means that a separate downstairs cloakroom can be omitted.

Fireplaces in bedrooms are not really worth while. It is usually cheaper to install a radiator worked from a back boiler fitted to a fire in another room, than to build a separate fire-place and a flue. If flues from all the fires in a house can be collected in one central stack,

it helps to keep the house warm and reduce building costs.

As to details, plaster can be omitted from certain inside walls, and the brickwork left exposed. Some conservative builders may oppose this suggestion on the grounds that there is a shortage of bricklayers capable of laying a 'fair-face' wall; but skilful plasterers are also hard to find.

* * *

Dead-locks are not necessary on inside doors. They are fitted automatically by builders, but are hardly ever used. A catch is all that is necessary, with a locking 'snib' on w.c. and bathroom doors.

* * *

The pendent light-point in the centre of the ceiling is often redundant. It is more con-venient to have a switch by the door controlling a skirting plug.

* * *

Employ an architect experienced in domes-tic work, and listen to his advice. Not only will he save enough money to pay for his fees, but he will also help to avoid time and worry. Further, the finished house will have extra comfort, more character and be more valu-able should it ever be necessary to sell it.

A Number of Original Ideas to Give You

Harmonious Lighting

INTERESTING lighting is like a discreet and very subtle beauty treatment for a room. It gives character and depth, playing down the bad points and high-lighting the attractive ones.

Apart from the decorative value of light in the right places, there is the important question of avoiding eyestrain. And there is the choice of the right wattage for each type of lamp. This in itself needs careful studying if you really want to get the best from your lamps.

One centre light in the ceiling is not good enough for reading or sewing. Take into account one important factor—the colour of the walls. All colours have a definite reflection factor. White has the highest of all —84 per cent.—and an all-white room with one 100-watt bulb would be adequately lit, while the same room decorated in warm pink would absorb twice as much light.

Peach has a reflection factor of 50 per cent., eggshell blue 45 per cent., deep cream 70 per cent., eau de nil 50 per cent., light grey 45 per cent., pale cream 73 per cent. Dead matt walls absorb light and painted walls reflect it. Remember this when you are re-decorating, and plan your lighting scheme accordingly.

Choose lamps with the same care as you would your dress accessories. They are the final, personal touch in a room and should fit in with the general atmosphere.

A modern-style flat with plain furniture, and with curtains and covers in rough-textured folk-weave, would need lamps with pottery bases decorated with bold colours in a simple pattern. Or classical-type bases, which would show up well against the rough fabrics and austere lines of the furniture.

Adjustable lights are a necessity for the happiness of a home. This is a hand-made hollow-stem wooden lamp with a brass fitting making it adjustable in length and angle. It rests on a two-feet stem five degrees off vertical line . . . an original and practical design

Designed by Nigel Walters

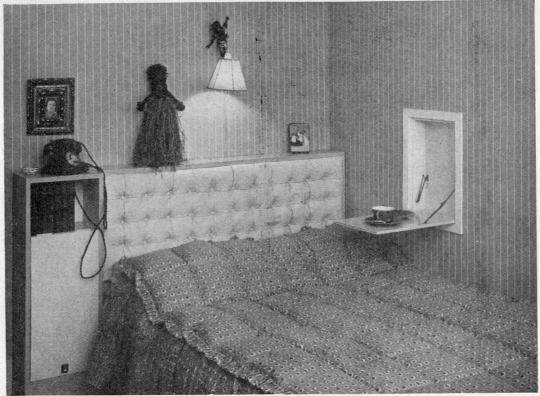

Designed by A. V. Pilley, F.R.I.B.A.

An overhead light above the bed must not be too high and must shine down. Note the unusual little hatch for the early morning cup of tea. The gay 'buttoned' bedhead and quilted bedspread give a kind of highly modernised Victorian air to the room. What could be just an ordinary corner of a bedroom becomes bright and interesting with original ideas

Flower-sprigged bedroomy lamps are out of place here.

Shades should balance the lamps. Choose them with an eye to the proportions of the base. So many attractive lamps are smothered in heavy parchment shades which are not very pretty and give out a yellow diffused light.

Dark Shade, White Lining

If you want something really new and elegant, try the American "drum" shapes in rich dark colours that are white-lined for clear light. Particularly lovely are shades in dark plum against smoke-blue walls, bottle-green against peach, cherry against dove-grey. Checked taffeta is very effective in this shape, poised on tall, slim, white bases and flanking a mirror in an entrance-hall.

If you cannot buy these shades in your local shops, there is no reason why you should not get plain ones and paint or distemper them, edging them with heavy white cord.

Keep frilly shades for the bedroom.

If you do a lot of reading or sewing, pay attention to the lamp you will use most. A "study"-type lamp is a very good buy indeed. It is fitted with a reflector-diffuser and a semi-opaque shade with a low surface brightness. It is a wonderful lamp for close work.

Here is a general guide to help you in judging the correct wattage for various parts of the house, assuming the background is fairly light. It is variable, of course, according to personal taste, but the wattage suggested is the lowest which it is advisable to have.

Hall 60 watts, passages 60, bedroom (reading lamps) 100, living-room (reading) 100, nursery (over-all) 150, bathroom 100, stairs 60, lofts 40, cellar 40, kitchen (over-all) 200, dining-room (over-all) 120.

Trick Lighting

From the purely decorative point of view, you can do some very ingenious tricks with lights. If you have lovely curtains, the evening is the time when they should come into their own by being illuminated. Velvet looks wonderful with a clear light gleaming over the rich surface, throwing up the lovely colour and texture.

Heavy satins, damasks, brocade and some of the better rayons also come to life this way. Or an elegant patterned chintz which lies hidden at the side of the window during the day can become the focal point of the room at night.

The best way to light curtains is to have a strip of fluorescent tube lighting along the inside of the pelmet board, throwing the light down over the fabric. Fluorescent lamps are cool burning and there is no danger of the material being singed. This form of lighting is not cheap, but it lasts three times as long as an ordinary tungsten-filament bulb and gives a clear white light which cannot alter the colour value of the material.

Alternatively, if you do not wish to go to this expense, try picking out your nicest piece of furniture—a desk or a sofa table—and placing it in front of the window with your most decorative lamp. This will give a certain glow of light on to the curtains and make a very pleasing picture on its own. If your curtains are not outstanding, it is better to let them merge quietly into the background of the walls.

Light in Dark Places

For the sort of dark corner you just don't know what to do with, a strip of fluorescent light will create a glowing background for a collection of china. Place glass shelves across the corner in front of the lamp and arrange china figurines on them. Or a collection of glass looks wonderful with the light shining through. Flowers, too, can be used with charming effect.

Another good idea is to have a small cupboard with a top of frosted glass. Inside the cupboard put an ordinary bulb. Place flowers or a statuette on the top and light it up at night.

Bookshelves, too, can be accentuated by good lighting. Tubular lighting along the top of the shelves throws up the bright covers. (Books, in themselves, are one of the best forms of decoration.) This is especially good in a large room with long low bookshelves at the far end.

Remember, too, that a large room with a high ceiling (such as one often finds in old houses converted into flats) lends itself for more daring experiments in light. The size

Heal & Son, Ltd.

A toddler cannot be too small to begin having her own little 'suite' for clothes and other belongings. A two-foot wardrobe, a baby dressing-table with room in the drawer for soft toys; a half-side bed with removable side for when she is older, and a cupboard chest. It is ideal when the bed light can be switched on and off by the child, as it gives her confidence

can be minimised by throwing far corners into shadow and concentrating, during the winter months especially, on making the fireplace the focal point of light.

Strong Enough Bulbs

A pointer here is to remember that unless the table holding the lamp is higher than the arm of the chair in which you are sewing, don't use lamps with a short, squat base. Have tallish lamps which will throw the light down to the book or sewing. Standard lamps are excellent for this purpose as they are more mobile and can be moved around to suit. Make sure that the bulbs are strong enough and that the light is not too diffuse, a very common fault with most standard lamps. They stand disconsolately in a corner with one small overworked bulb trying hard to give adequate light. Standard lamps should have a cluster of three bulbs really, to do their work of illumination.

Flood-lighting Alcoves

Alcoves and archways light up beautifully. Ordinary lamps can be used, or strip lighting, but must be placed so that the bulb cannot be seen.

Light should focus direct on to a dining-table. If you make an effort to be *too* artistic, your guests may sometimes be eating practically in the dark!

Wall brackets look delightful, especially with period furniture and good pictures, and they are perfect for decorating a long bare wall, especially when flanking an attractive group of old prints.

The brackets must be fixed *before* decorating a room, as a small channel has to be made in the wall for the flex to run up.

Originality in colour and light, if used imaginatively, is half the success of interior decoration.

If you keep your eyes open you will find many attractive lamp-bases . . . used fruit-squash bottles of original design; brandy tubs of china; wine decanters; your favourite ornament, all can be transformed by the handyman for use with a suitable shade. Children will love it if you stencil the design of several houses around a plain parchment shade, let them paint them, then cut out the little windows, and paste red or yellow cellophane over, so that the windows are apparently lit up when the light goes on.

Danger! Watch Your Step!

LEASES AND AGREEMENTS

When Buying a House or Renting a Flat

WHEN renting a flat, or buying a house, if you are a normal, honest individual, it is only too easy to imagine that everything is plain sailing . . . or else, of course, to be too suspicious when there is no need to be, and then to lose the residence you were after! The happy medium is always right. Without expecting too much, such as hoping for a brand-new house for the price of a dilapidated old one, at least check exactly what you are doing step by step.

For those *selling* a house or letting a flat, one could say: The moment you get even the firmest offer, do not turn away all applicants from your door. Things can fall through at the last moment.

When Leasing a Flat

It will pay you to have a solicitor look at even the most regular agreement. Clauses that are irregular, such as 'This agreement can be null and void with a month's notice from either party'—which means it cancels out any agreement at all—can be sandwiched in and get past those to whom all legal language is anathema. This can hardly be imagined but such things do happen to the unsuspecting and unbusinesslike! Also you should really have your copy of the agreement or lease before you take possession, as until you have this, you are not in a position to claim protection as legal occupier. However, if a solicitor is looking after your interests, or you are dealing with a reputable agent, it is not so necessary.

Here are some things to look out for.

PURCHASING A HOUSE

Freehold Property

When submitting an offer to purchase a freehold, make sure that you make your offer 'subject to contract,' as if at a later stage in the negotiations your solicitor decides it is not a good proposition, you are able to withdraw and obtain refund of any deposit paid. If, when you make your inspection, you deem it necessary to have a survey, your offer for the property concerned should be '£——, subject to contract and satisfactory Surveyor's Report.'

At an early stage one should ascertain what outgoings are payable and the date vacant possession will be given. If a mortgage is required, your Building Society or Bank will of course survey the property automatically to ensure that everything is in order, and your offer can then be made 'subject to contract and to a satisfactory mortgage being arranged.'

Leaseholds

A similar procedure can be adopted as when purchasing a freehold, but one should, of course, find out the date of the expiration of the lease, ground rent payable, and, if you desire to use the premises semi-professionally, whether there are any restrictive covenants prohibiting the same. A Building Society, or Bank, will usually grant a reasonable mortgage on leasehold premises providing the lease has a minimum of 60 or 70 years to run. This, how-

ever, should be checked by the prospective purchaser with the Society before entering into negotiations for buying. If a short lease is being acquired, ask the agent to check up with the ground landlord to find out definitely on what terms and for what period a new lease would be forthcoming.

Purchasing at Auction

When buying a property in the Auction Room remember that before leaving you will have to sign a Memorandum of Contract incorporated in the auction particulars and that this *is a binding contract*. Before attending, therefore, your solicitor should vet the

Cocktail cabinets had practically disappeared from contemporary furnishings a few years ago. Now they are coming back in a most important way, in a wide variety of moods and designs, from the plain bar fitment with stools, to the cabinet itself

This striking piece is a 'cocktail' of woods, since the outer frame is of burbinga, the inside lined with sycamore. The woods used for the front include burbinga, sycamore, makore, rosewood, marble gaurea, keyasinga and mazur birch

Designed by Christopher Heal, M.S.I.A.

conditions of sale, and you should get your own surveyor or builder to make an inspection prior to the auction.

LEASES AND AGREEMENTS

Renting An Unfurnished Flat

When opening negotiations for an unfurnished flat, by checking several important points with the lessor (or his agent) beforehand, a great deal of wasted time at a later date can be avoided both on your own behalf and from the legal point of view. Ascertain:

(a) The length of the lease if a new one is being granted, and whether it is to be 'internal repairing' or 'fair wear and tear.' With 'fair wear and tear,' you take the flat in its present state, and are not liable for decoration, unless damage has been caused.

'Internal repairing' implies that the landlord has the flat decorated upon entry, and you are either liable to have it put in the same condition upon leaving, or else a sum of money to cover this is mentioned in a clause in the lease.

(b) If you are taking an assignment of a lease and the unexpired portion is negligible, ask whether a new one is likely to be forthcoming and on what terms?

(c) Find out if the rental asked is inclusive, or whether excess rates are payable.

(d) If you propose using the premises for part professional purposes, enquire if this is permitted in accordance with the terms of the lease.

(e) If you wish to keep a pet on the premises during the tenancy, check if this is permitted.

Having satisfied yourself on these and any other points which occur to you, you may then be requested by the lessor or his agent to sign a form of offer setting out the agreed terms. Either communicate the wording of the form of offer to your solicitor and obtain his sanction before signing, or if this is not possible have the words 'subject to my solicitor's approval of the lease,' or a similar clause, added before signing.

If a premium is being paid, make quite certain how this sum is made up, i.e. whether fixtures and fittings are included, etc. Remember that a premium can only be asked under certain circumstances depending whether the flat is rent controlled and other factors, and legal advice should be taken on this point.

Renting Premises Furnished

When renting a furnished flat, the prospective tenant is usually required to sign an agreement. Before signing this agreement the

A Monk's Diner (reproduced from the Table Settles of the mid-17th century) is useful to have in the hall, as it can serve for an occasional meal, for a buffet when dispensing hospitality, or for an additional sideboard

Wood Bros. (Furniture), Ltd.

prospective tenant should make sure that the correct terms and rent have been inserted, and familiarise himself with any restrictive covenants contained therein. For instance, if he wishes to keep a domestic pet on the premises, or if he desires to use the flat for professional purposes, it should be ascertained that this is not prohibited. If the landlord agrees to your being allowed to keep your pet or carry out professional duties, a clause should be inserted to this effect. Before signing the agreement read it through carefully and if necessary obtain legal advice on any clause not understood. It should also state how rental is to be paid, i.e. monthly or quarterly and the amount. If the flat is taken through an estate agent, a standard form of agreement is used by him in most cases, and this has usually been approved in principle by many different legal firms, although of course the actual terms differ in each case. When signing, your signature should be witnessed in the usual way by a competent person who should add his name, address and occupation in the space provided.

Any inventory should be carefully checked that all the contents are really there (or you may have to supply the deficiency when your term is ended) and that the condition, if bad, is noted.

When Letting Your Flat Furnished

Have an inventory made (estate agents will send an inventory clerk along for about £2 2s. a day), arrange for meters to be read, and telephone calls checked up to date of entry of the tenant. See that your insurance carries some clause so that, if burglary or fire occurs while the house or flat is let, you are covered. Insist on a banker's reference. Check that the agreement prohibits your premises being sublet or used for any purpose other than as a private residence. Do not leave valuable china or goods about; it is not really fair to the tenant, as breakages *can* occur. Charge a sum to be paid as a deposit against breakage or damage, returnable if premises are left in good order with no breakages.

This need not be an unduly large amount, and depends a great deal on whether the use of china and linen is included. Nevertheless, it is as well to be covered in case of an unpaid telephone account, or any excessive wear and tear by inconsiderate tenants.

An 18th-century carved dresser. These, whether antique or ultra-modern, make a wonderful background for colourful pieces of china or pottery, bowls and unusual dishes

Bits and Pieces

A very high percentage of the furniture sold today is not finished in French polish but a clear **cellulose lacquer**. Instead of using an ordinary furniture cream use a polish that is sold specially for cars that are finished in cellulose. (There are several makes on the market.) The material actually polishes the surface of the cellulose, giving a higher glow to the furniture.

* * *

Scrub your **wicker furniture** with salt and water instead of soap; the salt not only cleans well but stiffens the cane besides. Coconut matting can also be cleaned in the same way.

* * *

For Pianists. If piano keys seem to be dull and discoloured, a rub down with a little piece of rag soaked in methylated spirits will bring back their own sparkling appearance.

* * *

Sunblinds will not blow about if you fill a small bag $1\frac{1}{2}$ in. wide and the length of the width of the blind with sand and stitch it along the bottom.

Your Caravan Home

IT is not so many years since caravans were only associated with nomads of the roads, the gipsies. We realise now that they must have had a good deal of fun, for the caravan represents something in life for which perhaps many of us are seeking, a kind of simplicity, with everything within reach, no rates, no enormous light and warmth bills, the world outside your front door.

Yet the caravan has progressed from the early, rather bleak models to miracles of comfortable living that often compare favourably with modern flats and houses. Your finances often dictate just how much in the way of luxury you can command; but so also does initiative. For many of the fitments can be fixed by people with a creative and mechanical turn of mind.

The housing shortage established the caravan as a home. You could obtain caravans complete with furniture and mattresses, but you couldn't find a house. The caravan

Courtesy of 'The Caravan'

THE LONG AND THE SHORT OF IT

Above: The roof lifts to 7 ft. 6 in. and the Tent Trailer holds two single beds, table, meat-safe, large front locker

This is the Berkeley Statesman with stairs to top storey inside. Two-storey models have not caught the public fancy

Courtesy of 'The Caravan'

Two vans are bolted together here to make one large home. Each travels separately on the road to the site. Such units together can be as much as 44 ft. long

was obviously a far better idea than living with 'in-laws' or paying exorbitant rents for dingy, one-room furnished flats.

Now members of every profession with their wives and children have become keen on a caravan home or occasional caravanning: admirals, lawyers, doctors, journalists, members of Parliament, artists, shop assistants, labourers—the list is endless. Even the Queen Mother solved the accommodation difficulties at Balmoral by providing a living-van for her guests.

Take Your Home Along

Other reasons have attracted people to caravanning—servicemen, actors, commercial travellers, whose work requires a constant change of location, have been quick to realise the advantages of a mobile home. Then a large proportion of the owners of caravan homes are retired folk. Why have the bother of maintaining a house with few home helps available and tied to one place? A caravan can be parked somewhere in the country or outskirts of a town. When they have ex-

To take your own home or hotel with you does avoid a number of difficulties during travel, not to mention the expense saved. This was taken during a 10,000-mile trip around the Mediterranean. While a 'touring van' is not a living-van, at the same time, it comprises most of the comforts of home

Courtesy of 'The Caravan'

hausted the pleasures of that living-place, they can move without all the usual bother of changing houses.

The caravan is limited in size by transport regulations to 22 ft. by 7 ft. 6 in. In consequence, the manufacturers have devised some ingenious methods of putting the proverbial quart into a pint pot. For one thing, some caravans have soared upwards like minor skyscrapers and a second storey has been added to give a bedroom or two above the lounge, kitchen and bathroom. So far, this type has not captured the caravanning public's imagination. Then another van has telescoping side walls that expand on the site

When holiday time comes along, if the site is inland, the main caravan is left there; the second trailer 'bedroom' is hitched to the back of the car, a tent is added to the equipment for the children and the family drive down to the sea.

Despite the many clever advances in luxurious design, somehow the ordinary caravan remains the most popular. Yet they come in all shapes and sizes, varying in price between £200 and £2,000. Obviously, the more expensive types are hand-finished, and include such equipment as refrigerators, television sets, electric light, cocktail cabinets—all the refinements of Mayfair for a hardy, outdoor life!

View from the kitchen doorway. There is a folding bed above the table; china cabinets at the end. Lantern roof gives good ventilation. Solid-fuel stove right centre, linen cupboard above. Two extra beds can be seen

Courtesy of 'The Caravan'

when the owner winds a handle. Another method of increasing house room is to bolt two caravans together so that, if required, the mobile home can be 44 ft. long. These are taken to the site separately. Then another of the latest models has end walls which extend when the caravan is not travelling to provide a further 12 ft. of living-space, and gives sleeping accommodation for six people.

Using Two Vans

Some caravanners like to have two vans in use. The larger van provides a kitchen and a lounge for the whole family, plus a bedroom for mother and father, and the small touring van provides a bedroom for the children.

Second-hand caravans are always available. but must be well considered before buying, Be sure you know what you are looking for. See that it is weather-worthy, that there are no cracks in walls or roof; but also, of course, do not expect a luxury model if you can only pay a little—for repairs can be done and additions made so long as the trailer is in reasonable condition. You get, in fact, what you pay for. The best new 'buy' is a caravan that is of stout construction, well painted and as large as you can afford. A living-van for four people should not be less than 17 ft. or 18 ft. in length, although those of less length will do, if necessary, for only two occupants.

The Berkeley Governor-General is one of the most luxurious living-vans, smoothly streamlined. When the caravan is not travelling, the end walls extend easily to give another 12 ft. of living-space, and an extra bedroom. No van is allowed to be more than 22 ft. long by transport regulations

Heating and Ventilation

The exterior walls of a van are usually made of the best hardboard or aluminium, and some form of insulation, like glass wool, is placed between the outside wall and the inner hardboard or veneer panelling. This does not sound like a very thick wall; nevertheless, a caravan in winter is a great deal warmer than the average suburban house. The insulation materials and a solid-fuel stove see to that. Such a stove is really an essential item of equipment. Otherwise, in a poorly insulated van, moisture in the air condenses on the cold surfaces and the walls will produce a miniature waterfall. In many vans a water tank or airing cupboard is built round the flue pipe of this stove. In a small or holiday van a paraffin or gas heater gives ample heat for the cold spring or autumn days. Paraffin stoves can also be used to cook some excellent meals. With these, on hot days, the cooking can be done out of doors in real camping spirit.

Ventilation in a caravan is naturally very

The studio-couch makes up into a double bed. There is a separate table between couch and sideboard, also another table in the extending end. It boasts a bathroom with full-length bath (the toe of which runs into the end of a kitchen unit); also a wash-bowl, a chemical closet and hooks for wet clothes

Berkeley Governor

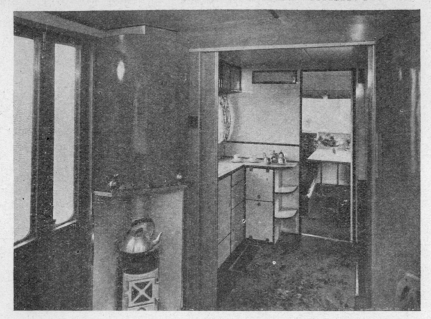

This is a centre-kitchen model; the carpet covers a concealed bath. The kitchen divides the end room (with two single beds) from the double-bed lounge, an excellent arrangement where there are children. There is a solid-fuel stove in the 'hall,' which will also heat an extra kettle

Courtesy of 'The Caravan'

important. There is less air space in a van than the ordinary bedroom of a house, so the air must be changed. Outlets must be provided at the highest point of the roof so that the stale air can escape, and there must also be provision for the intake of fresh air. The larder, toilet-room and immediately above the cooking stove should have ventilators.

The general method of cooking, lighting and, in some cases, heating is by butane gas— a by-product of refining petrol—supplied in this country by Boltogas or Calor Gas. It is in compact steel cylinders. Although it is as easy as town gas to use, appliances must be specially designed for it. Refrigerators, gas fires, irons, cookers, lights—all work very efficiently on butane. Some of the more expensive vans are wired for mains electricity, but, unfortunately, there are few sites with this power available.

And So To Bed

Because of the limitations of space, beds have to serve a dual purpose. There is the settee which pulls out at night to form a double bed. The dinette—a table between two settees—converts either into a double bed or two singles. Then there is the surprisingly comfortable bunk-type bed—a settee that turns into two single beds, one above the other. The fold-away bed, which is dropped down from the wall, may serve as the bulkhead between the lounge and the kitchen.

This type has the advantage that it can be stowed away with the bed already made; unlike the settee or dinette that has to be put together last thing at night. The bedding is usually stowed during the daytime in lockers under the mattresses.

Despite the many different caravan layouts, they narrow down to a choice between two themes: a kitchen in the centre of the van or at the end. The latter gives a large lounge that can be divided into two rooms at night by a folding partition. With a centre kitchen van, the lounge is small, but the children's room is farther away from parents staying up late with the radio on.

Everything is handy in the caravan kitchen. The sink and drainer, made of plastic, aluminium or steel, is next to the cooker. A working top, perhaps over a cupboard, the larder, and pots and pans on the shelf are all within easy reach. Some vans have elaborate plumbing systems designed to give hot and cold water direct to the sink. Water, however, still remains the biggest problem of caravan life. Few people are lucky enough to be connected direct to the main town supply. So it is hubby's happy task, before going to work, to collect the water in cans from the nearest stand-pipe and fill up the caravan's tank. On most sites the washing-up water runs from the sink via a length of rubber hose to a drain or soak-away. Otherwise a waste bucket has to be emptied.

Toilet rooms with a chemical closet form an integral part of the caravan. In larger vans this room incorporates a bath and wash-basin.

Lightweight for Touring

For touring, when a large-size van is not required, there is the very modern caravette, which can be towed by a 7-h.p. car or a 500-c.c. combination. It will serve as a sporting headquarters or as a spare room for those with a house or a living-van already, with sprung seats for daytime travelling or a bed at night. Additional tents can be carried to make more accommodation. This is not a folding model, although it has a top over an open truck base, which can be lifted off by two men quite easily, if necessary. The shell is aluminium outside, insulation board inside; it has a ventilation system and a detachable kitchen unit, and costs just under £100; so that from caravette to a super living-model practically anyone can find something to suit their pockets.

Choice of a Site

Before a caravan is bought, somewhere has to be found to place it. The demand for land round large cities is very high and it is here that there is an acute shortage of residential sites. Fortunately, the caravan dealer should be able to help. All caravan sites must have planning permission; it is not possible to park your van just anywhere. The good commercial site has hard roads, proper drainage and water-supply. There will be a toilet block which contains flush lavatories and either showers or bathrooms. The same building may also have a laundry-room. There will be individual storage huts and bins for anthracite or coal. The vans will be sited among attractive gardens, and the tradesmen will call. It is a garden city of its own kind.

Some caravanners prefer a secluded site where they can 'keep themselves to themselves,' but such a site still requires planning permission, and before a health licence is granted the local council will satisfy themselves that the sanitation facilities are all that are to be desired. A caravan can only stay on one site for 28 days; application for longer periods has to be made to the local council.

The Government has recognised the need for such social units as caravan sites, and gradually the standards are being vastly improved. Nowadays, if you asked most caravanners if they would like to go back to bricks and mortar, they would answer emphatically, "NO!"

Organisations that will help the caravanner are: the National Caravan Council; the Caravan Dealers and Agents Association; the Caravan Advice Bureau; and the Caravan Club for Touring Vans.

Trailer Tips

Give the illusion of greater space in the caravan lounge by fixing mirrors to the end wall.

A doorstep into the van can be combined with a scraper and box for tools, shoe-cleaning kit, and various oddments.

* * *

If the gas cylinder is placed outside the van it needs to be protected against the cold weather, otherwise the liquid gas will freeze up. A box or an old tin trunk filled with straw or glass-fibre insulating material makes a good cover.

* * *

Inside the van make sure that the gas-cylinder locker is ventilated at the bottom. If it isn't, bore a hole in the floor.

If the gas in the oven goes out, do not apply a match immediately. Turn off the gas, open the oven door to let the collected gas disperse, then re-light the oven.

Always ensure that there is a skylight or window partly open. Never block up the wall ventilators.

Earwig trouble? Cut the grass under the van and spray liberally with DDT. Sprinkle it on ledges and between mattresses and covers. You will soon be insect-free.

* * *

If you are preparing to move from your site and the caravan has no jockey wheel, don't try to lift the draw-bar of a heavy van by yourself. Lower the front legs of the van to take the nose weight, back the car under the coupling, raise the front legs of the van until the coupling on the draw-bar falls on the ball on the car's towing bracket.

* * *

Pressure cookers in the kitchen are an economy as they save butane gas.

An underfloor locker, drilled with holes, can be built into the van (near the axle to save ground clearance) and will make a very good place to keep milk and butter cool in the summer.

PASSE-PARTOUT BORDERS

*An economical hobby
allowing for decorative
self-expression*

Such borders can be used in gay colours in the kitchen and cloak-room, to relieve the bareness of tiling. Dull rooms can be brightened by a well-thought-out design, which, however, should be planned on the table first. If you do have a failure, then the binding can be removed by several applications of hot water. Try your hand at the wall of an unimportant room or a rarely seen wall to begin with! The effect is often of a hand-painted border. One, two or more colours can be overlapped, used in narrow to wide widths, and corners, curves and patterns all being possible. For curves, the bindings must be thoroughly moistened, and stretched gradually in order that the binding becomes pliable to use. Pelmet-boards can have strips put on in straight lines, with a geometrical design at each end. Plain furniture gains with an edging to drawers or top of a suitable colour.

A VERY interesting hobby is to think out designs, either quite simple and effective, or more elaborate, for the use of passe-partout in decorating your home. A low room will gain height with a band of passe-partout binding *blending* with the wall-shade (not contrasting), put around the top of the wall flush with the ceiling, and another band at the bottom around the skirting-board.

Skirting-boards of stairways can be treated in the same way, but here a contrasting colour may be used quite happily. In the illustration, plain distempered walls have encouraged the use of two shades of wood-grain binding, three strips being laid side by side to give a wide border of just on three inches. This border scheme is carried out at a suitable height, rising along the stairway wall and breaking up a large area of wood as is shown in the stairway wood panel. The skirting-board could also be treated, but in this case it would be better to reduce the width of the main border.

A Guide for You

If a guide line is required for mounting individual pieces of passe-partout, a strip of adhesive tape may be applied so that the wall surface provides a guided edge for mounting the work. When the job is completed the tape may be stripped away without leaving any residue. Self-adhesive tape will be found most useful in the case of working out corner schemes. Alternatively a line may be ruled with pencil if such a line is to be ultimately covered with material. Panels may first be prepared with adhesive tape and the work built inside or outside the tape.

LINEN
AND CHINA

MANY housewives today still have linen that belonged to their great-grand-mothers, bought in the days when things were made to last more than a lifetime. Strangely enough, it was also in those days that such enormous quantities of household linen were bought on marriage; yet the inter-changing of linen in use did also mean that it was not subjected to so much wear and tear.

There is a case both for the buying of linen or cotton. Linen is strong, for it is made from flax, the strongest of all vegetable fibres. How-ever, today, the young housewife who can afford only cotton is not interested in whether it will last her for ever, so long as it will be satisfactory for a few years. Linen has a cool touch, like a benediction, is moisture-absor-bent, and conducts heat *away* from the body. But cotton, too, is soft to the touch, freely transmits water vapour and prevents it from accumulating. So you take your choice.

Linen is preferable for kitchen tea-cloths, since there are no short ends to work loose, making polishing glasses a difficult task. Cotton dusters are best. Wash before using.

How to Buy

When buying cotton, make sure that it is closely woven, of fine, balanced threads. Hold sheets or cloth to the light to see that the threads are even, and that it is free of knots and weak places. It should, of course, be snow-white, without a tinge of grey, yellow or blue. Look at the selvedge, too. It should have a firm, closely-woven tape-like look which indicates that the fabric will not break and tear at the edge. Hems should be straight and neatly-sewn, with back-stitching to pre-vent ravelling.

Rub two parts of a sheet together over a dark surface. If it has been over-dressed, a white powdery substance will appear. This means that sizing has been used as a 'filler' to give the sheet a good appearance. The first washing, however, may prove that you have bought a loosely-woven fabric which will not stand up to hard wear.

It is very important to be sure that you get the exact size that you need when buying bed-linen. Many marital quarrels have been caused by too small sheets!

Mostly, sheets bear their actual size in inches, but occasionally they are sold as 'Single-bed size' or 'Double-bed size.' Since a single bed can be anything from a two-foot bunk to 3 ft. 9 in., and a double bed from 4 ft. to an antique Spanish double-bed of 9 ft. (although unlikely in this day and age!), it is obvious that a little accurate measuring is the order of the day, before shopping.

Sometimes sheets intended for single beds are made shorter than those for double beds, which is not founded on common sense, since beds very rarely vary in length.

Allow for Tuck-ins

Measure your bed, allowing for a certain amount of sheet-shrinkage after the first washing. (About 5–6 in. in length and 2–3 in. in width.) Allow for a good turn-over at the top, since many folk do not like the feel of a blanket against the face. A good portion must be taken into account to tuck in at sides and foot. Some qualities of sheet are fully-shrunk when sold, but it does no harm to err on the generous rather than the too-small size. Measure your pillow, as a too-tight pillow-case makes the pillow feel hard. Allow an extra inch all round.

When buying blankets (they should be pure wool), allow for the thickness of the mattress, plus 6–8 in. at the sides to tuck in. It need not be quite as long as the sheets, since there is no turn-over necessary, but remember that on cold winter nights enough length will be needed to fit well over the shoulder and under the chin! Bear in mind that heaviness is not necessarily a sign of warmth. Very light weaves are often cosier. Some people prefer blansheets (a mixture of blanket and sheet), which are ideal for children, being soft and fluffy to the touch, and can be boiled without injury to the fabric. If you have a blanket that is too short, stitch on a piece of flannelette, to use as the 'tuck-in.'

Even towels need to be the right measurement. Small towels are adequate only for drying hands or face. If a bath-towel is not

Shore Sheets, Ltd.
A white sheet with a gay frilled edging made in ten colour-fast shades; pillowcases match

used, then make sure that the hand-towels bought are long enough to stretch across your back when drying. All these small things add to the comfort of life, and add up to smiles instead of frowns. Tiny irritations such as too-short sheets, a too-small towel which gets soaked quickly when drying, become a mountain of annoyance eventually, instead of a lot of little molehills!

New Attractive Bed-linen

Manufacturers are busy these days with new versions of sheets and pillowcases, coloured frills, pretty candy-stripes, and attractive embroideries making the life of the homemaker gayer. Some sheets are embroidered with flowers, lilies-of-the-valley, roses, cornflowers, and chrysanthemums, and blankets can be chosen in a colour to match up with one of the shades in the flowers. The superstitious housewife can choose her 'lucky' flower!

Linens almost ask for a rather important-

looking monogram, and these can be worked at home, the shade chosen according to the colour of the sheet and some attractive contrasts worked out. Black and white is always smart. Rayon is also used as a fabric for sheets, has a luxurious effect, and wears quite well.

It is difficult for the bride to judge just what she will need in the way of sheets, tablecloths, and so on, when faced with the formidable list of her grandmother. But it is something that should be worked out very carefully. Not only the minimum she can buy (if expense is important), but a note of the decorating schemes she has decided upon, so that sheets, towels and eiderdowns can be chosen with a view to blending. Not to buy something because it is 'so pretty,' and then to find that it is the wrong length and is the odd man out where colour schemes are concerned.

It really does pay to buy, not the most expensive, which may mean very fine but not necessarily durable, quality, but the best of its class. Well-known manufacturers back their goods with the guarantee of their own reputation.

Vantona, Ltd.
A sumptuous-looking counterpane with a velvety face forming the design, which looks almost like heavy lace

Your sheets can be embroidered with your favourite flower—roses, lily of the valley, cornflowers or chrysanthemums

Barlow & Jones, Ltd.

List for the Bride

Here is a list that may act as some guide to the girl who is setting up house for the first time, whether it is a two-roomed flat or a house. It implies the minimum, which can naturally be enlarged as the purse permits.

Sheets	Three pairs for each bed.
Pillowcases	Three for each pillow.
Blankets	Four for each bed. You *can* manage with three and a flannelette under-sheet, if necessary.
Bath towels	Three for each member of the household.
Face towels	Three for each person; two or three spares for guests.
Guest towels	Half a dozen. (*They are often received as a wedding-gift. They can also be made at home, embroidered gaily, quite cheaply.*)
Bath mats	Two.
Tablecloths	Four.
Table-mats	Two sets.
Table-napkins	One dozen.
Dusters	Six or eight.
Teacloths	Three.

If coloured sheets and pillowcases are preferred to white ones, then try to stretch to the price of coloured, which always cost rather more than white. If you buy white, intending to change to coloured ones later on, you will miss the pleasure you would get from having your choice; or if you can soon afford coloured ones, then the white will 'rest' in the airing-cupboard. All sorts of attractive colours are available these days: deep pink, peach-pink, saxe-blue, pale blue, lemon, lavender, rose, eau-de-nil, jade and black.

Treat Them Gently

It is a good idea to buy an extra pair of sheets and pillow-cases every year, whether needed at that moment or not. It eases the strain on the budget when suddenly you may need several pairs at once. Do not pull sheets roughly when stripping the bed

Candy-striped pillowcases and sheets in fine Egyptian cotton with a lustre finish are delightful. The frill adds a note of frivolity

Richard Haworth & Co., Ltd.

or removing them to launder. Ease them loose first, as a sudden jerk strains them, causing them to wear out more quickly. Always put your freshly-laundered sheets and pillowcases at the bottom of the pile, so that you rotate the wear on them evenly. Go through all household linen when laundered, mending the very smallest tear at once. It will save bigger tears, a good deal of needlework all at once, and your eyesight!

The top part of the sheets gets the most wear, so put the top to the bottom sometimes when using them, to equalise the wear. Keep lavender sachets among the linen, and put different sizes in separate piles, so that they can be easily found, if you are working against time.

The eiderdown is one of the comforts of bedtime, helping us to be really snug. They can now be obtained backed with a slightly rough material that stops their slipping off the bed in the middle of the night. Many people like to put the eiderdown under the bedcover when the bed is made, especially if the room is used as a bed-sitting-room. But as eiderdowns can be obtained in shades to match or complement the bedspread, it is not necessary when the bedroom is to sleep in only, and not used as a dining-room or lounge by day. Even in this case, it is better to put the quilt away during the daytime, as the suction from a loose cover on top of it causes particles of down to be drawn through the quilt covering.

Covering and Filling

It is most desirable to buy a quilt filled with a good down, which can be made over with a new cover when the old one wears out. Also, it combines heat retention with a lighter weight. However, where price is a factor, then down and feathers can be combined successfully to make a satisfactory covering. An 'eiderdown' is really, if one is being scrupulous, a quilt filled with down from the Eider Duck, which comes from Iceland, and whose price is practically prohibitive, especially as about a third of the weight is lost in purifying.

Fashions vary for coverings, chintz being always in favour, and it is charming for a child's or young girl's room. Satin beauté, rayon satin and taffeta, especially in rich colourings, give a luxurious effect. Crepe, especially in a plain shade. is quieter, lending itself to more modern, straight-lined furnishing schemes. Manufacturers find that rose is the most popular shade, while green is not a favourite, especially in some country districts where it is superstitiously imagined that it invites the stork to visit the house too frequently!

When buying, see that the filling is distributed evenly, and that the centre is not

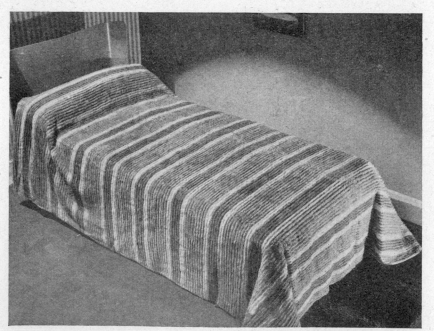

Tufting was improvised by the early settlers in America, who used up the odd lengths of cotton wicks left over from making tallow candles. Candlewick has come a long way since those days, attracting foremost designers to use distinctive colour combinations and patterns in the most modern spreads. This is in tan, green and gold

Everwear Candlewick ,Ltd.

A luxurious bedspread with thick tufting and an unusual floral design in varied colours. Its chevron centre-piece is a distinctive note

This is a multi-coloured, all-cotton bedspread called 'Nonsuch,' the tapestry design taking its name from the Surrey palace of Queen Elizabeth I. The woven design is of flowers, fruit and leaves ringed on a buff ground

Scottish Folk Fabrics

Barlow & Jones, Ltd.

between the folds. Do not wash a down quilt —have it dry-cleaned.

Bedspread Fashions

Bedspreads vary considerably, for there is both a rejection of the bedspread as it was known in Victorian days for much more modern designs, and yet a harping-back to some candlewicks and tapestries of a much earlier period. In fact, the bedspread must not be 'ordinary.' Most people prefer a cover fitted and made in a material matching their colour-scheme, but such charming bedspreads can be bought that cannot be resisted. There are tufted candlewick covers that fit in with period furniture, or simple designs that carry a more modern note. When these are woven instead of machine-tufted (the tufts being formed from the weft in the construction of the fabric) they are tied in more firmly, and result in an extremely hard-wearing bedcover.

There are mock-quilted bedspreads, or brightly striped seersuckers that require no ironing; mixtures of pastel-coloured rayon and cotton; multi-coloured quilts in tapestry design; woven tweed effects.

Measure your bed when it is made up, to

neglected. Spread out the quilt in a warm room after it has been delivered. Gradually its buoyancy should improve with wear.

Take care of your quilt. Do not grasp it by its decorative 'front' but by the under-facing. When you have a party, do not put visitors' clothes on top of it, as they are heavy and may soil it. Lift up the quilt if you want to sit on the bed. If the filling has floated down to the bottom, gently tap it back into place, while it is spread out on the bed. Brush it periodically so that dirt cannot find a home

Here are three cloths, 14½ in. by 20 in., from a set of six, gaily printed with country scenes and wild geese flying

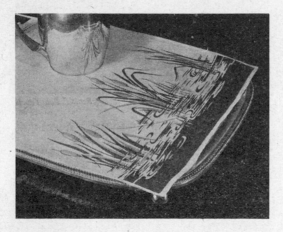

Such cloths can be put to many uses. At the top, as a guest-towel. Above, as a traycloth

On the left, the cloth is used as a place-mat. When there is a meal to be laid for just one person, a colourful mat is all that is necessary. These could also be used for trolley-cloths or chair-backs

decide how large you wish your cover to be, to allow for a drape at sides and the end; a skimpy, dragged look spoils the appearance of any bedspread.

When buying, avoid a bedspread with an open hopsack type of weave, or with long, loose 'floats' of surface yarn. These may catch on corners or odd points and be pulled out. A weave must be compact enough to stand up to everyday use over a period of years.

Dressing Up the Table

Now for the table. While meals served look so much more appetising when they are 'presented prettily,' so does an attractive table give pleasure and relaxation to a repast. Some people eat just to keep alive, hardly noticing what is put before them, or they consider the time spent eating just so much waste of time. Yet a meal at a beautiful, colourful table can represent a period of rest and refreshment that counts both as a conservation of energy to be used later, and a happy social occasion.

Tablecloths are used more often than tablemats on the Continent, but mats still hold pride of place here. Yet some housewives are apt to 'follow the Joneses' and if their friends use only mats, they will, also. If you like a tablecloth, whether it is a rich damask, lace, or gaily checked, then bear in mind that nothing can look more lovely with flower-decorations and shining silverware or plate.

You are liable to have an artistic clash if you put French provincial or 'cottage-y' red-checked tablecloths with a Regency interior of silks and satins, but if your decorative scheme is modern or non-committal in period, either a damask cloth, or one in gay, modern

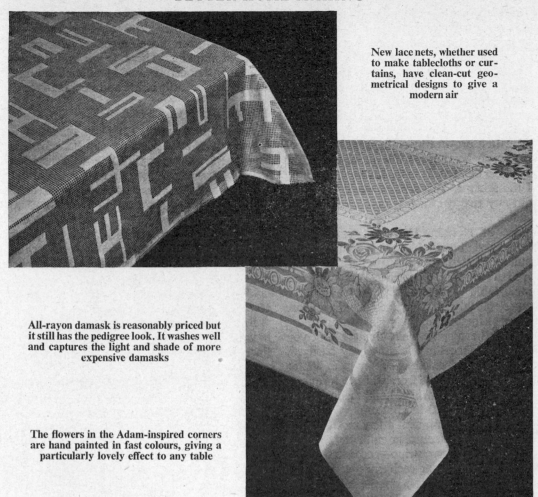

New lace nets, whether used to make tablecloths or curtains, have clean-cut geometrical designs to give a modern air

All-rayon damask is reasonably priced but it still has the pedigree look. It washes well and captures the light and shade of more expensive damasks

The flowers in the Adam-inspired corners are hand painted in fast colours, giving a particularly lovely effect to any table

colours, or elegant mats will be suitable according to the mood and the company.

Organdie is to be avoided for table-mats, since it is inclined to roll badly, and the least that can be demanded of a mat is that it shall lie flat. Some woven materials for tablecloths are likely to shrink badly in the wash, and to lose their shape. Seersucker in gay colours is easily washable, and the right note either for the nursery, or to start the day at the breakfast-table in a cheerful mood. Linen is always one of the best fabrics. White is practical in that stains can be easily removed. However, colour does lend itself to such charming schemes, that the question of stains becomes a matter of taking the thorns with the rose. Rayon is easy to launder, has a soft silky look somewhat like damask, and drapes well. It can also be obtained in many lovely pastel shades.

Original Ideas Count

The success of many table-schemes is due to their originality. If you have a red linen cloth, then table-napkins can be three of red, and three of black, put at alternate places on the table. Or table-mats can be of two alternating shades, say yellow and blue, with a blue napkin opposite a yellow mat and vice versa. Little square neck-scarves sometimes furnish amusing and colourful napkins for the informal gathering, and can be used with a plain cloth catching up one of the mixed colourings in the scarves. To the imaginative mind, nothing need be labelled only for one kind of use. A linen guest-towel may make a very attractive mat for the solitary diner, or a tray-cloth. The napkin may make a pretty guest-towel.

Well-known *couturiers* dress their tables

as carefully as their clients, and some of their ideas are easily copied by any home maker. There is no reason why each department of everyday life should not be pleasing to the eye.

To take a bed-clothing scheme chosen by Hardy Amies . . . the sheets are white Irish linen with brown cording and monogram, covered by a heavy brown linen counterpane, with white cording. The morning tea-tray is laid with a brown tray-cloth, napkin and tea-cosy, each bearing a white monogram. The gay china detracts from the severe masculinity of the scheme. This scheme could be varied with any two contrasting or complementary shades.

One of Norman Hartnell's choices is a Wedgwood blue tablecloth, with a white appliqué pattern that made a perfect setting for his Wedgwood tea service. A more formal dinner-table was laid with a white linen damask cloth, with plain linen napkins of rose colour to match the lovely glassware.

If you have some white damask that you want another colour, it can easily be dyed. A tablecloth decided upon by Mr. Victor Stiebel had been dyed from white to turquoise blue, and a heavy white, hand-made curtain fringe sewn around the bottom.

Kitchen towelling with a gay motif can be made into curtains, supper cloth and napkins to match. Or two strips—necessitating no sewing save hems at each end—can be put crosswise, like runners, on the table. Little guest-towels, trolley-cloths—and, of course, kitchen towelling!—can all be made from this fabric.

A really gay, Continental breakfast scene is favoured by Madame Champcommunal, of the famous dress-house of Worth. A plain lemon cloth has little circular mats of chartreuse-green linen, together with cerise checked napkins. There is no end to the ingenuity that can be used in table-colour and design, with a little effort and imagination.

Renovations in Gay Mood

A tired bedspread of a plain shade, or a tablecloth or even curtains, can be refreshed and smartened by appliquéing near the edge large patterns cut from cretonne or chintz. A wide band of colour catching up some tone in the cretonne can then be put on as a border.

The same idea can be followed with table-mats. If you cut, say, a rose from an odd piece of cretonne, each mat can be appliquéd with the same flower either in the centre or to one side. If you can find some reasonably-priced coloured glassware, you can choose a shade to tone in with the flower-motif.

Braid in a contrasting tone can be stitched in various criss-cross patterns to enliven faded linen, furbish up rugs and so on.

BEAUTIFUL CHINA

Craftsmanship, while still existent and possibly increasing, declined considerably during the years when so few materials were available. China and pottery especially suffered a blow, sending up the value of old decorated china. However, once again there are lovely designs to be found, and while modern taste inclines to sharper tones, more vivid colours, or else completely plain pastel shades, there are still the British potteries whose names are world-wide turning out designs often redolent of a past age, yet abreast of modern taste.

Designs like this one of multi-coloured flowers around a honeycomb centre bring out the cosiness and richness of chenille tufting. The honeycomb motif is repeated again in the border

Andriesse, Ltd.

For instance, take the Copeland-Spode works where old handicraft methods are still followed and there is no mechanisation. Some of the designs are almost exact copies of the earliest ever made in the factory when it began in 1770. The rose sprays designed by William Billingsley, the well-known flower painter of the eighties, still bloom on dinner-services all over the world. There are romantic stories connected with many of the designs. One series of shapes was copied from a silver service used by Queen Charlotte (who chose her own services after a visit to the factory). The 'Almond Blossom' pattern was copied from the decorated papers used to wrap the chests of tea which the first Copeland imported from China. Simpler, freer versions have emerged from many of the old designs used by various famous potteries.

China and Earthenware

Many people are a little vague as to the difference between china and earthenware, yet others are quite definite that a cup of tea tastes much better in china—and the finer the better!—although they are willing to concede that a cup of coffee with milk or cream 'goes with' pottery!

The term 'china' is applied to a wide variety of ceramics. Technically, china is a hard, vitreous porcelain, translucent and cold to the touch. In selecting fine china, the first consideration must be quality, for no amount of decoration can make up for faulty texture.

The best pieces of old chintz curtains or loose covers can be used for renovation by adding bands of the material

Instead of using strips, the pattern can be cut from cretonne and appliquéd on to dull or worn covers, cloths or curtains, and a band of plain colour added as a border

While really famous makes of china are extremely expensive, some stores sell dinner sets piece by piece, so that a valuable and beautiful heirloom can gradually be collected.

Earthenware is entirely without translucence, and less cold to the touch. Many of the same kind of designs are used as on china,

Susie Cooper

This gay design in crimson earthenware with a gold edge is called 'Regency Feather'

but often earthenware is more effective in plain colours. For breakfast-tables, or dinner-tables in an informal atmosphere, such plain pottery can be used with table linen to form an attractive colour contrast. Such as vivid blue pottery with a lemon cloth, or two tones of the same colour. Sets are often built up of a similar design in a different shade for each piece, which does lend variety.

Quite apart from the charm of its design, china and earthenware should be bought with due consideration for the part it is to play in the life of the household. Handles should be well-placed and easy to hold; cups should be high and narrow if you like a very hot cup of tea. In America more low, wide cups are sold than in Britain, which would indicate our island reverence for the cup that cheers! Tea-pots should have spouts that pour smoothly; jugs should be easy to clean and not have unexpected dips and crevices that make them difficult to wash.

Visits to museums will bring learning about china, which is an open window on to the centuries in which such pieces were made. It is amazing how very 'modern' many china designs appear; that is, modern in this age as well as the age in which they first made their appearance! By studying the history of the china, much romantic history comes to light, and taste is moulded and understanding of design deepened.

Care of Your China

When you have lovely things, do take care of them. China must be warmed evenly, not have sudden applications of great heat, either by cooked foods being poured in at boiling point, or standing a china pot on a stove. It can be stood on a firm, woven wire cake-rack, if it must be on the stove at all. Where food acids or fruits such as vinegar, lemons, and so on have been in contact with the china, it should be washed at once, in case the sheen of the coloured decoration may be damaged.

Harsh washing powders or soda in the washing-up water should be avoided for the same reason. A hot, mild, soap-flake solution is the best cleansing agent, although china and pottery should not be left too long to

Susie Cooper

A more conventional, graceful coffee-set 'Pink Pride,' in bone china. Pink with a gold edge

soak. Washing machines should be used with caution and the directions followed implicitly. Plates can become scratched if they are handled carelessly or roughly stacked. Cups should always be hung on hooks, as putting them one inside the other causes damage to both cup and handle. A little household bleach diluted will remove tea-stains on china in a matter of seconds, although it is best to use a little borax for cleaning the decorated part.

Repairing China

Broken edges of china must be clean, and where the break is an old one, the edges should be roughened with sandpaper before applying cement, plastic resin or glue, so that it holds. The join should be tied to hold it firm while drying. A little powdered alum can be melted instead of glue and put over the broken edges; press them together and keep firm with adhesive tape. Another adhesive is to mix gum arabic with plaster of Paris.

Pieces of beautiful china can of course be used as a wall decoration, or one or two pieces displayed in a cabinet to show them to their best effect. Gone are the days of crowded cabinets; a much more attractive scheme is achieved by the use of a simple grouping of a few pieces of charm.

Students' Progress

Time marches on, and with it come changes that sometimes take us forward, and often back a long way into the past. After all, nothing can rival the Greek statuary of hundreds of years B.C., and the drinking-vessels found among the ruins of ancient Roman civilisations are very similar to those we use today.

While many of our well-known firms concentrate on the continuation of patterns they have had for decades, others, both here and

These interesting new fabrics are, reading downwards: A heavy Jacquard folkweave with a design of Elizabethan figures and Windsor Castle. National emblems form a charming design on Jacquard satin. The 'M' design, a contemporary hand print on Dobby figured-satin cloth. Modern version of a Regency stripe in three colours

W. Foxton, Ltd.

Story-book king and queen in unglazed pottery in biscuit and white by a student, shows a romantic imagination at work

esteem—they go forward into new fields of decoration.

Fresh Design

One excellent sign is that, both in textiles and china, the names of designers are being more featured than for a long time, and this is an encouragement to the art student, in whose hands lies the future of our china design. Wedgwood, whose name has been a byword in our homes for two centuries, employs free-lance designers and takes on promising students direct from the Royal College of Art, which makes for a 'recharging' of original freshness. Small pottery firms also are producing work of great vitality.

Italy has always had a name for vivid and graceful china and glass and has had an influence on that of other countries. About the year 1500, emigrant Italian potters started a flourishing industry at Antwerp, which later moved to Holland; Italian potters from Antwerp, too, came to London about 1570. Wandering Italians also set up in Germany and France, but not with so much success, though in Switzerland there grew up a thriving manufacture of painted stove-tiles. This delightful art is being revived very slightly today . . . let us hope it develops.

Chinese porcelain has its periods of rare beauty; in fact, so few pieces reached Europe in the 15th and 16th centuries that they were mounted in silver or gold and treated as precious stones! Today, we have a return to simplicity, as if by ruling out the complicated although charming patterns liked by a

in other countries, are producing colourful and original designs that fill a positive craving for colour and new shapes. Many of these appear to take their inspiration from primitive work, but incorporate new techniques and materials. Instead of being tied to traditional effects—although these still continue to have a deservedly high place in our

The left-hand vase is eloquently named a 'handkerchief' vase; the middle is a conventional design, and that on the right is an ultra-modern design in green, deriving its inspiration from centuries ago. All are in Venetian glass

Right: These vivid, attractive dishes are of cut glass in blue and red, both by English students. Below is a leaf-shaped dish with fine white veins, a sample of today's Italian craftsmanship

previous age, we can begin to build anew a different conception of what constitutes both beauty and practicality.

There are tiles to be found, sometimes from Mexico which have drifted over here; or old ones usually vaguely labelled Staffordshire ware, and these make charming decorations either for the wall, or to be used as teapot stands. Modern tiles can also be bought and used in the same way. Mainly, of course, they are used in bathrooms or fireplaces.

The characteristic grey or whitish German stoneware, which reached full development in the 16th century, was mostly used for beer-jugs and tankards. Today there is a revival of this type of pottery, both mugs and vases, of a light opal-grey which forms a lovely background for flower-arrangements.

Colour and Purpose

In fact, when buying china, bear in mind not only the colour-scheme with which it is to be used but the purpose. Breakfast pottery can be gaily bright and it does not matter if it is on the thick side. China for tea-parties

needs to be thinner and the best you can buy ... but there again, make a note of the colour of your teacloths so that it can be bought to blend. Fragile china naturally does not look well with a brightly patterned peasant-type cloth. Vases of grass-green, mauvy-greys and cream are nearly always an excellent choice. It is very rarely that a very brightly coloured vase makes a good background for flowers, since they should provide all the colour needed.

Ornamental Glassware

Glassware can be bought quite cheaply again, and there is a liking for buying coloured glass, not only the expensive antiques, but modern glass that is not a strain on the purse. But there, too, it is wise to bear a very general colour-scheme in mind, with your table glass, candlesticks, fruit bowls, tankards, all matching or blending. Purple glass will blend with pink shades, or green; blue with amber ... but map it out in your own mind before buying, do not choose haphazardly. Make sure, too, that you can match up any set you buy. Nothing is more annoying than to spend money on beautiful glassware and then find that you cannot replace anything that is broken.

If you keep in mind the various colour-plans of your whole house or flat, you will be able to interchange things for a fresh appearance ... occasional change is beneficial to all of us! For instance, your glass candlesticks will look lovely with your table glass, but they can also be used on your dressing-table with a quite different colour-scheme so long as they have been carefully chosen to be happy with both.

A slightly surrealist influence pervades these dishes in black and white and brown and blue, made by English students

However modern glassware may appear, its shape can nearly always be traced back a long way in time for its inspiration. It seems impossible—and maybe unnecessary—to find a new form. Although the rather heavy and ornate cut glass still accounts for about fifty per cent. of glass sales, plainer ware in a variety of shapes makes up for the other fifty per cent.

There are some very cheap candlesticks to be found in the shops, mostly in a flat disc shape in various colours. These are ideal for

These striking figures in black and white, used as candlestick-holders, are the product of a famous Venetian glassworks

the dinner-table, since, even when holding long, slender, decorated candles, they do not make a barrier behind which people have to dodge to see one another. The original wares of foreign countries are again on the market, but of course, these products come in small batches, and can very rarely be found in the same designs another time.

England seems to lead in decorated candles. Shortish, rather fat candles with gold patterns are on sale for a few shillings a pair, and look remarkably elegant in the plainest holder. Many visitors buy them here to take back abroad with them since such candles, as we know them, are not easily obtainable outside this country. Candlesticks and candles not only lend charm to any grouping, but gain themselves from being put with the right companion-pieces of ornaments or flowers.

China in Filing Cabinets

Living certainly does become more stream-lined these days. Wedgwood have all their designs sold from filing-cabinets . . . later, we may buy all our china and earthenware that way! It does mean that plates, cups and

Another effective and decorative piece of work by a student; a very modern black-and-white coffee-set

There are many attractive modern designs for soup-sets to be found in the shops. This one, also by a student, is in pinky-grey with black stripes

saucers of varying designs can be seen and compared at a glance. 'Sample' dishes, even ornaments, are on display in meticulous order. Any existing patterns can happily be matched up almost immediately, which does not make the housewife quite so afraid of a breakage. Other non-current designs may, of course, take months to match.

Popular Fancy

The china that people mostly think of as Wedgwood—the blue jasper with white pattern in relief—is still made, but only in tea- and coffee-sets and small ornaments; it is still a favourite. Black-and-white patterns are modern and popular. The black vases and bowls that were in fashion in the late twenties are on show again, and can be a wonderful contrast for flowers or fruit. It is strange, with all the new designs, that the old ones have such a hold on our hearts. One of the most liked is still the 'Napoleon Ivy' design, so called because it was originally designed for Napoleon. One of the newer patterns, called 'Travel Throughout the Ages' (designed by Eric Ravilious, who was killed in the last war) was chosen by Princess Margaret. It features all the aspects of travel —aeroplanes, cars, balloons, ships—all in a quiet, contemporary, discreet yet colourful design.

China Shelves

An old bookcase can be painted a gay colour and, standing on top of a bureau or chest, makes an excellent 'display cabinet' for your favourite china pieces. Line the back of the shelves with the reverse side of printed linen or cretonne—it gives a muted, tapestry-like, effect.

One or two brightly coloured ornaments of good design are always a happy choice for book-shelf or mantel. The cock and hen in opaque coloured glass come from Italy, and are original flower-vases

PATCHWORK POTTERY

Make Coloured Pots and Plates

Save all your broken plates and cups, for if you are tired of plain ware, you can make coloured pots and plates for ornamental use, at home. It will cost little more than your own industry. Patchwork pottery resembles patchwork quilting, only instead of pieces of cloth you use fragments of brightly coloured china and glass!

Odd Bits and Pieces

To make a patchwork pot or vase you will need a stone jam-jar with straight sides, some putty, a small quantity of paint, a fine-pointed brush and, of course, your china and glass patches. First cover the outside of the jar with putty, not too thickly. Then take each piece of china or glass in turn and press into the putty until the jar is covered. Take care to leave only cracks, not spaces, between the pieces. As a finishing touch, cover the cracks with gold paint. Leave the work to dry for several days.

You can make plate in the same way, and the cheapest of tin dishes will serve to work upon. Patchwork plates look well as wall decorations, round a plate-rail, or, if really large, upon the mantelpiece. You may like to wait until you have collected a great many pretty fragments of china and glass before you begin on your patchwork ware; then perhaps you will be able to make a matching set of six lovely dishes, repeating the same basic design upon each.

SILVER FOR THE COST OF PLATE

Anyone who has a flair for furnishing richly at the minimum of cost, haunts markets and antique shops where old silver may be picked up for a reasonable price. Naturally, one has first to be armed with some knowledge, but there are books to be bought on silverware, and a little study of designs and marks will be useful when buying in unguaranteed markets.

For instance, collecting piece by piece, spoon by spoon, a service of George III silver can be built up for the same cost, or less, as good-quality silver plate, and about a quarter the price of modern silver, which bears a heavy tax. Victorian silver is even cheaper. It is an intriguing pastime . . . something like a detective story, only instead of clues, you have missing forks! Then the effort put into bringing it together is not wasted, for the set complete is worth very much more than it has cost collecting it in separate pieces. First choose your pattern. You can either do this by preference for simple Old English or a more ornate design, such as King or Queen's pattern, with shell at top and scrolled engraving running down the handle, or by finding some wonderful bargain of perhaps half a dozen forks or spoons of some particular pattern, and deciding to complete the set.

Gifts for Abroad

Then for that difficult task of sending presents abroad without putting either oneself or recipient to enormous customs charges, did you know that anything made before the date 1829 is considered 'antique' (with which label it is hard to quarrel) and therefore can be sent to the United States and all the Commonwealth duty-free? There are also many lovely things that can be found with a little persistence which make wonderful presents for friends at home, too.

For instance, a slender, flat, narrow-bladed George Third meat skewer makes an ideal gift for a man to use either as a paper-knife or, being both heavy and decorative, as a paper-weight. This should cost not more than £2 10s. to £3. George Third snuff-boxes make cigarette containers for handbag or table. A flat object that can be put inside a letter (or Christmas card) is an old silver decanter-label for whisky, gin and other liquids, costing about 35s. each.

An unusual thought is an antique French wine-taster, which makes a delightful ashtray, or container for sweets, sugar or trinkets. Babies' antique silver mugs cost no more than modern ones, and if sending across the Atlantic to a friend who has been 'blessed eventing,' are duty-free.

Keeping Silver Bright

Silver needs to be used to be kept free from tarnish. It can be laid away carefully wrapped in black tissue paper. Some people pack their silver away in flour; or with a piece of camphor. Soapy water, used for washing, brings up the brightness without polishing, or a little borax or ammonia can be added to the washing-water. If slightly tarnished, boil in an aluminium saucepan filled with salt water, rinse and polish with a chamois leather.

Courtesy of Richard Ogden, Piccadilly, London

At the top of the page is a George III tea-service dated 1809. It is easy to recognise the chaste and lovely lines of this period

A Georgian pierced sweet dish (or rather 'comfits' in those days!) dated 1770

An embossed sugar sifter of the same period, 1765

A salt cellar with a blue liner, 1802. These are usually bought in pairs

A pepper pot, 1776. A cruet-set can be built up from pieces bought separately

A George II meat-skewer of solid silver. When these can be found, they make paper-knives or excellent paper-weights, as they are heavy

Antique chased snuff-boxes can be used for cigarette cases; the smaller ones, or patch-boxes, are ideal for carrying saccharine

Old French wine tasters make charming sugar or sweet dishes or can be used as ash-trays

It is useful to know that antiques of a date before 1829 can be sent abroad duty-free. This is an aid to the solving of the present problem for overseas friends

THE ROSE BASKET

Here is another lesson in arrangement. This time it is roses and irises, a design by Moyses Stevens, which the beginner can copy by following the illustrations with care. First, choose your attractive basket with a container inside. Place your materials and basket on newspaper to protect the surface of the table

Begin to form the outline with the smallest roses, and an iris placed low in the basket. Remove alternate leaves from the stems, for foliage saps up the moisture needed to keep the blooms fresh

Put the wet moss in the basket, building up from the brim. Remember that the end of each rose stem should be cut with a sharp knife slantwise before placing it in the moss

These are the directions for the full-colour reproduction on the opposite page

Fill in the floral outline, still keeping all your flowers low in the basket, and dipping over the edge. Ensure that the moss is really damp and covers a generous portion of the stalks

Build upwards now, giving height with leaves. Guard against any unsightly gaps. Complete with the inner cluster of irises as seen on the left. See that the flowers do not stand level with each other, or the effect will not be 'carefully careless'

Fill a bowl with crumpled chicken-wire, and make an outline of your design with fairly tall twigs. Build up with daffodils, seeing that some tilt forward. Place some small bunches of violets centrally. They need not reach the water, as they absorb moisture through their petals when sprayed

An old china teapot that has lost its lid makes an effective background for a few choice blooms

Directions for building this arrangement are on opposite page

A bookcase placed out into the room forms a dining-alcove on one side. The pots are in a moss-packed trough, and thin wire can be used for plants to climb. Flower bulbs can be mingled with the greenery to give variety

Ivies are attractive when combined with a larger plant. Pots which are not sunk in moss, peat or packed around with newspaper will require more watering, although too much water is bad for most greenery of this type

TRAILING BEAUTY

Above:

The heart-shaped leaves of Philo-dendron scandens look delightful trailing from a wall-vase. This one has been placed just below the wall lights to make a pretty grouping, especially when the lamps are lit

Right:

One corner of a hall could be treated like this; any handyman can make a wall-trough long enough to carry a drifting curtain of green confetti. Strip lighting can be fixed just above the trough to achieve a little home flood-lighting, with fairylike effect

Climbing plants are especially fresh and decorative in a hall. By the stairs is a Ficus decora; in the window, ivy and Philodendron scandens. On the shelf, Philodendron with Canary Ivy and Cissus Antarctica

A GARDEN INDOORS

Flowers arranged with imagination and originality give a note of extra charm to any room

FLOWERS have been used throughout the ages in various parts of the world as a link with religion, as a language of love, and their arrangement has been, in the East, an elaborate ritual.

For some decades past, however, a stiff bunch of expensive blooms put into a Grecian urn were considered the height of artistic decoration. Money value, rather than artistry, was the criterion of their value.

Nowadays there is an ever-growing interest in the art of flower-arrangement. Those who can paint arrange their own 'still-life' with flowers and branches. Books on arrangements to be made with flowers, shrubs and berries have become best-sellers; schools of flower arrangement exist; flower-arranging societies flourish.

It is no wonder, really, for nothing can add to the charm of a room like a bowl of happily arranged blooms. Even a few wild flowers in a colourful milk-jug can light up a dull corner of a cottage living-room.

A room, of course, must be planned to stand alone, to be as gracious without any addition, but a carefully planned miscellany of flowers must be the finishing touch, the benediction to the whole.

Your Equipment

It is necessary to have a collection of variously sized vases and bowls. They need not by any means be expensive. These days unusual containers are used to give piquancy to the scene. An attractive teapot without a lid; a painted shopping-basket or toy wheelbarrow, each with a zinc container inside (sometimes a cake-tin will serve); a brandy glass for that one perfect bloom; a vegetable dish; a witch-bowl; a bread-bin can hold masses of long-stemmed flowers or shrubs, such as Michaelmas daisies, rhododendrons, gladioli. A water carafe is ideal for other flowers.

However, even those who love flowers often consider that they have an 'arrangement' when they have set a bunch in a vase, just seeing that the shorter stems lead up to the longer stems in a pyramid effect at the back or middle of the vase. While pyramid effects have their place, there are other designs to be aimed for, crescents, low clusters at the side of a bowl. A scheme can be built up from one central vivid flower, or 'trailing clouds of glory' from a wall-vase. A perfect bloom or two floating in a bowl of complementary or contrasting colour, with a piece of china or candlestick close by, makes a picture of great charm. As you experiment with flowers and other materials, it is rewarding to discover not only new arrangements, but that you can evolve your own effects of genuine artistry and have a means of creative self-expression.

While a blending of various colours is perhaps more interesting to arrange, a patch of one particular shade can be just as effective, and in some cases more so. A splash of yellow flowers that rival sunlight, for example, is always a happy choice in a dull room.

Original Groupings

Do not be too ambitious when you start. In the East, one flower decoration rule is to put the flowers as they grow: that is, a spray of apple blossom would sweep high over clusters of violets or primroses at the foot of the grouping. It is useful to bear this in mind, even if you discard it sometimes in favour of your own ideas. Clusters at one side of a bowl may be flanked by stones to help hold the grouping in place. The stones may be on view if they blend with the decorative scheme as a whole, or hidden by foliage if they are there only as ballast.

You will need various types of flower-holder. There are pin-holders, glass and wire holders, all to be bought for very little. One of the most useful is perhaps a piece of large-

There are many flower-holders to be bought but some are apt to give a stiff effect. Large-mesh wire netting is one of the most successful ways of keeping flowers in position

Buy a yard of the netting and a pair of special flower scissors. When you have cut a piece of netting, crumple it so that it fits but comes just above the rim of your container. Have your scheme of arrangement and colour definitely in mind before you make a beginning

A ring container is very useful for making low arrangements for a dinner-table so that the guests can see each other across the table. Short odd flowers fit into such a ring, but they need not be crowded next to one another —here is a charming arrangement of white roses set to one side

mesh wire-netting crumpled into the shape of the top of the vase you are using and hooked over the edge. This can be hidden by foliage. Crumpled wire-netting can also be used in the bottom of a shallow bowl, and kept in place by plasticine or modelling clay. Then some raffia—dark green is the most useful as being easily mingled with stems and foliage—to tie back branches or to keep a bloom in place. Where this is not suitable, you should have to hand some long pieces of wire. One of these can be inserted into the head of the flower and twisted around the stalk to bend to position in a formal floral scheme. Paper can be crumpled to put in the bottom of a vase—although not a transparent one, of course—so that short-stemmed flowers gain height.

Frame for the Picture

Background is as important to the finished design as is a frame to a picture. Should you use a small teapot without a lid, it may look forlorn and rather ridiculous marooned in the centre of a large table. But on a shelf, reflected in a mirror, it comes into its own. Dark red roses are going to be lost against very dark panelling or a highly patterned wallpaper. Set against cream walls or light panelling, they become a poem of beauty. If you set blooms next to a heavy, black, eight-day clock, the effect is ruined. Bright, vivid colours, such as marigolds or cornflowers, are more at home in lounge or dining-room, while the softer shades tone in better with a feminine bedroom. Even that is, ultimately, a matter of taste.

Then flowers can be used to pick up some motif in a colour-scheme or blend or contrast with a design in a furnishing material.

Vary Your Materials

There are many different mediums of decoration—pine leaves, ornamental gourds, even mushrooms can be used with effect; cones, pomegranates, kale, ripe corn, grasses, branches of red berries startlingly effective with vivid blue or white flowers. Gardenias and camellias, while they make a particularly lovely table-decoration, have to be handled with care, since they bruise and discolour easily.

In the autumn, gather beech leaves, and put them in a jug with one part glycerine to two parts of water, leaving them for about three weeks. This will preserve them for the rest of the winter. Other leaves can also be kept shiny in this way. Fern leaves dry well if they are placed between sheets of newspaper and left for some weeks under a mattress or unused carpet. As berries are likely to fall once in a dry, warm atmosphere, it is best to paint over the berries, branches and coloured leaves with thin, clear varnish, also to preserve them and give a shiny appearance.

Take a Little Care

Remember that flowers respond to a little care in an almost human manner. Draughts are bad for them. Plunge drooping flowers up to their heads in a pitcher of lukewarm water. Watch needs to be kept on the water in vases, as some flowers drink so quickly and greedily. It is not necessary to change the water every day, unless it becomes a little stagnant, which may be caused by leaves below water-level, which are better plucked off. A charcoal tablet may be dropped in the water to absorb poisons. The water can be just 'topped up' with fresh each day. Large-surfaced leaves should be placed flat in water for some hours to revive them and keep their shape. Violets, primroses, camellias and gardenias need only the blooms sprinkling.

Perhaps those folk who are said to have 'green fingers' because flowers respond to their handling are just those who love them.

CLIMBING GREENERY

Climbing greenery, while it has become more popular recently, has not been used, except in very modern, luxurious homes, to the extent that it could be. Yet it is of all indoor garden decorations the least trouble and expense once it has been arranged.

There are so many ways in which this kind of greenery can be used, apart from trailing from a container on the wall, or left simply as a pot plant.

Ivy can be trained to trail up the side of

To form a decorative arrangement of flowers, it is necessary that background and adjacent ornaments are taken into account as well. The candles flanking these lovely anemones give a finishing touch, and the three silver goblets that look as if they 'just happened' to be there are all part of the finished picture

A miniature plastic greenhouse makes a charming and interesting addition to a window-ledge. This one is length 7⅞ in., width 5¾ in., height 5⅜ in. The transparent top is removable for watering the tiny plants, which can be in small pots or grown in the tray itself

a window, with a single curtain drawn to the other side, to make a balanced foil for its fresh-looking charm. In this case, thin wire is used, and if you do not care for ivy, then *Cissus Antarctica* is a frail-looking, pretty plant to have in its place. It thrives well in all normal house temperatures. If you have wrought-iron gates to divide sitting-room from dining-room, then ivy can be trained happily over these.

In the bathroom, climbing plants give an effect of bathing in a forest pool, if you are of a romantic turn of mind! With a little wire and some artistic imagination, you can arrange the ivy to grow in swirling designs that hide any bareness caused by lack of expensive fitments or to cover the inharmony of old-fashioned interior arrangements. There are several varieties of ivy. The soft yellow-leaved ivy may blend with a colour-scheme

An attractive holder for plants. Other holders can be bought to hang on walls. Or a standing container with two 'troughs' for plants can be used instead to hold bottles when friends drop in for drinks, the plants being replaced afterwards

Put your glossy leaves into unusual jugs. Give the leaves a good bath before you use them and occasionally rub over with an oily rag. They can, for decorative purposes, be varnished different colours

If your room does not look out on to an agreeable view, a lattice of unpolished wood can be placed just before the window, and greenery trained to climb to one side from a moss-filled trough at the bottom. It would block out the light if growing all over the lattice

This chair has a frame of Australian walnut, is upholstered with 1½-in. foam rubber and covered with grey hide tooled in an all-over design

better than the dark green. Wash the shiny leaves occasionally, or rub them over with an oily rag, as this will conserve their moisture.

Potting Ivy

Pull a little ivy so that some of the roots remain on it. Pot it up into a little sand until more roots are formed and then pot it into good soil, for as a pot plant it can be used to great effect in narrow halls that would not take a larger flower.

Climbing greenery does not require much light and thus can be a gay curtain between two rooms; or employed to brighten a dull corner. Along the top of a bookcase or shelf, the pots can be in a moss-packed trough. In this way, bulbs can be added to add another note of colour. The heart-shaped *Philodendron scandens* is another pretty and robust plant.

When you want a big, important-looking pot plant that goes well with a severely modern decor, then choose a *Ficus decora*. Placed next to a staircase, vividly contrasting with the white wall of a hall, or flaunting its rich-looking leaves against a sunblind, it is an acquisition in the home. They cost so little and give such an expensive air.

A wooden lattice can also be fixed on a wall near a plain, large window and give a garden impression even against the dullest town view. Your excess greenery can be put into some unusual container, either plain or with its leaves lacquered to different colours.

BUILDING A MINIATURE GARDEN

THERE is a romantic appeal about a miniature garden, for it appeals to the child in each of us. It need not be only a garden, but we can become quite feudal and build a whole village. There can be flowers, bridges, houses, little mountain huts, even people! And we are monarchs of all we survey.

Such gardens should appeal especially to flat-dwellers, who cannot indulge their floral creativeness out of doors, providing both interest and a decorative note. These tiny gardens can be purchased ready made, but the imaginative will want to build their own, or at least to buy one that is large enough to welcome additions. They can be used, also, as window-boxes, or as the 'centre-piece' on a stone stand in the middle of a lawn.

Most of the miniature shrubs are known

From ' Miniature Gardens '

This delightful garden was planned for the Queen when she was Princess Elizabeth
by Anne Ashberry, who also made a replica for the 1951 Festival of Britain. Note
the arbour, and the tiny trees reflected in the pool

as alpine plants, and the places from which
they come sound romantic, and provide us
with a mental picture of towering mountains,
flower-sprinkled alpine meadows, rocks and
gorges . . . coming now from the Himalayas,
Greece, Palestine, Switzerland, Austria, China
and Tibet. Although such plants are now
grown and sold by nursery gardens, to begin
with, many famous explorers were responsible
for discovering them and introducing them
into this country.

These flowers, shrubs and tiny trees can,
of course, be planted in a proper rock garden,
but the advantage of a miniature garden in
an old stone trough, or a sink, is that it can
be looped on a support that brings it nearly
to eye-level, and can be gazed at and enjoyed
at leisure.

Here are some suggestions for plants to
buy. Dwarf conifers: *Cedrus libani Comte de
Dijon*, a lovely dwarf form of the Cedar of
Lebanon. Rather rare; 15 to 18 inches.

Juniperus Sanderi has enchanting blue-grey
foliage. The branches spread upwards and
the tree gradually forms a dense pyramid.

Chamoecyparis obtusa tetragona aurea has
dense foliage of a brilliant yellow. A rather
irregular shape, reaching its most attractive
when about six years old.

Chamoecyparis pisifera plumosa aurea com-

pacta Rogersii is a little tree with foliage of
pale green, tinged with gold. Very slow
growing.

Juniperus Coxii has branches that hang
down gracefully rather like a weeping willow,
and it looks at its best overhanging a small
pool. This unusual tree was introduced from
China. At six years old it is only about four
inches in height, although at ten years old it
becomes quite high.

Picea excelsa Clambrasiliana is a lovely
little pine which, in the spring, puts forth new
foliage of a fresh vivid green. It gradually
darkens towards midsummer. It has a true
pine scent.

Here are some plants which should not be
difficult to grow:

Anagallis tenella, the bog pimpernel, is
frequently found in marshy places in Britain.
It is a creeping plant, flat, with round leaves,
on a long stem, from which rise little cup-
shaped blooms of shell-pink.

Asperula suberosa comes from Greece and,
though it is hardy, looks fragile and delicate.
It has pale green, almost silvery, foliage, and
pink trumpet flowers from May-August.

Campanula fieldi has mauve hanging bells,
and bronze foliage.

Erinus Dr. Hanele has gay cerise flowers.
May–June.

Viola Yakusimanii, which comes from Japan, is a violet half an inch high, with white flowers shaded to lavender.

Wahlenbergia tasmanica has little bell flowers of lilac shading to white, on 2-inch stems. July–September.

There are not many bulbs small enough to go into the miniature garden, but those that will are among the loveliest blooms of all. There is *Anomatheca cruenta* from South Africa, like a salmon-pink gladiolus, with crimson centres. There are also some of the crocus species. The crocus 'Snow Bunting' is white with a golden centre and purple-brown markings on the outer petals, flowering January–February. The dwarf cyclamen will flower happily when well established. Dwarf daffodils are sheer delight.

Then few people will be able to resist their own dwarf rose garden. These fairy roses, of which there are many varieties, flower for longer than their larger rose sisters, although giving an effect of fragility. They look almost unreal, as do so many of the Lilliputian shrubs and flowers.

The best soil for a general collection of alpines is:

1 *part fibrous loam*
$\frac{1}{2}$ *part coarse sand*
1 *part leaf-mould or moss peat*
$\frac{1}{2}$ *part grit* (*granite or limestone chippings,* or *fine gravel* $\frac{1}{4}$-*inch grade, from which the dust has been washed or sieved*).

This is a general guide only, as much depends on the soil or loam available. All worms must be removed, as they can cause a good deal of damage. With the exception of a few, most alpines thrive in soil with lime in it. They need the maximum of light to help their growth. It is necessary that the bowl or trough should be of porous material, as well as having a small drainage hole at the bottom, otherwise the soil will become stagnant and the plants unhealthy.

A landscape that is to be indoors most of the time needs one or two dwarf conifers, some shade-loving plants, and a variety of the miniature roses.

Keep Them Moist

The garden should be placed in a window where the amount of light is not reduced, even net curtains can do this. Some balconies also do not get enough light. An indoor garden must be close to the window-glass and not on a table which is lower. As the foliage does not get any dews indoors, it is necessary to spray the plants, as well as to give sufficient moisture to the roots. Out of doors the amount of watering depends on the weather. A good guide-rule is that the soil should be kept slightly moist but not saturated.

From 'Miniature Gardens'

In this 'Olde Worlde Garden' Anne Ashberry has placed a hand-carved model of a well in weathered oak. There are ducks on the Green (a carpet of Scleranthus biflorus) and roses growing against the fence

LESSON

IN

ARTISTRY

If you have some natural talent for design, you will be able to map out your own ideas, then carry them out step by step. Here are three stages of a simple but beautiful line arrangement

A pin-holder is used on which to spear leaves of different lengths. They are, as you see, arranged symmetrically, leaving room for other material. You will find that it is nearly always best to arrange your background material first in a design of this kind

Next, the pin-holder (or whatever other type of holder you are using in a similar grouping) must be covered. Here, larger-surfaced leaves are used both to camouflage the holder and provide the background for the blooms

Now you have the complete arrangement, with the blooms—three florets from the
top of a spike of gladioli—unifying the whole. The picture has been built up, for
you will observe that no part of it is complete without the other

Shallow saucers, shells and low bowls can be used for this type of flower decoration. Large blooms which are still fresh when the lower blooms fade, can be cut
down to use in this way. Two or three separate blossoms can be blended for a striking colour effect. There are many delightful containers in the shops, of white glazed
pottery lined with pastel shades, that are particularly suitable for the use of short
or broken-stemmed flowers

If you have iris, either all of one colour or a blend of primrose and mauve, you can arrange them conventionally in a bowl by placing a pin-holder in the bottom, and impaling iris and leaves on to it, making sure that no head is level with another. The shorter stems are naturally at the bottom, and one centre tall one at the top in a pyramid effect. However, above you see a different and more original arrangement. The pin-holder can be covered with pebbles

This delightful arrangement is excellent for a centre-piece for the dinner-table, or on a sideboard. The platter can be of unpolished wood or gaily coloured pottery or glass. It is achieved simply by placing a few sprigs of Cupressus on a holder and arranging the fruit around it. Toothpicks will help to keep oranges in position

Modern tables with polished or unpolished tops demand modern decoration.
Here is an outline of pale green leaves, and mushrooms wired to rhododendron
leaves, a scheme which keeps fresh for some weeks. With a tall jug it is best,
as shown here, to cover the rim, or the result is apt to be ungainly. Do not be
too conventional in your choice of material. Fruit often gives a vivid effect;
berries are decorative; leaves are many-coloured. Pine-cones, wheat, heather,
toadstools, vegetables, all have their place in colour and design

The low cluster of pink camellias hides both the pin-holder and the base of the branches of horse-chestnut in bud. This is an Oriental type of arrangement.

Below:

One or two single blossoms can look very beautiful, especially on top of a bureau or desk. These two red flowers of Hippeastrum were the last from a well-spent stem, and used with bright green leaves

Make Your Own Curtains

CURTAINS are to a home as an overcoat or cloak is to a woman—it sets off the whole, is the final touch to the *ensemble*, screens from view, and also reveals whether she has taste or otherwise !

There are so many charming curtain-arrangements these days; so many pastel-shaded nets that filter the light, softening harshness of outlook; so many different rich brocades, rayons, gay chintzes, that it would be a very difficult person who could not find something both charming and to their own taste.

Curtains are also, in the main, fairly simple to make, if a few rules are followed. As usually they last for years, a good deal of care should be taken with the making.

Buy Enough Material

Let's say with emphasis that good curtains are an economy in the end, especially for large sash or modern horizontal windows, for these look better, wear better, wash or clean better. Also, if you move to a different house with smaller windows, they can be cut down easily.

Another point which makes for thrift in the end is not only to choose good material but to be *generous* with it. Amply large curtains with plenty of fullness in them when drawn across look and wear far better than those that have been skimped. So economise somewhere else in the house, if money is not too plentiful, but budget liberally for curtains.

When curtaining casement windows or small sashes, however, this does not apply so much. Such draperies are usually much washed and liable to blow out when windows are opened and to fade readily. Also, if you move to a larger-windowed house, they cannot be made bigger. Thus for curtains of this kind it may be better not to overspend, but to renew them fairly frequently.

Carpets, Curtains and Furniture

Carpets and furniture have to be taken into account when choosing the fabric for your curtains. Usually, printed linens, chintzes, rough-texture plain or solidly-patterned materials go well with dark oak. Gleaming golden yellow satin, cream, pale green, or wine-coloured damask or brocade show off the depth and richness of mahogany; period furniture of Regency or Louis IV type of gracious fragility needs glazed stripes, materials with neat and delicate designs, or copies of designs of the actual period. Very modern furniture looks best with vivid shades of scarlet, jade, royal blue, and is ruined by a 'pretty chintz.' It can take bold geometric patterns, and it says much for the progress of modern fabrics that designers' names are now featured, thus bringing it away from the anonymity of dull or unoriginal patterns. Cretonnes and chintzes nearly always blend in well with furniture that is of this age, but not what might be called ultra-modern. If curtains are patterned, then carpets should usually be plain, and vice versa, or at least one design should blend in and not 'fight with' the other. Too many designs cancel each other out, and none shows to advantage.

Naturally curtains, in size, material and make, must suit the windows of the particular room where they will hang, or the entire effect is ruined. So consider the main different types of windows and the special needs of each. We can divide the windows in our houses into:

- (*a*) Sash
- (*b*) Casement
- (*c*) Very large horizontal
- (*d*) French
- (*e*) Bow or bay
- (*f*) Special, uncommon types, such as round-topped, oriel, transom, etc.

Types of Windows

Let us consider each type in turn.

(*a*) **Sash windows** are old-fashioned and very few modern houses are likely to contain them. But there are so many sash-window houses in the older suburbs of large cities and in country towns that a very large number of housewives have to curtain windows of this kind. Sashes have many practical advantages. Their chief drawback from the curtaining standpoint is that—especially if large, which they mostly are—they are rather bare and gaunt-looking and need curtains which give them grace, cover up their bareness and are dignified and decorative. Good and fairly heavy materials do this best. A flimsy curtain fabric at a solid sash window looks unsuitable and poverty-stricken. Have plenty of fullness, too, because folds clothe gracefully the rather bare outlines of sash windows.

Another way of relieving the bare look of sashes is to hang two sets of curtains—outer ones, of one of the fabrics suggested above, to draw across and for colour, and a glass curtain, hung close to the actual pane, so that it is covered when the outer curtains draw across. This glass curtain diffuses a hard light, gives softness and grace to the sash and ensures privacy in town windows which are overlooked.

Two sash windows set close together should be treated as one unit, with one long curtain at each end.

(b) *Casement windows* are much found in the country and in town houses built twenty or thirty years ago, especially those of the semi-detached villa type, also in many blocks of flats. They were the reaction in building from the tall, bare sashes and consequently are somewhat small as a rule and rather low up from the floor. They also open right out or on a pivot (occasionally, in old cottages, right *in*) and there are usually small top and larger bottom panes which open separately. Where there are small top panes they are generally not curtained, though a pleated or gathered valance frill may hang partially over them. Casement windows have a friendly, informal, countrified effect which should be reflected in their curtaining. As they are small and one alone would not give much light, they are often set several closely in a row or round the curve of a bay window. In this case, they should be curtained as a unit and the same applies when two small casements are set one on each side of a French window.

As casement windows are not formal or stately, their curtains should be simple, gay, easily washable and plainly made. They must be short, too, hanging only to the sill, or just below. Suitable materials are lightweight cretonnes with *small* designs on them, cream or coloured casement cloth, cottage weave, many rayon fabrics, check gingham, glazed chintz and printed dress cottons. Transparent glass curtains of net (cotton or rayon) marquisette or muslin are sometimes hung close to the panes in addition to draw-curtains. But they are not really necessary unless the windows are overlooked by other houses or have an ugly view which it is pleasanter to hide.

In old cottages with very small casements the problem often is to make them look larger and more important and to gain all possible light. In this case, curtain materials with *narrow* vertical stripes give an impression of greater height. If the ceiling does not come right down on the window-tops (as it may do in old cottages), arrange for a pelmet frill to be hung *above the window-tops, with its bottom edges only reaching just to the top of the glass. Similarly, hang the curtains on the wall just outside the panes, so that they frame the glass closely without dimming any of the available light.* Remember, if you adopt these enlarging arrangements, to allow extra width and length when measuring for quantity of material and to buy rods or wires longer than the actual windows, so that they meet well when drawn.

(c) *Modern horizontal windows,* very large and with a maximum amount of unbroken-up glass, make rooms most attractively light and bright, for often a whole wall may consist almost entirely of glass. The large, clear panes can also give a rather hard, bare look to the room and in some cases a trying glare of light. So curtain such windows in a way to make the most of their advantages and minimise their drawbacks.

Here are some hints. All-over transparent pane curtains, hung between the coloured side curtains on an inner rod, diffuse the light softly, prevent glare and screen the room from passers-by. They likewise remove the bareness you often get with these windows. Provide also draw curtains of ample fullness, of heavy material or of a medium fabric lined, both because such large windows need weight in their curtaining and also to make the room warmer and cosier on winter evenings. If the curtains are patterned (although a vivid plain shade usually looks effective in this type of window), rather large flower designs or geometrical patterns, horizontal stripes and large checks are suitable; so are Paisley designs and curtains of Jacobean inspiration.

(d) *Bay or bow windows* are a group of windows (usually three, but sometimes five)

Courtesy of Chippendale's Workshops, Ltd.

This delightful drapery is known as 'swag and tail,' the swirled top being achieved by short pieces shaped and affixed to a backboard. Heavy furnishings should be lined to give additional weight. This scheme is in midnight-blue velvet with white fringe, curtains and bedspreads harmonising. The walls are silver-grey and white. Note the space-saving, built-in corner dressing-table

set close together and projecting outwards from the room in more or less of a curve. If built in a true curve they are called bow windows; if the effect is more squared, with definite angles, they are known as bay windows. True bows are found only in genuinely old houses and a few modern ones with horizontal window lines, bays being much more usual. Where there is a trio of windows the centre one is usually much wider than the side pair.

The windows in a bow or bay may be of sash, casement or modern horizontal type. Therefore in the main they should be curtained according to the suggestions already made for each type. But because in each case they are a *group* of windows instead of single ones, they must be treated as a group, not individually. This is not merely a case of curtaining them all alike. You must consider the curve of the bow or bay as a whole and think out a treatment which gives it grace and dig-

nity in its entirety. For example, most bays are more effective if framed with a floor-length curtain at the outer edge of each outermost window, these two being connected, in frame fashion, by a matching pelmet or frill running along the top of the bay. Inside this framework the intermediate curtains may be short ones hanging only to the sill or may be alternately of the 'frame' material and of net to give a lighter effect.

Never run long draw curtains across the inner line of a bay or bow, so that the projecting window part of the room is entirely cut off from use at night. It is quite easy to get hanging fitments which go efficiently round the curve of the windows. And remember—this curve was *planned* to give more space and a handsomer shape to the room and you lose these if it is shut off after dark. The bow or bay is both a complete unit in itself and an essential part of the room by day or night.

(e) *French windows* are, of course, actu-

Chippendale's Workshops, Ltd.

Window-curtains to soften the light can be of various pastel shades, and made of net, nylon, lace net with modern designs, or voile. The utmost use has been made of this recess, with its built-in desk, little cupboards and bookshelves each side

ally glass doors which, in many country or suburban sitting-rooms, open direct into the garden. In the older small houses this may be the only window in the room, and you can curtain it on its own merits.

If there are other windows in the room, take care that the French window is curtained to match the others. If the other casements have short curtains, those at the French window should match but be long with a similar pelmet or frill. If the view from the French window is not attractive and you like the glass screened with net or muslin, fully gathered on to rods both at top and bottom, then any other windows in the room should have net glass curtains as well, to give the right unity of effect.

The reason for making glass curtains for a French door with a heading and casing both at top and bottom, and rods or wires to hold them in place in both positions, is because long net curtains held only at the top blow out so far when the French window is open and get soiled, torn or in people's way.

(*f*) *Special, uncommon windows.* A window of an odd kind or unusual shape gives individuality to a room and so should be welcomed, even if it is more difficult to curtain than a plain sash or casement. Spend a little extra trouble to make your quaint little window look its best.

An oriel window projects from a room like a bay, but as it is built only into an upper room, it is not on solid ground like a bay but overhangs space. It may be semicircular like a bow, but is more often triangular, with two windows meeting in a point and perhaps a three-cornered window-seat filling in its space. As this sharp-pointed arrangement does not give a good framing result, curtain a triangular oriel with two long curtains hanging just outside it on the flat part of the wall. These draw across at night, if wished, and shut off the small projection. Treat a round oriel as an extra-small bow window.

Round-topped sash windows, with outlines that remind you of churches, are frequent in Victorian houses. Because of the semicircular top, round which curtains will not hang and draw, these windows often seem terribly puzzling to 'dress.' Actually the difficulty is easily overcome by special treatment of the pelmet—a valance frill is unsuitable for these windows.

Choose the curtains according to the rules already given for sash windows. Remember that they must be cut long enough to hang from a wire rod or other support placed (horizontal) immediately above the *topmost* point of the round-topped part. But if this kind of window has a separate small pane (fanlight) in the semicircular part which opens *inwards* on casement lines, then measure your curtain to hang from just beneath the fanlight, which should be left uncurtained.

Types of Curtains

We can divide curtains into three main types, according to the method of making. These are:

(1) Unlined curtains
(2) Lined curtains
(3) Transparent glass curtains

All 'fancy' kinds of curtains are variations of one or other of these three types.

(1) *Unlined curtains* form the majority of window draperies. They are the usual non-transparent curtains made of only one thickness of material and they may be used for casement, sash and practically any kind of window. They are nearly always made wide enough to draw right across the windows at night, if wished. They may be sill length (i.e. finishing an inch or two below the actual window) or floor length. For convenience of cleaning a room and to keep them from getting soiled, floor-length curtains should actually end about 3 in. above the floor.

Before you can calculate how much material to buy, you must, of course, decide on the length of your particular curtains. Sill or floor length?

Do not, if you can possibly help it, choose short curtains just on the ground of economy when long ones would look better. Decide whether you want your room to look gay or dignified, pretty or sober.

(2) *Lined curtains* have very definite uses and advantages. To begin with, for very cold or exposed rooms in the country or on the sea-front, where strong winds may be expected, lined curtains are cosier and as their two thicknesses makes them heavy they will not blow about annoyingly. Their double folds make them hang better and look handsomer at large windows. Also they wear a great deal

longer than unlined curtains, because the lining gets most of the wear and exposure to sun, keeping the main fabric in good condition. Select as expensive a material as you can manage for the actual curtains, lining them with something cheaper, such as casement cloth, sateen or Bolton sheeting. When this lining wears out, the curtains themselves should be sound enough to be relined and give you good service for years longer.

If you do decide to line your curtains, finish the windows with a stiffened pelmet of self or contrasting material or a wooden pelmet. Frilled valances are too frolicsome to combine with the dignity of these important-looking draperies.

(3) *Transparent glass curtains* hang right against the glass of a window, from a separate inner rod or fitment which is quite distinct from the one supporting the draw curtains. For this reason they must always be of transparent fabrics which will diffuse the light softly but not darken the room noticeably. Suitable materials are cotton or rayon net, nylon, voile, muslin, marquisette and furnishing ninon. Net curtains with a frill at the edge can be bought ready-made or by the yard.

Remember when choosing glass curtain material that the quality of light you get through it will vary, not only according to the fabric, but with its colour. Have you a sunless north room? Then give the cold light coming into it a sunshiny glow with transparent draperies of golden net or softly tinted peach organdie. A sunny south room, on the other hand, will look cooler and fresher in hot weather if screened with a very light cream or, if it blends with your other thick curtains, pale green or blue.

Glass curtains should never be made floor length. They would wear and soil easily if hung too near the ground and are too ethereal to look their best in large chunks.

Measuring Windows for Curtains

Use a yardstick. You can stretch this up to high windows without having to get on a step ladder and it is more exact than a tape measure, which is apt to stretch or slip. (*If you haven't a yardstick, stretch a tape measure along a broom handle and secure it to the wood with a drawing-pin at each end.*)

Have ready also a small notebook and pencil and write down each measurement as taken. This not only saves inaccurate remembering when you get to the shop, but the book can be kept. Then you needn't take the measurements again next time you need new curtains.

Write down the width of each window and the exact length the curtain is to be *when finished*. Afterwards, on a separate piece of paper, add the allowances for each curtain and reckon the total amount required for the window or windows.

FINISHING (MAKING) ALLOWANCES FOR CURTAINS

(In each case the allowance given is per *curtain* or *curtain width*, if it contains more than one width, not per pair.)

Unlined Curtains	*Inches*
Floor length, with top heading ..	9
Floor length, without heading ..	6-8
Sill length, with top heading ..	4-7
Sill length, without top heading ..	3-5

Lined Curtains	
The actual fabric (any length) ..	4-6
Lining of curtain (any length) ..	3-5

Glass Curtains	
Long, with top hem	3-5
Long (for French window) with top and bottom headings and casings	7-8
Short, with 1-in. heading	4-5
Short, with 1-in. heading and casing	5-6
Short, with casing	3-4
Short, with casing and bound bottom edge	$2\frac{1}{2}$-3

Also remember:

(*a*) If the curtains are to hang just outside the actual glass to make the window look larger, then see that your measurements and calculations include the bit of wall each side that will be covered by the curtains, as well as the actual area of glass. This may mean making the curtains wide which in some cases involves using more than one width.

To get the minimum curtain fullness at large windows it may be necessary to use a width and a quarter, or, more commonly, a width and a half—even two whole widths, occasionally.

(*b*) Width of material is another point to consider before giving your order. Suppose for a window measuring 36 in. in width and needing curtains 2 yards long, you intend to use 50-in. wide material (damask, taffeta,

velours, etc., sometimes cretonne, are apt to be this width). In that case you will need only one and a half widths per curtain—that is, three yards plus the usual allowances.

You may want a material that is not the ideal width for your purpose, although it *is* ideal in colour, design or price. Or you may be matching curtains to loose covers or bedspreads in the same room and have chosen the particular width best for your chairs or your beds. Very often you do not know till you get to the store and survey the stock what materials at what widths will be available.

In this case, it's a wise plan to make two calculations before going out, one giving the total quantity required in double width (46-54 in.), the other what you will need if you buy single width (usually 30 or 31 in., but in linen and a few fabrics 36 in.). Then, whatever width your chosen fabric may turn out to be, you know exactly how much to order.

(*c*) If you intend to have a matching valance frill or stiffened pelmet with your curtains, then buy enough for this at the same time.

(*d*) Some of the more expensive materials have a large pattern or medallions or sprigs at wide intervals. These must be matched to come in the same place on the two curtains of a pair, or the two widths of a wide curtain, otherwise the effect is lopsided and unsightly when hung. As this matching may involve some waste of material, allow about $\frac{1}{2}$ yard extra per *pair* of curtains (or per curtain if of more than one width).

How to Start

Before starting, clear the largest table you have and collect what you will need: a yardstick—or the home-made substitute already suggested; *large*, sharp, cutting-out scissors; plenty of pins (preferable steel ones); your sewing machine newly oiled; sewing cotton matching the background or main colour in the material; matching Rufflette tape to finish the curtain tops, sewing needles and thimble. Sometimes, but not often, you may need lead weights or weighted tape as well.

Making Unlined Curtains

These are a simple job but, like so many simple jobs, depend for good effect and good wear on being made with real care and accuracy. Don't picture yourself 'running up' curtains like lightning on your machine, unless you are a very quick and skilled needlewoman.

If they are merely 'walked up' at no great speed you will achieve a much slicker, more professional look.

The first job is to measure off and cut the various lengths required.

Besides the finishing allowance (for hems, headings, casings, etc.) in some cases it is wise to make a shrinkage allowance as well, so that you don't find your curtain, after a laundering or two, giving the impression that they are doing their utmost to climb up to the ceiling and have been rather successful at it! Shrinkage allowances apply chiefly to glass curtains. But many unlined curtains are washable and some at least of them are made of fabrics with an inclination to shrink. So if your particular material answers yes to these two points, I should advise you to cut with an eye to possible shrinkage. A reasonable shrinkage allowance for the average unlined washing curtain is $1\frac{1}{2}$ in. per yard of length. Thus, on the two-yard long curtain already mentioned, you might allow 3 in. for shrinkage in addition to the ordinary finishing allowance.

When making up the curtains, this surplus may be disposed of in various ways. The easiest, though not the prettiest in effect, is to finish the curtain bottoms with the usual hem and tolerate their hanging a little long until laundering has shrunk them to the correct length.

You may prefer your draperies to look 'made to measure' from the very start. Then one plan is to take up the surplus in an extra deep hem and to let this down when shrinkage has done its work. Another is to make the extra deep hem and then correct the length by running a tuck on the wrong side of the hem to shorten the curtain and make the hem only normally deep. If you hand-sew this hem, it will be very easy to unpick when extra length is needed. On the other hand, if the expected shrinkage does not occur, or while waiting for it to take place, the curtain is just the right length and no one, looking at it from the right side, will suspect that hidden tuck! A third plan is a visible, right-side tuck the same depth as the hem, if possible, and an inch or two above it. The effect is quite decorative.

Cutting Curtain Lengths

Curtains depend for much of their effect and wear on hanging perfectly evenly and on the two in a pair being of exactly the same length, so take time and trouble when cutting off your lengths.

First, measure accurately. This is particularly necessary when making big curtains which are more than a yard long, so that the yardstick has to be used twice in measuring them.

The edge cut off in the shop may be a bit jagged or crooked. Begin by straightening this, for it is the base from which all your measuring is done. Draw a thread right across in linen, casement cloth or any material in which a thread can be drawn. From this measure along one edge the length required and mark with a pin. Measure the same length along the other selvedge and mark it similarly. Now check your length by measuring back from each pin to the cut edge and check by your written length, plus the allowances you have decided upon.

When measured and checked, fold the material across from pin to pin (or draw a thread starting from a pin) and cut across very evenly. Cut like this, your curtains when made up will *really* be twins in appearance and won't develop that amateurish tendency to droop at one corner or sag somewhere in the middle.

Are you using more than one width of

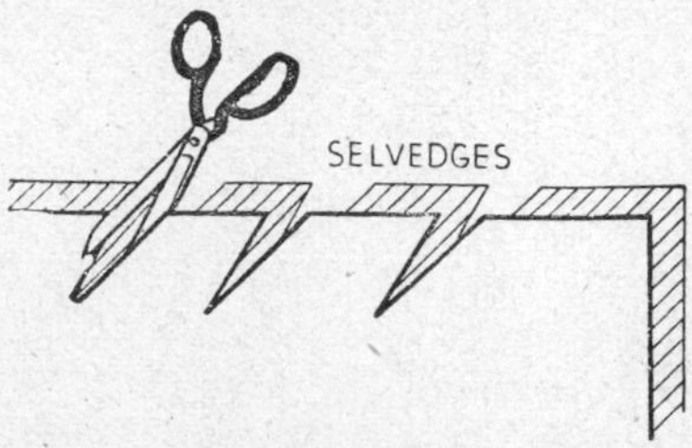

SELVEDGES

Fig. 1. Tight selvedges should be slashed diagonally at intervals before seaming

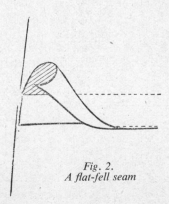

Fig. 2.
A flat-fell seam

material per curtain? Then match up the design as nearly as possible on the two widths to be joined.

This joining is the first sewing to be done. When both edges are selvedges, use a plain seam with the whole of each selvedge as turnings, because the selvedge is usually either a different colour or more tightly woven than the fabric. Slash tight selvedges diagonally at intervals before seaming, otherwise your curtain may hitch up where the seam occurs. Press the seam well. (*Fig. 1.*)

If the curtain does not need two full widths and you have a cut edge to join to a selvedge, use a flat-fell seam, which is very neat and flat and washes well. To make it, first stitch a plain seam with wide turnings. Press both turnings the same way, and trim off the under one as closely as is safe. Make a narrow single turn in the wide turning, tack it down flat over and concealing the narrow one and from the right side stitch along the tacking. Press well. The flat-fell seam has the advantage of looking just as neat and unnoticeable on the wrong as on the right side. (*Fig. 2.*)

Another point to remember when joining a half-width to an entire one is to make the seam (or at any rate to hang the finished curtain so that it comes) on the outside of the curtain nearest the window frame. This means that the curtains must be made up as a pair, not identically with the half-width on the same side in both. The seam is less conspicuous thus than if it occurs near the centre of the window when the curtain is drawn across at night.

How you finish the curtain top depends on how it is being hung. If a pelmet or valance frill will conceal its top edge, this should be finished inconspicuously and with economy of material—faced in with tape, or with a simple casing through which a wooden or wire rod is threaded.

Top with Casing. A casing is merely a hem with the supporting wire or rod run through it. Fold and stitch a hem in the ordinary way along the curtain top. If this is of washable material, remember that the casing may shrink when laundered and should therefore be folded deep enough to take the rod loosely when it is new.

Casing and Heading. When you want to run your rod or wire through a casing and yet have a top heading above it for decorative purposes (this is actually more apt to happen with glass curtains than with ordinary unlined ones), you will need a casing with a heading immediately above it. Remember when folding down the turn which serves for both heading and casing that the top of the casing marks the real top of the curtain as far as length is concerned, the heading being an ornamental finish which is extra to the actual length. (*Fig. 3.*)

Top without Heading. Along the curtain top make a single turn, $\frac{1}{2}$ in. deep, to the wrong side. Lay along this, $\frac{1}{4}$ in. below the folds, a length of Rufflette tape an inch or two longer than the width of the curtain. The tape, when laid in place, must conceal the raw edge of the turn. Stitch down the tape along each of its edges. Be careful when doing this to keep your stitches quite clear of the double line of cord threaded through the tape.

Extra Deep Heading. If the curtain is a long or important one or is hung from an ugly fitment you wish to conceal, you may need an extra deep heading, $1\frac{1}{2}$ or even 2 in. in depth. Such deep headings are inclined to droop in wear. Then they collect dust, look uneven and do not hide the fitment properly. You can slightly stiffen the heading to prevent this by running several rows of machine stitching across it, through both thicknesses. They give just enough extra body, in most fabrics, to prevent sagging and if evenly spaced about $\frac{1}{2}$ in. apart look quite decorative. Another plan is to insert a strip of canvas in the heading.

The bottom hem should only be turned up when the top is finished. Measure the exact curtain length required downwards from the middle of the Rufflette tape (because the heading is not part of this length) and mark it with pins. Make the fold of the hem along this pinned line. Stitch a double hem in the usual way and remember to overcast it together at each end, so that dust will not penetrate and it will hang without getting caught on window-catches and so on.

Occasionally curtains of lightweight material at exposed casement windows need weighting to prevent their blowing outside too much. For this buy weighted tape from a haberdashery department and insert a length of it all through the bottom hem. If the material is washable, leave one end of the hem open, so that the tape can be removed before laundering and replaced afterwards. When ready to hang, pull up the cords on the tape to the exact width of the window or hanging fitment. Knot their ends together and tuck them in (on no account cut the long ends off). Slip rings or hooks (according to the type of window fitment you are using) at intervals into the pockets in the tape and hang from their 'opposite numbers' on the fitment.

Side edges on the great majority of curtains are left as selvedges and if you are joining on an extra half width you should seam it by its cut edge, leaving the selvedge for the outer edge. But if the selvedges 'draw' or are unpresentable in any way they should be cut off and the cut edges be narrowly hemmed, faced with matching bias tape or bias strips cut 1 in. wide, or bound. Facing or hemming is best for a neat, inconspicuous finish. When binding is used it is a decorative idea to have a contrasting bind which gives an attractive colour scheme and trims as well as finishes the edges.

Making Lined Curtains

I have seen lined curtains quickly made like a cushion cover or a bag—by seaming material and lining together on the wrong side and then turning them right side out. This seems a perfectly simple method but it is also decidedly unsatisfactory. Curtains made in this way never hang smoothly as if fabric and lining belonged together and they are apt to balloon out in a wind and to bulge at the seams at all times.

The proper method is a special one, used only for lined curtains, which give beautiful results—draperies that hang perfectly together in long, graceful folds, flat edges and hems and real hard wear. It's not a difficult method, either, but it does need time and care and is mostly done by hand. Only the joining of widths, if this is necessary, and the attaching of the Rufflette tape at the top can be stitched in the sewing machine.

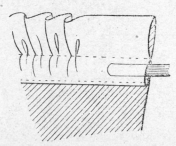

Fig. 3. Your glass curtains look prettier when your rod or wire is run through a casing with a top heading

Read through the foregoing directions for the making of unlined curtains, as a number of points are the same in the case of lined ones. For example, both your material and lining should be measured and cut, with great care as to straightness and accuracy. *When measuring and cutting the linings, make them an inch or more shorter than the curtains.* You see, in order that the lining shall not sag and show below the outer fabric at the bottom, it is made rather shorter and not brought down right to the turn-up of the hem.

After cutting out the necessary fabrics, seam the widths together if you are using more than one width. Use plain seams with ½-in. turnings. Now both curtain and lining are the correct width, but they are still entirely separate from one another.

When your curtains are really large ones, from now onwards it saves time and makes the job easier to handle if two people work at the making together; so arrange this if you can. You will also need a table (or two small ones pushed together) large enough to take the whole curtain out flat. Failing this, you can use the floor spread with newspapers or a clean dustsheet, but in that case you will have a lot of tiring bending to do.

Spread a curtain length out quite flat, wrong side uppermost. Spread over it a lining length right side uppermost, so that the two wrong sides are touching. Using both hands and working in outward curves (two pairs of hands are still better) smooth out the two materials till the lining lies completely flat and smooth over an equally unwrinkled curtain.

Now you must lock the two layers together, so that even when hung or in a breeze they will continue to hold perfectly together, without ballooning or puckering anywhere. It is on this locking process that the success and good appearance of lined curtains chiefly depend.

Locking is easy and quickly done, for it simply consists of buttonhole stitching the two layers invisibly together. Fine, close buttonholing is quite out of place on a curtain, of course. You space your stitches 4 in. apart (in velvet curtains there should be only 2-in. spaces) and so the work gets on with remarkable speed.

Still keeping curtain and lining laid out flat together, begin by folding back lengthwise, from top to bottom, one-third of the lining width, leaving the curtain still flat. Thread a needle with an extra long length of cotton, matching the curtain material (or its chief colour if patterned) as closely as possible.

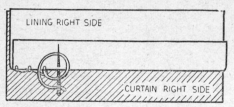

Fig. 4. Work all down the curtain, catching the fold of lining to the curtain fabric with a tiny buttonhole stitch

Now work all down the curtain, catching the fold of lining to the actual curtain fabric with a tiny buttonhole stitch every four inches. Take up only as much of each material as will hold the thread and you'll find that on the hung curtain it is very difficult indeed to find the stitches, let alone see them from a little distance. (*Fig. 4.*)

Don't worry about the very long pieces of cotton connecting one stitch with the next. They lie between the two fabrics and will be completely concealed when the curtain is made up.

Now fold the lining back similarly one-third from the other side and lock again. Thus the locking divides the curtain-width into three equal sections and so holds the two materials together evenly. Make two similar lockings on curtains a width-and-a-half. But those consisting of two full widths need an additional locking down the exact centre. Do this centre locking first by doubling the lining over in half; then the two side ones.

Have a hot iron ready and with it press in a single turn to the wrong side down each side edge of the curtain material—the turn should be 1 in. deep. Also press up the bottom edge singly to the depth you have allowed for when cutting and press this. Lay back flat on the curtain the folded-back sides of the lining and turn in the side edges of this to face the curtain sides, but ½ in. inside them—again to prevent the lining possibly showing on the right side. Slipstitch the two materials together down the curtain sides. There can be very long slips between the stitches. (*Fig. 5.*)

Top Finish. Measure upwards from the finished bottom edge of the curtain the exact finished length it is to be and at that point turn down both curtain and lining together to the wrong side. Lay a length of Rufflette

tape along the wrong side, covering the raw edges of the turned material; you must trim these off shorter if the turn is so deep that the tape comes too low. Stitch and draw up the cords in the tape for hanging as described for unlined curtains.

If you wish to sew on rings for hanging instead of inserting them in the tape (this may be better for an old-fashioned curtain rod which requires very large rings), finish the curtain top similarly but with a length of strong curtain braid instead of Rufflette tape. To this braid sew the curtain rings at about 3-in. intervals. Take care to place the first and last rings close to the side edges, otherwise these may droop in an ugly fashion when hung. If the curtains are really heavy (as, for instance, when they are very long or made of a thick fabric like velours) their weight will put a great strain on the rings, which will tend after a time to pull away from the braid. Result, the curtain top sags at this spot and perhaps a bit of fabric is torn away with the ring.

To avoid this tiresome mishap, in the case of heavy curtains sew each ring to the braid in two places instead of in only one. This distributes the strain and gives far better wear.

MAKING GLASS CURTAINS

In general, glass curtains are made in very much the same way as unlined ones. As they are made of transparent materials they present one or two problems of their own.

So, while generally following the rules for making unlined curtains, here are a few extra remarks.

Joining Widths. The materials — net, ninon, voile, etc.—used for glass curtains are so flimsy that very ample fullness is needed for a graceful appearance; allow from $1\frac{3}{4}$ times to twice the width needed. Glass curtain fabrics are usually fairly wide and so it is not

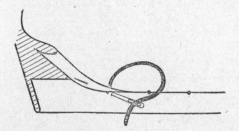

Fig. 5. Slipstitch, used for joining two materials down the curtain sides

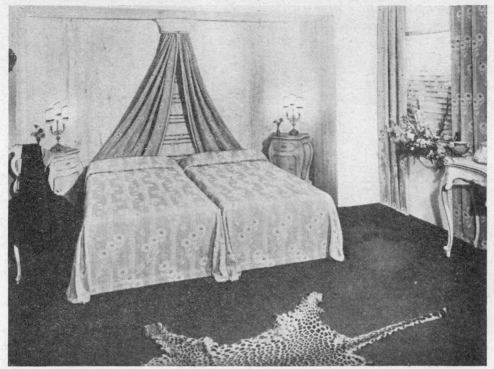

Vantona Textiles, Ltd.

The bed drapery is very reminiscent of French Empire, and this effect, together with bed coverings and curtains, is achieved by the use of six single bedspreads! Note the charming flower arrangement in the wall-vase by the window

often that more than one width is needed in these curtains. But when it is, make the join with the narrowest possible French seam, which is fairly unnoticeable and washes and wears well.

Curtain net ready frilled down each selvedge is very successful used across half the window, as the frills increase the length available when the material is reversed and the bottom frill (as one of them will be made up this way) weights the net nicely and provides a pretty finish. The top frill should be hemmed down to half its width, thus providing an attractively bunchy top hem through which the rod is run.

Top Finish. In exceptionally well-lighted rooms, or when a complete screen is wanted for the window, sheer curtains are hung from top to bottom of the glass.

With these curtains the top finish is well in view—not hidden by height or by a pelmet or frill, as full-length curtains often are—and so it should be decorative. A top heading does just what is needed and takes very little extra material.

You can't hang transparent half-length cur-tains from railway fitments or easily use Rufflette tape or rings, all of which would be too noticeable when hung against glass. So a hem or casing is needed immediately under the top heading to take a wooden or spring-wire rod.

Bottom Finish. A plain $\frac{1}{2}$-in. hem is the simplest and most usual. In transparent materials a hem should always be three-ply— that is, the first (raw-edge) turn should be the full depth of the hem. If you want to know why, fold an ordinary hem with a narrow first turn and hold it up to the window, noting the ragged, untidy edge that shows up clearly against the light. (*Fig. 6.*)

French windows are sometimes fitted with all-over glass curtains. These long draperies, if left to hang free, would blow about, catch in furniture or plants growing outside and be a general nuisance. So they should be fulled on to a rod not only at the top, but at the bottom as well. Finish the bottom just like the top, with a heading (perhaps we ought to call it a footing in this case!) and a casing for the rod next to it.

But how can one allow for shrinkage in

such a case? An easy way is to cut each curtain with 2 in. shrinkage allowance over and above that allowed for finishing. Make up the curtain at top and bottom. Then, just below the top casing and just above the bottom one, hand-run a tuck $\frac{1}{2}$ in. deep—thus taking up 1 in. on each tuck. When shrinkage occurs, unpick the bottom tuck. If the curtain shrinks further after more washings, unpick the top one also. Meanwhile the tucks will be quite ornamental.

SPECIAL TYPES OF GLASS CURTAINS

There's no need to get into a rut about your transparent window furnishings. Sometimes the hung-all-over type of curtain looks too ordinary and then you can give life and originality to your windows by choosing a more uncommon kind of glass drapery. Let's consider some of these and how to make them.

Crossover Frilled Glass Curtains

At the right window these give a specially soft and graceful effect and, as they are partly double, an extra amount of privacy. You can regulate how much of the window is screened and how much left exposed by the height at which you loop back the curtains and the length of the loopers. (*Fig. 7.*)

They should be $1\frac{1}{2}$ times the glass width. Allow only about $2\frac{1}{2}$ in. for top and bottom finishes, but extra length (from 3 to 6 in., according to the height of the window) to be taken up in looping. Unless you buy a ready-frilled fabric you will require additional material, of course, for making the frills. They will need to be cut 3 in. wide (including turnings) straight across the material from selvedge to selvedge and to measure, when joined, $1\frac{1}{2}$ times the length down the inner side and along the bottom of each curtain. From these measurements you can calculate how much extra stuff to buy.

Join the frill lengths with tiny French seams and stitch very narrow hems along one edge. (By the way, if you find open-mesh net difficult to stitch in the machine, lay a strip of tissue paper under seam or hem, stitch through this and afterwards tear the paper away). Fold a narrow single turn along the other frill edge and run a gathering thread along it. If the length is too great to be gathered on one thread, divide the frill edge with pins into 18-in. lengths and the curtain edge into 12-in. lengths. Gather each section on a separate thread, afterwards drawing up each thread to fit a 12-in. section on the curtain. Join the gathered frill down one side and the bottom of each curtain with a French seam. And by the way, be careful to frill a *pair* of curtains —not two both frilled on the same side.

Lay the two curtains exactly over each other, each with its frill a different way. Measure upwards from the bottom of the bottom frill the finished length required and at that point at the top fold down both curtains together into one top hem that will take the rod. Stitch this double hem, so that the curtains are joined together all along their tops, but are quite separate everywhere else.

To hang the curtains, run a rod through the hem. Fix a small cuphook in the window frame each side at the height you want your looping to be. Experiment first to find the effect you like best, looping the curtains one-third of the way down from the top, then half-way down, then two-thirds down and fix your cuphooks accordingly. Make loopers from coloured cords, strips of the curtain material, ribbons or strips of the draw curtains hung in the room, finishing each end of the looper with a curtain ring which will hang over the cuphook. Catch up one curtain each side with the looper, of course, so that its frill is towards the centre of the window.

Waterfall Glass Curtains

This pane arrangement gives a new and rather charming line. Curtains made in this way are very useful at windows where you want a certain amount of privacy without shutting out all the view and they are economical of material. Actually there is only one curtain halved diagonally to give a triangular effect. Waterfall draperies suit best square or squarish windows (or glass areas if only half

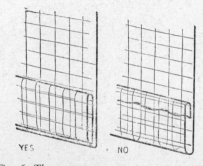

Fig. 6. The turn-up on net curtains should be the full width of the hem or an untidy edge will show up against the light

CLEVER CURTAINING *for* CORNERS

In a small room corners need to be put to use, and this can best be done by curtaining in such a way that they look as decorative as possible, and not 'makeshift.' Recesses, too, can provide a great deal of extra space when fitted up with shelves. A dull corner brightened by attractive draperies can lift a room out of the ordinary

These curtains are of rose-sprigged rayon, giving an air of silken luxury at very little cost. Note the pretty way the pelmet is draped and tied in the middle with a bow of narrow velvet catching up the rose colour in a deeper shade. Hats, bags, gloves, shoes, each have their own niche and anything needed can be picked out in a minute without turning a drawer upside-down

A recess has been used to take a towel-rail (which so often juts out from the wall to provide an unwanted bruise!); shelves hold bottles, lotions, beauty requisites or shaving tackle. An adjustable mirror could be put on the wall, if the recess is near a window. Curtains are of plastic, and gaily striped. A pattern can, of course, be chosen to blend with the colour-scheme you already have

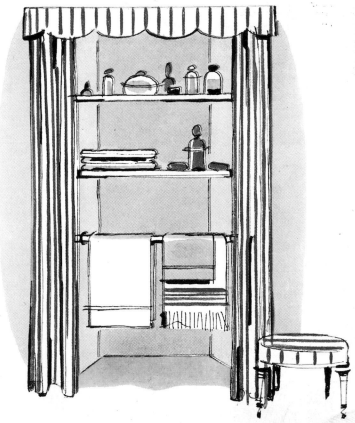

An ordinary window can have curtains reaching to the ground and the divan beds so placed that the effect is one of height and elegance. Stripes are always fresh-looking, and while in this case cotton was used both for curtains and bed covers, if the same idea was carried out in a garden room, one of the softer, striped deck-chair canvases could be used. In that case, a small padded ottoman at each side of the window would provide both seat and storage space

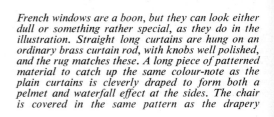

French windows are a boon, but they can look either dull or something rather special, as they do in the illustration. Straight long curtains are hung on an ordinary brass curtain rod, with knobs well polished, and the rug matches these. A long piece of patterned material to catch up the same colour-note as the plain curtains is cleverly draped to form both a pelmet and waterfall effect at the sides. The chair is covered in the same pattern as the drapery

Tubs of geraniums do not always have to be out of doors. Old Christmas-tree tubs, re-painted, make excellent plant-holders. Against the pale grey of these spotted starched cotton curtains, with the simple scalloped pelmet, the vivid pink of the geraniums contrasts charmingly. The green-painted tubs, too, strike a note against the pink striped rug

The gay arrangement shows up delightfully on a sunny day, and provides its own brightness when clouds obscure the sun

Fig. 7. Cross-over glass curtains are more in vogue, both for bedrooms or lounges, according to the type of furnishing

The frill can be a different shade, either catching up a colour in long, patterned curtains, or a paler tone of plain-colour curtains

Choose palest primrose for a room with a north aspect or peach. Cooler greens and blues are better in a room that catches the sun

the window is being covered) and require reversible material—most transparent fabrics *are* the same on both sides. Here's an excellent way of using a remnant of net, voile or ninon, picked up at a sale.

You will need a square or oblong of material with these measurements. Its length should be the curtain length desired, plus enough allowance for *two* top headings and casings. Its width should be ⅞ths the width of the window. Thus, if the window area to be curtained is 38 in. long by 32 in. wide, your curtain

material will need to be 38 in. long by 28 in. wide. But you must add to the length, *twice* over, a finishing allowance for, say, an inch-wide heading and a ½-in. casing. Allow 3½ in. for this or 7 in. when doubled and add to the bare length of 38 in. Thus you must actually provide, for a window of the size given above, a piece of material 1¼ yards long (38 plus 7 in.) and 28 in. wide. (*Fig. 8.*)

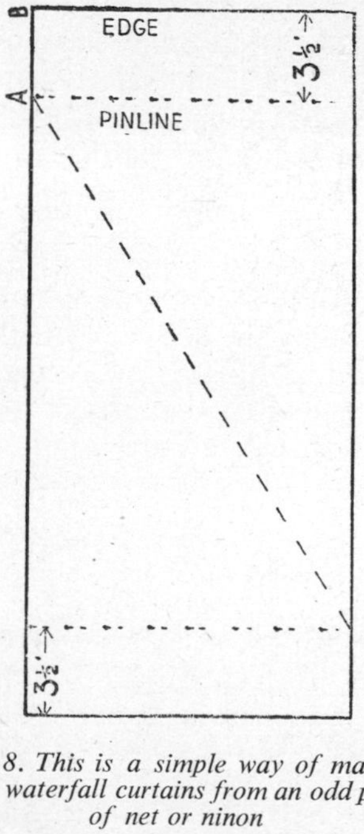

Lay the material out flat and begin by marking off with pins along both top and bottom edges sufficient depth (say 3½ in.) for the heading and casing. Now from one line of pins to the other (not from edge to edge) pin or tack a diagonal line joining opposite corners.

Lay bias binding, matching or contrasting with the curtain fabric, along each side of this diagonal line, with the two bindings just touching. Seam each into place as when starting a bind. Cut the fabric through on the diagonal line, exactly between the two bindings. At each end, from pin-line to edge (A to B in the diagram) make an upright instead of a slanting cut. Complete the binding of each edge by machine.

By starting the binding in this way before cutting you prevent the bias edge from becoming wobbly through stretching. Binding is used as a finish because hems are always unsatisfactory on a diagonal edge. Also the effect must be reversible.

Place the two curtain halves together, one reversed, to give a triangular space between them. Join them in the centre along their short straight edges, using a flat-fell seam. Now make the heading and casing in the usual way.

Fig. 8. This is a simple way of making little waterfall curtains from an odd piece of net or ninon

TRIMMINGS FOR CURTAINS

In general, curtains are best left untrimmed, especially if they are of patterned material. But on occasion a trimming of some kind is needed to provide a colour or texture contrast, break up the unbroken expanse of very large plain curtains or eke out a too-short remnant of material. Again, curtains which are not quite right for a room but have to be used on account of expense may be brought into harmony with the other furnishings by having a trimming added of the same material as some of those other furnishings. Lastly, when renovating worn curtains for further wear, you will find that judicious trimmings are invaluable for brightening faded colours or covering worn edges.

Don't, in any case, overdo the adornment of curtains. Trimmings should be as plain in themselves and as sparsely used as possible to give the desired note of contrast or relief. Here are some suggestions.

Piping can outline the shape of pelmets.

Frills along curtain edges naturally look best in a very feminine room or bedroom. Washing draperies of lightweight chintz, silk or rayon accord well with the informality of a frill. The frill can be of a deeper shade, and the curtain tied back with bows of the deeper shade. Frilled gingham or chintz looks well in the kitchen, too.

Binding is suggested, for severely practical reasons, for the bias-cut edges of waterfall curtains. It's very useful, too, if you are short of material and have none for bottom hems of curtains. And on draperies of rather jazzy or fidgety pattern—some checks and chintzes or very spriggy or 'patchwork' cretonnes— a plain binding, preferably matching the darkest colour in the pattern, does pull it together and increase its restfulness.

For narrow binds on cotton materials, cotton bias binding is excellent and time-saving. Wider binds should be made from straight strips of suitable fabric. Fold in single edges (this is already done on bought bias binding), double the binding lengthwise over the cut edge, pin or tack into place if necessary and machine-stitch on, both sides at once.

Bathroom curtains made of oiled silk or thin rubber sheeting (both excellent because steam does not wilt them) or plastic material may be left with cut edges, as these fabrics do not fray. But they look neater and more decorative if the edges are bound with matching or contrasting bias tape.

Contrasting bands are really facings applied not to finish the edge of a curtain but to trim it, usually a little above the bottom hem. Three bands placed close together, each of a different colour, brighten up too-dark draperies or cream or neutral ones which are lacking in life. The colours chosen for the bands should be bright and pick up tones that are used in cushions or loose covers in the same room. (*Fig. 10.*)

Use straight strips of material as bands. Fold in a narrow turn along each edge. Lay the band in position on the curtain, taking great care that it runs in a straight line without wobbles, and stitch down along each fold. It is usually best to have as much space between the bands as the width of the bands themselves.

Another idea is to have all three bands of one colour but graduated in depth. For example, the lowest one on a curtain of medium length might measure 2 in. wide, the second 1½ in. and the third and highest 1 in. There are numerous other banding arrangements, varying in depth, number, position and colouring which you can work out for yourself to suit your own particular draperies. Silk or cotton pyjama cord can be used in the same sort of lines.

Fringe can give a handsome effect on large lined curtains of non-washing material, especially when the accompanying pelmet is also fringed along the lower edge. Adding fringe to the bottom of a curtain, too, is a useful method of giving extra length if curtains have to be rehung at a longer window when

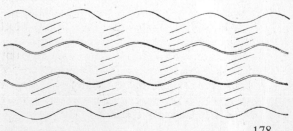

Fig. 9. Rickrack braid can be used in different colours, and with a zigzag or diamond effect. It is pretty for nursery or kitchen curtains, giving a simple cottagey air

moving house. The kind of 'bobble-braid' used on Victorian mantelpiece covers can be used with amusing and chic effect.

Rickrack braid can be a charming adornment for small curtains of casement type, particularly in the less formal rooms of a house, such as kitchen, nursery or bathroom. White rickrack looks particularly well on check gingham, while the coloured varieties are delightful on plain-tinted casements or other cottons. (*Fig. 9.*)

Be liberal with your rickrack. It is inexpensive and owing to its zigzag silhouette a single line of it is seldom strong enough to be really telling against the light. Besides, you can build up such attractive open diamond patterns by using two or three rows with the points just touching each other, or a firm, impressive zigzag by fitting two or three rows closely into one another. For thick zigzag rows, as for banding, each line of braid may be in a different and well-contrasted shade—say, three graduated tones of blue on a primrose curtain.

Darning in embroidery thread or wool is pretty and quick to do on casement, glass and other small curtains. Simply darn in and out in large stitches and straight rows (or zigzags), using several lines of darning placed close together an inch or two above the bottom hem. The colours used should contrast well with the curtain. On net glass curtains, darn in and out of the mesh, using embroidery wool.

CURTAIN RENOVATIONS

Well-made curtains of good material are worth renovating or recutting at least once before they are discarded. You may need to alter them to fit different rooms in a new home or hide worn places so that they will give longer service at their original windows.

In the first place, renovate only sound material. An odd burn or hole can be concealed, but if there is wear all down the edges the curtains can only be cut down for a smaller window so that all the worn parts are removed. If they show signs of wear all over, leave them as they are till past further use.

You need no hints for cutting down curtains to fit smaller windows. A much more difficult problem is lengthening, either because the curtains must be used at bigger windows, owing to shrinkage or because you have had to cut off worn portions. Here are some suggestions.

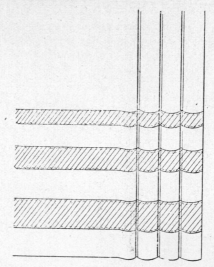

Fig. 10. Contrasting bands can be used to decorate your curtains or to lengthen them, if necessary. The bands should catch up colours used in other furnishings in the same room

(1) If only a few inches extra are needed, let down deep hems to their full extent and face or bind the edges. If the let-down shows badly, cover it with contrasting bands or darning.

(2) Has your window a top pelmet or valance frill? If so you can add an extra strip (which perhaps doesn't match exactly) to give more length much more inconspicuously at the top (where pelmet or frill will hide it) than at the bottom. If the top is worn (perhaps by rings or the pull of tape), substitute a new top portion. If it is the bottom that has gone, reverse the curtain, add a new strip to replace the cut-off bottom part and hang so that the good (original) top is now at the bottom where it is in plain sight.

(3) Cut up the matching valance frill to add on at top or bottom and replace it with a wooden pelmet or a contrasting frill or fabric pelmet.

(4) For a bay window, use the inner curtains to lengthen the outer ones and hang new inner curtains (printed if the outer ones are plain or vice versa or perhaps transparent ones 'framed' by the outer curtains and pelmet). Or use the old curtains as lengthened inner ones, providing new outer ones and frill or pelmet.

Side Edges. When these are only *slightly* worn or frayed, cut off the fray and turn in hems if you can afford a reduced width; if not, bind or face the cut edges.

Accidental Holes or Stains, not due to wear, can be concealed, according to their position, with the trimmings already described —contrasting bands, rickrack or darning, for instance, or appliqué of flowers.

Lined Curtains

Here the lining, which is exposed to the dust, sun and weather in general, gets nearly all the wear and such curtains are usually worth re-lining with a cheap material.

PELMETS AND VALANCE FRILLS

A pelmet (or its more informal sister, the valance frill) is to a window very much what the frame is to a picture or the trimming to a dress. That is, pelmets and valance frills can never be considered separately but only as appropriate finishes to the curtains with which they are hung.

You will see from this that a pelmet or frill should mostly be made of the same material as its curtains and have the same general characteristics. First of all, let's be quite clear

Worn places in curtains and chairs, accidental cigarette burns, or bad stains can be covered by appliqué of a design cut from cretonne. Here the same design is put on a plain screen to give an effect of unity

what a pelmet is and how it differs from a valance frill.

A pelmet is a straight or shaped strip fastened across the top of a window to hide the curtain rod or rail and the top of the window frame and give a decorative finish to the window as a whole. A pelmet, unlike a valance frill, is always stiffened and stretched flat without fullness. It may be plain or trimmed in various ways. Mostly it is made of the curtain material or of something which contrasts effectively with it (it may, for instance, be of plain fabric matching the main shade in a flowered curtain or a wooden pelmet, painted to match either the curtains or the other woodwork of the room). Wooden pelmets are, of course, a carpenter's job.

A valance frill is simply a wide frill, usually finished with a top heading like many glass curtains and drawn up into top fullness on curtain tape. It serves just the same purpose as a pelmet and, like it, is attached to a wooden pelmet board or metal pelmet rail fixed above the window-frame. Practically without exception a valance frill should be of the same material as the curtain and quite untrimmed.

The stiff, formal pelmet with its flat surface has a dignity that accords best with large windows and heavy, floor-length curtains, but it would look pretentious and top-heavy heading small casement windows.

A valance frill is, in comparison, soft, friendly and informal. This makes it ideal for old, low-ceilinged rooms with diamond panes, for modern casement windows in the villa and prefab type of house and for small, unimportant sashes such as one gets in the kitchens, bathrooms and passages of large, old-fashioned houses. As a frill is easily laundered, usually, whereas a pelmet (with few exceptions) must be taken down when soiled and sent to a dry-cleaner, frills are preferable for practical reasons to accompany curtains that will need frequent washing—say, at a nursery or kitchen window.

A pelmet, especially if trimmed, looks, when hung, a most formidable thing to make. Actually, it is one of the easiest jobs in home upholstery, though it is not a particularly quick one, because all work except the joining of any seams must be done by hand.

Frills are almost entirely machine work. They need a straight eye, but the job of making them couldn't well be simpler.

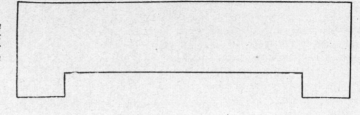

Fig. 11a. Patterns of pelmets can be bought, but a straight or box pelmet is simple to cut from your own pattern, made from kitchen paper

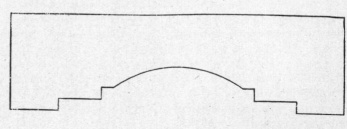

Fig. 11b. This is more elaborate still, but in the small house or flat it is wiser to keep to fairly simple designs, concentrating on colour and drapery

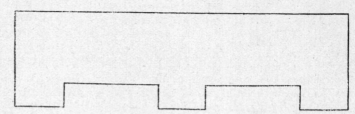

Fig. 11c. Another variation of the box-pelmet. These are very effective when curtaining two windows set close together, as the centre box falls just between the windows

Pelmet Making

First measure your window with a yardstick to find out the length required. The pelmet must stretch across the entire width occupied by the window—or across a pair of windows, if these are set close together. It must also be long enough to go round the thickness of the pelmet board or rail to which it will be fixed, so as to touch the wall on either side. This usually means adding 7 or 8 in. to the actual window width.

Paper patterns of pelmets can occasionally be bought. But as there is no standard size for windows, they may not fit yours or may not be available in a design you like. It is more satisfactory and not at all difficult to make your own pattern. Personally I like for this pattern-making a roll of kitchen paper, as it gives the continuous length wanted and saves pasting smaller pieces together. If you do have to join several sheets of, say, newspaper, be particularly careful that when fastened together they give an absolutely straight-in-one-line top edge—otherwise you'll have trouble with the pelmet made from this pattern when you start fixing it to the board or rail. You can test the continuous straightness of the top edge of the paper against your yardstick.

For fairly small and simple types of windows, a pelmet which is merely a straight strip, trimmed or untrimmed, often looks very well. In this case you have simply to rule out such a strip to the length you have already measured and a suitable depth. Its lower edge will, of course, be just as straight and unbroken as its upper one.

This brings us to the question of the best depth for a pelmet. That must depend chiefly on the height and depth of the window and, to a much less extent, on whether the room is well or poorly lighted. As a rough guide, a strip pelmet should be from 6 to 12 in. deep; on a shaped one, its drop ends or the deepest point of the design should be from 14 to 18 in. deep and the shallower parts from 8 to 12 in. in depth. A sound plan is to cut the pattern on the deep side at first. Then try it up against the window and make it shallower, if necessary, by taking off an inch or two along the straight top edge. This is much easier than trying to alter the shaped lower edge.

What design shall you choose, if you decide that a strip pelmet is too plain and ordinary for your particular room? At one remove from it, very easy to cut a pattern for, yet not quite as severe as a strip, is the box pelmet—a strip with a deeper rectangle or 'box' at each end. (*Fig. 11a.*)

One stage more complicated is a box pelmet with a slight arch in the middle and a little 'step' between the arched part and the box to make the descent at each end more gradual. (*Fig. 11b.*) When you are curtaining as one unit two windows set close together, it is often effective to use a box design with a centre box also to fall over the woodwork dividing the windows. (*Fig. 11c.*)

Remember, by the way, that unless your room is exceptionally well lighted, you should arrange the 'drop' parts of your design to fall over wall or woodwork, not over the panes, where they would help to darken the room.

From these three simple designs you can go on, if you wish, to much more complicated pelmet shapes with plenty of more or less elaborate curves (when patterning these curves, by the way, it's a help to outline partly round a large circular tray or round or oval dish). But in the average small modern house or flat it is fatally easy to over-elaborate pelmet shapes. Far better, in nine cases out of ten, to stick to a simple design of the type of those illustrated. If it should look too plain when made, it can be relieved with a little simple trimming.

When you have drawn out the pattern to your satisfaction cut it out and pin it to your pelmet board to judge the effect, viewing it from the far side of the room, not close at hand. Is it the right depth in proportion to the size of the window and the room as a whole? It should not look heavy and obscure too much light, but it should be deep enough to cover the curtain fitment and not appear mean or skimped. Is the silhouette of the bottom edge graceful and pleasing when seen against the light? If the pattern seems too deep, make it shallower as already explained. If too shallow or ugly in outline, cut a new one that corrects these faults.

Materials Required

Once you are satisfied with your pattern, you can ascertain from it the quantities of material the pelmet will require.

A pelmet consists of three layers—the visible surface, matching or contrasting with the curtains; the stiff interlining; and the lining, for which you should buy a cheap material such as casement cloth or sateen. For the stiffening you *must* use yellow-brown upholstery buckram. Dress buckram and other stiffish materials are unsuitable. Cardboard is likely to buckle badly or tear away from the pelmet board in wear.

Upholstery buckram, 36 in. wide, can be bought from furnishing departments of big stores. As a long shallow strip, nowhere more than half this width, is required for a pelmet, it is an economical plan to make two pelmets at once, each using more or less half the width. Or, if you only want one, you can buy half the length of buckram needed to stretch across the window, plus an inch or so for overlapping a join in the centre, after the buckram has been cut in half lengthwise.

The same economical plan may be followed for shallow pelmets when buying the material and lining. But remember that several inches are needed for turnings on these two layers, so this plan will not work for a pelmet which is to be anywhere more than 15 in. deep, if the material is less than 36 in. wide (velvets and cretonnes often are).

To give you an idea of quantities, a pelmet which is 2 yards long and has a greatest depth of 15 in. will require one yard of buckram and one yard each of 46-in. or 36-in. material and lining.

Cutting Out

If you have bought half the length of material needed, with the idea, mentioned above, of having a centre-front join, you must make this join before laying on the pattern. Cut the buckram in half lengthways. Overlap the two halves 1 in. down a short edge, taking great care to keep an unbroken straight line along the top—or woe betide your pelmet when you come to hang it! Test the straightness of your top line with a yardstick, as you did when making your pattern, then make the join with a large zigzag stab-stitch. Use a strong needle and thread, not cotton, for making the join. (*Fig. 12.*)

Lay the paper pattern on the buckram, with its centre-front edge (if you have cut the complete pattern you can find this edge by folding it in half exactly) to the buckram join. You cannot put ordinary pins through upholstery buckram, so hold the pattern in place for cutting with drawing-pins or slip-on paper clips. Mark the pattern outlines in the buckram with tailor's chalk. If you have cut only a half pattern, then turn it over at the join and similarly mark out its second half. Remove the pattern and cut out the buckram along the chalk lines, without turnings.

The red and white sprigged curtains have a plain red pelmet with a diamond design in white cord; the dressing-table stool catches up the curtain pattern

The furniture is of Australian walnut; the shelves and dressing-table top of plastic to be sponged clean easily. Notice the carefully planned fitment that takes radio (near at hand to turn on or off), books, tea tray, odds and ends

The gay patchwork quilt is both warm and cheerful. Directions for making a patchwork bed rug are on page 207

Council of Industrial Design

Should joins be needed at the centre-front of the material and lining, cut the fabrics in half lengthwise and machine-stitch and well press the seams before cutting out. Cut both fabrics out roughly with about 2-in. turnings, not following the pelmet shape precisely and laying the centre-front of the pattern to a fold of material made down the seam. Put the lining aside. It will not be wanted for the moment.

Making Up

Lay the cut-out material out flat, wrong side uppermost and smooth it out. If it is creased, iron it smooth at this point. Drawing-pin the cut-out buckram down on it, with the material turnings projecting beyond the buckram on all sides. See that all drawing-pins are at least 2 in. away from the buckram edges.

Upholstery buckram (and no other kind, which is one reason why you *must* have it) is stiffened with glue, so that a mixture of damp and heat will make it stick to the material and

save tedious sewing. Have ready a damp sponge and a hot iron. Wet the buckram edges all round with the sponge to a depth of about 2 in., then quickly iron down the material turnings on to the damped stiffening, to which they will stick firmly. At corners and along curves slash the turnings so that they will fold over and stick down flatly.

A good plan is to have two people doing this work, one damping and slashing while the other wields the iron.

Don't leave the pelmet long in this stage, but as soon as possible afterwards lay the lining, right side uppermost, over the buckram. Fold in the lining turnings to be slightly smaller than the pelmet (they may need trimming down a bit first) and slip-stitch them to the ironed-down turnings of the surface. Use a longer (and consequently faster) slip-stitch than in dressmaking.

Finish the lower edges with a matching pelmet fringe. Sew this on from the right side, with a line of running stitches along both the top and bottom of the unfringed heading. When turning corners, mitre the braid neatly and flatly; round curves, pleat it slightly so that it lies smoothly. If liked, a matching braid may be similarly sewn along the straight top edge of the pelmet.

Large pelmets in large rooms are sometimes trimmed with more braid sewn in patterns above the fringe. Pelmets in ordinary houses or flats mostly look best without this additional trimming, but if you use it stab-stitch it in place, through surface and buckram, *before* adding the lining, which will hide the stitches.

Rayon or Plastic Pelmets

There are some special points to remember if you think of making a pelmet from either one of the furnishing rayons or from plastic material, which is attractive for a pelmet because it can be sponged over when soiled. The gluing method, which is so labour-saving, can't be used for plastic fabric because this material won't stand ironing; and some types of rayon shrivel if damp heat is applied to them.

Test a scrap of your rayon first to see if it will tolerate sufficient damp heat to release the glue from the buckram. If it won't you must modify your method of making, and tack the rayon turnings to the buckram all round with stab-stitches before applying the lining. You can either make such small stab-stitches on the rayon side (with much bigger ones on the buckram) that they won't show when the pelmet is hung; or you can use larger stitches and cover them with fringe.

Another point. Should the rayon be at all flimsy, the hard edges of the buckram may cut through it in wear. To avoid this, pad those edges first with strips of unbleached calico. Or spread a layer of domette over the

Fig. 13. If you have a round-topped window, fix your pelmet board well above the top of the rounded part

buckram before laying on the material. The domette prevents the edges cutting through and also gives a much richer and more solid look to a thin surface material.

In the case of a plastic pelmet, the lining can't be slip-stitched to it, as the plastic fabric is apt to break away from any kind of hemming. A good remedy is to have both surface and lining of plastic (so that the whole pelmet will sponge over). Cut both surface and lining without turnings to the exact pattern size. Place all three layers smoothly together with the buckram between the two plastics and tack round the edges. Neaten and finish all round the pelmet with a binding of braid doubled over the edges and stab-stitched into place.

Pelmets for Round-topped Church Windows

This Victorian type of window, quite common today in the older built-up districts, presents a curtaining problem, especially when finishing off the top of the window. A valance frill is impossible, since frills, like streams, refuse to run uphill; and you may be puzzled how to fit a pelmet top to the rounded shape.

The answer is, 'Don't try.' Instead, as explained for curtains at this type of window, fix your rail or pelmet board horizontally well above the topmost part of the rounded top. Then cut a pelmet pattern with a straight upper edge long enough to go along the rail or board from wall to wall and a lower edge which follows exactly the semicircular top of the window. Make up the pelmet in the way already described. You then have a practical and attractive pelmet which finishes off the window successfully, and at the same time reveals the distinctive top curve. (*Fig. 13.*)

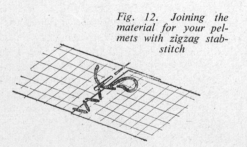

Fig. 12. Joining the material for your pelmets with zigzag stab-stitch

Fixing Pelmets

Fix above the window-frame, on brackets, a narrow wooden board or shelf only 3 or 4 in. wide. Nail or drawing-pin the top edge of the pelmet very tautly to the front thickness of the wood. Mark the centre of the pelmet and also that of the board and fix these two points together first, afterwards working outwards towards each side. If you prefer a metal pelmet rail, finish the lining side of the pelmet (before the top edge is slip-stitched down) with Rufflette tape as for a curtain. The pelmet is then hung from the rail in the same way as a curtain, but, of course, an inch or two outside it.

Should you want to use the tape-and-rail method for a pelmet in plastic fabric, it should be lined with ordinary material, not plastic.

VALANCE FRILLS

There is not much to say about making valance frills, because they are, in essence, extremely short curtains only a few inches in depth and are made in much the same way.

How deep should a valance frill be? Well, as in the case of pelmet depth, this depends on the size of your room, the height of your windows and the type of material you are using. Broadly speaking, the larger and more important the windows, the heavier the material you should use for curtains and valance and the greater you should make the depth of the top frill. As a general guide, valances should be between 4 in. (for small casements) and 12 in. deep. Cut a strip of paper the depth you think will be correct, pin it up over the window and stand well back to view the effect. If this is not pleasing, deepen or make shallower until you are satisfied with the result. Should you find that even a depth of 12 in. does not look important enough at your window, it is probable that it is too large and heavy a one to be suited by a valance frill. Consider whether a pelmet will not give a better result.

Quantity of Material Required

When the depth is decided, you can calculate the quantity of material needed. The frill strips should be cut straight across the width from selvedge to selvedge and for each strip you will need the depth decided on, plus 3 to 5 in. for top heading and bottom hem.

Thus for a frill 4 in. deep you should cut your strips 7 in. deep. But for a 12-in. frill allow the maximum extra and cut the strips each 17 in. deep. This is because the much larger frill needs a deeper heading and hem, to look well, than its baby sister.

You will join the selvedge edges of the strips, of course, to get the total length required for the valance. For a gathered frill allow 1½ times the finished length wanted. Thus, if your rail or board and your material are both 36 in. wide, you will need a total length (allowing for seams and hems at each end) of 57 in. Let's assume you are cutting your strips 8 in. deep. To get the length, you will need one whole strip and a good part of another—that is, half a yard of material.

Again, suppose your valance is a deep one and you are using for it a more expensive 54-in. material. If the strips are to be cut, say, 15 in. deep, to get your complete length for a large window (or a pair of windows) measuring a total of 80 in. (124 in. of frill), you will need two complete strips and part of a third—that is, 1¼ yards of material.

Of course, you must remember that in nine cases out of ten a valance frill matches the curtains it goes with. You will therefore be buying the material for both at once and so may effect some saving. For example, in the second instance given above, you require so little of the third strip (only about a quarter of the width) that you will probably be able to cut it out of a piece left over from the curtains, thus reducing the frill material needed to ¾ yard.

Making Gathered Valance Frills

Measure and cut your frill strips with the same care to get them absolutely straight and even in depth as described for curtain making. Join the strips together with plain ½-in. seams and press the turnings flat, one each way. Stitch a hem along the bottom edge. Fold a heading (¾ in. to 1½ in. in depth, according to the depth of the valance) and finish it on the wrong side with Rufflette tape. If the valance is to be fixed to a pelmet board instead of a rail (you may have the former fitting already in the room), make a casing below the heading, run a tape through the casing to gather it up to the required length and drawing-pin the valance to the pelmet board. When it is soiled remove the drawing-pins, pull out the tape and the frill can be laundered flat.

To put two quite bold patterns into a room needs some care to be successful. Here you have a gay modern curtain fabric with a Scottish printed linen on the chairs

The elegant furniture is of Australian black bean, inlaid with cherrywood, an unusual and striking combination

Design by Ian Henderson

Box-pleated Valance Frills

These are more tailored than a gathered frill, but much less so than a pelmet. They look well at largish windows, especially in a room like a dining-room which is rather formally furnished or in a lounge where the loose covers also have box-pleated frills. A man's den, too, is suited by the regular lines of box-pleating.

More fullness is required than for gathered frills, and for the best effect the valance should measure not less, finished, than 6 in. deep. When calculating quantity of material and cutting the strips allow about 2½ times the finished length wanted. Join the widths, press open the seams. Stitch a hem along to bottom edge.

Attractive pleats need accurate measurement. Starting 1 in. from one end of your length, mark out with pins along the top of the frill these three measurements, repeating them over and over again all along in the same order; first, ¾ in.; then 3 in.; finally 1½ in. Be careful to measure accurately, even if it takes time and care. Afterwards, starting at the same end, measure and pin identically along the bottom edge.

If your valance is a deep one to go at a large window, you may prefer rather more imposing pleats. For these, make your measurements a little larger, too—1 in., 4 in. and 2 in. respectively.

Now go along the frill taking up and pinning each 3-in. space as a wide tuck. Then spread it out flat into a box-pleat, making sure that one of its folds just touches the pin, at top and bottom, which marks off the neighbouring ¾-in. space. In this way each tuck, when box-pleated out, is centred accurately on the frill.

As each pleat is made, pin it in place at top and bottom. Keep two threaded needles going, one along the top and another along the bottom edge, and with these tack the pleats in position as you go along. Tacking finished, have ready a hot iron and two white pressing cloths, one dry, the other wrung out of warm water. Press two or three pleats at a time, using the following method, which sets them in very firmly. First cover them with the damp cloth and press heavily. While they are still steaming, whisk away the damp cloth, put the dry one in its place and press back the steam into the fabric. Pins, by the way, should be removed before pressing or they may mark the frill.

Now fold down and stitch the top heading and finish the frill, according as it will hang from a metal rail or wooden pelmet board, with Rufflette tape or plain curtain braid. As the fullness is already pleated to the length required, you will not draw up the cords on the Rufflette or run a tape through the curtain braid.

Lined Valance Frills

Generally speaking, lined curtains require a pelmet rather than a valance. But during the war, when most curtains were lined to provide blackout and chinks of light might escape above them, accompanying valances were often lined to match. Fortunately this necessity has now passed, but it may occasionally happen for some reason that lined curtains are hung with a valance instead of a pelmet. In this case, line the valance. So made, it will give a matching effect, and wear as long as the curtains do. Also, because single materials hang differently from doubled ones, it will 'set' in just the same way as the curtains and completely harmonise with them. The valance should be completely lined, using the method given for lined curtains, but without any backing, before box-pleating is done.

Trimmings for Valance Frills

This type of top-of-the-window finish has such a simple, informal air that trimmings are seldom needed. But as the valance matches the curtains and forms, with them, a frame for the window, any trimming used for the draperies should be repeated on the top frill. If the curtains have contrasting bound edges, for example, the valance should have them, too. This idea not only provides a note of contrast that is sometimes needed, but is a useful renovator when edges are frayed from much wear or laundering.

* * *

A Net Curtain Hint. When making net curtains a great difficulty is that pins supposed to hold the hems only too easily drop out of the open mesh. Get a packet of small invisible hairpins and use these instead. They are easily drawn out when the job is done.

Cotton Reels that Stay Put. How often one has an interrupting search for a reel of cotton that has rolled under a chair or got hidden under one's work. Here are two good 'stay put' hints. (1) Hammer long nails at even distances into a small board, hammering them only a little way in. The board stands on your work-table and on each nail a reel of cotton stays securely, yet can be easily threaded from when hand-sewing or lifted off to go into the sewing machine. (2) Buy two reels of each colour for a dressmaking or upholstery job— you usually have to, anyway. One of each goes in the machine. The other is threaded on to a length of tape, with other reels in common use. Make the tape long enough to double into a loop and knot at the top and hang it handily. When hand sewing or tacking your cotton is never lost.

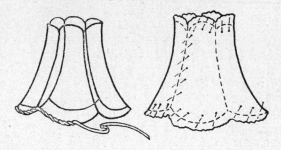

Left: Binding the frame of the lampshade.
Right: Pin your material into position, making quite sure that it is pulled taut

A CHARMING LAMPSHADE

TO MAKE FROM A REMNANT

THIS is a lampshade with an expensive look, but which can be made from an odd piece of lace.

You will need: $\frac{1}{2}$ yard 36-in. wide lace; $\frac{1}{2}$ yard 36-in. wide satin lining; $1\frac{1}{2}$ yards $1\frac{1}{2}$-in. wide looped fringe; $\frac{3}{4}$ yard $\frac{3}{4}$-in. wide braid ; 4 yards straight binding; 1 lampshade frame (6-sided bell shape 10 in. deep, 15 in. diameter base, 6 in. top); small pins.

To Make

Cover the entire frame with binding, then stretch the satin, on the cross, over one half and pin to binding with small pins to keep taut. Cut material away, leaving $\frac{1}{2}$ in. all round. Repeat on other half and join material at the sides.

Stretch the lace over the satin in the same way, attaching it into position over the pin heads. Remove the pins from top and base, also satin and lace cover, and french seam sides of them. Replace the cover over the frame and pin tautly into place. The seams should be directly over each frame support.

Stitch the cover to the tape. Then by folding the $\frac{3}{4}$-in. wide braid lengthwise, stab-stitch to the top of frame enclosing the raw edges of material. The lower raw edge should be turned back into a small hem which is covered when the looped fringe is sewn into position.

HOW TO MAKE A LOOSE COVER

You can pipe the edges of your covers with a colour that picks up a shade in patterned material; or use a contrasting tone with a plain material. Scarlet is attractive on dark green; yellow or white with navy; brown on creamy beige. A darker tone of the same colour is also very effective

FIRST of all, of course, you must find the exact amount of material needed, and this is how you do it. Add together the following measurements.

Place tape measure over the inside back of chair 1–2 and add on 5 inches for tuck-in; measure outside back 1–8 allowing 1-inch turnings. Inside arms, add 1 inch at 5, measure over to 4 with 5-inch tuck-in, double the amount to allow for the other arm.

Measure front of chair seat 3–7, allowing 1 inch at 3. The pleated frill is 3 inches wide, so allow a 4-inch width and length twice the circumference of lower edge of chair. Take similar measurements for cord.

To Cut and Fit Cover

Placing material on chair back, pin centre of material to 1 with 1 inch over the back.

Cut length 1–2 plus 6 inches and width 10–9 plus 3 inches. Pin round sides, allowing easy width and turnings. Mark with chalk the arm curve and allow 1-inch turning, widening to 3 inches at 12. Snip the edges of turning.

For seat, cut 2–3 plus 6 inches and width across 5 plus 10 inches. The inner arms cut from 4–5 plus 6 inches and 4–13 allowing good measurement and turnings. Cut to match material for second arm. Fit well the curved seat at arms and back, allowing 3 inches to tuck in on each side.

Pin, making it an easy fitting. Pin seat to back joining at mark 2, tack on right side. Then join inner arms to seat. Remove material from chair and with french seams machine curve 11–12, then along seat.

Place cover on chair, pin all round leaving turnings at 1, 4 and 3 round arm scrolls. Tuck in allowance round seat.

Cut a band of material for front of seat 3–7, measuring from 5 across plus 6 inches.

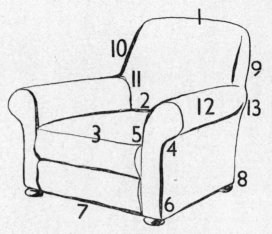

Diagram 1. This shows you quite simply how to measure the amount of material required. Place the tape measure over the chair at the points indicated in the instructions on this page

Diagram 2. Here you see the back view of the cover, when it is cut out and pinned on the chair. The outer arm piece is shown pinned to the inner arm

The outer arms are measured from 4–6 plus 2-inch turnings, and 4–13 plus 4-inch turnings. Pin along arm down the back and along

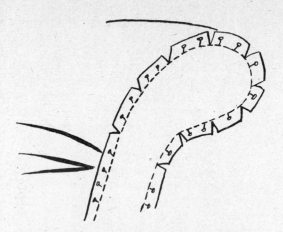

Diagram 3. Place your material on the arm scrolls and then mark around with chalk. Make it an easy fitting to allow for shrinkage. Then cut and tack into place as shown above

Diagram 4. This shows you the nearly completed cover, and also the position of the opening on the right-hand back seam. A placket is not really necessary on this type of chair

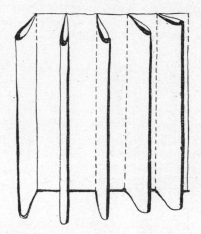

Diagram 5. The pleated frill is made as you see in the above diagram. The pleats are about 1 inch wide. If a frill is used, gather it evenly, and tack before stitching permanently

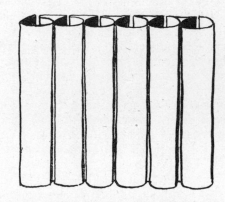

Diagram 6. This illustrates the right side of the pleating. Be sure to take care in measuring, and make pleats at even distances to get a professional effect. Press them well into position

scroll. Measure 1–8 plus 1-inch turning, pinning centre to centre at 1 and all round as shown in diagram 2; leave good turnings.

Cut material for scroll as diagram 3; leave 1½-inch turnings.

Finally, before removing cover to machine stitch, make quite sure the fit is loose to allow for shrinkage when laundered.

Now remove cover and machine all round on wrong side, leaving side opening as shown in diagram 4. To finish edge of cover make

pleated frill to fall at least 1 inch clear of floor.

To make frill, joins in the material will be necessary: make flat seams. Allow ¼-inch hem at lower edge. Box pleat as shown in diagram 5, tack, allowing turnings, then machine stitch. Press cover.

Fit on chair, mark position for sewing on press studs for fastening. Then sew cord on arms, seat and round the back of chair as illustrated.

Everwear Candlewick, Ltd.

These pretty little curtains are ready-made; the pelmet and side curtains are in one piece. They are in printed cotton, organdie and marquisette

DIVAN BEDS AND BOX OTTOMANS

Divans

In bed-sitting-rooms, or in a lounge where a divan is used both as a couch and as an emergency bed for a visitor, it must be provided with a neat, attractive loose cover which will fit not only over the divan itself but over the bedclothes as well. This is a very easy job for the home needlewoman—much easier, in fact, than a chair or couch loose cover, because the divan is merely an oblong without any curves, arms or back. If it has a head-board, this is not loose-covered.

When a bed has been converted into a divan and stands high enough from the ground to have things stored under it to save space, or has drawers fitted into it, a box-pleated frill is a good finish. The low modern divan, with frame reaching down to only a few inches above the floor, looks best made on very trim lines and without a frill. Use an extra-thick piping cord, covered preferably with definitely contrasting fabric, to relieve the plainness with a decorative note.

Remember when measuring for quantity of material and also when cutting out *to have the divan made up with an average number of bed-clothes*, so that the cover is large enough to go over them. Unless there is to be a frill, pieces will be only two in number—top and collar. Cut the top without a join, the length and width of the divan top plus the usual $\frac{3}{4}$-in. turnings on all edges; the collar a straight strip (or several joined) long enough to go right round the frame and $1\frac{1}{2}$ to 2 in. deeper than the finished depth required.

Notching is not needed, but after cutting out on a table by measurements, pin up the cover wrong side out and try it on to see that it fits the divan closely. It should slip on and off without a placket being needed. Pipe the join of top and collar and finish the bottom edge with the usual hem.

Box ottoman covers, being smaller and less formal in effect than those for divans, usually omit the collar and consist merely of an oblong top piece, with a gathered frill reaching to the floor joined directly on to it all round. Pipe the join of frill and top.

Furniture varies so infinitely in size, shape and the fashion of the moment that all instructions for loose-covering it must be fluid rather than exact. Loose covers provide more exceptions to rules than most things, and once you know the general procedure you can use your own judgment about details. The same position of a placket, for example, may be right on one chair and wrong or inconvenient on another. So, as you gain experience, make your own decisions in particular cases.

Secondly, unless economy is all-important, over-estimate rather than under-estimate the amount of material needed. It is seldom possible to judge to within a quarter of a yard, unless you have covered the same chair before in the same width of stuff. But if you calculate too closely, and then cannot match your stuff, the job is spoilt. Whereas half a yard or a yard over will never be wasted. You can keep it by you to use for repairs or 'collars and cuffs' when the cover loses its first youth. Or you can make from it an extra little cushion or a matching runner which will harmonise delightfully if used in the same room.

REPAIRS AND RENOVATIONS TO LOOSE COVERS

As loose covers use a lot of material and take a good while to make, it is sound economy to make them last and look well for as long as possible. Quite a lot can be done to keep them in good repair or smarten them up, especially if you have oddments of the material by you.

Backs and Arms Soiled or Rubbed

Greasy heads and grubby hands work this kind of mischief, and how tiresome to have to launder a whole cover because one or two spots only are soiled Far better, if you've that bit of extra matching stuff laid by, make a 'collar and cuff' set to prevent back and arm tops from getting soiled before their time, or cover up the damage if it's done already. If you've no self-material, use a contrast—printed on a plain cover or plain on a striped or floral one.

The 'collar' is a sort of deep cap which fits closely over the whole top back of the chair and comes down far enough to reach the neck of a person sitting in the chair. Use the loose cover as a pattern for this, making seams and pipings in the same places on your 'collar.' Or fit the collar direct on the chair itself, a trifle loosely so that it will go over the loose cover as well. Finish the collar bottom edge with a plain hem. Make the cuffs similarly to cover the front corners of the arms and extend as far back along their tops as is needed. Hem all unseamed edges, pipe all seamed ones.

Cutting Down

Just as a mother may cut down the best parts of a frock of her own to make a new garment for her little daughter, so a large loose cover which has worn through in a few places only, or faded very badly in spots, may take on a new lease of life if it is recut to fit a smaller chair—preferably one without arms or of the open-armed type, as then the arm portions of the old cover are available for cutting into. Or a couch cover may be transformed into one for a chair.

Don't waste time measuring the old cover on its new chair in the vain hope that a lot of the old seams will do again. They're seldom so obliging. Besides, it's the joined edges of a cover that get the chief wear, so re-seaming in a different place wonderfully removes the worn and shabby look. Also, unpick the cover *before* you wash it. It's so much easier to launder and iron in several flat pieces.

Also, make fresh piping from a contrasting oddment to brighten up the old material. Talking of brightening, a cover in reversible material generally looks much newer and more unfaded if you remake it wrong side out.

For cutting and making up the cover follow the general instructions already given. However, you may find that, as you are using fabric already cut out, you'll need more seams than are usually necessary, and perhaps not even be able to match the pattern where they occur. Never mind. Cut the most conspicuous pieces —seat and inside back—first from the best bits of material. Usually those which were originally the back and inside arm pieces are the least worn. Then piece together what is left over for the remaining portions, which are less noticeable. If you have to make extra joins, match the pattern if possible and in any case seam neatly on the straight thread and press well. Then don't worry if they're not invisible. After all, a re-make can never be quite as good as a new job.

The chair or couch now left coverless by your cutting-down operation may either have a new cover or, if that isn't possible, be given a 'collar and cuff' set made as already described. You can use any oddments or remnants of suitable material for this set and it will protect the most vulnerable parts of the permanent upholstery from wear and tear.

SMALL REPAIRS

Don't discard any otherwise good loose cover because it is worn in a few spots, faded in one area or someone has burnt a cigarette hole in a conspicuous place. If the cover is

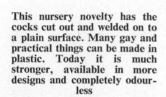
This nursery novelty has the cocks cut out and welded on to a plain surface. Many gay and practical things can be made in plastic. Today it is much stronger, available in more designs and completely odourless

Dunlop Special Products, Ltd.

191

generally in good condition, try mending the one or two bad spots.

Where's the self-material coming from for patching? Use a little ingenuity. Remember the very ample tuck-away round the seat of a chair or settee. This can't just be done away with, because it gives the necessary play to the cover when the springs are depressed by a sitter's weight; but you can go on the topping-and-tailing-a-shirt principle. The tuck-aways don't show, so cut off a strip 2 or 3 in. wide and replace it with, say, a bit of old shirt or curtain.

If bigger repairs are needed than can be done with narrow strips, a frilled cover may have to sacrifice its frill so that this can be used for patches and replacements.

Patching

On plain material this is rather too conspicuous to look well, unless in a quite unobtrusive spot on the cover—and you're generally not so lucky as that. But if the cover is floral or striped, by matching the pattern as exactly as possible you can get a quite unnoticeable effect. Hem down the new patch over the bad spot, without removing that bad part or hemming a second time as with ordinary patching. I suggest hand-hemming rather than machine stitching because it shows much less when pressed.

Replacing Worn Piping

The piping cord often rubs through the material of middle-aged covers, showing white at exposed edges and corners. On a long stretch, such as the whole seam joining the seat and front collar pieces, unpick the seam, and re-cover the length of cord.

For merely a small rub through at a front corner, first cut a bias strip of self or nearly matching stuff 1½ in. wide and 1 in. longer than the worn bit. Fold in each end. Fold one long edge in singly and hem it down to the cover just below the piping cord. Bring the strip over to cover the cord tautly and hem down the second edge as close to the seam as possible. If neatly done, this repair should never be noticed.

Cushion Cover Placket

From self-material or something as nearly matching it as possible, cut two straight strips, each 1 in. longer than the opening in the cushion cover. One strip should be 2½ in., the other 1½ in. wide. (*Fig. 14.*)

Double the wider strip lengthwise, turn in its edge at each end to face and stitch round the two ends and the fold. Fold in single turns to face along the remaining long edge. Sandwich between these turns the unpiped raw edge of the cushion opening and stitch in place from the right side. Face the piped edge of the opening by laying the narrower strip to it, stitching cover, piping and strip together. Then fold down the strip on the wrong side as a facing and stitch down again along its other (turned-in) long edge. Make the ends of the two placket halves exactly the same length and cross-stitch these ends neatly together. At 2-in. intervals sew hooks to the piped facing and corresponding bar eyes to the unpiped side, arranging them so that when the placket is closed its under edge lies exactly along the inner edge of the piping. (*Fig. 15.*)

SEAT, CHAIR PADS AND SQUABS

Sometimes a plainly made stool, wooden or dining-room chair needs a flat cushion on it, to give a little extra height, soften the hard surface of the seat or introduce a note of colour and decoration. Cushions of this type, which are to be sat upon, not leaned against, are known as pads and in certain points of their making vary from ordinary cushions.

They should always be kept rather plain and perfectly flat. Choose for pads hardwearing materials, plain-coloured, striped, checked or in some geometrical pattern. Floral designs

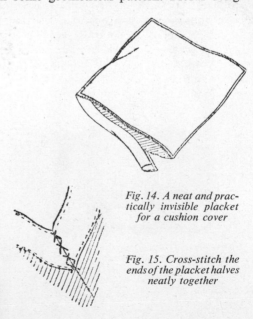

Fig. 14. A neat and practically invisible placket for a cushion cover

Fig. 15. Cross-stitch the ends of the placket halves neatly together

Boldly designed, colourful curtains, looped back for grace and light, go well with modern furniture

These bright golden curtains have a red pelmet, and the chairs match the pelmet. The ceiling is a pale primrose

This expensive-looking lampshade is made from a remnant of lace. Directions for its making are on page 187

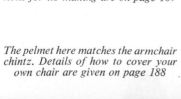

The pelmet here matches the armchair chintz. Details of how to cover your own chair are given on page 188

There are many lovely fabrics for curtains and covers to be found with a little seeking. These nine suggestions are, Top left: glazed flowered chintz, which looks 'right' with almost any furnishing. Centre: mercerised cotton damask, with a moiré finish. Right: hand-printed rayon with a simple, clean-cut design. Left: washable glazed chintz, excellent with Regency style. Back left: hand-printed linen. Centre: pen-and-ink print on rayon. Right: Continental glazed cotton. On floor, textured wool-and-cotton covering. Foreground, woven cotton with ribbed effect

seldom look right and need too frequent laundering. It is not comfortable to sit on trimmings, and they are apt to wear out quickly if they *are* sat upon; so for gaiety, if this is needed, rely on vivid plain colours (not too light) or dashing stripes or checks. A piped edge can give a bold contrast if desired.

A pad should fit precisely the seat it is to cover, following its curves and being indented to fit round the uprights of the chair back, if these exist, where they join the seat. To get the fit exact, lay a piece of white kitchen paper or newspaper on the chair seat or stool, hold it down with a weight and make an accurate pattern by cutting the paper all round the chair edges.

Pads usually consist of top and underside only. Cut these from the paper pattern, allowing ½-in. turnings on all edges. Occasionally, if a really thick pad is wanted, the cover may be boxed, but don't do this if the outline of the seat is at all complicated in shape. If boxing is used, it will be much thinner than an ordinary boxed cushion and the thickness strip should be cut only 2 in. wide (including turnings) and long enough to go right round the seat plus 1-in. turnings.

Stuffing for a Pad

Pipe and make up an ordinary cover, except that the *whole* of the edge which will go to the back of the chair (or one short end if the cover is for an oblong stool) should be left open for filling. If the cover is of washable material, finish this back edge with a placket so that it is easily slipped on and off for laundering. On a boxed pad cover the opening should come between the boxing strip and the underside.

Never stuff a pad with kapok or feathers. Feathers are too soft and kapok is apt to form uncomfortable lumps when sat upon. The correct stuffing is layers of some thick material cut to the exact size and shape and held together so that they cannot shift in wear.

There are several possible fillings. Perhaps the best is three or four layers of underlay carpet felt—six to eight layers if the cushion is boxed. Other satisfactory materials are old (but not too thin) blanket, especially Army blanket, or travelling rug or cheap terry towelling, which last has the advantage of being easily washable when soiled.

Use the paper pattern which fits the chair seat for cutting the filling layers, so that they

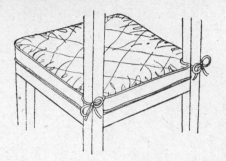

Fig. 16. Here is the chair-pad kept neatly in position by tapes

will be exactly right for both chair and cover. Cut them exact to the pattern, without any turnings. Lay them one on top of the other quite flat till you get the required depth, then hold them all firmly together by taking large tacking stitches through all layers. Tack first all round the edge, then across and across in several directions, so that no layer can ruck up anywhere in wear.

Place the padding flatly and exactly inside the cover, so that it fits precisely everywhere. Then sew up the open edge or fasten the placket, if you have made one.

A pad for a chair which has arms, even of the open kind, will usually stay in place of its own accord. But if the chair is armless or your pad is for a stool, it is apt to slide off should the person sitting on it shift about at all. So to keep it in position, sew tapes to the two back corners of a chair pad which can be tied round the uprights of the back. (*Fig. 16.*) For a stool put two tapes at diagonally opposite corners to tie to the legs.

Don't, with the idea of anchoring the pad more firmly, tie it down at all four corners, or the movements of the sitter will sooner or later tear the tapes loose—and perhaps a bit out of the pad cover at the same time! If preferred, the middle part of the tape may be stitched in with the cover seam, instead of being attached by hand afterwards.

Squabs

This is the name given to the very firm, mattress-like cushions which are used to cover the hardness of wooden window-seats. Sometimes, too, a squab is made to fit a wooden chair for which a considerable extra height is needed, as when, say, it is used for sitting at a typewriter. Squabs are a distinctive type of cushion, with similar covers (which are not

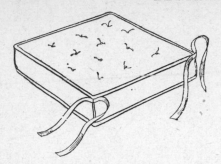

Fig. 17. Finishing off the squab

detachable) but different stuffing and methods of regulating it. For making them you will need a mattress needle (a giant of an affair, pointed at both ends), leather tufts and strong, fine string. You can get the needle and tufts from an upholsterer or soft furnishing department in some stores.

Cut a paper pattern the exact size and shape of the window-seat or chair for which the squab is wanted. Use this pattern for cutting four pieces with ½-in. turnings added on all edges. Two of these pieces should be in unbleached calico or some other strong cotton for the inner case; two in a decorative furnishing material for the outer cover. Cut also in calico four boxing strips, each 3 in. wide including turnings and as long as one side or end of the squab plus 1 in.

Lay the pattern on each shaped calico piece and mark the actual seam lines in pencil round it. Pin the boxing strips into place between the top and bottom pieces and exactly at each corner tack the boxing strip seams, straight and vertical. Then stitch these short seams, without unpinning them from top and bottom pieces more than just enough to get the stitching clear. Now tack the strips between top and bottom, over the pins, exactly along the pencil lines. When a corner is reached in this tacking, unpick the strip seam just to the depth of the turning and also slash the turning of the main piece to the same depth. Thus you will get good right-angle corners, which are important in a squab.

Leave most of the lower back edge of a seat squab or one end of a window-seat open for stuffing. Kapok is much too soft for squabs, which are continually sat upon, and rugging (bought at an upholsterer's or soft-furnishing department) should be used. Pick it over first a little at a time, to break up any lumps and remove loose dust. Then stuff the calico case as hard and tight as possible, putting the rugging in in handfuls and pushing it up well. It is most important not to stint your stuffing and to pack the cover just as full as it will hold, taking special care that the corners are hard and tight.

Sew up strongly the opening in the case. Then beat with a carpet beater or a stick to get it flat and even everywhere.

Make the outer ornamental cover in the same way, using the two pieces already cut out with boxing strips between them as already described. Be careful that the turnings are the same depth, so that the fit is exact. There are two differences only in making this outer cover—the seams should be piped, and at the two back corners the middle of a length of tape (to tie the squab in place, if it is for a chair—for a window-seat no tapes are needed) should be stitched in with the upper seam.

Draw the outer case over the squab, fitting it exactly everywhere. Sew up the opening. Now the squab must be tufted to keep the stuffing firmly in place and prevent it piling up anywhere in use. (*Fig. 17.*)

Tufting

Tufting couldn't be simpler. Thread your mattress needle with string. Mark out on the squab, on both top and underside, where the tufts are to come. They should be about 6 in. apart and in rows also 6 in. apart. Alternate the dots in the rows so that each comes half-way between and below those in the previous line.

The tufts are small leather discs. To tuft, thrust the threaded mattress needle through from the top of the squab, at a pencil dot, to the corresponding dot on the underside. It will need some hard pushing but you soon get the trick of it. Once it is through, re-insert it from the underside towards the top ½ in.

Fig. 18. Tufting

These are comfortable modern chairs of beech and cane, useful for the garden, a verandah, or even an extra chair indoors. You can make seat pads for your own plain chairs; they keep in place better than a loose cushion

Courtesy of Ian Henderson

away from where it came through. As the needle is pointed at both ends, it is usually easier to make the return stab with the eye end. Pull the needle through on the top, but while there is still a loop of string left on the underside slip a tuft under it. Then pull the string really tight so that it indents the under surface a little. The tuft is to give something strong to pull against and prevent the string from cutting the cover. (*Fig. 18*.)

On the top side, when first putting the needle through, leave only a short end of string sticking out. Now put a tuft under this, knot the end and the string in the needle firmly together over the tuft and cut off with quite short ends. Tuft every pencil mark similarly and the squab is ready for use.

PETTICOATS FOR DRESSING-TABLES

With the aid of pretty draperies easily made at home and a swing, hung or standing mirror, you can transform almost any shabby small table into a charming dressing-table.

Kidney-shaped dressing-tables are pretty but even in white wood they are apt to be comparatively expensive. If you want to keep down costs it is better not to be too particular about the exact size and shape of your home-made dressing-table. Instead, look among your household belongings or in secondhand furniture shops for a square, oblong or triangular piece of furniture that will serve as a solid foundation. Old-fashioned washstands are often priced very low, and even if the one you see has a hole in its top which once ensconced the basin it will serve if otherwise suitable, for

the void can be covered with a sheet of plywood cut to fit the top.

If not a washstand, look for a table of some kind. It may be an old kitchen table, of the old-fashioned kind with a wooden (not a porcelain) top, or some other battered relic which has seen good service already. As it will be completely covered, a scraped surface, worn paint or knocked-about legs don't matter in the least, provided the table is strong and stands firmly. But it should preferably have a rim which projects a little over the top edge.

If the room is tiny or rather crowded, a good space-saving idea is to have a triangular foundation fitted into a corner. You can use either the sort of three-cornered washstand already suggested or one of those corner wardrobe fitments which consists of a triangular wooden top ready fitted with curtain rod and rings. This, fixed at dressing-table instead of wardrobe height and provided with correspondingly brief curtains, makes an ideal space-saving dressing-table.

You may like to have a draped dressing-table in a more important room. In that case, use a larger table but give it importance and dignity to suit the room by making the petticoats of a rich material, such as taffeta or furnishing satin.

For the average small or smallish skirted table use a fabric which drapes softly and gives a fresh, youthful effect. Tiny-patterned cretonnes, many cotton or rayon summer dress materials, chintz, organdie, nylon and the more substantial curtain nets (pale net over a deeper coloured foundation is delightful) are all a good choice. Flowered transparent plastic fabric, though rather tiresome to sew, falls gracefully and is easy to clean. (*Fig. 19.*)

THE TABLE-TOP

When estimating the quantity of material required, you will need to decide first of all whether the table-top is to be covered in it, to match the petticoats, or not. Generally speaking, there are three possible treatments for the table-top. One, the most expensive but the easiest to keep clean, is to get a glazier to cut a sheet of heavy glass to fit it. Under this transparent cover, the table-top must either be immaculately painted or polished, or, if it is too shabby for either of these, be covered with a flat piece of the petticoat material laid under the glass.

A second plan is to cover the table-top with American cloth, picking up the main colour in the petticoats. This wears well, looks decorative and is easily cleaned by wiping over with a damp cloth.

The third method is to make a (not glass-covered) top of the petticoat material. This may have the frills joined to it all round, so that the whole drapery is in one piece and can be lifted off in a moment for laundering. The drawback of this plan is that the top always gets soiled very much sooner than the frills and yet can't be washed separately. Alternatively, the top may be made quite apart from the petticoats—a piece flatly fitting the table-top, with a border or thickness strip a

Fig. 19. The cheapest table and stool can be dressed up easily in flounced petticoats to give an expensive air

few inches deep joined to it all round with a piping. In wear, this border hides the tops of the skirts and the fitment by which they are attached to the table, and it can be removed instantly whenever it needs washing.

According to which table-top plan you choose, calculate the amount of stuff you will need. As one side of the table will be, probably, against a wall, this side, if you wish, need only have an ungathered strip about 6 in. deep. But it is preferable to reckon for frills right round, as then they can be reversed and put back to front from time to time, so that you get double wear from them.

The petticoats should be cut straight across the stuff from selvedge to selvedge. Measure round the table, calculate how many of these widths you will need to give the necessary fullness, add 2 in. on each strip for hem and turnings, and enough for the table-top if this is being covered in fabric.

The minimum fullness for a fairly substantial material like cretonne should be $1\frac{1}{2}$ times the measurement round the table, twice round in thinner stuffs such as dress cottons and $2\frac{1}{2}$ times round for thin fabrics—organdie, curtain net and the like. In fact, if you want a transparent stuff gathered fully enough not to *be* transparent, even three times round will not be too much.

If the table you are using is of normal height but small measurements, it may look too tall for its size. In this case you will get a prettier effect and cut the apparent height by using a double petticoat—the under one from the sill of the table to the floor and the one over it hanging from the top to from $\frac{1}{3}$ to $\frac{1}{2}$ of the distance down. If you intend doing this reckon the extra material needed before buying.

Has your table a front drawer which must be easily accessible? If so, arrange for two separate curtains which meet at the centre front and are easily pulled aside, clear of the drawer, when necessary. Or you can achieve a charming knee-hole effect with a pair of petticoats which end, one each side, just short of the drawer; such a dressing-table is very comfortable to sit at, as the kneehole space under the drawer gives room for the legs.

The drawer front may be shabby and unpresentable. In this case, cover it with material matching the petticoats or American cloth matching the table-top, fastening this in place with coloured drawing-pins or gilt chair pins.

MAKING THE PETTICOATS

This is easy, as they are merely short curtains of a simple type. Cut the straight strips for them with the turnings already suggested, seam the selvedge edges together with good turnings (nicking these diagonally at intervals if the selvedges are tight and inclined to draw) and press the seams well, one turn-in each way. Should you be joining part widths without selvedge edges, a French seam is usually best.

Finish with a narrow hem, edges which are to meet or give a kneehole effect in front.

Screw two cuphooks into the back of the table, just under its top rim and provide a wire spring rod which can be stretched round just under the rim, out of sight, from one hook to the other. Round the top of the petticoat stitch a hem (casing) deep enough (about $\frac{1}{2}$ in.) to take the wire comfortably. Thread the wire through the casing, fix in position and then turn up a bottom hem on the petticoat so that it just (but only just) clears the ground. Stitch and press this hem.

When the completed petticoat is put back round the table, adjust the fullness evenly and prettily on the rod. This kind of dressing-table curtain is the simplest of all to launder, because when released from the wire spring rod it is perfectly flat for ironing.

If you are making the two-tier petticoat suggested to reduce table height, after seaming together quite separately the widths forming the deep and the shallow frills, stitch a hem round the bottom of the shallow one. Then lay it over the deep one and fold both top edges together into the top casing, so that one wire will take them both. Finally, hem the deep frill just to clear the floor. Here again, laundering is made easy, since the joined frills are flat under the iron.

PETTICOAT WITH ATTACHED TOP

If you have decided to have the petticoat joined to a table-top cover, so that no rod is needed and the whole drapery can be just lifted off for washing, the making is a little more complicated.

Cut widths for the petticoat and join them as already explained. In addition, cut a piece of matching material the size of the table-top, plus $\frac{3}{4}$-in. turnings all round. This will be joined to the petticoat with a piping which follows the table edge exactly all round. You

Fig. 20. A window seat with squabs and a box frill looks effective but can cover a good deal of storage space

can pipe with matching material, with a contrast or with bias tape which picks up the main colour in patterned petticoats.

When you have enough piping prepared, gather the upper edge of the petticoat to fit the edges of the table-top piece.

To make sure you have the same amount of fullness all round and haven't to gather on awkwardly long lengths of cotton, work in this way. Find the total number of inches right round your table-top piece. Thus, if the table is 30 in. long by 16 in. wide, 30 + 16 + 30 + 16 in. gives a right-round measurement of 92 in. Divide this into four equal lengths of 23 in. each and mark these off with pins round your table-top edge. They won't come just at corners but this doesn't matter at all.

Now, by folding in half and then in half again, divide the top edge of the petticoat also into four equal portions and mark also with pins. They will, of course, be much longer than the table-top divisions, as you have allowed for plenty of fullness. If they are too long for each section to be gathered on one thread, it may be necessary to pin both table-top piece and petticoat in six equal divisions instead of four.

Gather each marked portion of the petticoat on a *separate* thread, leaving this loose and knotted at both ends for later adjustment. When all are gathered, tack the prepared piping round the table-top piece, raw edges facing outwards and flush with its raw edges. Draw up each gathering thread so that its section of the petticoat fits the corresponding section of the top piece, tack in position, then stitch as close to the piping cord as possible.

To get the seaming really close up, I always find it a good plan to run the presser-foot of

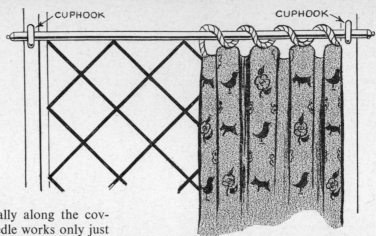

A cord looped over a wooden rod can be used for hanging Elizabethan curtains over a lattice casement. Use only one curtain for each window. The same method can be employed for door curtains. It is an exquisite way of showing off beautiful fabrics

the sewing-machine actually along the covered cord, so that the needle works only just clear of it. After seaming, put the cover on the table and turn up the bottom hem to just the right depth.

When this all-in-one cover is to be knee-holed in front to accommodate a front drawer, leave the right space between the gathered portions and neaten the piped edge between them with a wrong-side facing.

FITTING UP A WINDOW-SEAT

Old houses sometimes have picturesque built-in wooden seats which only need up-holstering to become real nooks of comfort and gay colour. In a newer house a broad wooden bench may be built in round a deep bay window, across a shallow one or under a small secondary window. Children especially love window-seats in their play-room or bedroom, and this sturdy form of seat will stand up to the liveliest scrambling about.

In a hall or on a landing where space is scanty, a window-seat fitted to a small window may take less room than a chair and serve many purposes.

Either a home or local jobbing carpenter can soon fix under any chosen window a plain, rather wide wooden bench. Be sure that this is placed about 2 in. lower than the actual height wanted, to allow for the thickness of its padding.

WINDOW-SEAT WITH SQUAB AND FRILL

It's a good idea to stain or enamel the wooden seat to match the paintwork of the room. Then the woodwork will keep cleaner and in better preservation, and if at any time the upholstered parts are removed for laundering, the seat itself will look neat and presentable. (*Fig. 20.*)

The fittings you need to make are quite simple—a firm, mattress-like cushion or cushions (if the seat is long) known as a squab,

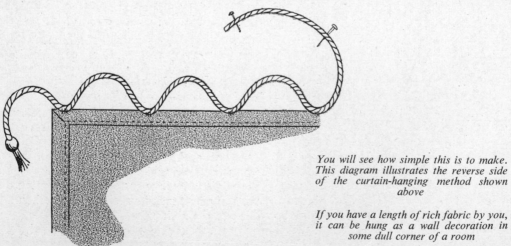

You will see how simple this is to make. This diagram illustrates the reverse side of the curtain-hanging method shown above

If you have a length of rich fabric by you, it can be hung as a wall decoration in some dull corner of a room

with a piped ornamental cover and a frill to match hanging from the front of the seat to the floor. If you have a door built across the front to make the seat into a cupboard you can omit the frill, otherwise it gives convenient hidden space under the window-seat which can be used for storage. It also lends a more dressed look to the general effect, and can still be used even if the window-seat is a finished little cupboard on its own.

Frill and cover may match the curtains hung at the window, or, if these are patterned, be of plain material in one of its main colours. Choose an easily washable fabric for preference, especially in a child's room.

Making the Squab

If the window-seat is more than 2 ft. 6 in. long, make two or even three squabs of equal size, as they are far easier to handle if not too large and heavy. For a small seat, say 30 in. long, only one squab is needed.

The Frill

If you decide on this to hang from seat to floor, provide a strip of material matching the outer cover of the squab. Cut this 3 in. deeper than the seat height and about $2\frac{1}{2}$ times the finished width required, if it is to be box-pleated; about $1\frac{1}{2}$ times if you prefer a gathered frill. Soft materials are best gathered, while stiffer ones should be pleated. Stitch a narrow hem along the bottom and each side edge. It can be box-pleated or, for a gathered frill, run two rows of gathers, close together, where the seat-level will come. Fix the pleated or gathered frill with drawing-pins to the seat edge. The squab will hide the pins and both frill and cushion are very easily removed for laundering.

Another plan is to affix the frill to one lower long edge of the squab cover, stitching its upper edge into this seam when made. In this case the frill need only be cut 2 in. deeper than the seat height instead of 3 in.

Multi-squab Window-seat

If the seat space is long enough to require two or more squabs instead of one, the good effect is lost unless these are absolutely identical in size and with true corners, so that they fit perfectly together. So take special care to be exact in cutting and seaming, and to stuff the corners very tightly.

When a window-seat is built all round a bay, you will need a separate squab for each section of the seat, and where two sections join there will be more than a right-angle. To fit this, each squab coming to the corner must have one end which slants outwards towards the window side, instead of being squared in the usual oblong shape. Take a careful pattern first in paper of the exact angle on the seat and be sure to get this accurate when cutting and seaming this end, so that the two squabs will fit together perfectly at the turn.

Roller towelling in fancy designs can be used for a multitude of purposes. This Irish linen towelling with an ivy-leaf design has been made into curtains, a supper cloth and napkins

Two strips used crosswise on a table make a decorative setting for four places. Cushion-covers, aprons, guest-towels can all match up from the same design

BAG EIDERDOWNS FOR CHILDREN

Babies' and small children's eiderdowns for cots and prams get such hard wear and need such frequent laundering that it seems hardly worth while spending much money on them. Besides, the kiddies grow so fast that these warmth-bringers are all too soon discarded as too small. So it's a good idea to economise by making these baby coverings very cheaply at home and thus having more money to spend on other juvenile items which must be bought.

A bag eiderdown for a baby's or a toddler's cot or to keep a small child cosily warm during airings may be made very easily, especially if you start well before it is wanted and treat it as pick-up work. If you have a piece-bag, the cost will be practically nothing—perhaps nothing at all—and yet the eiderdown will be warm, washable and pleasantly colourful to look at.

Briefly, the idea is to make a number of separate wee cushions or bags, warmly filled, of matching or contrasting material, and then to join these to form a quilt of the required size. A patchwork effect is generally best, as then you can use up economically all sorts of oddments from the piece-bag; but try to have enough matching ones to form the outer border or to make some simple and definite pattern.

For example, you might have a dark or plain-coloured outer border with the inside bags all lighter or patterned, though not necessarily matching each other. Another idea is to work on a colour basis, though materials may be different—say, a blue bag in the centre, varied pink ones encircling it and these again encircled by green ones forming the outer border.

Anyway, however varied the colours and patterns, for the sake of general wear and washability all the materials used should be of the same sort of fabric. Don't mix, for instance, rayon bags with cotton ones, and avoid any fabric which won't wash easily. The materials need not all be new. So long as they are strong and unfaded, good bags may often be made up from old summer cotton frocks or the best parts of discarded curtains. But if mixing old and new materials in one eiderdown, it is best to wash the new ones first, so that no problems of uneven shrinkage can arise after laundering.

The size of the bags does not greatly matter, as long as all are of exactly the same dimensions. These should partly depend on the size of the oddments you have available, remembering, of course, that a great many very small bags make a lot of work and may give a fidgety effect, with over-many seams for strength, while too large bags are extravagant of material and make it difficult to form an effective pattern.

A good size to choose, experience shows, is an oblong measuring 7 in. by $5\frac{1}{2}$ in. (these measurements include turnings). Each bag consists of two such oblongs. The two sides need not match, nor need the two sides of the finished eiderdown, which is reversible, be made up in the same pattern. But, of course, if you want a definite pattern of bags on both sides, you must work this out beforehand and seam your bag halves together accordingly. An easier plan, really, is to plan a definite design of bags for the top side and chance what sort of higgledy-piggledy arrangement of oblongs results on the underside.

Twenty-five bags of the size suggested, placed together in five rows of five, will make a quilt measuring approximately 32 in. by 25 in., which is a convenient cot size. For a pram this is too large, and it is better to reduce the bag size, in this case, to, say, 4 in. square, rather than to use very few large bags. A good idea is to draw beforehand on squared paper the size and design you want and the bag dimensions in which this can be best worked out.

Seam two oblongs together on three sides to form a bag. This is quickly done on the machine. Or if you want to make a bag or two at a time while on holiday or at odd moments, hand-sew them, using backstitch for greater strength. If you are making the bags a few at a time, store them flat as made and don't fill them until all are ready and can be put together. Be careful to make up all oblongs with exactly the same turnings and true, sharp corners, or they will not join correctly later. Press well after seaming.

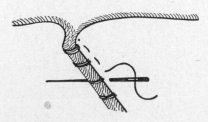

Fig. 21. Joining carpet edges

The use of brightly coloured mats, reasonable in price, can freshen up a jaded home. These rag rugs are woven in some of the old—but ever new — traditional Norwegian designs

Old rugs can be repaired, made smaller, and renovated by the use of braid and fringe

Norwegian Weavers

When enough bags are ready they must be filled. Kapok is the ideal filling and is not expensive. But if economy is very necessary, you can use all kinds of warm oddments, such as old woollen underwear and unravelled wool jumpers. All such filling must be shredded up really finely with scissors before use or it will mat up and form lumps when washed. Mix the various snippets well together before use, so that all bags will be uniformly filled.

Whether using kapok or shredded oddments, it is important only to fill the bags about half full, not to stuff them tightly. They are not cushions to lean against and it is plenty of air imprisoned with the filling which gives both warmth and lightness of weight to the eiderdown. As each bag is filled, turn in the raw edges of the open side and tack together.

Finally, sew the bags together in pattern order, first in long strips (five to a strip) and then joining the strips to give the width and complete the pattern. Make all joins by placing two bags face to face and closely and firmly overcasting them together, with corners matched exactly. The tacked open ends are closed at the same time by the overcasting. Arrange so that these ends do not come anywhere to the outside edge of the eiderdown.

When the quilt is all seamed together, press the overcast seams over a roller, so that the bags will fall away each side and the iron will not flatten them. You can make a roller by padding a length of dowel rod or thin broomstick. When soiled, launder the bag eiderdown just as you would an ordinary one.

REPAIRS TO CARPETS AND RUGS

When a fitted carpet is moved to a new house, it may require re-cutting in places to suit the new floor. The same need occurs if you move a worn carpet to a smaller room so that you can get rid of its bad patches, or decide to make the best parts of a really veteran floor-covering into a hearthrug. In each case, you must know the proper way of cutting the carpet and finishing the cut edge. Get the carpet cleaned first, if possible, otherwise your task will be a very dusty one

To cut a carpet, use sharp scissors. The cut, unless it is a slanting one to fit round some obstruction, should be exactly along a thread of the fabric. So, to ensure this, do your cutting with the wrong side of the carpet uppermost.

Binding Cut Edges

If these are to remain edges and not to be joined in a seam, they should be bound to strengthen them and prevent fraying. Use carpet braid as nearly matching as possible. Lay a length of braid to the underside, one of its edges flush with the cut carpet edge. (Some people prefer to pin the braid in position first, then cut the carpet along the braid edge.)

Secure braid and carpet edges together with large blanket (loop) stitches, making these $\frac{1}{2}$ in. long and $\frac{3}{4}$ in. apart. Pull each stitch really firmly with a slight but definite tug under, so that both the braid itself and the corded edge of the blanket stitch turn over somewhat to the underside of the carpet. Thus they almost cover and so protect the cut edge from wear.

If you find this pulling operation hard on your middle finger, hunt out a really *thick* old leather glove finger and wear it as a guard. At each end, turn in and overcast the braid to the carpet. Then hem down its free edge to the underside.

When a cut edge will get no wear—for example, if against the wall under a seldom-moved piece of furniture—it may be merely blanket-stitched without the use of braid.

Joining Carpet Edges

You will need to do this if making a rug from two good strips of an old carpet or re-fitting a carpet to a fresh room. If the joins needed are only short ones, they can very well be done at home to save time and expense. The following method is quite simple and gives a perfectly flat, unnoticeable join.

Unless the two edges to be joined are selvedges, first blanket-stitch the edges as already described. Then place the two pieces together, right sides touching, with the pile running the same way on both. First at each end, then at 6-in. intervals all along, match the two edges and firmly overcast them together with several stitches taken over each other in the same spot. This serves as a sort of tacking to keep the edges from slipping while being seamed. (*Fig. 21.*)

Sew the seam by hand with a running stitch stabbed to and fro. Keep the stitches the same size on both sides and $\frac{1}{8}$ in. away from selvedge edges—rather more from cut and bound ones. Press out the completed seam as flat as possible with your fingers, or hammer it if necessary. On the floor it will soon settle down quite smoothly.

Worn edges, or those which are frayed, especially at corners near doors, should be repaired quickly before they become really bad. Rugs with a fluffy or woolly pile are best mended with rug wool matching as nearly as possible. Cut off any fraying bits, then blanket-stitch over the worn edge, taking your stitches deep enough to reach well into the sound fabric. Or if you want a more definite and hard-wearing finish, hold a length of blind-cord or smooth, thick string along the worn edge and blanket-stitch over it.

Yet another good method with worn edges is to cut off any fray and then bind the worn edge with matching carpet braid. Double this over the edge, turning in the cut ends of the braid neatly, and secure in place, both sides at once, with stab-stitches.

All these carpet joins and repairs, except where otherwise stated, must be done with a proper carpet needle and a skein of waxed thread (not the thin kind sold on reels), which you should buy from a soft-furnishing counter or your local upholsterer.

FOR YOUR
NEEDLEWORK NOTEBOOK

Bent Knitting Needles. Knitting needles made of celluloid very easily get bent out of shape, making them awkward to work with. Soften them by holding them in hot water or in the steam of a kettle, and while they are flexible straighten them out between the fingers. Then harden them again by soaking in cold water. As celluloid is inflammable, remember that only hot water must be used to heat it; keep it right away from any naked flame or light.

Mending Lace. Torn lace can often be neatly mended by machine. Lay a piece of paper under the lace, bringing the torn edges as nearly together as possible. Thread the machine with very fine cotton, stitch backwards and forwards irregularly till the tear is firmly held, and then carefully tear away the paper. The mend will hardly show, provided the cotton used is a good match for the lace.

When Scissors are Blunt. It is so important to keep both scissors and cutting-out shears really sharp that you should take prompt action as soon as they seem the least bit dull. Here are three simple home remedies. (1) Try fifteen or twenty times to cut off the neck of a glass bottle with your scissors very briskly; of course you can't do it, but the slipping of the blades on the glass will sharpen them. (2) Use the scissors several times to cut a piece of coarse sandpaper. (3) If your scissors are new, they may be screwed up rather tightly, so that they work a little stiffly. Just draw your finger or thumb gently up the inside of each blade two or three times, thus dusting and slightly lubricating the metal from the natural oil in your skin. You will be surprised at the difference in smoothness that this makes. It will work, of course, only with scissors that are comparatively new.

How To Make
A RAFFIA LAMPSHADE

A wine bottle, a wire frame, and a little artistry are all you need

RAFFIA is always a modern note in furnishing, since it has an artistic simplicity that fits into many a decorating scheme.

Raffia can be bought in many colours as well as in its natural shade, so it is quite easy to make a lampshade in your favourite hue, but a natural shade will blend with any colour scheme.

There are special bottle lamp fittings on the market and these can be bought at most of the multiple stores for a few shillings, but if you prefer you can very easily make your own lampholder fitting to go into the top of any bottle you choose. For this you will need a strong cork which will fit tightly down into the bottle level with the rim—a plug of wood will serve the same purpose. Buy a lampholder with a round collar and make a disc to fit the collar: bore a hole through the wooden disc to take the flex. Wire the lampholder and pass the free end of flex through the bored hole, down through the straw, and out at the base. Attach plug. Screw the lampholder through the wooden disc and down into the cork.

Wire frames can be bought at large stores and are sold in various shapes and sizes, but whatever the shape or size, the frame must be bound completely with raffia before covering. It is quite easy to make the shade in two colours—if you buy an octagonal shape, cover the sides with natural raffia and the corners with a contrasting colour.

Bottles with a straw base can be bought at most wine shops for a few pence, but any fancy bottle will make a very attractive table lamp. So many things these days come in unusual bottles, that it is a shame to throw them away.

MATERIALS. *Wine bottle with straw base. Bottle lamp fitting and flex. Lampshade frame, ½ lb. of natural raffia, a length of straw fabric, 6 in. wide. 12 gilt studs.*

This can be made in any colour or a natural straw shade to blend with any background

First clean the bottle and dry thoroughly. Attach the fitting to top of bottle, taking flex down through the straw at base.

Bind the whole of the frame with raffia. Now cover the frame, tie end of raffia to top edge of frame and bring down and over bottom, then inside and back again to top edge. Continue in this manner until the frame is completely covered. Join raffia by tying ends into a knot, and, if possible keep the knot to the wrong side and trim off the ends neatly.

Turn in edge of the straw fabric along one edge and stitch to lower edge of frame all round, then fray out other end, for about 5 in. to form a fringe.

With 12 strands of raffia, make two plaits —one for top and one for lower edge. Bind each end of the plait securely, then sew to top and bottom edges.

Sew 12 gilt studs along the bottom plait at regular intervals.

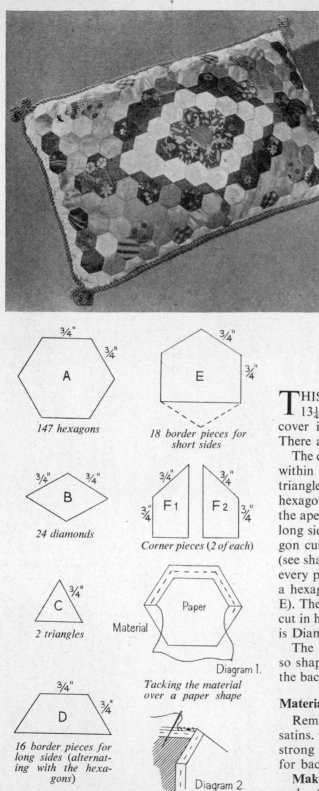

HARLEQUIN CUSHION

Made from remnants of silks and satins

A
147 hexagons

E
18 border pieces for short sides

B
24 diamonds

F1   F2
Corner pieces (2 of each)

C
2 triangles

Paper
Material
Diagram 1.
Tacking the material over a paper shape

D
16 border pieces for long sides (alternating with the hexagons)

Diagram 2.
Joining patches by overcasting

T HIS cushion measures 20½ in. long by 13¼ in. wide. The design of the front cover is composed of the shapes sketched. There are 211 pieces altogether.

The central portion consists of 25 hexagons within a border of 20 diamonds and two triangles. Outside this, the area is built up of hexagons with two diamonds end to end from the apex of each triangle. On the edges of the long sides every other piece becomes a hexagon cut in half through two opposite points (see shape D). On the edges of the short sides every piece except the corner pieces becomes a hexagon with one point cut off (see shape E). The corner pieces are made from shape E cut in half (see shapes F1 and F2). Triangle C is Diamond B cut in half.

The border pieces, D, E, F1 and F2, are so shaped to give the straight edge to which the back of cover is sewn.

Materials

Remnants of plain and patterned silks and satins. Cardboard. Stiff paper. Pure silk, or strong fine thread for sewing. Plain material for backing. 2½ yards of silk cord.

Making. Cut a cardboard template for each of the shapes shown and use to cut out

Continued on page 208

PATCH-WORK BED COVER

Make this to keep you snug in winter

PATCHWORK is usually thought of as being in silks or satins, but some very effective and warm covers can be made from thicker materials. This particular spread was first started from a scarlet wool-material house-coat; then pieces of an old grey tweed skirt that the moths had relished; some worn blue slacks, another grey coat, and a navy cloak.

First of all, of course, a bold repeating design of large, composite 20-in. squares was needed, which you see in the diagram. Four colours were to be used in the centre shapes; the corner triangles of each square were to be navy blue. The first intention was just to produce a thoroughly utilitarian piece of work, simple, to be made quickly and thriftily with whatever came to hand. But the joy of craftsmanship, of taking that little extra trouble which makes so much difference, soon took over.

Some of the materials were dull and cold in effect—very well, then, dyes could be bought, in any number of good colours. In the end, with the added touch of simple gay stitchery, the patchwork glowed like a panel of stained glass. But no new material was purchased—three or four packets of dye, some twopenny skeins of embroidery cotton, and braid to bind the outer edges of the spread were all the expense.

The slacks were unpicked and the pieces dyed, half a deeper blue, half deep green.

The scarlet gown, of course, needed no change. The light grey tweed was dyed deep yellow, and having been woven with mixed shades of natural wool ranging from white through grey to threads of black, the result

 BLUE   RED   GREEN   YELLOW   BLACK

was a pleasantly broken tone. Cuttings of several different materials, including part of an army blanket, were dyed navy, but this proved cold-looking; the pieces were finally re-dyed black, which set off the rest of the colours well.

Having sketched out the general plan, a template was then carefully measured and ruled up for the shapes which composed one large square; and three sets of pieces (for convenience in cutting out the material) cut in stout new brown paper.

The centre of each large square was made up of an octagon, four small squares and four lozenges (see drawing), using three of the four colours. To ensure an equal colour distribution there should be three of the 12 squares with the centre octagon in red, three with four small red squares and three with four red lozenges; and so on with each colour. This produces four different colour combinations, and these were arranged symmetrically in the whole plan, so that two similar squares never came next to each other, either across or diagonally.

The actual making adhered strictly to the traditional method. First the patches of material, allowing about ½-in. margins for seams, were cut out. Then, using the templates, a quantity of the shapes were cut out in paper. Old periodicals are thicker than newspaper, and if they are used will make it easier to cut out six or eight thicknesses at once. Then these paper shapes were pinned to the underside of the patches of material, and the material edges turned over and tacked down.

Every stitch of the sewing is by hand. First, following the plan, the edges of the tacked-up patches were closely oversewn together on the wrong side, until one whole large square unit was assembled.

Then, without removing the tackings and paper backing, herringbone stitch was worked in a heavy mercerised embroidery cotton, over all the seams on the right side, the colour used being always a brighter tone of the colour of material that did not appear in the square— i.e. on a red, green, yellow and black square, the herringboning was in bright blue; and so on. This stitching was made right through the turned-back seam edges of material on the underside, thus securing the seams flat open, and strengthening them.

When the three squares of the first row were completed, they were oversewn together in the same way as for the patches. Over the seams between the squares, the herringbone stitch was in lilac purple.

When two strips of the squares were made, they in turn were sewn together, and the seam stitched over in lilac; the third and fourth strips were added as completed.

The paper backing remained tacked in place until each whole square was finished and joined to its neighbours all round; then the tacking was pulled out, and the paper carefully removed.

To finish the edge, 1-in.-wide black woollen braid was oversewed all round to the turned edges of the outer squares, making small mitres at the corners. It was then turned over piping cord, securing this by small running and back-stitches as close as possible to the edges of material. Finally, the free edge of the braid was felled down to the wrong side of the work; done carefully, these stitches are practically invisible on the right side.

When all was joined up, and the tacking removed, the whole was carefully pressed under a damp cloth, on the wrong side. The size over-all is 6 ft. 8 in. by 5 ft., large enough to cover completely a single bed, or to use as a rug on a double bed, or even in a car.

The spread can, of course, be lined.

Harlequin Cushion—*continued*

the shapes in fairly stiff paper. Accuracy is essential. Then cut out the shapes in the materials, leaving generous turnings, and tack over paper shapes. Beginning with the hexagon in centre, build up the design.

Join the pieces by overcasting with tiny stitches on the wrong side. Work with a fine needle and short lengths of thread.

When the pieces are joined, remove tacking threads and ease out the paper shapes, *except* those on border. Cut backing material, allowing ½-in. turnings. Place right side of patchwork to right side of backing and overcast edges together on three sides. Remove paper from three sides sewn. Turn right side out and insert cushion before removing paper from remaining edge. Now remove paper and sew up the open end. Slip-stitch cord round edges, looping at corners.

Although you have to use the materials you have in hand, at the same time use only those colours that form a real harmony.

Homes for tropical fish have changed from mere tanks to aquaria both elegant and original. They form a definite part of the decoration of a room

Here the tropical aquarium is incorporated in a piece of contemporary furniture, with a cupboard underneath for storing equipment

START AN AQUARIUM

AQUARIA have been used for some years now as a colourful and delightful form of decoration, but few people realise how fascinating is the study of the fish. They can be bright, flashing, temperamental, they can quarrel and sulk. An aquarium of tropical fish is an ideal fitment for the lonely person.

From the first plain tanks have emerged designs both original and charming. For originality, there is the imitation street-lamp filled with fish; or one in a beer-barrel with the sides cut away and glass inserted. At the other end of the scale is a rather plain tank but mounted on a Chippendale stool to blend in with the rest of the large room of a country estate. A restaurant in the West Country has its ceiling of glass, and diners can while away any wait between courses by gazing upwards at the fish.

Make Your Own Aquarium

Your first requirement is, of course, a home for your fish. Do not bother with too small tanks, as they do not do justice to the fish or to their owners. A good average size is 24 in. by

12 in. by 12 in., which can be bought for about fifty shillings. Make sure that the frame is angle iron or at least an equivalent, as frames made from formed sheet steel are not so trustworthy. The cement holding the glass to the frame should be about $\frac{1}{8}$ in. in thickness.

You may prefer to make an aquarium for yourself, of the size mentioned above, and if so, this is how to do it. Obtain about thirteen feet of 1 in. by 1 in. by $\frac{1}{8}$ in. angle iron and cut into the following lengths: 4 at 24 in. long; 4 at 12 in. long.

Next, mitre both sides of the angle at 45° at each end so that a good right-angle joint can be made by welding. The local garage will usually undertake to do this for you quite cheaply. To prepare for the welding, lay two lengths of 24 in. and two lengths of 12 in. on the work bench to form a rectangle, and then insert into the frame thus made a board equal to the inside dimensions. This board should be cut away at the corners to give clearance for the flame. The same board can be used to make the other frame of the same dimensions. These frames form the top and bottom of the tank.

Bind wire around the outside to hold the frame square whilst the corners are being welded. The four 12 in. uprights can now be fitted and welded, either using a similar board or clamps to hold the frames in position for the welder.

Before actually making the board jig, check with the welder—he may have jigs for holding work of this nature, and so save you trouble. The completed frame should now be painted with a good-quality oil paint. Do not use enamel or lacquer as these tend to flake off eventually.

The frame is now ready for glazing. The glass can be 32 oz. for the sides, and either quarter plate or quarter rough cast for the bottom; these should not fit the frame tightly —allow about one-sixteenth of an inch all round.

The cement can be bought ready made in convenient tins and tubes, but if you prefer to make your own, use one part putty, two parts white lead, and two parts red lead, well mixed with a very small amount of goldsize. Spread the cement liberally on the bottom frame, making sure to fill the corners well, then lay the glass in and press firmly until approximately one-eighth of an inch of cement is left between the glass and frame. Clean off surplus cement with an old knife.

Repeat next with the two sides, and lastly, the two ends. A thin smear of goldsize on the frame and glass will assist adhesion.

Sand and Plants

Now that we have an aquarium, either bought or made, we consider the sand. Do not use ordinary builder's sand; this packs too tightly and is difficult to clean. The correct type can be bought from the local pet stores. This particular sand, in fact, is actually a fine grit, and although washed, should be washed again and again, and when you consider it clean, wash it once more. It is a frequent fault with novices to underestimate the importance of this somewhat tedious operation which, if not carried out properly, results very quickly in a cloudy tank.

The depth of sand can be varied to suit individual tastes, but two inches should be considered a minimum. To disinfect the sand, place it in a large bucket and boil for five minutes. This ensures that any germs lurking in the grit are destroyed, and if reasonable care is taken when introducing plants and other decorative devices into the tank, your aquarium will remain healthy.

Do not attempt to put soil of any nature under the sand in the mistaken idea that the plants will grow better, you would be welcoming trouble. The excreta from the fish will act as a fertiliser.

It is possible when adding new plants to an established aquarium that the water will become cloudy through disturbance of the 'mulm' on the floor. Leave this to settle and then syphon it off.

To Rival Nature

Now our aquarium set-up is beginning to take shape and rocks can be added next. Make sure that all sharp projections have been knocked or filed away so that fast-moving fish do not injure themselves accidentally.

The most attractive aquaria are those so designed to look as natural as possible, so with this end in view select rocks roughly similar in colour and shape. Highly coloured pieces of marble and similar types of stone are apt to look out of place in well-planted aquaria. Cumberland stone and the flat slaty-coloured rocks found in the streams of Devonshire are ideal types.

Arrange the rocks so that when the aquarium is viewed from the front they look balanced but not symmetrically so. They should not be too tall, as this tends to give a false impression of depth. Rocks can be made to form arches, terraces, and to hold banks of sand at higher levels.

They should be always well-cleaned by vigorous scrubbing with a stiff brush, and subsequent boiling.

A word of warning: As uneaten food tends

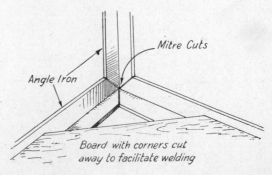

Mitre Cuts

Angle Iron

Board with corners cut away to facilitate welding

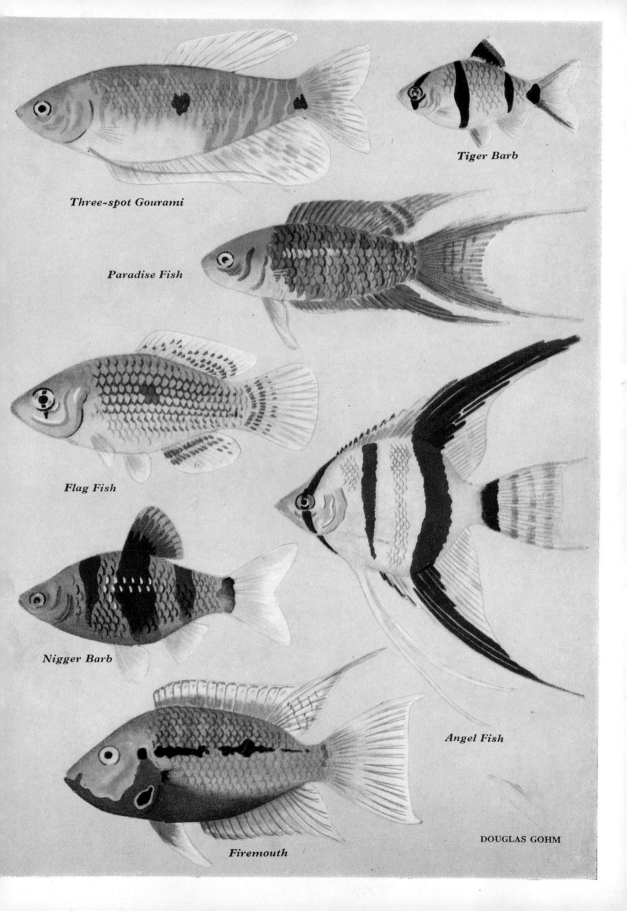

Three-spot Gourami

Tiger Barb

Paradise Fish

Flag Fish

Nigger Barb

Angel Fish

Firemouth

DOUGLAS GOHM

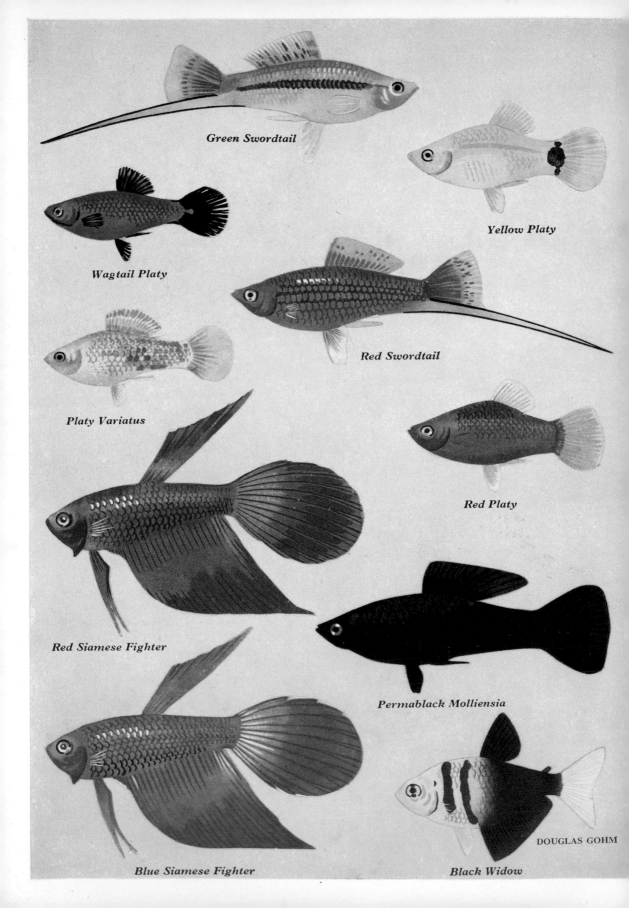

Green Swordtail

Yellow Platy

Wagtail Platy

Red Swordtail

Platy Variatus

Red Platy

Red Siamese Fighter

Permablack Molliensia

Blue Siamese Fighter

Black Widow

DOUGLAS GOHM

This is an attractive idea of mixing flower decorations with the aquaria. The fascination of keeping tropical fish soon grows, and other tanks are added. This is an effective way of displaying them. The plants have been chosen carefully and form a picturesque background for the colourful darting fish

Courtesy of 'Water Life and Aquarium World'

to pollute the water if it is left for any length of time, the possibility of this happening can be minimised if the rocks are pressed well into the sand, thus removing nooks and crannies where the food could otherwise become hidden.

Water and Plants

The moment has now arrived to fill the tank with water. This can be ordinary tap water, which is rather safer than pond or rain water, which may contain impurities.

If you live in a district where the water is hard, boil the amount needed for a while, allow it to cool, and then draw off the water from the top, using a piece of rubber tubing as a syphon. To prevent the stream of water disturbing the sand when filling, place a sheet of newspaper on the sand, this will then take the main force, and will rise with the water-level. Another means of filling is to use a saucer placed on the sand, or to use a clean watering can fitted with a rose sprinkler.

Plants can now be introduced into the scheme and arranged to suit individual tastes. The main precaution to be taken is to avoid covering the leaves of the plants with sand, as this tends to make them decay, or turn brown. Vallisneria and Sagittaria should not be grown in the same tank.

Here is a suggested selection of plants for a 24 in. by 12 in. by 12 in. tank:

20 Vallisneria	12 in. long
2 Indian fern	Medium
10 Ambulia	Medium

To Warm the Water

Tropical fish need water generally at a temperature of approximately 75° F. The easiest way to heat it is by electricity, using an immersion heater and thermostat to keep the water around the 75° F. range. This equipment is made specially for aquarists and can be bought quite reasonably from your local pet store. The heater can be laid on the floor of the aquarium and hidden by the rock scenery; the thermostat clips on to the side of the tank. A thermometer completes the installation. Details for connecting the electrical parts of our aquarium are supplied with the equipment.

A good basis for calculating wattage of the heater is to have 10 watts per gallon of aquarium water. To prevent the water collecting dust and the fish jumping out of their tank, lay a sheet of glass over the top or better still buy a cover specially made for the job. These covers have accommodation for electric lamp sockets, and provide by far the most satisfactory method of illumination.

Plants need light, otherwise they will turn brown, decay, and eventually die. A tank receiving little or no daylight requires a 50-watt lamp over it burning for nine hours a day.

Buying the Fish

OUR aquarium is now complete. It should be left for a few days to settle down, as this period also gives you the opportunity of checking that the temperature is being maintained satisfactorily.

The exciting stage has now been reached. We are off to buy our first fish. What are they going to be? We cannot mix fish indiscriminately; some species will want to eat others, some will destroy our plants and others just may not be suited to communal life. One rule is to try to keep fish of similar size in one tank. Large fish nearly always attack their smaller brethren, and even if they do not make themselves unpopular in this manner, they are apt to grab the lion's share of the available food.

The following list will give some idea of the types suitable for the beginner. It is, however, only a small selection when compared with the large variety of fish now available to the aquarist.

Courtesy of 'Water Life and Aquarium World'

A novel idea in which a street-lamp has been converted into a 'residence' for tropical fish. This is only practicable to accommodate a number of small specimens

Guppy	*Many-coloured.*
Permablack Mollienisia	*All black.*
Platy	*Yellow, or red, or many-coloured.*
Wagtail Platy	*All-black fins, body red or yellow.*
Swordtail	*Red or green.*
Black-line Tetra	*Silver with black line.*
Silver Tetra	*Mainly silver.*
Flame Fish	*Silver and deep red.*
Zebra Danio	*Deep blue and silver streaks.*
Pearl Danio	*Like mother of pearl.*
Tiger Barb	*Deep yellow, black bars over.*
Rosy Barb	*Mainly silver, blushes bronze.*
Dwarf Gouriam	*Red and blue-green striped.*
Three Spot Gourami	*Powder blue.*
Siamese Fighter	*Red, or blue.*
Angel Fish	*Brown-blue-silver with black markings.*

All the above fish can be put in one tank. It would not be advisable, however, to have two male Fighters together, as they would be certain to fight some time or another, unless of course the tank was very large, or the Fighters very small!

Large Swordtails, too, tend to become confirmed bullies, chasing and nibbling the fins of small inmates. If the specimens are large, limit the number to one only. The Silver Tetra is a very active chap and should not be put with fish that are easily scared. If you wish to gain practical experience first of all with inexpensive fish, try a tankful of Guppies. They are charming little chaps, easily bred (they are live bearers), easily fed, and offer a wide selection of colouring. No two male Guppies are ever exactly similar.

Food for tropical fish is very cheap. Dried shrimp, together with other dried foods, are made and supplied in inexpensive packets.

Dried foods only are not enough in themselves. They can form the mainstay, but foods like daphnia, tubifex worms, chopped earth worms, and mosquito larvae are in my opinion essential for strong, healthy fish.

From keeping fish, you can go on to breeding them, and then sell to the local aquarist or aquarists' societies.

More Tips on Fish-keeping

WHEN putting new acquisitions into your community tank, or any tank for that matter, float the container in the aquarium water for half an hour or so. This will ensure that the temperatures of both are more or less equal, and consequently the possibility of causing chills reduced.

* * *

Do not suddenly switch on the aquarium lights if the fish are in darkness. This frightens them, and sometimes causes them to dart about, hitting themselves on the rocks.

* * *

Do not overcrowd your fish, this will cause them to remain small and stunted. A surface area of 8 square inches per fish is an approximate formula.

* * *

Do not attempt to fertilise the plants, the fish provide all that is necessary. The addition of chemical fertilisers will invariably result in disaster.

* * *

Feed a little and often; sprinkle the dry food on the water surface with the fingers. The quantity should not exceed that which will be eaten within five minutes. Excessive feeding of dry foods causes the water to become cloudy. When feeding live foods, whether they have been purchased from a fish dealer or collected yourself, make sure that no Dragon-fly larvae or Water Tigers are among them. These are dangerous to small fish.

* * *

If the aquarium water should become cloudy, this is not necessarily a bad sign. If the colour is green it indicates an excess of light, but if the water is a brown or dun colour it is a danger signal, and immediate action is indicated. Clean out the tank and refill with fresh water.

* * *

Avoid putting metals into the water, the only really safe one is lead. Copper, brass, galvanised iron, etc., corrode and become poisonous.

Algae on the glass can be removed with a razor blade. A special long-handled holder is also obtainable from aquarist shops.

* * *

To avoid introducing into your tank fish that may be diseased, keep a small tank spare that can be used as a quarantine tank. The new fish are kept in this for a few days. If any fish are suspect add permanganate of potash to the water, $\frac{1}{8}$ grain per gallon.

* * *

Avoid planting Sagittaria and Vallisneria in the same tank, they rarely do well together.

* * *

Always use two nets when catching fast-moving fish, one to guide the fish into the other.

* * *

Never allow plants to become dry in transit: they should be wrapped in wet newspaper and then covered with a greaseproof paper.

* * *

Snails are excellent scavengers, they will eat algae and food uneaten by fish, but do not rely on them to remove all the undesirable matter. The 'mulm' on the floor of the aquarium should be syphoned off once every ten days or so.

* * *

Old weather-beaten rocks make the best ornaments. To obtain the desired effect if only new rocks are available, soak them in a strong solution of permanganate of potash.

* * *

Heaters left in contact with the sand collect a covering of lime, and this hard coat is detrimental to the efficiency of the heater. If the heater is placed on two stones so that the water can circulate completely around the glass envelope, this coating can usually be avoided.

* * *

Scum on the water surface can be removed with a sheet of newspaper. The paper is laid flat on the water and left for a few moments, then carefully peeled off.

DOUGLAS GOHM, F.Z.S

THE UP-TO-DATE
USE
OF
BRUSHES

Courtesy of Max Factor

Too many girls apply a hard outline of rouge, which looks feverish rather than healthy. The use of a sable-hair brush enables the rouge to be faded off to a natural flush

Lip-brushes can be obtained in cases for use on the dressing-table or in the handbag. It is much cleaner and more effective than using a finger, giving an even surface. Remember to finish the lipstick inside the lips

Both a brush and comb are needed for the eyebrows and can be obtained for a few pence. Brush the eyebrows the wrong way first, then smooth down in the right direction. When you comb them, it is easy to pluck out any that overlap the neat outline. Finish with a tiny touch of brilliantine. Always keep an eyebrow brush and comb on your dressing-table. They can be bought very cheaply

Courtesy of Max Factor

ON BEING BEAUTIFUL

'BEAUTY is in the eye of the beholder' is a very true maxim. We all know women whom we think are extremely plain, yet their husbands consider them quite lovely. Which is, of course, as it should be, and very lucky for a great many people! Nevertheless, it is hard for the most tolerant eye to overlook spotty skins, bad posture, dreary expressions and lank hair!

The woman who sets out to make the most of herself should remember the phrase, '*When you are born you have the face God gave you. When you die, you have the face you gave yourself.*' This is one of the first rules of beauty, for an amiable character, a smile *inside*, keeps the lines of the face upward, while depression, anger, bitterness drag down the whole structure. Just as the sea wears away a cliff, so does the most habitual expression shape the face.

So many things contribute to an impression of loveliness. There are stage and film stars, famous for their attractiveness, who are not strictly beautiful at all. But they give the *illusion* of beauty. They are well-groomed, their hair is shining and healthy, eyes bright; they may not have a great deal of make-up off the stage, but what they use defines their own personalities.

First Thing to Do

If you are not very satisfied with yourself, get out a notebook and pencil, take a good look at yourself in a mirror, and jot down your bad points. Is your hair bright, or does it need attention, a new style and the regular use of a tonic for a while? Is your make-up all it should be? Are your shoulders drooping? Have you rather a 'bread-basket' where a flat front should exist? Do you look charming except for dish-pan hands?

Either make yourself out a treatment sheet to be followed strictly and regularly; or else deal with one defect—assuming there is more than one—at a time, marking down your progress. When that is dealt with and vanquished, then proceed to the next. You are more likely to continue if you have not too much to remember.

BRUSH YOUR WAY TO BEAUTY

The use of brushes has become very widespread, so get yourself a set, and you will wonder what you have been doing all this time without them.

A powder brush is used to remove surplus powder when the face has been made up. Use a curved brush, as this follows the contour of the face. The skin is left very much smoother than if the puff alone is used, and it also prevents little patches of the powder caking on the skin as the day wears on. Also, powder stays on better if it is applied fairly heavily, and the use of the brush prevents an over-powdered look, which is not attractive.

Lip-brush. Buy an eight-inch sable brush, and cut it to a wedge shape, to apply your lipstick, making an outline before filling in. You can use your lipstick first, brushing it smooth with the lip-brush, or apply the brush direct to the lipstick and use the brush alone. A smoother, more satiny surface is achieved, although a little practice may be necessary at first.

You get a cleaner look to the edge of the lips with a brush, instead of a rather fuzzy or shaky line, especially if you want slightly to alter the shape of your mouth. A small mouth can have the lipstick brushed right to the edge. On a large mouth the lipstick can be skilfully applied so that it leaves off just before the edge. If upper or lower lips need emphasising to obtain more balance, then more lipstick can be brushed on to one than the other. There are also proprietary makes of lip-brushes, capped to carry in the handbag.

Complexion Brush. Some people are 'for' and some 'against' complexion brushes, but there is absolutely no doubt that they are necessary to the girl who suffers from blackheads. The brush is made soapy and briskly brushed with a circular motion around any area given to blackheads. This does clean the pores, which should, of course, be closed afterwards by dabbing with an astringent or pore lotion. The use of the brush also helps to prevent pores from clogging. Even if the face is never washed with soap and water in the usual way, a little brushing with a soapy complexion brush only of the area affected will be a great help.

Nailbrush. A complexion brush can be used for removing scaly skin from knees and elbows, but actually a nailbrush is better for this; also its gentle use on the fingernails prevents cuticle from having ragged edges. The remainder of the cuticle can be pushed back carefully, after washing the hands, with a soft towel.

Bath Brush. Body brushes tone up the skin, set the circulation coursing healthily, and aid to slimming. Long-handled bath brushes are really a necessity for keeping the back smooth and clean.

Eye-shadow Brush. The use of a brush for eye-shadow does mean that the touch is light. A heavy finger applying eye-shadow can drag the skin continually and help towards 'crocodile' lids! Dip the brush in the shadow, draw a line along the lash edge of the upper lid, and one halfway along the outer edge of the lower lid, then where the two lines meet at the outer corner of the eye, smudge them together, working the shadow up to the brow, and adding a little over the lid. A half-inch red sable brush such as you buy at any art shop is suitable.

Eyelash-brush. Naturally, you have one of these with your mascara, although it is a good idea to have two. Then when one becomes clogged through not having been wiped often enough after using, you can use the other, until such time as a little brush-cleaning can be done! Actually, your brush should be wiped clean each time, or instead of fine black lashes you will have what appears to be cocoanut matting surrounding your eyes! Your brows should also be groomed; little combs as well as brushes are available for this. Brush the brows the wrong way, then smooth them in the right direction. This will cause them to lie flat.

Rouge-brush. An artist's very large sable-hair brush is suitable for this. They enable the rouge to be put on much more naturally, fading off the colour to the merest flush.

Hairbrush. Hair-brushing has been recog-

Max Factor

Keep your eyelash-brushes clean or you will get a matted effect. Dip them in hot water before applying mascara

nised over the ages as a way to remove dead hair and to make the hair lustrous and healthy. There is a modern school of thought that claims only a comb should be used, but a brush brings the natural oil down from the crown of the head, stimulates the roots by the 'pull' on them. There are also brushes and combs made in one unit for the much-occupied woman! Two brushes used at once are good, brushing the hair over the face, head down, with a quickish sweeping movement of one brush after the other.

Notes on Brush Care. Do not buy very cheap brushes. Bristles should be firm and resilient, with an 'alive' springiness to them. Too soft bristles which do not rebound to their original position are of no use at all. Even a toothbrush should not be too soft, for it cannot properly clean the tooth-surfaces, and will do the gums no good. A good brush can be washed often, but a cheap one loses whatever firmness it started out with. Never boil a brush. Use *lukewarm* soapsuds and work them through the bristles until they are free from grease and dirt. Rinse in several clear, lukewarm waters.

Always dry any brush with the bristles pointing downwards, or moisture may seep into the anchoring foundations and gradually loosen them. Dry in sunshine and breeze, if possible.

CARE OF THE SKIN

WHETHER a woman is plump or slim, a lovely skin is always remarked upon. It is an extraordinary thing that more women have not beautiful complexions, for the poor, ill-treated epidermis does respond so quickly and gratefully to a little real care. While regular attention is the ideal, even some looking after can cause an indifferent skin to become radiant.

If, of course, you wash your skin in hard water and use harsh soaps; if you expose it to every element, wind and scorching sun that can toughen and dry; if you do not bother to clean it very thoroughly so that creams and dust can block the pores; if you do not bother to stimulate it so that the blood circulates freely and healthily, bringing life to tired, sallow faces, then naturally you will have a leathery covering to your face. Once it has got to this state, it will take some time to put right, and look most unattractive and unfeminine. After all, the first duty of any woman is to *be* a woman.

Basic Rules

Although to feed your skin, keep it thoroughly cleansed, and to stimulate it are the three basic things to remember, each woman needs one of these things more than another. The plump face very rarely needs too feeding a skin, or it becomes still plumper. Nor does the oily face respond to grease! The dry face, while needing to be kept clean, also has to have its natural oil content augmented.

Cream has to be put on in the right way, for just as constant expression moulds the flesh, even if it cannot alter the bone structure, so does constant pushing or pulling in a wrong direction do a good deal of harm. The movement should always be upward and outward. Actually, since the ideal is to keep the face in youthful lines, it is necessary to *maintain* rather than alter. Which is why one famous beauty firm believes only in tapping, and not in massage at all. It is why pressing is helpful in keeping the contour, too. This consists of putting the hands flat against the face and pressing firmly as if pressing into place, not *pushing* the flesh one way or another. Do this all over the face after cleansing. Press the fingers flat against the forehead; press for about six counts each time, take

away, then press again. Press the finger-pads very gently on the eye-lines. The inside flat of the fingers against the temples. The cupped palms of the hands under the jawline . . . you can press harder here, since your palms are against the bone. Two fingers of each hand against each side of the nose, palms against the cheeks.

What Is Your Type?

One of the first things that is noticed about a face, apart from its expression, is whether the skin is the 'English rose' type, or sallow and muddy . . . or dry or greasy. Though, treated properly, the greasy skin can look magnolia-like!

If you keep a beauty diary—in which you have made your notes already about any defects needing to be taken care of—then you should map out a daily routine for your especial skin.

Some women are not sure whether they have dry or greasy skins, and this is not as odd as it sounds. There are dry faces which nevertheless get greasy around the nose and chin, or even the forehead. This is a mixed skin and needs treating accordingly. Also there are 'between' faces which shine sometimes.

Do not push *the skin of your face;* press *the flesh firmly all over. When the hands are in this position, slide the 'heels' of the hands up towards the ears, without moving the finger-tips. This lifts the whole face*

Greasy or Dry Skin?

About an hour after you have removed your make-up, try this test. Press a face-tissue to your skin (or a piece of tissue paper) so that it has a chance to absorb any surplus oil. When you remove it, if it is greasy, then that is your skin-type. If just slightly greasy, your skin is normal and should always look well, provided care is taken of it; if the tissue is quite dry, then your skin is dry, too, and needs extra lubrication and feeding.

Enlarged pores indicate a greasy skin. Fine lines, too early wrinkles, pimples on a papery-surface complexion show that over-dryness is a fault.

Make-up may cover many complexion sins, but to look radiant the skin must be healthy and smooth. The house has to be right before you paint it! Cosmetics may be responsible for a good paint job, but the foundation has to be silk-smooth before the decorating begins.

After all, the skin is not just a protection to the flesh underneath. It is a living tissue. It is the secretions of its sebaceous glands which give it its elasticity, its firmness and texture. Cleansing, of course, gets rid of excess secretion, stale make-up and also as much dust and dirt as you would find on a piece of furniture at the end of a day!

Proper Cleansing

Proper cleansing is essential if it is not to be too drying. Many women do not wash their faces at all. Usually, too much soap and water *do* dry and age the skin. However, this is one thing that people respond to differently. Many women who look young have used soap and water all their lives. Others find their faces take on a 'grey' look, and fine lines appear. Usually if there is an excess of acidity, soap and water do not suit the skin. Many women say, "Oh, but I wouldn't feel clean if I did not wash in soap and water." This is a fallacy, for if they took a cleanser on a piece of cotton-wool *after* they had washed their faces, there would probably still be an amount of 'grubbiness' on it. Find the cleanser that suits you. There are many on the market. Excellent liquid cleansers; complexion milks which repair as they clean; liquefying creams. Most skins respond to the use of both a complexion milk and a cream.

Your Diary

Now for the treatment that will suit your skin.

Dry Skin: Cleanse at night with a liquefying cream, finish off by tapping briskly with a tampon of cotton-wool saturated in skin tonic. To save money, dampen the cotton-wool with water before applying skin tonic. In the morning, cleanse with swift upward strokes with cleansing milk, and follow with skin lotion. About six o'clock (fit in the time to suit yourself) cover face with cold cream or any skin food, and do some chores while you have it on for about half an hour. Pat with finger-tips fairly sharply all over to bring the blood to the surface, take off the cream with tissues, wipe over with skin tonic. Repeat every day. If your skin is very dry, use a liquid skin food to clean your face, in place of the milk, or use milk only three times a week, and cleansing cream the rest of the time.

Greasy Skin: Morning: Wash with hot water and sulphur soap, splash the face with cold water afterwards; pat over briskly with astringent. Use only a little powder-lotion as a powder-base. During the day take off make-up either with a deep liquid cleanser, or diluted eau-de-cologne. Wash again at night, still with hot water, followed by cold; or if your skin is not too greasy, then use a cleansing milk. If you are subject to blackheads, use a complexion brush round and round on the area affected. A pore paste applied at night will help. If your skin begins to feel taut, you are clearing up the greasy condition, and can use a liquid skin food three times a week. Skin balm will take off a surface dryness that even oily skins sometimes have.

Normal Skin: Cleanse with cleansing milk in the morning or during the day, and cleansing cream followed by skin tonic at night. Give yourself a soaking in skin food three times a week.

Mixed Skin: Not too easy to cope with. Apply skin food on the dry patches, use a complexion brush and soap on the greasy parts probably at the sides of the nose, maybe the forehead and chin. Otherwise cleansing milk and cleansing cream alternately. Skin food at night but not on the oily areas.

Ageing Skin: This depressing term can be applied to any skin from the age of 25 to 40. Some girls of 25 have faces that are more lined and sagging than many women of 40. So this category may not only apply to the middle-aged in years, but to those who have neglected their skins.

Cleanse in the morning according to your

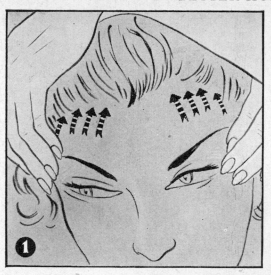

BASIC HOME-MASSAGE MOVEMENTS

1. Take the finger-tips of each hand alternately over forehead lines

3. Using a very light circular movement, follow the indicated lines, up from the chin to the cheek-bones, then to the temple. Do not pull the skin. Slap well with the back of the hand under the chinline

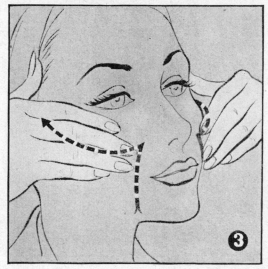

2. Draw your finger-tips right along the jawline, starting from the centre of the chin

4. Use a light tapping movement with the cushions of two fingers around the eyes, lifting the inner corner of the eyebrow

5. Cup your hands around your throat and draw them, one after the other, from the base of the throat to the chin. A light circular massage movement can be used, too

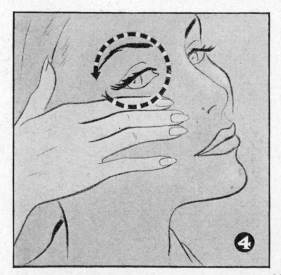

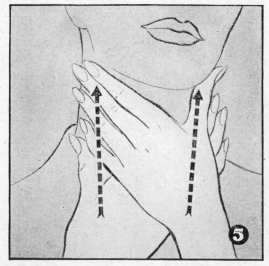

type, dry, normal or oily. Use at night one of the hormone or vitamin creams to replace the glandular substances that tend to disappear as the years roll by. Extensive medical research has produced creams and lotions with an effect far in advance of those even a few years ago. One of these creams or lotions can be used each day patted into the skin before the foundation and powder, as well as at night. If the skin is only a little 'tired,' then a hormone cream two or three times a week is sufficient. Lines under the eyes should always have a little feeding-cream tapped gently into them at night, but if they are quite marked, eye cream or muscle oil is indicated. Or a few drops of this can be worked into a small amount of skin food and patted around the eye area, not forgetting a little on the lids, applied with a very light circular movement, to avoid 'crocodile lids' later.

Stimulation

The older skin is one that needs stimulation more than any. If you have a dry skin, and the older skin does tend more to dryness than the reverse, clean your face, pat in a dry skin food, and leave it on while you do your ironing if possible, or while you cook a dinner.

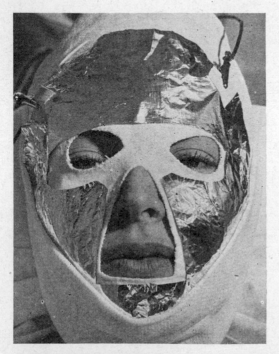

This kind of electrotonic mask, to iron out worry lines and wrinkles, is much liked on the Continent

The warmth will cause it to penetrate the pores. Take it off by pressing tissues to the face until it is all removed, and pat over with very cold milk (iced, if possible). Remove this after five to ten minutes with lukewarm water, followed by skin tonic.

Patting, of course, helps to stimulate the skin and to keep the blood coursing healthily. A patter can be bought at any beauty counter. Pat upwards and outwards. Along just under the jaw, outwards around the neck, from the chin across nose-to-mouth lines to the temple, very lightly with almost a whisking movement over lines at the corners of the eyes, fairly firmly on the forehead, along the lines. There are also stimulating lotions on the market, but the very sensitive skin will do best to avoid these. The skin can be slapped with a piece of cotton-wool soaked in eau-de-cologne, held loosely in the hand. This will make the face sting, so fan it with a magazine (or fan, if you have one!) afterwards—and again, remember, this is not for the very fine skin. Ice is wonderful held in the hand and rubbed all round the contours, under the eyes, under the jawline, over the cheeks, but it is better to lean over a basin as you do this, for the ice quite naturally melts. There are also little irons for the face, called ironettes, that have an excellent effect. Mary, Queen of Scots, and the first Elizabeth used hot wine in which to bathe their faces, to stir up the circulation, and this can still be done with good results. It is not as extravagant as it may sound, since it takes so little wine, and it need be only the very cheapest kind.

Masks

Every skin needs an occasional facial and mask occasionally after twenty-four. Let's say a mild mask once every three weeks up to thirty, once a fortnight to about thirty-four; once a week or ten days over that age. The greasy skin can always do with a mild pack once a week. Packs are simple to make, or there are a number of excellent ones already made for you to be bought.

Grain has been used as a beautifier for longer than one can trace back. The earliest records of ancient Egypt show barley, oatmeal, rice being used as a basis for beauty care. Leave a mask on for ten to twenty minutes. The quicker it dries, the healthier it shows your skin to be. If you have not the ingredients of a facial mask to hand, take

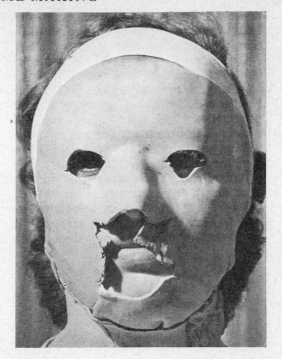

This is the plastic mask made of French mud from the Vichy springs. The lady may look gruesome now, but she hopes to look especially beautiful later

a handful of ordinary breakfast oats, mix to a paste with milk, add a few drops of lemon juice, and rub over the face. Most masks have just to be put on. This one needs rubbing, as it acts as a cleanser for the pores. It is difficult to keep on, so make sure it is the right consistency—like thin cream—and lie back for ten minutes. If the skin is very dry, add a teaspoonful of olive oil. Wash off with lukewarm water, in which you have put a little borax or a squeeze of toilet oatmeal to soften the water. A teaspoonful of benzoin will do this, too.

Fuller's earth is a good base for making yourself a pack. For oily skins mix with 10-vol. peroxide or astringent. Pearl barley mixed to a cream with wych hazel or rose water is also a mild mask for the younger woman.

Powdered starch may be mixed with wych hazel or astringent. It is excellent for the older woman. A double 'dose' should be put under the chin, adding the second coat when the first is dry. Rinse off with lukewarm water, dab the face with iced milk, leave to dry on, and leave for its tightening effect for as long as possible. You may sleep in it, if you wish.

An egg is the most refining of all masks and so, although well known, will be repeated here for those who have not tried it. Whip up the white, put on one layer, let it dry, then a second layer. When dry, add the yolk. This must not be left on too long as it dries very hard. Press a hot flannel to the face until it is loosened, rinse off, splash the face with cold water, dry, pat over a little skin tonic and your skin should rival silk. Even some white of egg, whipped up well, is a quick pick-me-up before an outing.

Try a hot wych-hazel pack. Make a 'mask' for the face of thin cotton wool, leaving holes for eyes and nose, and another covering for the neck. Heat some wych hazel, immerse the cotton-wool in it, press to face and neck, and closely around the nostrils. Leave to cool, then dip again in the wych hazel, which can be kept hot close by on a little spirit-lamp.

FACIAL BLEACHES
Fair of Face

NO list of facial bleaches would be complete without reference to the time-honoured honey treatment used by the leading and leisured beauties through the ages. Leisure, because a honey treatment just must not be hurried. For this reason it is generally avoided in beauty establishments, unless an operator has had much experience in its application.

Time and patience in 'acquiring the knack' should bring quite dramatic results.

Honey is the one thing that does not age; it has been found in ancient Egyptian tombs still in condition. It is supposed to impart some of its ageless qualities to the skin.

Cleansing cream is used for the first cleansing, which ensures complete removal of surface dirt.

About half a teaspoonful of clear honey should be enough for the whole face and neck, because only the lightest tapping touches should be used, and the honey barely touched for application.

These tapping movements continue on every part of the face and neck in an upward direction until the honey becomes discoloured. This decomposition shows that the pores of the skin are open and cleared. From time to time the finger-tips may be washed and dried, but water must not be allowed to touch the skin.

Cleansing cream is then used again and blotted off the skin with pieces of linen or old handkerchiefs to avoid any sense of dragging. Neither cotton-wool nor tissues are suitable, as cotton-wool sticks and tissues tear. The success of this treatment depends on lifting, without dragging, the discoloured honey from the pores.

A final cleansing is made with pieces of linen dipped in a saucer of water to which a few drops of gin or surgical spirit have been added. After this the skin is ready for its usual type of make-up. Very downy skins

Blend your skin food with some lemon juice

should avoid honey treatment, on account of the difficulty in removal.

Orange and Camphor Bleach

Strained orange juice—about 1½ table-spoonsful—added to 1 teaspoonful of finely powdered camphor and then strained again through muslin is a bleaching mask which is based on an old Chinese beauty treatment for a greasy skin. The mixture should be warmed over a saucepan of hot water and used nightly for several nights. It is patted on the skin and cleaned off about one hour after use. Pow-dered camphor needs orange juice to carry it into the pores, and orange juice itself has valuable properties.

The same ingredients, with the addition of half a teaspoonful of brown sugar or two or three drops of glycerine, would be an excellent treatment for a dry skin. Camphor and orange juice form a strong bleach, but need the help of a carrier to penetrate dry skin, especially the kind of dry condition which has been produced by slimming and too-reduced intake of fats.

As the effects of intensive reducing register on the skin of the face first, a corresponding nourishment must be used to feed the skin before lines make their appearance.

Soothing Bleach

When the face has become sunburned and painful an ordinary bleach may reduce the colour but not the pain caused by the inflam-mation. A sudden remedy must be applied. One that has stood the test of time is an easy-to-make bran bleach, which is soothing and healing at the same time. About 1 table-spoonful of bran is tied into a square of muslin about 7 in. square. This is soaked in a large cup of boiling water for several min-utes and squeezed now and then. A cup of hot milky water is produced and to this may be added a pinch of borax (dissolved first in a little boiling water). Thin pads of cotton-wool or scraps of old linen are soaked in the mixture and pressed lightly on the face. As soon as they begin to dry they are damped and replaced until the inflammation is reduced.

As a follow-up lotion the bran water should be warmed and beaten up with a few flakes of white Castile soap. This can be bottled but it will keep for a short time only, and being an inexpensive lotion, a fresh quantity can easily be made.

Herbal Face Lotions

From back in the past comes the use of herbs in treating the skin. A home-made lotion is generally better than a herb extract because the preservative used might be too strong for a delicate skin. To make a herbal pack, 1 oz. of herb is stewed for an hour or two and then strained and bottled carefully.

The two most helpful herbs are wild thyme and camomile, used together or separately; they refresh and heal. Parsley also clears the skin, boiled in the same way.

Herbal Packs

If any of these lotions are added to a table-spoonful of fuller's earth till it is of a creamy consistency, it makes an excellent pack. It can also be mixed with almond meal, making a beneficial pack for a dry skin. When it has remained on the skin for about half an hour and then removed, a few drops of English almond oil tapped gently around the mouth and chin and under the eyes will help to keep the complexion smooth. Almond oil cannot produce or encourage the growth of superfluous hair.

A Bleaching Pack for an Acid Skin

A skin which perspires too freely is usually one which is throwing off bodily acids. In many cases this excessive perspiration is a safety valve for bodily congestion and is often followed by patches of acid deposit, which is generally called 'nerve rash'.

Applications which clog the pores should be avoided and cleansing and cooling washes may be substituted. A pack which is healing as well as bleaching is half an ounce of best Epsom salts to one teaspoonful of powdered flowers of sulphur mixed together in a bowl with about one gill of boiled water and a teaspoonful of rose water added. This should be allowed to stand for an hour. Then the top liquid is poured off to avoid any specks of grit.

Pads of cotton-wool soaked in the liquid are then pressed over the surface of the skin. When the lotion is thoroughly dry it resembles a glazed shiny mask. Patting, not rubbing, with the palms of the hands will crumble off the mixture, until only a dusty surface remains. Very gentle rubbing with the finger-tips in an upward motion will remove what is left of the pack.

A clean, dry surface will be the result, as all the acid deposit will have been drawn away in the pack. Special attention should be given to the skin of the forehead where it joins the hair roots.

Every other day is a good interval for this bleaching pack. Acidity often gives rise to a grey look in the skin. Acid skins do not react well to soap and water and need a liquid cleanser.

An Acid Bleach

When acid conditions have left a discoloration around the mouth and chin, a 'wash' which might be used as a pack will help to restore the skin without burning it. The acid wash is prepared with the following:—

(Continued on page 226)

LEMON AID

ALWAYS have a lemon by you. Apart from using a slice in tea when you have given up milk, while slimming it has a myriad uses.

Nail-tips discoloured? Every time you wash and dry your hands dig the nails into a cut lemon which you'll keep beside the washbasin. You will find that the bleaching action of the lemon juice keeps them dazzlingly white. Or take an orange-stick, the tip covered in cotton-wool, and dip it in a little 10 vol. peroxide, with a few drops of lemon juice, and run it under the nail.

Your neck looks dingy after its winter hibernation under high collars? Give it a nightly massage with a creamy mixture of your favourite skin food and lemon juice. Blend them together in the palm of your hand before applying. Massage your neck with firm strokes.

Your complexion looks muddy? Don't worry, you can pave the way to a clear, blemish-free summer skin by cleansing your system. When you wake up each morning drink a glass of hot water to which the juice of a lemon has been added. You'll notice results in a few days. It will also help the slimming and brighten your eyes.

Freckles are your problem? Wrap a wisp of cotton-wool round an orange-stick, dip it into a cut lemon and dab each freckle in turn. To get results, you must carry out this treatment at least twice daily.

Your fair hair lacks highlights? A lemon rinse will make it gleam. After shampooing and rinsing your hair add the strained juice of a lemon to a pint of water and pour this over the hair several times.

Elbows red? Sit, while reading or studying, with each elbow in a nearly-squeezed-out half of a lemon, like little elbow-cups.

Dab your freckles frequently with lemon juice if you must get rid of them

ACNE

THE first rule with acne-vulgaris, which is the correct term for the commonest form of this skin trouble, is to keep greasy creams away from your face, whether they are the cleansing type or foundation creams.

Then try to find out *why* you get acne, and what you can do to fight it.

It most often affects teen-agers, who find that, as they begin to grow up, their skins get very greasy. This is because glands all over the body are waking up and starting to work. Some of them overwork, particularly the sebaceous glands in what you call the pores of the skin, but which are really tiny invisible hair follicles.

Unfortunately the acne germ thrives on grease, so the stage is set for it to make its first attack.

When the acne germ invades the pores of the skin it stops them getting rid of the excess oil the glands are throwing out, so the pores get blocked by oil which hardens and darkens with the action of the air on it. Then you have blackheads. Later, inflammation sets in and you have ugly spots.

Diet Can Help

The acne germ often attacks where there is dandruff, a condition that should never be tolerated for a moment. If you get acne on the upper part of your back and on your shoulder blades it is more than likely dandruff is to blame. Use a hair tonic to help clear up the condition and wash your hair and brushes at least twice a week.

One of your most powerful weapons in the fight against acne is a diet rich in fresh fruit and green vegetables, especially raw green vegetables. Drink a glass of hot water night and morning. Avoid greasy foods, cakes, puddings, pastries and chocolates. Deal with any tendency to constipation.

The very best external treatment is to keep the skin clean and free from grease by washing it with warm water and sulphur soap, which are the natural enemies of grease, using a complexion brush with a gentle circular movement. After a thorough washing the skin should be rinsed with warm water and then cold.

If the spotty condition is very bad, apply sulphur ointment at night. Sunshine or a few minutes a day with a sunlamp is helpful. If all else fails, the doctor may recommend a vaccine.

RED VEINS

It is not advisable to use strong stimulating lotions on red veins, or ice (unless it is wrapped in a soft, thin cloth, such as a fine butter-muslin).

Red veins are often caused by insufficient protection from the elements. A weather-lotion or foundation cream is excellent to use when out in rough weather, as some people have to be. Or a good suntan cream should be used in the sun's glare, with plenty of skin food or oil applied afterwards. Highly-spiced hot foods, too hot beverages, also produce these threadlike red lines, and sitting too near a fire does not help. The skins that have these veins (enlarged capillaries) are often very fine skins, and harsh soaps or even bad creams and cosmetics can do a good deal of harm. Most masks are not good for them, either, but a bland, mild mask will not cause any worsening in their state.

If these veins are very bad, they can be treated by electrolysis. This is a simple operation in the hands of a skilled operator. The veins are gently pricked to release the blood, then the current is applied to the surrounding area to prevent the swollen capillaries from filling again before they are healed.

Should they not be very noticeable, then your aid is a powder rouge adapted to the general skin-tone where the little veins are. The 'redness' is thus smoothed out and spread over till it appears as a healthy flush under make-up instead of a disfigurement. It is usually necessary to use a rather heavy powder-base to hide them completely, and not too fine a powder. Once the make-up is on, however, a very fine powder can be dusted over the whole to give a more glamorous effect.

Facial Bleaches—*continued*

Juice of half a lemon. *A pinch of powdered*
3 drops (no more!) of *borax.*
liquid ammonia. *1 oz. of boiled water*
  (1 tablespoonful)

The continued application of this 'wash' should produce a bleach, and as soon as the bleach is established—10–15 minutes—almond oil can be smoothed over the treated area.

Mashed potato, in very small quantities, can be used as a carrier for thin acid bleaches, and retains the moisture for a considerable time. Just mix the ingredients into about a tablespoonful of thinly mashed potato.

NECK AND CHINLINE

THERE are so many women who look younger than their ages, so long as you look only at their faces. But their necks! Hard, brown, or wrinkled . . . a signpost to *more* than their real years!

Why necks should be neglected in this way is extraordinary. Either the lazy do not give the neck a thorough cleansing such as they would give the face; or else they scrub it ruthlessly with harsh soap and hard water, and think the red turkey-cock folds are just something that 'happens.'

Some girls have lines round their necks at school, and they probably never will get rid of them. They are caused by a plump little kittenish neck that folds slightly. Even filmstars with all the beauty treatment there is at their disposal will have lines round the neck, too, sometimes. But it is not so much the lines, as the consistency of the skin, and the way the head is held, also the poise of the shoulders, that make a neck remarkable for its youth and beauty, or a sad feature that detracts from a good-looking face.

The First Rule

The first thing for contour of chin and firmness of neck is a daily exercise. This should always be kept up. It need not be done five times night and morning or any other set number of times. It can be done at any time when there is tension, or during the day when unobserved! Stand with feet slightly apart, arms relaxed by sides, chin on chest. Breathe in deeply, raising the head as you do so, then turn head to the right, and drop chin on right

shoulder, letting out the breath as you do so. Breathe in, lifting head, return to position and drop chin on chest again, letting out the breath as you do so. Repeat to left.

Another exercise is to stand about 20 in. from a wall, with the palms of your hands flat against the surface. Now lean forward and touch the wall with your chin, count six and return to position, but leaving your hands on the wall. Do it about ten times when you think of it. Either start with fewer inches or more, whichever you can manage, increasing the distance as you gain balance. This is also a good tummy exercise, drawing you into line.

It is an excellent thing when the head has been held in any one position too long, over either a sink or a typewriter, to rise, change your position, and move your neck about as if you were trying to work it loose from your shoulders. Put your head back, sticking out your chin as far as it will go. Twist your head from one side to another. Press the balls of your thumbs into the hollows at the base of the skull. A cramped neck is a sign of nervous tension, and works in a vicious circle, one contributing to the other.

Remember always to walk with your shoulders pulled down, and your head *up*.

Muscular Support

Massage your neck when you do your face, massaging upwards with the whole hand, first one, then another. The main influence in a firm neck is the behaviour of the sterno-cleido-mastoid muscle, which runs up the neck on either side. When your hands are well greased with feeding cream, take first your right hand up the left side of the neck from shoulder to just behind the ear, and then the left hand up the right side. To 'follow your hand up' sounds an odd direction, but it best describes just how to do the movement gracefully, and not as a 'push.'

Double Chin

The next rule is that most necks need a good feeding cream. The correct procedure is to

An excellent movement for raising a drooping look around the chin. Move first the fingers of one hand, then the other, alternately from the side of the chin to the corner of the mouth. Repeat each side ten times night and morning

use a massage cream, then apply a feeding, throat cream. However, once the neck is cleansed in any manner, with milk, soap and water (if you must), or cream, then you can do the massage with your feeding cream and leave it on for about 20 minutes after, before *blotting* off with cleansing tissues (not scrubbing or dragging over the surface).

Any tendency to a double chin needs to be severely dealt with. Slap under your whole chinline with the back of your hand any time you can, giving quite vicious, sharp little taps going from one side to the other and back. This can be done with a patter, on which you have put a cotton-wool pad soaked in astringent. If you have a double chin, when you give yourself a facial, lie for a while with a piece of cotton-wool damped in astringent under your chin, and kept in place by a fold of butter-muslin tied on top of your head. Chin-straps can be bought, if you wish, to wear at night.

The 'falling-away' chin is more difficult to deal with than a double chin, and the best results are accomplished by concentrating on massage that lifts the contour of the face. One that takes away nose-to-mouth lines, as well as helping the chinline, is to put the fingers of one hand at the side of the chin and slide them upwards, then follow by the fingers of the other, continuing the stroking movement, counting about three for the fingers of each hand . . . almost quick waltz-time!

Pressing and Lifting

Also when you are 'pressing' your face, palms on cheeks, fingers on temples, continue, after pressing, with this exercise . . . slowly slide the 'heels' of your palms upwards and outwards, so that your thumbs end by your temples, and your fingers are bent instead of straight. Slap those nose-to-mouth lines, too. Blow out your cheeks first, and then slap across them as sharply as you can take.

Kneading under a falling-away chinline is good, as well as for a double chin. Kneading can be done all over the face across lines, with the best effect. It is a movement of the closed fist, as if you were playing five-finger exercises with your knuckles. It needs a little practice, but is worth while, as you mould your face— but *do not pull the skin*. Always keep in your mind's eye a picture of what you want your face to look like (within reason!)—it will aid you to press and mould it to the right shape.

BEDTIME BEAUTY

THERE is no need to look lovely in the daytime and a fright when you go to bed. A permanent wave eliminates the need for curlers. If you pin your 'set' in very lightly for three nights after it has been done, it will last much longer. Also take your baths on the cool side, and wear a loose bathing-cap, not a tight one. If your permanent is at the awkward stage, then put in some pins or curlers, and tie a length of tulle over your head, either fastening with a knot at the back, or a bow on top, depending on how coquettish you feel. If you don't like pins or curlers, then wield a curling-iron, but not too hot, and rub in a little brilliantine afterwards.

As for your make-up, NEVER leave it on. A few nights with make-up on can soon make the most peaches-and-cream skin large-pored and leatherish. When your face has been cleaned, if you put a little cream rouge on the cushions of your cheeks, and rub some into your lips (being lighter than lipstick, it is not so likely to come off on the pillow) you will look blooming. Use some mascara on your lashes if you wish, but put on some white Vaseline or castor-oil first, so as not to dry them too much, and also to help them grow. If you are not the type to look well without powder, then put on a very light liquid powder (a herbal one will do your skin good), for it dries leaving a faint powdery surface.

Psychologists say that perfume can influence our dreams, so spray it on fragrantly at night and see what dreamtime will bring you!

Hand-creams all disappear into the hands these days, so night-time is best of all times for rubbing in a nice amount to work while you sleep.

Neck and Chinline—continued

The Right Cream

It is most important to pay attention to the cream you put on your neck. There are feeding creams which the double chin does not want, since just a light massage cream and an astringent are indicated; but the falling-away jawline does need feeding and sculpturing. The 'scraggy' chinline often shows that more rest is needed by its owner, and that perhaps your health needs keeping up to par. Hormone creams and lifting lotions are excellent for the tired-looking neck.

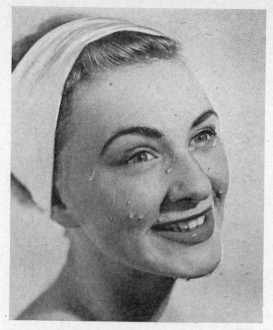

Cold tap-water—or rain-water if it is available —is at least free. It braces the skin, is a tonic for the eyes, tones the muscles

COLD-WATER TRICKS

YOUR greatest ally in your quest for loveliness is H_2O, that is, plain cold water from the tap. Drink two pints of it a day for a clear, radiant skin. Splash your face with it before you make up—it acts as a very mild astringent; sponge or spray yourself with it after a warm bath to make you feel fresh and glowing. Keep a firm and youthful bustline by sponging your breasts with it.

* * *

Your make-up will last longer if you set it with cold water. Do it this way. First of all, put on your foundation and powder as usual. Then take a piece of cotton-wool and wring it out in cold water. Dab the moist pad quickly all over your face. You will find that you will not need to be constantly re-touching your face, and you'll never have that artificial 'made-up' look.

* * *

If you want your face in summer to have the flattery and protection of make-up, yet, at the same time, to look as if your complexion owes everything to nature, give your skin a slight sheen—which is vastly different from

a shine! When you have smoothed tinted foundation on your face, wet one finger-tip under the cold-water tap and swiftly rub the drops of water all over the face. Powder while the skin is still slightly damp. This is especially effective if you are using a suntan foundation and powder, for it makes the tan look as natural as if you had been basking in brilliant sunshine.

* * *

The sparkle in your eyes will be helped if you remember that cold water is your friend. Splash it on to your eyes, trying to keep them wide open as you do it. If you make this a 'must' every morning you will not only be rewarded with bright eyes—you will also find that you start the day fresh and wide awake.

* * *

If you are troubled with hands which turn hot, red and sticky as soon as the fine weather starts, or on some important occasion, turn on the cold tap and, as the water flows out, hold your wrists under it. This will cool your hands at once, and they'll look much prettier.

* * *

Give your hair a treat—when you shampoo it, rinse it with water as cold as you can bear. It's going to do a lot of good by stimulating the flow of blood to the hair roots, and your hair will be healthier, lovelier. It closes up the pores of the scalp, too, so that you can safely dry your hair out of doors on fine days. You will find that this is a beauty treatment in itself.

* * *

Buy yourself a shampoo spray for a few shillings, and spray cold water not only over your head (with a brisk rubbing with a warm towel afterwards) but along your jawline, to brace it and keep at bay any tendency to droop.

* * *

After having a footbath, plunge your feet into cold water in which you have dissolved two tablespoonfuls of common salt. Dry very carefully.

* * *

If you cannot take a cold shower, wring out a small turkish towel on a warm day, and rub yourself all over very briskly with it. The circulation really gets going!

GLOSSY
HAIR

Courtesy of Richard Hudnut Ltd.

THERE is no doubt that the majority of women would agree that the single attribute which adds most to or takes away from attractiveness is the way the hair looks. Women who have bad skins, not-too-good figures, and who, in some cases even possess actual defects, owe a reputation for good looks to a shining, glossy, curly head of hair. After all, your hair is the one feature that *you* really can make beautiful. Nose, eyes and mouth all depend to a great extent on what Nature gave you, but hair is different— whether it is dry or greasy, fine or heavy, you can teach it to behave. If you brush and massage it into a healthy state, you can easily learn to style and set it or have it set, so that it enhances your features and adds glamour to your whole appearance.

Now to deal first with hairdressing at home. *Cutting and shaping* is not a home treatment. A good hairdresser will trim a wave into the ends of your hair, whereas you may get a shaving-brush effect. Choose your style, take it to him and ask him to copy it. Have your hair trimmed when it is due for a sham-

poo, as it is easier to shape then. Be careful, however, that you do not try a new style on the eve of an important occasion. It may not suit you. The first time should be when it will not matter a very great deal how you look.

If you have a salon set, ask the hairdresser to brush it all out and then comb it back into place, so that you can see how it should be done. (Far too many hairdressers send us out into the world with a mysterious hair style which we ruin as soon as we try to comb or brush it.)

Shampoo your hair every week to fourteen days. Dry hair, bleached hair, and permanently waved hair with dry ends should be given cream conditioning shampoos regularly, with a soapless shampoo for special dates. Always work cream shampoo over your hands so that it is applied thinly to the hair, and not in lumps which may resist all rinsing. Lather and rinse the hair *twice* and then, after several rinsings, use a tablespoonful of vinegar in a final rinse water if your hair is dark, lemon juice if it is fair.

Greasy hair needs regular soapless shampoos, with only an occasional conditioning shampoo. It should be washed at least once a week.

Set your hair immediately after your shampoo, while the hair is wet, and do the quick-drying hair at the temples first. As long as the hair is set while it is still really wet, setting lotion is not necessary. It can be used later for a re-set.

A beaten egg-yolk rubbed into the hair and left for five minutes, then rinsed out, is wonderful for the hair. If you wish to lighten the colour add a desertspoonful of peroxide.

If your hair is dry, brush brilliantine well in *before* setting it; all Paris hairdressers do this and it gives a lovely gloss.

Straight hair is easily remedied these days, but make sure that you are not robbing yourself of a certain distinction by having a permanent wave. There are many attractive styles for straight hair, both long and short; and it is far easier to get a glossy sheen on a head of naturally straight hair than it is on artificially curled hair.

If you wish for a permanent wave, you must choose between a salon or a home permanent. In either case, a test curl is essential to make sure you get the right strength of wave for your hair. If you select a home permanent, obey the instructions to the last letter, and if your hair is at all bleached don't attempt the full head until you have given a full-length perm to two test curls. Some heavily bleached hair takes only a few minutes with a home permanent.

Permanently waved hair is sometimes a danger because too many women accept a permanent as the only beauty treatment their hair needs, and therefore neglect their hair badly. Do not omit your brushing, combing, and scalp massage, just because you are lazy about getting your hair into shape again. Use a good hair tonic for a while after your permanent.

Never have a permanent wave when you are feeling off-colour.

Naturally curly hair needs nothing more than good shampooing and a comb wave to get a pretty effect. (You should not need to use a waving lotion, because dampness brings out the wave in your hair and a wet comb will give you all the set you need.) You can finger twist the ends up into curls if you like or accent the waves with setting combs. Don't try to improve natural curls with a perm,

although wavy hair with straight ends can have the ends curled easily.

Comb out carefully with a tail-comb if sculptured curls are wanted, or brush out and then comb into place if you prefer a loose style. If your hair is very soft always shampoo it a day or two before a party and re-set it the next night, using a non-greasy setting lotion.

A test as to whether all the soap is rinsed out of your hair or not—and if it is not, it means dull, lifeless locks—is to take a piece of hair in your fingers and squeeze it hard. If it squeaks, then you can stop rinsing. When doing up curls, take a piece of hair between finger and thumb and roll the curl round the protruding portion of your finger, pinning it into place. Do not roll directly from the end, there must be a little hole left, for too tightly wound hair is likely to split.

Coloured Rinses

Coloured and toning rinses are now available in such quality and quantity that no-one need have a mousy head of hair. If you choose a colour that you do not like, it will wash out quite easily next time. When you have rinsed your hair, put on a toning pack and work it in, then leave for ten minutes; rinse out carefully. For a coloured rinse, be very careful not to apply it too strong, unless you are expert at it. A very pale mauve tinge to grey hair can be extremely becoming—but the moment it is a patchy violet, well . . .! A pink rinse, which you can have at the hairdressers, is extremely becoming to the blonde. If it is only a suggestion, it is suitable for daytime as well as evening, for no-one is quite sure whether there is a tinge of pink or not. The colour will just be 'strawberry blonde'—romantic and pretty! You can also buy a puff spray that powders your hair with becoming glints for a special occasion.

Try massaging *the greasy head* with slightly damp common salt before a shampoo.

The right way to massage your head is not to slide your fingers over the head, but to move the whole scalp. Sit with your elbows on your knees, then you will not get tired, or lie on your back on the bed. When your hands are tired, shake them loosely from the wrist for a moment or two before continuing with the massage.

Very dry hair needs an oil treatment sometimes. Part the hair at one-inch partings all over, putting hot oil down each parting. Massage well in, and sleep with a towel around your head, or over your pillow. Wash or go to the hairdresser the next morning. If this is inconvenient, leave the oil for a good hour. The dry-haired lady should use a cream shampoo and a cream rinse to help cure a fuzzy, dull look. Brush in brilliantine every day, or at least every other day. This keeps the hair in good condition, and retains a gloss.

If your hair is greasy, strangely enough, to brush over a little spirit brilliantine replaces the greasy look with a glossy one.

Brushing is good for both dry and greasy hair. Use two brushes and lean with your head over the edge of the bed, lying first face down, and then on your back. This is invigorating to the scalp, lets the air through your tresses, and the blood flows to the roots. If a silk handkerchief is tied over a brush, this is excellent for the greasy-haired as the bristles get to the hair, and the handkerchief takes away some of the grease. Brushing also makes the hair manageable, as does thinning when it becomes too thick to cope with successfully. With a Taperette, you can cut it yourself. This is how you do it.

(1) *For thick, heavy hair* . . . lift up a layer of hair, starting about one inch from the parting, and secure with a clip. Do not cut this top layer. Now lift up a second layer of about one-inch thickness and, using a taperette, start from the scalp and taper lightly all the way to the ends of the strand. Take up each layer in the same way until sides and back of head have been completely tapered.

(2) *Medium-textured hair.* Repeat same procedure except that, when tapering, start halfway down the strand, and halfway down each subsequent strand.

(3) *For fine hair.* Take up the first layer and clip, then taper each further strand only an inch from the ends.

Now your hair will be easy to set yourself, and pin into curls. When you take your bath or bathe in the sea, slip in a few pins and let your hair be quite dry before taking them out.

Each morning take a hairbrush very slightly dampened with skin freshener over the contour of the cut, following the trend of your curls, then push into shape with your hand, pin a curl or two, slip on a hairnet until you have finished your toilette, when it will look as if you have had a new set, especially if you spray with a hairgloss or brilliantine.

Dandruff is annoying but a very common complaint. Part the hair at one-inch intervals and dab all along with an antiseptic. Massage, then brush out the dandruff. A little borax in the washing water helps. There are good dandruff lotions to be bought, as well. The old-fashioned scurf comb is not to be despised.

Tidy hair is quite ruined if there are stray wisps, and even a 'carefully careless' hairdo does not need a sudden straight 'rat-tail' hanging down. For the careful set, smooth up stray wisps with vaseline on the tip of your finger, tucking gently into the other hair, or use colourless lacquer. Solid brilliantine may do the trick. You can spray your whole set with lacquer to keep it tidy all day. A stray curl should be soaked in eau-de-cologne and either pinned up or put into a curler. It will dry very quickly. Water, of course, will not, so do not use it unless you have plenty of time.

Diet has an enormous amount to do with hair-health. Dry hair and dry skin both need fats in the diet, although this is awkward when dieting. However, make sure that some butter is eaten, do not cut it out altogether when trying for a new slim line. Vegetables, especially raw onions, chopped cabbage, watercress, fresh fruits, cheese, some milk. A course of halibut-liver-oil capsules is useful.

Lie with your head over the edge of the bed and brush your hair with one or two brushes. This aids scalp circulation

The Shape of your Face

While one follows the swing of the pendulum of fashion, from short hair to long, there are certain basic rules of suiting the face that must be followed if we are to make the most of ourselves. Each fashion can be slightly adapted to blend with our own type of features and individuality.

For instance, if you will admit to a receding chin, then your hair must not recede, too, but must be brought forward from the ear downwards to balance the profile. If your chin is pointed, then you do not want a small bun on top of your head that gives another angle, but to have your hair dressed in a soft under-curl, or wave, to soften any angular effect. When fringes are 'in,' it is commonly asserted that women with low or medium foreheads should not wear them, but here a question of personality comes in, for the woman with the *gamine* or piquant type of face that a fringe suits does not often have a high forehead! And the woman with a high forehead is usually the kind of person that a rather frivolous fringe would not become. So the question of hairdressing must be looked at, not only according to what we like, or our features, but our whole personality.

Square, Oval or Long?

Square faces do not need a roll right across the top of the head, or the broadness will be emphasised. The hair should be fairly high on top, and, when hair is long, rather low at the neck. If you have a pear-shaped face, round at the bottom, and tapering to a rather narrow forehead, a little bunch of curls on top will exaggerate this. A centre parting, softly waved out to curls at the side, will form a balance. Then a round face with curls in a halo effect looks even rounder. The hair worn fairly long, and with a 'crest' on top, makes the face more oval.

A perfect oval face, beloved of poets, should not have the lovely line cluttered up with hair coming from every direction. It should be drawn slightly or firmly back, whether curls are worn or whether the hair is straight, so that the hairline and outline of the face are visible.

The long face is not easy to dress, for with the wrong coiffure it can so easily look hard. The hair long in the neck, and flat on the top of the head, will give *more* length. Curls may not suit the long face, but if they do, then a

Richard Hudnut Ltd.

Busy women find the Taperette a boon when they are washing and setting their own hair, as they can shape and taper it at the same time

curly line at the temples will shorten it. If curls are not right, then a wavy, rather loose line—if liked, dropping over one side of the forehead—will be much prettier.

Touch of Time's Hand

If your hair is fading—and hairdressers remark that many girls start to have a few white hairs as early as thirty, these days—then do not rush to have it tinted. Many women, especially career women who find it necessary to look young as long as possible, do reach a stage where careful added colouring is a great help. But when it is just a question of a 'snowy touch' at the temples, then a tinted brilliantine can be brushed in, and washed out at shampoo-time.

SANDPAPERING

This fairly new development in the art of beauty proves the French proverb right, 'One has to suffer to be beautiful.' Sandpapering is so far used very rarely indeed in Britain, but was instituted and has gained popularity in the States. It is employed for getting rid of pitting left by smallpox or any other disease; the sandpapering gets below the scarred tissue. The operation necessitates a general anaesthetic, the whole face is bandaged and within three weeks, usually, the new complexion is ready to be shown to the world.

233

PLASTIC SURGERY

IT is not only society beauties, stage and film stars, and the very well-to-do who have facial surgery these days. Although fees are still high, many ordinary, everyday people who have saved a little money consider that a bad defect removed, or 'old age' pushed one stage further into the future, is worth a little sacrifice—say, instead of a fur coat or a piece of jewellery.

It is true that those with very bad facial defects are psychologically affected by them, and gain health, happiness and self-confidence when they are altered. The ravages of illness can also be smoothed away by a tuck here and a little pleat there. Gone are the days when 'face-lifting' was a music-hall joke.

While there are a good many practitioners whose fees come well within an average income possibility, economy for the sake of saving should never be made the main reason for choosing any particular surgeon. There are very satisfactory results in the hands of a highly skilled surgeon, but it is true that there are occasionally mishaps with the less experienced. Apart from those men who have gained high repute in this field, the best recommendation is to know someone who has actually been a patient of a practitioner.

The operations usually leave no visible scars, or scarcely visible, and the results are helped by manipulation and massage afterwards.

A New Nose

Nature, heritage and accident can produce a nasal structure of unpleasant or odd shape. The worry over an ugly nose may be the greatest limitation to a young person seeking work, where public opinion is concerned. Yet a beautifully shaped nose to replace the existing nasal organ can be made before the patient comes out of the anaesthetic. The bone of the nose is uncovered and carved or moulded into a better shape. The flesh is then replaced and sealed with no trace of the actual operation.

Removal of Deformities

With a similar type of operation, badly repaired scars from previous operations (or ugly growths) can be cut away and new skin grafted over the place, concealing the previous blemish.

Eyelid Lifting

Serious illness, as well as advancing years, can produce over-hanging eyelids and puffy underlids. The superfluous flesh is cut away and an invisible seam is made to restore the youthful shape. The same technique is employed with wrinkles.

Face Lifting

Face 'lifting' is a term covering either the removal of superfluous flesh at the sides of the face, lifting a sagging outline, or the complete removal of a large double chin. In each case a cut is made just before or just under the ear, when the unnecessary portion of flesh is removed and the seam closed with invisible stitches. To match both sides of the face is an operation which should be entrusted to none other than the most highly skilled expert. Cuts are sometimes made in the skin of the forehead, close to the hair, but never on the hair roots.

Outstanding Ears

Ears which stand forward in childhood can be lowered quite simply by a slight operation behind the ear, where it joins the flesh of the skull.

Reconstructing Legs

Legs are made straight and shapely by the removal of strips of flesh. Invisible or practically unnoticeable seams join the skin where the flesh has been removed. Great skill is needed for this type of work also, as after-effects may present a risk.

Bust Treatment

The bust can also be operated upon either to reduce the size and/or reform the contour. It is not now a particularly serious operation.

Birthmarks

Once upon a time nothing could be done about really bad birthmarks or 'port-wine stains,' as they were called, on the face. Nowadays, these can be dealt with by plastic surgery. A small birthmark, however, can be removed, in the same way as moles and warts, by electrical treatment.

Wrinkled Neck

Necks that have been neglected eventually often sag into wrinkled folds, which can be dealt with by being lifted from behind the ear.

Lovely Legs

If your legs are not your best point, here are a few simple rules to make them shapely and smooth

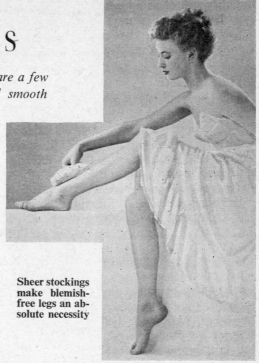

Sheer stockings make blemish-free legs an absolute necessity

IN these days of very sheer nylons, lovely blemish-free legs are important; even more so in the summer when stockings are often left off altogether.

Make an all-out attack on blotches and goose-pimples by scrubbing the legs as hard as you can with a soap-smothered loofah or soft nail-brush. Rinse thoroughly in cold water, and briskly rub them dry with a rough towel. Not only will you gradually banish the patchy look, but also the dead skin which flakes from over-dry legs will be loosened and removed.

You can counteract any tendency to dryness by massaging with a generous smearing of body lotion.

Hair on the legs is fairly easy to deal with. You can choose between using a wax or a cream depilatory.

There are two schools of thought about shaving. One school says it coarsens the growth and makes it worse. Others believe that it is quick, and discourages the growth as much as anything else does. You will soon know if you experiment once or twice. If you shave the legs with soap and water, they can then be 'touched up dry' every week or so, until they need to be done properly again. Whatever means you use to rid the legs of hair, dab them all over (but not immediately afterwards) with 10-vol. peroxide that has a few drops of toilet ammonia added. This both bleaches, and helps to discourage, further growth.

Using a Wax

If you decide on the wax method, first of all wash your legs to make sure there is no trace of lotion on them, dry them very thoroughly, and dust with powder.

An efficient hot wax outfit is sold with the wax in a little pan ready to be heated over a small flame. When the wax has melted it is spread over the legs—a small area at a time—in three layers. When it has set, the wax is lifted at once end and ripped off as quickly as possible, and the hair comes away with it.

Another type of wax comes in a jar, and the thinner it is spread the better the results, so soften it by standing the container in hot water for a few minutes.

When this creamy wax has been spread on the leg, a piece of cloth is pressed firmly on to it. As you snap off the cloth, the wax and the hair will come away with it too.

Both of these methods pull the hair out completely so the treatment should only need repeating about every six weeks.

Cream Depilatories

A cream depilatory comes in a tube and is spread over the legs, allowed to remain for a few minutes—the time varies slightly according to the strength of the growth—and then scraped away with a spatula, which is sold with the cream. This method dissolves the hair and is quicker than waxing, but the effects are not so long-lasting, and will have to be done about once a fortnight.

As the hair begins to grow again it's a good idea to rub the legs every other day with a soapy pumice stone or an abrasive mitt, to prevent the new growth from becoming stubbly.

Nothing you do will banish scorch marks immediately, as they are actually minor burns.

But they will clear up gradually if you give your legs a daily massage with a good all-purpose cream. In the meantime, disguise the marks with leg make-up.

A Little Massage

Any leg profits from a little massage, but more especially that which is too-thin or too-fat. Clasp both hands around your ankle and move them up firmly to the knee. If the thighs are not firm and lean, then sit on the floor and massage them, too, drawing each hand up (well covered in cold cream or body lotion) slightly cupped, one after the other in swift, firm movements. Walk about the house on tiptoe, as this will strengthen arches, pull the whole body into line and improve the shape of the legs. For puffy ankles (if *too* puffy, ask the doctor if there is any physical weakness causing this), massage, digging well into the puffy fat in a rotary movement with your finger-tips. Lie on the bed when you have time, or on your resting-board, head to the floor and legs raised, with cold-water bandages bound fairly firmly around your ankles. A third vinegar may be used with the water.

A good leg, and especially thigh, exercise is to stand, arms outstretched at sides, feet turned out. Jump, and as you jump, turn the feet in as much as possible, and put the arms over your head. Jump again, bringing arms to original position, and turning feet out again. Repeat ten times night and morning. Begin without moving arms, if it is easier.

HAPPY FEET

IF you take care of your feet, you may avoid many other ailments as well, for uncomfortable feet can cause a great deal of trouble. Change into comfortable slippers in the house, and you will not have so many 'strain-lines' on your face to guard against.

Most people complain that their feet feel bigger in warm weather. They get hot and sticky, and shoes that seemed quite roomy

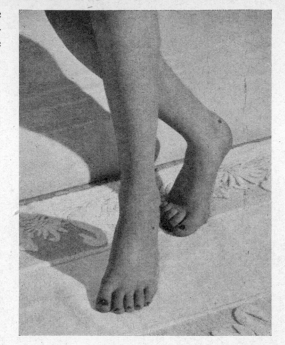

during the winter soon begin to pinch when their owners walk or stand about in the hot sun.

Walking in town, on hot, non-yielding pavements, or waiting for a procession to pass, tries the feet more than walking in the country does, along a shady, unpaved lane, or standing on springy turf.

Hot weather makes the tiny blood-vessels under the skin dilate and feet swell slightly, so they take up extra room in the shoes.

A tight shoe soon makes the small amount of swelling greater. This in turn means that the natural circulation is interfered with, blood cannot get away freely and then the feet will become worse.

Size is Important

In warmer weather, choose footwear which allows extra room for the feet. The actual weight of the shoe does not matter nearly so much as having the right size.

As those who climb or hike long distances

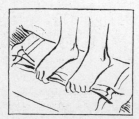

Right : Pick up a light cushion gripped by your toes to strengthen arches. Left : Pleat your bath-towel with your toes. Middle : After your bath, massage in cold cream or hand-lotion

know, heavy boots or shoes are more comfortable than flimsy, thin-soled footwear through which every stone can be felt. Socks are important, too, but see that they fit comfortably. Going without socks is nearly always fatal—particularly from the blister point of view.

If blisters do develop, prick with a sterilised needle to let out the fluid. Snip away the dead skin and clean the area thoroughly with methylated spirit. Then dry it and cover with a piece of adhesive tape.

If you intend to do much walking on your holiday, it is wise to prepare the skin for some weeks beforehand.

Soak the feet well and remove any rough, hard skin with the aid of pumice-stone. Dry thoroughly, particularly between the toes, then dab with methylated spirit. Finish off with a dusting of french chalk or talcum powder.

Do this each night before going to bed. The methylated spirit will help to harden the skin, so that it rubs and blisters much less easily.

If you buy new shoes or boots for the holiday, get them in plenty of time and wear them a little each day, so they will become moulded to the shape of the foot by the time you need them. But they should be reasonably comfortable when you buy them or it will be a question of whether you break in your shoes or your feet first. Too big shoes are also bad.

Nearly everyone has some slight individual variation—an extra-long or short toe, or a mild form of hammer toe, or a big toe that tends to turn in slightly.

Such toes have to stretch the leather and they must be given time to do so, before the new shoe will feel and be really comfortable.

Even if you are not planning to walk much, it is worth a little extra care to get your feet in good trim for your everyday life. Aching feet can ruin a good temper!

Always shake talcum powder into your socks or stockings in hot weather, and rub camphor ice or Frozoclone over your feet.

Foot Bath

Put your feet first into hot water with foot salts, then plunge into cold water into which you have put 2 tablespoonsful of common salt, changing several times. Dry and massage with cold cream and you will feel fairy footed!

ATTRACTIVE ARMS

BEAUTIFUL arms are always important, for in summer frocks, evening dress or bathing costume they are very much on view, yet usually they are singularly neglected.

The elbow is very much the Cinderella of the arm. It takes the weight off your shoulders, holds up your head when you are sitting at table, and it does all the bending!

The trouble is that elbows too often look as hard-worked as they are. If you let your elbow skin get horny, hard and discoloured, your arms are doomed to look ugly from the start.

Give your elbows a good hard scrubbing with a nail-brush daily. Dry them carefully and massage in a little hand cream, by cupping the elbow in the hand and working in a circular movement.

First moisten the arms liberally with cream right up to the shoulder, then, with more cream in the palm of the hand, massage firmly from wrist to elbow with long strokes; then from elbow to shoulder.

Upper arms can get very rough if circulation is bad and they are neglected. The best treatment, and the simplest, is to give them a daily friction with a loofah well damped with eau-de-cologne or toilet water.

Fat arms, which are inclined to be flabby, need exercise, and cold-water slappings daily. You can also use a slimming cream if you are trying to thin them quickly.

Here is an exercise which will do wonders if you repeat it daily: Stand erect, arms out at sides, palms down. Twist arms so that palms turn upwards, then raise arms, so that you can clap hands over your head. Still keeping arms up, turn palms out and clap backs of hands together over head. Lower arms to shoulder level. Twist arms again so that palms are facing upwards, then downwards. Repeat exercise twenty to thirty times.

Rest Helps

Thin arms need relaxation. Try to avoid straining them with heavy parcels, as this only accentuates muscles and makes arms look stringy. Do arm-dancing movements to music, since this will help to give graceful movement, and use lanoline or skin food at night.

Underarms are an essential part of arm beauty. Hair should be removed regularly, and do use an anti-perspirant. Put perfume inside your elbow as a finishing touch.

SLIMMING

Overweight can be due to a variety of causes, and there are many methods of dealing with it. Here slimming is dealt with comprehensively

THERE is no doubt about it, apart from the fact that clothes look much smarter on slim people than on fat, there are definite disadvantages to being very overweight.

Perhaps the most important is that, on an average, people who are slim live longer than those who are fat! There are certainly many complaints (diabetes is one of them) to which fat people are more prone than thin people.

Also, heart affections and high blood pressure are twice as common amongst fat people than thin, which is not difficult to understand. You see, all the *extra* tissue, whether it be a few pounds or a few stone, has to be nourished just like the rest of the body.

Consequently, the heart has more work to do. It has to pump harder to send the blood through the increased number of blood-vessels, and it is not surprising that 40 per cent. of all people who are overweight have high blood pressure.

Short of Breath

Fat people get out of breath quickly, and tire easily too. Neither is this difficult to appreciate. Supposing you were handed a 14-lb. sack of potatoes and told you must carry it around with you, all day, every day, wherever you went and whatever you did? And yet many people carry a far heavier load than this about with them by being overweight.

The fact that the weight is probably evenly distributed over the body doesn't make it any lighter! You don't notice it because it has crept up on you ounce by ounce.

First of all, are you absolutely sure that you are overweight? There is more to it than you think.

Your age and height must be considered, and *type* as well. You may be just as tall as your friend, and the same age too, but if you are large boned and she is small, something would be wrong somewhere if you both weighed exactly the same. The chart here gives the average weight of men and women at different ages, which is some guide, but you can add several pounds to the figure shown if you are the big-built 'athletic' type, and deduct several pounds if you are small-boned and 'petite.'

What Makes You Overweight?

You have found your ideal weight, and perhaps, it is not so very far out, yet still you are not satisfied. It is quite possible that you are not quite as fat as you think. The next time you have a bath, stand sideways in front of a long mirror.

What do you see? A tummy that is too big. A seat that sticks out too far. A sagging bust-line. Not very pretty, is it? But now stand up straight, and make yourself just as tall as possible.

Lift up your ribs, and pull in your tummy muscles hard. Tuck in your tail, just as if you were trying to squeeze through a very narrow space. Now take another look in the glass. Aren't you amazed at the result? Perhaps you can see that, after all, you are not as fat as you imagined. But maybe you still have quite a way to go. The first thing you want to know is What Makes Us Fat? Well, there is one answer, and one answer only. The body is not using up all the food that it takes in.

Metabolism

The whole process of taking in food—turning it into energy—growth—activity—repair, is known as metabolism.

(Continued on page 240)

TABLE OF AVERAGE WEIGHT

Age	20	25	30	35	40	45	50
5 ft.	7.12	8.1	8.4	8.7	8.11	9.1	9.4
5.1	8.1	8.4	8.7	8.10	9 st.	9.4	9.7
5.2	8.5	8.8	8.11	9 st.	9.4	9.8	9.11
5.3	8.9	8.12	9.1	9.4	9.8	9.12	10.1
5.4	8.12	9.2	9.5	9.8	9.11	10.1	10.4
5.5	9.2	9.5	9.8	9.12	10.1	10.5	10.8
5.6	9.6	9.9	9.12	10.2	10.5	10.9	10.12
5.7	9.10	9.13	10.2	10.6	10.9	10.13	11.2
5.8	10 st.	10.3	10.6	10.10	10.13	11.3	11.6
5.9	10.4	10.7	10.10	11 st.	11.3	11.7	11.10
5.10	10.8	10.11	11 st.	11.4	11.7	11.11	12 st.

CALORIE VALUES OF YOUR FOOD

Occupation	Calories
Work requiring extra strength (washer-women, machinists, waitresses, etc.)	2,500–3,000
Work which would be classified as light manual work, i.e. housework, or work involving walking and standing	2,200–2,500
Sedentary work (office work, etc.)	2,000–2,200
Leisured life	1,600–1,800

Food	Amount	Approx. Calories	Food	Amount	Approx. Calories
Almonds (shelled)	12	89	Lamb (chop)	3 oz.	320
Apple	1 small	65	Lard	1 oz.	250
Apricots (tinned)	4 halves plus juice	85	Lemon	1 large	43
Asparagus	8 stalks	40	Lentils	1 oz. (2½ tablespoonful)	105
Asparagus (tinned)	7 stalks	18	Lettuce	1 small head	12
Bacon	1 small rasher	30	Liver	1 oz.	40
Banana	1 medium	120	Margarine	1 oz.	226
Beans (baked)	2 tablespoonsful	129	Milk (whole)	1 pint	380
Beans (butter)	½ cup	131	Milk (skim)	1 pint	200
Beans (fresh, string)	½ cup (3 oz.)	12	Milk (condensed, sweet)	1½ tablespoonsful)	100
Beef (lean slice)	1 oz.	85	Mutton (roast, leg)	3 oz.	249
Beef (corned)	1 oz.	69	Olive oil	½ oz. (1 tablespoonful)	132
Beer	½ pint	200	Onions	1 medium	17
Beetroot	1 medium	21	Orange	1 medium	50
Biscuits (plain water)	1	37	Orange juice	½ cup	56
Bread (white)	1 thin slice	90	Peach (fresh)	1 medium	45
Bread (wholemeal)	1 thin slice	85	Peach (tinned)	2 halves plus juice	91
Brussels spr'ts (cooked)	9 medium	30	Pear (fresh)	1 small	70
Butter	1 oz.	226	Pear (tinned)	2 halves plus juice	86
Cabbage (cooked)	5 tablespoonsful	21	Pineapple (fresh)	1 slice	53
Carrots	1 large	24	Pineapple (tinned)	1 slice plus juice	90
Cauliflower	½ cup	25	Pork (loinchop, lean)	3 oz.	222
Celery	4 stalks	15	Port	2-oz. glass	67
Cheese (cream)	1 oz.	232	Potatoes	1 small	69
Cheese (Cheshire)	1 oz.	110	Prunes	5	141
Cheese (Cheddar)	10 oz.	120	Peas (fresh)	3 oz.	54
Cheese (Dutch)	1 oz.	77	Peas (dried, cooked)	2½ oz.	76
Cheese (Gorgonzola)	1 oz.	104	Peas (tinned)	3 oz.	72
Chicken (Roast)	3½ oz.	184	Quaker Oats	½ cup	60
Chicken (breast)	1 slice	60	Radishes	7–10	12
Chocolate	1 oz.	154	Rhubarb	3 oz. (approx. 1 cup)	3
Cider	½ pint	125	Rice (boiled)	½ cup	105
Cocoa (unsweetened)	1 oz.	128	Salmon (fresh, boiled)	3 oz.	171
Coconut (desiccated)	1 tablespoonful	40	Salmon (tinned)	3 oz.	117
Codsteak (steamed)	¼ lb.	90	Sardine	1 oz. (4 small)	84
Coffee (black)		nil	Soup (clear)	8 oz.	16
Cornflakes	1 oz. (approx. 1¼ cup)	104	Soup (tinned tomato)	8 oz.	83
Cream (thick)	1 oz.	115	Soup (vegetable)	8 oz.	42
Cream (thin)	1 oz.	61	Spinach	3 oz. (4 tablespoonsful)	21
Dates	3–4	93	Spinach (tinned)	3 oz. (4 tablespoonsful)	19
Egg	1	50–70	Stout	½ pint glass	142
Egg (fried)	1	120	Sugar	1 small teaspoonful	20
Endive	2 heads	9	Tea		nil
Figs (raw, dried)	2	90	Tomato	1 medium	14
Goose	3 oz.	276	Tomato (tinned)	3 oz. (½ cup)	20
Grapefruit (fresh)	½ medium	27	Tomato (juice)	3 oz. (½ cup)	18
Grapefruit (tinned)	8 sections	66	Turkey	3 oz.	168
Grapes	12	39	Turnip	3 oz.	9
Haddock (steamed)	3 oz.	78	Veal (cutlets)	3 oz.	182
Halibut (steamed)	3 oz.	85	Walnuts (shelled)	12	219
Herring	3 oz.	140	Water		nil
Honey	2 tablespoonsful	82	Watercress	3 oz. (1 small bunch)	12
Jam (strawberry)	2 tablespoonsful	74	Whisky	3-oz. glass	205
Jelly	1 oz. (1½ tablespoonsful)	90			
Kidney (beef)	1 oz.	35			
Lamb (roast, leg)	3 oz.	173			

Important: Be sure to include a certain amount of milk, green-leafed vegetables, root vegetables, and raw fruit, *each day.*

Every item of food you eat supplies a certain amount of energy—and can actually be measured, in units of heat, or calories. A calory isn't part of your food, like vitamins for instance, but the amount of energy *produced* by any particular food. Different foods have different calorific value. But every movement you make uses up a certain number of calories.

Ordinarily, the food you eat is used up by the body in twenty-four hours, the nourishment absorbed, and the waste matter disposed of by the bowels and kidneys. But here we come to a question of arithmetic. At the end of each day we have taken in a certain amount of fuel, and, according to our activities, we have used up a certain amount of energy. Now, if by any chance we have taken in more fuel than we have needed for the amount of energy used, then it goes into reserve, and the reserve is . . . FAT!

Of course, there is no hard and fast rule. Some of us use more energy than others just in standing still. Our bodies don't all work in the same way. Lean Mrs. X. *always* uses up every bit of fuel she takes in and none goes into reserve. Mrs. Y. who is plump doesn't, on the other hand, need so much. Her human machine can tick along on far less fuel, and so, every time she eats, something goes into storage.

Everyone has their own pet excuse as to why they are fat. Some say it is hereditary, and often a woman will accept her own plumpness as inevitable simply because she has a mother and a grandmother who are fat. What she really means is that the *tendency* to fatness is inherited, which may only be another way of saying that a large appetite, or a liking for fat-making foods, is inherited. Or perhaps good cooks run in the family, so that eating good food is second nature.

Glands

Another common excuse for obesity is 'Something wrong with my glands.'

It is very easy to blame the glands for everything, but they are not anything like as guilty as many people think. If a woman has some glandular trouble, she would have other symptoms which would worry her far more than being overweight. But here again, symptoms that appear to be due to glandular trouble are very often actually *caused* by the patient being overweight, rather than the other way round.

This has often been proved to be the case in menstrual or sex difficulties, lightly dismissed as 'glandular.' Some so-called cases of 'sterility' have been cured simply by putting one or both partners on a reducing diet.

The most popular excuse for obesity is 'thyroid trouble.' But if the trouble is sufficient to cause obesity it will cause other symptoms.

When the thyroid is inactive, the patient becomes sluggish, mentally dull, disinclined for exercise, and tends to be anaemic. Sometimes she puts on weight, but the fat is usually evenly distributed over the body, and the hands and legs are puffy. Also the fat does not keep them warm. People with this trouble are always cold—even in warm weather. Fortunately any real thyroid deficiency can be overcome by giving the extract by mouth.

The ovary is another gland that we think of in relation to obesity. Very often, if a woman has to have her ovaries removed, she puts on weight, mostly on her hips and thighs. Nowadays even this type of obesity can be dealt with. Certain hormones have been manufactured synthetically that act in the same way as the ovarian secretions. Supplied artificially, they have proved very useful in a number of cases.

There are some people whose obesity seems to be pituitary in origin. Their bodies are large, particularly over the abdomen, but usually their ankles and wrists are slim. Often the women who come into this category begin menstruation as early as nine years of age, and the periods are often profuse, prolonged, with a tendency to be irregular. The sex organs, however, are perfectly normal, and fertility is quite unaffected.

Fluid

There is one type of obesity that is entirely due to an increased amount of fluid in the body. Every cell of the body, as we know, needs fluid. This is absorbed as it is circulated by the blood stream. The surplus is passed out of the body, or given off as perspiration. But some people retain far more than they really need, with the result that what appears to be superfluous fat is really tissue that has become 'water-logged.' You find a perfect example of this in 95 per cent. of women who are pregnant.

An expectant mother may have gained as much as two stone by the time the baby is due.

240

The baby may account for 7 or 8 lb., the uterus itself for another $2\frac{1}{2}$ lb., and perhaps $2\frac{1}{2}$ lb. for the liquor. But even with an extra-large baby the sum total is rarely more than 14–18 lb. The extra weight comes from fluid that the mother has retained in her tissues. After the baby is born a large proportion of this fatty tissue disappears.

The people (other than pregnant women) who are fat because of this tendency to retain fluid are ordered special treatment. Usually their fluids are restricted and a substance is prescribed that enables the body to rid itself of unwanted fluid. Extract of thyroid is sometimes given in this case even if there is no thyroid deficiency; the amount given is not sufficient to affect the gland itself. *It cannot be stressed enough that thyroid should never be taken except under strict medical supervision.*

Adolescence

Overweight is very common during puberty and adolescence, and can cause more mental anguish than many adults realise. The fat teen-ager is usually unhappy about her condition, and she should never be teased, or her problem dismissed as unimportant. However, some parents go to the other extreme.

They are convinced it is 'glands,' and do all they can to persuade the doctor to prescribe 'glandular treatment.' It is, of course, due to the glands, in all probability, but treatment is rarely necessary. The glands and, in fact, all the organs are maturing at a terrific rate, and must be allowed to adjust themselves in their own time. If left alone, the bulges will eventually smooth themselves down into feminine curves.

But just the same, a great deal of puppy-fat *is* entirely due to faulty diet. Children need plenty of good, nourishing food at this time of their lives, and parents are apt to load them with starchy foods in order to fill them up.

If only young girls would realise that it isn't starvation they need, but the correct type of food. This does not mean going hungry; you can cut down on fattening foods, and lose weight, but still satisfy your appetite!

Worry

EMOTIONS certainly play a large part in obesity, although a great deal depends upon the individual concerned. You often hear of the woman who pines away with worry or unhappiness and goes as thin as a reed, but very often the reverse happens. It depends on her type.

It is true, worry and lack of sleep will take off the pounds quicker than anything, but so often eating is the only pleasure left in life, when everything else has gone wrong!

The same principle applies to people who are fat in spite of the fact that they swear they 'never eat a thing.' If this was true, they *couldn't* be fat. The answer is often snacks, which is quite the quickest way of putting on surplus weight.

Menopause

Many women complain of an increase in weight during and after the menopause, married women more usually than single. The cause of this is often the slowing down of some of the glands, but very often it is due to lack of exercise because of a general temporary off-colour feeling. Women who have put on weight to any extent at this time of life are advised to take matters in hand early.

The retention of fluid is common during the menopause, and restriction of fluids, omission of salt with food and strict attention to the diet will usually solve the problem.

Not too much Acid

Constipation is commonly associated with obesity, and is often aggravated by drastic diets. If the diet contains too many acid-forming foods it makes it more difficult for waste matter to be eliminated. It is the same if the food does not contain enough bulk.

The digestive muscles cannot grip, consequently the food cannot be moved on. It is important to avoid constipation when one is overweight, in order to make sure that the debris from the protein and carbohydrate foods (the fat-forming foods) is completely eliminated.

What is the best way to set about it? There seem to be so many different methods, and so many people who insist that their pet way is the *only* way.

We have seen that obesity is caused by too big an intake of food in relation to the output of energy, therefore, the most important method of all is diet.

Before we can summon up courage and begin to diet, we must understand something about the composition and value of different foods. Everything you eat comes into one of three groups, protein, fat and carbohydrate.

A balanced diet must contain these foods in correct proportions. In addition, there must be an adequate supply of mineral salts, vitamins and water.

Proteins are the body-building foods which are needed by every tissue of the body for growth and repair. They also supply energy. They are found in milk, eggs, cheese, lean meat, liver, heart, kidney, rabbit, chicken, pork, bacon, sweetbreads, game, fish (including sprats, sardines, herrings, roe, shellfish, eels, salmon), beans, lentils, carrots, nuts.

Fats are just as important as proteins. They supply more heat and energy than any other food. They are also used for building nervous tissue and cells. They are found in butter, suet, dripping, lard, cream, cheese, milk, egg yolks, all meat and bacon fat, herrings, mackerels, salmon, fish-roe, fish-liver oils and olive oil. But fats cannot be used properly without carbohydrates.

Carbohydrates are the starch and sugar foods and, combined with fats, are the energy-producing foods. They are found in bread, flour, spaghetti, macaroni, etc., sugar, oatmeal, potatoes, carrots, turnips, onions, etc., peas, beans, raisins, currants, sultanas, prunes, figs, dates, bananas, nuts, rice, tapioca, semolina, sago, honey, and cereals. Most foods do not consist *only* of protein, carbohydrate or fat. More often they are a mixture of each. A good example of this is milk. It is classified as a protein because this makes up the bulk of it, but it contains, in addition, carbohydrate and fat. You will often hear milk described as the perfect food, because it contains the different food groups in their correct proportions. It is, however, deficient in iron and certain vitamins and is not quite perfect.

Calcium and **Phosphorus** go together. *Calcium* is needed to build and maintain strong bones and teeth. It is essential to proper heart and muscular action and to ensure correct blood-clotting. It is found in milk, eggs, green vegetables, nuts, and especially cheese. *Phosphorus* is present in every tissue of the body, is essential for bone structure. It is found in most protein foods.

Iron is found in the red colouring matter of the blood and is essential for carrying oxygen. An insufficient supply results in anaemia. It is found in egg-yolk, watercress, oats, liver, dark green leaf vegetables, kidney, lean beef, whole wheat and oats, apricots, peaches and beans.

Sodium Chloride (common salt). It is essential that the correct amount of salt should be maintained, as too little results in muscular cramps. If your food is seasoned to taste it should be enough.

Potassium is needed for the muscles. It is present in nearly all foods, and a deficiency is never likely to occur.

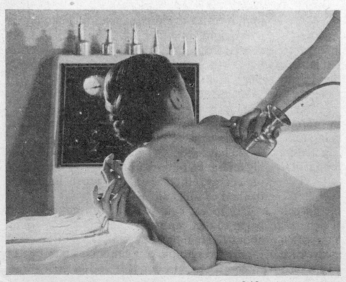

This is the 'Traxater' apparatus, invented in Denmark. It produces a vacuum force which is applied by metal cups of varying size. It is an effective means of slimming, and rejuvenates by stimulating the circulation and the lymph flow. It is also used successfully in the treatment of rheumatism

Magnesium forms part of the composition of bones and teeth. It also is present in all types of food.

Sulphur is needed for keeping the skin, hair and nails healthy. It is found in many proteins, also in egg-yolk, turnips, raw cabbage and brussels-sprouts. If you eat the usual amount of proteins you will get enough sulphur for a healthy diet.

Iodine is essential for allowing the thyroid gland to work properly. It is found in drinking-water, all sea-fish, fish-liver oils, watercress and vegetables (especially onions and watercress) grown in soil containing iodine. Any deficiency can be made up by using iodised table salt.

Vitamin A is especially needed for keeping the mucous membranes healthy, for resistance to infection and for good eyesight. It is found in green vegetables, tomatoes, butter, cream, carrots, liver, kidney, fish-liver oil, swedes, oranges, dried apricots, peaches, spinach, watercress, and the outer leaves of cabbage and lettuce.

Vitamin B keeps the skin healthy and prevents fatigue, loss of appetite, nerve troubles and constipation. It is found in yeast, hard fish-roe, oatmeal, brown bread, kidney, liver, lean meat, nuts, Marmite, eggs, milk, green vegetables, dried peas, beans and lentils.

Vitamin C is needed to keep the skin healthy, and also to keep the gums and mouth in good condition. It increases resistance to infection and helps the healing properties of the body. It is found in oranges, black currants, lemons, grapefruit, pineapple and in tomatoes and raw green vegetables.

Vitamin D prevents rickets and defective teeth and promotes strong bones. It is found in fish-liver oils, milk, butter, eggs, suet, herrings, sardines, salmon and tinned salmon. It can also be generated in the body by exposure to sunlight.

Vitamin E is often called the 'anti-sterility' vitamin. It is important to expectant and nursing mothers. It is found in milk and green vegetables.

Water. A large percentage of all food contains water, but extra fluid is essential.

The most important food is the protein, and at *least* 3-4 ounces must be taken daily.

Fruit is the plump girl's best friend, supplying necessary vitamins without bulk

THE 18-DAY DIET

THE following diet can be followed with confidence by active and healthy persons up to middle age. The diet has been carefully planned to give balanced menus with a nutritive sufficiency. The amount of weight lost will depend upon the individual, but it will reduce to a *normal* weight by supplying a *balanced* diet with adequate nutrition. Anyone *underweight* may gain on it, bringing their weight to normal! Don't be discouraged if some days you lose no weight.

The dinner menu may be taken at midday, and the lunch menu in the evening to suit the convenience of the individual. But it is important that the foods shown should be taken on the days given. If desired, shredded raw cabbage and carrots may be substituted for the salads mentioned. Saccharin should be used for all sweetening purposes. It is *essential* that the bread rolls are starch-reduced such as Energen, and that the ration is not exceeded.

Breakfast: Every day. (This will not be repeated.)

Starch-reduced breakfast flakes, average portion. 1 egg poached, boiled or scrambled, *or* 1 oz. lean grilled bacon, *or* 1 oz. lean ham, *or* 2 oz. white fish grilled, baked or steamed, *or* 1 kipper *or* 1 herring. 2 starch-reduced rolls with butter. ½ oz. marmalade. One cup of tea or coffee.

Milk allowance, ½ pint a day.
Butter allowance, 1 oz. a day.

First Day

Midday. ½ grapefruit. 1 hard-boiled egg, with lettuce, watercress and tomato. 2 Energen or other starch-reduced rolls with butter. 1 apple or pear.

Evening. 1 grilled chop, parsnips or carrots and cabbage. 2 starch-reduced rolls. Stewed rhubarb.

Second Day

Midday. Tomato juice. 3 oz. grilled white fish with grilled tomatoes. 2 starch-reduced rolls with butter. 4 oz. stewed prunes.

Evening. ½ grapefruit. 3 oz. stewed tripe, or baked rabbit, onions and cauliflower. 2 starch-reduced rolls. 1 slice fresh pineapple or 3 oz. stewed apricots, peaches or plums, with 3 tablespoonsful of junket.

Third Day

Midday. Clear soup. 4 oz. braised rabbit, cabbage and carrots. 2 starch-reduced rolls with butter. 1 orange. Small cup of coffee.

Evening. Tomato juice. 3 oz. grilled liver or kidney, tomato and sprouts. 2 starch-reduced rolls. 4 oz. stewed plums.

Fourth Day

Midday. ½ grapefruit. 2 oz. grated cheese with lettuce, watercress and tomato. 3 starch-reduced rolls with butter. 2½ oz. grapes, figs or 3 oz. fresh plums.

Evening. Orange juice. 2 oz. braised lean ham, onions and spinach. 2 starch-reduced rolls with butter. Stewed gooseberries with 3 tablespoonsful Enersem milk pudding.

Fifth Day

Midday. 4 oz. cod's roe grilled with tomato. 2 starch-reduced rolls with butter. 1 pear, apple or orange.

Evening. ½ grapefruit. 3 oz. stewed rabbit or boiled chicken, carrots and celery. 2 starch-reduced rolls. 2½ oz. grapes or figs, or 4 oz. fresh plums.

Sixth Day

Midday. Orange juice. 1 poached egg with spinach. 2 starch-reduced rolls with butter. 4 oz. stewed plums.

Evening. 1 lean grilled chop or 4 oz. lean roast meat, parsnips and cauliflower. 2 starch-reduced rolls. 1 pear with 3 tablespoonsful junket.

Seventh Day

Midday. Tomato juice. 1½ oz. lean grilled bacon or ham, tomato and cauliflower. 2 starch-reduced rolls with butter. 1 apple.

Evening. Lobster or crab salad with vinegar. Stewed apples or other fruit. 2 starch-reduced rolls with butter and a small portion of cheese.

Eighth Day

Midday. 4 oz. steamed fresh haddock, carrots and sprouts, 2 starch-reduced rolls with butter, 3 oz. stewed prunes. Small coffee.

Evening. 1 egg and ½ oz. cheese as soufflé with tomato. 2 starch-reduced rolls with butter. 1 slice of fresh pineapple, or 3 oz. stewed apricots, peaches or plums with 3 tablespoonsful of sago pudding. Coffee.

Ninth Day

Midday. 4 oz. cold lean meat with lettuce, watercress and tomato. 2 starch-reduced rolls with butter. Stewed rhubarb. Small coffee.

Evening. 4 oz. steamed fish with lemon juice, tomato and celery. 2 starch-reduced rolls with butter. 3 oz. stewed apricots.

Tenth Day

Midday. 4 oz. lean grilled ham, spinach and swedes. 2 starch-reduced rolls with butter. 1 pear. Orange juice.

Evening. Slice of melon. 4 oz. lean roast meat, cabbage and carrots. 2 starch-reduced rolls. 4 oz. figs.

Eleventh Day

Midday. Tomato juice. Prawn, shrimp or crab salad. 2 starch-reduced rolls with butter. Stewed fruit.

Evening. 1 oz. lean grilled bacon or ham. 1 oz. liver or kidney, with tomatoes and mushrooms, as grill. 3 oz. stewed plums with 3 tablespoonsful milk pudding. 2 starch-reduced rolls with butter and small portion of cheese.

Twelfth Day

Midday. 4 oz. lean meat, cabbage and carrots. 3 starch-reduced rolls with butter. 2½ oz. grapes or figs, or 3 oz. plums.

Evening. ½ grapefruit. 3 oz. braised rabbit, turnip and cauliflower. 2 starch-reduced rolls. 1 slice fresh pineapple, or 3 oz. stewed apricots, peaches or plums, with 3 tablespoonsful of junket.

Thirteenth Day

Midday. ½ grapefruit. 3 oz. herring roes, tomatoes. 2 starch-reduced rolls with butter. 3 oz. stewed prunes or figs.

Evening. Orange juice. 1 lean grilled chop, celery and sprouts. 2 starch-reduced rolls with butter. 1 fresh pear with 3 tablespoonsful of junket.

Fourteenth Day

Midday. Unthickened vegetable broth. 2 oz. grated cheese with lettuce, watercress, beetroot and tomato. 2 starch-reduced rolls with butter. 1 orange, or apple.

Evening. 4 oz. lean grilled ham, spinach and tomatoes. 6 oz. fresh strawberries, raspberries or stewed apple. 2 starch-reduced rolls and a small portion of cheese.

Fifteenth Day

Midday. Tomato juice. 4 oz. grilled white fish, carrots and cauliflower. 2 starch-reduced rolls with butter. 1 slice of fresh pineapple.

Evening. 1 egg and ½ oz. cheese as soufflé with tomatoes. 2 starch-reduced rolls with butter. 2½ oz. grapes or figs or 3 oz. fresh plums with 3 tablespoonsful of rice pudding. Coffee.

Sixteenth Day

Midday. 1½ oz. lean grilled bacon, french beans and turnip. 3 starch-reduced rolls with butter. Stewed apples.

Evening. ½ grapefruit. 3 oz. stewed tripe, onions and carrots (or lean meat). 2 starch-reduced rolls. Fruit salad made with 1 orange. 1 apple, 1 oz. of grapes. Coffee or China tea with lemon.

Seventeenth Day

Midday. ½ grapefruit. Prawn, shrimp or crab salad. 3 starch-reduced rolls with butter. 3 oz. stewed prunes.

Evening. 1 lean grilled chop, swedes and cauliflower. 2 starch-reduced rolls. 4 oz. stewed apricots or peaches, with 3 tablespoonsful of cornflour mould.

Last Day

Midday. 4 oz. stewed rabbit, carrots and cauliflower. 2 starch-reduced rolls with butter. 1 fresh peach. Small coffee.

Evening. 3 oz. cod's roe grilled, celery and tomato. 2 starch-reduced rolls. Stewed apple or fruit salad. Small coffee.

. . . and then you can stay that way with

The Weight-Control Diet

On Rising. Juice of lemon in half a cup of hot water.

Breakfast. Half grapefruit or one orange. One egg or two tablespoonsful of starch-reduced wheat flakes with milk. One cupful of coffee or tea—no sugar. Three starch-reduced rolls with two small pats of butter and one teaspoonful of marmalade.

Midday (may be exchanged with evening meal). Salad of tomato, lettuce, watercress (dressing of one teaspoonful of olive oil and lemon juice or vinegar) and either one egg, or portion of cottage or Cheddar cheese or small portion of macaroni cheese or slice of cold lean meat. Two starch-reduced rolls with small pat of butter. Orange, apple, pear, slice of pineapple, small bunch of grapes, or other fruit. One small cup of black coffee.

Tea. Cup of tea with milk, saccharine if needed. One biscuit.

Evening. Clear soup or ½ grapefruit. About 4 oz. of lean beef or lamb, or grilled white fish or small lean cutlets or steak or portion of chicken. Liberal helping of cabbage, cauliflower, spring greens or spinach. Two starch-reduced rolls with one small pat of butter. Baked or stewed apple or stewed fruit in season, or jelly or raw fruit salad. Coffee, or cup of China or weak tea with lemon.

Follow this if you can't manage the full diet.

NOW we have seen how our food is made up, we come back again to the question of calories. There is a table on page 239 showing *average* calorie requirements; but it is only a rough guide, and individual requirements must be considered.

When you are on a slimming diet, it isn't, strictly speaking, necessary to count the calories. The main thing to remember is to cut down on the carbohydrates and fats, and replace them by foods shown in the vitamin list.

Dieting need not be a hardship. The easiest way to set about it is to set a goal—and stick to it. The first few days are the worst, but once this stage is over, it is surprising how easily the habit of *correct* eating becomes. What is more, the results are encouraging, for not only do you lose weight, but you feel fitter, more alert, and have extra energy.

How fast should you lose weight? Here again, so much depends upon the individual,

SELF MASSAGE

Quick reducing may result in slightly flabby flesh. This is the way to keep it toned up. Hold the upper arm firmly with thumb underneath. Pinch the fleshy part from armpit to elbow until the flesh tingles

and naturally those people with little or no work to do can afford to lose weight more quickly than the others. It is generally accepted that men, housewives, and women who are out at business can safely reduce at a rate of 2 lb. a week. A more drastic loss should never be attempted without medical supervision. Too rapid a loss means sagging muscles and loose, wrinkled skin. But none of this happens with a slimming diet that is undertaken sensibly.

There are, of course, certain foods that are taboo during any slimming diet. These are: all fried foods, fat, and fat meat, sausages, oil and salad dressings, cream, pastry and cakes, thick soups and sauces, nuts, bread, biscuits, pastry, beer, wine and spirits, hot buttered toast, dripping, mineral waters—other than soda water, chutney, pickles, potatoes, chocolate and sweets, tinned salmon, fish tinned in oil.

SHORT CUTS TO SLIMMING

Perhaps all the time you have been reading this you have been thinking to yourself, 'Ah, it won't be so difficult for me, because there are those slimming tablets that So-and-So used to take. I can take those, too, and reduce in half the time.' But you won't, if you are wise, for *no* so-called slimming tablets should ever be taken except under medical supervision.

There are a large number of preparations under various trade names available on the market for slimming purposes. Many of them are nothing more or less than aperients, or rather a mixture of aperients, and drastic ones

at that. With a good diet, aperients are not usually necessary, and if they are, it is better to keep to an old, tried favourite. If you are considering taking a course of any slimming tablet—well, make sure you ask your doctor about it first.

Apart from the slimming tablets with trade names there are the glandular extracts which, unfortunately, can be bought without a doctor's prescription. There are thyroid tablets, for example, and pituitary tablets, but anyone who takes them without supervision is simply asking for trouble. In the first place, they come in different strengths, and secondly, it is quite impossible for you to know whether or not they would suit you. Glandular extracts taken without medical supervision can cause serious trouble.

There is a drug that is not a slimming drug, but, as far as slimming is concerned, its principal action is to reduce the appetite. But here again, it should *never* be taken unless recommended by a doctor, for it certainly does not suit everyone. If taken too late in the day, it will almost certainly produce insomnia, and may be responsible for 'nerviness' and 'the jumps.' To those people it suits, it is very good, *but* (and a very big 'but' too) do let your doctor decide whether it suits you or not ; it can be actually harmful.

A popular way of reducing is by taking Turkish baths, and very helpful they can be too, although not always in just the way people imagine. True, you lose weight immediately, but as soon as you eat or drink anything, back it comes, or at least some of it.

A Turkish bath, however, will encourage

the skin to breathe properly. It thoroughly cleanses the pores and rids them of all waste matter. Followed by a good massage, it is a quick way of getting rid of 'spots' of fatness, for instance, over the hips. You must definitely not take them if you have any heart weakness.

A roller, used regularly, particularly after a hot bath, whittles away the inches, particularly over the thighs and hips. A few minutes' treatment night and morning is sufficient to help considerably.

Another useful apparatus for home slimming treatment is one of the electrical apparatuses that 'massages' by vibration. They can be bought with different applicators for massaging the face and neck, the scalp, and the limbs.

Even if you cannot afford any of these appliances there is a great deal you can do for yourself. A daily rub-down is a 'must,' with or without a bath beforehand. A rough towel and a really hard rub will send the blood racing to the surface of the skin, helping to break up the fatty tissues.

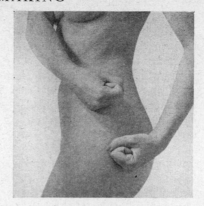

Clench hands, thumbs out, and pummel the fleshy part of the hip with the little finger side of the fist as hard as possible. Repeat other side

WHITTLE DOWN YOUR WAIST

IF you can put a tape measure round your waist and contemplate without dismay the inches it registers, then you're one of the lucky few. A stealthy inch or two encroaches so quickly upon our waistline, unkind witnesses to an over-starchy diet and a disinclination to take exercise. They urge us to do some immediate whittling down.

Exercise and careful diet are the main part of the waist-trimming story.

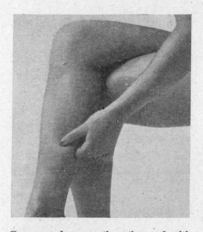

Cross one leg over the other and with finger and thumb pinch hard up and down either side of the calf. Repeat pinching on other leg

Six Minutes Every Day

It is important to approach them in the right frame of mind, which means realistically. Exercise and diet require discipline. One little lapse from grace quickly leads to another and all the previous effort goes for nothing.

That is the pill; the sugar coating is the fact that our figures really are what we make them, and that striving for a streamlined waist is well worth while because simple, inexpensive clothes will suddenly acquire a million-dollar look when they go in and out at the right places.

Here are three exercises especially designed to tone up the muscles and eliminate that

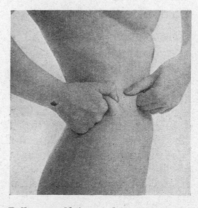

Pull yourself in as far as you can, then with finger and thumb of each hand catch hold of any loose flesh, pinching hard all around the waistline

spare tyre. Try them for six minutes a day; more if it can be managed. *With all exercises the breath should be held while in motion and expelled during the pauses.*

The Spiral. Sit on a stool, which should be low enough for you to have your feet flat on the ground and about twelve inches apart. If the stool is a little high, make a footstool with books.

Raise your arms above your head as high as they will go. Turn the palms upwards and entwine your fingers. Sit with your spine very straight and head erect; then bend slowly at the waist to the right; then back as far as you dare go without over-balancing; then over to the left, then forward. Don't hurry. It is the effort of balancing that contracts the waistline muscles.

Do this exercise ten times, then repeat, going the other way round. Each day you will find your balance improving and you will be able to bend a little farther backwards and a little farther to each side.

The See-Saw. Place your feet flat on the ground about eighteen inches apart. Let your hands hang loosely and naturally at the sides, with fingers extended. Stand straight, but not stiffly. Bend sideways to the right and try to touch the ground with the tips of the fingers (you won't, of course, but the object is to stretch the waist muscles). Repeat to the left side. Do this exercise ten times each side, always keeping the knees straight.

The Toe-Toucher. This is an old friend . . . hands above the head, knees straight; the target, to touch the toes without bending the knees. This must be done very slowly. On your way up, take your time and raise the torso smoothly and gradually.

Watch Your Posture

Wherever you are or whatever you're doing —walking, sitting in a train, sewing, or tapping a typewriter—give a little thought at intervals to your position. If you are slouching along or sitting slumped in a chair, check yourself smartly. Practise, from time to time during the day, pulling the abdomen muscles in, up, and in again. This discourages a sagging waistline.

Now for what we should, or should not, be eating.

Even if we are not following a strict diet, there is no reason why we should not be selective about what we eat, avoiding too many starchy foods which we know are fattening.

Dull? Not at all. Tomato slices and cheese between rusks or wheat biscuits are a nourishing and delicious substitute for ordinary sandwiches made with bread. When you do eat bread it should always be the whole-meal *or* starch-reduced variety. A second green vegetable or a salad in place of the inevitable potatoes is not only less fattening but makes a refreshing change.

Fresh fruit or a fruit salad winds up a meal just as pleasantly and much more healthily than a suet pudding. Eat it slowly, though, also your green salads, otherwise, they will cause flatulence, expanding rather than diminishing the waistline.

Unless you are on a very serious diet, sweets in moderation are good for you, giving you the energy to reduce your fat!

A little food and often is a better policy for waist control than going without for a long time and then eating an enormous meal. Snacks are bad as a habit, but if you must have something with your elevenses and at tea-time, a biscuit or two will do less damage than a sticky bun.

Hints That Help

Start the day with the juice of a lemon in a glass of warm water; end it with a glass of cold water. All simple rules, aren't they? But they're excellent waistliners.

So is a good foundation garment. It can literally take off inches—or, if it's a poor one, put them on. Flesh has to go somewhere, and a badly fitting girdle or corset, over-tight round the hips and diaphragm, will cause an unbecoming bulge.

Choose a firm foundation, but not one which causes discomfort. A corset which ends above the waist, so that the waistline is rigid, is a good buy for the girl who is plump.

And here are a few eye-deceiving tips to help achieve that trim-waisted look we're striving to acquire.

The natural waistline is curved, dipping at the back; skirt tops and belt should follow it.

Wear a wide, separate belt of petersham beneath your dress to nip in your waist.

Finally, keep a sense of proportion about other things besides your figure. Emotions that get out of control can cause chronic indigestion and puffiness. So try to combine an equable disposition with your exercises and a less solid diet, and you'll soon have the handspan waist all women envy and most men admire.

ARE YOU TOO THIN?

IT seems unbelievable to plump folk that some women really want to gain weight, but it is so, and it is not too easy.

You are probably a very active person, burning up food as fast as you eat it and turning it into energy.

To get those curves you covet, you must make a resolution to eat more of the fat-producing foods—starch, fats, sugar—and to try to get more rest.

It's not just an old wives' tale that placid, contented people put on weight, so do keep as cool, calm and collected as you possibly can. And always give yourself plenty of time to get from one place to another, so that you can walk instead of having to run. Do not jump up in the middle of meals to telephone.

You will find yourself on the way to being a more curvaceous beauty if you start each day with a cup of tea plus a slice of bread and butter. Follow it up with a hearty breakfast: porridge or cereal of some kind with milk, then a main course (sausages and ham are your allies), and finish up with as much toast, butter and marmalade as you can manage.

Have a milk drink or a cup of soup for elevenses, or if you really want to stick to tea or coffee have a buttered bun or sweet biscuits with it. A raw egg beaten up in milk is nourishing.

Eat a Good Lunch

No quickly snatched sandwich lunch for you unless you want to face an angular future. Have thick soup followed by a fat-builder like creamed fish and mashed potatoes, or a meat pie, with plenty of potatoes as well as green vegetables.

Suet puddings will also help you to get up to the wished-for weight.

Eat once again with your afternoon cup of tea, and be sure you have a full evening meal with all the starchy foods you can manage. But for your health's sake be sure you have your quota of green vegetables and fruit. Drink a bedtime beverage made with milk.

Drink fruit squashes between meals, and as much milk as you like. Eat and drink slowly, for much thinness is due to indigestion.

Relaxation should be the watchword of the too-thin. Don't run for a 'bus unless absolutely necessary, there will be another in a minute.

Exercises are a great help. Breathe in deeply before an open window each day, count six, let out the breath slowly. Develop the bust by the 'arms outward fling' exercise, or lie on the floor, hands clasped behind your head, bend the elbows to try to make them meet, then slowly push them back again.

BEAUTY POT-POURRI

IF your beauty preparations are mixed up in a drawer or on a shelf, buy an ordinary plastic knife-box, which costs a few shillings, and keep all your lotions, nail-varnish, remover and creams in it. It can be so easily lifted out of the drawer when you wish to tidy it; or a shelf can be so much more easily dusted, if the beauty containers can be lifted off all together.

*　　*　　*

If you run out of skin food one night, pat under your eyes with top milk.

*　　*　　*

If you are 'too tired to move' for no particular reason, go for a walk in the open air. It will set you on your feet in more senses than one. You are supplying yourself with oxygen by breathing in the fresh air, and letting out the stale, and thus relieving the toxic condition that led to your being so tired.

*　　*　　*

Do some deep breathing before an open window every day. Draw in a breath by pushing *out* your tummy, then as the breath rises, draw your tummy in, and your bust lifts. Hold your breath for six counts, then let it slowly out with a hissing noise until you have no more breath, by which time you should be well caved in in front.

*　　*　　*

If your nylons get mud-splashed just turn them down and wash the backs of your legs. You will find that as the mud has gone right through your stockings, no marks will show.

*　　*　　*

Girdles are hard to pull on when you are slightly damp after a bath or bathe, so shake some talc in your girdle and it will slide on easily.

HOW TO MAKE UP

MAKE-UP advice, when it relates to colour, is not easy to give, for very few women belong to a clearly defined type. There are brunettes with blonde skins, blondes with sallow complexions, red-heads with high colours. You also have to pay some attention to the clothes you are wearing, and there should really always be two 'slants' of make-up shades in the cosmetic wardrobe. Lipsticks with a slight orange tone to go with greens, yellows, brown, rust; and rouge and lipstick with a slightly blue cast to blend better when wearing blues, most pinks, mauve. The effect of the prettiest hat is spoilt if the lipstick its owner is wearing is of a violently different tone. If you have a coat of a very definite colour—say, a scarlet with a good deal of yellow in it—then wear it when you buy a lipstick and try it on the back of your hand. Look at it in the daytime. The charm of clothes is heightened with complementary make-up.

On the whole, very dark, red lipsticks are ageing, although there is a type of girl with a pale magnolia skin who can use them with great effect. Petunia tones are sometimes ageing, but, though from time to time they go out of fashion, there is also a rather pale skin against which they look always right.

Your cream and powder rouge must match your lipstick, although a medium rouge (of an ash-rose type) is always useful to keep on hand, since it blends most naturally with the genuine flush on a cheek.

What is Your Skin Type?

Dry skins should always be treated to a foundation that has properties which help the skin. The older dry skin needs both a cream and foundation with estrogenic properties, to replace the moisture that dries up as the years go by. The greasy skin should have only a good liquid powder as base for powder. The normal skin can use almost anything according to choice, but it is best to back the products of known makers, whose name carries a guarantee of purity.

Many women these days favour a heavier make-up which conceals flaws, red veins and pimples, such as the pancake varieties. While there is no doubt that these are glamorous in effect, sometimes they are apt to be drying. It is best to use another foundation or skin balm under them, so that the drying effect is offset.

Your Own Attraction

As for powder, very fine powders do not suit everyone, and some prefer a heavier one. Too heavy a powder is likely to clog the pores. However, some of the very fine powders give a veil-like illusion, and the combination of two powders is always successful. Use your heavier one in a fairly neutral shade first, and dust over with the very fine powder afterwards, in peach or rachel or a faintly rose cast, whichever suits you best. If you put a rosy powder straight on to a sallow skin, the effect is grey, but, once you have the covering of a neutral powder first you have a glowing effect. Both teen-agers and the not-so-young-as-they-were women should go in for light make-up. The teen-ager's standby is a clean, shining freshness, glossy hair, gleaming teeth, fresh frocks. The older woman needs chic, careful grooming, a nicely kept head of hair; heavy make-up is ageing, especially around the eyes. Beige eye-shadow suits both teen-agers and the older woman. On the one it gives the faintest shadow without any look of make-up. On the other it lightens dark eyelids. Sometimes the older woman looks well with a darker foundation, giving a warm, sunburned, healthy look.

You can apply cream rouge after your foundation—it spreads more easily this way—then press the powder well in and remove excess with a brush. The older woman doesn't want the ageing effect of powder nestling in wrinkles. You can then add the slightest rounding-off flush of powder rouge if you look more glamorous with a colour. Or none at all if to look 'pale and interesting' is more your *forte*. Actually, the idea used to be to use a powder darker than your skin. It is more becoming usually to choose a powder one shade lighter than your skin tone. Do not forget to put a foundation, as well as

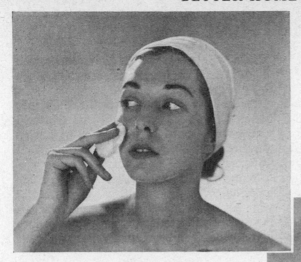

Clean the face thoroughly, using cleansing milk, cream or washing with soft water and a bland soap. Or wring out a piece of cotton-wool in water, dip it into your cleansing cream and wipe all over the face with upward strokes. Slap afterwards with a piece of cotton-wool soaked in skin tonic or astringent. You can also slap with iced milk and rinse off with lukewarm water, for an extra glow

Apply your foundation. Put little dabs of it all over the face, then smooth in very lightly with the finger-tips. Do not forget to put some on your neck. Powder applied direct to the skin is drying

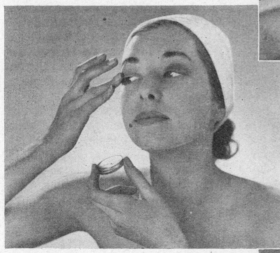

Apply your eye-shadow with a light finger-tip or a brush from the centre outwards for a normal eye. For deep-set orbs, put very little on the lid, but emphasise the shadow more towards the actual bone, so that the bone recedes and the eyes come forward. Protruding eyes can take a good deal of colour on the lids, eased off towards the brow

Use little tiny strokes of an eyebrow pencil to lengthen the brows. If your face is short, keep the brow straight or curved very slightly upwards. The long face needs the brow bringing down at the ends. If you have large eyes, draw a light line under the lower lashes and smudge a trifle. Smaller eyes need a line only at the outside of the lower lid

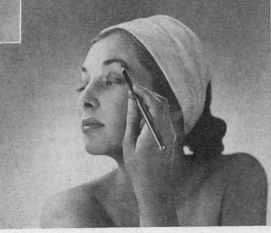

powder, on your neck, otherwise the powder alone will be drying.

Watch the Films

The way you apply your rouge can alter the shape of your face. The films are a good Charm School, especially the Technicolor ones, for you can study the make-up of the actress most like yourself. The long face should have rouge from the sides of the nose across the face, worked a little up towards the forehead. You can put a shadow of rouge also on your chin, ear-lobes and forehead to shorten the apparent length of the face.

If you use too small an area of rouge on a round face, it will show; so apply it on the cushion of your cheeks as you smile, easing it off towards the temples and to the merest flush in the lower cheeks. On the heart-shaped face, the rouge follows the line of the face, wide at the top, narrowing down to the centre of the cheek and fading off. The square face should be rouged on the outer parts of the cheeks; the oval high on the cheek.

When the cheeks are hollow, do not put rouge where they fall in the middle, or you accentuate this. Rouge around the outside of the hollow, just smoothing off where it occurs, and you have more appearance of fullness. High cheekbones should not use too bright a rouge, or the effect is hectic and feverish.

When you are made up, press firmly but gently over the whole make-up with a piece of cotton-wool dampened with eau-de-cologne. This 'sets' it.

The too-round face can have some darker powder used on the outside of each cheek, also the square face, but in this case it should come down diagonally to the point of the chin.

All successful make-up is the result of experimenting and adjusting well-known rules.

NECK REVIVER

To give your neck a treatment to help restore it, smother it in massage or cleansing cream. Massage well all over, working from the shoulder to the ear, then remove the cream with a face flannel dipped and wrung out in as hot water as you can bear. When it is all removed, spray with your astringent or skin tonic (if you keep it in a scent-spray), or slap with a piece of cotton-wool soaked in skin tonic. Put on light cream or skin balm, and powder lightly over.

POISE *for* PERSONALITY

IT is so often true that the woman who walks as if she is someone, is usually taken to *be* someone.

To be graceful pin-points the difference between a gauche young girl and a poised young woman. It implies smooth, unflurried movements, the serenity which springs from self-assurance and no fidgeting.

You say good-bye to grace when you make jerky, ungainly movements, when you flutter your hands in meaningless gestures as you talk, when you continually pat your hair into place, when you perpetually peep in your compact mirror to make sure your nose is matt and your lipstick unsmudged, when you sit tensely on the edge of your chair.

No Awkward Movements

Jerky movements can be corrected if you take time to practise walking gracefully. Try the old trick of balancing a book on your head and walking along a straight line. You will find that as long as your movements are elegant the book will remain on your head—the first ungainly motion will send it toppling.

Now put a chair in front of a long mirror —watch yourself as you sit down and rise up again. If your movements aren't smooth, keep practising.

Put a book on the floor and pick it up, looking in the mirror as you do so. Was your back straight? If not, try again.

Keep on practising in this way until it becomes second nature to you to walk, stand, sit and bend the *right* way. You will not be self-conscious when entering a room, because you will not be afraid of knocking your elbow, stumbling or dropping your handbag. Walk 'tall,' elbows slightly back, shoulders down like a coat-hanger.

An Air of Repose

Descriptive gestures with the hands are one thing, but fluttering hands are no aid to conversation—they distract other people's attention from what you are saying. So does fidgeting with your handkerchief. Cure both these habits by keeping your hands lightly clasped in your lap as you sit talking.

Knowing you're perfectly groomed gives you the self-confidence which is grace's greatest ally.

For instance, that hair-patting habit will vanish like magic if you *know* your hair is always in place.

Constant use of your compact springs from the feeling that your make-up is not going to last throughout the evening. If you're *sure* your nose isn't going to develop an unbecoming shine, that your lipstick isn't going to smudge, you won't be tempted to keep glancing in your mirror. 'Make your toilette,' as our French friends say, then forget yourself.

Learn to Relax

If you sit on the edge of your chair it's obvious that you're tensed up and find it difficult to relax, or you wouldn't choose such an uncomfortable position. So practise complete relaxation—once you've mastered this you'll find you won't be so tensed up, that you sit easily and gracefully. Every day, when you can arrange the time, lie flat on your bed for ten minutes and relax completely, going over every muscle to make sure it is not tense.

Bodily poise does aid mental poise, and exercises will help balance and assurance.

Almost any ballet pose done each day will do. Here are two adapted as exercises:

Stand on the flat of right foot, rest the left foot before you on the back of a chair, a low sideboard, or something at hip-height. Swing up your left arm, then bend both head and arm till you touch your knee with your forehead, your instep with your hand (you may not make it the first few times). Return to position, swing arm down, put your left foot to ground. Repeat exercise with the right side. This need be done only about three times each side and you will feel the strong pull right down your figure. Immediately you will stand better. You can graduate to standing with both hands clasped over your head, instead of one at a time.

Better Balance

Here is another that also supples you, and reduces the waist:

Stand on the flat of your right foot, with your left foot resting on a chair-back or high arm, *sideways;* your left arm is just curved with the hand in front of your diaphragm, your right arm curved over your head. Bend sideways as far as you can, return to position. Repeat the other side. This exercise should be done about eight times.

A very ordinary exercise that is excellent for balance is to lie on the floor, arms by your side, raise both legs together, circle widely five times to the left, return to ground. Relax for a few moments, raise, swing in a wide circle five times to the right. Repeat three times. You will find, when dancing, that you move more lightly and have an easier balance than before. Or put your arms above your head, clasp hands, rise on your toes, then very slowly sink to the ground. Repeat three times, if you can without wobbling, before returning arms to sides and beginning again.

When sitting, try—in imagination, of course!—to make the back of your neck meet the top of your head. This pulls you into line.

Grace and Charm

For grace of movement, take a basket, walk a few steps on the soles of your feet, put the basket on floor, reach up high on tiptoes to gather some imaginary fruit growing very high, lower the fruit into the basket keeping knees stiff; pick up the basket, give a little run on tiptoes; repeat the whole performance right around the room two or three times.

Poise of course implies that you are sure of yourself, which is why you must be *bien soignée*: all fluff taken off your coat-collar with a little petrol or cleaner; the heels of your shoes always mended in time; shoulder-straps kept under control with small loop and press-stud; hair combed at the back as well as front, no chipped nail-polish.

Acquire Confidence

This is where the business of curing any particular beauty fault comes in, for in tackling and overcoming it, you acquire confidence, both in your will-power and appearance. Once you have done your best with it, whether it is a middle-aged spread, round shoulders or drab hair, forget it. For instance, if you have large feet, make sure that they are well shod, and that your seams are straight. Never draw attention to your worst point. Do not try to push your feet under the settee when sitting talking to a guest and say, 'Oh, I know my feet are huge!' No-one will notice unless you mention it. And who cares, but you?

In fact, the girl who is poised carries an aura of serenity about with her, and other people relax happily in her presence. No wonder she is popular!

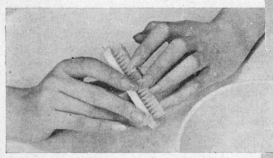

A HOME MANICURE

It does not matter how careful the general grooming, if the hands are uncared for. Put aside a definite half-hour once a week to give yourself a manicure

Arrange everything you need before you begin

Below: Scrub the nails thoroughly with a stiff brush dipped in warm, soapy water, or use a nail shampoo. Rinse them in clear, cool water. Push back the cuticles gently with a soft towel, or a little rubber 'hoof' you can buy very cheaply

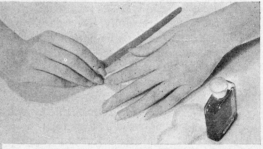

Above: Remove your varnish, then shape nails to a becoming oval with a nail-file. Finish off with an emery board to remove any roughness

Right: Whiten the nails by digging into a cut lemon, or dip a cotton-wool-covered orange-stick in peroxide and run under the nail-tips

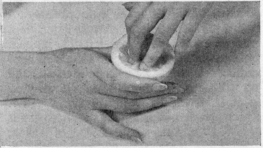

Left: Take your orange-stick with a fresh piece of cotton-wool around the tip and dip it into cuticle oil. Work around each nail, then dip finger-tips into soapy water, rinse and dry

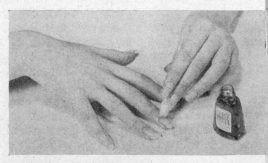

Right: Remove all dampness from the nails with varnish remover. Now apply varnish (apply a base coat first, if you wish) with long, sweeping strokes—one in the middle and then one each side. Make sure you have just enough on the brush. Some bottles have 'shoulders' on which to rest two fingers

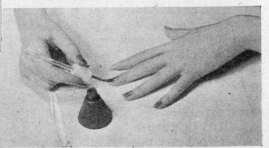

ELEGANT HANDS

YOUTH does not usually have any very difficult hand problems. There is redness, of course, the result of both a rather poor circulation and a particularly thin skin. There is no actual cure for this. The best that can be done is to practise flapping exercises for the hands; keep up your general circulation by means of sufficient outdoor exercise, and drink plenty of milk. (As this is inclined to be fattening, leave off some other food in its place.) Take a course of cod-liver oil. When you are going out, remember to wash a few smalls, dry your hands carefully, then rub in some hand make-up cream, smoothing it off carefully above the wrist to blend into the arm, and not to show a demarcation line. Also, while not affecting poses, such as crossing your hands on your breasts or striking any dramatic attitude such as clasping your throat, try to remember to keep your hands upwards. In this way, you help the blood to drain down and avoid that angry redness.

Shape of the Fingers

Shape is a poser at any age, if the gods have not been kind. As the twig is bent, so the tree is inclined, and there are young girls who wear a too-tight thimble on every finger while reading. It is quite possible that, carried out conscientiously, this might have some slight, ultimate effect. Otherwise shape cannot be changed. Firm massage with a hand cream and careful manicuring do give the impression of a beautiful hand, whereas the same hand neglected cannot appear anything but ugly.

It is as the hand gets older that it loses its satin-smooth suppleness. So many women think their hands do not get old along with their faces, and take no particular care of them until brought up with a shock one day when perhaps they see their own rather lined, loose-skinned extremities next to the plump, little puds of a teen-ager. It is then difficult to catch up with lost time, for so many hand creams, excellent as they are for leaving the skin fragrant and soft, do not remove lines. There are hormone hand creams which, used regularly, feed the skin and help to bring back youthfulness.

Daily Care

The first rule to remember is to wear your gloves when out, not just to carry them. A cold wind whips up a rough surface and etches other pen-fine lines. Even if you are a housewife and just running out to baby in the pram in the garden or to take in some washing, have ready a pair of mittens made from an old pair of gloves that are easy to slip on.

The second thing is to put an allowance of skin food on to your hands every time you massage your face. This must be massaged in with a firm stroke from the tips of your fingers to the wrist. At night, having wiped off any surplus, do not wash your hands again.

Housework of any kind is a fatal enemy to hand-elegance. It is useful to keep a bottle of hand-lotion by kitchen and bathroom sinks and fine yourself a penny for the poor-box (it's always something to fall back on) when you neglect to use it. *But it is not enough.* Ordinary hand-creams will not offset the effects of dust and dirt. They are excellent for keeping the cared-for hand in condition.

It used to be a clumsy device to wear gloves when doing grubby work, for the efficient housewife always likes to 'get down to it,' and gloves impede just that freedom of action necessary, that ability to search out corners and crevices. Barrier creams, however, form invisible gloves when cleaning the stove or gardening; and a different 'cream glove' for hands that may be in water for a long time. They also provide a protective barrier between

If your hands are discoloured, add some lemon juice to your hand-cream or lotion. Keep hand-cream by kitchen sink and in bathroom

the hands and irritant substances that may cause infection.

Always soak the washing-up in soapflakes or a detergent, and use a mop.

A bland soap is castor oil and zinc; it has always been unrivalled for baby's chafings, it also benefits the adult skin when constantly washing.

When the hands are in a really neglected state, a cream with honey and/or glycerine should be used constantly. A warm oil massage (olive-oil will do) twice a week. A hand-pack or facial mask is sometimes helpful to lighten brown hands, but is inclined to be drying for a tired skin. A little ordinary oatmeal mixed with a teaspoonful of lemon juice and milk, rubbed well into the hands and rinsed lightly off, leaves them in nice condition.

There are many lotions and creams on the market from which to choose. A violet-scented liquid that softens and whitens. A cream that you rub in *before* washing your hands during the day, and *after* washing your hands at night. Very excellent it is, too. A honey and almond cream in a plastic pack that squirts out just sufficient to use and does not run the risk of falling and breaking, and is easy to pack.

Breaking Nails

If your nails break, you may be anaemic, just run-down or there is perhaps a deficiency of calcium salts in the blood. Take some vitamin C, eat spinach, watercress, black-currant purée, drink milk. There is an excellent cream against brittleness in nails. Nail-polish is not harmful. In fact, a double or triple coat of nail enamel will help to guard them. Put oil around the cuticles at night, or cuticle cream. Dial telephone numbers with a pencil. File the nails all in one direction if you can acquire the dexterity. It strengthens them. If a nail has torn a little but not broken, bind it over with Dalmas strapping cut to the shape of your nail, then put polish on top of this. It will be unnoticeable. Usually it takes about six months to grow a nail, but they grow more quickly on those whose health is good.

Damp Hands

Moist palms are a burden to some people, but as they are a sign of nervousness, the nerves have to be calmed first. Then, when going out, dab the palms with a deodorant or strong astringent, and powder over with boric acid when dry.

When 'dressing' your hands, bear in mind that pale hands can take pale rose or deep red varnishes; the pinkish hand is made whiter-looking by contrast with a deep plum or dark red lacquer; the brown hand is suited better by a shade with more yellow in it, a rusty colour is best . . . mauve tones destroy its charm. There are pearl polishes that look delightful in the evening, and many new iridescent colourings in these.

Dry hands need oil, and a shilling bottle of olive-oil will not only do for salads, but will provide many beauty treatments! A hot-oil application to dry face, hands or neck, just wiped off after a few minutes and powdered over, is very helpful.

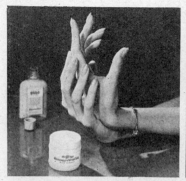  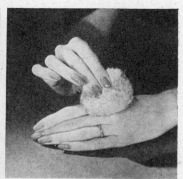

Courtesy of Damaskin

Coarse or badly coloured hands are difficult to disguise; use a special matt hand make-up that makes them good-looking and protects at the same time. Hands need care really more than the face, as they get rougher treatment. Massage in cream while the hands are still warm after washing; put a few dots of the hand make-up over the hands and smooth it in with quick, circular movements. If you are going out in the evening, dust over with a little powder

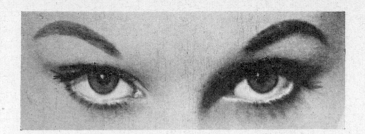

EYES

Eyes are the windows, either sparkling or dull, that reflect our health, our emotions, our hearts. Take care of them

IT is always a good beauty rule to play up your best feature, and this focal point would be their eyes for many women—if they took care of them. The eyes must not be tired or torpid, for nothing suggests age—and dispiritedness—so much. Diet greatly affects the clearness and sparkle of our eyes. Stodgy, indigestible foods lead to indifferent internal functioning, and constipation is the enemy of clear and sparkling orbs.

Ice-cold Compresses

Both winter winds and summer sun are apt to take toll of eye-beauty. It is a good plan to lie down immediately on reaching home either from a job or a shopping expedition, with icy eye compresses over your eyes (the kind that are kept ice-cold in an air-tight jar). You can, of course, use cotton-wool soaked in eye-lotion, or if you have none, then diluted wych hazel or a few drops of eau-de-cologne in an eggcup of water. (But *only* a few drops.) The coldness of the compress gives a bracing tone to the whole face, relaxing the entire body, and making you ready for the Second Instalment of your day, instead of a tired evening.

An eye-bath is an absolute necessity every day, using fresh lotion for each eye. People who would never hesitate to take a daily dip, often do not give a thought to their eyes collecting dust, facing winds all day long. Germs can enter through the eye-ducts, so it is obvious that cleanliness is essential. Catarrh also clouds clear eyes, so therefore take care of that complaint as well if you suffer from it. Styes are a sign of a run-down condition or an ingrowing eyelash. Foment with boracic lint dipped in very hot water and take a tonic. Do not rub your eyes with either a grubby handkerchief or a hand that is not too clean, because you may cause trouble where none, so far, exists.

Dealing with Lines

Laughter is inclined to make eye-lines, but do not worry about that, as laughter also exercises and lifts the muscles of the face, and helps the blood to course happily, gives relaxation in place of strain. For lines around the eyes, tap in a little nourishing skin-food or eye-cream every night. Remove in the morning with light little whisks of a tampon of cotton-wool dampened with skin-tonic. Whisk over the lines lightly as if you were whipping eggs or cream. When you are lying with pads over your eyes, you can also put cotton-wool dampened well with astringent over the lines underneath.

One coat of whipped white of egg makes a good pack for eye-lines, but it must be removed very carefully with lukewarm water.

When you have no opportunity of lying down, cup the palms of your hands over your eyes. It used to be the rule to 'think black,' but the latest dictum is that it is an effort to think, so be completely relaxed! Lying in the sun, with the sun playing direct on your closed lids for a while, is also good for them.

If you have been indulging in the luxury of a 'weep,' put a flannel wrung out in very *hot water* over your reddened eyes and press for several moments, then splash with cold water. Repeat several times.

Exercise

The muscles of the eye need exercising, for a fixed, strained look is the last thing you want. Stand still, raise your eyes to the ceiling, then back, straight ahead; look to the extreme side, and back to the front again; then to the other side, back; then down. Next, roll your eyes round and round slowly in one direction, relax, blink a few times, and roll them round in the other. If you are in a bus or train, let your eyes follow another travelling object without moving your head.

When you are sewing, lift your eyes occasionally to focus them on another part of the room; blink several times. When reading in bed, see that the light drops on to the page, and does not stream directly into your eyes.

Frown lines may be caused by short sight, so check with your oculist. Dark shadows under the eyes may be worry, a run-down state, or kidney or liver disturbance, so consult the doctor. Also make sure you are having sufficient rest, fresh air, and are drinking plenty of cold water. A smoky atmosphere is very bad for sensitive eyes.

Choosing Glasses

When choosing glasses, remember that pale blue frames are usually ideal for white hair. Yellow frames are a good colour contrast for the brunette. Scarlet rims are rarely as becoming as they may be thought to be. The blonde should wear darker rims, as the too-pale shades will make her look washed-out, but *very* dark rims are rarely becoming to a woman. If you want adorned frames for the evening, try placing an ear-ring at each further top corner.

Do not wear glasses that slip a little on your nose; they are ageing. Any oculist will make you some rims that fit the bridge of your nose firmly or that stay put if you haven't a great deal of bridge to your nose.

Your eyebrows must always be neatly trimmed. If you do not want them plucked to a fine line, at least keep them tidy, taking hairs from under rather than above the brow. The natural line is followed, leaving the brow slightly wider at the inner end, and tapering off. If you have them done by an expert once or twice, you will soon be able to keep them neat yourself.

Brush your lashes with castor oil, white vaseline or any eyelash-grower every night.

Eye-strain

Here are a few remarks on the medical side of eye-care.

Using your eyes for reading seems quite a simple matter, doesn't it? Yet, just to get to the end of this line of print, means that, already, they have had to perform all kinds of amazing mechanical feats, and as many as twelve separate eye-muscles have been in use —over and over again.

The eye is an extremely sensitive and highly complicated mechanism, and a doctor's advice should be sought at the first hint of trouble.

Tucked away in the outer corner of the eye is the tear-gland, which goes to work every few seconds—whenever you blink, in fact. This action draws tears from the duct (not noticeable, because there are insufficient to spill over) and keeps the eye fresh and clean. Once their job is done, these tears drain away down a tiny canal in the inner corner of the eye, which leads into the lower part of the nose.

Should this canal become blocked, a surgeon can clear it or make a new aperture. So if you have tears when not laughing or crying, see a specialist immediately.

The Long and Short of It

Then, maybe you have been surprised to find that while many middle-aged people need glasses for reading, their sight for distant objects is perfect. It is all a matter of focusing.

In order to focus at all, the eye-muscles have to pull the lens into a different shape. As we grow older, our lenses, like our arteries, tend to become harder. Consequently the muscles find that their job becomes more and more difficult, and eventually, very little focusing is possible.

What about 'eye-strain'? Reading in a bad light, going to the cinema, watching television; all these, we are told, are liable to 'strain' our eyes. But what we really mean is that these things will make a part of our brain tired, for it is the brain that carries out the actual process of seeing, and not the eyes at all!

Contact Lenses

Bad light and straining to see may make our eyes ache, but they will not harm them any more than constant smelling will strain our noses! More often than not, the trouble that we refer to as 'eye-strain' is faulty focusing due to astigmatism, the medical term for a slightly misshapen cornea—the window of the eye. Glasses will correct the vision of people with short sight, long sight or astigmatism, but they cannot cure it.

There was a time when nothing could be done for cataract—a condition where the eye's lens becomes clouded, as a result of injury, disease or old age. Later, surgeons discovered that it was possible to remove part, or whole, of the clouded lens. But even so, cumbersome glasses had always to be worn.

Now, when the lens is removed, a transparent covering, made of plastic, is inserted over the eye-ball, which does away with the need for glasses altogether and, what is more, is invisible.

Watch the Symptoms

There is no need to have an operation for cataract before you can wear contact lenses. They are becoming increasingly popular with women who, because of their work, perhaps, prefer not to wear ordinary glasses.

However, before you decide to throw away your horn-rimmed spectacles, remember that contact lenses are not as simple as they sound. You need patience and perseverance to get used to them, and they are far from cheap. Also, they cannot always be worn for more than a few hours at a time.

A disease that sends hundreds of people blind each year, simply because they deliberately ignore its stealthy symptoms, is glaucoma. With this complaint, the internal fluid of the eye cannot escape. Increased tension causes pressure on the optic nerve, giving rise to blurred vision, coloured halos round artificial lights and, in some cases at least, severe pain.

Once this disease has destroyed vision, nothing can replace it, although *treated in time* the disease can be arrested—one good reason why disturbed vision, or eye-trouble of any sort however insignificant it may seem, should never be neglected.

There is no doubt about it, good eye-sight depends a great deal upon physical fitness.

Haven't you noticed if you are run-down or convalescing after an illness, your eyes are the first to suffer? They tire more easily than usual, and the light out of doors always seems to be particularly bright.

In the same way, worry and emotional upset will affect your eyes. People suffering from psychological troubles nearly always complain of some kind of eye-trouble. Let the doctor decide whether your blurred sight is eye-trouble or emotional strain.

So take care of your eyes, for both beauty and health.

FOR BEAUTY HINTS

Get yourself a small address-book, and write down each beauty tip that you need to use, under the right initial . . . S for skin, E for eye and so on.

PERFUME

is a matter of individuality. What is your scent?

THE fragrance of a suitable perfume brings just the finishing touch to a becoming outfit. Unfortunately, some women never use perfume unless they are 'all dressed up,' then they use very little that is soon lost, and is not remarked at all. That is why a little handbag phial to refresh is so important.

Perfume should be applied at least with sufficient strength to be noticeable, although, naturally, not *too* obvious. However, there are times when a perfume or toilet water or perfumed cologne is almost necessary. What about in the kitchen, when the air is thick with cooking odours that cling in the hair and about the person? Keep a spray of perfumed cologne on the kitchen shelf, and just spray it around your head and neck, and a little in the air. You'll feel refreshed and less tired. Even listening to the radio in the evening, a light fragrance adds to the charm of the evening. Either put it on the corner of your handkerchief, in the crook of your arm or on your wrist, or tuck a piece of cotton-wool damped with perfume down your front. Your nostrils, from time to time, will be swept by a most pleasant wave of fragrance.

Magic Spell

Perfume was made much of as far back as 1300 B.C. Cleopatra might have been much less a *femme fatale* without it! During the Crusades, knights returned from abroad with foreign perfumed oils in alabaster containers —and even today's knights usually favour perfume as a gift for their fayre ladyes! In fact, in George III's reign there was an Act of Parliament passed making null and void any marriage contracted under the magic spell of perfume!

However, you cannot buy a perfume by just smelling it in a shop. It is a most extraordinary thing, but the same perfume can smell entirely different on two women. The chemistry of the skin is not the same, and therefore subtly alters the odour.

Therefore you must choose the perfume that exactly expresses your personality. While some women need a light floral scent, especially the very young, and others a slumbrous, musky perfume, at the same time, summer or morning clothes demand a slightly lighter scent than do winter furs, or clothes for late afternoon and evening wear.

How to Buy

When trying a perfume in a shop, test it on the inner wrist. Perfume applied to the pulse-spots gives the best effect. Keep your perfume in the bottle in which you have bought it, and put it somewhere cool and dark. This way the perfume will not evaporate or oxidise. Remember, too, that an extra half-turn to the stopper will help to avoid unnecessary evaporation.

Perfumes are most romantic in their make-up for, besides flowers of all kinds, there are many unusual ingredients from far-off places. Roses from Bulgaria; jasmin and orange blossom from Grasse; neroli from Algeria; narcissi and hyacinth from Holland; frangipani from the West Indies; from Manila the romantic ylang-ylang—which means 'flower of flowers.'

Then there are grasses. Lemongrass from India and Madagascar; citronella from Ceylon; gingergrass from the East Indies; palmarosa from India.

Spices and herbs, too, have their place. Caraway and cardamon from India; cassia, the Chinese cinnamon; cloves from Zanzibar and the Molucca Islands as well; ginger from Jamaica; pimento from Mexico; thyme which grows several thousand feet up in the mountains along the Mediterranean coast; vanilla from Java and Tahiti; lavender from England; rosemary from Spain and Dalmatia.

Lemons, Leaves and Lichen

Citrus oils. The lemon tree came originally from China and India, but now grows mostly in Sicily and California; bergamot grows in Calabria and gives that fresh, sharp tang to the cologne family; lime oil comes from the islands of Dominica and Montserrat in the British West Indies; petitgrain from Paraguay.

Woods, too, are used. Ingredients for scents are extracted from their bark. Sandalwood from the British East Indies, Mysore and from Sandalwood Island; cedarwood flourishes in the huge tracts of North America; rosewood —a tropical tree—comes from Brazil and Honduras.

From leaves and roots come other ingredients. Patchouli came originally from Kashmir but now grows in Singapore and Penang; geraniums are cultivated in Réunion and Algeria; vetivert in the island of Bourbon; orris on the southern slopes of the lovely Florentine hills; eucalyptus in Australia.

Gums and balsams—unlovely in themselves—each play a part towards the final bouquet. Labdanum from Crete; myrrh—a bitter, aromatic gum-resin from the myrrh tree which grows in Arabia and on the Eritrean coast of the Red Sea; galbanum from Persia. Then there are olibanum and benzoin from Southern Arabia and the forests of Siam; balsam tolu from South America and styrax from the dense forests of Asia Minor.

Lichen. Oakmoss grows mostly in Jugoslavia, with Morocco a close second. It has been grown, with some success, in Scotland.

Animal products. Strange but true—four members of the animal kingdom contribute to the making of fine perfumes. There's the Canadian beaver to provide us with castoreum; civet from the civet cat of Abyssinia; musk from the musk deer of Tibet; and the whale which yields precious ambergris. These animal products are primarily valuable as fixatives, for they hold a fine perfume together.

Remembering these things lends even more enchantment to our choice of perfume.

Here are a few suggestions to suit your type and purse:

THE TEEN-AGER should use the light flower and floral bouquet perfumes, such as *Endearing; Le Tréfle Incarnat; Wild Violets; Bocages; Muguet Fleuri; Coeur-Joie; Moss Rose Cologne.*

THE CAREER WOMAN could make her choice from perfumes which have a tang of leather or fern: *Avec Plaisir; Cuir de Russie; Miss Dior; Meteor; Le Dandy; Mischief; Saga; Mink.*

FIGURE TRIMMERS

To limber up each day is important. Jump up and down on your toes as if skipping. Swing each leg backwards and forwards, several times, then the arms

Waist-liner. Stand upright, legs apart, left hand on hip and right hand behind your head. Move trunk slowly to the left, keeping head and legs straight. Return to upright position, change position of arms, and bend other side. Repeat five times each side

Hip-reducer. Sit on the floor cross-legged, hands at sides. Rock slowly from side to side so that pressure is felt on hips. Uncross legs, take weight on your hands, lift hips from ground, lower them with a bump ten times or more daily

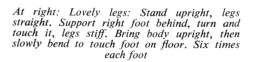

Above: Tone up those tummy muscles. Sit on the floor, knees bent, arms outstretched. Incline slowly backwards, straightening and raising legs. The arms, which will help the balance, should be drawn towards the chest. Keep movements smooth. Ten times

At right: Lovely legs: Stand upright, legs straight. Support right foot behind, turn and touch it, legs stiff. Bring body upright, then slowly bend to touch foot on floor. Six times each foot

Dressing-tables de luxe for next to nothing! An old writing-desk, re-lacquered, makes a wonderful hold-all for toilet articles

An old-fashioned wash-stand has lost its marble top to the kitchen for pastry-making; it has gained a candy-striped skirt to hide a shelf for all your shoes

Right: Cut an edging from flower-prints, glue to the glass of a mirror, cover with varnish

A wooden board on wall-brackets is covered in chintz. The little chests are covered in the same pattern, and an old mirror is rejuvenated with an edging of the same material

Right:
A shelf for a bed-sitting-room is covered with plastic material, and holds a lamp and tobacco-jars containing cotton wool! The bathroom medicine-chest is fixed next to the bookshelves and painted to match

THE OUTDOOR GIRL can find a lovely range of scents nostalgic of the countryside. Perfumes with a tweedy or woody note: *Tweed; Blue Grass; English Fern; Heather; Vivre; French Fern; Visa; Evergreen.*

THE SOPHISTICATED LADY should choose from the heavier, warmer perfumes with a tinge of musk or notes that come from the Far East: *Tabu; Blue Orchid; Midnight; Joy; Padisha or Bambou; Baghari; No. 5.*

WOMAN OF THE HOME should choose according to her type, yet the fresh, light, floral perfumes may suit her best most of the day. For evening and social events, scents with a more sophisticated, modern note: *Golden Age; White Lies; L'Heure Bleue; Passionement; Crêpe de Chine; Gardenia; Gemey; Je Reviens; Great Expectations.*

Many Uses

Perfumed cologne or toilet-water is not only useful for spraying on hair. You can take a piece of cotton-wool soaked in eau-de-cologne around your hair-line after powdering. Give yourself a rub over with toilet-water on a loofah glove after the bath. Part your hair all over on a hot day and dab the partings at half-inch intervals, give it a good massage, then comb it back into place cleaner, fresher and more fragrant. Sprinkle your pillow with raindrops of perfumed cologne, for this has the same effect as the old herbal pillows, bringing drowsiness and sleep. Take it on a journey to wipe sticky hands, or a hot forehead, in summer taking one of the frozen lavenders or colognes with you. Sprinkle some perfumed toilet-water in the water in which you rinse your lingerie, and also a little on the ironing-board when you iron it. Make a cover for your lingerie drawer of rayon, chintz or fine flannel, and sew a tiny triangle of ribbon at each corner. Put a piece of cotton-wool soaked in your favourite perfume in the ribbon triangles. Lay your lingerie on one side of the cover, then fold the rest over the top. Your undergarments are now enfolded in a fragrant nest.

Give your feet a brisk massage with eau-de-cologne after a footbath, especially if you are about to go walking or dancing. Spray perfumed cologne around the hem of your dance-frock, so that its scent rises as you dance. Do not put perfume itself on clothes, for it may mark them. If a room is likely to become heavy with cigarette-smoke, spray a floral

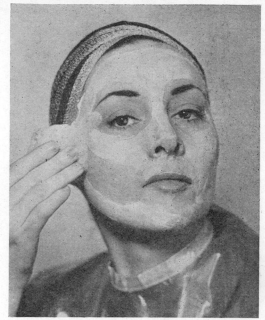

Courtesy of Max Factor

SILKEN SKIN

YOUR complexion-beauty is aided if you use a sponge for applying your cleansing lotion in a 'professional massage' fashion. Use a soft, fine, natural sponge. Cleansing cream, lotion—or soap, if you must—can all be massaged into the skin to do their work much more quickly and thoroughly than if the finger-tips are used. As sponges are so soft, even if you use considerable pressure there is still no danger of irritating the skin.

To steam your face occasionally gives a babylike skin. It is a very old treatment, but simple and effective. After cleaning your face, put on a bathing-cap, and lean over a bowl of steaming water, putting a towel over both head and bowl. Come up for air when you have to, add more boiling water, and steam again. It need not take more than five minutes, all told. Splash your face with cold water or astringent to close the pores.

---

essence on the light-bulbs. The warmth will throw out enough fragrance to combat the stuffy atmosphere. The very perfume-conscious can buy perfumed ear-rings, or even spectacles whose shafts can be perfumed! The inside of your lingerie drawers and cupboards can also be painted with scented lacquer which dries very quickly.

The Question of
JEWELLERY

JEWELLERY has as many trends as fashions in clothes. One year gold adornment is all the rage, another year nothing but bits and pieces belonging to our great-grandmothers are in vogue. Nowadays, there is rather a mixture of everything being worn, which is a help, since very few people can afford to change their jewellery at the slightest whim of La Mode.

There are always our individual tastes to follow, too. One woman will like dramatic jewellery with large semi-precious stones, another will fall for an original design rather than intrinsic value; yet the next girl will want to change all the time, buying an untarnishable choker one moment, and painted wooden beads the next.

It Must Be Becoming

Certain rules must be followed for jewellery to 'do something for you.' While a choker generally looks best on the woman with a long neck, the short-necked girl can also wear one if it appears to suit her face, by choosing one that is not too wide. Then when Fashion sweeps in with long strings of beads or pearls, the tall woman can carry

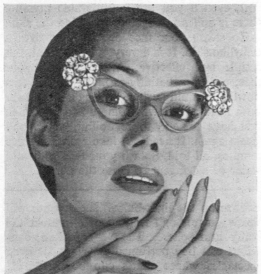

Courtesy Chen-Yu

Clips can be used on your frock, on your belt, your lapel, both to one side of your collar—or on your glasses to give them chic in the evening

them off successfully. The short hand looks best with a delicate *oval* ring rather than a marquise shape, which latter is long enough to emphasise the shortness of the hand, making it look squat! Long rings often look well on long hands. The little hand is not enhanced by large chunks of semi-precious stones, such as cornelian or bloodstone; they ask to have delicate designs. A thin finger will not do justice to a ring with stones arranged vertically; an 'eternity' ring is most suitable, or one more or less of that shape.

In fact, jewellery can do a great deal to flatter a woman.

Flattering the Arm

For instance, if a wrist and arm is below or above the average proportions, it should not be adorned with a bracelet which only exaggerates its defects. A too-slim wrist can be much improved by a wide, close-fitting bracelet, plain or gem-set, whereas a wrist of more generous proportions should wear a bracelet which allows for freedom of action. There must be no suggestion of tightness. Such a wrist may be adorned with one or more very narrow bracelets or a heavy, loose-chain bracelet with charms or coins attached. Another flattering type of bracelet for the not-so-slender arm is composed of chrome baguettes forming a narrow band, set in silver or gilt metal.

Colour is important, and neutral or dark clothes can be high-lighted by a vivid splash of colour to suit the individual.

Brunette. The exotic type can wear the heavy, gilt jewellery, particularly the massive chain type, with heavy gilt medallions. She can also wear the heavy gilt ear-clips, and the more fanciful long earrings. For her, too, are the pieces of costume jewellery—a choker necklace or chunky bracelet of deep red coral or vivid blue-turquoise. All the ruby-red gems, sapphire blue and emerald green.

Redhead (Auburn). She also can wear heavy gilt jewellery, but is most suited by the 'sherry' colours in costume jewellery, such as imitation amber, both opaque and clear, topaz and the bronze tones of gemstones.

Redhead (Ginger). Gilt jewellery again, and the clear tones of green gemstones, or the lighter tones of amethyst and imitation 'cat's eye' stones. Cornelians are especially good.

Blonde. The blonde needs to exercise especial care in the choice of costume jewellery, even more than real. It should be kept to the minimum and to the delicate colours, such as aquamarine, and the sparkle of rhinestones and zircons. Pearls are ideal for her. Vivid colours or heavy jewellery can overshadow her.

Tall Women. A tall woman can carry off jewellery to better advantage than a short, rather 'dumpy' type. She can wear long, chandelier earrings which are now made in very lovely designs, using both metal and imitation stones. Necklaces can be of the choker type, with a good deal of colour massed at the base of the throat.

Short Women. Their jewellery should be

Chunky jewellery shown here is untarnishable gilt, and is suitable for day, evening or even beach wear. The two necklaces are the same size but different design. The ear-clips and dress ornaments are interchangeable

Greatrex, Ltd.

Take your jewellery away with you in a proper case that will prevent scratching, has a place for everything and takes up little room

light and graceful and not overdone in quantity. Sometimes longer necklaces are becoming, but it is easier to decide if the article is tried on. Lapel clips should not be too large, too ornate and should not be worn *too* high on the shoulder.

One into Four

Adaptable jewellery is a help to have in one's jewel-case. For instance, the Coronation suite of jewellery, diamonds and palladium (a metal developed only in recent years) consisted basically of necklace, earrings and bracelet, yet it was so designed that it can be worn as twelve separate pieces. Much less ex-

pensive jewellery is also designed to fit many needs. There are brooches with a section to be swivelled out of sight, so changing the colour. Giant metal brooches with coloured 'refills,' to match various outfits. There are odd earrings, with a similar design but different coloured stones for each ear. The untarnishable metals can be worn as beach jewellery, a fashion that does not have a great deal of support in this country, though it can look very charming!

There are new methods of riveting which result in inexpensive jewellery which is practically indestructible. Fresh rainbow-coloured stones that catch all the shades in a sunbeam.

Yet nearly all modern designs owe something to the past; feather brooches, in gold with delicate fronds sprinkled with precious stones, are an echo from a century that is gone, as are flower-brooches and sunbursts. No doubt Cleopatra wore jewellery that would not look out of place today!

Ring the Changes

However, there is one rule and that is that one really good piece of jewellery can 'dress up' a frock or suit more than a lot of cheap bits and pieces. The sophisticated woman can wear more elaborate jewellery than, for instance, the outdoor girl. The first would lose her *chic* if she did not wear earrings or a smart clip, the second would have her charm spoilt by miniature chandeliers dangling from her ears, and a large paste ornament.

Nevertheless, the clever woman can always find something to suit her, but she will not always be content just with the purchase she has made. A clip can be fastened over the front of a necklace or choker, worn to one side, or in the middle. Earrings will do duty as clips and vice versa. Two strings of beads or pearls in two shades can be twisted together; a necklace can be twisted round a wrist and adorned with a flower in the evening. Necklaces can be worn under collars, over collars; a tiny jewelled pin on one side of an Eton collar. A velvet ribbon can be threaded through a choker and tied in a bow. Jewellery can also form a lovely colour contrast—for instance, a deep blue jumper or frock worn with coral necklace and earrings becomes an '*ensemble.*' Film-stars often find unusual ways of wearing or combining jewellery and should be watched for suggestions you can utilise. Yet, whatever the jewellery wardrobe consists of, it should be taken care of. So many women just dump jewellery in a drawer, or wrap it in tissue paper when they go away. This means that settings are soon damaged, stones lost, the pieces are tarnished and scratched.

Cleaning Your Jewellery

Jewellery, as a general rule, should be kept away from heat, as the settings may become warped, and packed into something soft, such as suede or velvet, which is where a jewel-case is useful.

Diamond brooches and other gem-set jewellery should be washed in soapy water and dried with a soft towel. A fine camel-hair brush dipped in eau-de-cologne will remove any dirt from the crevices. Where the setting has become tarnished or discoloured, a fine polish can be obtained by the application of a paste consisting of jewellers' rouge mixed with ammonia or warm water. The paste should be applied thickly, then rinsed off in water and dried by placing in sawdust or cotton-wool. A final polish may be given by rubbing on a little dry rouge with a clean cloth.

Pearls, real, cultured or simulated, should always be kept from contact with soapy water or other liquid. Pearls tend to dry out of the certain oil they contain and as they are absorbent, the natural oil from the human skin gives the necessary gloss to the stone. Many women sleep in their pearls, real or artificial, so that the necklace improves with age. Pearls should be wiped gently with a soft piece of chamois leather and care should be taken not to leave them in a box with sharply facetted gems which might scratch their surfaces.

Plain gold, silver, platinum and palladium jewellery will require to be washed only in warm water soapy, rinsed in clear warm water and dried with a soft cloth. It may be improved by a final polish with a chamois leather or silk handkerchief. If silver is badly tarnished it may be cleaned with jewellers' rouge or dipped in 'Silver Dip,' obtainable from jewellers' shops. In both cases the silver must be rinsed in warm water and dried with a soft cloth.

Artificial Jewellery

Coral, chalcedony, cornelian, lapis lazuli, etc., in necklets, earrings, rings and bracelets, may all be cleaned by careful washing in warm, soapy water, rinsed and dried and finally polished with a chamois leather.

Paste and other synthetic stones set in costume jewellery should not be washed in soapy water but dipped in methylated spirit or ammonia water, gently brushed and dried with a soft cloth.

Marcasite should not be washed, but brushed with a soft brush and polished with a chamois leather.

Rings should always be removed before immersing the hands in water as constant washing will loosen the settings and abrasives and powders will clog and subsequently damage the jewellery.

RELAX!

IF you see a woman over 40 with a practically unlined face, then you are looking at someone who knows how to relax. A woman who, when possible, bends before the storms of life and lets them pass over her, instead of fighting everything that comes her way, and breaking.

Don't Be a Martyr

So many women are tensed-up martyrs. They haven't a moment, they say. If you had as much to do as they have. . . .! Yet ANYONE can take just a few minutes to let go and relax completely, which sometimes is all that is necessary. It takes the nervous type longer, because they have to learn to let go. They are so often the ones who really could slow down, but have somehow hypnotised themselves into believing that the world would stop if they did.

In the days of ancient Rome, many women famous for their beauty reclined on couches, and got up only for public appearances. While this would be difficult for today's housewife or career woman, at least it shows the emphasis placed not on resting, but on being able to rest, which is a different thing. There are quite a number of women who could take a day in bed occasionally, but the idea of staying in bed if they are not ill savours of positive wickedness to them. Why? What is the virtue of wearing oneself to a shred, and then being irritable with all and sundry? To rest *before* it is necessary is a safety valve against over-tiredness. Nervous tension is nearly always the cause of insomnia. You must put back the force you give out, or your bank of energy will become overdrawn.

Check Your Muscles

To relax, lie on the bed and go over all your muscles to see that they are relaxed, not forgetting your mouth, neck, arms, ankles, tummy. Imagine that you are sinking beneath waves that are lapping over you and it is all very peaceful. Don't wonder if the milk is boiling over, and how you'll pay the school-bills. At the moment they don't count, and when you get up, none of your worries will seem so important, either.

Think of being bathed in a yellow or orange glow from head to foot, an electric glow that is invigorating you. It doesn't cost anything, and it can help. If you are in an office, then 'go limp' for even two minutes during the day, head down, arms like a rag doll. (Two minutes by your watch is a longer time than you think.) Then get up and stretch, arms, legs, neck.

Head Downwards

You can buy a resting-board on which your feet are higher than your head. This takes the strain off the heart, so that it does not have to pump blood up into the brain—the blood just flows down of its own weight. If you are not too large, you can use an ironing-board, propped up on a pouffe or low bed. Or a plank of wood wide enough for you, to the bottom of which some male member of the family has fixed a strap to hold your feet, is also an alternative. Ten minutes a day lying wrong way up should help youth and beauty.

The philosopher Nietsche said, '*No small art is it to sleep; it is necessary for that purpose to keep awake all day*.' Many women sleep late, take a nap after lunch, go to bed early and then wonder why they cannot sleep. Over-tiredness is bad, but that is usually mental tiredness. Real physical tiredness rarely prevents sleep. If you rise at an ordinarily early hour and work hard, then 10 to 20 minutes' complete relaxation after lunch is excellent. Try this exercise if you are the wakeful type:

Lie on your back, as relaxed as possible, with your arms by your side. Take a deep breath, really slowly, by expanding your tummy muscles as far as possible. (If you don't do it this way, it's no use.) When your lungs are really full, hold your breath for as long as possible. You will probably hear your heart beating, but it won't matter; be thankful you can! (In any case, palpitations and an occasional irregular beat are *not* symptoms of heart trouble, if this is one of the worries that keeps you awake!) Now exhale, very gently, through the mouth by pulling in your

BATHROOM BEAUTY

THERE are all sorts of baths, and many ways of taking a bath, and they may as well be made to pay beauty dividends. First of all, when the bathroom is warm and the temperature of the water just right, make *quite* sure that all your troubles are firmly parked *outside* the bathroom door. Make a resolute vow not to think of them, for there is nothing you can do while steeped nearly to your neck in hot water. If you relax, your mind may be so rested that the right solution to anything worrying you may just come to the surface . . . *after your bath!*

* * *

Secondly, put a few light pins in your waves and/or curls, and wear a loose-fitting bathing cap over them. A tightly-fitting cap is apt to make your head perspire, thus spoiling your hairdo.

If your skin is inclined to dryness, use a bath-oil. Also well rub in a body-cream after the bath.

* * *

A lukewarm bath is better for relaxing, if you are inclined not to sleep very well. A pine bath will take away the tired, aching feeling. Do not use cold water after the bath. Go to bed and slowly sip a warm drink. Ordinarily, either splash yourself with cold water afterwards, or use a cold spray. Dry briskly with a warmed towel, then give yourself a quick rub over with a loofah glove or knitted string glove soaked in toilet water or eau-de-cologne, working from your ankles up over your shoulders and down your back to your ankles again.

* * *

A packet of ordinary starch added to the bath will give your skin an alabaster glow. Half a pound of Epsom salts in a very hot bath, to which you constantly add fresh hot water during a quarter of an hour's bask, is reducing. Be sure that you react well to very hot baths, however. Go to bed immediately afterwards, so as not to catch cold. Wrap yourself in a towel, even after drying, as you may still perspire some of the fat away.

* * *

Rub all callouses with well-soaped pumice-stone. Put a thin layer of cold cream or skin food on your face. To soften the water, make some little muslin bags and fill with medium oatmeal, squeezing one out into each bath. They will serve more than once, if you use them afterwards for small quantities of water.

* * *

If you want to ward off an incipient chill, add a small tin of mustard to a quick, hot bath, wrap up well, and go to bed with a hot drink and two aspirins.

Use a stiff nail-brush on all goose-pimply areas, elbows, knees, the backs of your legs, upper arms, and do not forget a back-brush. Try doing a few exercises in the bath, leg-raising, deep-breathing, massaging briskly any surplus fat. Water aids their efficacy.

* * *

And last, throw in a handful of detergent, because it will make wiping round the bath half the trouble, and leave no rim.

Relax!—*continued*

tummy muscles, really slowly, until the whole of your body feels like a collapsed bicycle tyre. That is all. Repeat this once or twice, breathing ordinarily in between the exercises, but do remember to use the tummy muscles as if they were a pair of bellows.

Give Yourself an Order

You will find, once you have mastered the art of relaxing, that if you feel tense, if you have caught sight of yourself in a mirror with a tight mouth and worried eyes, and say sharply to yourself, 'Relax!' that your subconscious mind will get the message and you will automatically slump. The worried look will vanish, your shoulders go down, your arms slacken. It is auto-suggestion and, as it works, you may as well suggest the right things to yourself as the wrong ones. To keep telling yourself, 'Oh, I am so upset,' will not help. Say to yourself, 'I'm going to relax for five minutes, and when I get up I shall feel marvellous!' It's much wiser, and it's true!

Always remember, if you are worried, that *'Tomorrow is another day.'* Anything can happen. An optimistic attitude invites sunshine. Tense folk miss little happinesses for they are too 'strung up' to recognise them.

FOR YOUR PHOTOGRAPH

Your photograph will last through the years, so you must look your best when you have it taken

Courtesy of Max Factor

Would you believe this girl was the same as the one in the bottom photograph? If you are having your photograph taken, blemishes like uneven skin tones, redness and lines can be entirely covered by make-up. To change the appearance of too broad a jaw, a double chin or too wide a nose, highlight and shadows must be applied. A highlight should be three or four shades lighter than the foundation colour, a shadow similarly darker

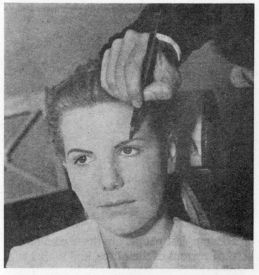

The face must be clean, free from grease. Apply shadows to the jaws, if necessary. Put on foundation, smoothing with a sponge. Then put in other shadows and highlights where necessary with finger or brush. Put on another layer of foundation, then pancake

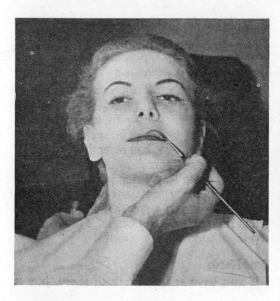

Moisten eyelids sparingly with cream, apply eyeshadow. Powder the entire make-up, buff the face with a puff. Make up the brows with a chisel-point pencil. Add a little line at the corner of the eyes; apply eyelash make-up, then lipstick. Carefully rub the areas that were shadowed and bring out just as much shadow as you wish

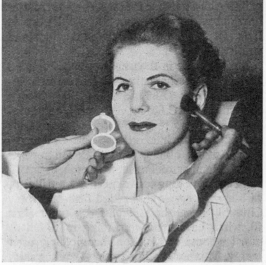

Brush on a little light dry rouge to make the eyes sparkle and model the cheekbones. To refresh make-up after several hours, use a lighter powder. Now you are ready for the camera!

'White Flowers' by Barbara Ringrose, which was exhibited in the Academy after only five years of 'Sunday painting' on the part of the artist

BE A SUNDAY PAINTER

THE happiest people are those who extend the horizons of their lives, and to that end, a really creative, interesting hobby is almost a necessity. So many people, both famous and unknown, duke and dustman, have found that painting at the week-end took them into another world of colour and form, and gave them a sense of achievement. The best of painting as a pastime is that it does not matter how old you are, you can still wield a brush. It is not like athletic pastimes that demand youth and resilience.

Many people in the public eye . . . Winston Churchill as perhaps the best-known artist-in-his-spare-time; Field-Marshal Sir Claude Auchinleck, G.C.B.; Noel Coward, and numerous film stars surprise those who see their paintings by their excellence and craftsmanship. Among others, a well-known novelist and a Member of Parliament each began to paint during a long convalescence from illness, with special easels that stood firm on a bed. Churchill began being a 'Sunday painter' at 40, when he needed something to which to transfer some of his then incompletely used energy. Titian was still painting—and he said, *learning* to paint—at 90 years of age. Grandma Moses whose paintings have been exhibited in, among others, the Vienna State Gallery and the Paris Musée d'Art Moderne, did not begin painting on her little American farm till she was nearly 80. When her neuritis became too painful, she tried to forget it by transferring the country scenes around her on to canvas. She worked out her own method of putting three coats of white over the canvas before she began the picture, which gave it an unusual luminosity. Two of her very small pictures sold for £600 each.

You, too, can work out your own method as you paint. First of all, however, you will want some idea of how to begin. Barbara Ringrose, who began painting in her spare time five years ago, has recently had one of her paintings (reproduced on this page) accepted by the Royal Academy.

These are her suggestions on how to start. They will save you a great deal of time spent on trial and error. Read what she has to say—and then see what you can do!

Your Needs

If you have some money to spare, buy a wooden paint-box complete with a palette that fits inside. The next thing is a small dipper (oilpot) that will fit on to the edge of your palette. A strong sketching easel will suffice for indoor and outdoor work when you begin. Later on, you may find it a help to have a small studio easel as well.

Medium (this is to dilute your paint). It is best to begin by using two parts poppy oil, or linseed oil, with one part turpentine. Turpentine dries quickly, linseed and poppy oil slowly; if you want your picture to dry slowly, use less turpentine. With too much turpentine, however, the colours lose some of their brilliance when dry. This question of medium is one with which you will experiment, gradually finding your own rules. Never paint with half-wet paint. Paint into wet paint or when totally dry.

Paints. Start with only a few paints at first, or you will be confused. Cadmium yellow, lemon yellow, alizarine crimson, permanent blue, cerulean blue, cobalt, light red and burnt sienna, ivory black and titanium white. Also a large tube of flake white, as you will use more white than anything else.

Brushes. One No. 6 hogshair brush; two No. 7; one No. 5; one No. 4; one No. 2; one small palette-knife for mixing paint and scraping off thick colour. If you have a minimum to spend on your equipment, instead of a paint-box you can use a tin box with a lid for the paints, and a flat piece of wood (well sandpapered), or a tin lid for a palette. Do not make the mistake of being too economical about your brushes. If they are too cheap, they will not last, they soon lose their shape and you will spend more in the end.

Canvas. Buy a block of oil canvas paper, about 14 in. by 10 in. or 12 in. by 16 in. Take off one sheet at a time, and drawing-pin it to a board or strong piece of cardboard. It is not worth while buying a canvas until you have had some practice in painting, for they are not cheap, and daler or canvas boards are excellent when you are ready for something a little more solid for work meant to last.

How to Start

Arrange your paints around the edge of your palette, beginning with the lightest colour, around to the darkest. It is, of course, a matter of personal choice how you arrange your colours, but once having decided the way you prefer them to be, always put them in the same order.

Now put a little medium in your dipper, clip it to the edge of your palette, near the end just above the thumb-hole. Have a piece of rag handy, and you are ready to begin the adventure of being an artist.

Subject. Do not be too ambitious to start with. As an idea of a still life with which to commence, choose a bowl, arrange it on a blue ground, and drape an off-white or grey cloth as a background. It should be kept fairly flat, as folds come later, being more difficult. Put in the bowl, perhaps, two red peppers, a small cabbage, a lemon or so. Place the subject where most of the light comes in from the left.

Monochrome. It is good practice to paint your first attempts using three tones of one colour. Place on your palette titanium white and burnt sienna only, obtaining a medium

Noel Coward is a spare-time artist and amusingly refers to his work as 'Touch and Gauguin.' This is 'Harbour at Sunset.' It is a healthy pastime if you have a talent for landscape painting, as it will serve to take you into the fresh air

Photo: Rosemary Macindoe

and light tone of sienna by mixing it with white.

How to Draw

Even if you feel you are unable to draw very well, if you have a sense of colour, you should achieve a happy effect. Many artists draw in the subject with charcoal, and fix it with fixative. You may find it simpler to put a little of the lightest tone on the brush, and very lightly indicate the main outline on the canvas. Use the rag with a little turpentine on it if you wish to alter anything.

Be bold. Attack your subject. Do not worry overmuch about a correct drawing; you will learn a great deal as you continue, absorbing knowledge and hardly realising it.

At first, brush in the darkest tones, follow with the medium tones, and lastly the lightest. Now work up each part of the picture. Stand well back from time to time, studying the subject and the picture for a few moments. Occasionally it is a help to go right away for five minutes. When you look at your attempt with fresh eyes, you will be surprised at the different things that strike your eye.

Avoid too much detail; brush in your first pictures in broad strokes; only lastly add the highlights. Work on the picture as a whole; to spend too much time on small portions of it will tend to detract from the effect. Work in the background as you go along, considering it as part of the picture, not just as a backdrop to the picture.

Now We Progress

For your next attempt, paint the same subject in full colour. Keep your colours bright and clean, do not mix them too much, and forgo too much shading. Later, when you are more adept, you will get excellent dark tones for heavy shadows or dark backgrounds by mixing permanent blue with light red or burnt sienna. You will seldom, if ever, need to use black; it should be avoided as much as possible.

A good brown is made by mixing light red and cerulean blue or cobalt. Each painter has his own ideas about mixing paints, and you, too, will find, after experimenting, that you evolve a method of your own. You will be wise, however, to keep to the basic colours mentioned, at first.

It is helpful to give yourself a time-limit. This keeps you from dabbing in too much detail, and aids you to approach the picture as a whole and broadly painted.

Landscape

If your tastes incline more to landscape than still life, try to find a spot away from the crowd, or you will find that you are considered as a passing entertainment. You can, if you wish, make little drawings and notes, endeavouring to paint the picture when you

REMEMBER

That you do not need a lot of expensive equipment. The thing is to get some paint on to canvas.

Not to be too ambitious to start with. Try simple arrangements, strong, contrasting colours.

That you may not be at all sure at first just whether you are a flower, landscape or portrait painter. You may have to try various styles before you find your own.

To tackle the work boldly, don't dab at it. Don't tell too many of your friends about it until you are fairly sure of your own skill; their comments may dissuade you from continuing!

To take a few lessons if you are interested and can manage to do so.

That you will not know what you can do till you try!

return home. However, until you are more experienced, you will lose atmosphere painting in this way.

Take a piece of cardboard, and cut a hole in it the same shape as your canvas. It will help you to select your scene, and decide how to place it on the canvas. You can also use this method with any kind of picture.

Half shut your eyes from time to time when studying your picture, for this will help you to avoid an excess of detail.

Portrait Painting

This does demand a sense of drawing, which you may have. When you begin, do a number of quick unfinished sketches until you feel confident of making a real beginning.

Transferring Design to Canvas

If you have a sketch that you wish to transfer on to a larger canvas, take a ruler and draw lightly over the sketch, dividing it up into squares. Now divide your canvas into the same number of squares and you will find it quite simple to draw or paint in the design or picture.

Design

Strive for balance in your groupings. If you have some objects on one side of the canvas and an expanse of space the other side, it must be only because that is how you wish to paint it . . . not because you have not bothered to see that each part of the design has some relation to the other. If you are painting a bowl of fruit, then try the effect of a piece of fruit to one side on the table. With a little effort, you will acquire a sense of proportion and balance.

Do not worry about mistakes. The pleasure of using oils instead of water-colours is that you can scrape off what you have already done with a palette-knife and rag, and begin all over again.

Canvases may be used again if reversed on the stretcher, and given a coat of white undercoating paint, matt finish.

To Clean Brushes

Dip in turpentine, wipe off, then wash them with soap and water, working out the paint with the finger-tips, rinse and ease them back into shape. Clean all the paint from your palette each time it is used, then wipe with an oily rag.

'Self Portrait' by Sir Douglas Fairbanks. Portraiture is not everyone's gift, but get out your materials, look in the mirror (or take a photograph) and see what you can do

Varnish

If a finished picture has become dull, or you wish to give it a protection against dust and dirt, cover it with retouching varnish. Use thinly and apply with a clean brush. Leave to dry flat and not in sunlight or draught.

A Final Hint

If you are easily swayed by adverse comment, then do not show your first attempts at painting to your friends. Also paint quietly by yourself. Friends' comments may not only be disturbing, but take away your confidence, which will be one of your most valuable assets!

You will find your observation heightened and visits to art galleries will give you a great deal more pleasure, as you study how each artist puts on the paint, and achieves his effects.

A Word about Frames

It is useful from time to time to try a frame around the picture on which you are working, to judge the balance. Some artists prefer to work with a frame from the beginning, especially with portraits, to avoid a 'crowded' effect.

Here is the delightful and very feminine bedroom,
in pale pink and blue

MATERIALS REQUIRED

Walls and Fixtures. Strawboard, sprigged wallpaper, checked shelf paper, white shelf paper, cardboard, Cellophane, coloured picture for 'view,' Scotch tape, looped braid for picture-rail and plastic rod for curtains.

Living-room Furniture, etc. 5 2-lb. sugar cartons, shallow cardboard box, cardboard, cellulose wadding, glue, material, cord for trimming, cork mat, 2 cotton-reels, 2 knitting-needles, 2 ice-cream cartons, small wad of cork from inside of small screw-cap, plaster of Paris, wire, tinsel ribbon, 6 birthday-cake candles, small medicine bottle, coloured plastic wire, handbag mirror.

Bedroom Furniture, etc. 4 shoe-boxes, 1 1-lb. sugar carton, cardboard, material, cellulose wadding, glue, braid for trimming, cotton-wool, Scotch tape, 4 corks, 3 small handbag mirrors, coloured plastic base of a lipstick, small essence bottle, narrow braid, small wad of cork, 'pearl' hatpin, rat-tail braid, 2 small buttons, hat elastic, plastic rod.

Kitchen Furniture, etc. 8 shoe-boxes, 2 small boxes, cardboard, dress hooks, small rings, metal screw-caps, wire.

NEXT time the children ask 'What can we play at?' on a wet day, let them give a little assistance towards making a collapsible doll's house. It sounds an ambitious undertaking, but nothing could be simpler.

The top secret is that the entrancing furniture is ingeniously made from clean white cardboard shoe-boxes of uniform size, and sugar cartons. (Most shoe-shops will give away empty boxes.) The three cardboard walls are 'hinged,' and so can be folded away when not in use. On one side they are covered with red-and-white shelf paper for the kitchen, on the other with pastel sprigged wallpaper which does duty for either living-room or bedroom. So, since we give directions for

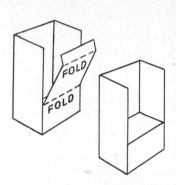

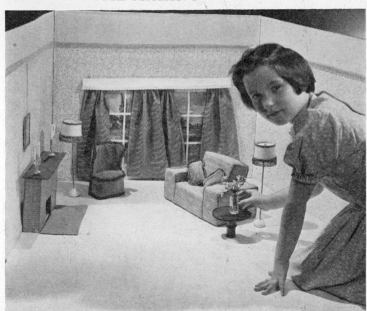

Above is the framework for the bedroom chair made from a sugar carton. Below, a 'fire' is lit in the 'brick' fireplace

The same framework furnished as a lounge

making furniture for all three rooms, it will depend entirely on the whim of the small proprietors which is to be the room of the moment.

Most materials—or substitutes—should be available in the average home, with perhaps the exception of the following: strawboard, Scotch tape, looped braid, plastic-covered wire, plastic-covered rod for curtains, thin cardboard; but these are obtainable for only a few shillings.

Walls and Fixtures

The strawboards used each measure 31 in. wide by 25 in. deep, but there are two or three standard sizes.

The boards are hinged together with Scotch tape. Lay them flat on the floor, side by side, allowing at least a quarter of an inch between each. Join the edges with cross strappings of tape, and over these stick a vertical strip the length of the 'walls.' Repeat for the other side.

Cover the boards on one side with sprigged or small-patterned paper (not over hinges) to within 5 in. of the top. Cover the remaining inches with plain white paper for a frieze, and stick braid over the join in the paper to serve as a picture-rail. Choose braid with a loose loop on which you can hang pictures and mirrors. Turn the boards over and cover with the checked shelf paper. A frieze is optional.

Note. The wallpaper can either be pasted on or fixed with Scotch tape round the edges. Finally, cover joins in the boards on both sides with tape and bind all edges.

The size of the windows depends on the picture and the amount of material available for the curtains. Cut the picture in half and stick each half on a piece of cardboard. Cover with Cellophane and cross strappings of cardboard about a quarter of an inch wide to suggest panes. Fix to the centre wall with tape.

Four rings to hold curtain rods are fixed to the wall with Scotch tape threaded through them; one at each side of the windows. It is advisable to have a rod for each window.

The pelmet is a strip of cardboard about 1½ in. deep, edged with braid. Fasten it to the

This is another corner of the lounge, which can of course have the furniture moved about to suit its small owner

The standard lamps are knitting needles with inverted ice-cream containers as shades. A charming colour-scheme would be brick and gold with a touch of sapphire blue

lose wadding, bedspread is of same material as bed-covering, frilled and trimmed with braid.

Dressing-table. Materials: 1 shoe-box, material, 4 corks, glue.

Mount the box on the four corks. Make a frill and gum this round the top of box. Cover the lid with material and place on top.

The **triple mirror** consists of three small handbag mirrors attached together with strips of Scotch tape, leaving a narrow space between the mirrors to allow them to 'fold.'

A miniature **mirror** and **brush and comb set** can be bought cheaply from one of the multiple stores. **A powder bowl** can be made from a coloured plastic base of a lipstick container with a tiny ball of cotton-wool with a bow on top.

Bedside Table. Made with strong white cardboard (four pieces 5 by 3 in., and two pieces 3 by 3 in. for top and bottom) joined with tape. Decorate with a flower cut from the chintz that covers the chair and stick rat-tail braid round the front $\frac{1}{2}$ in. from the edge.

wall, just above curtain fittings, with Scotch tape along top only, so that it can be lifted up for curtains to be changed.

THE BEDROOM

Bed. Materials: 1 shoe-box, covering material, cellulose wadding, glue, braid for trimming, cotton-wool, Scotch tape.

Note. 1-in. turnings must be allowed on material. This applies throughout.

Cover the outside of the box with material, sticking it down inside with the tape. This, inverted, becomes the base of the bed. For the bedhead, pad the inside of the lid, cut down, with cotton-wool to the depth required and cover with material. Pull it tightly and stick down with tape.

Mark the back of the bedhead cardboard with dots in diamond formation and sew a couple of stitches on each dot, pulling the needle right through the cotton-wool to the covering material and then back again. Secure tightly to give the padded effect.

Cover a thin piece of cardboard to fit over the back of bedhead, and sew on. Glue bedhead to one end of the shoe-box. Gum on narrow braid to cover stitching.

Mattress and pillow are stuffed with cellu-

The modern wing-chair and chesterfield are made from sugar cartons

Before sticking on the braid, pencil in where it is to go on the doors and cover the line with a tracing of gum. Stick the braid to this, to give a panelled effect.

Lamp. A small essence bottle, with a lamp-shade made of a pleated circle cut from thin cardboard 5½ in. in diameter. Stick a suitable trimming round the edge and round the centre. Push a 'pearl'-headed pin through the centre of the cardboard and then through a little cork wad with a good smear of glue on it. This is pushed up against the shade to hold it in place. The pin is then stuck firmly into centre of bottle-cork.

Wardrobe. Materials: 2 shoe-boxes, Scotch tape, rat-tail braid, buttons, hat elastic, plastic rod.

Stick two shoe-boxes together with tape. Cut off the rims of the lids, neaten with tape and stick on to the outside of each box to form doors. Decorate each with a flower cut from the chintz, and rat-tail braid to give the effect of panels. Buttons and elastic loops fasten the doors.

Fix a shelf of cardboard near the top with tape for dolls' hats. Make a hole near the centre partition just below the shelf, slip the rod through and attach to sides of boxes with the Scotch tape. Make tiny hangers from wire covered with white tape.

Chair. Materials: 1-lb. sugar carton, chintz material, cellulose wadding, cotton-wool, braid for trimming.

Cut the lid off and slit down the two front side corners to within about 2 in. of the bottom of the carton (see diagrams on page 275). Then fold back the loose front panel to join the seat and fold again 2 in. beyond the front crease. This will enable you to tuck the further inch down the back of the seat. Before tucking it in, smear it with glue to keep it in place. Slightly bend the top front corners of chair.

Pad, cover and quilt the front of chairback as for bedhead. Stick a piece of material across the lower front of the chair, and also the seat. Cut out a piece of cardboard to cover the whole of the back and sides for added strength. Cover with material and slip-stitch into position. Trim with braid to disguise seams.

THE LIVING-ROOM

Chesterfield. Materials: 4 2-lb. sugar cartons, cardboard, cellulose wadding, glue, material to cover, cord for trimming.

One box forms the seat, one the back, and two on their sides, the arms. Pad the seat, lower front, back and top by gluing on strips of cellulose wadding. Glue wadding over arm-tops and down fronts.

To cover, place a piece of material over the seat and lower front, glue it over the padding

The very up-to-date kitchen has red and white patterned wallpaper; red and white check gingham-covered seats; hygienic white fitments with scarlet borders

and stick the overlapping pieces down the sides and under the box. Now cover the two arms in the same way, but to strengthen their outer sides slip-stitch a piece of material-covered cardboard to the covers. Cover the back piece.

Assemble pieces (see sketch on page 276), stitching seat to arms and back to seat. Cut out a piece of cardboard to cover the whole of the back of chesterfield and arms. Cover with material and slip-stitch into position.

Slightly tilt the back to rest on the seat. Trim all joins with cord. Neaten the underneath with a piece of material-covered cardboard slip-stitched into place.

Make cushions as required.

Table. A cork mat mounted on two cotton-reels which have been stuck together, the entire 'piece' being stained.

Fireplace. Made from a shallow cardboard stocking-box. From the lid cut an opening for the fire. Put the lid on the box and cover the front and sides with brick-patterned paper. Make a mantelshelf by sticking a strip of stained wood (or cardboard) across the top.

The fire is devised from a few twigs and red Cellophane paper cut to represent flames. The hearthrug is a strip of felt.

Standard Lamps. Made from knitting-needles with knobs at one end. The shades are small ice-cream cartons inverted and trimmed with fringe and braid. The knitting-needle is stuck down the middle of the carton. The shade is held in place with glue. Make a base of plaster of Paris and, before it is quite hard, insert the needle.

Birthday-cake candles in a branched frame of wire covered with tinsel ribbon make the **candelabra.**

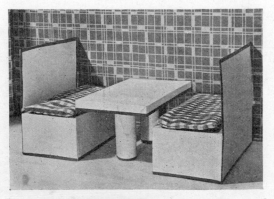

This attractive little dining corner would seat four

The **vase** is a medicine bottle; the **flowers** are of gaily-coloured twisted plastic wire. The **mirror** is a handbag mirror, mounted on a slightly larger piece of cardboard, the extra width serving as a base for the gummed-on braid edging. String for hanging is fixed down the back with Scotch tape.

Wing Chair. Materials: 1 2-lb. sugar carton, cardboard, cellulose wadding, glue, velours or plush material, braid for trimming.

On the carton, mark in pencil the shape of the wing chair (see diagram on page 276) and cut away, leaving only the frame.

Pad and cover the inside of the back and stick down the turnings at the back. Cover the lower front sides. Neaten edges by turning under and gumming firmly.

Cut a shape of thin cardboard to fit the back of the chair and little wing sides and cover with material. Cut in cardboard a seat to fit, pad and cover. Sew seat to lower front of chair, having filled in the hollow underneath with wadding. Sew on back and trim with braid at all edges.

THE KITCHEN

Cupboards and fitments are made entirely from white shoe-boxes, and it is essential to get six boxes exactly the same size.

Broom Cupboard. For the door, cut rim off lid of a shoe-box, bind three sides of the lid with red Scotch tape (to give the effect of a painted border) and hinge to the box with transparent tape. A shelf can be attached with strappings of tape. Sew on a red button for handle, and back with tape.

A loop of hat elastic attached to the side of the cupboard fastens it.

Sink Unit. Turn a box on long side. Cut a hole on top and fit in a white soap-dish as sink. Cut off rim of lid, using a short rim as a strut in front of sink to prevent sagging. Stick tape all down the back of the support with 2 in. left at both top and bottom to attach to the box. Cut the lid in half to make two doors. Trim a little off each end for a good fit. Bind the edges to match the broom cupboard and other units, and hinge to cupboard with tape. Buttons and loops of elastic make fasteners.

The next unit and the one opposite are plain boxes serving as work units. Trim the lids, bind with red tape and stick on.

Cooking Unit. Divide box into two com-

(Continued on page 281)

SPACE TO LET

A room can have its furniture arranged in a way that leaves no space to spare. With the arrangement slightly altered, another few feet of walking room is achieved, as in the placing of these two bunk beds

Above right:
Once the home handyman (or woman) has learned how to make shelves and drawers, there are many ideas for utilising space usually allowed to go to waste. This sprung mattress is placed on a cut-down chest of drawers at one end, with a fitment of two more drawers supplying the rest of the base

A dining-corner is cosy both for eating and writing letters, or even sitting, feet up, with a good book. This fitment is easy for the home carpenter to put together and yields a good deal of storage space

No Fresh
Flowers?

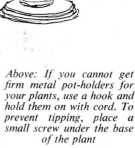

Flowers are sometimes beyond the reach of our purses, but plants (which can look dull) can be so arranged that they adorn a room as cheerfully as hothouse blooms. Use trailing Tradescantia, Begonia Rex with warm pinky leaves, or satin-leafed rubber plants. Try fixing them to a lamp-standard as shown on the right

Tall sprays of Ruscus are arranged with Cape Gooseberries in an ordinary flower-pot. Cord in the same warm tangerine shade as the Cape Gooseberries is wound round the pot. Stand it in a window, and give a treat to the passers-by. Wind braid or cord around any of your pots instead of using a bowl

Above: If you cannot get firm metal pot-holders for your plants, use a hook and hold them on with cord. To prevent tipping, place a small screw under the base of the plant

A mirror is always a happy background for flowers or plants. The iron wall-brackets hold pots or trailing Philodendron or ivy sprays; there is a rubber plant on the wall-table. If you do not care for the large-leaved plants, try a copper preserving-pan filled with autumn leaves of all shades of bronze, red and green, arranged with Cape Gooseberries and yellow Immortelle

Try These Ideas

HOW
to
MEND
a
FUSE

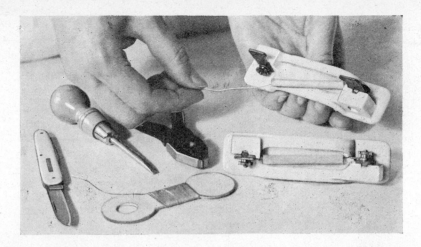

IT is very irritating when the lights fail at a time when it is too late to ring up the local electricity authority. Everyone ought to be able to mend a fuse, although it is unsafe to use some makeshift, such as a hairpin, when there is no fuse-wire in the house. So, first things first: see that there is always some 5-ampere fuse-wire on hand.

The first thing to notice is whether only one lamp is affected, or several lamps. If the former is the case, then it is almost certainly a burnt-out lamp. In a clear lamp the fracture of the lamp filament can be easily seen and, as you will have one or two lamps in reserve, it will be a simple matter to replace it.

If the lamps are not at fault, examine the fuse-box. In some types, the fuse-wire is visible and a break can be seen at a glance. In others it is necessary to pull out the china bridges and examine the wire at the back. *Before doing anything at all, turn off your main switch.* Use a torch or a candle to see what you are doing.

If the fuse-box is in order, but no lights can be obtained, yet there is light in neighbouring houses, it is possible that one of the company's fuses has gone. These are in sealed cases above the mains and may be opened only by the maintenance staff of the authority.

When you have found the broken fuse-wire, unscrew it, and be sure you get all the ends of wire out. Now take a piece of fuse-wire, wind it round the screw and screw it down *tightly.* See that this is in a clockwise direction, otherwise the tightening will push the wire away from the terminal. Fuses vary slightly; some are threaded through an asbestos tube, some go straight down a porcelain channel, others round a porcelain centre. Take your fuse-wire, stretch it in its place and wind it round the other screw. Screw down tightly and break off the wire close to the screw. Put back the china bridge, turn on the main switch, and all should be well. Look at the other fuses, however, in case both positive and negative fuses have gone.

Doll's House—*continued from page 278*

partments (cooker and cupboard) with cardboard down the centre. Black screw-top bottle caps make hot-plates on top of the 'oven.' Cut holes the size required, insert caps and fix down with tape.

Remove rim of lid, and cut lid into two pieces for doors. Cut to 1-in. strips, edge with red and fix one on extreme left for oven switches, and one in front of partition between doors. Bind doors with red tape and fasten with red buttons in the usual way. Sew on red buttons (different from door handles) for oven switches, backing them with tape.

Dresser. Fix a box with doors and strut,

finish as for sink unit. Make two small boxes into the top cupboards. Place in position, backing the whole with cardboard.

Table. Made from a shoe-box lid bound with red tape gummed on to two cardboard tubes from toilet rolls.

Seats. Shoe-boxes turned upside down with a piece of cardboard bound with red stuck on to make a high back. The arrangement for hanging pans by the cooker consists of a strip of cardboard attached by two dress hooks sewn on to curtain rings taped on to the wall. The pans hang on reversed hooks, and consist of metal screw-caps with red-bound wire twisted round and extending into a looped handle.

COLOURFUL
COVERINGS

WHEN you have an old chair that needs reseating, try using American cloth in a gay shade and paint the chair to match or contrast. The most expensive modern chairs have seats of plain or striped webbing, an idea from Scandinavia. Or old nylon stockings are strong for everyday use. Tacks and plywood are the only other things you need.

You will need 12 yards of strong 2½-in. webbing. Try royal blue or chrome yellow. In order to get the webbing taut and firm, you will have to use a small block of wood to pull it over very tightly (it needs a strong arm for this) so that it will not sag. The tacking must be very secure. A few shillings should cover the cost

Use one yard of oil-cloth or American cloth 36 in. wide, (wrong side). If the right side has already been worn, it will not matter. It will use it up, and be economical at the same time. Tack strips under the seat rail, very firmly, then thread the other strips through, pulling them taut and tacking the end firmly under the seat

This chair has a new strong seat made from 32 old nylon stockings. The colours can be left a harmony in beiges and browns, or you can boil the stockings till they are all one shade, or dye them. The seat should be a padded one of the 'drop in' type. Tack the stockings very firmly under the inner edge, then weave them closely in and out. Finish off the inner edge with a strip of thin plywood tacked over the stockings so that they do not fray

This little chair was a symphony in two shades of pink to use in the children's nursery. Altogether it took 13 yards of webbing, obtainable at any shop. The seat was a piece of $\frac{1}{2}$-in. plywood cut to the shape of the chair and then padded. The small padded back was covered to match. Different combinations of colours can be used: beige and brown; scarlet and cream; dark and pale green; or just one shade picking up a colour in the room in which it is to be used

MAKING THE FURNITURE FOR
A BACHELOR FLAT

(Illustrated on pages 18–19)

BEDSIDE CUPBOARD

Top and Bottom, A and B, are 15 in. by 8 in. by ½ in. with a shoulder joint, C, cut at each end.

Two Sides, D and E, are 28 in. by 8 in. by ½ in. and are glued and nailed to A and B with thin oval nails.

Back, F, is a piece of thin plywood glued and screwed into position.

Door, G, is a frame which just fits into the front of the cupboard and is made from wood 1 in. wide by ½ in. thick with mitred corners, and is faced both sides with thin plywood or composition board, glued and nailed to the frame with small panel pins. The door should be hinged on the edge farthest from the bed. A small knob is screwed to the door, also a ball catch.

Shelves, H. are ⅜ in. thick and should be just wide enough to stop the door level with the cupboard front; they rest on thin strips, I.

LINEN TRAY TO FIT UNDER BED

Sheets, blankets and personal linen may be kept in this. *Front and Back*, A and B, 5 ft. by 7 in. by ½ in. *Two Ends*, C and D, 3 ft. by 7 in. by ½ in. *Corner Blocks*, E, 7 in. by 2 in. by 2 in. Screw together as shown, then fit *two partitions*, F and G.

Bottom, H, ¼-in.-thick plywood screwed in position is best (but thin tongued and grooved boards can be used). Rubber-tyred castors are screwed through the bottom of the tray into E.

Handle, I, is a piece of wood 4 ft. by 2 in. by 1 in. with a strip 1 in. wide and 3 ft. long cut from one edge; screw this to the front of the tray (with heads of screws inside tray). If you wish, three thin plywood lids can be hinged to cover each compartment.

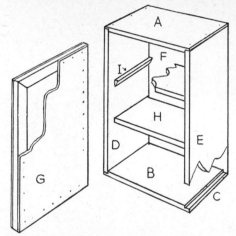

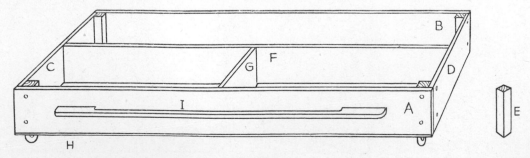

TABLE AND WALL BOX-SEAT

You can make more than one
of these tables if your room is
a large one

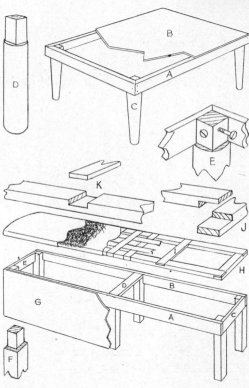

TABLE

Make a frame, A, 2 ft. by 2 ft. 8 in., using wood $1\frac{1}{4}$ in. by 1 in. thick. Fasten to the frame with glue and panel pins a sheet of $\frac{1}{4}$-in.-thick plywood or $\frac{1}{4}$-in.-thick plastic sheet, B (which can be obtained from most large timber merchants—is made in a variety of colours and is undamaged by hot plates, etc.). *Legs*, C, about 15 in. high, can be purchased ready made, or you can make chunky ones from rolling pins, D. Screw the legs into the corners of the table-top, as E.

WALL BOX-SEAT (in which may be stored brooms, shoes, etc.)

Top Frame, A, B, length is $\frac{1}{2}$ in. less than you will want your finished seat, 3 in. by $\frac{3}{4}$ in. C, D, E, 16 in. by 3 in. by $\frac{3}{4}$ in.—nail them firmly together. *Legs*, 15 in. by $2\frac{1}{2}$ in. by $2\frac{1}{2}$ in. Cut a $\frac{3}{4}$-in. shoulder joint as shown 3 in. from the top, F. Screw through the frame into the legs; also glue them. *Front and Ends*. A sheet of thin plywood or composition board, 15 in. wide, G, should be glued and nailed in position with panel pins (or you can just use curtain material frilled on a tape and tacked along the top edge).

Padded Seat. Make a frame, H (using wood 2 in. by 1 in.), the length and width of your box, with a cross piece, I, about every 16 in. Make half-lap joints at the corners, J. Cross-pieces should be jointed, K. Glue and screw together. Upholsterer's webbing is then interlaced tightly across the top of the frame, taken over the edges and tacked underneath. Over this a piece of hessian is stretched and tacked to the top of the frame (or you can just use thin plywood instead of webbing and hessian). On this is spread a 2-in. layer of upholsterer's hair (obtainable at upholsterer's). *Be sure to pad the frame edges.*

Then stretch over the covering-material. Tack it with a turned-in hem underneath frame. Two small blocks of wood, 2 in. long by 1 in. by $\frac{1}{2}$ in., can be screwed underneath the front of the seat frame and 1 in. from the front edge; these will stop the seat sliding forward.

BOOKSHELVES AND CUPBOARDS

You can either stain and polish your hand-made furniture, or paint it cream, combined with another attractive colour

BEDSIDE BOOKSHELF

Top Shelf, A, should be 9 in. wide by ⅝ in. thick and the length of your divan bed (when made with bedclothes) from the foot to the wall at the head, and a shoulder joint, H, should be cut at each end.

Ends, B and C, are 9 in. by ⅝ in. and the height is 13 in. above the top of your bed. Nail and glue them to A, as shown, with oval nails.

Shelf, D, is 9 in. by ⅝ in.—its length is the distance between B and C, and it should be nailed 10 in. below A. A *strip*, E, 5 in. by ⅝ in., is nailed in the position shown to support D. A *panel*, F, 10 in. by 9 in. by ⅝ in., is fitted at the bed-head end of the shelves.

Back, G, can be thin plywood or composition board, or you can just use the wall of your room.

BED-END CUPBOARD

Top and Bottom, A and B, are 9 in. wide by ⅝ in. thick and their length is equal to the over-all width of your bed plus the bedside bookshelves.

Ends, C and D, are 9 in. by ⅝ in., and the same height as those of the bookshelves. Assemble as shown.

Shelf, E, is 9 in. by ⅝ in., and is nailed 10 in. below A.

Centre Partition, F, is 9 in. by ⅝ in., and is nailed between E and B.

Back, G, is thin plywood or composition board nailed and glued to A, B, C, D.

Doors, H.—Make four frames to fit snugly in front of the cupboard, using wood 1½ in. wide by ½ in. thick. Mitre the corners, I, then nail thin plywood or composition board to both sides of the frames (use panel pins and a smear of thin glue). Glass-paper the edges level when finished, and screw small knobs into the frames. Then hinge the doors to C, F and D respectively.

Shelves, J, ½ in. thick, rest on two strips nailed to cupboard sides and should be just wide enough to allow doors to fit level with the cupboard front.

* * *

NOTE.—These measurements can be varied to suit individual needs. All nail heads should be sunk with a nail punch and the holes filled with plastic wood.

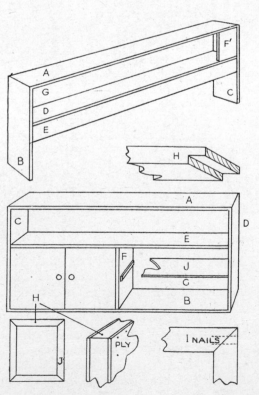

COOKING-CUPBOARD AND DRESSING-TABLE

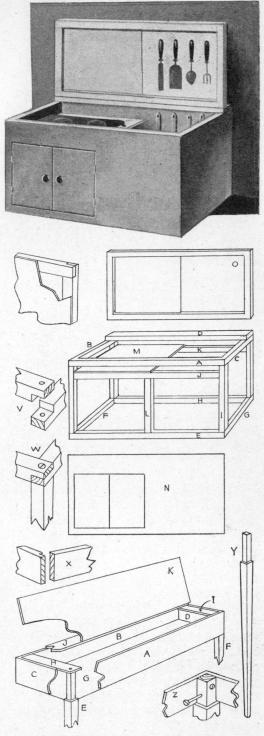

COOKING-UNIT CUPBOARD

Framework. A, 36 in. by 1 in. by 1 in. B and C, 15 in. by 1 in. by 1 in. A, B and C are joined with half-lap joints, see V. D is a board, 36 in. by 2 in. by 1 in., which is fixed on top of B and C. E and H, 36 in. by 1 in. by 1 in., and F. and G, 15 in. by 1 in. by 1 in., are joined at the four corners with half-lap joints.

Four Legs. I, 21 in. by 1 in. by 1 in., are placed one at each corner of the upper and lower frames and are held in position by a thin screw $2\frac{1}{2}$ in. long which passes through the centre of the half-lap joint and into the end of the leg, see W. This also applies to the back board, D, of the top frame, which has no joint: 3-in. screws should be used here. Drill the holes for screws in the frames but not in the legs. J and K, 34 in. by 1 in. by 1 in., are screwed into position shown, 4 in. below the top frame. L, 16 in. by 1 in. by 1 in., is screwed in the centre between J and E. A piece of plywood covered with asbestos, M, is screwed on top of J and K—on this rests your cooking unit. The front, back and two ends are covered with thin plywood or composition board. N shows how the front is covered.

Lid. Make a frame to fit on top of A, B and C and in front of D. Use wood $\frac{3}{4}$ in. thick, $1\frac{1}{2}$ in. wide—half lap corners and glue them. Cover frame with plywood $\frac{1}{4}$ in. thick, line the half of the lid which covers cooking unit with asbestos; fix clips for cooking implements inside lid. The lid is hinged to D and may have a folding stay at one end if desired.

Doors are made in the same way as the lid and are hinged in the opening below the cooker: buckets can be stored here. A row of hooks screwed into K and J are for pots and pans. The cooking unit rests on M, and a flexible pipe passes through a hole in the side nearest floor gas-tap.

DRESSING-TABLE

Front and Back, A and B, 36 in. by $\frac{1}{2}$ in. by 5 in.—cut shoulder joint at each end, as X. *Ends,* C and D, 12 in. by $\frac{1}{2}$ in. by 5 in. Glue and nail A, B, C, D together, using $1\frac{1}{2}$-in. panel pins. *Legs,* E and F, 32 in. by $1\frac{3}{4}$ in. by $1\frac{3}{4}$ in. Cut a shoulder on two sides only at the top of each leg, $4\frac{1}{2}$ in. down by $\frac{1}{2}$ in. deep, Y.

(Continued on page 300)

Make Your Own
GARDEN FURNITURE

IF you have a garden, you probably have a favourite corner in which to sit. It may have the best view, be shielded from observation, or just be a shady nook. Instead of dragging out an old deck-chair, and putting your book on the grass, make yourself this comfortable table and reclining-chair. This is the way.

Table. Cut two lengths of wood as A. Screw to these, 3 in. from each end, the four leg pieces, B, then screw the two horizontal supports, C, in the position shown. Now drive a piece of broomstick through the holes in the legs with 1 in. projecting on the outsides. Fix these as shown with a long thin nail driven through the edge of the leg as shown at D.

Finally, cut nine lengths of boxwood, 20 in. long by 4 in. wide and any reasonable thickness, E, and nail them to the supports, A. There should be a space of $\frac{1}{4}$ in. between each piece and they should, when fixed, project 1 in. all round.

Garden Chair. The main parts (two each of A, B, C, D and E) are cut from wood 4 in. wide by $\frac{3}{4}$ in. thick. The slats for the seat and back, F and G, are cut from old boxwood about $\frac{3}{8}$ in. thick and 3 in. to 4 in. wide. To assemble the seat, first screw the two side pieces, A, to the two pieces B, using screws at least $1\frac{3}{4}''$ long, then nail on your slats, F, to make the seat.

Next, bolt the two uprights, D, to the two sides, A, using bolts $2\frac{1}{2}$ in. long by $\frac{3}{8}$ in. diameter, K. (Use washers under the bolt heads and wing nuts.) Nail back slats, G, to uprights, D. The two legs, C, should then be screwed to

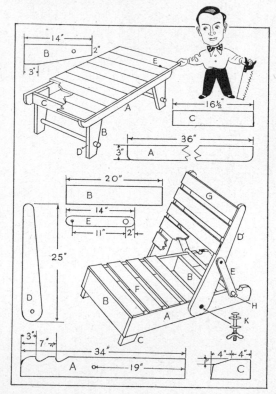

the inside corners of the seat. (See diagram.)

Then bolt the two supports, E, to the uprights, D (bolts $2\frac{1}{2}$ in. by $\frac{1}{4}$ in. with wing nuts and washers), and finally a length of broomstick, H, should be driven through the holes in the lower ends of the supports with a projection of 1 in. on the outsides; fix the stick with a thin nail driven through the edge of E.

Paint top of table and slats of chair in white, the rest of wood-work in another colour.

PERIODICAL EXAMINATION OF YOUR HOME

*'A stitch in time' can save a good deal of work or money
later on*

HUMAN nature being what it is, the hardest task to do is the simple one that may be done at any odd time. A piece of work urgently required is finished off, no matter how busy we may be, but the job we promise ourselves we will do next when we have half an hour on hand is the one that will be found still undone a month or two hence. The best way to overcome this human weakness is to fix a limit of time for such a task, provided of course it is worth the doing, and treat it as a matter of urgency to get it done within that time.

Of all such jobs, probably the easiest to postpone are the little odds and ends that need attention in the home. The screw working loose, the rusty piece of metal which needs repainting, the tile calling out to be re-fixed, the tap constantly telling us by its drip that a new washer is required.

If these things, seen every day, are neglected, what of those unobserved defects, the decayed wood, the damp patch, the broken slate, the cracked pipe. Only when the storm has come and the effect has become serious do we notice them at all unless we have formed that admirable habit of examining the house periodically, with the object, not exactly of looking for trouble, but of looking for *likely causes of trouble*.

Remedy Defects in Early Stages

It will be agreed that money and inconvenience can be saved by discovering and remedying defects in their early stages, but the difficulty for the person without much technical knowledge of building is what to look for. Here are a few suggestions.

THE EXTERIOR
Slates, Tiles and Chimney Stacks

The exterior is the part that has to resist the full force of wind and weather, and is therefore most likely to show parts dislodged or decayed and to cause damage if left in disrepair.

Commence at the top, for a peck of troubles can lie here unheeded. The slates or tiles—are any cracked, broken, slipped out of place or missing altogether? Does the ridge want pointing? And the chimney stacks, do they show any cracks, or are there any open brickwork joints to be pointed? The easiest place for damp to get in is at the junction of two kinds of material, where, for instance, the roof tiles join the chimney stacks. Such joints are generally covered with lead or zinc, the edges of the metal being tucked into joints of the brickwork and the other edges lying on or under the tiles. See if the lead or zinc has drawn out of the mortar joint; if so, water will assuredly trickle down inside. Also see if the leadwork needs dressing down flat on the tiling.

Are the Gutters Choked ?

Next examine the gutters—the roof is planned for water to flow into them, so if they are choked with leaves or an accumulation of dirt, or if creepers have grown over and into them, they will not function, and instead of passing on the water into the drains they will probably let it run down the walls and soak them as no driving storm would do. Birds take a delight in nesting at the top of a rainwater pipe (the vertical pipe leading from gutter to drain), and a nest will completely choke a pipe.

Some lengths of the eaves gutters may have dropped, and if so the rainwater will flow away from and not towards the outlets.

Cracked Gutters or Rainwater Pipes

It is worth while to see if any sections of the gutters or rainwater pipes are cracked. Such cracks will probably be on the side towards the house, not only because of the natural perversity of things, but because the casting of the pipe is weakest on the rough

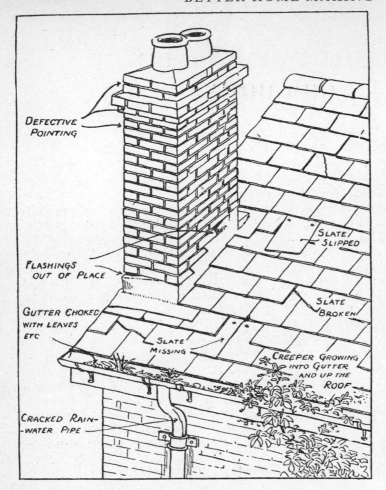

DEFECTIVE POINTING

FLASHINGS OUT OF PLACE

GUTTER CHOKED WITH LEAVES ETC

CRACKED RAIN-WATER PIPE

SLATE MISSING

SLATE SLIPPED

SLATE BROKEN

CREEPER GROWING INTO GUTTER AND UP THE ROOF

The first place to begin is at the top—with the roof. Here you see the main points likely to be in need of attention

sive, and particularly if they are near the corners of the building, the opinion of an expert is desirable. Brickwork should not get out of upright or develop bulges; if they are noticed, the advice of a person who thoroughly understands building construction should be sought, for if the defect has not gone far, it is often possible to effect a small repair and secure the wall from further movement.

Dampness

Dampness or damp stains should be looked for. Wet rooms are most unhealthy, also dampness in building materials hastens their decay, wood rots, brick and stone crumble, and iron rusts. Apart from defective gutters and rainwater pipes previously mentioned, frequent causes of damp walls are:

(1) Earth banked up for garden beds too high, reaching above the damp-proof course (a course of material such as slates or bitumen impervious to water) intended to keep the moisture from the earth rising in the substance of a wall. In brick-faced walls the position is shown by a wider joint than the others.

(2) Shrubs too close to a wall, especially around rainwater pipes.

(3) Open joints in pavings against walls, letting water run in without an opportunity of escaping.

(4) Cement plinths or skirtings intended to keep the bottom of the walls dry, but which have worked away from the face of the wall, so that water trickles down behind, leaving the walls damper than if there were no cement work at all. Such skirtings should always

part which the builder sets against the wall, also pipes do not get so well painted at the back.

How to Tell Whether a Pipe is Whole

A tap on the pipe with a penknife or anything else handy will indicate by the ring or the dull sound if the pipe is whole. Do not forget to look at the shoe which discharges over the gully: is it choked and is there a collection of leaves blocking the gully? The nails holding the pipe to the wall sometimes get drawn away, and then in time the pipe will drop.

Look at the Walls

Now give an eye to the walls and watch particularly for cracks, joints of brickwork to be pointed, any bulging parts and signs of dampness. Slight cracks may not be serious; all buildings settle down, and initial cracks are hard to avoid, but if the cracks are exten-

finish at a brick joint and be 'tucked' into the joint at least $\frac{3}{4}$ inch.

Blocked Gratings

Gratings or airbricks are usually to be found near the ground. They serve the useful purpose of admitting a current of air to the space under the lowest floor. If there were no ventilation, dry rot would probably appear in the floor timbers. The gratings readily become blocked; they should be kept clear of all obstruction.

Painting

The painting of woodwork and ironwork, looked upon by many chiefly for its decorative value—giving the house a well-cared-for look—or the reverse, has the very practical use of preserving the material to which it is applied. If this purpose is considered, attention will be given to the parts which do not show equally with those which all may see. If paint is much worn, or the material has perished, its protective value will have been impaired, and decay or rust will follow as a certainty.

Where to Look for Decayed Wood

The points at which decayed wood are more likely to be found are at the bottom of door frames, sills of windows, and the bottom rails of sashes and doors. The woodwork of half-timbered buildings of the 'Tudor' type is often badly protected from the weather and readily decays.

Outbuildings and Fences

The outbuildings, fences and gates should be examined even more frequently than the house, as perishable material enters more largely into their construction. An extra coat of creosote, or an application of paint, applied as soon as wanted, will save expensive repair and renewal later.

The falling down of fences may cause much annoyance and bad feeling between neighbours. This could be avoided if a little attention were given earlier on when the first signs of decay appear in the posts or the fence begins to lean over.

THE INTERIOR

The condition of the decorations and the repair of fittings in regular use will not need a special examination, as they will force themselves upon the attention of the householder who takes a pride in his house. What can be overlooked, and therefore is in need of some effort of will to examine, are the hidden things and the automatic appliances which ordinarily look after themselves, and only now and again require some little attention (which prevents more damage later).

Don't Forget to Go up into the Loft

The roof loft—what a glory-hole this usually is! There will probably be a trap-door, and perchance some high steps are handy, but it is a dark and dirty job to get up there, and yet that is where the cistern is almost sure to be. Frequently innocent of any cover at all, or a makeshift one at best, the dust and dirt can get into the domestic water supply.

Clean out the Cistern Once a Year

A certain amount of deposit from the main water supply is also inevitable, consequently, if the water drawn off for household use is to be pure, the cistern should be cleaned out periodically once a year; at any rate it should be looked to regularly. In cleaning out a cistern it is important not to stir up the sediment before running away the water through the pipes, else hard, sharp pieces of rust or grit will get into the pipes and will be most difficult to clear, and, in addition, it may be found necessary to re-washer taps, etc. On no account should water be drawn from any of the hot-water taps while the cistern is empty, or air may be drawn into the pipes and cause bother when the system is refilled.

Examine the Ball Valve

An overflow pipe is fitted to a cistern in case the ball valve does not act; it is rarely called into service, but it should be examined from time to time to see that it is clear for eventualities.

Cover Water Pipes with Felt

The water pipes in the roof are subject to attack by frost and should therefore be covered with a thermal insulating material. Various gas pipes, electric conduits, etc., run through the roof space and may get rusty.

Faults to Look for in Rooms

Within the rooms the chief things to look for are damp stains, signs of dry rot—decay of materials and settlement cracks. Damp

Look at the shoe which discharges over the gully. Here the earth is banked above the damp-proof course, blocking up ventilating grating; pipe cracked; nail loose; paving and plinth cracked by wall, allowing water to flow into the foundations

Dry Rot

Dry rot is a fungoid growth which attacks and saps the virtue from woodwork. The conditions that favour its growth are stagnant air and moisture, and so the space under the ground floor is where it is most frequently found. Before laying linoleum right over a floor the provision for ventilation under the floor should be examined. There should be a sufficient number of air bricks so arranged that a current of air will pass under every part. If any dry rot is discovered the wood must be cut away and burnt, otherwise the infection will spread rapidly and a large area will become involved.

stains are principally due to external defects which may not have been noticed when the house was examined outside.

Window-sills

Look under the windows, because faulty construction of window-sills is all too common. Rain gets in between the wood sill and the stone or tile sill unless a proper water bar of metal has been inserted between the two sills, and, not being seen, it is often omitted and the pointing is depended on to keep out the rain. This may be sufficient when all is new, but when the sun has shrunk the wood and the pointing works loose, the water easily finds an entry.

Damp Stains along Lower Parts of the Walls

If damp stains are noticed along the lower parts of the walls, suspicion should be cast upon the efficiency of the damp-proof course, or it may be the earth is too high on the outside, as mentioned already in the external examination of the house.

Dampness in Cupboards

Mildew and dampness are not necessarily due to a defective structure. Very often dampness in cupboards or other closed places arises from a lack of ventilation. If the joinery is well made and tight-fitting the circulation of air is less than with ill-fitted cupboard doors. Fortunately, lack of ventilation in such cases can soon be corrected by the boring of two or three small holes to give a through current of air.

Damage Caused by Wood Beetle

Another destructive agent is the wood beetle. The death-watch beetle confines its attention to hard woods such as oak. The beetle that does most damage in ordinary houses is the furniture beetle. It has a particular taste for sapwood, and is more rarely found in the heartwood which alone should be used in building. If any wood is found to be badly affected by the beetle—its presence can be detected by numerous small holes in the surface and a very fine powder in the wood —it should be cut out and burnt. If the wood is only slightly attacked the best plan is to creosote it thoroughly—provided, of course, creosoting is in keeping with the decorative treatment, if the woodwork is exposed. Another useful preventive is a coating of beeswax and turpentine.

The bottom of a door and frame (shown by the dark lines) are the places where rot is most likely to occur first

Cracks in Walls and Ceilings

Cracks in walls and ceilings are the cause of much fear and even alarm for householders and house occupiers. They may be due to movements in the structure, in which case they may be serious, or they might be due to slight shrinkages in materials, such as timber, which is unavoidable, and these cracks may be of no more importance than their unsightliness.

Hot-water Boiler and System

Of all the parts of a house and its fittings, the one that will almost assuredly be left last for examination is the hot-water boiler and system. Provided hot water can be drawn from the taps the system is allowed to go on undisturbed, and yet much trouble may be gradually—very gradually—accumulating.

It has been noted in the case of the cold-water cistern that sediment is deposited from the water. Similarly, in the hot-water system this sediment held in suspension in the water supply will gradually fall, and, more important still, the lime in solution in the water will be deposited by the constant heating of the water and form a crust or 'fur' in the boiler tanks and pipes just as furring takes place in a kettle. Hard water contains a high percentage of lime, and consequently the furring is more rapid with hard than soft water. It will be seen that boilers and tanks are provided with removable covers to openings, called mudholes or manholes, and thus the sediment that has been deposited can be removed.

DRAINAGE

It speaks volumes for the modern method of drain construction, how very seldom manhole covers are lifted and drains inspected. It is no uncommon thing to find such covers rusted in, or even with fences and other things built over them. It is, however, unwise, even with the best-laid drains, to allow them to pass unexamined for indefinite periods.

Where to Look for Faults

The points to be looked at in a drainage system are, briefly: First, the gullies receiving waste water from sinks, baths and lavatory basins; soap and grease constantly passing into or over the gullies are sure to collect, and if allowed to remain too long will eventually choke the gratings and block up the traps. The gullies should be cleared of

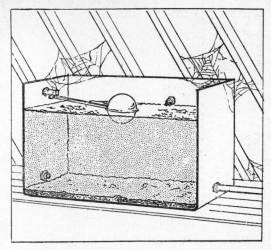

Before and After: Above is an uncovered and dirty cistern, overflow pipe choked, sediment collected on the bottom, pipes exposed to frost

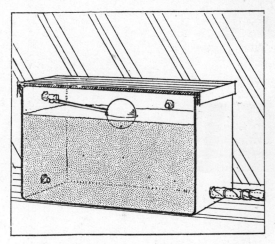

Now we have a covered and perfectly clean cistern, all scum and sediment removed, the overflow pipe clear, and pipes covered with felt

sediment and the gratings and pipes swilled out with either a hose or a bucket of water.

Lift Manhole Covers

The manhole covers should be lifted occasionally to see that water is running clear, that no material has got into the drain to choke or partially choke it, and that the cement work of the manhole has not cracked or fallen. When examining drains it is a good plan to allow water to flow through from a bath or sink to see if it is clear and free-flowing.

The fresh-air inlets, with their valves of mica, should also be examined. If broken or stopped with leaves, air from the drains can

When attending to the drainage system, examine the fresh-air inlets and their valves of mica. Here they are shown partly choked up. The mica flap cannot close to check foul air from drains

get out freely, and usually in places close to windows or to pavements.

Periods of Examination

Each owner should make his own schedule of times for examining his house according to the quality of the building, and his own circumstances. The following are merely suggestions:

Exterior. Twice yearly, spring and early autumn.

Interior. Roof, once a year; rooms, twice yearly, spring and early autumn.

Drainage. Gullies, once a month; manholes, yearly.

It may sound rather frightening to read of all the defects to which a house is liable, almost as fearsome as reading a list of symptoms of diseases; fortunately, in both cases one rarely experiences more than one or two at a time, and that at wide intervals. The worst danger for both body and building is *neglect*; timely examination and speedy repair soon put the defects right.

HOW TO FIT A NEW TAP WASHER

If a water-tap drips, the first thing is to obtain three or four washers of different sizes. Half-inch washers are those most frequently used, but as one cannot be certain of the exact dimensions until the water is cut off and the tap dismantled, it is just as well to be prepared with alternative washers measuring $\frac{3}{8}$ inch to $\frac{3}{4}$ inch.

Red fibre and treated leather washers are used for cold-water taps. Both kinds give good service. Leather and fibre must never be used for hot taps, because these rapidly deteriorate under the action of the hot water. Rubber-composition washers are essential for hot-water taps. Do not attempt to make washers; they may be purchased at any ironmonger's.

Turn off the Water

Before anything is done to the tap the water should be cut off. What this entails depends on the tap itself. If the water flows direct from the main, it is necessary to turn off the main cock and turn on the tap and wait a few moments for the connecting pipes to empty themselves. Sometimes this cock is near the kitchen sink, but frequently there is no other main cock except one in the front garden or in the street pavement. If the supply comes from a tank, shut the ball valve off by lifting the ball arm and tying it up, and then wait for the tank to empty itself. In the case of hot-water taps the source of heat must be removed or an explosion is possible.

A Useful Tip

A hot-water tap, or a tap fed from the cold cistern, can be unscrewed without stopping the water supply if one is ready with a large wet cloth to cover the hole as soon as the cap is withdrawn from the tap. It is not safe to attempt re-washering a main tap by this method because the force behind the water is too great.

Unscrewing the Tap

Taps are frequently difficult to unscrew, especially when they have been undisturbed for some time. A large adjustable spanner is the most suitable tool for unscrewing the tap in the absence of a plumber's wrench. The essential thing is to turn the spanner the correct way. Some taps have right-hand threads, that is to say, they undo when the cap is turned anti-clockwise, as seen from the top of the tap. A larger proportion of taps have left-hand threads. If it is not known whether a tap is left- or right-handed—try both ways before using too much force on the spanner.

Take extra care when unscrewing a tap which is wiped into a lead pipe or the joint may be damaged. The tap is firmly held in the free hand while the spanner is being turned. Care must also be taken in this way when the tap is backed with a tiled wall. Always unscrew away from the wall, so that a sudden slip of the spanner will not damage it. Basin and bath taps are easiest to deal with because their seating is firmer.

Chromium-plated Taps

Certain taps have a domed covering, fitted over the nut, and the nut is therefore invisible. All that is necessary with them is to unscrew the dome, to lift it up, and then the nut is revealed.

When the nut has been loosened the upper part of the tap can be lifted out of the fixed body, revealing the jumper.

The Jumper

The jumper is the portion of the tap to which the washer is fixed. Its object is to prevent the rotation of the washer when the tap

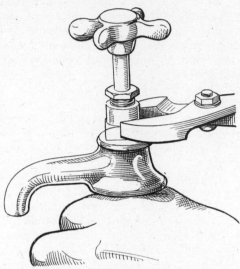

Fig. 1. The first thing to do after turning off the water at the main, is to unscrew the spindle of the tap. The tap should be turned full on before unscrewing as shown above

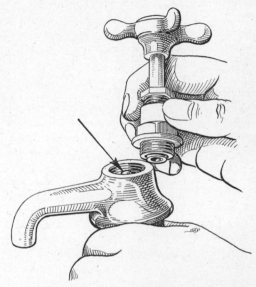

Fig. 2. Now lift off the spindle. The jumper will probably remain in the cavity, unless it is a tap of the type shown in Fig. 4

Fig. 3. Here is the jumper being lifted out after the top of the tap has been removed. The nut seen on the left must be taken off to enable the new washer to be placed on

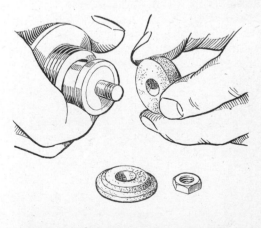

Fig. 4. Fitting the new washer on to the jumper. Some taps have a fixed jumper to prevent the washer sticking down. The only difference in the operations is that the jumper comes away with the top of the tap, and does not have to be lifted out

is turned. If the washer were to rotate with the tap, it would soon wear out on the seating. Some taps are made with the jumper separate from the cap of the tap; others are separate because the retaining-pin has broken. When the jumper remains in the tap when the cap is lifted off, it should then be possible to lift it out.

If the jumper will not lift out easily the spindle is strongly gripped in a pair of pliers, with a protecting piece of leather in the jaws of the pliers. The jumper is then forced out with the old washer attached. Care must be taken not to damage the jumper spindle; it is made of copper and is easily scored with the pliers.

Removing the Old Washer

The washer is held on to the jumper with a small nut. This unscrews anti-clockwise, looking down on the nut. If the washer nut is very tight it will be necessary to grip the flange of the jumper in a second pair of pliers in order to unscrew it. Hot-water taps frequently become corroded at this point, and are usually difficult to unscrew. The thread of the jumper may be so badly corroded that it breaks off. For this reason it is advisable to keep a spare jumper as a stand-by.

Replacing the Tap

When the new washer has been fitted to the jumper, examine the washer which provides a water-tight joint between the cap and the body of the tap. This washer is renewed if necessary. It is made of leather. Fibre should not be used for this, because it is liable to fray when the tap is screwed up. Do not put any paint or red lead on the cap thread with the object of making the joint water-tight, because

this will contaminate the water supply. Make sure that the jumper rotates freely in the cap of the tap before putting the tap together again.

Combined Tap Washer and Seating

To overcome seating wear there is on the market a special type of combined washer and seating for both hot and cold taps.

The washer, instead of being fixed at the end of the jumper, is inserted into the seating, flat side up. When the column is replaced and tap screwed up the jumper plate will then press the washer right into its seating.

It is claimed that this type of combined tap washer and seating outlasts the ordinary washer by years.

Other Faults

It may be that when the water supply is turned on, the tap is no better than it was at the outset. This will be due to one of three reasons:

(*a*) The washer has not been properly fitted. There is only one thing to do when this is suspected, and that is to go through the whole process again. Take particular care this time that the washer is pushed in perfect contact with the metal circle against which it is fitted.

(*b*) The washer is not the proper size. In such cases it is usually too small.

(*c*) The tap is worn out. This happens after a considerable amount of wear, especially in areas where the water is gritty. In such cases the inside of the tap becomes roughened, and the soft washer cannot shut down in absolute contact with it. Hence the water is able to trickle through, although the spindle is shut down to its fullest extent. The tap should be replaced.

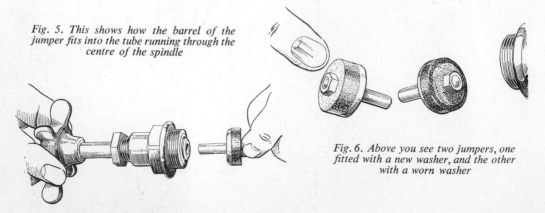

Fig. 5. This shows how the barrel of the jumper fits into the tube running through the centre of the spindle

Fig. 6. Above you see two jumpers, one fitted with a new washer, and the other with a worn washer

PAINTING *the* FRONT DOOR

TO paint the front door a new bright colour, or a conservative dark shade, improves the look of the whole house.

It is best to remove the door fittings: the knob, letter-box cover, knocker. If the surface of the door is in good condition, free from all defects, it may be safe to proceed without removing the old paint and varnish. In that case the door should be washed down with a good cleansing solution, such as Manger's sugar soap.

Rubbing Down

This is best done with either pumice stone or 'wet or dry' sandpaper and sugar-soap solution.

If pumice is used, two pieces will be required, one rather large piece rubbed first to a smooth face on a flat stone, and a smaller, shaped piece, which will be convenient for getting into the mouldings. If sandpaper is used, the same sheet will do for both level and curved surfaces. The parts under treatment should be kept well wetted, as the sugar soap acts as a lubricant to the abrasive. Special care should be taken to clean those parts of the panels immediately adjacent to the mouldings, as, owing to the shrinkage of the wood, ridges of old paint are sometimes found there. The object of this rubbing down is not only to smooth the surface, but to kill the gloss on the old material, providing a satisfactory base for the new paint. The rubbing being completed, the whole of the door should be swilled down.

If there are any open joints or other inequalities, these should now be stopped up. First brush a little paint into these places, allow this to dry, and then fill the openings with putty and smooth off with the knife. When this is quite hard, sandpaper the whole surface of the door and dust off.

In the majority of cases it is really necessary, before repainting, to remove the old paint.

It is simplest for the amateur to use one of the chemical paint-removers, of which there are several makes on sale, or a scraper can be used.

The tools required are a painter's duster, a large-size flat paint brush (not less than $2\frac{1}{2}$ inches wide), and a smaller brush (say 1 inch) of the same type.

Priming

The now bared surface of the door should next be well sandpapered until it is perfectly smooth. All knots require to be coated with shellac knotting to prevent the exudation of sap.

The whole of the door should then be 'primed,' which is the word applied to the first coating of a new or bared surface.

The best paint for priming, and indeed for many other purposes, is a genuine white-lead paint. Assuming that a 2-lb. tin of this ready-mixed paint has been opened, it will be found that part of the oil has risen to the top. This should be poured off into another vessel and saved for later use.

Sufficient of the paint for the priming coat should be poured into the paint kettle, and a very little turpentine added. The object of this turpentine is to enable the priming coat partially to penetrate the wood. The priming coat should then be applied. When it is thoroughly hard, the whole surface of the door again requires sandpapering. Then sponge the door down with clean water and allow to dry off.

Second Coating

Any of the white-lead paint that was not used for priming may be used for the second coat, adding, if too stiff, the oil previously poured off. All paint coats should be well brushed out, as thin coats are always better than thick ones. This coat, too, must have ample time to harden before we proceed further. Twenty-four hours is the minimum.

First Finishing Coat

The further processes will depend upon the kind of finish required. If a plain colour-scheme with a glossy surface is required, it remains to choose the colour. Visit the paint stores and get the paints mixed to your

(*Continued on page* 300)

When uncurling paper draw it over the edge of the table

Hang Your
Own Wallpaper

Many folk can put paint or distemper on a wall quite easily, but hanging wallpaper is not so simple, unless you bear in mind a few guiding rules

WALLPAPER hides a multitude of defects that are revealed on a distempered surface, and there are so many extremely beautiful patterns on the market these days that the home decorator might try her hand at papering a small room first. To calculate the quantity required, remember that English wallpapers are usually made in pieces of about 11½ yards long by 21 inches wide. Measure the whole of the surface to be covered, and reduce to the total number of square yards. The superficial area of a roll of paper or "piece" is about 7 square yards, so (making an allowance for waste) if we divide the total number of square yards to be covered by six, it will give us the required number of pieces.

Preparing the Walls

Newly plastered walls can be papered, if they are thoroughly dry. To allow for a 'hot spot' of lime in the new plaster, give the entire wall space a coat of vinegar size, made by mixing 1 pint of vinegar with 1 quart water. This will neutralise any active lime in the plaster.

Old wallpaper must be thoroughly soaked and removed with a wall-scraper, or stripping knife. Then a coat of size must be applied. Size must always be dry before new paper is applied.

Fill all cracks, crevices and nail-holes with a plaster filler, and when the surface is dry, smooth down with sandpaper.

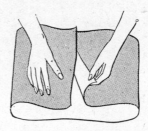

Carry the paper in a fold to the centre. Do not crease folded end

Check Your Paper

Although the retailer endeavours to supply you from one printing of paper, it is as well to check that there is no variation in shade.

When uncurling paper, draw over the edge of the table, pressing the curled part as it passes over the edge. Cut the first length slightly longer than the height of the wall and lay this face up on the table. Unroll the paper for the second length, but before cutting, place the left edge of the second length along the right edge of the first to ensure that the pattern is matched. Cut each succeeding length in the same manner.

Apply paste down the centre of each length and then brush outwards in a herring-

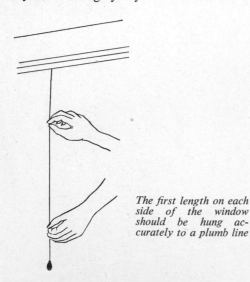

The first length on each side of the window should be hung accurately to a plumb line

bone fashion. Then fold the length by taking up the corner and carrying the paper over in a fold to the centre.

Where to Commence Hanging

Commence hanging on the right-hand side of the main window and continue round the room to the door. Then hang from the left-hand side of the window, continuing round to the door. This is to ensure that you hang the wallpaper away from the light. The first length on each side of the window should be hung accurately to a plumb line; great care should be taken with these lengths, as on their correct hanging, depends much of the success of the finished job. It would be as well to run the plumb line through chalk or charcoal, then snap a line against the wall

Cutting around an obstruction

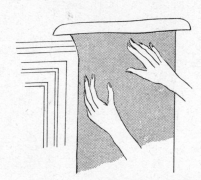

Slide the paper into position with the palms of the hands

approximately 20 inches away from the window.

Unfold the top of the first length and place the right-hand edge against the chalk line. As you unfold the paper along your guide line slide the paper into position with the palm of the hands. Smooth it down the centre with one stroke of the paper-hanger's brush, then sweep to right and left. Do this half-way down the wall and check to make sure the outer

edge is straight with the guide line. After the top half has been smoothed against the wall, unfold the bottom half, allowing it to hang down, then follow the same brushing procedure. Press the paper against the picture-rail and skirting-board with scissors and then trim. Afterwards brush the paper firmly down with a paper-hanger's brush. Any paste accidentally transferred to the paintwork must be sponged off immediately. Now carry on with the hanging of each succeeding length by butting each new length against the preceding one, being sure the pattern matches perfectly to obtain a satisfactory finish. It is very necessary to butt the edges of the wallpaper and for this purpose it is essential that the selvedge is trimmed on both sides. When each length has been on the wall about 10 to 15 minutes, roll the edges with a seam roller but do not press too hard.

When turning a corner trim the length so that it extends a little on to the next wall, the corners will then have a smooth, finished

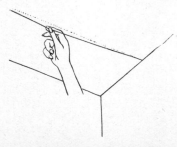

Snap a chalk line on the ceiling

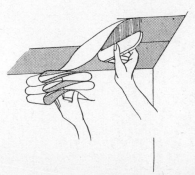

The paper unfolds as it is brushed into position on the ceiling

appearance. When only part of a full width is required, next to a door, it is easy to cut the paper a little wider than necessary, hang, smooth and tap into a crease and then trim with scissors.

The method of applying wallpaper when obstructions such as electric-light switches are encountered can best be described by illustration. Proceed with the hanging from the top as usual until the obstruction is reached. A horizontal cut is made to the edge of the paper closest to the obstruction and the hanging of the length is then completed to the bottom of the wall. A vertical cut is now made in the paper above and below the obstruction, the line of the vertical cut passing through the centre. These strips may now be cut off round the obstruction.

Papering the Ceiling

If the ceiling is to be papered then this must be done before the walls are begun.

First snap a chalk line on the ceiling a little less than a width of the paper from the wall, against which the first ceiling length will be hung. Use this as a guide to obtain your first length straight and work away from the light. Paste in the usual way but fold the pasted surfaces together as shown in sketch. This allows the paper to unfold as it is brushed into position. Support the folded lengths with an extra roll and apply the paper to the ceiling with the outer edge against the marked line. Use the paper-hanging brush right to left, smoothing the paper firmly into the joint between the wall and ceiling. You will find that the paper laps down on to the wall and can be marked and trimmed off with the scissors. When cutting your lengths, allow a little extra to enable the pattern to be matched, the surplus can again be trimmed with scissors.

Painting the Front Door—*continued from page 297*
requirements. One firm has a range of 999 shades produced from 16 basic colours. White lead as the basis should be specified, and the first finishing coat should consist, so far as the medium is concerned, of linseed oil and genuine turpentine in the proportions of two-thirds oil to one-third turpentine by measure.

When this coat is dry and hard, it must be sandpapered.

If the final paint coat is to be afterwards varnished, it should be more 'flat,' which means that the proportions of oil and turpentine must be reversed; viz. two-thirds turpentine to one-third of oil. Also the paint should be very well strained.

This having been applied and allowed to dry, the door is now ready for varnishing.

The varnish to be used will depend somewhat upon the colour of the paint used. If the colour is dark, the most suitable varnish will be either an outside copal front door varnish or an outside-quality carriage varnish. If the colour is pale, a pale decorative varnish (outside quality) is called for.

The work, after a light sandpapering with a very fine-grade paper, must be well dusted off so that no grit remains. Also, no varnishing should be done if there is dust about.

The brush with its charge of varnish should be applied straight to the door. In varnishing the panels, first brush downward, then across, and then finish up and down to spread the varnish evenly.

If the door is a panelled one, the panels should be done first, then the mouldings, thirdly, the upright centre stile, fourthly, the cross stiles and finally, the upright side stiles.

If a simpler process is desired, this is made possible by using one of the gloss enamel, suede finish, plastic or emulsion paints now available, instead of the final paint and the varnish coats.

A Bachelor Flat—*continued from page 287*
Gently taper each leg to a 1⅛-in. diameter at the bottom—you can round them by shaving off the edges with a plane or spoke-shave and glasspapering to finish. (Or legs could be bought ready-made.) Glue and screw the legs in the corners, as Z. Two pieces, H and I, 1½ in. wide by ½ in. thick, fit on top of each leg and flush with the top of the box.

Back Strip, J, is 36 in. by 2 in. by ½ in. and is glued and screwed to H and I from inside. **Bottom,** G—a piece of thin plywood is glued and nailed to the bottom edges of A, B, C, D. **Lid,** K—a piece of laminated plywood, 36 in. by 10½ in. by ½ in., rests on A, C, D and is hinged to the front edge of J; when opened the lid rests against the wall and on the inside can be screwed clips to contain brushes, etc. The table is either screwed to the wall through the back or can have four legs.

HEALTH IN THE HOME

These details are not a substitute for the doctor's care. They give an outline of symptoms and treatment for many common diseases, and will help you in emergencies

ACIDOSIS

SOME children have recurrent attacks of vomiting, yawning and headache, together with a smell of apples (acetone) in the breath. This suggests an over-acid condition of the blood, and is mostly brought on by rich food, excitement or sometimes no apparent reason at all.

Treatment. Avoid rich or fatty foods as are found to upset: fried foods, oils and chocolate. Keep the bowels open without the use of drastic purgatives. Counteract the acidity by giving an alkali, such as half a teaspoonful of bicarbonate of soda in a little water three times a day after meals over a period of time. Glucose should be taken by the mouth. In children prone to car- or train-sickness the attack may be anticipated and perhaps prevented also by the giving of glucose—a heaped teaspoonful in water or with food—before the journey.

ADENOIDS

Adenoids are spongy masses growing from the roof of the back of the nose and their enlargement or inflammation is both a result and a further cause of a run-down condition; mouth-breathing is caused by obstructing the free airway through nose to throat, and there is sometimes a cough. This may result in recurring colds and bronchial catarrhs. The signs of adenoids are a tendency to catch colds, difficulty in breathing through the nose or speaking properly. The child usually snores.

Treatment. Their removal. The operation is not dangerous and the improvement in health and appearance is often wonderful. After the operation the child should be encouraged to do breathing exercises night and morning. A diet of raw fruits, vegetables and plenty of milk and fresh air are necessary.

Adenoids are generally associated with enlargement or unhealthiness of the tonsils, and if this is the case the tonsils should also be removed at the time of operation.

ALVEOLAR ABSCESS OR GUMBOIL

A swollen and painful gum is usually due to an abscess or collection of matter (pus) forming between the root of a tooth and its socket. Consult a dentist about the removal of the tooth. It is unwise, however, to inject a local anaesthetic into the gum when an abscess is forming, therefore extraction must be either under gas or without an anaesthetic.

Temporary relief may be obtained with rinsings of the mouth with hot water containing tincture of iodine; painting the gum with tincture of iodine and heat applied to the face. One or two five-grain tablets of aspirin can be taken to relieve pain. A tonic can be taken after the abscess has broken.

ANAEMIA

Anaemia is a deficiency in the quantity or quality of the blood, and may follow severe bleeding or malnutrition. The deficiency, however, is frequently in the quality of the blood. The usual signs of anaemia are paleness of skin generally, mainly of the gums and lips and eyelids. There is also lassitude, loss of energy and appetite and breathlessness on exertion.

Treatment consists in taking plenty of fresh air, good food and proper rest. The diet should contain plenty of such foods as contain iron—for instance, meat, eggs, liver, wholemeal bread, green vegetables and especially spinach, cocoa, milk and fruits generally, and the anaemic persons should make themselves eat, as 'the appetite grows with eating.'

For medicine, iron must be given in the form the doctor recommends. In pernicious anaemia, liver injections or pills may be given.

ANGINA PECTORIS

This is the name given to severe paroxysms of heart pain occurring generally in later life and mainly in men. The attack comes on suddenly after exertion. The symptoms are severe pain over the heart, a feeling of deathly illness and a necessity to keep quite still. With these, there are the usual signs of collapse—blueness and tingling of lips, a grey face, sweating and difficulty in breathing.

Treatment. The sufferer should avoid exertion and, as much as possible, mental strain and anxiety. He should avoid heavy meals and cut down on drink and tobacco. Spirits are preferable to beer. He should carry with him some capsules of amylnitrite, one of which he may crush and inhale at the onset of an attack, or Testosterone proprionate have been recently recommended. Sal volatile (aromatic spirit of ammonia) may be given during the attack, a teaspoonful in a little cold water. This stimulates and also helps to dispel the flatulence which the patient feels.

APPENDICITIS

Inflammation of the appendix varies in degree. The signs are pain, usually sudden, in the abdomen, sometimes with vomiting and nausea. Tenderness is felt in the right lower quarter of the abdomen. Attacks are liable to be recurrent.

Treatment. During an attack the patient should go to bed at once and only water or fruit-juice should be taken and no aperient. A doctor should be consulted at once, as severe inflammation may cause the appendix to become the centre of an abscess. At the same time hot applications may be applied to the abdomen and continued as long as pain and tenderness remain. The appendix may have to be removed on the advice of a surgeon.

ASTHMA

A distressing complaint consisting of periodical attacks of difficulty in expiration and sometimes a cough. We speak of certain people as being 'asthmatic' or subject to attacks of asthma. The complaint often runs in families.

Prevention. The sufferer is usually allergic to such things as certain foods, especially seasoned dishes; grass-pollens; feather pillows; dust from cereals; foggy weather; some drugs. Asthmatics are also affected by locality;

they have attacks in one district but not in another. Today, emotional causes are considered most significant. A psychologist may trace the cause of anxiety. Any infection of nose or throat must be treated. Attention paid to diet, avoiding naturally all foods liable to bring on an attack. He should live in a cool, dry climate. Breathing exercises are valuable. The allergy should be investigated by a doctor. Some people are affected by the presence of cats or of horses or flowers and should avoid them. Children should be examined for diseased tonsils and adenoids.

Treatment. At the first warning a tablet containing half a grain of ephedrine hydrochloride should be given. Adrenalin may be given also by hypodermic injection to cut short an attack of asthma, both under the doctor's directions.

BED-WETTING (ENURESIS)

The cause of this can be psychological or some organic defect, or bad training in infancy. The wetting of the bed most commonly

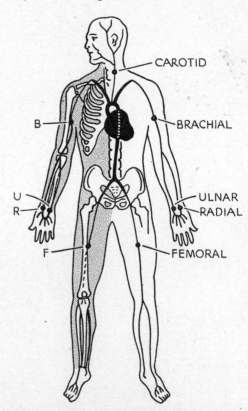

These are the main arteries of the human body. To control bleeding the artery is compressed against a bone at a point nearer the heart than the actual bleeding-point

happens in the early morning. The presence of a full bladder seems to be felt before quite awake and the semi-conscious urge meets with an involuntary response. There may be digestive trouble, or a tight foreskin; or the urine may be over-acid and irritating, as shown by its pink colour and a sediment.

Treatment. Some success has been claimed for benzedrine and ephedrine in difficult cases, under doctor's care. Attendance at a Guidance Clinic is useful. Never give a full or indigestible meal to a child in the evening, or too long a drink.

If the child is old enough to appreciate it, give him a word of praise when his bed is dry in the morning, or even give him some small reward. In bed-wetting there is often some insecurity or resentment in the child's mind; the removal of some—maybe imaginary—grievance, or the establishment of better understanding between child and parent, may result in a cure.

BITES AND STINGS

Insect stings are not dangerous unless very numerous or in a dangerous part, such as the tongue.

Gnats are a particular nuisance to some people, especially to those with delicate skins. Gnats can sometimes be repelled by smearing exposed parts with oil of citron or lavender. Witch-hazel jelly makes a helpful application, or dabbing with a solution of soda and water, or an antiseptic.

Bees and Wasps. Cause swellings which are painful at first and afterwards itching.

Treatment. Cooling lotions such as calamine should be continued as long as swelling and itching persist. A bee leaves its sting embedded in the skin; the sting should be pulled out with tweezers or lifted out with the point of a sterilised needle.

Thorns. Pricks with thorns in the garden should never be neglected. Rose-thorns in particular can cause a deep puncture, and not infrequently introduce septic material. Weak tincture of iodine should be applied immediately; and subsequently hot fomentations of boracic lint used. Red streaks appearing on the arm are a sign that septic material has got into the lymph-stream; the streaks should be painted with the weak tincture of iodine. A running sepsis of this kind might become serious and medical advice should be taken if it occurs.

BLOOD PRESSURE

A variation in blood pressure in individuals is quite compatible with perfect health. However, our blood pressure is evidence of our condition, and there are states of health in which it is higher or lower than the normal. Blood pressure is likely to be *lower* than normal in conditions of debility, especially after illness such as influenza. It can also occur in some forms of heart disease, in tuberculosis or even be due to the weather. The signs are weariness, loss of energy, headache, depression and perhaps dizziness. It may be also due to lack of sunshine and good food. A tonic and good food are helpful.

Due to the gradual thickening of the arteries, blood pressure is *higher* than normal in people past middle life who are of sedentary habit, eat and drink too much or work too hard, worry and are constipated. Repressed emotional disturbances can be a cause. Common signs are headaches, with sense of fullness in the head, giddiness, noises in the ears, flatulence, fatigue and palpitations. There may also be bleeding at the nose, which in such cases is a natural safety-valve.

Treatment. Mainly by diet, eating very little meat and abstaining from all alcoholic drink, also from hot sauces, pickles and highly seasoned foods generally. Over-exertion and excitement must be avoided. It is most important to ensure regular functioning of the bowels. The patient must endeavour not to worry or be excited to temper.

BOIL

A boil is a localised inflammation around a hair follicle, resulting from an infection by a germ known as *Staphylococcus*, and the slough or core represents the corpuscles which have been killed in their battle with the microbe. It usually occurs only in people with lowered vitality.

Treatment. Do not poultice boils; such treatment weakens the surrounding skin and makes it liable to infection with the same microbe, with the result that more boils form. If a warm dressing is desired, the kaolin poultice is the one to choose. When pus shows through the skin, a small incision with a sterilised needle should be made to help the pus escape.

BREAST, INFLAMMATION OF

Swelling and tenderness of the breast occur in quite young girls, and even in babies. In very young infants, the condition may be due to ignorant handling, in a mistaken effort to 'draw out the nipple'—an unnecessary and wrong proceeding.

In older children the inflammation may be spontaneous or the result of a blow.

Treatment. Fomentations of boracic lint wrung out of very hot water, and covered with cotton-wool and a wide bandage, may be applied two or three times daily; or a kaolin poultice may be put on and left for twenty-four hours. Sometimes an abscess forms. The treatment of abscess will be a small incision by a doctor in a direction radiating from the nipple. If it is not opened, the abscess will eventually burst, in which case a scar is more likely to be left than when an incision is made.

Nursing Mothers

In nursing mothers an inflammation of one or both breasts may occur from imperfect emptying, especially if the mother is run-down.

Treatment. Hot fomentations may be applied, and the milk removed with a breast pump; if the breast pump is too painful the milk may be gently pressed out by stroking towards the nipple with a sponge or pad of lint wrung out of hot water. Penicillin should also be given. It is not wise to feed an infant from an inflamed breast.

The same remarks as above apply to an abscess.

BRONCHITIS

Bronchitis is a catarrhal infection of the large air tubes in the lungs. There may be some predisposition to this illness. The first stage is a dry and irritable condition of the bronchial tubes, resulting in a hard cough, a feeling of rawness behind the breast bone, which may be very painful. Later the inflamed lining of the tubes throws off mucus, and the cough then becomes looser and less irritating. The expectoration, which was at first scanty and frothy, now becomes more plentiful. In children it is often the result of measles. It often results from a chill or from sinusitis.

Treatment. Put the patient to bed in a warm room and keep him in an even temperature of 65–68° F. Food must be very light, mainly milk, until temperature subsides. The chest and ribs may be rubbed with camphorated oil or a white liniment or a Radlin poultice applied. An expectorant mixture can be given. Relief may be obtained from inhalations of Tinct. Benzoini Co. (two teaspoonsful to a pint of hot water).

BRUISES

A bruise is the result of a blow, and the blue colour and swelling are due to blood oozing beneath the skin from torn blood-vessels.

Treatment of a bruise is to rest the part and to apply lint soaked in a cooling lotion, or a handkerchief wrung out in cold water, or an ice-bag. Either of these should be renewed frequently.

A badly bruised surface will respond to a few minutes occasionally under an infra-red lamp.

In a generally bruised body, if the patient is well, a warm bath can be found soothing.

BURNS AND SCALDS

A burn is an injury caused by dry heat; a scald is caused by wet heat. Burns and scalds vary from a reddening or blistering of the skin to a deep destruction of the substance of the body.

The first danger is shock, then sepsis.

Treatment. Get the patient to hospital as soon as possible. Meanwhile get the clothing off a burnt person quickly. Cut around any clothing adhering to a burnt part. In scalds, tear or cut off clothing which may be saturated with boiling water. Keep the sufferer covered with warm blankets and give hot sugared tea or coffee.

For minor burns to be treated at home, immerse the burnt or scalded limb in warm water to which bicarbonate of soda (cooking soda) has been added in a strength of two teaspoonsful to the pint, or apply lint or cloths soaked in this lotion. Penicillin injections prevent infection.

(1) Tannic acid in jelly form is useful for superficial burns or scalds on the surface of body or limbs; it is not so good for fingers or toes or at the bends of joints. It may be applied directly to the skin, or thickly spread on linen or on lint (the 'cloth' side, not the 'fluffy'), and it forms a protective coating which may be left undisturbed for a week or more. Some application for burns should be part of every home medicine chest.

(2) An emulsion of acriflavine in liquid paraffin applied on lint, but should not be used on children.

(3) Lint or gauze soaked in a warm solution of picric acid, in a strength of 1–1,000.

If blisters form they may be snipped with sterilised scissors and a new dressing applied.

As healing proceeds, the limb must be moved each day, because the scars which form after burns and scalds are liable to contract. If there has been a considerable destruction of skin, it may be wise to have grafts of skin applied to the healing areas; this, of course, is a matter for an expert surgeon.

CARBUNCLE

Though of the same nature as a boil, differs from it in that several hair follicles are involved, and the carbuncle discharges through several openings, whereas the boil has only one. In carbuncle a doctor should be consulted, as both boils and carbuncles are liable to occur in diabetes, kidney disease and gout.

Treatment. Good general health is most important. Constipation and anaemia must be corrected, skin cleanliness insisted on; fresh air is essential. Tonics such as iron may be given, with plenty of green vegetables and fruit in the dietary, and quantities of water should be drunk. Meat should be reduced, alcoholic drinks avoided. The advice of a doctor should be sought regarding intra-muscular injections of penicillin. Ultra-violet rays are beneficial.

When the boil or carbuncle is open and discharging, moist hot dressings of boric lint soaked with a saturated solution of Epsom salts are excellent.

CANCER

Cancer is a disease usually attacking the elderly. It does not occur at all among some races living on natural foods. Skin cancer is caused generally by some trades.

If a person has a hard swelling or a lump where no lump should be, or a sore that will not heal; or a discharge, and especially blood-stained discharge, where no discharge should be—for instance, from nipple or bowel or genital passages—then the advice of a doctor should be sought. Some harmless reason may be found for the symptom; but if not, the patient will have the satisfaction of having taken advice early. With modern methods a cure is most likely to be effected.

CHICKEN-POX

The child who has chicken-pox has often only a little loss of appetite and a disinclination to play. The illness, however, is highly infectious. The spots take the form of small raised pimples, which develop a watery head. They are scattered, appearing first on the body, often below the collar-bones, and become widely spread in the course of two or three days. New spots may be seen while the older ones are developing their watery heads and then drying up, and no part of the body seems exempt except the palms of the hands and the soles of the feet; indeed the spots can be very irritating among the hairs of the head and inside the mouth.

Treatment. Keep the child warm; give a cooling mixture and keep the bowels active; milk of magnesia does very well. Dust the spots with a mixture of boracic powder, and those on the head should be kept moist with olive-oil.

It is well to keep the child in bed until the spots are drying; diet should be light. When all spots are dry, warm baths may be taken; but the child must not be allowed to pick off the scabs which form as the spots dry. The time between exposure to infection and the development of the rash is long—from seventeen to twenty-one days. The child should be isolated until all the scabs have fallen off.

A simple arm-sling is made by putting one end of a triangular bandage over the shoulder of the uninjured side and round the neck. Carry point behind the elbow of the injured limb and place the forearm over the centre of the bandage. Carry the second end up to the first and tie. Bring the point forward and secure with a safety-pin

CHILBLAINS

They occur mostly in children and in persons whose general health is below the average, and are associated with a deficiency of calcium (lime salts) in the blood. It is better to prevent them by not wearing tight shoes and gloves, not 'toasting' feet at the fire or sitting in a draught and by taking plenty of exercise to keep up the circulation. Try wearing old-fashioned bed socks at night.

Treatment. Some sunlight treatment will help. Diet should contain plenty of vitamins and calcium (Vitamin 'C' tablets will help and also Vitamin 'K'). Relief of itching may be found in painting the skin with collodion or surgical spirit.

For broken chilblains use a zinc and salicylate ointment (Lassar's paste is useful; it may be applied spread on lint). Paschki's Paint is also helpful.

COLIC

The word 'colic' is used to describe severe irregular and spasmodic griping pains in the abdomen. It is usually due to the taking of some unsuitable food—green apples and unripe plums are proverbial examples—or the presence of some irritant material in the bowel.

Treatment. If the pain is not localised to any one spot, a dose of castor-oil may be safely given. This quickly empties the bowel of undigested material; and when evacuation has taken place, a dose of twenty drops of chlorodyne (for an adult) and abstinence for a few hours from solid food will usually be enough to effect a cure. During the paroxysms of pain, hot applications may be made to the abdomen—such as a large hot fomentation of lint, wrung out of boiling water, or a partly filled rubber hot-water bottle. A glass of hot water with a few drops of oil of peppermint may bring relief. An enema is also beneficial.

Children can be given lime or dill water. Repeated attacks which do not yield to treatment should be referred to a doctor as they may be a symptom of poisoning, or of a growth.

Renal Colic or Kidney Colic

In this form of colic there is a sudden severe pain in the loin, running down one side of the body and into the groin. The pain is accompanied by a desire to pass water, and the urine may be stained with blood. In most cases it is caused by the passage of a small stone from the kidney down the tube (the ureter) to the bladder. The pain stops when the journey of the stone into the bladder is complete, though there is likely to be soreness in the affected loin for a day or two.

Treatment. Rest and hot applications to the loin. Aspirin or chlorodyne may be taken, but kidney colic is a condition which calls for the attention of a doctor or surgeon.

Gallstone Colic or Biliary Colic

This again is a condition requiring the advice of a surgeon. The pain is severe and felt acutely about the margin of the ribs on the right side of the abdomen, through to the shoulder-blade on the same side. It results from the passage of a stone from the gall-bladder along the tube which leads the bile to the bowel; thus jaundice is not uncommon.

CONCUSSION

This is a complication of a head injury, very frequently seen. It should never be treated lightly, as there may be possibility of brain damage. The symptoms, in conjunction with the history of the accident, vary from momentary giddiness to complete unconsciousness. There may be headache and vomiting.

Treatment. In the absence of the signs of more severe head injury, such as twitchings, bleeding from the ear, or prolonged unconsciousness, cases of concussion usually recover quickly if allowed to rest quietly in bed for a few days. An ice-bag may be applied to the head, but no stimulants given. A concussed child should be kept away from school and lesson books for a few weeks. Any case of real head injury should be seen by a doctor.

CONSTIPATION

Constipation can be at the root of many ailments and is unfortunately a very common ailment.

Treatment. Enough fluid and good food must be taken. Drink hot water before breakfast and at night. Eat plenty of fruit and green vegetables and foods containing 'roughage' —such as oatmeal, wholemeal bread, potatoes cooked in their jackets. Make it a rule to visit the lavatory at the same time every day, preferably after breakfast in the morning. Laxatives should not be relied upon, but are necessary sometimes. Liquid paraffin is a lubricant which mixes with the food masses and can be taken plain, or in emulsion form. It is not a purgative medicine. Of medicines, the most useful are senna pods (from five to ten steeped for a day in a cup of cold water); cascara (conveniently in tablets of two grains of the extract); and syrup of figs or lixen for children. Many people prefer a small dose (from half to one teaspoonful) of 'salts' first thing in the morning. To produce a rapid clearance of the bowel in illness, castor-oil is used. One or two tablespoonsful for an adult or one or two teaspoonsful for a child, may be given, either on a little hot milk or on orange juice.

An enema can be given when purgative medicines have been taken without result, or when it is not advisable to give a purgative. Enough exercise must be taken. Walking is excellent, and bending and twisting in the 'daily dozen.'

CONVULSIONS

In infancy a convulsion may be set up by such various causes as indigestion, constipation, teething, worms and a tight foreskin. A convulsion also may occur at the beginning of some acute illness, such as measles or bronchitis; and though repeated convulsions may be a feature of some more serious trouble, such as meningitis, in most cases the convulsions of infancy have a cause such as mentioned above. Where there is no apparent cause, there may be rickets. Sometimes there are warnings such as twitchings and irritability; other times the onset is sudden. There are grimaces, consciousness is lost, limbs stiffen, the face becomes blue.

Treatment. The baby should immediately be undressed and put in a warm bath; at the same time apply cold-water compresses or an ice-bag to the head. When the child is quieter an enema of soap and water may be given slowly. When the baby is better, it should be allowed to sleep; but a dose of castor-oil should be given and a dose of bromide mixture (two grains of the bromide of soda for an infant of one year) every four hours for a couple of days.

CROUP

Croup is characterised by a crowing sound with each intake of the breath; it may be due to spasm of the larynx or to swelling as a result of catarrhal inflammation, and is associated with rickets. It sounds more dangerous than it is.

Spasmodic Croup

This is seen in infants when the nervous system is upset—for example, in teething or indigestion—or in some form of irritation such as worms or the need for circumcision. It occurs without other signs of cold or sore throat.

Treatment. Give the child a hot rubber bottle (not *too* hot) on its chest to relieve spasm, and an expectorant cough medicine. Clear out the bowel by castor-oil or enema, give a hot bath, and then a dose of bromide of soda (two grains for a child a year old) or antipyrin (one grain for a child of the same age). Have a steam kettle by the bedside. Give the child cod-liver oil three times a day, reduce the starch in the diet and see that he has plenty of fresh air. When the child is well, have him examined for rickets, unhealthy tonsils and adenoids.

DEAFNESS

Deafness can be a condition of hysteria; otherwise it may be a common accompaniment of advancing years, the drums becoming stiffened and the internal mechanism of the ear less mobile. In such cases a deaf-aid may be a comfort and its use should be persisted in as it eliminates the feeling of aloneness so many deaf people feel. In younger life, deafness is sometimes due to an accumulation of wax. A little diluted hydrogen peroxide dropped into outer ear may help. Its use every week or so may prevent the trouble. Wax can be removed by syringing the ear, but must be softened first with olive-oil or glycerine. Water for syringing should not be above blood heat. Where the patient cannot help himself, it should be done by a doctor.

Deafness may also be due to catarrh. Often a quick but forcible puff out of the cheeks, with the nose held closed, will be enough to clear this little tube, but this manoeuvre must not be tried if the throat is inflamed or if there is earache. When children have earache, a drop of warm olive-oil put into the ear may be a relief. Deafness in children, with earache, and especially with a tenderness behind the ear, should certainly be a sign for seeking immediate medical advice.

Heat, such as a rubber hot-water bottle in a cover or towel, held over the ear, may relieve acute pain.

Deafness is often due to an affection of the middle ear, and a specialist should be consulted.

DIABETES

Diabetes is characterised by the presence of sugar in the urine, due to a defect in the action of the pancreas, a gland which lies in the abdomen behind the stomach.

The signs are thirst, an increased output of urine, and weakness accompanied by loss of weight. Diabetics are also prone to itching and to boils and carbuncles.

Sugar in the urine is detected by boiling the urine with an equal quantity of Fehling's or Benedict's solution in a test-tube; if sugar is present the blue colour of the solution changes to brick-red. Under proper and continued treatment diabetes may be regarded as curable.

Treatment is twofold.

(1) Carbohydrates must be reduced gradually, the intake of sugar-producing foods withdrawn or reduced. These are sugar itself, all sweetened things; also all starchy foods such as rice, tapioca, sago, bread and cakes. Eggs, salads and green vegetables may be taken; also bacon, cheese, fish and meat; and there are various diabetic breads and biscuits which may be used instead of the ordinary. The diet should be fixed by a doctor for each patient.

(2) *Insulin.* The discovery of insulin, a substance prepared from the pancreas (sweetbread) of various animals, has quite altered the outlook in diabetes. Insulin is necessary if the urine is not free from sugar after dieting on a 1,500-calorie diet. The patient may administer insulin to himself once the correct dose has been decided by a medical man.

DIARRHOEA

Diarrhoea may be due to many causes, hysteria, poisoning, intestinal catarrh, chill or bacterial. Sometimes it is Nature's way of getting rid of improper food. While some foods are mildly laxative, as for example prunes, others may act as purgatives, as unripe plums may do. As the cause may be due to some disease, it must not be too lightly regarded.

Treatment. If the taking of indigestible food can be remembered and diarrhoea has followed, then a dose of castor-oil (one or two teaspoonsful for a child and one or two tablespoonsful for an adult) will be likely to prove a safe remedy.

An Inflamation of the Bowel

Under this heading may be mentioned the summer diarrhoea of infancy. A catarrh of the bowel may be set up by microbes taken in milk.

Treatment. A dose of castor-oil is again a useful treatment, but the sufferer should be restricted to a fluid diet until the inflammation has subsided, together with rest and warmth. The fluids should be sweetened water or meat extract and water given lukewarm or cold. If these are vomited, cold boiled water, with half a teaspoonful of common salt to the pint, may be given. Astringent drugs such as ipecacuanha or opium are useful. The taking of oatmeal gruel is also a help. Antibiotics, such as M & B and penicillin, can be given.

DISLOCATIONS

In a dislocation the bones entering into a joint are partially or completely separated from their natural position. A dislocation differs from a fracture in that the limb is fixed instead of being unusually movable. There is obvious alteration of the shape of the joint

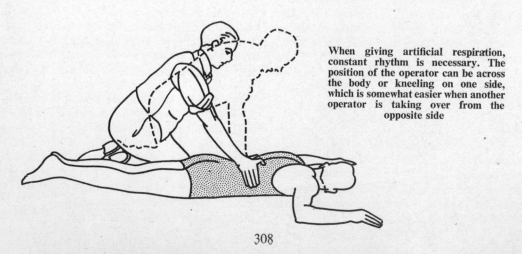

When giving artificial respiration, constant rhythm is necessary. The position of the operator can be across the body or kneeling on one side, which is somewhat easier when another operator is taking over from the opposite side

and change in the length of a limb. It is always wise to have a joint injury X-rayed.

A fracture may coexist with a dislocation and more damage may be done if roughly handled. Do not attempt to reduce a dislocation if a doctor or hospital is available. Put patient in bed, apply cold compresses to relieve pain, and support dislocated joint on a pillow.

DOG-BITE

Mad dogs are rare, and a bite from a dog known to be healthy should be treated as an ordinary wound, which may be likely to be septic, and bruised from the animal's teeth.

Treatment. Wash with soap and water, then apply tincture of iodine. As a precaution the wound should be cauterised either with silver stick (solid nitrate of silver in pencil form) or with pure carbolic acid on a probe wrapped at its tip with cotton-wool. An antiseptic wound-dressing is then applied and the injured limb kept at rest. A bite from a mad dog —a dog suffering from rabies—is a more serious affair. Tie a tourniquet between the wound and the heart. The patient should suck the wound, spitting out the blood. Wash, then cauterise freely as above. The patient should then have anti-rabic treatment.

DROWNING

Swift action is necessary when attempting to revive the apparently drowned. Do not stop to remove any clothing. Immediately the person has been lifted from the water, turn him head downwards to allow water to run out of air passages. Then lay him on the ground face downwards with arms above head and the face turned to one side. Quickly loosen any tight clothing such as collar, waistcoat, braces. Swiftly wipe out the mouth and nostrils in case water or weed is present, and draw forward the tongue so as to give free airway. Gentle but firm action is needed. Roughness may cause more injury.

Kneeling across the buttocks of the patient, place your two hands on the lower ribs and lean forward, throwing your weight on your hands so as to compress the chest, counting slowly—one, two—meanwhile. Relax the pressure and the chest will expand by its own elasticity, as you count: three, four. The counting should be about the rate of seconds. Repeat the movement, avoiding hurry, but aiming at twelve to fifteen complete movements of compression and relaxation in each

minute, without pause. Continue until natural respiration is restored, or if not, persevere with the movements for at least two hours. When tired, hand over to somebody else without a pause. There must be unhurried, uninterrupted perseverance. While this is going on, if possible, warm blankets should be brought, the patient covered and hot-water bottles packed around him.

When the patient draws a breath for himself, this may be felt beneath the hands which rest upon the ribs, and possibly heard. Efforts should not be relaxed until rhythmic breathing is well established.

The patient should be kept in bed for a day or two until danger of bronchitis and pneumonia has passed. Similar treatment by artificial respiration is useful in cases of suffocation and of coal-gas poisoning. Get the patient to the fresh air and proceed with the movements above described. Stimulants will be necessary.

DIPHTHERIA

Diphtheria is an acute infectious fever of childhood which has lost much of its terror since the introduction of the diphtheria antitoxin, and especially since the discovery of 'immunisation' or rendering the child proof against diphtheria by inoculation. Milk is frequently the mode of infection.

The symptoms of diphtheria are a general appearance of illness with rise of temperature and sore throat. In most cases the child does not have great pain with the throat; but the characteristic greyish-white or greyish-yellow patches may be seen on the tonsils, soft palate and uvula, or on the back of the roof of the mouth. The breath is offensive, and the glands of the neck are enlarged.

Treatment. Diphtheria is a serious disease; antitoxin is given as early as possible, and absolute rest in bed is necessary for at least three weeks. Every case of diphtheria should be under medical care.

DYSPEPSIA OR INDIGESTION (Atonic)

Atonic indigestion is due to inadequate secretion of the gastric digestive juice and arises mainly towards middle age.

The signs are weight and distension in the region of the stomach, that is, between the lower end of the breastbone and the navel, a discomfort which may amount to actual pain; wind may be brought up and there is often a feeling of sickness, and pain in the heart region. The appetite is poor and this state is mostly due to errors of dieting and consequent constipation. Nervous indigestion is brought on by mental anxiety.

Treatment. Hot water—a teacupful taken to drink as hot as comfortable—often brings ease; a few drops of essence of peppermint form a popular remedy; or, better, a level teaspoonful of bicarbonate of soda in a tumblerful of warm water. Medicinal charcoal alleviates distension, as it absorbs gas. Food should be simple; milk, soups, steamed fish, not too much starch or heavy meals at all. A little tonic may help.

Indigestion (Acid)

This is dependent upon an excess of hydrochloric acid in the gastric juice. Highly strung people have a tendency to this type of indigestion. Main symptom is a burning pain an hour or two after meals; a sour or burning fluid may arise into the mouth.

The same treatment as above should alleviate immediate discomfort. Proteins and fats should be increased, starch intake diminished. All food *must* be well masticated. Avoid highly seasoned food and alcohol. Outdoor exercise helps nerves and digestion. The acidity should be controlled with alkaline powder.

DRUG ADDICTION

Drugs which may become habitual in certain people are opium, morphia, heroin, cocaine, and addiction often occurs accidentally. A drug is prescribed perhaps for insomnia and becomes a habit.

Treatment. Drug-takers are secretive about their habit and resent interference; secretly they are ashamed. Sudden withdrawal of the drug may result in a state of health which gives rise to alarm, depression, sleeplessness, loss of appetite and loss of interest. This result must be countered by companionship, encouragement, frequent light feedings, and if necessary rest in bed. If the craving does not go, treatment should be in an institution, as there are so many new ways of dealing with this addiction—resulting in the gradual deterioration of the individual—that a cure is more than possible.

ECZEMA

Eczema is an inflammation of the skin and may appear on any part of the body. It is seen as an outbreak of small spots on a reddened area of skin; the spots being either open, wet and discharging (weeping eczema) or dry, scaly and crusted (dry eczema).

Eczema is always accompanied by itching and the scratching that is provoked makes it worse. Like asthma, it may be allergic in nature, and is sometimes caused by external irritants used in certain trades—flour, plants, chemicals, etc.—though naturally only a few are affected. Injections can help to immunise the sufferer to the effect of the irritant.

Treatment. In the red, inflamed stage, calamine lotion, dabbed on and allowed to dry, is soothing. In the dry and scaly stage Lassar's paste may be used, with or without 20 minims of the liquor picis carbonis (tar solution) to the ounce of the paste. X-ray treatment often results in a cure. Eczema is often associated with some other form of ill health, autointoxication caused by constipation, or a tendency to rheumatism or asthma. The

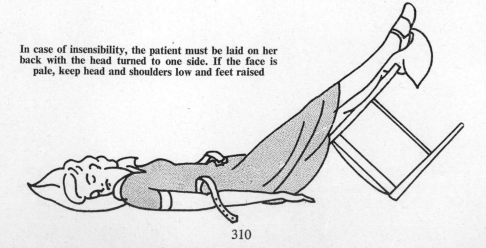

In case of insensibility, the patient must be laid on her back with the head turned to one side. If the face is pale, keep head and shoulders low and feet raised

general health must be considered. Very little meat should be taken, or none at all; and alcohol avoided.

ELECTRIC SHOCK

If there be contact with cable or wire, switch off current if possible and free the patient, but whilst sufferer is in contact he must not be touched by the naked hands of the rescuer, unless the latter be insulated upon an india-rubber mat or pile of *dry* clothes. Push the sufferer away with a piece of dry wood, or catch hold of him by covering hand with an empty india-rubber tobacco pouch. India-rubber gloves are, of course, better, but not always handy. Dry clothing or a mackintosh coat can be thrown around patient, but do not touch his clothing which may be damp. If necessary, perform artificial respiration, and do not cease until patient comes under medical attention. Treat burns in usual manner.

ERYSIPELAS

A local febrile disease producing a deep red colour of the skin, associated with a feverish condition. Erysipelas usually affects the face. A patch of skin becomes red and shiny and small blisters may appear on it; the redness spreads rapidly and there is a general feeling of illness and aching body pains. Germs have nearly always entered through an abrasion of the skin.

Treatment. Rest in bed; diet should be fluid; attend to the bowels; keep the affected part covered from the air. An antiseptic dusting powder or lanolin is useful; but a better application is a paint of ichthyol in glycerine (one part in ten). As erysipelas is a septic infection liable to produce general and possibly serious illness, one of the products known as Sulphonamides or Sulphapyridine is usually given under the direction of a doctor. The eyes should be protected by instilling a few drops of argyrol, twice daily. Injections of penicillin should give the quickest cure.

EYE, COMMON DISEASES OF THE
Conjunctivitis

This is an inflammation of the external membrane of the eyeball. There is a sensation of 'sand in the eye,' with heat, redness and a flow of tears. The condition is caused by cold winds, dust or other forms of irritation, and sometimes by an inturned eyelash or a germ. It may also be associated with catarrh and hay fever.

Treatment. Bathing the eye with a boracic lotion two or three times daily is enough to cure in many cases. Use absorbent cottonwool to wash the eye, not an eyebath. If the smarting is severe, relief is obtained by two or three drops of a solution of hydrochlorate of cocaine (four per cent). Penicillin eye-drops are very helpful.

Inflammation of the Lids (Blepharitis)

This should be treated by careful and thorough cleansing with boracic lotion, and the application of the ointment of the yellow oxide of mercury—known as golden eye ointment—or penicillin cream.

Stye

A stye is an inflammation of one of the glands at the margin of the lid. It commences with redness and pain, gradually becoming a yellowish swelling with an eyelash at its centre. It can sometimes be prevented when it is

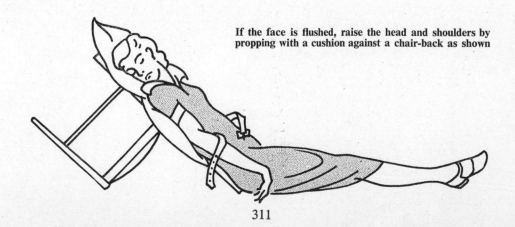

If the face is flushed, raise the head and shoulders by propping with a cushion against a chair-back as shown

beginning by pulling out a lash at the tenderest spot.

Treatment. By application of hot antiseptic compresses. A mild ointment, such as boracic or a diluted golden eye ointment, may be smeared along the lids, and this may be continued after the stye has discharged. If the abscess does not subside it should be lanced by a doctor. A tonic may be needed, as a stye is usually indicative of a run-down condition. Penicillin injections should be given.

Squint

Squint in children should never be neglected. Suitable glasses cure many cases, and exercises are nowadays prescribed to help bring the eyes into correct line. Surgery is sometimes indicated.

Cataract

Cataract is a disease of advancing years or the result of an injury, in which the crystalline lens of the eye gradually becomes cloudy and opaque. Thus the eye slowly loses its sight.

Treatment. A change of glasses may have some effect, otherwise a simple operation, rarely needing a general anaesthetic, is necessary to restore sight.

FAINTING

Fainting is due to a deficient supply of blood to the brain inducing unconsciousness. Usually lasts only a minute or less. The face is white, respiration quiet, and pulse hardly to be felt. If the fainting fit is prolonged, a doctor should be called.

Treatment. The treatment is to get the head lower than the body or down between the knees immediately on beginning to feel faint. It is important to be in open air or by an open window. A drink of water should be given—the mere act of swallowing is a stimulant to the heart—or take a teaspoonful of sal volatile in a wineglass of water; or use smelling-salts. Brandy acts as a stimulant.

If actual fainting has occurred, immediately lay the patient flat with head low; loosen tight clothing; dash cold water on the patient's face, or flick gently with a wet cloth. Smelling-salts may be held to the nose. Sal volatile can be given on return of consciousness only.

FIBROSITIS

This is a form of rheumatism affecting muscles and fibrous tissues, such as in neck and shoulder. The state of the constitution must be taken into consideration when deciding the cause.

Preventive Treatment. Avoid draughts of cold air and damp living-quarters; change clothing and shoes if wet; attend to the general health. Avoid constipation. High colonic irrigations may help.

Treatment in the Attack. Rest is necessary for the affected part. Take no meat or seasoned foods; drink plenty of fluid (alkaline waters). For medicine, sodium salicylate in four-hourly doses of ten to fifteen grains is useful; or aspirin may be taken for relief. One of the preparations of menthol and wintergreen sold in collapsible tubes can be used for massaging the affected part. Apply heat; a bran-bag or hot-water bottle will do; but better still are the forms of electrical heat, either diathermy or radiant heat (infra-red rays). The teeth should be X-rayed, as infected teeth are often a cause.

FITS
The Epileptic Fit

The subject of epilepsy usually gives a cry and falls to the ground. He is unconscious, grey, his teeth are clenched and he makes jerky movements with face and limbs. The eyes are open, fixed and staring; often froth on the lips. There may or may not be convulsions afterwards. The jerky movements are followed by a general stiffness and this in turn by relaxation and drowsiness. Many epileptics sleep for hours after their fits. Epileptics often have warnings of an attack by itching arms, flashes of light, sickness or even a particular smell which enables them to lie down in time.

Treatment. Loosen tight clothing, especially round the neck; put a roll of handkerchief between the teeth to prevent biting of the tongue, or hold a thin piece of wood between the back teeth till fit is over. Restrain movements just sufficiently to prevent the patient from injuring himself. If he has fallen in the roadway, drag him to a place of safety. Nothing can arrest the fit. Do not attempt to give the patient anything to drink.

Drugs are prescribed for each individual patient which, if persevered with, should bring a successful cure.

The Apoplectic Fit

An apoplectic fit or 'stroke' or 'seizure' results, as a rule, from the interruption of the normal circulation in the brain. It occurs mostly in later life. The fit is usually sudden, the patient is unconscious, flushed and breathing stertorously, and has probably vomited.

Treatment. Loosen all clothes, turn the head to one side. Do not move the patient if possible, until the doctor arrives, or if it is necessary, then it must be with the utmost gentleness. Remove any false teeth and apply an ice-bag to the head. Do not give anything to drink during unconsciousness.

As consciousness returns an aperient may be given (Epsom salts, or three grains of calomel) and milky drinks or barley-water given to quench thirst. Use a feeding-cup; moving of the head and sitting up are unwise. After a few days the immediate risk of further thrombosis has passed; but rest in bed must be insisted on for two or three weeks. Massage of paralysed limbs is helpful when consciousness has returned.

When apoplexy is due to haemorrhage into the brain, it is sometimes fatal. When the cause is a clot in one of the blood-vessels, the patient recovers but must live an abstemious life, and be relieved as far as possible from worry.

The Hysterical Fit

The subject of an hysterical fit is almost always a girl or young woman. It always occurs in the presence of onlookers, since its psychological reason is a craving for attention and sympathy. Laughing and crying are often parts of an hysterical seizure, but consciousness is not lost. As a rule the pulse is good; the patient can be roused, and a brusque application of cold water to the face revives. The patient should be spoken to sternly, as sympathy may cause a relapse.

Treatment. The treatment, when the fit is over, is the attempt to discover, possibly by hypnosis, the cause of the hysteria. Any errors in bodily functions must be corrected; the mind must be occupied, a tonic taken and a healthy open-air life enjoined. A complete change of environment may help.

FOREIGN BODIES

Foreign Bodies in the Eye

Treatment. If a speck of grit is on the lower lid, draw the lid down and wipe away the grit with a clean piece of cotton-wool moistened with warm water. If it is beneath the upper lid, draw the lid down over the lower lid. If this does not succeed, place a penholder or knitting needle horizontally along the lid and roll the lid back by grasping the eyelashes. When the particle is seen it may be wiped off with the moistened corner of a handkerchief.

If there is a foreign body embedded in the eyeball, it is more serious, and the help of a doctor should be sought. If a doctor is not available, a drop of two per cent solution of cocaine may be placed on the eye, and the speck extremely gently wiped off with a probe wrapped with cotton-wool. Great care must be taken not to damage the transparent portion of the eyeball. The eye must be washed afterwards with eye-lotion. If acid or quicklime is splashed in the eye, it must not be rubbed. After bathing with warm water, a little castor- or olive-oil should be dropped in, and the eye bandaged. Naturally, if the damage is serious, a doctor must be immediately consulted.

Foreign Bodies in the Nose

Children sometimes put things up the nose; beads, bits of pencil and so on.

Treatment. If it is fairly large, sometimes the article can be seen and can be gently hooked out with a bent hairpin, passing the loop of the hairpin carefully beyond the foreign body and drawing it gently down. A sniff of pepper may cause the foreign body to be sneezed out, or blowing the nose is sometimes sufficient. Tweezers may be of use. If it is out of reach, then expert attention must be sought.

Foreign Bodies in the Throat

Pieces of food, or small objects held in the mouth, may become drawn into the upper part of the throat or the windpipe by sudden coughing or laughter. Or a fish-bone or lump of food may become lodged there.

Treatment. Thump the patient hard between the shoulder-blades. Children should be turned upside down and slapped on the back. The fingers may be passed to the back of the throat in an effort to hook up anything lodged there. A fish-bone that can be seen can be removed with forceps. If not, give a piece of bread to eat; this should carry it down. A large object should be pushed on down towards the stomach.

Foreign Bodies Swallowed

Swallowing a small object, such as a cherry-stone or button, is seldom followed by trouble;

the foreign body is enclosed in the food, and passes along the bowel to be discharged with the evacuation. Larger objects, such as coins, or sharp angular things like pins, pieces of pencil, and toy whistles, can be dangerous. It is desirable to locate the foreign body by X-rays, as it may be too large to pass from stomach to bowel, and will remain in the stomach until removed by operation.

Treatment. Give the patient meals of pasty material such as bread and milk, rice pudding or bread and butter. If a child, keep him at rest. No opening medicine must be given, damage may be caused to the intestine by setting up violent movements. When the bowels act, the material evacuated must be examined carefully.

Foreign Bodies in the Ear

Children sometimes put small things into their ears, or an insect may fly in.

Treatment. If this happens, fill the ear with warm olive-oil, and turn the head down to the affected side, so that the oil runs out. If this does not succeed, the ear must be syringed gently with warm water. This should be done by a doctor, as ineffective syringing may leave a moistened pea or other seed to swell in the channel of the ear. Insects in the ear usually float out if the ear is filled with warm olive-oil.

GASTRO-ENTERITIS

An inflamed state of the stomach and bowel, characterised by pain, vomiting and diarrhoea. It is frequently epidemic, but can also be caused by food-poisoning. It is often seen in infants; the 'summer-diarrhoea' is a gastro-enteritis.

Treatment. If vomiting has not occurred, an emetic should be given, and a purgative. Hot applications should be made to the abdomen. The danger in gastro-enteritis is in the loss of fluid from the body, therefore endeavour to make good this loss by giving water or sugar-water by the mouth. Penicillin should be given.

To adults, a dose of ten grains of carbonate of bismuth with twenty drops of chlorodyne may be given; but chlorodyne should not be given to infants. For these a simple bismuth mixture is best. During the attack it is best to give no milk.

GASTRITIS

Gastritis is an acute catarrhal inflammation of the stomach. It may result from indigestible foods, over-indulgence in alcohol or influenza. Vomiting and severe stomach pains are the prominent symptoms, the tongue is furred, there may be some fever.

Treatment. Patient should fast for twenty-four hours, except for warm water sipped, and repeated ten-grain doses of the carbonate of bismuth. The patient should be in bed until pain and vomiting have ceased, and a hot-water bottle applied to the stomach. When pain and vomiting have ceased the patient may be put on light milky foods, eggs and barley-water. If pains are severe, the doctor may prescribe tincture of opium.

GERMAN MEASLES

This is an acute infectious fever. The rash consists of small closely-set spots, appearing first on the face. There is an association between German measles in the first three months of pregnancy and some congenital defects. The spots are, as a rule, more separated than scarlet-fever spots, and smaller than the spots in measles.

Spots may be seen on the roof of the mouth. The throat is inclined to be sore and the eyes hurt slightly. The rise of temperature is slight. The appearance of small hard glands at the back of the neck is a characteristic feature.

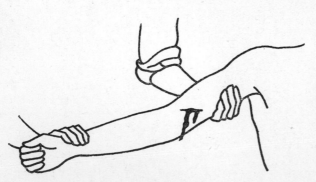

Digital pressure is here applied on the brachial artery to stop bleeding from arm or hand. The pulse is being tested at the same time

Treatment. Isolation until the spots have faded, which should be within a week. Bed and opening medicine (milk of magnesia); light diet. Fluid diet if there is a temperature.

GOITRE

Goitre is an enlargement of the thyroid gland in the neck; it may or may not be accompanied by ill-health. Simple goitre is prevalent in mountainous areas and is the result of a deficiency of iodine in soil (and hence in foodstuffs grown therein) and in the water. The swelling is visible; a rounded mass on each side of the voice-box and wind-pipe.

Treatment. Thyroid extract or iodine is given with care. Iodised lozenges are often given as a routine to children in mountainous districts where goitre is prevalent. Iodine may be added to drinking-water or table salt. Simple goitre is not dangerous in itself; but it is a disfigurement and may cause distress from pressure on the trachea (the windpipe). If it does not improve under general tonic treatment—plenty of green vegetables, iron and cod-liver oil—a portion of the gland may be removed by operation.

Exophthalmic Goitre (Graves' or Basedow's Disease)

The enlargement of the thyroid is accompanied by signs of ill-health due to the over-activity of the thyroid gland. This disease sometimes follows a nervous shock, and the signs of ill-health are palpitations, trembling of the hands, prominence of the eyes, loss of weight and nervousness.

Treatment. Rest is essential, both mental and physical. Administration of iodine drops should be under the direction of a doctor. Other lines of treatment sometimes used are X-rays, thiouracil or the removal of the enlarged gland by operation; but these are questions for the expert to decide.

HAEMORRHAGE

This means bleeding, but usually is taken to signify bleeding of a dangerous character. If the bleeding is from wounds and injuries, apply pressure with a thumb, or one thumb on top of the other, to the injured part if it can be done safely. If the haemorrhage is from a limb it can be controlled by compressing the artery against a bone at a point nearer

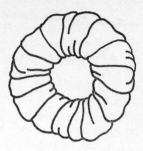

For scalp wounds, make a ring pad from a bandage by rolling the end round the fingers, then passing the remainder over and under this until it is formed. Tuck in ends

to the heart than the actual bleeding-point. Arteries may be felt as 'pulses.' Examples are the artery on the inner side of the upper arm, and the artery in the front of the thigh just below the fold of the groin. Bleeding from injuries to arm or leg may be controlled by pressure at these places. Keep the patient lying down. No stimulants should be given until bleeding is controlled. Afterwards a sterile pad can be applied, kept in place by a firm roller bandage or in the case of excessive bleeding, by a tourniquet.

In bleeding from wounds of the scalp—for instance after falls from a height or injuries from falling objects, if there is a possibility that the skull is injured—no direct pressure should be applied to the wound, but a pad of firmly rolled lint should be used, shaped as a ring and the head bandaged with this, with the wound within its centre.

HAY FEVER

This is an allergic disorder consisting of sneezing, running at the nose, redness and watering of the eyes, occurring chiefly in the early summer at the time when the grasses are flowering. It is due to the sensitiveness which some people have to plants, grasses and trees; or to dust and emanations from animals.

Prevention. A course of inoculation with the appropriate pollen vaccine gives the best hope of preventing hay fever. (It is possible by skin or eye tests to discover which grass or flower or other substance is the responsible cause.) The inoculations may have to be repeated every spring until middle-age.

Any abnormality of the nose should be rectified. Nasal sprays of ephedrine are useful. The membranes of the nose may be treated by white vaseline, and the eyes by dark glasses. Antihistamine pills and nasal sprays are most helpful during an attack. Electrical treatment, such as zinc ionisation, or ultra-short wave to the sinuses, is a valuable prophylactic.

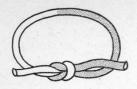

When tying a bandage a reef knot should be used. The diagram shows how this is made

HEADACHE

Headache can be a symptom either of some trivial or important health derangement.

Occasional Headaches. Can be caused by 'liverishness,' indigestion, constipation or fatigue and colds.

Persistent and Recurrent Headaches are most often due to eyestrain. They can also be caused by nose trouble, emotional upset, rheumatism or neuralgia, kidney disease, meningitis, brain tumour, etc.

Treatment. If constipation is present a laxative should be taken. A hot drink and a compound aspirin tablet may be taken on an empty stomach. Lie down in a darkened room. If headaches come on after certain articles of food, these should be avoided.

Headache of fatigue or cold is treated by warmth and rest, and a hot drink, such as milk, with a compound aspirin tablet is desired.

The headache in eyestrain is usually in the forehead and often on one side only; it commonly takes the form of 'bilious headache.' Avoid eyestrain, pay attention to an adequate diet, try not to overwork or worry. Consult an oculist, or doctor, if pain continues.

HERPES

An eruption of blister-like spots on the skin, following the line of a nerve, commonly seen on the lip in the course of a cold. When they follow the line of an intercostal nerve (the nerve which runs at the lower border of each rib), the condition is known as *shingles*. Herpes is usually associated with a run-down condition. They are often accompanied by neuralgic pain.

Treatment. A zinc ointment may be applied to the spots, and a tonic taken. Tonics are needed for the run-down condition which is often present. A one per cent ammoniated mercury paste is a suitable application.

Patients with shingles should be careful not to catch cold, to which they are liable. Shingles are related to chicken-pox. A sterile dressing should be applied and the spots kept dry with talcum powder. The doctor may

recommend an injection of pituitrin to shorten the outbreak and alleviate pain.

HICCOUGH

Hiccoughs can arise from indigestion, nerves or anxiety.

Treatment. Sipping very hot water, or ice-water, may relieve these spasms. Chewing of a lump of sugar on which five drops of essence of peppermint have been placed may help; or bending right over a cup of water and drinking from the far side. Remain quiet and still for a few minutes; take a long, slow breath.

Hiccoughing may be a troublesome condition in certain long illnesses, such as those affecting the heart or liver; in such cases the doctor in charge of the case should be informed, as the patient becomes exhausted.

IMPETIGO

A contagious skin disease, of flat, pustular sores. Impetigo is a disease usually associated with dirt, but need not necessarily be so. It is most commonly seen on the face, and may come from head or body lice.

Treatment. Soften and remove the crusts with warm olive-oil. Apply lint spread with ammoniated mercury 2·5 per cent ointment. The spread lint should be kept in place by bandage and renewed twice a day, and sores should clear up in a few days. The general health must also be attended to. Penicillin cream usually produces a rapid cure.

INFANTILE PARALYSIS (Poliomyelitis)

This is an inflammation of the spinal cord caused by an infecting virus; it is a disease which particularly attacks young children and is most prevalent in summer.

The complaint in its earliest stages may be taken for a feverish cold with flushed face, severe headache and stiffness of the neck and back. The paralytic stage may develop on the second or third day of the illness, affecting arms and legs.

Treatment. The patient must be isolated once disease is diagnosed. If cases are known to be in the neighbourhood, children must gargle with a mild antiseptic and spend as much time in the open air as possible. A doctor should see every child with feverish cold and stiff neck; this is important. A bromide may be given for relief of pain. The affected limbs must be kept in position by light splints. There must be rest and quiet and the patient's morale must be kept up. Extraordinarily good results are now obtained in the treatment of this disease, for which the doctor will prescribe.

INFLUENZA

This disease may be divided into three types, according to the seat of chief symptoms. These are the catarrhal, the gastro-intestinal or of the nervous system.

The Catarrhal Type, the commonest type of 'flu,' begins with headache, pains in limbs and back, sore throat, loss of appetite and often dizziness and a feeling of lassitude. It comes on rapidly, the temperature rises, and the patient is prostrate. There is often a dry hard cough or loss of voice. After a few days the headache and the pains are better, and the temperature normal; after a day of normal temperature the patient may get up. Pneumonia is a common complication in the elderly and should be guarded against.

The Gastro-intestinal Type has a similar onset, with nausea and vomiting, and possibly diarrhoea.

The Cerebral Type has as its prominent symptoms intense headache, with drowsiness, possibly nose-bleeding, and vomiting.

Treatment. Bed is necessary in a light and airy room, preceded by a hot bath if the patient is able. A hot drink with a couple of aspirin tablets should be taken, a dose of opening medicine, plenty of warm fluids for diet and no solid food until the temperature is normal. Cough, headache and joint pains may be ameliorated by a stimulant cough mixture for the one and aspirin compound or Dover's powder for the other.

Influenza leaves the patient weak and 'washed-out,' despondent and without energy. One of the various tonic food-drinks should help to restore energy.

Prevention. Anti-influenza vaccine, given with a hypodermic syringe at intervals of a week, is often helpful. Fresh air is important, also gargling every day with an antiseptic. The best time for protective inoculation is in the autumn and the protection lasts for about six months.

INGROWING TOE-NAIL

In this condition, caused as a rule by the pressure of shoes, the flesh at the side of the nail becomes inflamed and swollen and bulges over the edge of the nail. The name, therefore, is not quite accurate; the nail itself does not alter, but, being hard and resistant, is enclosed by the inflamed flesh. The great toe is usually the one affected.

Treatment is first of all preventive. Shoes must fit well, and nails must be cut properly, i.e. straight across.

The treatment of the condition is to get the foot well soaked in disinfecting lotion. Then cut a piece the shape of a 'V' out of the middle of the top of the nail at the ingrown corner, lift up the over-growing flesh by tucking a small piece of boracic lint soaked in glycerine beneath it. This should be repeated two or three times daily. If the over-growth is very heavy, it may be touched with a piece of bluestone (sulphate of copper). This treatment should succeed; if not, a piece at the side of the nail must be cut away. If still very painful after a few weeks, a surgeon should be consulted.

INSOMNIA (Sleeplessness)

Insomnia is very debilitating to mind and body, but it is not in itself a danger to mental balance. It is necessary to trace the cause. Pain naturally causes sleeplessness, so does a cough. High blood-pressure is another cause. Overtiredness can cause wakefulness. Sometimes it is persistent worrying. If so, after supper, the patient should take a walk for half an hour, then perhaps sit listening to music. A cup of a warm milk-drink will help; or a warm bath relax. Reading before sleep does not suit everyone as it excites the brain and imagination. In some cases a person will sleep quite soon, but wake up after a couple of hours or less, unable to get to sleep again.

Very few people realise that dyspepsia, especially with flatulence, is a chief cause of disturbed sleep. The taking of an alkali will help. Suitable alkalis are bicarbonate of soda (from a half to a full teaspoon in water), milk of magnesia, or one of the various alkaline stomach powders.

Sleep in a well-ventilated room. Do not take tea or coffee last thing at night. Try sleeping with a very high pillow. Where insomnia is wearing a person out, the use of a drug to restore sleeping habits becomes necessary. A doctor will prescribe this.

JAUNDICE

The cause of jaundice is an obstruction of the entry of the bile from the gall-bladder to the bowel; the bile is then absorbed into the bloodstream.

Jaundice may be catarrhal, when the small bile-ducts in the liver are inflamed, caused by a virus, and often epidemic. It can last up to three months, and a complete change of air is necessary to bring back complete health. Or jaundice may be obstructive, as in closure of bile-duct by a stone or a growth.

Treatment is according to cause. For catarrhal jaundice rest in bed, hot applications or a mustard poultice to the liver (i.e. lower ribs on the right-hand side), avoidance of oily and starchy foods and gentle aperients. If it is severe, only fruit juices should at first be taken. Patients with jaundice of this type catch cold easily.

For obstructive jaundice, the stone may pass naturally, or, if the stone is too big to pass, must be removed by operation.

LARYNGITIS

An inflammation of the larynx or 'voice box,' which may be catarrhal, or due to excessive use of voice. The signs are pain in the throat with dry cough and a squeaky or whispering voice.

Treatment. The voice must be completely rested and it is better to go to bed. Inhalation of steam is useful (with or without a few crystals of menthol or a few drops of friar's balsam in the boiling water); cough sedatives may be taken; damp compresses may be applied to the front of the throat. The patient should remain in a room at an even, warm temperature.

MASTOID DISEASE

The mastoid is the bony prominence behind the ear. Inflammation or abscess in the mastoid is a result of inflammation of the middle ear. It is a serious condition. Pain and tenderness is felt at the back of the ear, possibly with some swelling over the bone. The temperature is high, there may be vomiting and delirium; the patient—usually a child—is obviously ill. A surgeon must be called in

at once as the inflammation may spread to the brain membranes. Early mastoid inflammation may clear up with application of heat and sulphonamide drugs, but sometimes an operation is necessary, usually with excellent results. Penicillin or the other modern antibiotics cure most cases.

MEASLES

A common infectious disease mostly incurred in childhood, though adults are not exempt.

At first there is acute nasal catarrh, feverishness and a dry cough. After three to five days the spots begin to appear, and the eyes are red and watery. The spots are of a dusky colour, appearing first as small flat red spots, grouped in clusters of crescent shape. They come firstly on neck and face, and spread within a day or two to limbs and body, often very profuse on the back. The cough is hard and painful; sometimes almost incessant. The face is swollen and the temperature soars. After two or three days the rash fades, the temperature falls, the cough is looser and the patient is convalescent.

Treatment. Put the child to bed in a warm room, and shade lamps to protect the eyes from glare. Allow fresh air, but no draughts. There must be a fluid diet until the fever subsides, such as barley-water flavoured with lemon, or sweetened orange juice and water; milk and water, or milk and barley-water.

For medicine, a simple cooling mixture may be given. The patient may be sponged down with warm water, avoiding draughts, during the feverish stage. Bed is wisest until the spots have faded; then up in the bedroom at first and out of doors when all spots have faded and the cough has gone.

Measles take about fourteen days to develop after exposure to infection. Infectiousness soon ceases after the temperature has fallen and the spots have gone. Isolation must be maintained, however, from other children until three weeks from the first sign of illness. Complications often arise and, if so, sulphonamide drugs will be prescribed by the doctor.

MUMPS

Mumps is an infectious disease, seen mostly in childhood and adolescence, occasionally in adult life. It is characterised by an inflammation of the salivary glands.

The signs are swelling in front of and below

the ear, extending on to the cheek, on one or both sides, but usually on one side first, followed in two or three days by the other. The swelling is tender and is accompanied by pain which is worse on moving the jaw or eating. In some cases there is no feeling of illness; in others, there is feverishness with general malaise. The swelling subsides usually in four or five days.

Treatment. Keep the patient in bed until swelling has gone down, with a silk handkerchief or scarf to keep the neck warm. In boys and men an inflammation of the testicle, or in girls of the ovary, is sometimes a complication, thus the rest in bed is a wise precaution. Light diet, attention to the bowels, and warm fomentations of glycerine of belladonna to the swelling to relieve pain, are other points in treatment. Mumps is a very infectious complaint, particularly at the onset, when the swelling is beginning. A child in contact with mumps should be kept from school for three weeks.

NEURALGIA

Neuralgia or nerve pain may vary from a mere twinge to an unendurable agony. It occurs in run-down states of health and affects various nerves, of which neuralgia in the face or head is the most prevalent. The pain is often precipitated by cold draughts, or may come on without obvious cause. Decayed teeth or an unerupted wisdom tooth may be the cause. There may be pressure on a nerve, caused by local disease.

Treatment. Relief may be obtained by the application of warmth, and the administration of some pain-relieving substance such as aspirin or phenacetin. At the same time the general health must receive attention; worry avoided as much as possible; aperients may be required and a tonic taken. A dentist should be seen if the pain continues, also an ear, nose and throat surgeon.

NEURASTHENIA

This may be described as a state of tiredness of mind and body. It is a nervous debility, illustrated by worry over trifles, imaginary ailments, and an inability to concentrate. Complete change of scene is the best line of treatment, with rest for mind and body; and plenty of good food. If it continues, psychological treatment may help to reveal underlying cause.

NEURITIS

The term means inflammation of the structure of a nerve. Such inflammation may be due to injury or exposure to cold; rheumatism, septic teeth, any condition of malnutrition of the body. Too free indulgence in alcohol over a long period, or a lack of vitamin B from the diet, may also be responsible in certain cases.

The signs of neuritis are 'pins and needles' in the affected nerve, with perhaps cramp, pain and numbness.

Treatment is by rest and warmth and the treatment or removal of the cause if a cause can be found.

Vitamin B1 may be given either in tablet form or in foods, of which the richest are unspoilt cereals, although a vitamin B1 concentrate should be taken over a prescribed period. Two tablets of yeast daily should also help. Plenty of fresh air and exercise is necessary. Any focal infection must be dealt with. Pain-relieving drugs may be taken while pain is severe and cause is being sought.

NOSE-BLEEDING

A child is often frightened by nose-bleeding, which often has no apparent cause and soon stops, or maybe it is due to his having pushed something up his nose.

Treatment. Rest in a chair or bed with the head raised. If the bleeding does not stop, apply ice-water compresses to the nose and forehead, and to the back of the neck. Give ice to suck. If bleeding persists from one nostril, plug that nostril with a strip of gauze soaked in a solution of witch-hazel, or use adrenalin gauze tape, which is sold in tins. When bleeding has stopped, give children and young adults calcium in some form for a while. Calcium increases the coagulability of the blood, and this makes the bleeding less likely to recur. In adults it may be due to high blood-pressure, kidney disease, anaemia and nasal growths, but the commonest cause is an injury to the nose.

PHARYNGITIS

This is inflammation of the throat, affecting the whole of the back of the throat and not merely the tonsils. There is pain on swallowing; the whole arch of the throat looks reddened. There may be slight fever; the glands in the neck may be enlarged and tender.

Treatment. Inhalation of steam gives relief;

or two or three small crystals of menthol, a few drops of friar's balsam or pine oil, may be put in a quart jug half-filled with boiling water, and the fumes inhaled two or three times daily. Gargling with aspirin in hot water (ten grains to the wineglass) alleviates pain. A hot bath and rest in bed help at the outset.

PSORIASIS

An intractable, non-infectious, skin disease recognised by its silvery, scaly patches. It is often hereditary, its actual cause is unknown. The patches may occur on almost any part, but they follow places where clothing presses and are frequent on backs of elbows, knees, waist and scalp.

Treatment. There is no ointment which can be said to 'cure' psoriasis, though zinc ointment with tar (twenty minims of the liquor picis carbonis to the ounce) may alleviate the condition. Arsenic given internally (as prescribed by doctor) is useful. The patches disappear under the action of sunlight; treatment with ultra-violet light may be tried.

POISONING

The effective treatment of poisoning depends on the kind of poison swallowed; but if the patient's mouth is not burned, a good general rule is to give an emetic to make the patient vomit as quickly as possible. Common emetics are a tablespoonful of common salt in half a pint of lukewarm water, the patient to drink this amount or more; or mustard and water. Vomiting may be produced by tickling the back of the throat. Also give an aperient, castor-oil or Epsom salts. Exceptions to this rule are:

(1) When there is unconsciousness, in which case swallowing is impossible, medical aid must be sought for the washing out of the stomach with rubber tube and funnel.

(2) When corrosive substances such as strong acids have been taken. Neutralise the acid by giving an alkali such as chalk or magnesia or bicarbonate of soda or alkaline stomach powder, two teaspoonsful to the half pint. Corrosive alkalis, such as caustic soda or strong ammonia, should be neutralised by vinegar and water.

In poisoning by carbolic acid give Epsom salts; this forms a harmless compound with the acid.

Shock and collapse following poisoning are treated by rest and warmth. A stimulant may be given; sal volatile—half to one teaspoonful in a tumblerful of cold water—a teaspoonful to a tablespoonful of whisky or brandy (diluted); hot tea or coffee.

PYORRHOEA

An inflammation of the gum and the sockets of teeth with some oozing of matter. Bone absorption takes place, and in time the teeth fall out.

Treatment. Pyorrhoea is a common condition and in some cases the only possible cure is extraction of the affected tooth or teeth. Direct application of penicillin helps sometimes. The precise cause of pyorrhoea is unknown. Some consider it purely local, due mainly to eating soft, sweet and starchy foods. Others blame the general health. If the proper food and sufficient lime salts have been supplied in childhood, and attention paid to small tooth troubles which have arisen, young people have a good prospect of owning a sound set of teeth when they become adults.

Pyorrhoea can sometimes be arrested first by having the teeth thoroughly scaled. The pus pockets must be thoroughly sprayed with hydrogen peroxide, and some antiseptic such as iodine used to dry up the condition and harden the gums. Very hot water in which common salt has been dissolved, held in the mouth three or four times a day, will relieve inflammation. A tooth extracted where there is a bad condition may be all that is necessary, without the indiscriminate extraction of all teeth, which is mostly unnecessary.

RHEUMATISM

Rheumatism varies in severity from a twinge of pain on movement of a joint or muscle to universal joint pains and swellings accompanied by high fever (rheumatic fever); or from a mere passing stiffness to a state of complete crippling. The general health must first be built up to raise resistance. Though rheumatism is brought on by cold and damp, the real cause is a micro-organism. Diseased teeth, infected tonsils, sinus or intestinal trouble can cause rheumatism.

Treatment. A hot bath with $\frac{1}{2}$ lb. Epsom salts and a brisk rub-down after, then a warm bed in a warm room, as rest for the affected muscles, is essential. The affected parts may be rubbed with the analgesic wintergreen and menthol balm; aspirin in ten-grain doses may be taken three or four times a day. Heat applied helps to relieve pain, and exposure to infra-red rays is beneficial. Diet must contain no meat; alcohol must be restricted. Milky foods are allowed, and fluid (alkaline waters) may be taken *ad lib* as it assists the working of the kidneys.

Recurrent Rheumatism

Damp houses and damp beds can cause recurrent rheumatism, or the neglect to change damp clothing.

Rheumatic subjects should live on dry ground, preferably on gravelly soil and in places where the water is not too hard. There should be plenty of open-air exercise. The bowels should be kept open by small doses of salines.

Rheumatoid Arthritis

This is a painful and crippling form of chronic rheumatism characterised by morbid changes in the joint membrane and surrounding cartilage and bones, often causing deformity.

Treatment. Cod-liver oil, iron and yeast should be given for the anaemia with which it is often associated. Diet should contain a good deal of fat, fresh fruit and greens. Anti-rheumatic vaccine is not so much used these days but may be injected in increasing doses at intervals of from five to ten days, by a doctor. Myocrisin (a gold salt preparation) is a drug that has been found of much use.

Electrical Treatment. Radiant heat (the infra-red or ultra-violet rays) and diathermy and special baths help. Light massage is also used for the relief of stiffness.

RICKETS

Rickets is a deficiency disease of infancy and young childhood, causing the bones to become soft. There is lack of fat in the diet and insufficient fresh air. The signs are enlargement of the wrists, small swellings on the ribs near the breast-bone, paleness of skin and sweating of the head.

Rickets is less frequent since the improvement in child care generally and with the discovery of vitamin D, which prevents rickets. Rickets seldom occurs in children who have been breast-fed. The chief sources of vitamin D are cod-liver oil and halibut-liver oil; either of these may be given daily to bottle-fed infants—cod-liver oil one teaspoonful, of halibut-liver oil three drops daily. Calcium

is also needed and ultra-violet rays aid a cure.

When signs of rickets are seen, such as softness and bending of the bones, the child should not be allowed to walk for fear of deformity. A pint of fresh milk daily, and cream added to a generous diet, is necessary.

RINGWORM

A skin disease of childhood, due to the microsporon fungus. It is characterised by small circular scaly patches on the scalp and thinning of the hair. Broken hairs should be examined under the microscope to make the diagnosis certain, as the fungus can be detected. There is also ringworm of the beard and the body.

Treatment. The scalp should be shaved and washed daily, then ointment applied. Useful ointments are those of sulphur or nitrate of mercury. This treatment takes months, and watch must be kept for the irritation and soreness which these ointments may produce. Exposure to X-rays effects a quicker cure. Care must be taken not to spread the infection and children must naturally have their own towels, washcloths, brushes and combs.

SCARLET FEVER

The incubation period is usually three to four days. In scarlet fever the spots take the form of a fine red rash which may appear as a general flush on the face, and minute red spots over the body. In contrast to the flush, the part around the mouth looks pale and this is a characteristic appearance in scarlet fever.

Scarlet fever begins with headaches, sickness, feverishness and sore throat. Rash appears on the second day. Temperature is high and pulse unusually rapid. By the second day the tongue begins to show a 'strawberry' appearance. The tonsils are usually swollen. There is difficulty in swallowing. The temperature falls gradually after about four days. In the second week 'peeling' begins, but as time passes flakes are shed from all parts of the body and lasts about five weeks. Scarlet fever varies in severity, but complications may set in, such as kidney or ear trouble, which must be guarded against.

Treatment. The patient must be isolated in a warm room; fluid diet; a cooling mixture. Sponging with warm water daily, a limb at a time, is soothing, especially if temperature is above 104° F.

Every case of scarlet fever should be seen by a doctor, and the child must be kept in bed for three weeks, however quickly he may seem to recover from the acute stage. Chill must be guarded against. A weak antiseptic ointment should be used when peeling sets in.

Home nursing of scarlet fever is difficult, and the child is best in a fever hospital. Special treatment may be necessary in the form of drugs and injections of serum, which, injected at once, often mitigate the symptoms. The child must be regarded as infectious until all peeling has ceased. A course of penicillin is helpful.

SCIATICA

An inflammation of the sciatic nerve. Chills and damp, sitting on wet grass or cold stone, may be starting causes. Sciatica is also associated with unhealthy teeth, or other points of infection. The main symptom is pain in the hip and legs.

Treatment. If acute, rest in bed is necessary. The application of heat to the affected hip, aspirin or phenacetin will relieve pain. Electrical treatment is also useful in sciatica, and spa treatment or a visit to a warm, very dry climate can help. Nowadays the most common cause of sciatica is regarded as being a slipped intervertebral disc. If rest and manipulative treatment do not effect a cure, an operation may be necessary.

SEA-SICKNESS

Travel sickness is due to a stimulation of the labyrinth of the inner ear. Psychological factors are also present. Those who know they are likely to suffer in this way often imagine they are sick before the journey has started. Begin your journey as healthily as possible. Keep the bowels open, avoid greasy, heavy meals. Do not take much alcohol. If the journey is short, go and lie down with the head low. If the journey is a long one, it is best to keep about in the fresh air. Keep warm. Walk about and do not watch the waves. If well enough to go to the dining saloon, keep to the plainer dishes. If constipated, take a cascara at night or a dose of an effervescing saline in the morning. Some sedative such as phenobarbitone taken on prescription for two days before the journey will help. Also a doctor may prescribe in severe cases hyoscine hydrobromide in a one-hundred and fiftieth grain dose; but if you can brace yourself to get your sea-legs without taking drugs or medicines so much the better. Will-power does have an effect on avoiding sickness. Try to become interested in a book, a game, a conversation, if possible, keeping your mind off your own reactions.

SPRAIN

A sprain is an injury of ligaments, or muscles, not sufficient to cause dislocation. In a sprain, some of the binding fibres of a joint may be torn and not merely stretched. The immediate effect is severe pain; swelling follows and any attempt to use the sprained joint is painful.

Treatment is to apply cold compresses as quickly as possible, renewing them frequently; cover the compress with a bandage firmly applied, but not so firmly as to interfere with the circulation. If outdoors, bandage firmly over the shoe.

The joint must have complete rest until it can be moved without pain, and the affected limb should have a well-padded splint applied. A common injury during exercise, such as running or tennis, is the tearing of a few fibres of a leg muscle. This causes immediate and severe pain; there is tenderness at the injured spot, and walking is painful.

Immediate rest for a few hours is necessary; but the treatment is to apply a firm supporting bandage and to begin to use the limb as soon as possible. Some sprains are allied to fractures, and where there is any doubt, it is as well to have an X-ray of the injury taken.

A sprain with no swelling should be treated with immediate massage.

SUNSTROKE

This condition is a result of over-exposure to direct sunshine; it is more properly called heat-stroke, for it is an effect of heat, and can also occur in any exposure to high temperatures, as in very hot rooms. Wearing unsuitable clothing, and alcoholic habits, predispose to this. The onset is sudden; the patient feels faint, with giddiness, headache and maybe vomiting. Unconsciousness may follow, with flushed face and high temperature.

Treatment. Remove the patient to a cool atmosphere and spray with ice-cold water. Ice, or iced water, should be applied to the head and neck. This should be continued until the temperature has fallen to within two degrees above the normal; the patient should then rest in a darkened room, with a cool compress on the forehead. If severe, rectal injections of ice-cold water with sodium chloride should be given. Large quantities of saline must be given to the patient to drink, when he can swallow.

SWELLINGS AND LUMPS

1. **Enlarged or Inflamed Lymph-glands.** These are frequently found in the neck, especially in children, due to absorption of poison from unhealthy tonsils, adenoids, ear-trouble or teeth. If a child has such lumps or glands in the neck the cause of infection must be found. A doctor should be consulted, as the enlarged glands may be tubercular. These do not necessarily indicate tuberculosis, and the condition may be completely cleared up.

Treatment. Once the infection has been dealt with, the general health must be built up with good food, cod-liver oil, tonics and fresh air. Enlarged and tender glands may also be found above the inner side of the elbow and in the armpit and also in the groin, caused by infection brought to the glands by the different lymph-vessels. In such cases the cause of infection must be treated when discovered; matter from whitlow let out by incision; sores dressed with antiseptics; or the skin over gland swellings painted with the tincture of iodine. All doubtful lumps or swellings should be seen by a doctor as, although they may be quite harmless, they may be also a danger signal that leads to the arrest of a serious condition.

2. **Ganglia.** A ganglion is a hard cyst or swelling which may develop on a tendon sheath, commonly seen on the wrist or back of the hand. A ganglion may give a sensation of weakness in the wrist. It is painless, harmless and may disappear of its own accord. If it is unsightly it may be removed by a surgeon.

On the course of the fifth nerve, there is the important Gasserian ganglion, which may be divided in case of severe trigeminal neuralgia.

TETANUS (Lockjaw)

Tetanus is an infectious disease which occasionally develops after wounds have become contaminated with dirt, especially from roads and manured ground. As the tetanus bacillus does not like air, it is more likely to grow in deeply punctured wounds. From the wound, the bacilli make their way up the motor nerves to the brain and spinal cord. Usually within ten days of the infliction of a wound, the patient has a feeling of stiffness in the muscles that move the jaw or the neck.

These symptoms should never be neglected. They lead to spasms of the facial muscles, which extend to other muscles.

In all wounds soiled with dirt a dose of anti-tetanus serum should be given immediately or as soon as possible, by a doctor. The wound must be thoroughly cleaned with an antiseptic. By this means the prevention of tetanus is fairly certain. Once it has occurred the patient should be kept in a darkened room and sedatives given for the relief of paroxysms; sometimes chloroform may be necessary. Large doses of tetanus anti-toxin should be injected.

TONSILLITIS

In tonsillitis the tonsils are swollen and reddened. It may be caused by an infection or a general run-down state of health. There is pain in the throat and difficulty in swallowing.

Treatment. Gargles during the acute attack should be used hot and frequently. If the glands in the neck are tender and swollen, keep the neck wrapped with a wool or silk muffler. If very severe, apply a kaolin poultice and leave it on for twenty-four hours. The patient should be kept in bed in a warm room and a mild aperient given. Sulphonamide drugs or penicillin may be prescribed.

Alarm may be caused by the appearance of white or yellowish spots on the inflamed tonsils, as they may be confused with diphtheria. In diphtheria the spots are likely to appear on the palate and walls of the throat as well as on the tonsils. A doctor will be able to tell the difference.

TOOTHACHE

As a means of relief in toothache, rinse the mouth with a solution of bicarbonate of soda (a teaspoonful in a teacup of warm water), paint the gum with iodine, and if there is a hollow tooth aching, place a small piece of cotton-wool soaked in oil of cloves in the cavity of the tooth after removing food particles. Heat, such as given by a hot-water bottle, held to the face sometimes relieves pain. Dental treatment should be sought.

TUBERCULOSIS

The tubercle bacillus usually enters the body through being inhaled, or may be swallowed in infected meat or milk.

The early signs are lassitude, a slight but persistent cough, and a feeling of feverishness with rise of temperature in the evenings. There is loss of weight and sometimes anaemia. A staining of blood in the mucus which is brought up in coughing may also be an early sign. These symptoms should induce any sufferer to be X-rayed.

Treatment is by fresh air, complete rest and plenty of good nourishing food, especially the fatty foods such as milk and butter. Cod-liver oil is valuable.

This is not a disease in which recovery is quick; the health must be built up very thoroughly or relapse may occur. After recovery a fresh-air life, free from too much exertion or worry, is important. In these days there are many advanced methods of treatment and modern drugs which vastly increase the chances of complete recovery, however advanced the disease may be before it is discovered.

URTICARIA (Nettle-rash)

This is an itching eruption on the skin, occurring in patches of spots or wheals. Some people are liable to repeated attacks.

Urticaria is usually caused by an allergy to some foods which act as a poison to the individual, such as shell-fish, tomatoes, strawberries, some tinned and potted foods. Drugs, such as tetanus anti-toxin, even aspirin, quinine or penicillin, cause urticaria.

Treatment. Restrict the diet and remove the cause. This means that if the urticaria follows some form of food, a purge should be given. Allay the irritation. Calamine lotion may give relief; or an antiseptic dusting powder may be used. In severe cases a solution of boric acid should be dabbed on—a teaspoonful to a $\frac{1}{2}$ pint of water. People who are subject to urticaria may be benefited by a course of glucose. Calcium salts or anti-histamine drugs are helpful. When very severe, injections of adrenalin alleviate the condition.

VACCINATION

After vaccination, a slight papular elevation appears after about three days, over the point of inoculation. Vaccination is to gain immunity to small-pox, and is now quite free from harm or risks. The lymph is obtained from a similar eruption in healthy calves, and glycerine added. The best age to vaccinate a baby is between two and four months.

After five or six days a redness appears around each point of inoculation, and by the end of a week a 'vesicle' has formed, with some soreness and inflammation around it. There may be an associated enlargement of the glands in the armpit. If the skin is dusted with an antiseptic dusting-powder, the vesicle will dry up after ten days or so and form a scab. This will have fallen away by the end of the third week, leaving a 'vaccination mark' which remains throughout life. Re-vaccination should be performed every seven years or when exposed to infection.

VERTIGO (Giddiness)

This may occur under many different circumstances. It may be associated with head noises or diseases of the inner ear. It may occur on suddenly rising from a chair or on first getting out of bed in the morning, and may be accompanied by nausea, and it means no more than anaemia and a general loss of tone. Dizziness is often due to circulatory disorders, anaemia or exhaustion.

Attacks of sudden vertigo may be a feature of minor epilepsy, occurring at intervals, with a loss of awareness of surroundings.

Heart weakness may lead to giddiness, also high blood-pressure. Heavy smoking may cause it. Derangement of the liver often results in mild giddiness. It can also arise in brain disease, although in serious disease there are other symptoms which the doctor will recognise. Eyesight troubles may also lead to giddiness. The only cure is to consult a doctor with a view to finding the cause and dealing with it.

WHOOPING COUGH

This is an infectious fever mainly incurred in childhood. Whooping cough begins like an ordinary cold with slight fever and this is the most infectious stage. A dry cough begins early, but it is not until a week or so has passed that convulsive coughing develops with the characteristic 'whoop' accompanied by bronchial catarrh. The child is not usually very ill except for the exhaustion which follows the frequently repeated spasms, and the vomiting which the coughing sometimes causes. Bronchitis and convulsions are possible complications. The child should be kept quiet as any excitement acts as a stimulus.

Treatment. Though the cough may be to some extent kept under control by sedative cough mixtures, there is no medicine to 'cure' whooping cough. Plenty of fresh air is good, and the child should sleep in a well-ventilated room, and be out of doors by day if it is not too cold. A fumigating lamp should be kept burning in the bedroom; a teaspoonful of coal-tar inhaling fluid vaporised over the lamp allays spasms of coughing. In a child's room, it should be placed out of reach. Treatment by a vaccine, both preventive and curative, is used nowadays. The strength must be built up after with good food.

A child suffering from whooping cough should be regarded as a possible carrier of infection for six weeks from the onset.

WOUNDS

All wounds should be immediately cleansed by washing in a warm disinfecting solution, such as Dettol or tincture of iodine. Then the cut or torn edges must be brought together as closely and neatly as possible. If stitches (by a surgeon) are not necessary, the wound may be closed satisfactorily with an adhesive strip dressing. If the wound is clean and the dressing applied carefully, the dressing may be left unchanged for as much as a week, by which time healing will have taken place. A wounded member should be completely rested to allow it to heal. If there is still throbbing pain after the first day, especially with redness appearing beyond the dressing, it indicates some inflammation. The wound must be redressed. If the wound is found to be red and inflamed, a dressing of boracic lint wrung out of boiling water may be applied. Bruised and lacerated wounds may have a dressing of warm boracic lint from the start. A wound which is bleeding fairly copiously should be bandaged with sufficient pressure to control the bleeding, but a tight bandage should not be left on for more than two or three hours, when the bleeding should have ceased, then a dry dressing can be applied. See also 'haemorrhage' and 'tetanus.' All small cuts and scratches should be painted with the weak tincture of iodine.

PEOPLE WHO ARE

ALWAYS FEELING ILL

NEVER really ill—but never really fit. Lots of us feel like this these days.

We will pretend we are talking about one particular girl—let's call her Joan.

Joan is always tired. She also gets odd aches and pains in her limbs, which she puts down to 'rheumatism.' Backache is another of her complaints, which is much more difficult for her to ignore, because her tiredness makes it far worse than it would normally be.

She gets constipated very easily.

Headaches worry her a lot. At times she has a dull ache in her head for days on end.

What worries her more are horrible attacks of depression and nerves. Joan often feels that everyone is against her. She wants to cry at the slightest thing.

Of course, it goes without saying that Joan suffers from insomnia. Hundreds of little problems rear their heads, assuming gigantic proportions until, tortured and restless, Joan finally drops into an exhausted sleep.

If she *really wants* to get well, she should allow herself a month or six weeks for a concentrated 'Get Fit' campaign.

The first step is a good iron tonic, because in all probability she is a little anaemic. She must keep the tonic at home and at work so that she can take it *regularly*.

Secondly. Early to bed each night.

Step three. Curing the constipation. There is a certain type of constipation, due to a hold-up in the intestines, that means a lot of waste matter is present which should have been got rid of days before.

This accounts for biliousness, headaches, odd pains in the arms and legs, and most troublesome of all, a really bad backache.

Joan should take a good walk each day.

There are many aperients on the market that are non-habit forming, and Joan should choose one of these, because at the beginning of her campaign she may have to take one regularly. Six glasses of cold water a day will also help.

When Joan is beginning to feel better, she won't have to worry so much about nerves. Nerves and really good general health rarely go together. There is one other very important thing: a healthy body needs a happy, healthy mind, and Joan needs her share of outside interest and recreation.

All aches and pains are more noticeable when we are bored or unhappy.

INVALID COOKERY

The invalid needs the appetite tempting; careful cookery
and a prettily laid tray help to do this

INVALIDS' appetites need tempting, and a daintily arranged tray will often mean that the meal is eaten with relish, instead of being pushed away. As far as is possible, food intended for the sickroom should be prepared the day it is to be eaten, and it looks far more appetising if served in individual dishes. Never overload an invalid's tray, for nothing is more likely to discourage a capricious appetite.

Be sparing with seasoning and flavouring when preparing food for the sickroom, and serve hot food really hot and cold food really cold.

Arrowroot Gruel (1 large cup)

1 *heaped teaspoonful*   1 *teaspoonful sherry or*
  arrowroot.   *brandy.*
½ *pint milk.*   *Teaspoonful sugar.*

Mix the arrowroot to a paste with a little of the milk, boil the rest and pour over the arrowroot, stirring as you do so, return to the pan and boil for 5 minutes, stirring constantly. Add the sugar, and sherry or brandy before serving.

Arrowroot Pudding (1–2 people)

1 *tablespoonful arrowroot.*   ½ *pint milk.*
1 *teaspoonful castor sugar.*   *Small egg.*
Brandy to taste.

Mix the arrowroot to a smooth paste with a little of the milk, boil the rest and pour on to the arrowroot, stir well, return to the pan and cook for 5 minutes, stirring constantly. Take off the heat, add the well-beaten egg and brandy, pour into a small warm greased pie-dish and put into a quick oven for a few minutes to brown the surface.

Barley-water

1½ *pints boiling water.*   2 *oz. pearl barley.*
Rind and juice of a   1 *oz. loaf sugar.*
  lemon.

Wash the barley in cold water and put into a saucepan, cover with cold water and bring to the boil. Then strain and put the barley back in the pan and add the sugar. Peel the lemon thinly so that none of the white pith is removed, put the peel with the barley and sugar and add 1½ pints of boiling water, then simmer it gently for about 15 minutes. Strain into a jug and use when cold. The juice of the lemon is added when cold.

Beef Tea

1 *lb. lean shin of beef.*   1 *pint lukewarm water.*
Pinch of salt.

Cut the meat up into very small pieces and put it in a double saucepan over boiling water with the water and salt. Cover over and let it simmer for at least 2 hours. If to be used at once, strain it and take off the fat with a piece of soft paper. Otherwise stand in a cool place uncovered and remove the fat when cold.

Beef and Sago Broth

1 *lb. gravy beef.*   1 *yolk of egg.*
1 *oz. sago.*   *Salt to taste.*
1 *quart water.*

Cut up the meat finely and stew it very slowly in the water for 3 hours, strain, add salt and sago. Cook gently for 30 minutes. Remove from the heat. Beat the yolk of egg in a basin, add a little of the broth, stir well and then pour into the broth. Re-heat but do not let it boil.

Black Currant Tea

1 *dessertspoonful black*   ½ *pint boiling water.*
  currant jam.   1 *teaspoonful castor*
1 *teaspoonful lemon*   *sugar.*
  juice.

Put the jam, sugar and lemon juice into a jug, pour on the boiling water and stir well. Cover over with a plate and let the jug stand on the hotplate for 15 or 20 minutes, then strain.

Serve hot as a remedy for colds.

Brain Scallop (1 person)

1 *set of brains (calves'*   1 *gill white sauce.*
  or sheep's).   *Few drops of lemon*
1 *teaspoonful chopped*   *juice.*
  parsley.   *½ oz. butter.*
Breadcrumbs.

Wash the brains several times in salted water, then carefully remove the skin. Put them in boiling water for 2 or 3 minutes to blanch them, then drain carefully. Simmer in the white sauce for 20 minutes, add the parsley and lemon juice and put into a greased scallop shell. Scatter some breadcrumbs over the top, put the butter in tiny pieces on them and either brown under a hot grill or in a quick oven.

Bread and Milk (1 person)

1 *slice of bread.*   ½ *pint milk.*
Pepper and salt.

Cut the crust off the bread, then cut the crumb into squares. Boil the milk, pour over the bread, cover and leave for a minute or two. Add a dash of salt and pepper and serve at once.

NOTE. If liked, half a teaspoonful of meat extract or Marmite can be dissolved in the boiling milk before it is poured over the bread.

Chicken Broth

Use the liquor from a boiled fowl, add the chicken bones and bring to the boil, then simmer for 2 or 3 hours. Strain through a sieve, remove all fat and season to taste. If liked, add a very little cooked rice.

To make the broth more nourishing, add a beaten yolk and a tablespoonful of cream or top milk to ½ pint of the strained liquor and re-heat without boiling.

Chicken Panada

Take a lean chicken and wash it clean. Boil gently till the bones can be removed, then put the flesh into the liquor again and cook gently till tender. Strain off the liquor. Put the meat twice through the mincer, add a little of the liquor to thin it, and serve either hot or cold, according to the taste of the patient. A little minced onion can be added, if liked.

Cornflour Soufflé (1–2 people)

½ *pint milk.*   ½ *oz. cornflour.*
Grated rind of ¼ *lemon.* ½ *oz. castor sugar.*
1 *egg.*

Eggs, milk, white fish, chicken, custards are all standbys for meals on the way back to health

Mix the cornflour to a smooth paste with a little of the milk, boil the rest and pour on to the paste, stirring as you do so. Return to the pan and cook for 5 minutes, stirring all the time. Let it cool a little, then add the sugar, lemon rind and beaten yolk and stir well. Whip the white of egg stiffly and fold into the mixture as lightly as possible. Turn into a greased pie-dish and bake in a fairly slow oven till a pale brown. Serve at once.

Egg Flip (1 person)

½ *pint milk.*   1 *oz. castor sugar.*
1 *egg.*   *Sherry or brandy.*

Dissolve the sugar in the milk. Beat the egg well and stir the milk on to it, add sherry or brandy and pour into a glass.

Eggs and Noodles au Gratin (3 people)

6 *oz. noodles.*   2 *oz. chopped ham.*
Salt.   3 *oz. grated cheese.*
1 *oz. butter.*   3 *tomatoes.*
1½ *oz. flour.*   *Parsley.*
Seasoning.   3 *eggs.*
⅛ *pint milk.*

Drop the noodles into salted boiling water, cook for 10–15 minutes. Strain into a colander and keep warm. Melt the butter in a pan, stir in the flour, season. Add the milk, stirring well. Slice the tomatoes, chop up the parsley. Grease a casserole and arrange alternate layers of noodles, ham, cheese, tomatoes and white sauce, finishing off with the white sauce. Break an egg into a cup and gently place it on top of the dish, then do the same with the other eggs. Sprinkle all over with cheese. Bake for 20–25 minutes near the top of the oven. Decorate with sliced tomato and chopped parsley. Serve at once.

Fish Cream (1–2 people)

4 *oz. fresh haddock.*   ½ *oz. butter.*
1 *tablespoonful milk.*   1 *egg.*
½ *oz. breadcrumbs.*   ½ *gill cream.*
Salt and pepper.   *Squeeze of lemon juice.*

Wipe the fish and shred it finely, removing any bones or skin. Melt the butter in a saucepan, add the yolk, milk and breadcrumbs. Cook till thick without boiling, then add to the fish. Mix well together, then put through a fine sieve. Add seasoning, lemon juice and cream, and then the white of egg stiffly beaten. Turn into a greased basin, cover with greased paper and steam very gently for about 40 minutes. Turn out carefully and serve at once.

Fish in Custard (1–2 people)

2 *fillets of sole or plaice.*   1 *small egg.*
Pepper and salt.   *Water biscuit.*
1 *gill milk.*

Beat up the egg with the milk and the biscuit crushed to powder, then add seasoning to taste. Put the fillets one on top of the other in a greased fireproof dish and season them. Put in a hot oven, and when the fillets are hot add the custard mixture. When the fish is cooked and the custard set lift the fillets carefully from the dish and put on a hot plate, with the flakes of custard on top.

Ginger Pear Shake (2 people)

3 *fresh pears.*   1 *pint milk.*
Ginger ale.

Peel the pears, then pass through a fine sieve. Mix with the milk and three-quarters fill the glass with the mixture. Fill up the glass with ginger ale. Serve very cold.

Milk Jelly (3–4 people)

1 *pint milk.*   ½ *oz. powdered gelatine.*
Rind of half lemon.   1½ *oz. castor sugar.*

Put the ingredients into a saucepan and stir over a low heat for 10 minutes or so until the sugar and gelatine have dissolved. Do not let the mixture boil. Take out the lemon rind. Pour the milk into a basin, stirring now and again until it is the consistency of thick cream. Then pour into small wetted moulds and leave to set.

Rabbit Cream (1 person)

2 *oz. raw rabbit.*   ¼ *oz. butter.*
¼ *oz. breadcrumbs.*   ¼ *gill milk.*
½ *white of egg.*   ¼ *gill cream.*
Pepper and salt.

Put the milk, butter and breadcrumbs into a saucepan and heat till the butter melts and the breadcrumbs swell. Put the rabbit four times through the mincer, and then add it to the milk, etc. Beat the white of egg to a stiff froth and fold lightly into the mixture. Add the cream and seasoning. Three-parts fill two little dariole moulds with the mixture, cover with greased paper and stand in a saucepan with boiling water half-way up the sides. Put on the lid of the pan and steam them gently for 40 minutes, then turn out and serve. Chicken can be served the same way.

Crême Aurore

2 *oz. butter.*   2 *oz. cream of rice or flour.*
1 *tablespoonful tomato purée.*
1¼ *pints veal or chicken bouillon.*

For the Garnish: 1½ tablespoonsful finely diced red carrot, the same of french beans or shredded cabbage, and half the quantity of celeriac or head of celery.

Melt the butter, add the flour, cook two or three minutes, then draw aside and stir in the purée and bouillon. Bring to the boil and simmer 30–40 minutes. Meantime, cook the carrot in a little bouillon, add the celery and beans in water; strain. Then skim the soup, season lightly, add a nut of butter off the fire and finally add the cooked vegetables.

The Invalid's Tray

Lay a tray with a little imagination. A pretty traycloth, a couple of flowers in a small container, gives the one who is ill a feeling that life can be pleasant, that she is being cared for, and is not a nuisance.

The FIRST BABY

It is not only new mothers who will find these suggestions helpful

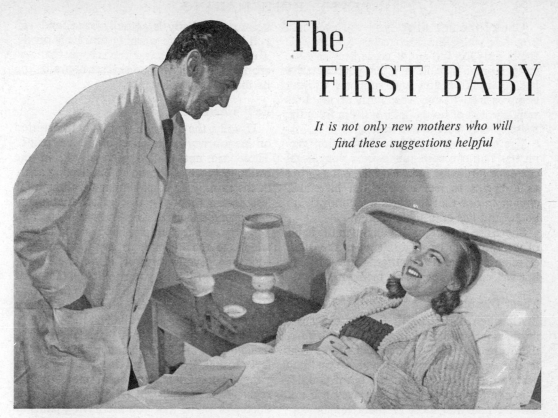

Choose your doctor with care, for much of your peace of mind depends on the confidence you have in him

HAVING a baby is an ordinary enough occurrence—unless you happen to be the mother. Then, of course, it becomes *the* event of the year. Whether the waiting months are to be happy or tedious depends upon your attitude of mind.

Do remember that pregnancy is not, in any sense, an illness. It is a perfectly natural process, and the majority of women discover that during this time they feel, and look, better than ever before.

The first thing you will want to know is the date of your baby's arrival. Take the date on which your last period started, and add nine months and seven days. For example, if your last period began on February 1, then you can expect him to arrive round about November 8.

But babies aren't always punctual! If you are going to a hospital or a nursing home, have your bag packed two weeks before The Day, and don't be surprised if you are still at home two weeks after it!

Friend Doctor

Choose your doctor carefully, making quite sure that he is interested in midwifery.

Some doctors just aren't, and while you would still be in perfectly safe hands, you must be able to look upon your doctor as a friend.

Once there was an idea that the expectant mother should 'eat for two.' Now we know that this is completely unnecessary.

Eat, just as you always do, three normal meals a day. You need one to two pints of milk a day and plenty of fresh fruit, vegetables and green salad, butter, eggs.

It is essential to have your teeth inspected, for if any of them are decayed they will undoubtedly get far worse during the time you are expecting your baby.

Clothes are always a problem, for the nicer you look the better you will feel; and pay attention to your posture. Don't slouch or sag. Hold yourself as tall as possible, with your tummy muscles drawn well in, and you won't need those maternity clothes for quite a while.

When you do begin to get bigger, don't go straight into smocks. Choose a cross-over dress, preferably in a dark colour (navy blue is best) with white at the neck, and an expanding waistline, with a long cross-over collar.

One of the first things you will need is a brassière with adjustable straps, for as a rule the breasts feel full and become heavier quite early in pregnancy. Be sure that your brassière has an uplift action and supports without compressing. It must be worn at night as well, for it is of no use taking strain from the muscles only part of the time.

The same rule applies to foundation garments. You can continue to wear your usual corset or girdle for quite a while, but as soon as it begins to feel the slightest bit small, change to one that supports the tummy from below and has adjustable lacings.

Shoes are important. If you are in the habit of wearing high heels, don't go to the other extreme and wear real 'flatties.' Choose roomy but well-fitting shoes, with medium heels.

Minor Disorders

Although it is true that most expectant mothers feel better in health than ever before, there are one or two minor disorders that tend to arise during pregnancy. You may never experience any of them, but if you do, it is comforting to know that they are not serious, and that most of them can be corrected quite simply.

Heartburn, for instance; a teaspoonful of bicarbonate of soda dissolved in a glass of hot water and sipped slowly will usually put matters right straight away.

If you find yourself wanting to 'spend a penny' very frequently during the early stages of pregnancy, there is no need to be alarmed, for this is not a 'disorder.' As pregnancy advances, the uterus no longer presses on the bladder, and the 'symptom' goes.

As the day when your baby is due to be born draws near, time begins to drag. All your final preparations and arrangements are made. Now there is nothing to do but wait. . . . No easy matter, if patience is not one of your virtues!

These last weeks mean a monotonous, day-to-day existence. You cannot plan anything ahead, simply because you do not know for certain where you will be this time tomorrow!

Some young mothers are almost afraid to go out shopping, or even to be alone in the house, for fear their baby might arrive before they can contact their doctor or get to the hospital.

There is no need to curtail your activities to this extent. A great deal has to happen before your baby is actually born, and you will have adequate warning that he is on the way. Even if you know for certain that you are in labour, it will be several hours before he makes his appearance.

Baby's Arrival

Usually, the first sign that baby has started on his journey is the onset of labour 'pains.' These are not really pains at all, in the ordinary sense of the word, but fleeting aches in the tummy or back similar to, though far less severe than, the discomfort that many women experience during the monthly period.

If any of these things happen you should telephone the hospital to say that you will soon be on your way; or, if you are having your baby at home, you should contact your doctor. You will not need his help for a very long time, but a warning gives him a chance to make his plans accordingly.

When first you think you feel a labour pain, make a note of the time, and again when you feel another. Even though they are very slight, you will find that they occur more or less regularly, and you will be able to tell your doctor or nurse that you are having pains at half-hour, fifteen-minute or five-minute intervals.

The First Stage

With a first baby, this first stage of labour may last anything from twelve to fourteen hours, or even more. But don't let this worry you, for, in the initial stages, usually the contractions are very slight, and you can relax with a cup of tea, carry on with your household tasks, or knit, sew, read or listen to the wireless. It is better to have somebody with you to talk to, if you can manage it, for it helps the time to pass more quickly.

It helps a good deal to understand exactly what is happening during labour. For nine long months your baby has been curled up in the uterus, and until you go into labour the entrance to the uterus, the cervix, is closed. Before the baby can really start moving on his journey, this entrance has to open up wide enough to allow his head to pass through. This is what is happening during the whole of the first stage of labour.

Every contraction means the cervix is opening a tiny bit wider, up and over the baby's head, until it fits across the widest part. It is easy enough to relax in the beginning, but as the contractions get stronger it becomes very difficult. You need to use every bit of your will-power if you are to resist the temptation to tighten up inside, just as you would with any kind of tummy-ache; but if you have been practising regularly throughout your pregnancy it will be easier.

Do As You Are Told

Once the cervix is fully dilated, the whole character of the labour pains changes, and you know that you have started on the second stage, which, with a first baby, lasts from half to one hour.

Now, instead of wanting to tighten up, you will find yourself taking deep breaths and pushing down for all you are worth. No doubt you will be encouraged to do so, but listen carefully to what your doctor tells you, and do exactly as he says. Each organised effort that you make means that the baby is being propelled farther and farther down the birth canal.

This is when you can help, but it is sheer hard work, and the true meaning of the word 'labour.'

But however tired you may feel, don't give up, for it means that with your co-operation you will hear your baby's first cry any time now, and you will be allowed to see him before he is bathed and tidied up.

Once the afterbirth is expelled, all your efforts are over. Now you really *can* lie back and relax—this time without any difficulty!

Varying Anaesthetics

Until the middle of the last century, nothing whatever was done to relieve women of pain and discomfort during childbirth. But in 1847 the first step was taken when Dr. James Young Simpson introduced chloroform.

Even then people were sceptical, and it was not until several years later, when Queen Victoria chose to try this new discovery, that it became popular.

But how little doctors knew about it in those days! The anaesthetic was used so indiscriminately that dealing with its after-effects was one of the major difficulties of a confinement!

But it was obviously considered better than nothing, for no further steps were taken until as recently as 1906, when from the Continent came news of a wonderful new discovery known as Twilight Sleep.

For quite a time it seemed to be the perfect answer to the problem. But the fashion didn't last, because it was discovered that this method of conducting a confinement prolonged the time of labour, encouraged 'complications' and, not only that, endangered the life of the baby.

Since then, medical research has made colossal strides.

Today we have a whole range of analgesics and anaesthetics that can safely be used to assist women in this age-old business of having a baby.

Muscular Contractions

You see, it is not quite so simple as it sounds. It is easy enough to remove pain—a general anaesthetic will do that most successfully—but the 'pains' of labour are really the contractions of the womb muscles which are propelling the baby on his journey.

If we remove the 'pains' altogether, then we may interfere with the contractions and, consequently, do far more harm than good.

This is where analgesics come in, for—unlike an anaesthetic which produces full unconsciousness and muscular relaxation—an analgesic is something that will relieve pain without interfering with the strong muscular contractions that are so necessary during labour.

A good example is the 'gas-and-air' machine which is available (during hospital *or* home confinements) to all mothers.

Perhaps the best feature about this apparatus is the fact that it is constructed in such a way that the mother can give *herself* the gas and air mixture whenever she likes, in perfect safety.

All over the world you will find many women who will tell you that these machines are 'useless' and that they 'don't help at all,' but this is usually because they have not had sufficient instruction in the *right* way to use them.

You see, the effect of inhaling this gas is not instantaneous, therefore you must begin inhaling at least twenty to thirty seconds before the 'pain' begins, which is not as difficult as it sounds when they occur so regularly.

By doing so the gas will give its maximum benefit when the contraction is at its height, and you will know nothing about it.

The majority of women find that this form

of analgesia is all they need during the entire confinement.

Other Pain-killers

In recent years a substance known as Trichlor-oethylene, or 'Trilene' for short, has received a great deal of publicity.

It is given in the same way as the gas-and-air machine, but has a deeper effect. Until recently it was used only in hospitals or nursing homes, but now it can be administered in private houses, under the supervision of a midwife. Then there is the anaesthetic known as 'caudal' anaesthesia. 'Caudal' means 'tail,' and in this method of relieving pain a substance is injected near the tail-bone, which temporarily paralyses the nerves that convey sensations of pain from the womb.

Caudal anaesthesia is popular in America, but although the effects are quite remarkable, this method has certain disadvantages—one of the reasons why it is not so widely used in Britain.

When you discuss your confinement with your doctor, be sure to ask him about analgesics, and which he recommends. Don't be afraid of sounding afraid! Why *should* any relievable pain be suffered? You want to be as comfortable as possible. He will help you.

Natural Childbirth

Then there is the method somewhat ambiguously called 'Natural Childbirth.' Actually, it is a system first introduced by Dr. Grantley Dick Read, in his book *Childbirth Without Fear*, which introduces the theory that if women were taught to relax and work *with* Nature in producing a baby, they would suffer a great deal less than when they may be, through tension and fear, resisting the rhythm of what should be a natural process.

Fear tenses the muscles and produces more pain, therefore fear must be abolished. Relaxation, which so many find difficult, has to be learnt. Exercises are prescribed especially for controlled breathing and diet. Many women who have tried it claim that they have suffered only discomfort, not pain, when the baby arrived. Careful diet can avoid many discomforts, such as a kind of poisoning that makes the whole of the waiting-period miserable, and deficiency—rickets, anaemia—in the baby. But each case has to be guided according to the subject. Women

are individual creatures, and cannot be treated as though they were on an assembly line. Some are more sensitive, others more nervous. The medical profession now believes that it is just as mistaken to withhold some form of drug to a woman who needs it, as it is to insist on anaesthetising women who do not need or want it.

Natural childbirth is alleged to minimise the need for drugs.

Read all you can about childbirth and choose your own way of coping with what is, after all, a *very* normal event.

Let the doctor and hospital help you—and never, *never* listen to old wives' tales!

THE FATHER OF YOUR CHILD

Maybe, to your husband, pregnancy seems to be such an exclusively feminine matter that, although he would like to help you as much as possible, there seems to be little he can do until the baby actually arrives. *Then*, things will be different, and he has every intention of pulling his weight as far as bathing his son and heir is concerned!

But really, you need his help *now*, in the form of love and companionship, more than ever before.

We all know that having a baby is a perfectly natural and normal occurrence, but at the same time it is a tremendous experience for a woman.

Because it is all so new, there will be times when you will be scared and apprehensive, especially if you fall a victim to those people who delight in passing on old wives' tales.

In An Adventure Together

It won't help if your husband dismisses your feelings lightly, or tries to laugh you out of them because 'it has happened to thousands of women before.' That may be so, but right now it is happening to you—and that is quite a different story!

Neither will it help you if he goes to the other extreme, and becomes worried and panicky at your slightest ailment, so that you feel that perhaps after all there *is* something wrong; no, a happy medium is what is needed at times like this. Quiet confidence from him and a sympathetic ear (because it is wonderful to be able to *admit* that you feel a bit tired or jittery, or your legs ache) and you won't feel that you are all alone in your adventure.

The attitude of the baby's father can help the lady-in-waiting to pass the time happily. A little sympathetic help goes a long way

Things He Should Do

There is another point. During pregnancy your husband should see that you have just as much recreation, or even more, than usual. Resting or not overdoing it is all very well, but nine months is a long time to wait, and the latter months can become very tedious.

Visits to the cinema or theatre, and other *joint* outings, will help to relieve the monotony.

Not only that, knowing that he is proud to be seen with you will have a wonderful psychological effect.

It is no laughing matter for you to find your figure becoming more and more heavy and clumsy, even though you know that the ultimate result is well worth it, and just telling you that 'it hardly shows at all' won't cut much ice!

What you need most is to be reassured from time to time that, however ungainly you become, your husband loves you for yourself, and that your companionship and affection are really important to him.

One word of warning to your husband: Complimentary references—however casual —to another woman's figure are unnecessary, unkind—and tactless!

The aim of every couple who are expecting their first baby should be to lead as normal a life as possible.

Physical relationships need not be avoided, except perhaps in the first three months of pregnancy, at the times when a menstrual period would normally be due, and for a few weeks before the baby arrives. But when such relationships do occur, the desire *must* be mutual.

If, to your husband, you seem averse to lovemaking, it does not mean you have changed—nor that it is a permanent state of mind. He should be patient, and respect your wishes without criticism, and you will love him all the more for his understanding.

Now a word of warning to you: Don't take an unfair advantage of your condition, and insist that your poor husband shall know every single detail of what you are going through for 'his sake.'

He gets home at night after a hard day's work and shouldn't have to listen to long descriptions of every minor discomfort you have experienced during the day. He's not heartless—just tired!

The Confinement Begins

Luckily, most of us realise that pregnancy is a woman's *job*, and even if (secretly) we do think we are being rather brave and clever, we know that we must not inflict *too* many details on the menfolk!

The worst time for 'expectant' fathers is during the confinement.

When you first tell your husband that your baby has started on his journey, more likely than not he will be filled with a sense of panic, and, for the first time, realise the full significance of the situation.

Best Way To Help

Your calmness may surprise him, but the least he can do is to hide his emotions, rather than add to your worries.

As time goes on the hours of waiting seem endless to him. Nothing much happens, and no one seems to *do* anything. He feels helpless, in the way, and certain that you are being neglected. Not only that, he is by now quite convinced that the doctor or nurse is hopelessly incompetent.

There seems to be nothing but an army of strangers keeping him away from his wife at the one time when he feels you need him most!

A first confinement is usually a long business, and this doesn't mean that there are complications.

He should keep away, but in touch, and, sooner or later, he will be told that he can announce your baby's arrival to your family and friends.

Many husbands are present at their wives' confinements these days, but that is a matter for mutual decision.

TO KEEP COMFORTABLE

KEEP a good large bottle of eau-de-cologne on hand (it can be obtained in various perfumes), as it freshens up your hair, your hands, your feet. Press chamois leather dampened with cologne over your face on a hot and tiring day . . . it blots up moisture without upsetting your make-up. To be completely fresh takes off some of the 'ungainly' feeling.

* * *

You may dance up to about six months, but gentle dances, not a Scotch Reel!

* * *

Wear suspenders, not garters, for the latter increase any tendency to varicose veins.

* * *

Remember your deep-breathing exercises. They help to decrease any nervous tension.

A walk a day is a 'must' for radiant health, whether it is striding over a heath, walking to business instead of taking a bus, or pushing the pram a little farther than the shops

PERSONALITY GLANDS

HAVE you ever wondered why it is that each of us is 'different'; not only in physical appearance, but in personality and temperament too? Some women are thin, excitable and highly strung. However much they eat, they never seem to put on weight. They have abundant energy, most of which they use up in worrying about anything and everything.

Other women are just the reverse—easygoing, carefree and placid. They take life as it comes; nothing, and nobody, seems to ruffle them. Even the fact that they tend to put on weight easily, and early in life, is never a *major* problem.

Your glands are the main cause of these differences. Not the lymphatic glands (those in your neck, for example, that swell up when you have a sore throat), but the ductless, or endocrine glands, such as the pituitary, thyroid and adrenals.

It is the secretions from these that are mainly responsible for our physical appearance, and which, at the same time, have a profound effect on our personality, well-being, and whole attitude towards life.

These glands are not mere isolated organs.

A Few Homely Talks on Everyday Ailments

They are all part of a team. If one works faster, or 'goes on strike,' the effect will be noticeable.

Glandular Types

Think of the thyroid, the important gland that lies at the base of the throat. If this gland does not produce an adequate amount of secretion, the person concerned becomes sluggish, mentally dull, and disinclined for exercise of any sort. She puts on weight, all over her body, and her hands and legs become puffy.

On the other hand, if the thyroid gland is working too hard, the person becomes irritable, unreasonable, and emotional. Her heart beats rapidly the whole time, and there is a tendency for the eye-balls to protrude.

In most of us, one gland seems to dominate the others.

Suppose you have been called the 'adrenal type.' You are gay, kind, good-hearted, sympathetic, and never moody. The weather doesn't bother you, and you eat and sleep well.

Your hair is thick, and, as you grow older, you may tend to put on weight. Your feet are small, and your fingers and toes are short. If you are married it is quite likely that you will have a large family because, for you, childbirth is often an easy business.

Adrenal—or Pituitary?

Perhaps the 'adrenal type' doesn't describe you—it may be the thyroid that is your dominant gland. You are nervy, worried, always on the go, and one of your greatest difficulties in life is relaxing.

In all probability, you are tall, and flat-chested. Your features are small and well-moulded, and your hair is fine and soft. Although you cannot help worrying about most things, you are rarely concerned about your figure, for, try as you may, it is difficult for you to put on weight.

Still not you? Then possibly, in your case, it is the pituitary that is top-dog. If so, you are artistic, and have an uncanny knack of jumping to the right conclusion. You know what you want, and, as a rule, the best way to get it. Physically, your frame is large, and you are tall, with long arms and legs.

These, then, are the three main glandular types, but there are other glands that also play their part.

The thymus, for instance, has been described as 'the gland of childhood.' It is thought that this gland more or less controls a child until puberty, after which it decreases in both size and activity. Its work having been completed, responsibility is then assumed by the other endocrines.

Don't Blame Your Glands!

Sometimes the thymus refuses to 'retire gracefully,' and we get a type of woman whom we know well.

She is dainty, with a pink-and-white complexion. She is scatter-brained and 'helpless,' and tends to dissolve into tears.

One important point: none of us is dominated *exclusively* by one gland. Our personalities and physical appearances are usually a mixture of two or more types, so you cannot blame your glands for your shortcomings! But knowing to which type you tend will help you watch for your shortcomings and make an effort to correct them. Your virtues can be taken for granted!

WHAT IS A SLIPPED DISC?

'SLIPPED disc' is certainly a fashionable complaint. So fashionable, in fact, that some of us may be reluctant to admit our doctor's diagnosis for fear that our friends may accuse us of 'shooting a line' or making a fuss about nothing.

There are older people who go so far as to maintain that there is no such complaint— that a 'slipped disc' is merely a new-fangled name for common or garden old-fashioned backache, caused by kidney trouble, lumbago, faulty posture and so on.

Nothing could be farther from the truth.

Of course, in the large majority of cases, backache *is* due to other causes. Nevertheless, a slipped disc is often the answer to many severe pains in the back that in the past could not be explained.

Pads between Vertebrae

What are these discs that seem so fond of giving us the slip? To understand this, it is necessary to know something about the anatomy of the spine.

This is not, as so many people seem to imagine, one long, flexible bone. It consists of no less than thirty-three small bones, known as vertebrae, that are placed one above the other, and held together by cartilage and ligaments.

In the centre of each vertebra is a hole, and these holes form a continuous channel through which the spinal cord passes.

Each one of these vertebrae is separated from the next by small 'cushions'; these are the discs that we hear so much about.

Their job is important. They act as shock absorbers, so that every time we twist, bend or move the spine at all, the vertebrae are prevented from grinding and grating against each other.

The outer casing of these discs is extremely tough, and the filling consists of an equally tough jelly-like substance.

Sometimes something goes wrong. Strain, injury, or a sudden movement may tear the outer covering. The jelly-like contents bulge out and the trouble begins.

Pain Is Localised

Why should this cause pain? Simply because the spinal cord gives off nerves that pass through spaces in the spinal column, and run to other parts of the body. When the discs are in place all is well, but if one bulges out, then it is bound to press on the nerves in the vicinity. Consequently we get severe pain in the part that is 'served' by that particular nerve.

For instance, if the troublesome disc is low down in the spine, it may cause lumbago or sciatica. If it is much higher up, then the pain will be in the shoulder or neck. It will not clear up until the disc is back in its proper place.

How can you tell whether or not your backache is due to a slipped disc? Unfortunately, *you* can't—but your doctor can. When he diagnoses your trouble, do please believe what he says, and don't write him off as not knowing his job just because he says it is due to fibrositis or lumbago, while your friend, whose symptoms are identical, has got a slipped disc.

You see, all the muscles of the body are encased in strong fibrous tissue. If, for some reason or another, these muscle-sheaths be-

come inflamed, then we have the condition known as fibrositis. It can affect almost any muscle in the body, and at the same time can be extremely painful and disabling.

Fibrositis Is Similar

Fibrositis, giving pain that resembles a slipped disc, can be due to a wide variety of causes. Strain, damp and draught, and teeth or tonsils that need attention, are the most common.

When you remember this fact, it isn't really surprising that so many people imagine quite wrongly that they are suffering from a slipped disc. If your trouble is constant, see your doctor; it may be a slipped disc, which can be cured.

FEARS AND PHOBIAS

EVERY one of us is afraid at some time or another. If you hear someone described as a 'wonderful person—doesn't know what fear is,' you can rest assured this remark isn't true. The person in question can be just as afraid as any of us, but she has probably trained herself to control her emotions so that nobody else suspects how she feels. She has probably taken the trouble to find out *why* she feels afraid, and having discovered the cause, knows how to deal with the situation when it arises.

The trouble with most of us is, that when we are afraid, we get into a panic that makes clear thinking impossible. In addition, the things that frighten us are so often childish, or we think they are, that we refuse to admit to them in case we are laughed at. Consequently, we try to bury our fears and pretend they are not there.

Unfortunately, if we do this, they have a nasty habit of popping up their heads just to remind us they are there, when we least want or expect them! But if we bring our fears out into the open and examine them, we stand a better chance of killing them stone dead!

Based on Ignorance

Fear is one of the oldest human instincts, and originated in ignorance. In primitive times there was so much that man could not understand. Thunder, lightning, darkness and death just couldn't be explained. These things made the poor primitive man feel powerless and weak, and, of course, he did all he could to please the gods who he imagined were responsible, in order to protect himself. That is how superstition began, because once a man had any degree of success, through a coincidence, the idea caught on, and all his neighbours followed suit.

It is a mixture of protective fear, primitive religion, and superstition that is responsible for many of the nervous troubles of today.

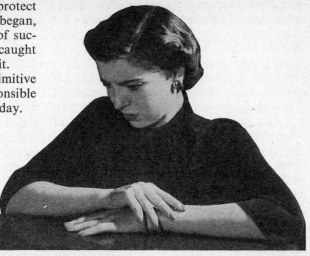

Nearly everyone has some fear, but if it is repressed it is apt to grow out of proportion

False Symptoms

Then again we may be perpetually haunted by a fear of illness. The palpitations that we experience so often convince us that we have heart disease, and we live in constant fear of sudden death.

That irritating cough, or a fleeting pain in the chest, is sufficient to confirm our suspicions of tuberculosis.

With a physical and mental effort that few people could appreciate, we muster our courage to visit a doctor, only to hear that there is nothing wrong with us.

But does this bring relief? Only temporarily, for after a while we are sure that the doctor was mistaken, and that we are, in fact, doomed!

On the other hand, we may experience attacks of panic for no known reason. We don't know why we are afraid—or of what. All we do know is that we are terrified. Our limbs tremble and become weak, and our heart-beats race uncontrollably. We feel cold, sick, and our vision is blurred.

A Feeling of Tension

These attacks, lasting anything from minutes to hours, or in some cases days, leave us exhausted and apprehensive, simply because we cannot explain them.

Not surprisingly, this confusion brings about a feeling of tension in the head, a muzziness as if the brain were made of cotton-wool, or in a 'skull-cap' of pressure.

It is hardly to be wondered at that such mental chaos gives rise to a sense of unreality, as if we, or other people, were living in a

dream. Once we reach this stage we are certain that we are going out of our minds —and so another very common fear is set up —the fear of insanity.

What is the difference between these feelings that come on for no *apparent* reason, and those felt by a primitive man confronted by a wild beast, or come to that, a burglar who suddenly sees a policeman? It is all due to fear—a sensation of helplessness because 'something' has us in its power.

Like many of us today, savages had a fear of death. They couldn't understand why anyone should die unless they were attacked. If anyone showed signs of dying it was because that person was 'possessed by evil,' and the only cure they knew was to try and 'suck out' this evil, quite literally.

Why do we always feel more comfortable eating at a table by the wall in a restaurant rather than at one in the middle of the room? Only because our ancestors, having had to hunt for their food, always ate it under the shade of a rock so that there was no chance of being attacked from behind by animals or enemies!

It is the same with people who suffer from agoraphobia (a fear of wide open spaces). In primitive times, if you were in the middle of a large plain, with no rocks or trees for shelter and protection, you were liable to be killed, or anyway severely wounded, by any wild animal or enemy you happened to meet.

Alone in the Dark

A fear of the dark—very common, although few people admit to it—can also be accounted for quite easily. In the same primitive times, animals could wander about unmolested only when it was dark, because *they* could see, whereas their enemy, man, couldn't. Consequently, any human roaming abroad after dark was courting certain death, and was quite naturally afraid, for very good reasons!

In those days, to be alone was dangerous, and this accounts for the morbid fear of being alone that some people have today. If they discover they are quite by themselves anywhere, even in their own homes, they get all the feelings of panic that I described before. Once they see another human being, or know that there is someone within calling distance, all is well, and they feel safe.

When we are children, we sometimes *learn* to be afraid because some new experience shocks our sensations and we do not know how to adjust ourselves to it. For instance, a child touches a perfectly ordinary looking box, and suddenly, a clown's head pops out on a spring, or a mechanical toy suddenly moves about. It is the unexpectedness that startles, and so every box or toy is regarded with suspicion. It is the same with ugly masks, insects, mice (especially mice), spiders, furry animals. It is not the things themselves that are frightening, but what they are liable to do next.

This sort of childhood experiences creates a feeling of apprehension, that often stays with us all our lives, and becomes what doctors call phobias. Just think of the sort of things that frighten *you*. There is always an explanation if you go back far enough.

Why We Are Superstitious

People do all sorts of things to give themselves moral support! Some men never feel 'right' unless they carry a walking-stick. This is a throw-back from the time when a man was never safe unless he carried a club.

You often hear of nasty accidents happening to people after they have lost their special mascot or charm. The reason is generally because they pin so much faith to the object, that when they find they have lost it, they are in such a panic that they don't pay any attention to what they are doing, and get knocked down by a bus, or meet with some similar accident.

The thing to remember is that *everyone* is afraid at times, and most of us have our pet fears. They are nothing to be ashamed of, nor on the other hand, should they be a source of pride.

A fear of heights, enclosed spaces, cats, snakes, knives, insanity, illness, blood, crowds, defying superstitions . . . all have their origin in primitive times.

You can generally work the cause out for yourself, and having once discovered it, you will find that you will be able to see it in its right proportion. It is possible that a phobia intrudes to such an extent that it may interfere with your mode of living, and prevent you from enjoying life to the full. Then you know that the time has come for you really to face up to your phobia and get right down to the cause.

If you cannot do this unaided, a medical psychologist is the person to help you. By these few examples of present-day superstitions and fears, we can see that however civilised and balanced we are, there is a little of the savage hidden somewhere in *all* of us.

If we take the trouble to work out the cause of our fears and phobias we are already nearly cured, as it is only the things we do not understand that we fear.

JAUNDICE

JAUNDICE is the name we use to describe an illness in which the skin takes on a yellow discoloration. Actually this may happen in quite a number of diseases. It can happen in certain rare diseases of the blood where the red blood cells are destroyed and broken down. The colouring matter of these cells is then set free in the circulation and gives the skin a yellow tinge.

By far the most common variety of jaundice, however, is that brought about by some sort of trouble in the liver or gall-bladder. Anything, in fact, that interferes with the free flow of a fluid called bile.

Bile itself is made by certain cells in the liver and is normally stored in a small sac-like organ, called the gall-bladder, tucked away on the under surface of the liver.

It plays a big part in the digestion of fats, and when needed the bile is poured from the gall-bladder along a duct which opens into the duodenum where it mixes with our food in its journey through the intestinal canal.

If, however, the liver is diseased, or a stone blocks up the exit from the gall-bladder, the bile stagnates and its yellow pigments begin to show in the skin, instead of being carried out of the body with the rest of the waste materials of the digestion.

The Symptoms

One of the simplest kinds of jaundice follows a chill on the liver. Catarrhal jaundice, we call it.

An attack of this sort very often starts with a feeling of being a bit 'under par,' loss of appetite with, perhaps, a feeling of nausea, slight shiveriness and even a mild rise of temperature.

The skin may feel itchy—often maddeningly so—and this may happen before any discoloration appears.

When it does, the typical yellow of jaundice is usually first noticed in the whites of the eyes and then spreads rapidly all over the skin surfaces, although the actual illness occurs before the change in the skin-colour, which begins usually when the patient has passed the worst stage. It may vary very widely from a pale lemon-yellow to a really quite deep orange colour in intensity.

Another sign to watch for is the change in the colour of the urine, which becomes a very dark orange, almost red in colour.

Sometimes this sort of jaundice breaks out in small epidemics.

Another very similar variety, called infective hepatitis (which means an inflammation of the liver) is caused by a virus.

This illness was quite common in the Forces during the war and had much the same effects as the catarrhal jaundice already described.

Blood Diseases

None of the common kinds of jaundice permanently damages the liver, as a rule, and most people recover without any ill effects.

In most medical circles it is, however, usually considered wise not to take any form of alcohol for the following six months, so as to rest the liver and give it the best possible chance of complete recovery.

Now for a bit more about some of the blood diseases mentioned at the beginning as being a less common cause of jaundice.

Destruction of the red blood cells can produce a yellow skin. One of the causes of such blood destruction is a specially severe kind of anaemia called pernicious anaemia, where the trouble is caused by the red blood cells being destroyed at an early stage in their development before they become fully mature.

The skin in this particular disease becomes a very characteristic lemon-yellow colour.

Another fortunately rare form of jaundice caused by blood-cell destruction is known as haemolytic disease of the newly born.

Rhesus-negative Babies

Perhaps you have read about these rhesus-negative babies. The majority of them, and first babies at any rate, escape this disease completely, but every now and then a second and subsequent child born to a mother of the rhesus-negative group may stimulate its mother's blood to produce certain substances that attack and destroy the blood of her unborn infant.

When this occurs, the child may be born with jaundice due to the destruction of some of its blood cells before birth. The destruction may be so severe as to call for a blood transfusion.

In moderate or mild cases, however, the jaundice disappears within a week or two as soon as the baby has made sufficient new blood of its own and has got rid of the products of blood destruction from its system.

HINTS *on* PACKING

IF you have to go into hospital, you may look on packing as a bore, but actually it can be a pleasure, if methodically done. Put all the heaviest things in the bottom of your case. Anything likely to crush, *roll* with tissue-paper between the folds. If you have to buy extra nighties, remember that nylon does not need ironing to look nice. Take eau-de-cologne to damp your hair, and hairpins to twist it into quick curls that will set and dry in a few minutes when you want to look specially nice.

* * *

Put adhesive tape around the necks of any bottles, so that the contents cannot spill. If buying new bottles, get the plastic kind. Take a pretty tin, to keep 'offerings,' such as cakes and biscuits, in. Put in a notebook in case you need to make jottings of recipes given you by a bed-neighbour, something you read in a book or the address of a new friend. Take a specially luscious tablet of soap, to give you a luxurious feeling.

WHAT SHALL WE CALL THE BABY?

THERE is one rule, and that is do not call a girl-baby by a name which will 'date' her! There are not only fashions in names, but also those that link up with some historic event. Avoid these, if you want to be popular with your children later. Some parents like plain names, others romantic ones. It would be very dull if we were all called by the same kind of name. Many famous people have a name that adds to their distinction; others have lent glory to an everyday name.

Adam—Man (*Hebrew*)
Adrian—Black (*Latin*)
Alan, Alain—From Welsh bard of harmony (*Celt.*)
Alaric—Noble ruler (*Teut.*)
Alexander—Helper of men (*Greek*)
Alfred—Counsellor (*Teut.*)
Alvin—Elf friend (*Teut.*)
Ambrose—Immortal (*Greek*)
Andrew—Manly (*Greek*)
Angus—Great strength (*Celt.*)
Anselm—Divine helmet (*Teut.*)
Anthony—Inestimable (*Latin*)
Arnold—Strong as an eagle (*Teut.*)
Arthur—Noble (*Celt.*)
Asa—Physician (*Hebrew*)
Ashley—Craftsman (*Teut.*)
Athelstan—Noble stone (*Teut.*)
Aubrey—Ruler of spirits (*Celt.*)
Austin—Contraction of Augustus, august (*Latin*)

Adela, Adele, Adeline—Of noble birth (*Teut.*)
Adrienne—From Hadrian, a town in Picenum (*Latin*)
Alice, Alicia, Alys, Alison—Truth (*Greek*)
Aline, Aileen—Noble (*Teut.*)
Alma—A maiden (*Hebrew*)
Amabel—Lovable (*Latin*)
Amanda—Lovable (*Latin*)
Amber—Precious (*Arabic*)
Angela, Angèle, Angelina—Angelic (*Greek*)

Anne, Anna, Annette, Annabel—Fair grace (*Hebrew*)
Anthea—Grace (*Hebrew*)
Antonia, Antoinette—Inestimable (*Latin*)
April, Avril—April
Arline—A girl (*Teut.*)
Audrey—Noble threatener (*Teut.*)
Aurelia—Golden (*Latin*)

*

Baptist—A baptiser (*Greek*)
Bardolph—Distinguished helper (*Teut.*)
Barnaby—Son of exhortation (*Hebrew*)
Barnard, Bernard—Bold as a bear (*Teut.*)
Barry—Straight as an arrow (*Celt.*)
Bartholomew—Friend (*Hebrew*)
Basil—A king (*Greek*)
Benedict—Blessed (*Latin*)
Bertram, Bertrand—Bright raven (*Teut.*)
Beverley—Beaver meadow (*Anglo-Saxon*)
Boris—A fight (*Russian*)
Brian, Bryan—Strong (*Celt.*)
Bruce—From Bruys, town in Normandy
Bruno—Brown (*Teut.*)
Burgess—Freeman (*Old Eng.*)

Barbara—Foreign (*Greek*)
Beatrix, Beatrice—Joy-giver (*Latin*)
Belinda—Beautiful snake (*Latin*)
Bella, Belle—Beautiful (*Fr.*)
Berenice, Bernice—Bringing victory (*Greek*)
Bernarde, Bernardine, Bernadette—Bold as a bear (*Teut.*)
Bertha—Bright (*Teut.*)
Beryl—Precious stone (*Anglo-Saxon*)
Blanche—White (*Fr.*)
Blodwyn, Blodwen—Security (*Celt.*)
Bridget—Strength (*Celt.*)

*

Calvin—Bald (*Latin*)
Carl—A man (*Teut.*)
Cary—Walnut tree (*Teut.*)
Caspar, Casper—A horseman (*Persian*)
Cecil—Blind (*Latin*)
Cedric—War chief (*Celt.*)

Charles—Strong (*Teut.*)
Christian—Belonging to Christ (*Latin*)
Christopher—Bearing Christ (*Greek*)
Claude—Lame (*Latin*)
Clement—Merciful (*Latin*)
Clifford—The ford by the cliff (*Teut.*)
Clive—A cliff (*Anglo-Saxon*)
Clyde—Glorious (*Greek*)
Conan—Wisdom (*Celt.*)
Conrad—Resolute (*Teut.*)
Constant—Faithful (*Latin*)
Cornelius, Cornel—A horn (*Latin*)
Crispin, Crispian—Curly haired (*Latin*)
Cyril—Lordly (*Greek*)
Cyrus—The sun (*Persian*)

Camille, Camilla—Servant of the temple
    (*Latin*)
Candace—Glowing (*Latin*)
Candida, Candy—Glowing (*Latin*)
Carlotta, Charlotte—Strong (*Teut.*)
Carol, Carole, Carola, Caroline—Strong
    maiden (*Latin*)
Cassandra—She who inflames with love
    (*Greek*)
Catherine—Pure, clean (*Greek*)
Celeste, Celestine—Heavenly (*Fr.*)
Celia, Cecilia, Cecily—The heavens (*Latin*)
Charity—Charitable (*Saxon*)
Charmian—Handmaiden (*Greek*)
Chloe—Blooming, verdant (*Greek*)
Christina, Christine—Christ's messenger
    (*Latin*)
Clare, Clarice—Clear (*Latin*)
Claudia—Lame (*Latin*)
Cora, Corinne, Corinna—Maiden (*Greek*)
Cynthia—From Mount Cynthus (*Greek*)

*

Damon—To rule or guide (*Sanskrit*)
Dana—Darling (*Celt.*)
Dennis—From Dionysus, a god of revelry
    and wine (*Greek*)
Dominic—Born on Sunday (*Latin*)
Douglas—Dark grey (*Celt.*)
Drew—Skilful (*Teut.*)

Daphne—A bay-tree (*Greek*)
Deirdre—Mystic (*Celt.*)
Delia—From the island of Delos (*Greek*)
Della—A princess (*Teut.*)
Denise—From Dionysus, god of wine (*Greek*)
Diana—Goddess of light (*Latin*)
Dinah—Judgment (*Hebrew*)
Dolores—Sorrows (*Spanish*)
Donna—Mistress (*Latin*)

Dora—A gift (*Greek*)
Doris—A sacrificial knife (*Greek*)
Dorothy—Gift of God (*Greek*)
Drusilla—Grace (*Anglo-Saxon*)
Dulce, Dulcia—Sweet (*Latin*)

*

Earl—Nobleman (*Anglo-Saxon*)
Edgar—Rich spear (*Anglo-Saxon*)
Edmund—Happy protection (*Anglo-Saxon*)
Edward—Rich ward (*Anglo-Saxon*)
Eliot—God's gift (*Hebrew*)
Ellis—God is my salvation (*Hebrew*)
Elmer—Famous and noble (*Anglo-Saxon*)
Emile—Industrious (*Latin*)
Eric—Ever king (*Scand.*)
Errol—Wanderer (*Latin*)
Ethan—Strength (*Hebrew*)
Eugene—Well born (*Greek*)
Eustace—Steadfast (*Greek*)
Evan—Young warrior (*Celt.*)

Edith—Rich gift (*Anglo-Saxon*)
Edna—Rejuvenation (*Hebrew*)
Edwina—Rich friend (*Anglo-Saxon*)
Eleanor—Bright (*Greek*)
Elizabeth—Oath of God (*Hebrew*)
Elodie—Music (*Greek*)
Eloise—Famous holiness (*Teut.*)
Elsa—Noble maiden (*Teut.*)
Elvira—White (*Spanish*)
Enid—Spotless purity (*Celt.*)
Erica—Royal (*Scand.*)
Ernestine—Serious (*Teut.*)
Estelle—A star (*Latin*)
Eugenia—Well born (*Greek*)
Eunice—Good victory (*Greek*)
Evelina—Life (*Greek*)
Evelyn—Pleasant (*Celt.*)

*

Fabian—A bean grower (*Latin*)
Felix—Happy (*Latin*)
Fenelk—Of the fens (*Celt.*)
Ferdinand—Leading an adventurous life
    (*Teut.*)
Floyd—Grey (*Celt.*)
Francis—Free (*Teut.*)
Franklin—A freeman (*Teut.*)
Frederick—Peaceful ruler (*Teut.*)

Faith—Fidelity (*Latin*)
Felicity—Happiness (*Latin*)
Fidelia—Faithful (*Latin*)
Frances—Free (*Teut.*)
Freda—Peace (*Teut.*)

*

Gabriel—Man of God (*Hebrew*)
Gary—Spear-bearer (*Teut.*)
Gaston—Hospitable (*Teut.*)
Gene—A diminutive of Eugene
Geoffrey—God's peace (*Teut.*)
George—Farmer (*Greek*)
Gerald—Spear wielder (*Teut.*)
Gerard—Firm spear (*German*)
Gilbert—Bright pledge (*Teut.*)
Giles—A kid (*Greek*)
Glenn—A dale (*Teut.*)
Godfrey—God's peace (*Teut.*)
Gordon—The triangular hill estate (*Teut.*)
Gregory—Vigilant (*Greek*)
Guy—A leader (*Fr.*)

Gabrielle—Of God (*Hebrew*)
Gail—Father's joy (*Hebrew*)
Georgia—Feminine form of George
Geraldine—Spear wielder (*Teut.*)
Gilda—Golden (*Anglo-Saxon*)
Gillian, Jill—Downy-faced (*Latin*)
Gladys—A Welsh form of Claudia
Gloria—Fame (*Latin*)
Greta—A contraction of Margaret
Griselda—Stone battle-maid (*Teut.*)
Gwendolen—White-browed (*Celt.*)

*

Harold—Powerful warrior (*Scand.*)
Harvey—Progressive (*Celt.*)
Hector—Holding fast (*Greek*)
Henry—Ruler of the home (*Teut.*)
Hilary—Cheerful (*Latin*)
Hiram—Noble (*Hebrew*)
Howard—Guardian of the hedge (*Teut.*)
Hubert—Of bright mind (*Teut.*)
Hugo—Thought (*Scand.*)
Humphrey—Support of peace (*Teut.*)

Harriet—Ruler of the home (*Teut.*)
Hazel—From the tree so named (*Anglo-Saxon*)
Helène, Elaine—Bright (*Greek*)
Heloise—Famous holiness (*Teut.*)
Henriette—'Riette' is a pretty abbreviation. Ruler of the home (*Teut.*)
Hermione—Maiden of high degree (*Greek*)
Hester, Hesther—A star (*Hebrew*)
Hilda—Battle-maid (*Teut.*)
Hildegarde—Battle-maid of war (*Teut.*)
Honoria—Honourable (*Latin*)

*

Ian—Scottish form of John
Ivan—God's grace (*Hebrew*)
Ivor—An archer (*Teut.*)

Ida—Happy (*Greek*)
Ilka—Every (*Gaelic*)
Imogen—Beloved child (*Greek*)
Ina—A Latin suffix meaning 'little'
Inez—Portuguese form of Agnes
Irene—Messenger of peace (*Greek*)
Iris—A rainbow (*Greek*)
Irma—A stranger (*Teut.*)
Isabel, Isabella, Isobel—Variations of Elizabeth

*

James—A supplanter (*Hebrew*)
Jason—An atoner (*Greek*)
Jasper—Master of the treasure (*Persian*)
Jeffrey—God's peace (*Teut.*)
Jerome, Jerry—Holy name (*Greek*)
Jesse—Wealthy (*Hebrew*)
Joel—Strong-willed (*Hebrew*)
John—Grace of the Lord (*Hebrew*)
Jonathan—The Lord's gift (*Hebrew*)
Julian—Belonging to Julius (*Latin*)
Justin—Right (*Latin*)

Jacqueline—A supplanter (*Hebrew*)
Jane—A variation of Joan
Janet, Janette—A diminutive of Jane
Jean, Jeanne, Janine—Variations of Joan
Jeannette—A diminutive of Jeanne (*Fr.*)
Jennifer—White wave (*Celt.*)
Jessica—God's grace (*Hebrew*)
Joan, Joanna, Johanna—Grace of the Lord (*Hebrew*)
Jocelin, Jocelyn—Merry (*Latin*)
Josephine—Addition (*Hebrew*)
Joyce—Merry maid (*Old English-Latin*)
Judith, Judy—Praised (*Hebrew*)
Julia, Juliet, Juliette—Downy-faced (*Latin*)
June—Ever youthful (*Latin*)
Justina, Justine—Right (*Latin*)

*

Keith—The wind (*Gaelic*)
Kendall—Chief of the dale (*Celt.*)
Kenneth—Handsome (*Celt.*)
Kent—Chief (*Celt.*)
Kirk—A house of worship (*Gaelic*)

Karen—A Scandinavian form of Katherine
Katharine, Katherine, Kathleen—Pure (*Greek*)
Kay—I rejoice (*Greek*)

*

Lancelot—A boy servant (*Latin*)
Laurence, Lawrence—The laurel (*Latin*)

Lee—A shelter (*Anglo-Saxon*)
Leo, Leon—A lion (*Greek*)
Leroy—The king (*Old French*)
Leslie—One who leases (*Teut.*)
Lester—Shining (*Anglo-Saxon*)
Llewellyn—The lightning (*Celt.*)
Lucian—Light (*Latin*)
Luke—A contraction of Lucian or Lucius
Lyle—An island (*Teut.*)

Laura—The laurel (*Latin*)
Lavinia—A woman of Latium (*Latin*)
Leila—Darkness (*Arabic*)
Lenore—Bright (*Greek*)
Leola—Dear (*Teut.*)
Leslie, Lesley—One who leases (*Teut.*)
Lilian, Lillian, Lilas, Lily—A lily (*Latin*)
Lilith—A snake (*Hebrew*)
Linda—Handsome (*Latin*)
Lois—Better (*Hebrew*)
Lola—Originally a diminutive of Dolores
Loraine, Lorraine—Sorrowing (*Latin*)
Loretta—Little learned one (*Teut.*)
Lorinda—A derivative of Laura
Lorna—Lost (*Anglo-Saxon*)
Lucia, Lucile, Lucille, Lucinda—Light (*Latin*)
Lydia—A woman of Lydia (*Greek*)
Lynn, Lynne—A cascade (*Teut.*)

*

Malcolm—Male servant of Columbia (*Celt.*)
Mark, Marcus—Hammer (*Latin*)
Martin—Warlike (*Latin*)
Matthew—Gift of Jehovah (*Hebrew*)
Maurice—Dark in colour (*Latin*)
Michael—Godlike (*Hebrew*)
Miles—A warrior (*Teut.*)
Morgan—A sea-dweller (*Celt.*)
Mortimer—Dweller beside still water (*Celt.*)
Myron—Myrrh (*Greek*)

Madeline—A variation of Magdalene
Mae—A kinswoman (*Anglo-Saxon*)
Marcella—Shrewd combatant (*Latin*)
Marcia—Brave (*Latin*)
Margaret, Margot, Marguerite—A pearl (*Greek*)
Maria, Marian, Mariana—Bitter tears (*Hebrew*)
Marietta—Derived from Maria
Marjorie—A pearl (*Greek*)
Marlene—Derived from Magdalene
Martha, Marta—A lady (*Aramaic*)
Mary—Bitter tears (*Hebrew*)
Maureen—Dark (*Celt.*)
Maxine—The greatest (*Latin*)

Melanie—Dark-complexioned (*Greek*)
Melinda—Gentle (*Greek*)
Melissa—A bee (*Greek*)
Merle—A blackbird (*Fr.*)
Miranda—Admirable (*Latin*)
Miriam—Exalted (*Hebrew*)
Mona—Unique (*Greek*)
Monica—An adviser (*Latin*)
Muriel—Fragrant (*Greek*)
Myra—The admirable (*Greek*)
Myrtle—Token of victory (*Greek*)

*

Napoleon—Of the new city (*Greek*)
Neal, Neil—A champion (*Celt.*)
Nicholas—Victory of the people (*Greek*)
Nigel—Black (*Latin*)
Noel—Christmas (*Latin-French*)
Norman—Niord's man (*Teut.*)

Nancy, Nannette—Derived from Anna or Anne
Naomi—Pleasant one (*Hebrew*)
Natalia, Natalie—Born (*Latin*)
Nina—Goddess of the sea (*Babylonian*)
Nita—Bright (*Latin*)
Nona—The ninth (*Latin*)
Norma—A square (*Latin*)

*

Oliver—The olive (*Latin*)
Oscar—Bounding warrior (*Celt.*)
Owen—Young warrior (*Erse*)

Olga—Gracious (*Slav*)
Olive, Olivia—An olive (*Latin*)
Olwen—Dreamer (*Celt.*)

*

Patrick—A nobleman (*Latin*)
Paul—Little (*Latin*)
Percival—Courteous (*Greek*)
Perry—Precious gems (*Teut.*)
Peter—A rock (*Greek*)
Philip—Fond of horses (*Greek*)

Pamela—All honey (*Greek*)
Patience—Patience (*Latin*)
Patricia—Of noble birth (*Latin*)
Paula, Paulette, Pauline—Small (*Latin*)
Peggy—Derived from Margaret
Phoebe—Radiant (*Greek*)
Phyllis—A green leaf (*Greek*)
Priscilla—Ancient (*Latin*)
Prudence—Discretion (*Latin*)
Prunella—Harvest (*Celt.*)

*

Quentin—The fifth (*Latin*)
Quilla—Herb (*Anglo-Saxon*)

*

Randolph—House wolf (*Gothic*)
Raphael—Medicine of God (*Hebrew*)
Raymond—Wise protection (*Old Frankish*)
Rex—A king (*Latin*)
Richard—Stern king (*Anglo-Saxon*)
Robert—Bright in fame (*Teut.*)
Roderic, Roderick—Famous ruler (*Teut.*)
Rodney—Road servant (*Anglo-Saxon*)
Roger—Spear of fame (*Teut.*)
Roland, Rollo—Fame of the land (*Teut.*)
Ronald—A contraction of Reginald
Roy—A king (*Old French*)
Rudyard—Famous rod or wand (*Teut.*)
Rufus—Red (*Latin*)
Rupert—Bright fame (*Teut.*)

Regina—A queen (*Latin*)
Rita—Courageous (*Sanskrit*)
Roberta—Bright in fame (*Teut.*)
Rosa, Rose—A rose (*Latin*)
Rosamond, Rosamund, Rosalind—Famous protection (*Teut.*)
Rowena—White skirt (*Celt.*)
Roxana, Roxane—Dawn of day (*Persian*)
Ruth—Beauty (*Hebrew*)

*

Sebastian—Awe (*Greek*)
Seth—Appointed (*Hebrew*)
Silvester, Sylvester—Belonging to the forest (*Latin*)
Simon—He who hears, famous (*Hebrew*)
Stephen, Steven—Crown (*Greek*)
Sterling—Genuine (*Teut.*)

Sara, Sarah—A princess (*Hebrew*)
Selina—Moon-goddess (*Greek*)
Serena—Tranquil (*Latin*)
Sheila—Irish form of Cecilia
Shirley—Dweller in the sunny meadow (*Teut.*)
Sibyl, Sybil—A prophetess (*Greek*)
Sonia, Sonja—Wise one (*Slav*)
Stella—A star (*Latin*)
Stephana, Stephanie—A crown (*Greek*)
Susan, Susanna—A lily (*Hebrew*)
Sylvia—Dweller in the forest (*Latin*)
Sybilla—A prophetess (*Greek*)

*

Terence, Terry—Smooth (*Latin-Greek*)
Theobald—People's prince (*Teut.*)
Theodore—God's gift (*Greek*)

Thomas—A twin (*Aramaic*)
Timothy—Honour God (*Greek*)
Tobias, Toby—The Lord is good (*Hebrew*)
Tybalt—Form of Theobald

Teresa—A reaper (*Greek*)
Theda—Divine (*Greek*)
Thelma—A nursling (*Greek*)
Theodora—God's gift (*Greek*)
Thyra—Belonging to Tyr, god of strength (*Teut.*)

*

Una, Unity—One; together (*Latin*)
Ursula—Little-bear (*Latin*)

*

Valentine—Healthy (*Latin*)
Vernon—Flourishing (*Latin*)
Victor—The conqueror (*Latin*)
Vincent—Conquering (*Latin*)

Valeria, Valerie—Valiant (*Latin*)
Vanessa—A butterfly, from a mystic divinity (*Greek*)
Vera—True (*Latin*)
Veronica—A flower (*Latin*)
Victoria—Victorious (*Latin*)
Vida—Life (*Latin*)
Vina—A Hindu musical instrument (*Sanskrit*)
Viola, Violet, Violette—A violet (*Latin*)
Virginia—A maid (*Latin*)
Vivian, Vivien—Lively (*Latin*)

*

Walter—Powerful warrior (*Frankish*)
Warner—Protecting warrior (*Teut.*)
Warren—A protecting friend (*Teut.*)
Wilbur—Bright resolve (*Teut.*)
Wilfred—Desire for peace (*Teut.*)
William—Helmet of resolution (*Teut.*)
Winston—Dweller in the friendly town (*Teut.*)

Wanda—A shepherdess (*Teut.*)
Willa—Resolute (*Teut.*)
Wilma—Resolute contender (*Teut.*)
Winifred—White wave (*Celt.*)
Wynne—White (*Celt.*)

*

Yolande—Dreamer (*Latin*)
Yvette—Little ivy vine (*Teut.*)
Yvonne—Grace of the Lord (*Hebrew*)

*

Zelda—From Griselda, of stone (*Teut.*)
Zita—Mistress (*Hebrew*)
Zoe—Life (*Greek*)
Zona—A girdle (*Greek*)

ALL CHILDREN LOVE

DRESSING-UP

Suggestions for making impromptu fancy dress and how to make wigs

'Dressing-up' for the Children

You are likely to want fancy costume from time to time for the children and a splendid plan is to keep a trunk or large box into which you can cast all sorts of oddments to be ready when you need them. Almost anything which you might consider pure rubbish really does 'come in useful some day' where fancy dress is concerned. So save old garments which are capable of being easily adapted, bright papers and tinfoil, odd skeins of wool, buckram, vivid ribbons, gay American cloth, cardboard, and miscellaneous showy beads.

What use will they be? Aprons and peasant blouses can be cut from white summer frocks. Cardboard, coloured papers, tinfoil, American cloth, and beads are all useful when it comes to making crowns and fairy wands. Brown and black wool are easily transformed into beards, moustaches and the long plaits of peasant girls and fairy-tale princesses.

Little Dutch girls are always pretty, but a blonde wig with plaits adds a certain something the others haven't got

Oddments of black velvet or silk can become masks for masked dances or for highwaymen.

All gaily coloured scarves, on being discarded, should go into the theatrical box. They are most adaptable for turbans, pirates' head scarves, and gipsy sashes or cummerbunds for children. An old tablecloth of thick dark material is worth saving, too, for it is easily pleated up at one end to fit the neck and so becomes a highwayman's or period cloak. You can cut a most regal-looking crown from a strip of gold oil blaze, shaped into 'strawberry leaves' along the top edge and ironed off on to upholstery buckram. It can be jewelled showily with large bright gums from the sweet shop, surrounded by pearl beads. American cloth, too, has sufficient 'body' to be twisted into a sugar-bag cone for a mediaeval lady's tall headdress.

Don't forget crêpe paper, which may be pleated into a waist tape and sewn to it to form a kilted skirt. It can be tacked together very quickly, and though its life is not long, many fancy costumes are, after all, worn only once. For this reason all fancy dress, whether of paper or material, should be only quickly run up and not finished any more than is necessary to give a good effect. Aim at something that will hold together for a few wearings and look impressive in a showy way.

King Richard . . . but his crown is not worth a ransom! The 'jewels' come from the sweet-shop and the tunic is an old blouse of Mother's

Seen at a Distance

When making stage costumes, allow for the fact that the dress will be seen only at a distance, and therefore all trimmings and accessories need to be somewhat exaggerated. Delicate finishes or fine embroidery would simply be lost under these conditions, and the state of the wrong side does not matter in the least. Often seams need only be tacked together with large stitches, and a line of big running stitches in matching cotton will serve to hold a hem.

Crêpe paper does not need hems at all, as its edges are firm and non-fraying. Stitch it by machine, as it is apt to tear under hand sewing. To get pretty flared or fluted effects on frills or the bottoms of skirts or sleeves, cut them across the grain and stretch the edges a little between finger and thumb.

Keep one or two old sheets and pillow-slips for dressing-up purposes. With a few stitches or pins they are so easily draped into last-minute representations of nuns, ghosts, and other dramatic figures garbed in flowing white.

Ruffs are needed for many costumes, such as those of Elizabethan days, as well as for Harlequins and Pierrots. The easiest way of making them is to cut several straight strips of book muslin, theatrical gauze, or crêpe paper. Make each strip about 12 in. wide and quite twice the length round the neck. Place several strips one over the other, and run a gathering thread through the lengthwise

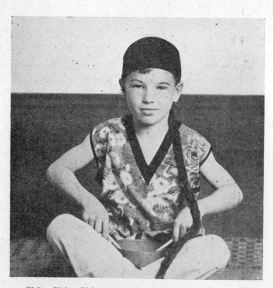

Chin, Chin, Chinaman—but unlike the rhyme, he doesn't look very sad. An easy and effective costume to put together

centres of all at once, drawing it up to fit the neck. Either attach it to a white band which fits tightly round the neck by means of a hook and eye, or sew ribbon over the gathering thread, with ends long enough to tie the ruff in position.

The edges of the frills should be left raw or may be bound with contrasting material or crêpe paper. This ruff is effective and much more quickly and easily made than a formal pleated one.

A pie-dish frill, slipped over the head and held in closely to the neck with an india-rubber band, makes a good small ruff for one wearing only! Invention can run riot, and use all sorts of odd things to represent something quite different.

Always try first what can be done with things already to hand or easily borrowed. For instance, an attractive Biblical costume, suitable for Nativities or such plays as *Jonah and the Whale*, can be simply contrived from a plain night-gown, an old-fashioned kimono dressing-gown stored in the acting box, a striped scarf and a square of butter muslin. Get the silhouette and general effect right, without worrying too much about details.

Making Wigs from Wool

Often the simplest home-made fancy costume is given just the right air by an appropriate wig. A short-haired child does not look right as a Dutch peasant minus the long pig-tails, nor can short hair be powdered to give, not only whiteness, but high-piled curls to a *poudré* costume. Wigs are extremely expensive to buy or hire, and often hot and heavy to wear. Grandma in a play may be still in her teens but a white wig will add years!

Fashioned at home from ordinary knitting wool, they are very cheap and easy to make, and exceedingly light and comfortable on the head. Don't confine yourself to 'natural' hair shades; for many romantic, jazz, or comic costumes coloured 'hair' is extremely effective and adds to its wearer's good looks. Generally speaking, most of the pastel shades and some bright colours are very becoming to girls, while for men orange, crimson, and bottle-green are amusing and effective.

As these wool wigs are easily washable, they may be laid by after use, and worn again later, either as they are or adapted to a different costume.

For a foundation, use a well-fitting net

shingle-cap. Even easier to sew the wool on to, provided it is in sound condition and fits down well over the ears, is an old hat lining. For the wig itself you will want, according to the style, from two to four 1-oz. *hanks* of 4-ply knitting wool. Wool ready wound into balls is useless for this purpose.

A Girl's Wig

To make a girl's wig in whatever style, you must start in the same way. Open out two hanks of wool, without cutting them, and loop them over a small table. Spread out the part lying on the table-top smoothly to form a thin, even layer, and then put in the parting with a long embroidery thread in flesh colour.

To do this, start at the end of the hank farthest away. Slip half the thread under the first half-dozen strands of wool. Bring it up and tie it once to the half on the top. Go on knotting and tying each little group of strands together, working towards you, till all the wool is 'parted.'

You will need some kind of head-block to hold the foundation cap out while you are sewing on the wool. A saucepan of suitable size does very nicely! Fasten your net-cap firmly round it, padding out the flat bottom of the pan with a little tissue-paper, so that the cap is kept taut. Then lay the 'parted' hanks of wool over the front part of the cap, with the parting at centre-front or side, as seems more appropriate or becoming.

Working from the parting down to where the ear will be, lightly sew the wool, in thickness of about a dozen strands at a time, down to the cap. Use rather sketchy tacking stitches. They will sink into the wool and be lost. If the wig is for a girl, as you stitch, push the wool into becoming waves with your fingers as a hairdresser does when she sets your hair.

By the time, waving and stitching, you reach about to the crown of the head, the two hanks will be exhausted. Put the wig on the wearer to judge where the hanks should be cut. On the left side leave the wool long enough to twist into a small 'ear-phone.' On the right side cut it much longer, so that the strands, when plaited later, will be long enough to go across the back of the head. Plaiting shortens the wool, so allow for this when cutting.

From the wool cut off, lay aside enough for the right-side ear-phone. Use the rest to fill in the back part of the wig. Do this with

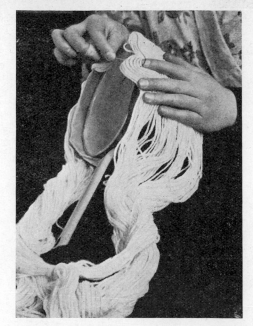

Here is a wig being made with a saucepan as the 'model'

loops about twenty strands thick, placing each loop inside the previous one until the space is all filled up. Plait the long end of wool that was allowed for the purpose on the left-hand side, and bring it across the back of the cap, just above the neck, so that it covers the cut ends of the loops.

If long plaits are wanted, as for a mediaeval character, use another hank of wool for each plait, and sew one end of it in place under each ear-phone, which in this case should be kept as small and flat as possible.

For *poudré* costumes, curls can be fixed in the same way, twisting shorter lengths of wool into spirals, and holding them with paste or spirit gum. They will stay in sufficiently for a stage appearance, but cannot be recommended for an evening's dancing, which would probably soon straighten them out.

A 'bun' at the nape of the neck or a Greek knot high on the head are both easily twisted up from a length of wool and sewn or hair-pinned into place.

A man's wig is simplicity itself to make. Proceed just as already described, but lay the wool straight instead of with waves, and cut off at the correct length all round. The short bob is right for fairy princes and the 'hair' cut off just clear of the shoulders correct for an ancient Egyptian. Pirates need a short pigtail.

CHOICE of a CAREER

There are no special technical qualifications for being a kennel maid. Common sense, patience, love of animals, good health are necessary

BOYS are not so anxious to be engine-drivers these days as to pilot the fastest plane in the world. Girls in their teens are still attracted by the glamour of the stage, although this is apt to wear off. To be an airline hostess has a glamour appeal, and the very hard work entailed may be forgotten. However, if there is some difficulty in thinking of the right career for the young son or daughter to follow, it is often because many types of work are forgotten. The following suggestions may aid a decision on a momentous point—perhaps the most important anyone can make, since work takes up at least half of our lives, and it is as well that it should be a happy choice.

AGRICULTURE. For responsible jobs in this sphere a degree is necessary, and financial assistance is available. Whether aiming for a degree, or just wanting an outdoor life, the local Employment Exchange have up-to-date details of the Ministry of Agriculture's plans for training and employment. The need for land workers is urgent.

ACCOUNTANT. Good general education essential, university degree unnecessary. Must have aptitude for mathematics and write legibly. Articled as clerk for five years to a chartered accountant (premium may be asked). Full particulars from the Society of Incorporated Accountants and Auditors, Incorporated Accountants' Hall, Victoria Embankment, London, W.C.2.

ARCHITECT. Aim is to register with the Architects' Registration Council. This comes

C.O.I.

Foresters are urgently needed. Here is a student learning to measure a tree. A course normally takes two years, and board and lodging is free in residential schools

preferably by way of full-time course of five years, or three years up to intermediate examination standard, then work whilst studying part-time for the final examination. List of schools obtainable from the Secretary, Board of Architectural Education, Royal Institute of British Architects, 66 Portland Place, London, W.1.

AIR STEWARDESS. Girls between the ages of 21 and 35 are selected. Must be smart, capable, able to speak at least one other language and have a knowledge of First Aid. Medical examination necessary. Great advantage to have worked in a hospital, or have had experience of catering or welfare work. Apply to one of the air lines such as B.O.A.C., Stratton House, Piccadilly, London, W.1; or B.E.A., Keyline House, Ruislip, Middlesex.

ALMONER. This is hospital work. Training takes two years at a university school. Must be at least 21 years old for this work. The Institute of Almoners, Tavistock House (North), Tavistock Square, London, W.C.1, have up-to-date details.

BANKING. Apply when 16 years old, but not much older. Big banks have a waiting list and their own training schools. These are free. There is earlier promise of promotion to managerships than in the past. Apply to any well-known bank, or to Institute of Bankers, 11 Birchin Lane, London, E.C.3.

BEAUTY CULTURE. It is best to attend a beauty school for a short course of about six months. Or apply to a well-known salon when about 25 years old. Competition very keen. Alternatively, apply for work in the cosmetic department of a large store; no previous training will be required. Must be cheerful, good mixer.

BLIND, Home Teaching of the. Good general education necessary; experience of social work useful. A career for those between 25 and 35 years old. Training begins in the autumn for a certificate of the College of Teachers of the Blind. Medical Officer of Health at the Town Hall will be able to give individual advice.

BUYER. Factory Buyer is usually a man; store buyer often a woman. Most stores take

B.E.A.

A charming Air Stewardess on the tarmac at Northolt welcoming passengers on board the aircraft

would-be buyers as apprentices. Thorough experience as saleswoman best grounding. Part-time evening classes can be taken. Apply to large stores, or get addresses of possible factories from the Employment Exchange.

CATERING. *Canteen.* Considerable demand for qualified candidates. Full-time course of training sponsored by the Institutional Management Association. Or apply for work in the canteen of a large establishment. The Industrial Catering Association, 140 Park Lane, London, W.1, will answer enquiries and give advice.

Demonstrator. Variety of jobs in connection with manufacturers of food products or gas and electricity supply authorities. Domestic Science students have first chance. Education Officer at the Town Hall has information about the various courses.

School Meals. General cooking experience and a liking for children required. Education Officer at the Town Hall welcomes applications and knows where there are vacancies.

CHIROPODIST. The course is full-time and takes two years. The Society of Chiropodists, 21 Cavendish Square, London, W.1, has details of local centres and offers advice about setting up in private practice.

Beryl Grey in *Sleeping Princess*. To follow an artistic career, stage, art or literature, usually means that life is all ' feast or famine,' but those with talent find the opportunity for self-expression makes it worth while

CIVIL SERVICE. Variety of jobs from work in a Post Office to posts in the Foreign Service and Colonial Service. Most entries by way of competitive examinations. Details about examinations and recruitment from Civil Service Commission, 6 Burlington Gardens, London, W.1.

CONTINUITY GIRL. *Films.* She is responsible for the continuity of every scene in the film. Secretarial training and acute observation essential for this exacting work. Write to the major film companies.

COURIER. Opportunities occur with travel bureaux. Rarely are women employed as couriers. Advisable to apply direct to travel bureaux such as Messrs. Thos. Cook & Son, Ltd., Berkeley Street, London, W.1, or to the

British Travel and Holidays Association, Queens House, St. James's Street, London, S.W.1, which will provide details about registration. Women can find employment as hostesses to look after travellers in various resorts. Knowledge of languages useful.

DENTIST. Specialised training starts at the age of 17 years, and gaining the diploma admits one to the Dentists' Register. Refer enquiries to The Dental Board, 44 Hallam Street, London, W.1.

DISPENSER. Short course of nine months for the Society of Apothecaries' examination. Booklet on this career obtainable from the Society of Apothecaries of London, Black Friars Lane, Queen Victoria Street, London, E.C.4. Messrs. Boots, the Chemists, run apprenticeship schemes: apply to 82/83 High Holborn, London, W.C.1, for details.

DRAUGHTSMANSHIP. Mainly for men, but occasional opportunities for women. Must be good at lettering, and skill at map drawing a help. Apply to Association of Engineering and Shipbuilding Draughtsmen, 96a St. George's Square, London, S.W.1.

DRESS DESIGNING. Attendance at an Art School before applying to well-known fashion houses, or passing an entrance examination to Royal College of Art, London (age 17–25) for Diploma of Design; or can work three years for National Diploma of Design awarded by Ministry of Education. Positions as designers may be in industry, films, *haute couture*, wholesale dress trade. Local Employment Exchanges give help in the choice of progressive firms.

ENGINEER. *Civil.* This branch appeals to those with a scientific leaning and desire for open-air life. May begin as an apprentice with a firm of civil engineers plus part-time study; or an apprenticeship, then a University course; or go direct to a University on leaving school. Official body to which to refer is Institution of Civil Engineers, Great George Street, London, S.W.1.
Electrical. Electrical engineer deals with all equipment from heavy power to light current apparatus. Full-time courses of about three years, also student apprenticeships, all lead to membership of the Institution of Electrical

Engineers, Savoy Place, Victoria Embankment, London, W.C.2.

Mechanical. Training is normally five years' full-time practical work with evening study, or three years full-time. The trend is to specialise in aeronautical, automobile or marine. Details of examinations obtainable from Institution of Mechanical Engineers, Storey's Gate, St. James's Park, London, S.W.1.

FARMS AND GARDENS. *Herb Farming.* Women of all ages can undertake this work. Usual to train with idea of starting a farm of one's own. A year's training gives experience in the practical herb-farm cycle. Details from the Herb Farm, Seal, Kent.

Market Gardening. Application for training is made to the local offices of the Ministry of Labour and National Service. Small wage whilst training.

Milk Recorder. For details, write to the Milk Marketing Board, Giggs Hill Green, Thames Ditton, Surrey.

FORESTER. Must be Matriculation standard, commencing 18–20 years of age. Three years' training of part-time study and practice. Payment and housing. Apply Forestry Commission, 25 Savile Row, London, W.1.

HAIRDRESSER. Now an essential, not a luxury business. Best to take an apprenticeship with a first-class salon. Individual advice given by Incorporated Guild of Hairdressers, Wigmakers and Perfumers, 33 Gt. Queen Street, London, W.C.2, or National Hairdressers' Federation, 20 Cranbourne Gardens, London, N.W.11.

FOOTBALLER. Apply to one of the well-known clubs. Cannot sign an agreement as a professional until at least 17 years old. Full details in the booklet obtainable from the Football Association Publications, 22 Lancaster Gate, London, W.2.

GIRLS IN GREEN. These are drivers employed by the Government, chiefly by the Home Office, to drive cars used by officials. Write to Ministry of Supply Official Car Service, Kingston House Garage, Knightsbridge, London, S.W.7, stating driving experience and whether prepared to go abroad.

INTERIOR DECORATOR. For the artistically minded this career is full of scope. Practical and theoretical training detailed in programme issued by the City and Guilds of London Institute, publishers John Murray, 51 Albemarle Street, London, W.1.

JOURNALISM. One way is to enter a newspaper or periodical office in clerical capacity. Or try to join local or provincial paper as journalist. Read advertisements in 'Situations Vacant' in daily Press and journalistic papers. Consult the Institute of Journalists, 2–4 Tudor Street, London, E.C.4,

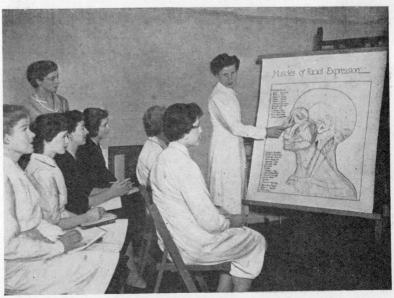

A thorough knowledge of bone structure is necessary for the would-be beautician. Courses last anything from three months to a year. Good health, cheerfulness and the right touch are essentials

Courtesy of Innoxa (London), Ltd.

or the National Union of Journalists, 22 Gt. Windmill Street, London, W.1, about training schemes.

KENNEL WORK. Few large-scale kennels, but sometimes possible to obtain work with dogs combining this with odd jobs. Training available at the Bell Mead Training School, Priesthill House, Old Windsor, Berks. See also the canine Press—*Our Dogs* or the *Dog World*. Work, for which little or no training is required, can sometimes be obtained in the kennels of the dog-racing stadiums. Love of animals is an essential.

LECTURER. For lecturing in Teachers' Training Colleges a good degree and teaching experience are necessary. Information can be obtained from Local Education Authorities. There are also lecturing agencies for those who wish to capitalise on specialised knowledge. A course in public speaking may be a help.

LIBRARIAN. Especially for those with literary tastes. A useful summary of the prospects and qualifications required compiled in a free leaflet issued by the Library Association, Chaucer House, Malet Place, London, W.C.1. Applicants should be between the ages of 16 and 19.

MANNEQUIN. Training is necessary, but the course lasts only about a month. Go to a school with good connections, because work is booked through the school. Only follow this career if you have the right appearance, personality and excellent physique, otherwise, the odds are against anything like continuous employment. One of the well-known agencies and schools is Lucie Clayton Ltd., 449 Oxford Street, London, W.1, or Gaby Young, 37 Panton Street, London, S.W.1.

MEDICINE. High standard of education. Must pass pre-medical examination in chemistry and physics. This is followed by five years' full-time study in a recognised medical school for a degree. Refer to British Medical Students' Association, B.M.A. House, Tavistock Square, London, W.C.1.

METEOROLOGIST. The Meteorological Offices of the Air Ministry, Kingsway, London, W.C.2, and the Colonial Service, Church House, Gt. Smith Street, S.W.1, recruit staff annually. Must be prepared to spend time overseas.

Medicine in all its aspects is wide open to women these days

NAAFI. This is usually work in canteens, but there are also vacancies in bakeries, factories, warehouses, clubs, offices, and transport in connection with the Navy, Army and Air Force Institutes, at home and abroad. Address application to Imperial Court, Kennington Lane, S.E.11, or the Employment Exchange.

NURSE. Training lasts three years, after which one can specialise. Can enter a hospital as a student nurse from the age of 18 years to 30 years; some hospitals take older women. Payment whilst training. Advice and information from the Nursing Recruitment Service, 21 Cavendish Square, London, W.1.

NURSERY NURSING. Can train in a college from the age of 17 years or in a nursery from the age of 15 years, for the National Nursery Certificate. Information regarding colleges from the Association of Nursery Training Colleges, 6 Grange Gardens, Pinner, Middlesex. Medical Officer of Health at the Town Hall will provide names of local nurseries where students are trained and paid whilst training.

OCCUPATIONAL THERAPY. Training takes $3\frac{1}{2}$ years, and though there is no upper age limit, students are not accepted before they are 18 years old. Sympathetic nature and psychological understanding are a help. Association of Occupational Therapists, 251 Brompton Road, London, S.W.3, provide information about scope, schemes, fees and so on.

PHOTOGRAPHER. Many branches in this sphere, from newspaper, commercial, scientific, portraiture to medical and agricultural. The Institute of British Photographers, 49 Gordon Square, London, W.C.1, provide comprehensive information and literature to would-be photographers. Or apply to newspaper.

PHYSICAL TRAINING. Attractive career for the young athlete. Men take a degree course followed by a year specialising in Physical Education. Women take a special three-year course. Some colleges are grant-aided, and the Educational Officer at the Town Hall has details of local training centres.

PHYSIOTHERAPY. This term indicates physical means by which health may be maintained and restored, such as massage, remedial exercises and electrical treatment. Good education, physique and condition of the hands are important. Students accepted from the age of $17\frac{1}{2}$ years for the three-year course. Details from the Chartered Society of Physiotherapy, Tavistock House (North), Tavistock Square, London, W.C.1.

POLICE. Men must be 5 ft. 10 in. tall; women 5 ft. 4 in. Age limits: men, 20 to 30; women, 20 to 35. Initial three-months training. Statement of conditions of entry obtainable from the local Chief Constable, Police Headquarters. A policeman can rise to be Assistant Commissioner of Police, and there are many attractive openings and wide scope for the ambitious.

RADIOGRAPHY. Two-year course for the student who is at least 18 years old. Qualified radiographer works in a hospital or clinic. Notes for students available from the Society of Radiographers, 32 Welbeck Street, London, W.1.

SCIENTIST. *Metallurgy* offers responsible posts in research and production. Demand is increasing. The Institute of Metallurgists, 4 Grosvenor Gardens, London, S.W.1, will supply information about examinations and courses.

Geology. Employment is in universities and museums. Degree is necessary, and the Education Officer at the Town Hall can supply information about specific courses of study.

Analytical Chemist. Analysts employed in Government laboratories, laboratories of public analysts and private laboratories. Degree is required, and the address of the appropriate university can be obtained from the Education Office, local Town Hall.

SKATER. Must start training very young. On leaving school, practice is full-time. Success in competitions and championships leads to professional status, if desired. Training is given at well-known rinks.

SPEECH THERAPIST. This is a medical auxiliary service and the course takes three years. Examinations are conducted by the College of Speech Therapists, 68 Queen's

Gardens, London, W.2, which will also advise about training-schools.

SPEEDWAY RIDER. First step is to purchase bike and equipment—approximate second-hand price £75, or new as much as £200. Then comes a trial at a well-known stadium. Courage, plus sound ability, is needed. Usually, an agreement with a promotor is signed and there is then a retaining fee. Speedway publications, such as *Speedway Gazette*, give helpful advice about scope, where to train if necessary, purchase of the bike, and other up-to-date information.

STAGE. *Acting.* A career for those with outstanding talent. The Royal Academy of Dramatic Art, 62 Gower Street, London, W.C.1, will provide details of scholarships. Or apply for an audition to local or touring repertory companies.

Ballet. Training must start at a very early age. Application to the Secretary, Royal Academy of Dancing, 154 Holland Park Avenue, London, W.11, will bring informative literature.

Designing. This is a career for an art student. The Central School of Arts and Crafts, Southampton Row, London, W.C.1, provides opportunities for theoretical study and practical work in the theatre.

STEWARDESS. Must be a trained nurse, at least 25 years old and unmarried. Apply for an interview to one of the large shipping companies, such as Cunard White Star Line, Cunard Building, Liverpool 3.

STENOTYPIST. This is typing phonetically and is a form of secretarial work for those who wish to travel. Many secretarial colleges teach stenotyping, including the Palantype College, 229–231 High Holborn, London, W.C.1, which also has lists of vacancies.

TEACHER. Great demand for teachers. It is now possible to train even after having entered another profession. Tuition is free. Full details found in Notes for Intending Teachers, issued by the Ministry of Education, Curzon Street House, Curzon Street, London, W.1.

TELEPHONIST. The Telephone Manager of the local G.P.O. interviews likely applicants. Paid whilst training.

TRICHOLOGIST. Trichology is usually part of the stock-in-trade of the hairdresser (care of health of the hair); permanent waving equipment manufacturers also appoint these specialists. Training is generally by way of a three-year course at a technical school. There are various private schools. The Institute of Trichologists, 47 Vale Road, Sutton, Surrey, will supply a syllabus and all regulations for membership.

VETERINARY SURGEON. Professional status is by way of a Diploma of the Royal College of Veterinary Surgeons. Training takes five years. Details from Royal College of Veterinary Surgeons, 9–10 Red Lion Square, London, W.C.1.

WINDOW DRESSER. An art student is most suited to the work. Apply to large stores for full-time work, addressing application to Staff Manager. In the smaller shops, window dressing is combined with selling or clerical

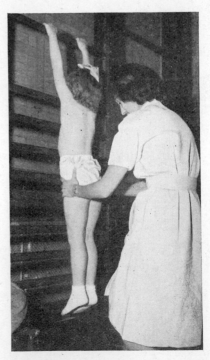

A physio-therapist needs personality and initiative, for no two patients are alike. This little girl is having posture training for a curved spine

work. Courses in window dressing are also given by the College of Distributive Trades, 107 Charing Cross Road, London, W.C.2.

YOUTH EMPLOYMENT OFFICER.
Duties vary from giving advice on careers and the administration of the office to help to young people during the first years of their employment. This post is obtained through the Civil Service, whose headquarters are at 6 Burlington Gardens, London, W.1.

HER MAJESTY'S SERVICES

NAVY. In general, officers enter as naval cadets and attain the rank of lieutenant at the age of about 22 years. Boys of 15–16 can enlist as seamen. Address of local Recruiting Office obtainable from the Post Office or the Employment Exchange.

ARMY. Opportunities for skilled and unskilled men. Entry usually through an army apprentices' school or enlistment. Initial training at any Army Basic Training Unit. Post Office or Employment Exchange will supply local address.

AIR FORCE. Training is in flying and a wide variety of trades and duties. Volunteers accepted from the age of $17\frac{1}{2}$ years. Preliminary interview with appropriate Recruiting Office, whose address can be obtained from the Post Office or the Employment Exchange.

* * *

WOMEN'S ROYAL NAVAL SERVICE. Recruits must be between 18 and 28. Enrolment is for four years. Main recruiting office, Queen Anne's Mansions, London, S.W.1. Apply for illustrated booklet, enrolment form and list of vacancies.

WOMEN'S ROYAL ARMY CORPS. Sign on for three or four years, at any age between $17\frac{1}{2}$ and 36 years. Illustrated booklet available from the local Army Recruiting Office; Post Office will supply this address.

WOMEN'S ROYAL AIR FORCE. Eighteen groups of jobs in the W.R.A.F. Volunteers accepted for a minimum of four years from $17\frac{1}{2}$ to 36 years, and the Royal Air Force,

There are many exciting and important jobs in the police. Here a revolver is being examined for finger-prints. A policeman can rise to be Assistant Commissioner of Police

Victory House, Kingsway, London, W.C.2, will supply up-to-date literature.

Your Qualifications

To have a desire to follow a particular career is at least a pointer in the right direction. When you have found just what abilities are required, be ruthless with yourself and find out if you really have these qualifications. It may be possible with study to make up for some lack. Some characteristics, however, might make a chosen job impossible. You cannot be a pilot if you dislike heights, or a chef if you are allergic to being shut in a hot atmosphere. You will fail in the jobs necessitating human contacts—journalists, beauty operators, airline hostesses, advertising, hotel employment, travel-agency work—if you do not care for your fellow creatures. And if forestry, civil engineering, agriculture, the police force sound right for you, then you must be happy leading an outdoor life.

Make out a list of careers that attract you, with a column for abilities needed and another column for frank remarks on your own capabilities. Write down your state of health, finances or any circumstance that might affect the choice of a career. In fact, quiz yourself honestly. This will be a guide.

WHAT ARE THEIR FEARS?

Some children show their feelings, others repress fears and childish worries

IT is a dreadful thing for a child to be afraid, and yet it is often the parents themselves who are directly responsible for many of their children's fears—quite unwittingly, of course.

A very young baby experiences fear only if he hears any sudden, loud noise, or if he has the sensation of falling. Any other fears he shows as he grows from a baby to a young child are acquired generally through a misguided adult! The tendency to develop various fears and phobias seems to begin, as a rule, when a child is around three years old.

As he gets more venturesome, his mother, quite naturally, has to show more anxiety in an effort to protect him. This so easily turns to over-anxiety, expressed by frequent cries of

alarm such as, 'Oh, don't do that, you'll hurt yourself!' or, 'Mind out, else you'll fall!' until the poor child is reduced to a permanent state of nervous apprehension and sees danger in everything.

For instance, so many children are afraid of dogs—quite unnecessarily really, for as a rule children and dogs get on very well together. How is it, then, that you very often see a child screaming with fright if a dog comes near him? Often because in the past his mother has said, 'Don't go near that doggie, darling; he might bite you.'

Better by far to explain, at a really early age, that all animals are friendly, but only with people who are friendly towards them, and that because of this it is better to stand quite still and talk nicely to an animal instead of trying to touch him, just in case the dog misunderstands.

Explain, too, that any dog may bite if he is touched when he is eating, not because he is unfriendly, but because he thinks his food is going to be taken away.

Nice Policeman

It is quite wrong to threaten a child that if he is naughty the policeman will lock him up, although there are still people who do it.

Just imagine the effect this sort of threat has on a child. Apart from the fact that it instils in the child a real fear of policemen—who should be looked upon as friends, in case at any time the child is lost—there is another side to it.

It gives a child a guilt complex, so that he lives in permanent dread of being punished for some tiny 'crime' that perhaps only he knows about, and which in his own mind has become magnified out of all proportion.

What Do They Read?

When it comes to children's literature, you can't be too careful! Everything that a young child reads should be scrutinised beforehand by a grown-up, because book titles can be most deceptive.

The fact that a book is described on the cover as a 'fairy tale,' or a 'story about children,' is, unfortunately, no guarantee that it is suitable for a child to read, for many of these so-called 'children's' books seem to be written by people who have little or no understanding of the workings of a child's mind.

It isn't so much the wicked fairies, the dragons or giants that cause the trouble, for, deep down, most children are well aware that these characters are only make-believe, and therefore quite harmless.

It is the stories that feature cruelty by human beings that are most likely to do the damage, for children know that such people exist and therefore, they reason, it is possible that these terrible things *could* happen.

Uncanny and weird creatures are just as bad. Recently an eight-year-old girl had two books given to her on her birthday. In one was the picture, in vivid colours, of a large, savage-looking fox devouring the mutilated body of a rabbit. In the other book was a poem about a bogey-man who 'caught naughty children.'

And these were books that were sold as being 'suitable for young children!'

A Bad Influence ?

What about comics? Many parents forbid their children to spend their pocket-money on these, because they are afraid that the children's minds will be badly influenced, and their taste for 'good' literature completely destroyed.

There is a good deal of truth in these arguments, but there is another point to be considered. When anything is so universally popular, it is obvious that it fills a need of some kind.

When a child is very young his imagination will turn him into a soldier or an engine driver at will, and he is perfectly contented.

But at ten years old, he has to face up to the realities of school. Now he wants to see himself performing miraculous feats of daring and courage; but he cannot express himself.

That is why, at this age, comics and comic strips are regarded by children as the 'breath of life.' Stories of space ships, and men from another planet with a certain amount of violent battle thrown in, provide an outlet for their imagination.

These rarely do any harm because, if you notice carefully, it is always a case of good finally triumphing over evil. It may seem, to a grown-up, a somewhat crude way of bringing home a moral, but at least it is one that a child can understand and appreciate.

Unfortunately, *all* comics do not express these principles, and any that a child reads should be supervised by an adult just as carefully as his books.

The literature we read when we are very young often creates impressions that stay with us for the rest of our days.

Exciting, but Harmless

Fortunately, not all authors imagine that children delight in the fantastic, the horrific and the macabre. There are numerous books on the market that are ideal for young people. They are exciting, yet harmless, and many of them carry a well-disguised moral that sows a worthwhile seed to flower later.

Films, too, should be well 'vetted,' for some full-length cartoons have most horrifying episodes that not only result in immediate nightmares but repressed fears that burgeon in adulthood.

There are some parents who take the line that even if a child is nervy there is no point in protecting him from such books or films, for he is bound to come across them sooner or later, and in any case he will grow out of it when he is older. This may be true in certain cases, but with a highly-strung child a fear may persist, and attach itself to other objects as he grows older, until when he is grown up he is still afraid, but the original cause of the trouble is quite forgotten.

It's Catching

If a child is afraid, whether it is of water, the dark (which fear often springs from some story) or anything else, never try to laugh him out of his fears. Ridicule only makes matters worse, and drives the fear deep down. If your child is afraid, encourage him to try to tell you why. Whenever possible explain to him *why* he is afraid, and let him know that you, too, had just the same sort of troubles when you were his age. This alone is often enough to start a cure. If ever *you* are afraid, well, do your best to hide it, for there is nothing more catching than fear. A child usually trusts an adult, especially the adult closest to him, and if she is not afraid, then he will be inclined to relax and feel that there is nothing really to worry about.

Morlands, Ltd.

WHAT MAKES BABY CRY?

The sun may be in his eyes; he may be hungry; there must be a reason, but it is very rarely serious

WHEN your baby keeps crying, naturally you *want* to pick him up and comfort him, but you have heard that this will 'spoil' him, and that all babies must be allowed to cry because it is the only way they can exercise their lungs.

What do you do? Difficult, isn't it?

In time, you will get to know what his different cries mean, for there is no doubt about it, they do vary. But the exercise theory is nonsense, and there is always a reason why a baby cries, even if it is only because he dislikes his own company!

Perhaps the most common cause of all is 'wind.'

All babies, whether they are breast-fed or bottle-fed, swallow a certain amount of air during their meal-times.

Unless you make quite sure that it has all been 'burped' up again, before he is put back in his cot, it will get into his intestines, make his tummy hard and distended, and cause him a great deal of pain.

A Contented Child

Incidentally, this 'burping' business isn't as simple as you might think. Some mothers bang their babies on the back really hard and then wonder why they are sick!

Baby should be held upright against your shoulder and his back *gently* rubbed (not patted), the whole length of his spine. It may take as long as ten to fifteen minutes to get results, but if you want a quiet, contented, *comfortable* baby, it is essential.

When baby cries, it is only natural to wonder if he is hungry. If he is, then not only does his cry sound different, but he begins, *consistently*, some time before his feeds are due.

If he is crying really hard, there is no harm in feeding him a little early (for we all get hungry at times for no apparent reason), but make sure that he is having sufficient food.

Correct Feeding

During twenty-four hours, most babies need $2\frac{1}{2}$ oz. of milk mixture for every pound of their body weight. For example, if he weighs 10 lb., then 10 multiplied by $2\frac{1}{2}$ gives you 25 oz. Divide this by five (the number of feeds in the day) and you find that he needs at least 5 oz. at each feed.

If he is breast-fed, then arrange to have several test feeds done. Even if he is gaining weight regularly, it may be that he can do with a little more.

And don't worry too much about the danger of over-feeding. In spite of what you may have been led to believe, it is by no means a common condition.

Bodily discomforts are another cause of crying that may easily be overlooked. For instance, is baby cold? It is no good feeling his hands, for they are never a true indication. Feel his feet. If they are cold to the touch let him wear bootees—yes, even on a fine day—for feet that are warm will mean a warm body too.

On the other hand, he may easily cry because he is too hot. If you can see tiny beads of perspiration around his nose, or on his forehead, remove some of his covers, or at any rate loosen them, for it may be that he has got hot through struggling to move about. Or is the sun streaming right into his eyes and worrying him? See that he has a canopy for shade. There are some very pretty ones to be bought for the pram.

Napkins should, of course, always be changed as soon as they are wet or soiled although, oddly enough, babies don't often complain for this reason. What worries them far more is a nappy that is pinned too tightly, or if he is chafed or sore—soreness sometimes resulting from acidity. For chafing, boracic ointment mixed with castor-oil is most soothing.

How old must a baby be before he cries through boredom? Even a baby of four or five months gets tired of staring at the same old ceiling or sky.

He Needs Amusing

There is no harm at all in propping him up just a little so that he can see what is going on. Talk to him by all means as you go about your work, but don't rush over at the slightest whimper. If you do, he will soon discover that, in spite of his size, he is the boss!

There is a type of baby who is as good as gold all day, yet between the six and ten o'clock feeds yells consistently—especially, or so it seems, when you have visitors!

Thank your lucky stars that he chooses this time rather than in the small hours of the morning, but see if the trouble could be caused by over-excitement.

Baby needs a play-time, of course, but in some houses the early evening is the time of a great deal of activity. Father comes home, and naturally wants to see his son, and because of this, baby is very often allowed to stay in the living-room after his feed.

Too Excited to Sleep

But voices, radio, table-setting and clearing away, all help to make him over-tired, so that when finally he is put upstairs he finds it difficult to settle down.

So if your baby seems to cry a great deal, do all you can to discover the cause. If the trouble persists, then talk to your doctor.

But don't worry too much for, in a very young baby, crying is rarely a sign of anything serious. Quite a bit of the time he is just seeing how much he can ' get away with.' You will soon learn to know when he is shamming.

THE MIDDLE CHILD

SOME time back, a mother was worried about her little girl, aged six.

The other children in the family were no trouble at all, but Jennifer was 'different.' Just lately she had taken to showing off dreadfully. She indulged in tantrums, and every now and then she had bouts of bed-wetting.

Now the mother realised that all these things were symptoms of a feeling of insecurity, but she couldn't see why Jennifer should act this way.

They hadn't moved house; she and her husband rarely had any differences of opinion —certainly not in front of the children. True, there was a baby, but he was eight months old, and Jennifer had shown no sign of this trouble when he was born.

A Happy Family, but . . .

In any case, they had taken great care that neither of the children should feel at all neglected or 'out of things' as soon as they knew the baby was on the way.

Well, there was certainly a clue to all this— Jennifer was the middle child.

It is easy to say that psychologists, child-guidance doctors, and people who write about children always have an excuse for their difficult behaviour. If the child is an only one,

She took to showing-off and indulged in inexplicable tantrums. She needs to feel important

that explains everything. If he has a younger brother or sister, well then, he is obviously jealous. If he comes in the middle, that, too, is the cause of his difficulties. In fact, it seems that whatever position a child holds in the family, it is bound to lead to trouble sooner or later.

It is not really that bad. There are many children who never give their parents cause for anxiety. The others do, nearly always because of this underlying sense of insecurity we hear so much about.

He Has No Privileges

There is no doubt about it, the middle child has additional disadvantages. For a long time he was the 'baby,' and you can't get away from the fact that a baby, of necessity, does take up a large proportion of his mother's attention. You may say that the eldest child is just as likely to feel out of things, but it is not quite the same for him.

You see, he has had much more time in which to adapt himself. He stopped being the 'baby' when the middle one arrived, and now he is very conscious of being the eldest of the family, and consequently thoroughly enjoys all the privileges that his superior position brings. But the middle one doesn't seem to have any privileges at all.

Too Intense

Sometimes matters are made worse, if the mother knows that the third child will be her last. She tends to get rather more intense about this baby than she did over the others; she is making the most of him, because everything she does is for the last time.

An older child may easily sense this extra attention, and because he doesn't understand the reason for it, he may well imagine that his mother prefers the baby to him. That in itself is enough to give him an overwhelming feeling of jealousy, and would account for bouts of 'babyish' behaviour.

He feels, subconsciously perhaps, that by imitating the baby he may get the same amount of attention. The fact that it never works out that way at all certainly doesn't help matters; it merely emphasises the fact that, as far as he can see, there is no justice anywhere!

Another common, but often overlooked, cause of trouble is 'handed-downs.' If the middle child is the same sex as the eldest, he is painfully conscious of being the only one who doesn't get new clothes. His mother buys his big brother new outfits and gives presents to the baby. But what does he get? The things his elder brother has grown out of!

Is there anything that can be done to make the middle child happier about his position in the family? A great deal. He should be made to feel an individual in his own right.

Let Him Help You

Show interest in his own pet activities, and he will respond. Encourage him to help you, not just because you need an extra hand, but because you value his assistance.

In fact, make him feel important. It never fails. Give him certain privileges for no other reason than that he *is* the middle one, and if finances will run to it, something new, in the way of clothes, especially for him. These are the little things that help to establish his identity.

Some parents think that if they treat all the children exactly the same they are being fair and just. But that isn't strictly true.

Each an Individual

Each child is an individual in his own right and his position in the family must influence his personality. After all, having an older and a younger brother is a very different thing to having two younger or two older.

It is a tricky job, for a mother must never appear to favour one child more than another. It may need thought, but it is well worth it, for no one knows the misery that a child suffers once he is allowed to feel out of things.

CUTTING-DOWN

WHEN making an adult's clothes into something for a child, fresh trimmings will often give a new air. *A Skirt* will make girl's skirt, pinafore frock, small boy's knickers, child's cardigan. *Day Dress* will make girl's frock or blouse, skirt, dressing-gown, or boy's blouse or knickers. *Blouse* will recut as little girl's knickers, blouse. *Slip* will make knickers, frock for baby, slip or nightie for little girl, blouse for small boy. *A Coat* turns into skirt or dungarees for girl, knickers or jacket for boy. *Man's Shirt* can be turned into shirt for boy, blouse or pinafore for girl, or rompers for toddlers. *Man's Trousers* can be recut as skirt, slacks, coat for girl, coat or knickers for boy.

HE WON'T EAT!

Mummy may have taken a long time to prepare the meal—but bang, it goes on the floor

MOST of us have had experience of 'nightmare' meals with children at some time or another, and there are several reasons why a child may lose his appetite.

If he is just off-colour—over-tired, perhaps, or affected by the weather—the desire to eat will soon return quite spontaneously. If he is 'sickening' for something, then the trouble is easily explained once the complaint develops. On the other hand, if the problem is of long standing, it may be the child's mother who, quite unconsciously, of course, is the cause of the trouble!

This is the kind of thing that usually happens. Little Tommy announced that he doesn't like what is on his plate. Mother tells him, quite sweetly, to 'eat it up,' otherwise he will never grow up to be 'a big man.'

Tommy couldn't care less. He doesn't like his food, and he has made up his mind not to eat it. He clamps his teeth together, and pushes his plate across the table.

Avoid a Battle

Mother immediately scolds him for his bad manners, and this makes him more resentful than ever. With a slight edge to her voice she announces that there is a lovely pudding to follow, but he can't have any unless he finishes his first course.

Tommy is furious. He wriggles with annoyance and slides down in his chair, which irritates his mother almost beyond endurance. By this time, her nerves are becoming frayed. She finds it difficult to disguise her feelings, and the scene is set for a first-class battle.

How long it lasts will depend upon her next move. If she packs up the plates, dismisses him from the table as if nothing has happened, all will be well. Tommy will be ready and waiting for his next meal—providing, of course, it isn't the same food heated up!

They Crave Attention

If, on the other hand, his mother belongs to the 'you'll-sit-there-until-you-do-eat-it' school, the battle may well last the rest of the day, punctuated by harsh words, tears, a great deal of emotional tension, and finally, complete exhaustion on both sides.

She may feel that the 'moral' victory has been worth all the fuss, but she can rest assured that the trouble will occur again. After a little while Tommy may develop a food complex that could easily stay with him for the rest of his life. Many of our adult 'fads and fancies' are due to being forced to eat things we disliked as children.

Then again, if the child is fit and well, a refusal to eat may be nothing more than a desire to gain attention. Small children aren't slow to realise that one of the quickest ways to become the centre of attraction is not to eat what is put before them.

If a mother is the over-anxious type who has read just a little too much about proteins, carbohydrates and vitamins, little Tommy has only to keep his mouth tight shut at mealtimes to enjoy the satisfaction of her undivided attention. He is well enough, but he delights in her anxiety about his health and nourishment. He knows that she is worrying about him and it makes him feel important.

SHOULD THEY BE PUNISHED?

Of course they should, but how much and when, and does it do any good?

Again, apparent loss of appetite may be due to 'fussiness,' not of health, but table manners. Tommy uses his fingers instead of a spoon, because it is easier, and his mother objects. Or he spills something on the floor and she gets really angry because of the 'mess on the carpet.'

Poor Tommy comes to expect a scene at meal-times, and not eating seems the easiest way out.

Sometimes a child will refuse to eat simply because he is not hungry. If he looks pale, or not as fat and robust as his mother would like him to be, he is often made to drink quantities of milk, or given cod-liver oil, which can so easily take the edge off his appetite. Stopping these foods for a day or two will often put things right.

Rules for Encouragement

These, then, are some rules which should ease the problem: Small servings on a plate—nothing takes away the appetite so quickly as the sight of too much food at once. Cheerful indifference as to whether he eats or not. No fussing—he will eat soon enough when he is hungry. No sweets or snacks in between meals.

If things get really difficult, the companionship of other children will often solve this very tricky problem.

PETER is a small boy of ten, and if there is ever any 'trouble' in the neighbourhood, you can pretty well guess that *he* isn't far away. He is disobedient, untruthful, and at times vicious and cruel. Not only that, the other children detest him because he is a bully and a sneak.

Yet, believe it or not, his parents are anything but lenient. They say that they believe in discipline, and bringing children up strictly.

Every time Peter is *very* naughty (and that is pretty often!) he is severely punished. More often than not, the punishment takes the form of a sound thrashing.

But it never seems to have the desired effect, for very soon he is doing just the same old things all over again.

He Is Never Thrashed

On the other hand, Paul, a youngster of the same age, has never been thrashed in his life, simply because it hasn't been necessary.

He is by no means a goody-goody, and can be as tough as the next, but he is obedient, kind, and (the hall-mark of a good job of work by the parents) popular with other children.

Does this prove that punishment is unnecessary?

Not really, for most children need it at some

time or another, but usually it shows that if a child needs *frequent* punishing, the fault may lie in the way the parents are handling him, rather than with the child himself.

Respect Is Essential

If a child is on friendly terms with his parents, that is, if he loves and (most important) respects them, without in any way being afraid of them, then it stands to reason that they will be able to guide and control him without finding it necessary to use force.

When he is very young, a child will obviously slip up from time to time, but when the relationship between parent and child is on the correct footing, then *severe* punishment is rarely necessary.

If it is, there are one or two questions you must ask yourself.

First of all, does it achieve the results you want without breaking his spirit, or making him afraid, defiant or rebellious?

Secondly, are you really punishing him because he deserves it, or merely to relieve your own feelings?

Sometimes it isn't easy to tell. It is only natural to feel like slapping Tommy good and hard if he accidentally breaks your most cherished piece of china, but be fair, and ask yourself if your treatment would have been the same had it been an old, unwanted article that had got smashed.

Remember, children cannot assess the value of such things, unless it has been pointed out to them beforehand.

Again, are you consistent? A child cannot be expected to know right from wrong if an incident that caused no comment yesterday suddenly becomes a 'crime' today.

Try, whenever you can, to avoid threats— particularly those you have no intention of carrying out.

Children are quick to hit on the truth, and once they discover that your words are meaningless, they will interpret them as a challenge and please themselves all the more!

These days, everyone knows how wicked and harmful threats of policemen and 'bogeymen' can be, but there are other forms of punishment that should also be avoided.

For instance, if you shut a child up in his bedroom when he has done wrong, he will only become resentful and sulky. Not only that, the room itself will eventually have unpleasant associations for him, and later they may affect his sleep and give him nightmares.

Fear Makes Him Lie

Spanking? Well, it is certainly better than nagging, sneering and drawn-out disapproval, for at least it is over and done with quickly.

But smacking should never be used as a punishment for lying, for it will only make matters worse. Usually, if a child lies, he does so out of fear of punishment, and if he is frightened still more, well, it will only make him lie harder than ever next time.

A most important step in dealing with children who always seem to be in the need of punishment is to try and discover *why* they behave as they do.

The child who 'plays up' for no apparent reason may be doing so simply to attract attention.

Why He Is Naughty

He may have had his nose put out of joint by the arrival of a new baby, or perhaps his mother has been exceptionally busy and made him feel that his presence is tolerated rather than enjoyed. In cases like this, a little extra 'mothering' and attention (though not, of course, too soon after the 'crime') may be all that is necessary.

On the other hand, he may behave badly simply because making adults lose their temper gives him a sense of power. Extra praise for his own achievements is often sufficient to restore his self-confidence.

There is one other point that is important. Never resort to the 'I'll tell your father when he comes home' technique. It is unfair all round. If the child comes to regard his father as the person who always deals out punishment, their relationship is not likely to be easy when he is older. However, Daddy should take his part in maintaining 'order' or it will be Mummy who is regarded as the dealer of punishment.

But remember, a good child is a happy child. If yours is constantly naughty, try to find out the cause.

MINI-MINIATURE GARDEN

IF a child wants to make a miniature garden (see page 153), he can make a very small one in almost any receptacle, even an earthenware pie-dish will do. He can experiment with a few rock plants, and decorations of shells and pebbles.

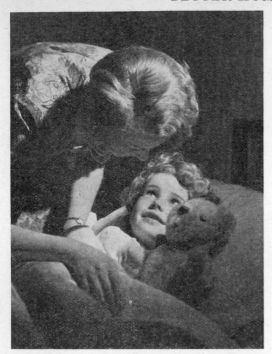

The child's mother and father are the most important persons in the world to her; she may begin to feel she is disappointing them

The BACKWARD CHILD

THE term 'backward' can mean anything —or nothing. There are people who use it to describe the child whose brain (through some congenital illness perhaps, or an injury at birth) can never develop normally. Others employ it to excuse the fact that little Tommy is never in the running for a prize at school!

They may be right or wrong in their diagnosis, but whatever they mean, the term implies some degree of mental slowness.

There is no disgrace whatever in being backward. It is nobody's fault. We are not personally responsible for the amount of intelligence we are blessed with, any more than we are responsible for the colour of our eyes, or the size of our feet. It is just another of those things that are decided at the time of conception.

Misguided Parents

On the other hand, the child who is not so quick-thinking as the majority of children at the same age is often made to appear far more backward than he really is, by the misguided treatment of his parents.

With the best intentions possible they have, perhaps, studied books on child welfare which state, quite dogmatically, what the 'average' child should be able to do at various stages of his development. And, to their horror, they discover that, according to the book, their own particular offspring is nowhere near average. Therefore he must be 'odd.'

Something must be done, and thinking they are helping and encouraging him to 'catch up,' they more or less force him to do all the things that, apparently, he should be able to do. Feed and dress himself, perhaps, or, if he is older, do the lessons that other children of his age seem to manage quite simply.

A Great Deal Can Be Done

They may even see to it that his companions are older, more advanced children, in the hope that he will be encouraged to copy them.

But it doesn't work out that way at all. He continues to play on his own, or stand around watching the others with a somewhat blank expression on his face which seems to confirm his parents' worst fears.

The reason is not difficult to understand, though. Just imagine how *you* would feel if you found yourself amongst a group of people who did nothing but talk about subjects that were way above your head. High finance, perhaps, or the intricate details of atomic research—you would probably have a perpetually blank expression, and feel more than a little tongue-tied.

And yet, when you are with companions who share similar interests to your own, you are quite animated and, at times, even eloquent!

So it is with the backward child. If his playmates are at the same level of intelligence— irrespective of age—he will be far happier, and not only that, stand a much better chance of getting on.

What abilities he has will be exercised and, consequently, developed. He will rapidly gain confidence because he is not made to feel 'different' or out of things, for, goodness knows, there is nothing that destroys one's morale quicker than a constant sense of failure.

When the parents of a backward child are prepared to acknowledge the fact, without fuss or worry, that he is a little 'slow,' a great deal can be done.

The Danger

He may be slow, but if he is allowed to develop in his own time without constant nagging (and sometimes anger, for slowness appears to be deliberate disobedience sometimes), he will catch up in the end, even if he never becomes a genius.

After all, who wants a genius? They are not at all 'comfortable' people to live with!

The danger lies when parents have already set their heart on a certain career for the backward child that is far beyond his ability.

Because it is obvious that he will never be able to fulfil their ambitions, they feel frustrated, and (quite mistakenly, of course) ashamed.

They are continually apologising, or making excuses for him, for feelings of this kind cannot be hidden.

He Needs Your Love

Sooner or later the child will become conscious that his mother and father, the most important people in his world, are disappointed in him. Once this happens, it will be difficult for him to be happy again, for the backward child needs, above all, love and gentle appreciation. He may even become a 'nobody wants me' martyr, and that can last a lifetime.

Of course, if a child's mental development is seriously retarded—so much so that at eighteen months he can do little more than he could as a tiny baby—then it is a different story, and a difficulty that needs expert advice and guidance.

Even so, the outlook is by no means as black as it was some years ago. The important thing to remember is that the term 'average' is relative.

So many of the people who really matter today are quite honest about the fact that at school they were more than a little backward. Newton, who discovered the Law of Gravity, did not begin to talk till he was three years old, and Einstein was a little backward. Backward children may catch up swiftly later on.

TABLE-MATS

A PIECE of left-over (or old) linoleum makes an excellent mat to protect the nursery table from too-hot dishes. It can be cut to fit under the tablecloth, or plate-sized mats can be shaped from it.

TRAVELLING
with
CHILDREN

HOLIDAY-TIME is always problem time for mothers of young children, especially if it involves travel, and most mothers think twice before they take a baby on a long journey. Visions of heating bottles (if the baby is not breast-fed) and coping with damp nappies is enough to deter any woman.

However, travelling need not be a headache if plans are made well in advance.

Young babies usually travel well; if they are made warm and comfortable they will sleep most of the way.

Put the baby in a Moses basket if he is under four months—he will not feel the draughts this way. Easter time means warmer weather, so don't overdress him. Light clothes and warm coverings will be quite ample.

Good Stand-bys

The bugbear of soiled napkins will disappear if you take a packet or two of disposable ones.

Let her take her favourite toy with her, or it will be the one thing she wants

Cellulose wadding is another excellent stand-by. You can buy a roll at any chemist's. Place a large strip of this inside the napkin to save it from becoming soiled and damp. The wadding can then be thrown away.

Added protection can be given by plastic knickers. Generally speaking, protective knickers are not good—especially rubber ones—but they are quite permissible for a journey.

Prepare the required number of bottles on the morning of the trip and wrap them up well in layers of newspaper. Take a thermos flask of boiling water and a jug.

Heating the Bottles

When the baby requires a feed, stand the bottle in a jug of boiling water until it gets to the right heat.

Purées and broths can also be heated in this way.

Don't worry if the baby seems disinclined to take his bottle—he probably finds his surroundings very odd. It won't hurt him to take less than usual.

Babies on a mixed diet can have tiny, thinly cut sandwiches of meat or vegetable extract, or honey followed by light sponge fingers and milk.

Don't give a baby food prepared in the restaurant car—it is usually unsuitable.

As babies get thirsty when travelling, always take a thermos of cold, boiled water. *Never* use the drinking water provided on the train.

If you are taking an older child up to six years, the food problem is not quite so difficult. The main thing to remember is to keep him from getting bored. Once boredom sets in he gets fidgety and fretful and, if susceptible to travel sickness, may feel bilious.

On the morning of the journey, give him a light but nourishing breakfast—no fried foods such as bacon and tomatoes. Let him have cereal with milk and sugar (or glucose), toast with marmalade or honey. Don't give him too much milk—a drink of water is much better.

It is a good plan, a day or two before the journey, to give young children drinks of fruit juice diluted with water, to which glucose has been added. These are excellent in helping to combat travel sickness.

Food for Older Children

Constipation should be avoided, and if there is a tendency towards it a mild aperient, such as milk of magnesia, given.

During the journey they can eat fresh sandwiches with plain but nutritious fillings, and fruit. Give them fruit drinks if they are thirsty.

Take plenty of barley-sugar sweets and give them one about every twenty minutes to help keep any biliousness at bay. They can have plain boiled sweets as well. No rich chocolates or creamy sweets.

Children of six or seven years can have lunch on the train, but if the journey is long, don't let them eat a heavy meal. Soup is not always a wise choice if they are inclined to be bilious.

Symptoms of travel sickness are not difficult to diagnose some time before they actually produce sickness. The child will yawn a lot and produces a good deal of saliva. The skin will feel cold to the touch and the child look pale, with a tinge of green in the skin. He will probably complain of a slight headache and general squeamishness.

Keeping Boredom at Bay

As soon as these signs appear, wrap him warmly and give him plenty of *fresh air*. A fruit drink will often help. Keep him quiet and don't move him around too much.

It is as well not to discuss a child's tendency to travel sickness in front of him, or he thinks it is expected of him, and as soon as the journey begins he will complain of feeling ill. Some children are more open to suggestion than others.

Lastly, to keep children from being bored, play games such as 'I spy' with the older ones and provide crayons and colouring books for the younger ones. Babies will be too engrossed in everything going on around them to require any special distraction.

DOLL'S BOOTEES

IF a little girl is learning to knit, she can make a pair of doll's bootees. These are for a doll about 10 or 11 inches high, but can be made larger. A left-over of wool will do for them.

Cast on 14 sts. and work in garter stitch for 16 rows. **17th Row.**—Cast off 6, and work 4 rows. **21st Row.**—K. 6, inc. once in next st., k. 1. **Next 3 Rows.**—K. **25th Row.**—K. 7, increase once in next st., k. 1. Work 3 more rows without increasing and cast off. Work a similar piece and sew up seams of two pieces. The other bootee is, of course, the same.

HE
TELLS
FIBS

Sometimes he is trying to avoid punishment. Other times, it is an over-active imagination seeking outlet

What can you do about a child who is untruthful? It is a problem that worries some mothers tremendously. They discover that little Tommy has been telling fibs, and their first reaction is that some drastic step must be taken straight away in order to prevent him growing up with a bad moral character.

In all probability they inflict a severe punishment to stress the seriousness of the situation, and, quite unwittingly, make matters a thousand times worse.

What is the Reason?

You see, things may not be as serious as all that. All children tell fibs at some time or another, but what is important, is to discover just what *type* of fibs they are telling, and why.

Take Peter, for example. His mother was most embarrassed when a neighbour stopped her in the street, and asked if she could come round some time to see the wonderful new television set that she had heard about.

They haven't a television set at all, but Peter had described it in great detail to his little playmates, and—well, you know how things get around.

Now, believe it or not, there is no wickedness in this kind of lie. Peter told it with one object only—to impress.

It was important, however, to find out exactly why he should feel that such a step was necessary. This kind of behaviour indicates that for some reason or another the child is harbouring a sense of inferiority.

He struggles to overcome it in the only way he knows—by boasting, and giving the others something to think about.

In Peter's case, the reason was obvious. He was an only child, his parents hadn't much money, but they were over-anxious to keep up appearances. With the best intentions, they sent him to a 'superior' nursery school (that they could ill-afford) in order that he should have 'suitable' playmates.

It was a little too much for him. The other children came from homes that had far more than Peter's, in the way of things that money could buy, but Peter was far too young to realise how little that matters, and he wasn't going to be outdone!

Understandable really, for when you come to think of it, even grown-ups are sometimes guilty of this type of exaggeration!

He Doesn't Count

It isn't just a lack of material things that can cause this feeling of inferiority and subsequent boasting. Very often it is because the child's parents are too busy to give him enough undivided attention, and consequently he feels neglected. It may be that there is a new baby in the family, and his nose is put a little 'out of joint.'

The treatment is simple—extra fussing to restore self-confidence, at the same time pointing out how silly it is to make statements that cannot be substantiated.

Harmless Lies

Very small children spend a great deal of time in a world of their own, which can give the impression that they are telling fibs.

It sometimes worries a mother to hear her child describing what 'my friend, Ermyntrude' did today, particularly if it is 'Ermyntrude' who is blamed for the milk that was spilt on the carpet, or some other 'crime.'

Here again, these lies are quite harmless—even natural—and the best way to cope with them is to enter into the spirit of the game, stressing what fun it must be to have such nice 'pretend' friends. Children grow out of this phase as soon as they enter a world where school, and school friends, can take the place of imaginary companions.

The only kind of lie that really matters is the one that is told out of fear. Even then, it may not be so much the child's fault as the parents'.

The Way to Prevent It

Perhaps such severe punishments are inflicted that he will lie, rather than be found out and face up to them. Unless the fear of his parents is removed he will certainly never be cured of his untruthfulness.

It may be, too, that, quite unwittingly, he has been set a bad example by his mother giving the impression that truthfulness is not really so important after all.

It isn't difficult to do. You know the sort of thing: 'Oh, say I'm out,' when an unwelcome visitor calls, or 'I will be back in a few minutes,' when you know perfectly well that it will be a few hours. They cannot understand why, in the case of grown-ups, there should be such a difference between theory and practice.

Children are literal creatures and have no way of assessing degrees of truth. If they hear us fibbing because it happens to suit us to do so, well, you can hardly blame them for doing the same when they find themselves in a tight corner.

The best way of all to prevent fibbing, is to see that you are on really good terms with your children.

If they feel that you can be relied upon to try to understand their point of view, you need have no fear that their moral character will suffer.

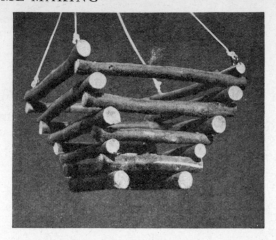

A Rustic
Hanging Basket

YOU don't have to be a carpenter or even particularly clever to make this original hanging basket to give Mother to cheer up the porch or verandah. It is quickly and simply made and will cost you next to nothing, which is a help, isn't it?

Collect some branches about 1 inch in diameter, and saw them into the following straight lengths:

Two pieces 6 inches long.
Four pieces 8 inches long.
Four pieces 10 inches long.
Four pieces 12 inches long.
Four pieces 14 inches long.

You will also need a piece of flat box-wood 4 inches by 6 inches; four 1½-inch nails; twenty 1½-inch screws and four cup-hooks. To hang it you will need some small-linked chain, although wire or cord will serve.

Nail the flat piece of box-wood lengthways across the two 6-inch pieces so that they support it as a base, and so that it sticks out about an inch on either side. Then build your basket criss-cross with the other pieces of branch wood, ascending 2 inches longer each time. Put the screws about an inch and a half from each end so that they are never one over the other.

When you have fixed the last piece of branch, screw your cup-hooks at each top corner, and then attach the chains. If you find screws difficult to manage, make a hole in the right place for each one first.

DANGER IN THE HOME

THESE days, most mothers are very conscientious about instructing their children in road safety, to give them protection against street accidents. Yet many of these same 'careful' mothers quite unwittingly expose their children to serious danger simply by not taking sufficient precautions to guard against accidents in the home. Many serious accidents could be avoided if only certain simple precautions were taken *as a matter of course*.

Of all indoor accidents, the most common are burns and scalds, and it is a sobering thought to remember that *every year* more than four hundred babies or young children die in this manner, to say nothing of the dozens who are left disfigured.

Even so, the mothers of these children are not necessarily 'neglectful.' They may have done their best to protect their children, not realising that the precautions were inadequate.

Think, for a moment, of fireguards. No one would be foolish enough to leave a young child alone in a room where there was an unguarded fire, but the usual run of fireguards are more or less useless unless they are securely fixed. Many of the strongest can easily be knocked over by a dog or cat.

For complete safety, all fireguards should have a small mesh, be covered at the top, and fixed to the wall on the 'hook and eye' principle. Not only that, they should be as deep as possible, otherwise the wire will become hot and dangerous to touch.

Burns and Scalds

Electric fires, portable or fixed into the wall, are another source of great danger. A child's clothes can so easily catch fire through touching the lighted bars unless the fire is covered by a securely fixed mesh guard.

A common cause of scalds is over-turned saucepans. Young children are inquisitive creatures, and if they see saucepan handles sticking out, they may easily reach up and 'grab,' just to find out what is inside.

But that isn't the only danger. A mother may hurriedly turn and knock the protruding handle, with disastrous consequences.

Even if the pan doesn't fall off the stove, there is a danger that boiling water or fat may fall on a child.

Prying Fingers

In the same way, teapots, and anything containing hot liquid, should always be kept in the middle of the table. 'Inquisitive' fingers, or merely one tug at the cloth, may be sufficient to upset the lot.

When there are 'toddlers' in a house, it is better to use tablecloths that cover only the surface of the table, and don't hang down at all. If you think they are ugly, clips round the table legs are next best.

Another common cause of accidents in these days of television sets and labour-saving devices is electricity.

Too often worn flex is left unrepaired, or lamps that are not in use left with the switch on, but without a bulb. Electric irons, too, can be a source of danger, and they are used often enough when there are children in a family!

No Shocks for Anyone

If you have to answer a door-bell while you are ironing, do take either the child, or the iron, with you! Or, at any rate, see that there is a closed door between them! Leave them together, and even though the child may have been trained 'not to touch' he may easily get caught up in the flex and bring everything crashing down on him, with not only burns as a result, but possibly concussion, too.

Then again, so many houses are built with electric points in the skirting boards. What youngster, just beginning to crawl, could resist exploring these sockets with his fingers? Even older children may be tempted to investigate with the help of knitting needles, pins or nail files, not realising the danger of the contact with metal.

If the points in your house are used often, or if they are not of the special safety pattern, adhesive tape right over the point is better than nothing.

Another precaution that is sometimes overlooked is hot-water bottle covers. A child who is sleeping heavily may not be immediately conscious of a too-hot bottle. Matches and cigarette-lighters must be kept well out of reach on a high shelf, or children may 'experiment.' Matches are especially dangerous.

The Truth About Twins

There is more than one kind of twins. Some have a separate personality
from the 'other half.' Many have an extraordinary bond

THE birth of twins is nearly always the occasion of surprise and, sometimes, of consternation. People are most curious about the cause of their birth.

If twins regularly or frequently had twin offspring, you would say that twinning was hereditary, but this is not the case. In fact it is extremely rare for twin parents to have twin children. For the most part twins come unexpectedly to parents who were both singly born. There are two distinct and different kinds of twins as recognised by biologists: one-egg twins (two yolks in one egg) and two-egg twins (two eggs and two yolks). One-egg twins are duplicated editions of one another, and are always same-sexed twins, either both males or both females, and are usually so much alike that even their friends have difficulty in telling them apart. Two-egg twins are related to each other in exactly the same way as ordinary brothers and sisters, except that they are of the same age.

Two-egg twin pairs may consist of two boys, two girls, or a boy and a girl. They are, taking into account the matter of age, only as similar in their mental and physical characteristics as are ordinary brothers and sisters. The mental bonds of one-egg twins, however, seem to be definitely stronger and harder to analyse. The members of a pair of one-egg twins seem to regard themselves as one unit and often, if not always, tend to submerge their individual personalities in the pair-personality. This frequently results in a feeling of incompleteness on the part of such twins when they are temporarily or permanently separated.

Reared Apart

For example, there were twins, Edward and Fred, separated in infancy and reared apart unknown to each other until they were grown and married men. Each of them had always felt that once he had a brother who died.

Mental telepathy, or thought communication with others, has for a long time been regarded by some people as little more than superstition.

Telepathy

However, one cannot be closely connected with one-egg twins without discovering that many of them regard themselves as having something like telepathic powers. Twins often claim that when they are separated they can tell what the other is thinking about, or that one can feel when the other is sick, hurt or in danger.

Another interesting story is told about two sisters who wrote examination papers in biology. When the teacher examined the papers they were so much alike that she suspected them of copying. The girls, however, having been previously unjustly accused of collusion in examinations, had adopted the practice of sitting far apart, and they proved that they had done so on this occasion. The teacher accepted their explanation and admitted that she was powerless to prevent mental telepathy—as she termed it.

The only way to explain this is to say that if you take two watches with similar cases and works, take a wheel out of one and exchange it for the identical wheel in the other, the watches go on ticking in just the same harmony. Maybe it is the same with twins. Twins must have brains and nervous systems which are so very much alike throughout that they cause the appearance of mental telepathy.

Primitive Superstitions

Among primitive peoples the birth of twins is commonly regarded as a portent of either good or evil. Among some tribes of Upper Guinea, for example, twins are welcomed and cherished as a good omen, indicating that the god of fertility and plenty has seen fit to bestow his favours upon the family, or even the tribe, into which the twins are born. In fact, all over the world twins are a subject of great interest.

SOUND SNAP-SHOTS

for the family album

Photo: Diana Waring

SNAPSHOT albums are always fun. 'Did we *really* look like that?' is often asked. Yet these days whole albums are built up, not of photos but of records. For right from baby's first word (even though it may be only an incoherent gurgle), throughout the schooldays, the twenty-first birthday party, the wedding, these records are a complete sound-track of the milestones of the years.

The child's awakening intelligence and character are conveyed by the way questions are answered; or the difference with which various members of a family will sing or recite.

On birthdays, children can make a record for Mummy or Daddy. The little ones are not always easy subjects to record, as they often do the wrong thing at the right moment with unfailing avidity. John says, 'Hullo, Daddy darling!' in his most enchanting voice, but puts his hand right over the microphone as he says it! Or he kicks it with his foot, and it makes a noise like thunder on the recording. If he and his baby sister are a twosome, he smacks her and she cries.

The patience of a Job is often needed, but most recording-studios have someone around who knows just how to handle children.

One Hundred Years Ago

It is just about a hundred years ago since the first daguerreotype photographs were beginning to be in common use. A nervous young man and a blushing girl would seat themselves stiffly before a terrifying apparatus and have their coy attitudes or simpering smile set for ever on a shiny piece of card.

People do not enter a recording studio with quite the same self-consciousness, but at the same time nervousness is still there to make a gay, happy voice sound strained and unnatural. Or 'sweet nothings' are whispered too close to the mike, so that they sound like nothing so much as a storm at sea! Sometimes a photograph or snapshot of an event is taken at the same time or on the same day as a recording is made to celebrate some event, thus linking up the visual and the oral memory of a fleeting moment.

Recording a Party

At parties, recording equipment is taken to a private home or to an hotel, recording speeches, remarks, entertainment, idle chatter. Single recordings at a studio are quite inexpensive, but a recording of a whole ceremony naturally sends the cost up, although to have a happy day brought to vivid, pulsing life at any moment in the future by putting on the gramophone may be worth it. There are many other things that can be recorded— a message of thanks for a favour; the sound of a friendly voice to someone alone; a greeting.

Perhaps such records could act as peace-makers. If the middle-aged couple pull the curtains, turn the lights down low and put on a recording made on a honeymoon; listen to the warm, lovelit voices, the pet-names with no meaning for anyone but themselves—and how many quarrels might vanish into the mist?

Modern Laundering

*Wash-day need not be a chore. With up-to-date appliances
or without them, the right way of tackling the work makes
everything run smoothly*

EVERYTHING becomes easier if it is tackled in the right way, and laundry is no exception. Clothes that are washed properly are a joy to behold, and last much longer. Once clothes and linen are rolled down, they should be ironed as soon as possible, as they have a much fresher appearance.

It is not everyone who can afford a washing machine, but if you can, here are a few notes about them:—

If only the smalls are to be done at home, a washing machine may be unnecessary, but if the family wash is done, even for two people, a washing machine should go as high on the list of essential equipment as the vacuum cleaner.

Washing machines vary greatly in size and type and in the conveniences they offer. The smallest machine of real value takes 3½ lb. of dry washing. It will take a single blanket, or its equivalent, but not a double-size one. This size washer is large enough for a house-hold of two, three or even four people, but will not take all the household washing, such as long heavy curtains and loose covers.

Another washer, which occupies little more floor space than the first, will take 6 lb. of dry washing. This size machine is suitable for most families of two to four people, and will take a double blanket and medium-weight curtains and loose covers, which is an obvious advantage.

The least expensive machine of this capacity has a hand-operated wringer, which accounts for the low price. Another, which is more costly, has independent water heating, so that boiling can be done in the machine. This one also has a hand-operated wringer. A third has water heating and a fully-powered wringer, which gives it almost all the conveniences of a large washing machine, but makes it the most costly for its washing capacity.

Next come the full-size family washers, offering invaluable features. Most important is washing capacity, which in general is 9-10 lb. of dry clothes. This means that a machine of this size will take almost any household soft furnishings and cope, of course, with the weekly family wash in the minimum of time. All machines of this size are fitted with a fully-powered wringer. Some have independent water heating, so that water temperature can be raised in the machine to the required washing heat or to boiling-point. Many are now equipped with a rotary ironer as an optional, but most valuable, accessory.

A new development is the production of wash units to convert an existing wash-boiler into a washing machine. One has hand-operated paddles fitted into a lid. Another is made on the lines of the old dolly stick. It is an ingenious design, electrically operated by connection to the motor of a vacuum cleaner. The action of this machine is very gentle and should prove no harder on the clothes than careful hand washing.

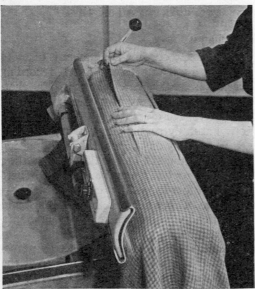

English Electric Co.

The rotary ironer is mounted on the washing machine. The garment is kept straight by smoothing it with your fingers. Here pleats are being pinned into place ready to press

This washing machine has a 10-gallon tub capacity and will take 8 to 9 lb. of dry clothing per load. It has an automatic overload device to prevent straining the motor

There is also a power-wringer fitted which may be positioned at eight different angles, so that wringing may be done over the tub or the sink

English Electric Co.

Which Iron to Use

When considering buying a washing machine that will cope with the soft furnishings and sheets, the time spent on ironing should be borne in mind. The rotary ironer already referred to is ideal for finishing a big wash quickly and efficiently, and can be operated sitting down; but it is not essential for a small family. The new light-weight hand irons are a delight to use. They vary according to make from about 3-4 lb., and some are so well-balanced that they feel lighter than they actually are. The new-type element heats the whole surface of the soleplate quickly and evenly, and little, if any, hand pressure is needed. The ease and speed of ironing is impressive in comparison with an iron of $5\frac{1}{2}$ or $6\frac{1}{2}$ lb. All these light-weight irons have automatic heat control.

An iron that tips up automatically on to a cool flat heel is a new idea. It is less comfortable to use than those already described, but for a busy mother of young children the safety tip-up device may prove helpful in preventing scorching when she is called suddenly to cope with some emergency.

An oil iron is of great value to many country dwellers. It is simple, safe, efficient and well-balanced. With occasional pumping to maintain pressure, it retains adequate heat for ironing a big family wash.

There is another electrically controlled iron that looks like two ironing boards that shut together. The operator just sits down to the pile of work and pulls a lever.

An ironing-board must stand perfectly steady and the feet must not scratch the floor surface—some are rubber-shod. Height should be comfortable for ironing without stooping, and the board as wide as possible, allowing for double garments such as shirts to be slipped over easily. The end should be curved and well padded for pressing sleeve-heads and shoulders. Some ironing boards have a sleeve-board attached. For large flat household articles an ironing board is too narrow. Use a wooden or enamelled kitchen table-top covered with two thicknesses of blanket and a piece of old sheet. Fix both firmly to the table corners with clips designed for the purpose.

And now for home laundry without a washing machine

Light-weight and light-coloured summer clothes need frequent washing, not only to keep them looking fresh, crisp and cool, but to preserve the fabric. The dusty soil of summer, which quickly makes clothes look grubby, is unimportant, as far as the welfare of the fabric is concerned, in comparison with body acids contained in perspiration. Acids, when allowed to remain in the fabric, will quickly cause rotting of the fibres and will also bleach out the dyes. Frequent washing in hot weather will lengthen the life of clothes and save laborious mending, provided the right washing and ironing methods are used for different types of fabrics.

The first precaution, when buying ready-made summer clothes or material by the yard, is to look for a fabric which is pre-shrunk and branded with the name of a well-known manufacturer, or for a reliable washability and colour-proof guarantee, which will probably be in the form of a tag attached to the garment or fabric.

Natural and White Cottons and Linens

In natural colour and white, cottons and linens are easy to launder. Soak them over-night in hot soapy water. This loosens the dirt and saves rubbing, which is harder on the fabric than normal wear. In the morning, rinse thoroughly and wring out well. Wash in hot water, using good-quality soap-flakes, oil-base washing soap or soapless detergent powder to give a good lather. Rub badly-soiled parts lightly, taking care to rub fabric against fabric. Rinse and wring thoroughly and hang white materials to dry out-of-doors in sunshine if possible.

If starching is necessary, steep the garments in a hot-water starch after rinsing. The strength of starch depends on the degree of stiffening required and the quality of the material. A firm, closely-woven fabric will probably need less starch than a loosely-woven, thin or worn one. To obtain a glossy finish and good stiffening, iron non-starched fabrics when evenly and thoroughly damp.

The Gas Council

These irons are used as a pair. While one is being heated, the other is transferred to the trivet for use. The ironing set can also be supplied for use with bottled gas

Coloured Cottons and Linens

If a colour-fast guarantee is supplied by the manufacturer, it is safe to follow the washing method for white cottons and linens. If there is no guarantee, test the fastness of the dyes before washing for the first time.

Testing for Colour Fastness. Wet an incon-spicuous corner of the garment with cold water. Place it between two pieces of white cotton material and press with a hot iron. Any loose dye will immediately mark off on to the white cotton, and is a sure sign that washing, however carefully and expertly done, will affect the colours. Dry cleaning is better for fabrics in which dyes are loose.

Washing fabrics which are not colour-fast

1. Avoid long immersion in water.
2. Avoid high temperatures.
3. Avoid use of alkaline soaps and bleach-ing materials.

Washing process

1. Have washing and rinsing waters ready before wetting the material. Treat one gar-ment at a time, washing, rinsing and hanging it to dry without pause.
2. Wash only in warm water with pure soap-flakes or a soapless detergent powder to form a good lather.
3. Avoid rubbing, but squeeze gently with the hands in washing and rinsing waters.
4. Final rinsing water should be cold and slightly acid. Add 1 tablespoonful of acetic acid to each gallon of water used.
5. Stiffen with boiling-water starch used cold or warm, as for white cottons and linens.
6. Remove all surface water in the wringer, placing a layer of old clean cloth between each layer of the fabric. Hang to dry in a shady place.
7. If colours are very loose, lay the garment out flat to dry on an old piece of white material. This should prevent bleeding of colours.

Silk and Wool

1. Soak overnight in warm water, with enough soapless washing powder to give a good lather. Rinse in the morning. Fold care-fully and pass through the wringer or squeeze out the water by hand, but avoid twisting the fabric.
2. Wash by squeezing in warm water with soapless washing powder or soap-flakes to give a good lather. Avoid rubbing. To remove

Many housewives get irritated by the flex being tangled. This soothing gadget supports the flex away from the work, following every movement of the iron. It is of all-metal construction, thus lasting for years, and costs only a few shillings

Flexaway

obstinate soil, rub on a little of the powder and leave for a minute or two.

3. Squeeze out the water and rinse twice in warm water. There is a school of thought that does not believe in rinsing woollens. It is best to select your own method.

4. Fold and pass through the wringer, supporting the material in the hands to avoid undue strain.

5. To dry woollens—shape them flat to the original measurements and dry flat at a moderate temperature, indoors, or in a shady place out-of-doors.

To dry silks—dry flat, as woollens, or hang over a line out-of-doors, but never suspended from pegs.

6. Iron woollies and silks slightly damp on the wrong side with a warm iron.

Rayons

Rayons are weakest when wet and should not be soaked. They are washed exactly as silk and wool and must be handled carefully.

1. To dry—roll rayons in a towel and leave till evenly and slightly damp. Do not damp them by sprinkling.

2. Press with a warm iron, stretching the fabric slightly to the original measurements. For a glossy surface iron on the right side, for a dull finish on the wrong.

3. Avoid ironing over double parts such as seams, and pressing the iron hard into hems and gathers. Press seams first on the wrong side, and fold them back out of the way when ironing the main part of the garment. Ironing

over seams gives a sharp glossy line on the material and causes holes.

Fine Woollies

Light-weight woollies, particularly Shetland, pull out of shape very easily when washed. To preserve the shape of a woolly of this type, tack it carefully on to double butter muslin or a piece of old white material, easing or pulling it to the exact measurements. Then carry out the whole washing process, undoing the tacking stitches only after pressing. The woolly should, of course, be turned inside out before it is tacked to the base.

Washing Sheets

Soak sheets and pillowcases overnight in cold water.

Use a reliable washing powder and follow carefully the maker's instructions as to quality, temperature and so on. Be sure that whatever the cleansing agent used, it is completely dissolved in the water before any article is immersed in it. Rinse thoroughly. Many a dingy cotton sheet is due to insufficient rinsing. Spread the sheets full width on an outside line. When dry, remove them, pull them to straighten them and fold them lightly to avoid unnecessary wrinkles, damp and roll down.

Shake out each piece; bring selvages together with right side of the sheet out. Bring centre fold to the selvages and iron the top fold. Next fold end to end, bringing hems together; continue double folding to the size desired, ironing the surface as it comes to the top.

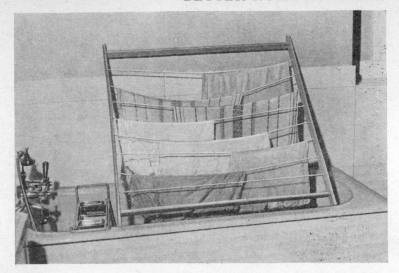

A light-weight fitment that is of inestimable use in the small flat, a drying-rack to stand over the bath

There are other space-saving telescopic racks which fold up; or some are out of the way, on a pulley to the ceiling

Use a moderately hot iron. If it has heat control, turn to 'Cotton'. Start ironing pillowcases at the closed corner from side seam across the case, gradually working towards the open end. Turn the case over, then iron the other side. Never press directly on the fold as this tends to weaken the fibres. Lift iron when you reach the edge of the fold and smooth it with your hand.

To equalise wear at the folds, fold sheet or pillowcase in halves one time; in thirds the next.

Be sure all articles are thoroughly aired before putting them away, otherwise mildew may form.

Towels

Put white towels to soak in cold water for a few hours before washing. Coloured towels should not be soaked, nor should they be boiled, but washed in hot, soapy water.

Rinse thoroughly and bear in mind that a little salt or vinegar added to the final rinsing water will brighten coloured goods. Hang towels on a clean clothes-line to dry, preferably in the open air. Terry towels should not be ironed, as this flattens the pile. When the towels are dry they should be shaken loose, folded and put away.

Never store any household linen article unless it is completely dry, or mildew will form.

The Care of Turkish Towels

Trim off any loose threads in your towels that may occur from time to time, then they will not get pulled further.

Rotate the use of your towels by placing the freshly laundered ones at the bottom of the pile in your linen cupboard. Thus you will spread wear and tear over a number and give each one a rest period between use.

Try Some Home Dyeing

If once or twice a year you look over all your blouses, light frocks and lingerie, you may be able to freshen them considerably. If you are doubtful about your capability of doing a garment yourself, it is better to send it to the cleaners. For instance, a grey frock could be dyed brown or black, given a new set of collars and cuffs, have the sleeves cut off, a new belt. A light-colour suit might be dyed black or brown. If brown, give it a leopardskin collar and edging to the pockets. If black, a black velvet half-collar, and flaps to the pockets, or else a big velvet button (or buttons) and a velvet cravat.

Wool or pure silk takes dye easily. Rayons and artificial silks are very absorbent and need great care. They do not all respond in the same way. Experiment with a belt of the same material, if you have one. (If it is spoilt, you can always wear a contrasting belt.) Or perhaps you may have a square of the material somewhere.

Patterned materials can be freshened with a dye over the whole, but it should not be too dark a dye. If there is black in the pattern, it will still come up black, but the other shades will be brighter.

A cold-water dye should be used for fine silks, organdie, muslins, chiffons, and all pastel shades. A hot-water dye is suitable only for things that are not likely to be harmed by high temperatures. Dyeing should not shrink any garment more than ordinary laundering would do. It is safer to remove all buttons, zips, plastic or metal fastenings. Put in some odd pieces of the same material if you have them, then whether it is a loose cover you are tackling or a garment, you have a piece at hand to reinforce it at any time. Put in some cotton, too, so that it can be sewn with the right shade. You *can* have a dark material dyed lighter but as this usually means bleaching first, it is a professional job. It is safer to have a darker shade, but it need not always be a very dark one. A pastel frock or coat may easily dye a deeper shade of the same colour quite successfully.

Care of Your Clothes

Do you know that after about six months of ordinary wear, a suit weighs a quarter of a pound more than when it was new? This shows how much dirt and dust it can acquire during those months! Have your clothes cleaned when they need it, otherwise the dirt works its way into the fibres of the cloth. Pressing too often without cleaning forces dirt into the fibres, too.

Shake your clothes and suits every night, brush where needed, and put them on hangers. A man's suit should have the pockets emptied, otherwise it soon acquires a sagging look. Clothes that have been worn on a hot day, or in a very smoky atmosphere, should be hung in a draught for an hour or so before being put away.

When clothes are put away for a season,

There are irons for all uses; no one need 'make do.' On the left is the Tilley oil-iron; right, the Victor safety-iron, which falls back on its own end, thus avoiding scorch risk. At the bottom, the G.E.C. lightweight iron

they must be absolutely clean. Examine for any signs of moth. Put them between layers of newspaper and pack with an anti-moth powder, or crystals sprinkled well between the garments. Take out occasionally and shake, examining for any damage.

HOW TO REMOVE STAINS

IF you are doubtful about removing a stain it is better to take the garment to the cleaners and ask their advice. You may rot the material or cause harm to a dress that could be cleaned safely or, as a last resort, renovated or dyed. The difficulty, sometimes, of using a home cleaner is that rubbing part of the garment with a wet or dry solvent removes any underlying dirt from the area of the stain. The place where the stain was, having been partially cleaned, will then appear lighter than the rest of the garment. It is usually necessary, therefore, when removing stains, to immerse the garment completely so that these light patches do not occur. When you take the garment to the cleaners it is best to tell the manageress what the stain is, so that she can notify the works and the stain can then be tackled from the start with the correct process.

When a stain becomes old it becomes more obstinate and difficult to remove. Bleaches will rot delicate materials if they are not washed out immediately they have done their work. Great care should be taken when removing marks from some synthetic fabrics. For instance, acetone or nail-varnish remover will possibly remove nail varnish from silk, wool and so on (though the dye in the varnish may linger on), but a synthetic fabric, such as rayon, will tend to 'melt' if acetone or varnish remover is applied.

When the mark is small and you feel safe in trying to remove it yourself, here is the routine:

Alcohol. Apply cold water. To prevent any water-rings, dry quickly with an iron, putting the garment under a cloth. If you leave to dry slowly it will tend to leave a mark.

Ink. It is best to leave this alone if it is on a dress and send to the cleaners. A white tablecloth may be saturated in milk and salt. If this is not satisfactory, a diluted household bleach will finish the job. On clothes, the fat content in milk may leave a stain which is equally difficult to remove. A detergent in hot water will nearly always remove ink from a carpet. Rub the soap or detergent well into the stain. You may have to wash some more of the carpet to get an even effect. Do not use a bleach on anything coloured or the colour will go with the stain.

When ink stains are old they are more difficult to remove. On white materials use a hot solution of oxalic acid, salts of lemon or chloride of lime. As salts of lemon and oxalic acid are poisonous, apply them with a bone, glass or wooden spoon and wash out the utensil afterwards. Wash the garment thoroughly afterwards to remove the chemicals.

For a small stain, melt the end of a wax candle, or put some soap, over the spot, press to it, leave for a day, then remove grease and clean or wash in usual way.

Lipstick. Very small lipstick stains can *sometimes* be removed by the use of most of the home cleaners on the market. However, a considerable lipstick stain, where the ingredients of the lipstick are built up on the surface of the garment, presents a more difficult problem. If treated with large amounts of lighter fuel or petrol the stain will spread over an area much greater than its original size. Furthermore, the garment will have been stained with the red dye which is contained in the lipstick itself. It is impossible to remove this red dye without the aid of chemicals which do not come within the normal usage of the home.

Biro Ink. Water won't remove it, although methylated spirits may do so. The uncontrolled application of petrol home cleaners, while removing some of it, tends to spread it over a much larger area. The only way to remove large areas of biro staining is by soaking in a strong detergent for a considerable time.

Food. This is a water-soluble stain and requires the quick application of cold water, with the garment rubbed reasonably vigorously, depending on the type of the material. Wool will stand more pressure than silk without being damaged. Here, again, quick drying is essential to prevent water marks.

Blood. There is only one home treatment for blood and that is the quick application of cold water. It is better to immerse the garment completely rather than to rub the particular area of the blood stain, unless it is a very small spot. Allow the area of the stain, in this case, to dry slowly, because once blood has been in contact with heat it is all the more difficult to remove should you decide eventually to send it to your cleaner. Blood will oxydise on

being in contact with the air, and more particularly when in contact with heat. Old blood stains can be bleached with chloride of lime or peroxide of hydrogen. Do not use on colours.

Grass Stains. On non-washable garments methylated spirit can be used to remove them. White garments can be washed with ammonia and water, or the affected part of linen or cotton soaked in a bleach. Rub washable garments stained with grass with paraffin or glycerine, washing afterwards in the usual manner.

Tea and Coffee Stains. Sponge with cold or tepid water to which a drop of glycerine has been added.

Wines, Spirits, Fruit Juices, Milk, Ice Cream, Most Foods, Grass, Trees. Sponge with a very mild solution of one of the modern detergents and cold or tepid water, having rubbed off as much as possible with a dry, clean cloth, or apply some powdered starch first, which will absorb most of the stain. Soak old fruit stains in glycerine.

Paint, Tar, Motor-car Oil. Sponge with a clean cloth dipped in turpentine or one of the reputable home cleaners.

To apply first-aid methods as quickly as possible to a stain is the most important thing to remember. The longer a stain is left to set into the fabric, the more difficult it will be to take it out later on. So, to make your clothes last, when you get home, however tired you are, do, before going to bed, make a quick examination of them and, after giving them a good brush, do your best to remedy any damage that may have been done. A stitch in time really does save nine.

Crude Oil Stain. Crude oil washed up from the sea sometimes sets on swim suits, dresses, coats or shoes. Some seaside town councils have gone the length of setting up special cleaning stations on the beaches where unhappy people queue up for a rub down before returning home- and hotel wards. The trouble is that the oil has a tar base, so no amount of first-aid cleaning will completely remove the brown stain it makes, although cleaners have a special solvent.

The best emergency treatment is to fill a saucer with one of the well-known home cleaners and gently squeeze the stained area in it to dissolve the solid matter as much as possible. Be careful not to rub, for this will spread the stain and drive it deeper into the fabric.

DO A LITTLE
EMBROIDERY

MANY women do not like dressmaking, but a little embroidery is something that can be picked up in an odd moment. It is not only soothing to the nerves, it can be done while listening to the radio, or talking, and more especially allows scope for the creation of lovely colour-schemes, giving just that individual note to the home that is so satisfactory.

Embroidery Equipment

The tools you will need for this attractive craft are surprisingly few and inexpensive.

Needles. Except for a very few stitches, such as diamond hemstitch, which are carried out in ordinary sewing cotton, sewing needles are not used. Instead, supply yourself with a packet each of *crewel* or *embroidery needles* (about the same size and shape as sewing needles, but with large eyes to take the thicker thread used); and *wool needles* (with blunted points, useful for wool embroidery or for doing tapestry or other work on canvas).

Scissors. Your ordinary sewing scissors are rather too large and clumsy for most kinds of embroidery, especially where, as in scalloping and cutwork, part of the material has to be carefully cut away. So invest in a really good pair of slender, sharp-pointed embroidery scissors and keep them for embroidery purposes only. A pair of curved manicure scissors is also a great help for cutting out neatly the points between scallops, but they are not essential.

Hoop Frames. Many kinds of embroidery are more easily and quickly worked if the material can be held well stretched, instead of having to stretch it over the fingers of one hand. Hoop frames consist of two rings of wood or metal, one of which fits closely within the other. The material is laid on the smaller hoop, then the larger one is pressed over it, holding the stuff stretched. It is useful to have two hoops, one of medium size and one small, but the medium one only will do very well. The best hoop to buy is one which has some kind of screw or tension arrangement to keep the material from slipping anywhere.

Tweezers are in no way essential, but they *are* a help in pulling out the threads of canvas after cross-stitch embroidery on ordinary material is done. They also handily draw out threads for hemstitching. Get the ordinary small toilet tweezers.

Corks. Keep a few corks of various sizes in your workbox. By putting the points of embroidery scissors, knitting needles, stilettos, and mattress needles into them when not in use you will save your fingers many an unexpected jab, and the lining of your workbox will wear far longer. In addition to these permanent tools you will, of course, according to the work in hand, need from time to time supplies of suitable transfers (or a sheet of black carbon paper for transferring your own designs), with material and threads suited to the particular job you are doing.

Embroidery should be Spotless

Embroidery is delicate stuff; it is very easy for it to lose its charming first freshness before it is finished. For this reason keep a bag of washing material which will hold your work whenever you are not busy on it. In addition, if you do much white work or delicate embroidery for underwear, it pays to wear a clean overall or pretty little apron while embroidering, or to spread a clean white square of material on your lap. Try always to wash your hands just before starting work, even if they don't look grubby.

Choosing and Using Transfers

Bought transfer designs are the greatest possible help to home embroideresses, and are very inexpensive. To get the best out of them, there are certain points to remember. To begin with, from the very wide choice available, pick out a pattern which is suited to the fabric and to the type of embroidery you intend doing. Before you buy a transfer you must also decide whether you will have it printed in blue or yellow—the two colours available. Use blue whenever possible, as it is kinder to the eyes and obtainable in a larger range of designs. Yellow is necessary for all dark colours and for blue and mauve, as on these shades a blue transfer will not show up.

It is also best for dark greens or browns which have a decided yellow tinge; but it will not show too clearly on such shades, so work as far as possible by daylight.

The transfer must be correctly ironed on to your material if you are to have a clear outline for your work. A smooth, padded surface, such as your ironing-board, is necessary, as any hollows, however slight, will prevent the transfer from marking properly. Lay your material smoothly on the ironing-board, right side upwards.

Cut away from the transfer any lettering, numbers, or parts of the design not wanted, and *use these to make a sample stamping on an oddment of the same material.* This is always advisable, because varying heating of the iron is required on different fabrics. If the transfer does not mark, or does so only very faintly, the iron is too cool. If it marks blurred, heavy and thick, the iron is too hot—assuming in both cases that the material is a suitable one. An iron of the right heat gives a clear, firm outline. Uneven marking generally means an uneven surface under the material, or that the iron was allowed to cool noticeably between start and finish.

Arrange the transfer, face downwards, against the right side of the material, taking care that it is straight and in the right position. Pin it down, well away from the outlines, so that the iron need not go over the pins and leave marks of them on the stuff. Iron off with an iron of the tested heat. This applies to blue transfers. Lift a corner to see that the outline is good before removing the whole transfer.

As a rule yellow ones require less heat to mark well. It is a good plan to put two thicknesses of newspaper over the transfer, to absorb part of the heat, when ironing it off. Press more slowly and evenly than for blue outlines. If the transfer does not mark well, press again, with only one thickness of newspaper under the iron.

Most smooth materials take a transfer very well, but there are a few fabrics which require special treatment.

Stamp organdie and voile on the *wrong* side. The outline will show through clearly and not be so heavy as if on the right side. Thinner transparent materials, such as georgette, chiffon, and net, should not be stamped at all. Instead, tack the transfer underneath the material, so that it shows through. Work through both transfer and fabric, afterwards tearing the paper away.

There are two methods for velvet and other pile materials. Pile will not take a transfer as it is, so the first plan is to press the material on the right side to flatten the nap. Let it cool, then stamp off the transfer. After embroidering, raise the flattened nap by steaming it from the wrong side.

If you do not want to flatten the nap on velvet, or to mark a beautiful material with outlines, tack the transfer over the right side of the material, work through transfer and stuff, as for transparent materials, and afterwards tear away the transfer.

Sometimes you may want to remove a stamped outline ironed on by mistake. This can usually be done, though not from white and pastel satins. Different methods are successful with different transfers and materials.

If the fabric is easily washable, first try washing and well rubbing with good soap flakes. If this does not succeed, or if laundering would hurt the material, rub the outlines hard with benzine. Methylated spirit works better in some cases.

Transferring Designs

It may happen that you have drawn or traced your own design, for which there is no transfer, and want a way of marking it clearly on your material. This is easily done with the aid of a sheet of black carbon paper, which costs a few pence from any stationer. *Be careful to get an embroidery carbon, not a typewriter one.*

Place your material flat on a pastry-board (if you haven't a drawing-board) or the kitchen table. Lay over it the carbon, black side downwards. Over this again place your design, and secure the three layers to the board with drawing-pins, to prevent any slipping.

Carefully go over the outlines of the design with a steel knitting needle, embroidery stiletto, or orange stick, pressing evenly and rather hard, and you will find the design clearly marked on the stuff. For dark materials a white carbon is needed.

This method is also excellent if you want

to use a second time a transfer design which has been stamped off once. Trace its outlines through carbon paper as many times as you wish (or as long as the transfer will hold together!).

A Little Practice

If you want to do embroidery, know your stitches. Never attempt to do a stitch, even of the simplest kind, with which you are unfamiliar, straight on to a piece of embroidery, or you run the risk of spoiling it. No one works a stitch as well as she might the first time she tries it, and you should always do a little practising first on an odd piece of the same or similar material, just to get your hand in.

Make a Sampler

The idea of the old-time samplers, which we now consider as antiques, was to teach a little girl her stitches, and the first samplers were really 'samples' of different stitches. This is a good plan to follow today, at any rate with the dozen or so most-used stitches. It gives you practice in forming the different stitches really well, and it serves as a reminder, for you can pack your sampler in your week-end suitcase, or take it about with you, when it would not be convenient to carry a large book for reference.

Linen is the best material for a sampler, and a good size, which will hold all the stitches you are likely to use often, is about 9 by 12 in. To keep the edges from fraying, as linen so easily does, practise overcast cross stitch and the various buttonhole stitches round them, while the centre can be devoted to rows or groups of such everyday stitches as outline, stem, chain, lazy-daisy, French knots, feather stitch, and the simple hemstitches. Linen is suggested because it has threads which will pull, and so hemstitching can be worked on it as well as surface stitches.

If you haven't done much embroidery, don't attempt to fill your sampler all at once, for learning so many stitches quickly will only muddle you. Practise two or three first, then do a piece of embroidery, using these two or three. Practise another, use this as well in your next fancywork job, and so go on gradually, always trying a new stitch first on your sampler and then using it on an actual piece of work. In this way you will learn a large number of stitches gradually and thoroughly.

If you use linen in a pretty shade, and work your stitches in varying colours which harmonise or contrast with the background, the sampler will be ornamental as well as useful. Leave a space at the bottom where you can add your name and the dates of beginning and ending the sampler (these will give you practice in embroidering lettering and numbers). Then perhaps in years to come your grandchildren will frame your 'practice piece' (as we have framed our grandmothers') as a treasured example of the beautiful work done at the present time!

By the way, when writing or reading about stitches confusion often arises from the fact that many stitches have two, three or four different names, and that often any particular person knows only one of these names and her neighbour may know only another of them. Again, the same name may be applied by different people to two quite distinct stitches. All this often makes it difficult to identify a stitch that may have been read about or mentioned by someone else. As far as possible, alternative names are given.

Back Stitch

This is an elementary and important stitch in both embroidery and plain sewing. In embroidery it is used for outlines for which a definite, yet broken rather than smooth, look is required, and also for very indented outlines, as it goes easily round even sharp curves.

To work. Hold the work so that the outline to be back-stitched is across the fingers. Bring the needle out on to the line, not quite at the extreme end. Take a straight backward stitch along the line to the extreme end. Then take the needle under this stitch (on the wrong side and under as much more space as a second stitch the same length will occupy). Bring the needle up and take another back stitch from this point to the end of the first stitch. Continue similarly, alternating a short back stitch on the surface with a double-length one underneath. All the back stitches should connect neatly, be the same length, and be worked loosely enough not to pucker the material.

If short back stitches are worked in coarse thread, not quite touching each other, almost a beaded effect will result.

Barb Stitch (8)

This is bold and handsome, for borders and the veins of leaves. It is one of the buttonhole-

Below: Overcasting

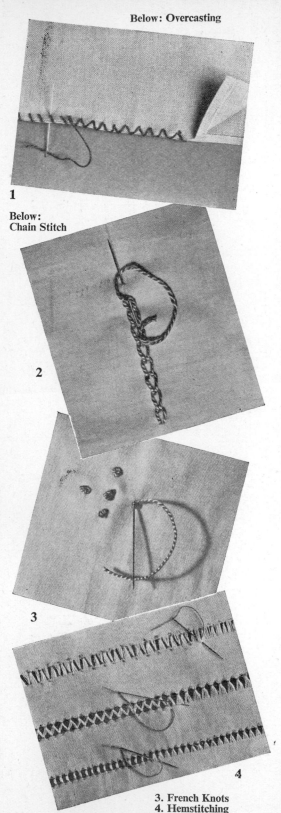

1

**Below:
Chain Stitch**

2

3

4

3. French Knots
4. Hemstitching

stitch variations, enriched with a whipping stitch in a contrasting colour. It takes time to do, but is not difficult.

To work. Work a row of open or spaced buttonhole stitch and then another row back to back with it, the spikes of both coinciding to form vertical bars. Whip over the double centre-line with a second contrasting thread,

Blanket Stitch

This name is often wrongly given to any form of open buttonhole stitch, but really it belongs to a diagonal-type work in groups of three stitches, which was originally used for blanket edges. It makes a pretty edging for many purposes.

To work. Fold and tack a hem on thin material. On woollens, especially if they are at all thick, turn only a single fold or work to the cut edge. Work as for buttonhole stitch, but take the first three stitches all into the same hole at their inner end. This means that two of them will be diagonal and only the centre one upright, the three forming a triangle with a line down its centre. Work all along in the same way in groups of three stitches, the end of each triangle touching the beginning of the next.

Some people find it easiest always to work first the centre stitch of each group.

Buttonhole Stitch (10A)

This, with its many variations, is one of the most important stitches in embroidery. In fact, whole pieces of work are often carried out entirely in this stitch. It is also very important in *broderie anglaise*, appliqué and hardanger, where it finishes cut edges firmly and prettily. Many small flowers in outline embroidery are quickly worked in open buttonhole stitch. It also, alone or with other stitches, makes innumerable pretty borders for dress purposes.

The open variety of buttonhole stitch, in which the stitches are well separated, is sometimes referred to as blanket stitch. Actually, blanket stitch is simply one variety of open buttonhole stitch.

Every type of buttonhole stitch is best worked with a twisted thread.

To work. If working over a hem, tack or crease this in place first. The best width for the hem is $\frac{1}{4}$ in. wide, as a rule. Fasten the working thread inside the hem, where it will not show; then bring it up to the right side

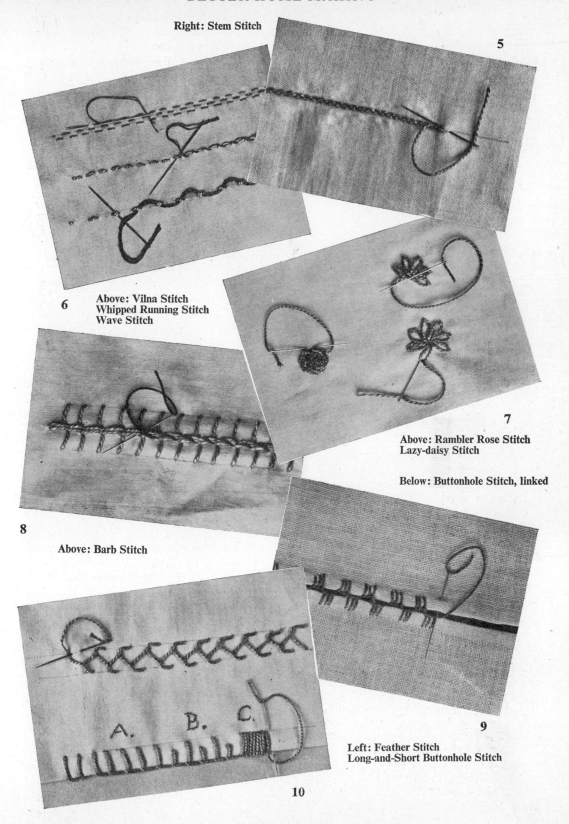

Right: Stem Stitch

5

6 **Above: Vilna Stitch**
Whipped Running Stitch
Wave Stitch

7

Above: Rambler Rose Stitch
Lazy-daisy Stitch

Below: Buttonhole Stitch, linked

8

Above: Barb Stitch

9

Left: Feather Stitch
Long-and-Short Buttonhole Stitch

10

11

Left:
This is a fascinating and amusing early motor-car worked in green, red and blue. It is worked in tent stitch

Below:
Here you see two ways of working tent stitch in tapestry. Colour and design are important

on the hem edge at the left-hand end of the hem. To start, make a straight upright stitch the width of the hem. Put the needle through to the wrong side at the end of this stitch, bringing it up again on the hem fold, where it originally came through. Make a second upright stitch, this time downwards towards the hem fold, ¼ in, or so from the first, holding the thread down with the left thumb so that it is *under* the needle. Pull up the thread, and it will form a bar along the hem edge, known as the purl—continuous, yet starting afresh with every stitch. This purl is the distinguishing mark of every type of buttonhole stitch.

Continue to take upright stitches ¼ in. apart all along, always keeping the thread under the needle. When turning a corner, make a diagonal stitch going, at its inner end, into the same hole as the last upright stitch, and take the first upright stitch on the new line also into this hole; this gives a symmetrical effect.

Sometimes in buttonhole stitch the stitches are worked close enough to touch (10C).

Buttonhole Stitch—Linked (9)

A very pretty form of buttonholing, useful when a seam or two widths of material are to be joined in a decorative way. It may be used for seams of bedspreads, two-material cushion covers, underwear, or for adding contrasting hems to tablecloths and traycloths.

To work. Fold in narrow hems along the edges to be joined, and tack them down if necessary. Place the two edges closely side by

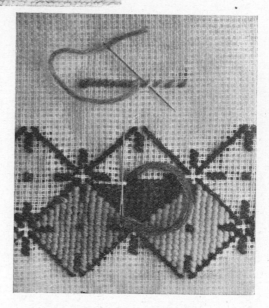

side, either in an embroidery hoop or by tacking them down to a strip of brown paper. Take three narrowly spaced buttonhole stitches over one hem, making them the depth of the hem. Then, without fastening off or cutting the thread, take three more just below, but in the second edge of stuff. Continue alternating three stitches in each edge till the seam is complete. The stitch may be varied by taking only two each side.

Buttonhole Stitch—Long-and-Short (10B)

Long-and-short buttonhole stitch is a simple and popular edge finish suitable for almost any piece of work. It should be boldly worked with a thick thread.

To work. Make narrowly spaced buttonhole stitches (see this heading) which are alternately long and short. A bolder version of the stitch uses spikes of three heights, either going up from short to tall and then starting again with the short, or gradually descending from the tall through medium to short. The groups of graduated stitches may be continuous or with a noticeable space between each.

Chain Stitch (2)

For bold outlining or for filling the double outline of stems quickly and effectively, this stitch is excellent. It is also a good padding stitch to use under scalloping or satin stitch. Remember when buying working threads for a piece of work using chain stitch that it is rather extravagant of thread.

To work. Work downwards or towards yourself. Bring the needle up from the wrong side at the top of the line or design. Put the needle in close to where it came up, holding the thread down under the needle with the left thumb to form a loop. Pull up the thread. Now insert the needle inside the loop, bringing it out again a little lower down the line. Pull up the thread to form a small loop as before; this gives the series of links from which the stitch is named.

Work chain stitch a little loosely or it will pucker the stuff. Keep the loops of even size.

This design is worked in lazy-daisy stitch for **12** leaves and long and short satin stitch for the flower

To work. Simply place two stroke stitches of equal length one over the other at right angles, so that a cross or multiplication sign ($\times$) is formed. All cross stitches in a given piece of work should cross over the same way, and when a number close together are being worked, it is simpler to work one stroke of each cross all along the line, and then return crossing each stroke with a second. A line of touching cross stitches, worked X-wise, and enclosed in two rows of outline stitch in the same or a contrasting colour, makes a pretty decoration for babies' frocks.

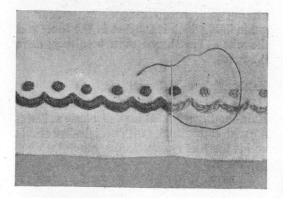

Padded scallops being closely buttonholed

Cross Stitch

One of the easiest and most popular of all embroidery stitches, it has given its name to one type of embroidery, carried out entirely in this stitch. It is also often combined with other stitches in simple coloured embroideries or worked in rows or groups of joined or detached stitches as a trimming.

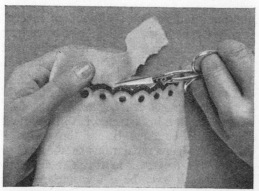

Cutting away the material carefully from the buttonholed edge, with sharp embroidery scissors

Cross Stitch—Overcast (1)

Also known as criss-cross overcasting. This is a simple and very useful adaptation of cross stitch to a hem or doubled edges. It makes a bold and effective trimming for the joins of cushion covers or to finish the hems of runners and traycloths. When finely worked, it is very pretty to hold the rolled edges of handkerchiefs or underwear. Tack down the hem or edges to be joined (with their raw edges folded inwards face to face) before starting the cross stitch.

To work. Keep the right side of the material towards you, and start working from right to left. Make a row of slanting overcast stitches right over the hem or edge. Make them ¼ in. deep, or a little more (except on handkerchiefs and underwear), and keep the stitches an even distance apart. When the line is finished, return in the reverse direction, slanting the stitches the other way and working into the same holes as in the first row. Thus a series of cross stitches over the edge is formed.

Even working gives this stitch its effectiveness. A good way to ensure evenness is first to stitch the hem by machine, with fine cotton, loose tension, and a long stitch. Preferably use an extra-large machine needle. This machine-stitching takes the place of tacking, and has the additional advantage of giving even spaces for the overcasting. Work the first slanting row through *alternate* machine stitches; when returning, use the stitches missed before. This makes the work very quick and regular. The machine-stitching may afterwards be pulled out, if liked; if left in, it will hardly show.

Darning Stitch

In embroidery this quick stitch is simpler, and varies more than when used for mending. It consists of rows of running stitches, the in-and-out of the stitches alternating in each row. The term 'darning stitch' also sometimes denotes a single row of running stitches used to outline a design. Stitches do not run both ways, as they do in mending.

The chief use of darning in embroidery is to fill backgrounds or fairly large parts of the design. When a background is to be darned, this should be done before the design is embroidered, and the darning should be close enough for the rows to touch and strictly alternated. It may be either horizontal or vertical; the first is commoner. If petals or other parts of a design are first outlined and then filled with very widely spaced rows of darning, they will have more body and colour than if merely outlined, yet still look light and open.

To work. Make rows of straight stitches with spaces between the same length as the stitches. In alternate rows go under where the previous row shows a surface stitch, and vice versa. Keep the lines very even. If a much-filled-up effect is wanted, pick up only a thread or two each time, leaving long stitches lying on the stuff. Thus almost continuous lines are formed with a minimum of thread and work.

Feather Stitch

This is quick and pretty when a bordering effect is wanted, giving an open, rather lacy result. Use it to finish the hems or edges of embroidered articles, or work it inside a leaf outline when you want a natural veined look. It is also a favourite stitch for adorning in a simple way children's frocks and underwear.

To work. The beauty of this stitch depends very much on its evenness. So if you are not used to it, a pencil line to work along will prove a help. Hold a line of feather-stitching upright, and you will see that it is really a simple form of buttonhole stitch, with the stitches below each other instead of alongside. Simply work a buttonhole stitch first to the left and then to the right, at different levels, placing your needle diagonally towards the guide line, which it touches at the bottom of the stitch. The thread must be always *under* the needle.

Feather Stitch—Triangular (10)

This variation has a more formal look than plain-feather stitch. It is particularly suited to use with embroideries with straight-line effects, and is the best type of feather stitch for crazy patchwork.

To work. It must be very evenly placed, so use two pencil lines as guides, placing these lines about ¼ in. apart and parallel. Bring the needle up from the wrong side. Take a stitch exactly along the left-hand line, pointing towards you, and keeping the thread *under* the needle. Take the next stitch in the same way down the right-hand line, making its top level with the bottom of the first stitch. Remember that, as in buttonhole stitch (of which feather stitch is really a variation), the thread must be kept always beneath the needle.

French Knot (3)

This is a favourite stitch, with a great many uses. French knots, varying in number according to the size of the flower, make the best of all centres for small blossoms. Sometimes whole outline designs are carried out in French knots, giving a beaded effect. Clusters of small berries should be embroidered with a French knot for each berry. The stitch is also used in rows as a simple trimming for children's frocks, or to hold hems which are to be let down later, as it does not mark the stuff. When building up borders from simple stitches, French knots look well, worked inside ladder stitch, herringbone stitch, or the prongs of open buttonhole stitch.

To work. Bring the needle up to the right side at the point where the knot is to be. Twist the thread once, twice, or three times (according to the size desired) round the needle, at the same time holding down the slack of the thread, above the part twisted. Push the needle through to the wrong side as close as possible to where it emerged, holding the thread down until it is all drawn through.

Should the knot be inclined to 'topple,' it is a good plan to take a tiny extra stitch over the loose side of the knot after making it, thus: bring the needle up close to the loose side and put it down through the centre of the knot. The effect gained is particularly suitable for berries.

Hemstitch (4)

This is the favourite of all drawn-thread stitches, and is extensively used as a fancy hem on linen embroideries. It is also very popular as a simple trimming for fine underwear, linen frocks, and coats.

To work. If it is being used as a hem, first turn in and tack the hem; then from the hem inwards draw consecutive horizontal threads to a width of $\frac{1}{8}$ or $\frac{3}{16}$ in. If the hemstitching is to come in the interior of the stuff, where there is no hem, simply draw the thread at the right spot. When the hemstitching is not to go to an edge of stuff, but stops short at a given point, cut the threads at this point before pulling.

Hold the stuff with the wrong side towards you and work from left to right. With a fine thread in the needle, bring it through at the inner edge of the hem, hiding the knot in the hem. Take up on the needle four vertical strands in the drawn part; then insert it again diagonally behind the four strands, emerging in the edge of the hem. Thus the thread in order to pass behind the strands a second time will first pass in front of them, completely encircling them. Pull up the thread and the part round the strands will pull them tightly together. Make a little stitch into the solid edge just beyond the four strands to hold the pulling thread firmly. Then put the needle behind the next four strands and repeat.

Hemstitch—Bar

This stitch is simply a more finished version of ordinary hemstitch, and is used for much the same purposes. It is also known as double hemstitch, owing to the double line of working.

To work. Proceed exactly as for hemstitch (see this entry). When the hemstitch is completed along the hem edge, turn the stuff and hemstitch the inner edge similarly, catching up just the same groups of four threads. These, instead of forming triangular shapes as in hemstitch, by the extra line of stitching are turned into straight narrow bars—hence the name.

Herringbone Stitch

This stitch plays a part both in plain sewing and in embroidery. In dressmaking it is chiefly used for holding down a hem made in flannel or other bulky material in which a double turn is not advisable. A single turn is made, and the raw edge held down by herringbone stitch, which prevents fraying.

It is used for turning in babies' flannels and sometimes in upholstery sewing when dealing with felt. Ordinary sewing cotton is used on flannel.

Herringbone may also be worked in embroidery silk as a simple border trimming for children's garments, or may be used as an ornamental casing on underwear through which to run a ribbon or trimming band.

To work. Work from left to right. Use two parallel lines to guide the stitches, and bring the needle through from the wrong side at one end of the upper line. Take the thread forward and downward to the lower line, on which pick up a small horizontal stitch with the needle pointing *backwards*. Pull through, take the needle diagonally upwards to the upper line and make another backward stitch there. Continue stitching alternately on the two lines, so that a kind of cross stitch is formed.

Left:

Antimacassars may be out of date, but 'chairbacks' (another word for the same thing) seem to be coming back into favour! They do avoid one part being continuously rubbed. This is a checked glass-towel worked in red spiders' webs

Below:

Wheel stitch, or spiders' webs, can be used to fill any kind of space simply by making the spokes of the wheel longer or shorter

13

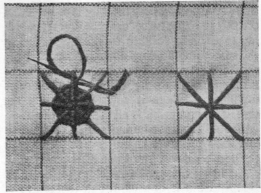

When working herringbone over a raw edge, every slanting thread must pass over that edge, the upper line of stitches being worked on a single thickness of material, and the lower on the doubled turn.

Honeycombing

This is one of the simplest of the various stitches used in smocking. Like all smocking stitches, it is worked on rows of gathers instead of on the usual flat surface. It is quickly made, and is a pretty stitch for trimming children's simple garments or for adorning fullness sections, such as vestees, in grown-up clothes.

To work. Prepare the material in gathers. The stitch is worked on two rows at once, a stitch being taken alternately on the upper and lower rows. Bring up the needle from the wrong side through the left-most pleat of the second or lower row, starting with a very large knot that cannot possibly pull through. From the starting-point, make a back stitch which catches together the next pleat to the starting one, in the same row, and the starting one itself.

Insert the needle into the second of the two pleats (the right-hand one) behind the back stitch just made, and carry it up inside the pleat—so that it does not show on the right side—to the row immediately above. Now, as before, back stitch together this pleat and the one next to it to the right (actually the third pleat from the left, as this stitch was started on the second). This time put the needle downwards inside the third pleat, taking it down to the lower row.

Continue in this way back-stitching to-gether two pleats alternately in the lower and upper rows, the second pleat in one stitch always becoming the first in the next (though higher or lower), so that a diamond pattern is formed.

Lazy-daisy Stitch (7)

This may not be a lazy person's stitch, but it is a very quick one, for each stitch accounts for the entire petal of a flower or a small leaf! It is a very popular stitch for small flowers or leaves in designs embroidered in outline. It is also known as picot stitch.

To work. Lazy-daisy is really a form of chain stitch in which each link in the chain is detached from the others and held down with a small extra stitch. Starting at the centre of a flower or the stem end of a leaf, bring the needle through from the wrong side. Hold down the thread with the left thumb, and put the needle back into the stuff where it came out, bringing it up to the right side again at the outer end of petal or leaf. Keep the needle over the loop of thread just formed, and pull up the loop fairly loosely to cover the petal or leaf outline. Secure the loop down by making a little bar stitch across its outer end, which takes the needle back to the wrong side ready to start the next stitch.

Outline Stitch

This is often confused with stem stitch, but, although very similar, the position of the thread and stitches differs in the two.

To work. Embroider upwards, starting at the bottom of the outline to be covered. Bring the needle through from the wrong side, and take a stitch, needle facing downwards, a little higher up. Keep the thread to the left of, and underneath, the needle. Pull up the thread. Pick up a second stitch from above downwards, making the bottom of this come out just at the top of the first stitch. Continue thus till the line is covered.

Rambler Rose Stitch (7)

This offers a quick and easy way of making an informal-looking small rose in a design. Designs in which small flowers are simply indicated by a circle look well worked in this stitch. If roses so made are grouped in twos and threes, with a few lazy-daisy leaves, they make a charming scattered decoration for a little girl's frock.

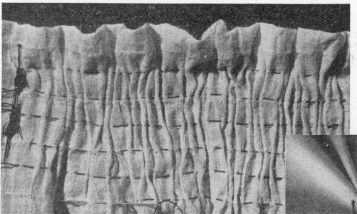

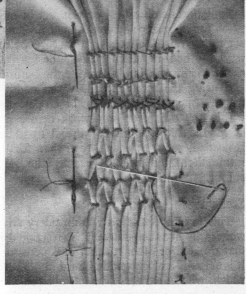

You will see how to begin by gathering your material. Smocking is delightful on children's clothes

14

Right: This simple illustration of a piece of smocking shows honeycombing, single cable, herringbone and outline stitch

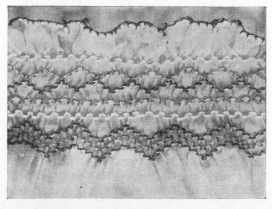

Smocking can be worked in several blending shades by following a pattern like the one shown above

To work. Start with a French knot in the flower colour. Then go closely round and round it in spiral formation with ordinary outline stitch until the rose is large enough or the circle on the design is filled. If an oval is to be embroidered instead of a circle, start with two French knots side by side and work round these. A pretty plan is to make the French knot and inner coils of outline stitch a deeper shade than those outside.

Satin Stitch

This is one of the half-dozen most useful embroidery stitches. It should be practised until it can be worked to look as smooth and satiny as its name! It is used for filling where a solid, all-over effect is wanted, as in much flower embroidery.

To work. Satin stitch is a series of stroke stitches lying side by side so closely that none of the fabric shows between them. Bring the needle through to the right side on one edge of the outline to be filled, and put it in again exactly opposite on the other edge of the outline, making a straight line of thread across the space. Bring the needle up again as close as possible to the start of the first stitch, put it in again beside the end of the first stitch, and so on till the space is filled.

The effect is often prettier if the stitch is worked slanting across the outline, instead of directly up and down and across. This plan is generally used for leaves and stems.

Satin Stitch—Padded

Sometimes embroidery carried out in satin stitch looks bolder and handsomer if there is a slightly raised effect. In this case before working the satin stitch, pad the design with chain stitch, working just inside the outlines, and using the same thread. When padding round shapes, chain stitch in circles, one within the other: do not work across and across the shape. If only a rather flat padding is needed, use a thinner thread than for the satin stitch, but keep it exactly the same colour.

Scalloping

This is almost the only embroidery stitch which will give such a firm finish to raw edges that no hem or other turning in is necessary. It is actually a close, padded buttonhole stitch which, when used on edges, is called scalloping. Usually, but not always, the edge is shaped into a series of semicircles, either by marking half round a coin or with a scalloping transfer. Scalloping is a great feature of *broderie anglaise*. It is best on firm materials.

To work. Allow at least $\frac{3}{4}$-in. turnings on edges that are to be scalloped, placing the scallops that distance from the edge. Pad between the double outlines of the scallops with a line of chain stitch or with closely set running stitches—the chain stitch is much quicker. Then work close buttonhole stitch across the scallops, with the purled edge covering the outer edge of the curves.

When buttonholing is completed, with very sharp embroidery scissors cut away the turnings of stuff as close as possible to the buttonhole edge, taking great care not to cut the stitches.

Smocking

This decorative way of holding rows of gathers in place is never out of fashion. It gains its name from the fact that it was originally used for the smock-frocks or overalls worn by English farmworkers in bygone times.

Smocking has a great deal of elasticity, and smocked children's garments readily stretch as a child grows.

As much fullness is needed, smocking is most successful on cotton and silk fabrics which are firm but comparatively thin.

The evenness and regularity of smocking depend almost entirely upon the same qualities in the preliminary gathering, so this must be carefully and unhurriedly done. It is not safe to trust to the eye for keeping the rows level and equal distances apart. Either mark out a series of dots on the material, carefully measuring them with a ruler—or, better, iron off on the wrong side a smocking transfer, which consists of rows of dots ready spaced out.

Transfers may be bought with the dots various distances apart for different types of work, the distance between the rows being the same as, or greater than, that between the dots. An average space between the dots is $\frac{3}{16}$ or $\frac{1}{4}$ in. Allow from two to four times as much smocking width as the width it is to be when finished, according to the distance apart of the dots. The farther apart they are, the greater the width required.

To mark the material with dots, whether in pencil or with a transfer, stretch it quite taut on a drawing- or pastry-board, and hold it down with drawing-pins. If you are doing your own marking, prepare a long strip of cardboard with two complete rows of dots very accurately marked on it. Pierce each dot with a stiletto to make a hole through which the point of a pencil can be inserted. Lay this card on the material, make a pencil mark through each hole in the two rows, then shift it to mark the next two rows. Keep the card after use, as it will form a permanent marker.

When the material is dotted, start gathering with a long thread and a good knot, making a commencing back stitch in addition in case the knot pulls through. Gather by running the needle from dot to dot in a row, picking up your dots very accurately. At the end of a row pull up the thread to the width required. Do not cut off the surplus, but hold it by winding it round a pin placed upright at the end of the row. Gather each row on a separate thread and wind this on a separate pin.

For the smocking use a firm mercerised or cotton working thread.

The simplest smocking stitch is honeycombing. This is a little different from other smocking stitches in that most of it is invisible and hidden in the folds, whereas the usual smocking stitches are simply ordinary embroidery stitches worked on the surface of the gathers.

Here are some of the principal stitches used.

Outline Stitch. This is a favourite for the top row of a panel or to separate more elaborate stitches. Two rows in two different shades are often placed close together. Starting in the pleat at the extreme left, and holding the gathers sideways so that you work downwards, work as for ordinary outline stitch exactly over the gathers, taking one stitch in every pleat. Remember that in outline stitch the thread must be kept to the left of, and underneath, the needle.

Single Cable Stitch. A simple arrangement of back stitching. Take a back stitch in each pleat along a row of gathers, placing the thread alternately above and below the needle when making the stitches. Thus, first stitch, thread above needle; second stitch, thread below needle, and so on.

Wave Stitch. One of the most decorative and imposing of smocking stitches, worked from left to right. Bring the needle through from the wrong side between the first and second pleats, and take up the first dot. With the thread *below* the needle, now pick up the second dot and draw the two slightly together. Repeat with the third, fourth and fifth dots. Now you have finished the upward slant of the wave and must carry on, making a corresponding number of downward stitches, with the thread *above* the needle. Three rows of wave stitch are often worked close together.

Stem Stitch (5)

This very useful stitch for all kinds of outlines looks a good deal like outline stitch (see this heading), but is worked a little differently. Another name for it is crewel stitch. Strictly speaking, in stem stitch the stitches are overlapped more than in crewel stitch; but in practice the two are slightly different variants of the same stitch.

To work. Bring the needle through from the wrong side at the bottom of the outline, as working proceeds upwards. Work as for outline stitch, but keeping the thread to the *right* of the needle instead of to the left. Also, in true stem stitch each stitch should be started half-way down the previous one, whereas in crewel stitch it starts at the top of that just worked.

Tent Stitch

This has a confusing number of names, being also known as petit point, needlepoint, half-cross stitch and tapestry stitch. Actually, it is the best known of the many stitches used in tapestry work or needlepoint, and many pieces of such work are carried out entirely in tent stitch.

To work. The name half-cross stitch is an accurate working description. Simply make the first slanting half of a cross stitch (see this heading), working over either one or two threads of the canvas, according to the size of stitch desired. Work these slanting stitches closely side by side, so that they cover the surface. Always put the needle in upright.

Vilna Stitch (6)

This is really more a narrow border than a stitch, as its other name, triple border, suggests. It is a dainty and quickly worked simple decoration specially suited for children's clothes. If neatly begun and finished off it is reversible and so particularly useful for 'both side' items such as scarves, handkerchiefs and traycloths.

To work. Make a line of running stitches with the stitches equal in length to the spaces between them. Run a similar line each side of the first one and quite close to it, making the stitches in these two lines alternate with those in the first one.

Wave Stitch (6)

This is a simple and particularly graceful variant of running stitch, using two separate threads, which look prettiest when of different colours. It makes quite an important-looking border for household linen or curtains; if worked all in one colour it gives a realistic effect of waves in a seascape or ship design. It is also useful for holding tucks on a child's frock in a decorative way, yet so that they are easily let down when the child grows.

To work. Make a row of running stitches with the distance between the stitches about twice as great as the length of the stitches, which should be short. With a second thread, preferably contrasting with the first, take the needle under each running stitch but without catching the material. Go under the stitches alternately from the upper and the under side and leave the thread loose enough to give the wave effect.

Wheels—Darned

These, with their slightly more elaborate variation, overcast wheels, are used in many kinds of embroidery to fill effectively either round or square spaces. As they can vary very widely in size, simply by making the spokes longer or shorter, their uses are many.

To work. Make a large cross stitch by placing a horizontal stitch over a vertical one. Work over these two diagonal stitches, so that you now have eight spokes of a wheel. With the same or a contrasting thread, start at the centre where the long stitches intersect, and darn round and round, over one spoke, and under the next alternately. The darning may be continued to only half the depth of the spokes or right up to their ends, according to the solidity of the effect wanted.

Wheels—Overcast

These have the same uses and much the same appearance as darned wheels (above), but take a little longer to work and have a more definitely wheel-like appearance. This stitch is a realistic way of working spiders' webs also, and these are sometimes worked on alternate squares of a soft canvas checked in two colours or on large-checked gingham.

To work. Make the spokes just as for darned wheels, but instead of darning them, go under two spokes (between spoke and material) and then overcast *back* over the last spoke. Continue round and round till the spokes are half or completely filled. For borders, half-wheels, with five spokes instead of eight, give pretty results.

Whipped Running Stitch (6)

Also known as twisted running stitch. This makes an attractive alternative to outline stitch for stems and tendrils or to finish hems on embroidered articles or children's clothes. It is very quickly worked, preferably in two well-contrasted colours.

To work. First make a row of running stitches, making the distance between the stitches about twice as great as the length of the stitches. Then, with the same or a second colour, pick up each running stitch by passing the needle between the stitch and the material. Always insert the needle from the same side of the running stitch, and leave the thread somewhat loose.

APPLIQUÉ

Embroidered Appliqué

The colours of applied materials must be fast if the article is an often-laundered one.

The applied portions are held down to the background with embroidery stitches, and the interiors of the appliqués have their details embroidered. For instance, veins are worked on to leaves, stamens on to flowers, doors and windows on to cottages, and so on.

There is a choice of two plans when doing embroidered appliqué. In the first the applied pieces are cut out roughly, buttonhole-stitched in place, and then their edges are cut away close to the purl of the buttonhole stitch, as in scalloping; in the second and more popular, the applied pieces are cut out exact to their outlines, which are then covered and prevented from fraying with buttonhole or some other stitch.

The first method is preferable for appliqués of material which frays very easily. Otherwise the second is better and easier. The first method requires two copies of the transfer, one for ironing on the background, the other for cutting up and stamping on the various appliqué materials. By the second method only one is needed, as the transfer may be first stamped off on the background and then the appliqué portions of it may be carefully cut out and used as paper patterns for cutting out appliqués (except where there are details to embroider on these).

Buttonhole stitch, worked closely, must be used to fasten down appliqués cut by the first method, as no other stitch has an edge that will allow of the material being cut away right

Riot *of* Colour

A riot of colour is lovelier sometimes than a formal display of expensive blooms. These mixed flower-heads were first arranged in two shallow dishes, which were raised on folded newspaper inside the trough. Wild and garden flowers, poppies, daisies, roses, all nestle happily together. The posy in front is set, with the help of a floral pin-cushion, in a saucer! Choose your embroidery shades from such groups of flowers

Stiffer blooms, such as chrysanthemums, demand a more formal arrangement, but contrast can be achieved by choosing differently coloured heads. These eight flowers and a spray of beech are grouped on a ' pin-cushion ' in a vegetable dish. In winter, use these to help with scarce plants . . . sprays of ivy, wild grasses, ears of corn, dried hydrangea heads tinted pink and blue, mixed with blue teazle and honesty

'Daisy' Table Mats

These charming mats, so easy to make, look wonderful against a dark, polished surface. The flowers have other uses, too

You can arrange these crisp dog daisies round the bottom of a dark summer frock, or around the low neck of a summer blouse. One or two at the high neck of a dress, or just on the pockets, are delightful

*   *   *

Then trace off three petals . . . one small, one large and one small, with the large one in the middle, to form a little design . . . on to waste-paper baskets, furniture, lampshades. They can be painted in gipsy blues and reds, with an occasional green and yellow one to give a gay effect. Arrange a border of each little group of three leaves with about two inches' space between each

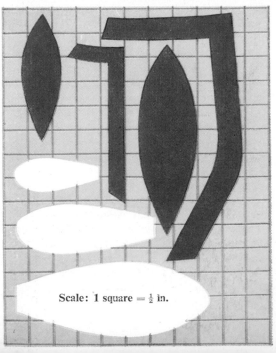

Scale: 1 square = $\frac{1}{2}$ in.

up to it without fraying further. Work this outwards from the appliqué, so that the purl edge lies exactly along the join of the appliqué to the background.

In the second method, by which the appliqués are cut out to their exact shape from the start, lay each, as cut, precisely over its corresponding outline on the background, and pin or tack it down, taking great care that it lies perfectly flat and unwrinkled. To help in getting this result, it is a good plan with a large appliqué to put a thin coating of rather dry paste over the centre of the *background*. It is better not to paste the appliqué itself, as this sometimes wrinkles it. Be careful not to paste anywhere near the edges of the appliqué portion on the background, as the paste would be stiff and hard later for the needle to go through.

If pins are used for fastening down oil baize appliqués, remember that they leave permanent holes in this fabric, so they should only be inserted near the edges, where the holes can be covered by the applying stitchery.

Use a twisted embroidery thread for the buttonholing, either matching the appliqué in colour or, preferably, a shade or two darker. Close buttonholing is needed for all fabrics which fray, but American cloth and felt may be appliquéd down with a well-spaced stitch which is much more quickly worked. The open stitch also gives a lighter effect.

In machine-made appliqués chain stitch is often used to hold down appliqués, but in handwork, though sometimes used for materials which fray very little, it is not very satisfactory, as it does not hide the edges properly.

Blind Appliqué

This is the name given to appliqué which is not embroidered, but is secured to the background with slip stitch or blind stitch.

This is the simplest and quickest kind of appliqué, and so is excellent for very large pieces of work, such as wall hangings, bed-spreads and cushions. To make it, cut out each appliqué piece with narrow turnings. Pin or tack the appliqué in position (keeping pins or tackings away from the edge). Slip-stitch down all round to the foundation, turning under the surplus edges with finger and thumb, or with the needle-point as you go along. Use sewing cotton matching the appliqué. Afterwards well press.

'Daisy' Table Mats

(Illustrated on opposite page)

THEY'RE gay and different, and they'll add a bright, Continental touch to special meals.

For your home, they provide table mats that are really individual, and single you out as a hostess with discerning taste. On a polished wooden table they bring sunshine to your room and add an air of luxury to even the most ordinary lunch.

They would also make a wonderful present for that girl you know who is getting married shortly—and one she is not likely to receive from anyone else!

In fact, with these daisies you just can't go wrong. They have one hundred and one pretty and decorative uses.

Materials. For a set of four place mats, four glass mats, and centre mat, $\frac{3}{4}$ yard of 36-in.-wide white cotton material; $\frac{1}{8}$ yard each of yellow and green cotton material; matching sewing threads. Bias binding, for centre mat, $\frac{1}{2}$ yard yellow, 6 yards white; for one place mat, one glass mat, $\frac{1}{2}$ yard yellow, $1\frac{1}{2}$ yards green, $7\frac{1}{2}$ yards white.

To make. Yellow centres: cut $3\frac{5}{8}$-in. circle for centre mat and $3\frac{1}{8}$-in. for place mats, $1\frac{3}{4}$-in. for glass mats. Overcast all cut edges to prevent fraying. Cut a stalk and a leaf in green for each glass and place mat.

Petals: for centre mat, cut 19 large petals; 21 medium petals for each place mat, and 18 small petals for each glass mat.

Prepare bias binding by folding the binding lengthways not quite in half, but just to where it is double. Then, with sharp pair of scissors, cut off about half of other double side. This makes less bulk to sew.

Bind yellow centres with yellow binding, green parts with green binding. Bind petals with white binding, overcasting lower straight edge. Press all parts well before assembling. Stitch petals at back of yellow binding, slightly overlapping each other.

Do not stitch them at any other place, as they will fall into position when put on the table.

Arrange green stalks and leaves as shown in illustration, secure with a stitch at back of mats and press with a warm iron.

'Fruit Cluster' Table Mats

THESE mats are very simple to make and the embroidery in red, purple, green and gold is enchanting. Linen is perhaps the most suitable material to use. You will need $\frac{5}{8}$ yd., 36-in. wide, and $7\frac{1}{4}$ yds. of edging. There are many pretty edgings to be bought in the shops, or of course you can crochet round each mat; use lace if you wish (it would have to be coarse and very plain); or bind with bias binding in a shade to catch up one of the colours in the fruit cluster.

Lay your material flat and cut one piece of material 20 in. by 19 in. Cut this into four, which will give you your four mats 10 in. by $9\frac{1}{2}$ in. each. Then cut another strip of material 12 in. by $19\frac{1}{2}$ in., which provides you with your centre mat.

Your Embroidery

You will need these embroidery cottons: 2 skeins of red; 2 skeins purple; 2 skeins mauve; 2 skeins gold; 2 skeins green; 1 skein brown.

Transfer the design to your mats as indicated on the opposite page, then work the embroidery as follows:

Apples. Main stem brown satin stitch and stem stitch; fruit stems and leaves in green satin stitch. Apples to be filled in with red chain stitch, the eyes in brown chain stitch.

Pears. Leaves and stems as before; fruit filled in with gold chain stitch, eyes in brown chain stitch.

Plums. Leaves and stems as before. Fruit filled in with mauve chain stitch.

Grapes. Main stem brown satin stitch, fruit stem green satin stitch. Leaves and tendrils green stem stitch. Grapes outlined with three rows of purple chain stitch. (Work overlapping grapes first.)

When filling in the solid fruits, begin working from the outside edge, leaving the highlights. Do not pull the stitches too tightly or the material will crinkle in the centre. Three strands of the cotton are used throughout for the embroidery, but only two are required for grape tendrils.

The colours chosen show up well on a cream-coloured or very pale yellow linen. You can then have the edging in golden-yellow, or purple. If you choose pale green linen, then see it blends with the green embroidery cotton for the leaves. It is best to buy your material and take it with you when you go to choose the fruit colours.

Trace this fruit on to a piece of tracing-paper, then trace on to your material with an embroidery carbon. Or you can prick around the design on your tracing-paper with a fairly thick pin, lay it on your dinner mat, and shake powder over the holes. Draw in lightly where the powder has outlined the design and embroider

These outlines are for you to trace as described above.

397

Needlework Notions

Making a Screen

A screen is indispensable where there is a baby in the house, is very useful in a sick-room, or for more comfortable living. It is an expensive item to buy, but it can be made quite cheaply at home.

Wooden frames for screens can sometimes be bought ready for staining and covering, or a home handyman can make them. Sometimes a shabby existing screen only needs re-covering. Again, a fair-sized wooden clothes-horse makes an excellent screen frame, if brass hinges are substituted for the webbing straps that join the panels. Enamel the frame any colour desired. Another idea is to hinge together the frames of two old deck-chairs to make a four-fold screen.

The most practical covering is the ' French door' curtain, as this is easily removed for laundering. Use any suitable washing material such as cretonne, printed linen, or check gingham. Make a curtain for each panel, with a heading and casing at both top and bottom, arranging the length so that the casings will come against the top and bottom edges of the frame, with the headings extending beyond them. Through each casing run either a light spring wire rod, screwing this in position on each upright of the panel; or, if the screen is small, run a tape through, and fix this to the frame with drawing-pins stuck at intervals through both tape and casing.

If the curtain material used is not heavy enough to break any draught effectively, an excellent plan is to 'line' the screen with panels of coloured plastic material fixed with matching drawing-pins to the wrong side of the frame. These are easily wiped clean with a damp cloth when soiled.

For a baby a screen with pockets in which toilet articles are kept is useful at bath-time. In this case, cover with plain panels of cretonne, as described for the plastic material. Before fixing these in position, make and attach to them whatever pockets are wanted, drawing up the top of each pocket on an elastic-run casing. Fix similar straight but unpocketed panels on the other side.

Re-cover Your Eiderdowns

If your eiderdown is only faded and not worn, it is sufficient to envelop it in another cover which will hide the discolorations. Extra strength and durability are not required, so, as eiderdowns should always be as light in weight as possible, it is best to make a thin, semi-transparent cover of such a fabric as voile or furnishing net or nylon.

Net can match the eiderdown or contrast with it; in the latter case you will get a delightful shot effect from the eiderdown colour being glimpsed through the net.

The new cover is made like a very large cushion cover. Make it on the large and loose side for your eiderdown, because both net and voile usually shrink when washed. Allow, too, for the amount taken up by the thickness of the feathers.

Seam up the cover on three sides and part of the fourth, inserting a narrow contrasting piping between the two thicknesses. Lay the new cover out flat on a large table and put the eiderdown into it, spreading it out well so that it fills the new cover evenly. Pin here and there through eiderdown and cover to keep the eiderdown spread out, and sew up the open end.

Now secure the new cover permanently in place by fixing it down to the eiderdown along the original lines of stitchery in the latter. There are two ways of doing this fixing. One is to put the whole thing in the machine (a treadle machine is the best) and stitch through all thicknesses of both. This is a bit tricky if you work alone, as you must keep one hand constantly moving about underneath the eiderdown to see that the under-lay of the new cover is not getting creased or folded in the machine. A better plan is to have one person machining and a second to do the smoothing and spreading out.

The other method is to quilt by hand in running stitch.

If your eiderdown is wearing through, the new cover must be of thicker material—say down-proof sateen. Make it and fix it on in the same way as for the transparent cover.

Make Your Own Gifts

Vantona

Make out a list of birthdays and friends to be remembered at Christmas well in advance, so that you can be prepared

THERE is something so personal about a gift we have made ourselves, whether it is just a casual present to please, or to mark an anniversary, birthday or Christmas. It is an excellent plan to keep a 'Gifts' box, into which you pop from time to time left-overs of material, remnants of ribbon and lace, half-skeins of embroidery silks, and other 'wherewithal' for making presents. Then, at odd moments, you will enjoy creating some charming novelty for the right occasion.

The following suggestions are inexpensive, made without much labour, and yet have that air of 'something different' which makes a present welcome.

Shampoo Cape

For the girl who washes her hair at home, giving protection without getting in the way.

Required. Three thick face cloths, coloured or with coloured borders, matching or contrasting shades; a press-stud.

To make. One face-cloth forms the back of the cape. The other two are slightly overlapped on to it, one over each top corner, so that they fit snugly round the neck and overlap each other a little in front, where they fasten with a press-stud. Make the overlaps at the back twice as deep as they are wide, so that they form oblongs, not squares, and sew them together.

Desk-set in Oil Baize (American Cloth)

A schoolgirl, or a young student, will appreciate this desk outfit.

Required. ¼ yard (or less) of bright-coloured oil baize—say orange; 1 oblong of cardboard, blotter size; 2 sheets of coloured blotting-paper; 1 skein of brown embroidery wool; 1 large orange bead; a small cylindrical tin; oddment of cotton material the same colour as the oil baize.

To make. Decide on the blotter size, folding the blotting-paper to fit. Cut an oblong of cardboard this size and from coloured cotton material—say casement cloth—cut another oblong the same size plus turnings. Cut two strips of American cloth the same length as the width of the cotton oblong and 3½ in. wide. Turn a narrow hem along the sides of the cotton oblong, then join to each end the ends and one side of an oil-baize strip, so that these form a pocket each end by which the blotting-paper is held. Edge the free sides of the strips with spaced buttonhole stitch in brown wool. Slip first the cardboard and then the blotting-paper in place.

The Pen Vase. Enamel the tin inside and along its bottom rim orange or brown. Cut from the oil baize a strip ½-in. deeper than the tin and long enough to go round and overlap a little. Turn in the ½ in. along the top, and buttonhole-stitch the folded edge in

399

A desk-set in American cloth. A friend's initials or name on it is a nice personal touch

brown to match the blotter ends. Glue the strip smoothly round the tin.

The Penwiper. Outlining round a small saucer, cut 4-in. circles, one in oil baize and three or four others from oddments of felt or thick cloth. Buttonhole round the oil baize circle in brown wool. Place it over the other circles and secure all together in the centre by sewing on a large bead.

Camphor Sachets

Hung in a wardrobe or placed in drawers, these guard against the ravages of moths. Three, each in a different pastel shade, tied together or put in a dainty box, make a charming gift or sell well at bazaars.

Required. Oddments of organdie in pale

Guest towels are always welcome for the housewife or girl who lives on her own. A little embroidery makes them smart

colours; 1 camphor cube; ¼ yard of baby ribbon; and 1 needleful of stranded cotton for each sachet.

To make. Cut two matching 4-in. squares of organdie for each sachet. One inch in from the outer edges, sew them together with large running stitches in stranded cotton. Before sewing the fourth side slip the camphor cube between the two thicknesses. Double the ribbon into a loop to hang the sachet by, and secure it at the fourth corner.

Lavender Sachets

These are not unlike the camphor sachets just described, and may be sold or presented also in sets of three.

Required. Oddments of organdie; 1 needleful of embroidery silk; ¼ yard of baby ribbon; and 1 teaspoonful of dried lavender flowers for each sachet.

Cut two 3½-in. circles for each sachet. Place them together, and 1 in. inside the edge all round work an inner circle of an embroidery stitch close enough to prevent the lavender working through. Before completing the circle put the lavender between the two thicknesses. Add a ribbon loop, putting its ends inside when completing the embroidery-stitch circle.

Embroidered Guest Towel

A welcome gift and so quickly made.

Required. ½ yard of pastel-tinted linen or huckaback; a small oddment of white linen; 1 skein of white stranded cotton; 1 needleful of yellow stranded cotton.

To make. Cut the towel 16 in. wide and hem the long sides. To each end add a doubled white hem, 1 inch deep when finished. Pencilling round a penny, mark five circles in a row 2 in. above one hem. Inside each circle work a lazy-daisy flower in white, with a centre of yellow satin stitch or French knots. Naturally you can vary the colours, or embroider a name or initials.

Breakfast Cloth

This is a very quick piece of work with a simple, attractive gaiety.

Required. 1 yard of 36-in. linen, casement cloth, or even unbleached calico; odd cotton scraps in bright colours from the piece-bag; oddments of embroidery thread.

To make. Turn in a hem all round the square of material and run this with large black darning stitches. Cut circles 2 in. across from oddments of gay cotton; twelve circles will be needed, but they need not all be different. In each corner of the cloth arrange three circles of contrasting colours in a row, each overlapping the next, and buttonhole-stitch them down with coloured thread.

A Bib for Baby

A set of three, with a different design on each, is a useful gift or soon sells at a bazaar.

Required. ½ yard of coloured linen (this will make three bibs); sheet of black carbon paper or three transfers; 1 skein of white embroidery cotton; 3 yards narrow white tape.

To make. Divide the linen across the width into three, to get three oblongs each measuring 15 in. deep by 11½ in wide. Along the bottom of each bib make a 2-in. hem and finish it with hemstitching. At the top end, scoop out the curve for the neck and narrowly hem this and the sides; or bind the neck curve with cuttings from the linen or with cotton bias tape. A design (different for each bib) may be traced through black carbon paper from a child's picture book—a bird or animal is suitable. Or use transfers. Work the design in your favourite embroidery stitch. Sew on tape ties.

An Amusing Glass-towel

For a household stall or for a bachelor girl, two or three of these motto glass-towels make a welcome contribution.

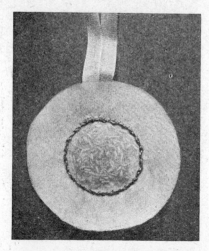

Lavender sachets to hang in the wardrobe make a pretty small present in a cellophane box

Required. For each towel, 1 yard of 18-in.-wide glass-towelling with coloured borders; embroidery threads; and 1 yard of cotton bias tape matching the borders.

The coloured borders go only down the sides of the towelling, so complete the bordered effect by turning up a single hem along each cut end and covering it with a right-side coloured facing of bias tape. An inch above this at one end write a slogan in pencil in your largest round hand, such as 'To Avoid Dis(h)order!' Work it in stem stitch.

Cold-cream Cap

Any woman interested in giving herself beauty treatment will be glad of this gift.

Required. ¾ yard of blue checked glass-towelling (this quantity is enough for two caps); white tape; blue embroidery cotton.

To make. The cap is triangular in shape. Cut a 25-in. square in half diagonally; each half will make a cap. Turn in the long cut edge and face it with tape, stitching this preferably by machine, as it is less likely to stretch the bias edge than hand sewing. Before taping, take in a pleat at each side, over the ear, to make the cap fit the forehead snugly. Using the blue squares of the towelling as a guide, work a simple pattern at the front in blue feather-stitching—for instance, a square (or rather, diamond) consisting of four blue checks, with a cross in the middle, and a straight line raying out from each point of the diamond.

The cap is fitted snugly round the head, the corners tucked in at the back and secured with a small safety-pin. It protects the hair from grease during cold-creaming or massaging.

An Original Neck or Head Scarf

It has the advantage of using oddments of material and of being non-bulky at the back of the neck, so that it fits very snugly under the big fur collar of a winter coat.

Required. Two ½-yard squares of silk, both plain but of different colours, or one plain and one patterned.

To make. Have the squares machine-picoted all round or work overcast cross stitch over tiny rolled hems. Overlap one square on to the other at a corner, forming a double square measuring 2½ in. Machine the two squares together and the scarf is complete. Two vivid shades, such as scarlet and blue, or neutral ones, such as stone and brown, or pastel-blue and rose, make a very elegant accessory.

Lightning Handkerchief Sachet

Made in ten minutes and decidedly attractive!

Required. Two white handkerchiefs with wide coloured borders; needleful of white embroidery cotton.

To make. Turn back the coloured border along one side of one handkerchief towards the centre, and on the flap thus formed write large in your own handwriting in pencil the word 'Hankies.' Work this in white, in outline or chain stitch. Place the labelled handkerchief exactly over the other one. Leave the embroidered side open, but join the other three sides into a sachet by stitching invisibly through the two lines of hemstitching by which the coloured borders are joined to the white.

Lavender Cracker

It takes very little stuff and very little work.

Required. ¼ yard of mauve organdie; lavender blossoms; ½ yard of mauve baby ribbon.

To make. Cut a strip of organdie 12 in. long by 7 in. wide, and some extra strips 3 in. wide to make frills that will billow out the open ends nice and fat. A ¼ yard of one colour, as suggested above, is most economical for a single cracker; but if several are being made get several ¼-yards of different colours, and make the 3-in. frills in each cracker contrast with the main part.

Seam up the main piece of organdie into a tube 12 in. long. Three inches from one end gather the tube up closely to form the bottom of a bag, which must be filled with lavender. When this is in place, run a similar gathering thread 3 in. from the other end, to close the bag and hold the lavender securely. Fill each end of the cracker with 3-in. frills, fully gathered. Tie the ends of ½ yard of narrow ribbon round the two 'waists' to form a hanging loop.

A Bright Apron

Give it to a friend who is her own cook and bottle-washer!

Required 1 yard of 36-in. Japanese crêpe or other rather loosely woven cotton; embroidery threads; ¾ yard of narrow ribbon the same colour as the material.

To make. Stitch a line of machining 1½ in. from two neighbouring edges of your square of stuff, and fray out the edge up to the stitching. Slope out the other two sides in a slight scoop to give a better fit round the armholes, and bind these two edges with the

GIFTS THE CHILDREN CAN MAKE

Hem three sides of a square of hessian for a gardening apron. Gather into a felt band. Cut the flower-pot from red felt and stitch on. Embroider flower and leaves

Make a scarlet felt ball, filling with cotton-wool, for a pin cushion. Roll a small piece of green felt for the stalk, and cut out a leaf. Stitch to top of the ball and fix in pins

same or a contrasting bind. Try the apron on diamondwise, with the fringe at the bottom, and at the top turn down the point becomingly to the right side. Embroider it with a simple motif. To each point of the turned-down piece stitch one end of the ribbon, which holds the apron round the neck. Fasten the back points, where fringe and binding meet, with a press-fastener.

Gingham Runner

Just the thing for a seaside bungalow or country cottage.

Required. ½ yard of check gingham (or 1 yard will make three narrower runners); skein of embroidery silk matching the colour of the check.

To make. Make the width of the material the length of the runner and cut it 15 in. wide (12 in. if you are making three fro   a yard). Make a narrow hem all round: ᴗne inch inside this all round work a row of continuous cross stitches, keeping them straight by the line of the check.

A Graceful Collar

Very little work—very good results!

Required. Either a 12-in. handkerchief or

a square of silk or other suitable material measuring 13 in.; ¾ yard of bias binding; embroidery wool or silk.

To make. If a handkerchief is used, the edges are already finished. In the centre of it (without cutting through the edges at any point) cut out an elongated oval, roughly about 9½ in. long and 3 in. wide in the middle. The square is used diamondwise and the cut-out oval should extend to within 1 in. of the back corner of the handkerchief. The oval must be big enough to slip comfortably over the head. Bind it with bias binding. Press a pleat towards the centre down each side of the neckline, holding it with an invisible stitch or two, and the collar is complete.

If a square of material is used, tack and press a narrow hem all round the edges and adorn these with underlaid buttonhole stitch. The small portion of the underside which is exposed by the pleating should be threaded on the wrong side to give a uniform effect.

Waterproof Sponge Pochette

So convenient for a traveller or week-ender. For economy in material, make three of these at a time for gifts or bazaars.

Required (for three pochettes). ¼ yard of

Good-morning Toothbrush. Paint a smiling face on to a white toothbrush, varnish over. Drape a face-cloth round the handle and secure with a gay bow of ribbon

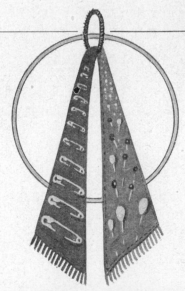

Cut two strips of coloured felt, as shown, Join, then fringe one end of each. Work running stitches with coloured wool right round. Cover a curtain-ring with blanket-stitch. Pass felt through ring, decorate with safety-pins, and some fancy pins

Runners are extremely simple to make, or a plain woollen scarf can be used instead, with running stitches worked in a good contrast as an attractive finish

one side with the silk chosen. They form the base of the sachet.

For the bag part, cut a strip of silk 11½ in. deep and 27 in. wide. Make it into a cylinder with a narrow French seam. Gather one end of the cylinder to fit the cardboard base and sew it to the edge of the covered cardboard circle intended for the bottom of the sachet. Place the other circle, right side upwards, over the raw edges, and stitch it down all round.

Finish the top of the bag with a ¼-in. heading and a casing below it, as for short pane curtains, but on a smaller scale. Insert the ring into the casing before stitching its lower edge.

This case will hold lots of handkerchiefs, keeping them flat and uncreased on its firm cardboard base. To close the sachet, hold it with the bag part fully extended, and twist the ring half-way round before letting it drop. It will fall neatly in position, in a series of charming pleats, over the base, and keep the handkerchiefs entirely free from dust.

Vivid Wool Posies

These are so cheap and quick to make that you might well turn out a dozen in varying colours.

Required. 12 in. of green wool braid, 1 in. wide; oddments of coloured or rainbow wool; a tiny scrap of buckram.

To make. Cut a wee circle of buckram the size of a halfpenny, and work loops of yellow (or any other coloured wool) rather larger than the circle, all round, from the centre

black American cloth (oil baize); 1 card of green cotton bias binding; ½ yard of thin white rubber sheeting; oddments of coloured rubber sheeting for appliqués; white and black embroidery threads.

To make. For each pochette cut a strip each of black oil baize and white rubber sheeting, making both the same size—15 by 7 in. Lay the sheeting inside the oil baize as a lining, and fold one end of the double layer to form a pocket 5 in. deep, which leaves a flap the same size. Bind the two materials together with the green binding, securing the sides of the pocket at the same time. Stitch the binding on with long (¼ in.) running stitches in thick green embroidery cotton, then complete wave stitch with black thread.

Use coins of various sizes to cut appliqué circles in coloured rubber sheeting; enough may be obtained in good condition from discarded rubber aprons (which should always be kept). Overlap these on the pochette flap in any simple pattern and stick them down with seccotine. Or make this in any other colour you choose. Black is unusual.

Twist Handkerchief Sachet

A gift as pretty and useful as it is novel.
Required. Round embroidery hoop, measuring 6 in. across; ⅜ yard of soft silk in any pretty shade; a small piece of cardboard; an oddment of flannel.

Use one ring only of the hoop, the latter thus serving for two sachets. For each sachet cut two circles of cardboard the same size as the ring. Lay them together, pad them with a circle each of flannel, then cover each on

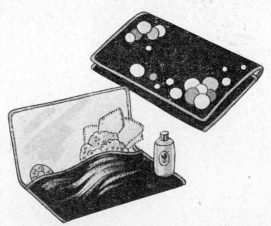

A bright waterproof pochette in black and white or a pastel shade for the traveller. Three can be made for very little money

If you make an early-morning tray-set of cloth and tea-cosy cover in this smart broad stripe, use white linen for the traycloth and sew on a portion of the striped material to two corners

outwards, until all the buckram is concealed. Now go round again with orange wool, making just a loop here and there to contrast with the yellow. Three blue or brown French knots form the flower centre, and a loop each of yellow, orange, and green wool should be left hanging to simulate stems.

Cut the 12 in. of braid into three 4-in. lengths. Double and fold back each length to give a pointed-leaf effect at one end, and secure it with a few invisible stitches. Arrange the three leaves artistically as a background for the flower, and stitch them to the back of the buckram.

A Flower Bed Jacket

Very quickly made, very dainty and so handy for breakfast in bed.

Required. 1 yard of 36-in. flowered voile or silk; 6½ yards of baby ribbon matching the main colour in the flower sprays.

To make. The material will be an exact square. Cut it diagonally from one corner to the very centre, to make the front opening. Then cut out enough in the middle to fit the neck. This makes a four-pointed jacket, the points coming at the front (two of them, as this corner has been cut), at the back, and over each arm. Bind all edges with ribbon. Face the neck with a bias strip of binding or white material. Make sleeves by the very simple process of catching together the arm pieces, 15 in. from the points, with bows of ribbon. Use the rest of the ribbon to make ties at the centre-front.

Child's One-piece Pinafore

Every child can use an extra 'pinny.'

Required. ¾ to 1 yard (according to the size of the child) of 36-in. zephyr, nurse-cloth, or linen; embroidery threads; two buttons.

To make. No pattern is needed. Cut an oblong 32 in. wide by 20 in. long, and out of one of the long edges cut the armholes, 9 in. deep, leaving a point at each end that will just take a buttonhole. This leaves between the armholes a centre-front about 10 in. wide, out of which you must hollow the neck, 4 or 5 in. deep, and sloping up to two more points between it and the armholes. These points will take buttons to fit the buttonholes on the back points, giving a crossover back and fastening on each shoulder.

Hem all edges and trim them with bright-coloured feather stitching or some other suitable embroidery bordering; make two buttonholes, and sew on two buttons. The pinafore measurements given are toddler's size, but they are easily enlarged for older children.

Linen or Gingham Cloth and Cosy Cover

Just the thing for a tea-table set in the garden, or for the children's meal.

Required. 1¾ yards of green checked gingham; an oddment or left-over of plain green cotton; a skein of green embroidery cotton.

To make. Cut the cloth a yard square in gingham. Then decorate it and make it a little

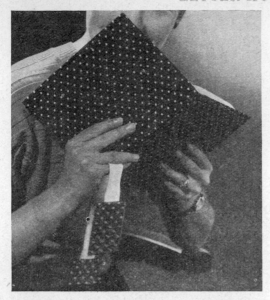

Make a book-cover (and marker) by cutting two pieces of cardboard ⅜ in. larger than an average library book in a smart strong material. Join a narrow piece of canvas between the two pieces, using adhesive tape, leaving ¼ in. space between. Now place a canvas piece each side of the board, fasten with adhesive tape. Spread glue and cover with material, cutting level when dry. Cover other side allowing ¾ in. turnings and glue to wrong side. Fold in each side to wrong side and stitch top and bottom edges

larger by adding a broad double hem in the plain green material. Make a cover to slip over an average-sized tea-cosy in the gingham, with a 2-in. bottom hem of plain green.

Trim both items with simple pine-tree appliqués. No transfer is needed for these—just cut three 3-in. squares of the plain green. Divide each in half diagonally and you have two tree appliqués. Place three in each corner of the cloth, on long thick trunks made of green chain stitch. The middle tree should spring exactly from the corner, with a shorter one each side of it. Buttonhole-stitch the appliqués down to the cloth. On the cosy cover there should be three trees rising from the green hem in a descending row, each a little shorter than the last.

Long-handled Back Powder-puff

Any friend who goes much to dances will appreciate this for powdering her back easily when she dons evening dress.

Required. A good-sized wooden spoon; several yards of ½-in. baby ribbon; a scrap of silk; a swansdown powder puff; two tiny flowers from an old artificial spray.

To make. Wind the ribbon, well overlapping it, over the wooden handle so that it is completely covered and finish each end with a bow. Cover the bowl of the spoon smoothly on both sides with silk matching the ribbon. Sew a swansdown puff of suitable size to the silk covering the inside of the bowl. Cover the outside with gathered frills of ribbon, arranged in diminishing ovals until the centre is reached. Finish this with the small artificial flowers.

THREADING NECKLACES

It is seldom worth while to spend the time necessary to re-thread a broken necklace that only cost a very small sum; it is better to buy a new one. But accidents happen to necklaces which are old, particularly lovely, or of a unique type, perhaps bought abroad. These cannot be replaced, and therefore the only remedy if their thread breaks is to re-thread them.

Again, you may have loose beads given you, or beads of a special colour you cannot get again, and wish to assemble these into a necklace or chain for a present.

If the beads are large *and* have large holes (the two things do not always go together!) you can use an ordinary fine darning needle threaded with a thick mercerised embroidery thread, which will carry a good weight and not break easily. In the case of finer beads, often no ordinary sewing needle is slender enough to go through their tiny holes and yet carry a thread of sufficient strength to bear the weight of the necklace.

In this case use a beading needle, which is particularly fine, and yet has a good-sized eye. You can buy a packet at any fancy-needle-work shop. Or you may prefer a ready-cut fine yet strong silk thread, with a wire threader attached to one end, which can be bought all ready to use; it is specially suited for threading pearls.

In order to make sure you have a good arrangement and enough beads to complete the necklace, plan half of it on the table before starting to thread. As you place each bead in position for the half you are planning, drop another matching one into a saucer. In this way you will be sure of having sufficient of the right kind and colour for the second half of the work.

Remember that big, expensive beads should be eked out by having one or two much smaller ones placed between them. If the big beads are bright, black or neutral-coloured small ones will throw them up best. This plan not only economises the expensive beads, but actually looks prettier, as the variation of size prevents any monotony. Again, concentrate your showy beads round the front half of the neck, making the back part of much smaller ones, for big beads are not only wasted under the collar of a dress, but prevent it from setting well and are usually uncomfortable.

Comfort is Everything

Cylindrical beads are often more comfortable than round ones for the back half of a necklace, from collar bone round to collar bone.

To knot or not to knot when threading beads? Well, as knotting not only prevents your losing more than one bead if the string breaks, but spaces out the beads and so uses fewer, it is always to be recommended for any beads you value at all. Many women hate the bother and unevenness of knotting, but that is simply not knowing just how to do it. You'll get quick and perfect knots if you thread in the following way:

Cut two threads, much finer than you would ordinarily use, and thread each into a separate fine needle. (Remember, by the way, that knotting greatly shortens the threads, and therefore they should be cut very much longer than the necklace is to be.) Knot the free ends of both threads together about 3 in. from the ends, and thread your beads on to both threads, passing the two needles, if fine enough, both together through each bead.

After slipping on each bead, just tie the two threads into a knot close up to the bead and thread on the next. Isn't it simple? You'll have no uneven spaces of thread between the beads this way.

Naturally, where you have a knot after each large bead, this will take the place of the small bead you would ordinarily use after it. Remember when making a knotted necklace that the thread will show at the knots and be definitely part of the colour-scheme, so its shade must be chosen accordingly.

MORE NEEDLEWORK NOTIONS

Replacing Torn-out Buttons. Sometimes, especially on children's clothes, a button is torn away, bringing a piece of stuff with it and leaving a hole in the garment. The best method of mending is first to sew a fresh button on to a square of stuff larger all round than the hole; or cut such a square, with a button attached, from an old garment of the same colour. From the back push the button through the hole, leaving its square of stuff on the wrong side to form a patch, which is hemmed down, and the torn edges of the hole caught to it.

* * *

Renovation. Cover an old brassière with material from the top of an old summer frock and thread elastic in the waist of the lower half for a skirt. Result: one sun-suit as short or as long as you like.

* * *

Making Vests Ladderproof. While the vest is new and unworn, use a fine mercerised embroidery thread to work round the bottom edge: one double crochet, two chain. This keeps the edge unbroken, and it is broken edges which start ladders.

* * *

Really Effective Tea-cosies. For lining a tea-cosy, nothing is better than ordinary chamois leather, for this is remarkably good at holding in the heat.

Take a pretty small basket and make a top of covered board, allowing ¼ in. to protrude. Sew on a ring to hold scissors; make a pincushion of cotton-wool and material to match. Line basket, fit out with sewing cotton

If You Can Make Good

OMELETTES

Then, with fruit and coffee, you have an excellent meal always to hand

Allow three or four eggs to each two people, according to size of egg and appetite of person! Break into bowl, season, beat well until yolk and white are blended

*   *   *

A small frying-pan especially for omelettes is best for one person, but a larger one when making an omelette to be divided

Get your butter or oil very hot in a clean pan, with a faint smoke just starting to rise

*   *   *

Now pour your eggs into the pan. They will sizzle slightly. Stir quickly for a second, then leave to set. As it is setting, push the mixture away from the sides with a fork, allowing the unset mixture to flow into the space, tilting the pan slightly

*   *   *

Left: Continue until the top is just moist. Too dry an omelette is not ... an omelette! The cooking must be swift

Below: Tilt the pan, fold over quickly and serve. Remember, ' You may wait for an omelette, but an omelette must not wait for you '

HOME COOKERY

This is a complete cook-book with simple recipes for plain tastes, economical and appetising recipes for the family and other rather more elegant recipes for very special occasions

A TASTY meal, well served, is one of the real enjoyments of life, yet so many people content themselves with the same dull repasts, such as watery cod, boiled potatoes and prunes and custard, day in, day out, when a little imaginative *interest* in what is being eaten would bring the level of home cookery much higher.

After all, as the biologists say, 'we are what we eat.' So, apart from the interest in its taste, the three functions that food we eat should fulfil are:

(1) To build and repair the body.
(2) To give it warmth and energy.
(3) To protect the body and regulate its working.

The principal body-building and repairing foods, known as proteins, are: meat, milk, cheese, eggs, fish, pulse foods (dried beans, peas, etc.). Of these, the first five are what are called first-class proteins, the pulse foods second-class.

The warmth- and energy-producing foods are: (i) carbohydrates, which include starches and sugar, and (ii) fats, both animal and vegetable. The carbohydrates consist of: oatmeal, bread, flour, potatoes, rice, tapioca, sago, sugar; the fats of suet, lard, dripping, margarine, butter.

The foods containing vitamins, all of which have their particular function to perform, and which are contained in the two following groups: (i) milk, butter, vitaminised margarine, cheese, eggs, herrings, liver, salmon (fresh or tinned); and (ii) potatoes, green vegetables, salad vegetables, fruit (both home and foreign), carrots, tomatoes, wholemeal bread. Vitamin C, which is present in fresh

---

BE AN ARTIST

There are more ways of being an artist than by painting pictures. There are people who look on a meal as just something to keep them alive; others who take a keen interest in finding new ways of presenting old favourites or trying out fresh recipes. Many folk in Britain feel that a liking for good food is not to be admitted, yet why should artistry in cooking not be of the same value in life as playing the piano or a game of golf? After all, we eat two or three meals every day!

A genuine pleasure in a task makes it half the trouble. It is not a bad idea for the amateur to learn to prepare one or two dishes exceptionally well, then she will always have a menu ready to surprise and delight her guests. Let the chef above then wish her, '*Bon appétit, Madame!*'

---

fruit and vegetables, is apt to be destroyed or weakened by cooking, hence the importance of including a certain amount of raw fruit and vegetables in the daily menu. These provide in addition the roughage which should form part of everyone's daily food.

SOUPS

There can be nothing more warming or delicious than a really good soup. It can be a meal in itself. An appetising soup always makes a happy beginning to a winter meal.

Stock-making is really a very simple process and no one need be daunted by it. Let us take, first, brown and white stocks made from meat. Brown stock is made of the bones and meat of beef: that is, beef is the foundation of it, though a knuckle of veal is sometimes added; white stock of the bones and meat of any white meat, such as chicken, veal, rabbit or turkey. Vegetables are added to flavour, and also seasoning.

In the ordinary way, stock can be made of he remains of joints, chicken, rabbit—anything you have in your larder and want to utilise; but if you want really clear soup, such as a consommé, then it is better to buy fresh meat or bones.

Both brown and white stocks should be made the day before they are needed, if possible. When the stock is made, put the saucepan uncovered in the larder and do not remove the fat until you are going to use it. Then take a knife, loosen the fat round the edge and lift it off. Remember that the fat on the surface acts to some extent as a preservative, but no stock keeps for long, especially when vegetables have been boiled in it, so do not make more than you can use up in a day

EMERGENCY MEASURES

Liquids:

Small teacupful	¼ pint (or 1 gill)	
Breakfast cupful	½ pint	
Tumblerful	½ pint	
6 tablespoonsful	¼ pint (or 1 gill)	
1 pound	1 pint	

Solids:

Flour, sugar, rice, oatmeal:

Slightly-rounded teaspoonful ..	¼ oz.	
,, ,, dessertspoonful	½ oz.	
,, ,, tablespoonful	1 oz.	
Level teacupful (small)	4 oz.	
Level breakfast cup	7 oz.	
4 level teacupsful	1 lb.	
Golden syrup, treacle, jam, butter:		
1 tablespoonful	2 oz.	

or two. In the summer avoid using vegetables until you are actually making the soup.

As a change from fried dice of bread or toast, sometimes serve Rice Crispies or Puffed Rice, warmed in the oven; or grated Parmesan cheese is a delicious addition to many soups.

Allow 1-1½ gills of soup per head, if it is part of a several-course meal, ½ pint per head otherwise.

Ordinary Brown Stock

Allow a quart of water and half a teaspoonful of salt to a pound of bones (cooked or uncooked), and add any scraps of meat you may have, cutting off any fat. Let it stand for half an hour, if possible, before bringing it very slowly to the boil; skim, then add a few slices of carrot, turnip and onion, and some herbs tied up in a muslin bag. Thyme, a bay-leaf, parsley, mace and marjoram can be used— dried, if you are not able to get them fresh. Simmer very slowly for at least two hours, covered over, then strain into a basin and stand it in a cool place in the larder, uncovered.

For white stock proceed in exactly the same way, using knuckle of veal and any scraps of white meat instead of beef.

These two stocks can be used for all ordinary soups requiring stock as a foundation.

There are occasions, however, such as dinner parties, for example, when something rather extra specially good may be needed, and so here are recipes for making clear soup stock, and white stock made with fresh meat or uncooked bones.

Stock for Clear Soup

Allow 1 quart of water to a pound of shin of beef (meat and bone together, or mixture of beef and knuckle of veal). Break up the bones and slice the meat thinly, removing any fat. Put into a saucepan with the water and a teaspoonful of salt and bring slowly to the boil. Skim, then add a small carrot and onion, a piece of celery cut small and some herbs tied in a muslin bag. Simmer very gently for about 3 hours, covered over. Then strain through a fine cloth and put in a cool place, uncovered. (The meat can be boiled up again for a second stock.)

If it is not absolutely clear, pour the liquid on to some broken eggshells and add a beaten white of egg. Heat it slowly, whisking it well

Put the milk, stock, butter and seasoning in a saucepan and bring to the boil. Then add the chestnut purée and re-heat.

Just before serving add some whipped cream. This, be it mentioned, is a very rich soup, and not for the dyspeptic.

Cream of Onion Soup (6-7 people)

1 *quart milk.*	1 *tablespoonful brown*
6 *large onions.*	*or wholemeal flour.*
2 *oz. butter.*	2 *yolks of egg.*
A little salt.	*A little cream.*

Peel and scald the onions, cut them into slices and stir them into the melted butter. Simmer slowly for half an hour.

Heat the milk. Add the dry flour to the onions and stir constantly for 3 minutes over the fire. Then turn the mixture into the milk, and cook for 15 minutes.

Put the soup through a strainer, re-heat and add salt.

Beat the yolks well, add the cream to them, and stir into the soup. Cook for a few minutes, stirring constantly. Do not let it boil. (If liked, use milk instead of cream, in which case add a tablespoonful of butter at the same time.)

Haricot Bean Soup (5-6 people)

1 *breakfastcup haricot*	*A few bacon rinds.*
beans.	1 *gill milk.*
1 *onion.*	½ *oz. butter.*
1 *stick of celery.*	*Blade of mace.*
1 *quart white stock or*	*Pepper and salt.*
water.	

Wash the beans well and soak in water overnight. Then rinse well. Put the beans, blade of mace, cut-up celery, bacon rinds and sliced onion into the stock or water, cold, and bring to the boil. Simmer gently for about 2 hours, stirring now and again. Rub through a sieve and put back in the pan, adding the milk, butter and lastly pepper and salt, stirring well all the time.

Italian Soup (3-4 people)

4 *oz. macaroni.*	1 *quart white stock*
3 *oz. Gruyère or Par-*	*or water.*
mesan cheese.	1 *oz. shredded suet.*
Pepper.	2 *oz. butter.*
	Small tin of tomatoes.

Boil up the stock or water with the suet and a pinch of pepper, add the macaroni broken into small lengths and cook for 20 minutes till it has doubled its size. Add some cold water to stop it cooking any more. Drain and keep both macaroni and liquor hot.

While it is cooking, grate the cheese. Put the tomatoes and juice into a small saucepan with half the butter and cook for a few minutes. Put some of this mixture into a hot tureen, add a few small pieces of butter, then put a layer of cheese, next some macaroni; repeat these layers till all are used up, pour over the liquor in which the macaroni was cooked and serve.

Kidney Soup (5-6 people)

½ *ox kidney (or ½ lb.*	1 *oz. dripping.*
liver).	*Small turnip and carrot.*
1 *quart brown stock*	*Pepper and salt.*
(or water with a	*Any mushroom trim-*
very little Marmite	*mings, or 1 table-*
added).	*spoonful mushroom*
1 *tablespoonful flour.*	*ketchup.*
Large onion.	*A few mixed herbs.*

Cut the kidney or liver into pieces. Prepare the vegetables and cut them up and put them with the meat into the hot fat. Fry till brown. Then add the stock and bring to the boil. Skim well. Put the herbs in a muslin bag and add them to the stock. Then simmer it very gently for one hour. Rub the kidney, etc., through a sieve, and put it back in the saucepan.

Make the flour into a paste with a very little water and pour it into the stock, stirring well. Boil it for a few minutes. Then season. If desired, add a tablespoonful of mushroom ketchup just before serving.

Leek and Potato Soup (5-6 people)

2 *leeks.*	2 *or 3 potatoes.*
1 *tablespoonful flour.*	1 *quart water.*
½ *pint milk.*	1 *onion.*
Salt and pepper.	*Butter.*

Melt a little butter in a saucepan, stir in the flour and cook for a few minutes, then add the milk, stir and heat. Add the water, the potatoes peeled and cut up and the leeks and onion cut small. Bring to the boil and boil for 15-20 minutes till the vegetables are tender. Put through a coarse sieve, pressing the vegetables through, put back in the saucepan, re-heat, season and serve. (If the soup is too thick, thin it with a little more milk.)

Minestrone (Italian) (4-5 people)

1 *lb. haricot beans.*	*A small onion.*
3 *tablespoonsful tomato purée.*	*Parsley.*
A little cabbage.	*Stick of celery.*
3 *potatoes.*	*A sausage.*
Rice.	*Olive-oil.*
1 *clove garlic (shredded).*	2 *oz. spaghetti.*

Soak the beans overnight. Then put them in a casserole with water to cover them well and let them simmer gently until quite soft.

Chop up the onion, parsley, celery and sausage and fry in olive-oil until the onion is cooked and brown.

Rub the beans through a sieve and put them back into the water in which they were cooked. Add the onion, etc., and oil, the tomato purée, chopped cabbage and sliced potatoes, garlic, spaghetti, rice, and simmer gently till tender.

Mulligatawny Soup (4-5 people)

1 *lb. lean mutton or rabbit.*	1 *apple.*
1 *quart brown stock or water.*	1 *teaspoonful chutney.*
2 *onions.*	1 *oz. dripping.*
1 *carrot.*	1 *teaspoonful lemon juice.*
1 *turnip.*	*Curry powder to taste.*
1 *tablespoonful cornflour.*	1 *dessertspoonful shredded cocoanut.*

Cut the meat up into small pieces and fry quickly in the dripping till brown. Then add the stock or water, the vegetables and apple chopped small, and the cocoa-nut. Simmer for 1-2 hours, and sieve. Put back into the pan.

Make a paste of the cornflour and curry powder mixed with a little cold water and pour slowly into the soup, stirring well. Add the chutney and boil up. Add the lemon juice at the end.

A dish of boiled rice should be served with this soup.

Mushroom Soup (4 people)

½ *lb. mushrooms (or mushroom stalks).*	2 *oz. flour.*
1 *slice of onion.*	2 *oz. butter or margarine.*
1½ *pints milk and water.*	*Salt and pepper.*

Stew mushrooms with onion for 40 minutes. Rub through a sieve. Melt butter; add flour, and seasoning, then the mushroom purée, and fluid in which mushrooms were cooked. Add a little top milk or cream. If mushroom stalks only are used, decorate soup with a few slices of mushroom caps.

Onion Soup (4-5 people)

3 *Spanish onions.*	1 *flat tablespoonful ground rice.*
Stick of celery.	*Pepper and salt.*
1½ *pints of water.*	1 *oz. grated cheese.*
1 *pint of milk.*	
2 *oz. butter or margarine.*	

Slice the onions and celery and place in a saucepan with 1 oz. of butter or margarine; cook for a few minutes, then add the water, and allow to simmer gently for about an hour, or until the vegetables are soft. Stir now and again to prevent burning. Add the milk and bring to the boil. Shake in the ground rice, stirring all the time, and cook till it thickens. Add seasoning. At the last moment put in the rest of the butter. Serve with a scattering of fried crumbs and cheese.

Pea or Lentil Soup (Dried) (3-4 people)

½ *lb. split peas or lentils.*	1 *oz. butter or margarine.*
1 *onion.*	1½ *pints of water (or part water from ham or bacon boiling).*
Small carrot.	
Small turnip.	
Bacon rinds to flavour.	1 *teacupful of milk.*
Few outer leaves of celery.	*Salt and pepper.*

Wash the peas or lentils well and soak overnight in the 1½ pints of water. Next day bring to the boil with the bacon rinds and simmer for 1 hour. Cut the vegetables into slices and add, cooking till they are soft. Put through a sieve, or mash up with a wooden spoon. Replace in the saucepan with the milk, re-heat, stirring all the time, put in the margarine or butter, and pepper and salt and serve.

If water from ham or bacon boiling is used, do not put in any salt.

Potato Soup (5-6 people)

1 *lb. potatoes.*	1 *tablespoonful cornflour.*
1 *quart of milk.*	1 *teaspoonful of salt.*
Fair-sized onion.	*Pinch of pepper.*
1½ *oz. butter or margarine.*	*Teaspoonful of chopped parsley.*

Boil the potatoes and mash in the usual way. Scald the milk, to which the onion has been added, then remove onion. Add the milk and the butter to the mashed potatoes, and stir well. Mix the cornflour to a paste with a little milk and pour into the hot soup, stirring well. Simmer for 3 minutes, add the seasoning, and sprinkle chopped parsley on top when about to serve. Serve with fried dice of bread.

Parsnips and carrots can be used instead of potatoes, but in this case add bacon rinds or a ham-bone to give flavour.

Spinach Soup (3-4 people)

1 *lb. spinach.*	1 *teaspoonful of*
1 *pint white stock.*	*cornflour.*
½ *pint milk.*	*Pepper and salt.*
1½ *oz. butter or*	1 *small onion.*
margarine.	

Wash the spinach in several lots of water, then cook with the onion, in its own moisture, and rub through a sieve. Bring the stock to the boil. Make the cornflour into a smooth paste with the milk, add it to the stock and again bring to the boil. Then add the butter or margarine and seasoning. At the last moment add the purée of spinach and remove from the fire the moment it boils or the colour of the soup will be spoiled. Serve with puffed rice heated in the oven or fried croûtons.

A little cream adds to the flavour, and a little finely-chopped parsley improves the appearance.

Tomato Bisque (4-5 people)

1 *quart milk.*	*Bacon rinds.*
2 *onions.*	*Salt and pepper.*
Small tin tomato purée.	¼ *teaspoonful carbonate of soda.*
1 *dessertspoonful cornflour.*	

Slice the onions and add with the bacon rinds to the milk, keeping back just enough milk to mix the cornflour into a paste. Boil up. Strain and boil up again. Add the cornflour paste, boil up again and season. Blend in the purée. At the last moment put the carbonate of soda into a warm jug and pour the hot liquid on to it. This makes the soup have a fluffy appearance. Serve at once.

Tomato Soup (3-4 people)

1 *lb. fresh or tinned tomatoes.*	1 *oz. butter or margarine.*
3 *shallots.*	*Pepper and salt.*
1 *pint white stock or* ½ *pint milk and* ½ *pint water.*	½ *oz. finest sago.* *Sugar to taste.*

Put the shallots cut up into a saucepan with the butter and let them simmer slowly for 5 minutes, stirring carefully. Add the tomatoes and boil together for about 20 minutes. Rub through a sieve and put back into the saucepan. Add the stock. Bring to the boil. Then add the sago, the sugar and simmer for 5 minutes. Season and serve. A little top milk or cream improves both taste and consistency.

White Vegetable Soup (4 people)

1 *moderate-sized carrot, turnip and onion.*	1 *tablespoonful cornflour.*
1 *parsnip or swede.*	1½ *pints water.*
1 *stick celery.*	½ *pint milk.*
1 *oz. dripping.*	*Pepper and salt.*
1 *leek.*	*Pinch of dried herbs.*

Wash and prepare the vegetables and cut them up into small dice. Put in a saucepan with the water, the herbs, and a pinch of salt and bring to the boil. Simmer gently for half an hour. Then add the cornflour mixed to a smooth paste with the milk, and stir well while it thickens. Lastly, add the dripping and pepper and salt to taste.

Zuppa Verde (Italian)

Spinach.	*White stock.*
Beet-leaves.	1 *egg.*
Carrot, celery, onion and parsley.	*Grated Parmesan cheese.* *Pepper and salt.*
Tomato purée.	*Butter.*

Boil some spinach and beet-leaves together, and when cooked chop them finely. Cut up the carrot, celery, onion and parsley and fry them in a little butter. Add a little tomato purée and the chopped spinach and beet.

Add some white stock and at the last moment beat up an egg and add to the soup with the grated cheese and seasoning. Beat them well in, but do not let the soup boil.

Serve with fried croûtes.

Cockie-Leekie (7-8 people)

An old fowl.	2 *onions.*
6 *large leeks.*	1 *oz. pearl barley*
Pepper and salt.	*(soaked overnight).*
Prunes.	

Boil an old fowl with the onions for 3 hours, then strain it and take off the grease.

Wash the leeks, removing any coarse green leaves, and cut into inch lengths. Put the stock in a saucepan, add the pearl barley, bring it to the boil and simmer gently for an hour, putting in the leeks for the last quarter.

Cut the best bits of meat off the fowl and

cut them into fairly large pieces. Put them into the stock with pepper and salt and re-heat without boiling.

Stew some stoned prunes in a little of the broth and serve separately.

Oxtail Soup (8-10 people)

1 oxtail.	A bay-leaf.
2 quarts of brown stock (or water with a little Marmite added).	A few dried herbs. 6 peppercorns. 3 cloves.
1 turnip cut small.	About ¼ teaspoonful
1 carrot cut small.	celery salt to taste.
Salt and pepper.	1 oz. flour.
Butter.	

Wash the tail well, wipe, break up into pieces and put into a saucepan with enough butter to prevent burning. Shake about till brown. Then add stock or water, vegetables, celery salt, and the bay-leaf, peppercorns, cloves and herbs tied up in a muslin bag. Simmer gently for about 3-4 hours, season and strain, putting back the smaller pieces of the tail. Re-heat and thicken with the flour made into a paste with water, adding a little browning if necessary. Leave overnight and skim off fat. Serve with a few croûtes of bread.

Pot-au-Feu (4-5 people)

1 lb. shin of beef.	1 cabbage.
1 quart of water.	2 oz. sago or tapioca.
1 leek.	Bunch of herbs.
1 parsnip.	Blade of mace.
1 carrot.	6 peppercorns.
Stick of celery (or a few celery seeds).	Salt to taste. A few cloves.
1 turnip.	

Wipe the meat and tie it with tape so that it does not lose its shape. Put in a saucepan or casserole with the water. Bring to the boil, add salt to taste and skim well. Simmer for half an hour.

Get ready the vegetables (the cabbage goes in later), cut them up and add, together with the herbs, peppercorns, mace and cloves tied up in a muslin bag. Simmer gently for 1½ hours.

Clean the cabbage, cut it in half, and tie together with a piece of tape. Add it to the liquid and simmer gently till the cabbage is tender. Take out the meat, untie it and put on a hot dish, with the vegetables round. The cabbage should be served separately.

Strain the liquid through a colander, using some of it for gravy. Leave the rest to get cold, and when it is to be used take off the fat, bring it to the boil and throw in the sago or tapioca. Cook gently till transparent. Serve.

Scotch Broth (5-6 people)

1½ lb. neck of mutton (lean).	1 oz. rice.
3 pints cold water.	Chopped parsley.
Small carrot, onion and turnip.	Salt and pepper.

Stand the mutton for half an hour in the water, having first removed any superfluous fat. Bring slowly to the boil and skim.

Wash the vegetables and cut them into small pieces, and add them with the rice and seasoning. Simmer for about 1½ hours, skimming at intervals. Take out the mutton, cut off the meat and dice it, and put the dice back into the broth. Add the parsley right at the end.

If desired, 1 oz. pearl barley can be used instead of rice, but in this case it should be soaked overnight. A leek can be added with advantage.

SAUCES AND BUTTERS

Sauces are a very important part of the menu. It is no exaggeration to say that they either make or mar it. A well-made appetising sauce brightens up many homely dishes, while it gives additional piquancy to the more elaborate ones. The French philosopher, de la Rochefoucauld, was alleged to have said that 'the English have one hundred religions, but only one sauce.' A truly smooth, creamy sauce is a culinary poem.

White Sauce (4 people)

1 oz. butter or margarine.	Pepper and salt.
1 tablespoonful flour or 1 dessertspoonful cornflour.	½ pint milk or white stock.

Method 1. Put the milk or white stock into a saucepan, leaving out just enough to make the flour or cornflour into a smooth paste. When it boils remove the pan from the fire and add the paste, stirring well. Then bring slowly to the boil. Let it cook gently for 5 minutes, then season. Remove the pan from the fire and stir in the butter.

Method 2. Melt the butter, add the flour or cornflour, sieved, very slowly, stirring all the time, and cook till smooth. Remove from the fire, beat in the milk or stock gradually with a whisk or wooden spoon. Put it back on the fire and bring to the boil, stirring all the time. Then season and cook it for 5 minutes.

NOTE. If you want a thick coating sauce, allow a little more flour or cornflour and an equal quantity of fat.

This foundation can be used for the following sauces:

Anchovy, Béarnaise, caper, cheese, Dutch, egg, Hollandaise, horse-radish, lemon, mustard, onion, oyster, parsley, shrimp and tartar.

Sweet Sauces. Exactly the same method can be used for making sweet sauces, omitting the seasoning and adding sugar and the desired flavouring instead. Lemon and orange sauce can be made by adding a little juice to sugared white sauce; in the case of sauces such as ginger, treacle, coffee, chocolate, etc., the flavouring is added while the sauce is actually being made.

If you want something a little richer than the ordinary white sauce, either add a little more butter, or beat in a yolk of egg, being careful first to remove your sauce from the fire as it will curdle if it is boiling; or add some cream, or some unsweetened condensed milk.

When adding brandy, rum or sherry, it is better to add it right at the end, sherry particularly being very liable to curdle the sauce.

Amber Sauce (4 people)

½ pint stock (or water with Marmite or meat extract added).	1 dessertspoonful cornflour.
1 teaspoonful tarragon vinegar.	Teaspoonful lemon juice.
1 tablespoonful sherry.	Chopped pickled gherkin.

Put the stock or water in a saucepan, leaving out just enough to make the cornflour into a smooth paste. When it boils add the paste, stirring well, and bring slowly to the boil. Let it cook gently for 5 minutes. Remove from the fire and add the vinegar, sherry, lemon juice and chopped gherkin. Re-heat but do not let it boil.

Anchovy Sauce (4 people)

½ pint white sauce, anchovy essence, pepper and salt.

Make some white sauce, omitting seasoning, and when cooked add anchovy essence, pepper and salt to taste. A yolk of egg can be added and the sauce re-heated, being careful it does not boil.

Apple Sauce (4 people)

1 lb. apples.	Grated rind of half lemon.
½ oz. butter.	1 tablespoonful brown sugar.
½ gill water.	

Peel and core the apples, slice them thinly, and put them in a saucepan with the water, lemon rind and sugar. Cook them till they become pulp, stirring frequently. Add the butter and mash them up well with a fork.

Béarnaise Sauce (4 people)

2 yolks.	1 dessertspoonful tarragon vinegar.
3 tablespoonsful chopped shallots.	1 gill vinegar.
1 tablespoonful cream or a little butter.	1 gill white sauce. Salt and pepper.

Boil the shallots in the vinegar and strain. Put the vinegar and sauce into a saucepan, and at boiling-point add the beaten yolks, remembering to remove the pan from the flame. Season and add the tarragon vinegar and cream or butter right at the end.

Béchamel Sauce (4 people)

½ pint milk.	5 peppercorns.
1 small onion or shallot.	1 tablespoonful flour.
Small piece of carrot.	1 oz. butter.
Piece of celery.	¼ gill cream.
1 bay-leaf.	Salt.

Put the milk into a saucepan with the vegetables, bay-leaf and peppercorns, and bring to the boil. Allow them to stand for 5 minutes with a lid on. Then strain. Make a white sauce in the usual way with the milk, flour, and butter and bring to the boil. Let it cook for 5 minutes. Add the salt and cream at the end.

Black Butter Sauce (3-4 people)

2 oz. fresh butter.	Vinegar to taste.
Salt and pepper.	

Melt the butter and heat till it is a good brown. Be very careful not to burn it. Add the vinegar and seasoning and re-heat, stirring well, but do not let it boil.

This can be served with grilled fish, especially skate. It can also be served with French beans or with old broad beans which have to be skinned before being sent to table.

Bread Sauce (3-4 people)

Small onion.	2 peppercorns.
½ pint milk.	Salt and pepper.
2 oz. breadcrumbs.	2 cloves.
½ oz. butter.	

Put the onion, cut in half and stuck with the cloves, with the peppercorns and a pinch of salt into the milk and simmer for a few minutes. Strain and put the milk back into the saucepan. When boiling stir in the bread-crumbs slowly, and bring up to boiling-point. Add butter and seasoning.

Caper Sauce (4 people)

½ pint white sauce.   1 teaspoonful of the
1 tablespoonful capers.   caper vinegar.

Make some white sauce and when cooked add the capers chopped; remove from fire and add the vinegar, stirring well.

Celery Sauce (4 people)

1 small head white   1 teaspoonful cornflour.
celery.   1 tablespoonful cream
½ pint milk.   or a little butter.
1 small onion.   Seasoning to taste.

TIMELY TIPS

Stained vacuum. If you have a vacuum flask that is becoming very stained inside by constant use, place some crushed egg-shell inside and add a drop of vinegar. Shake briskly for a few minutes, empty and rinse and the inside of your flask will look perfectly clean and new again. Water-bottles, wine decanters or pickle-jars that are stained, answer to the same treatment. Sand can be used instead of egg-shell.

A tip to clean aluminium teapots. Cut up two or three sticks of rhubarb and put them in your teapot; fill to the top with boiling water and allow to stand two or three hours. Empty and rinse out with boiling water.

When putting away a 'best' tea or coffee pot, put two lumps of sugar in it. This will avoid mustiness.

If hot fat is spilt on the kitchen table or floor, pour cold water on it immediately. This hardens the fat at once, prevents it sinking in, and it is far easier to scrape off at once carefully with a knife. Wash with hot water and detergent, polish.

Put mushrooms into boiling water for a minute or two before you fry them. This prevents them from shrivelling in the frying.

When you have washed and cleaned **celery stalks,** to stand them in a jug of cold water to which a little common salt has been added keeps them crisp.

To keep a lettuce fresh, put it in a pot with a lid on.

Mix the cornflour to a paste with a little of the milk. Wash and cut the celery into small pieces, and cook it in the rest of the milk till tender, with the onion. Remove the onion and rub the celery through a sieve. Put the purée back into the pan and add the paste, stirring well. Bring to the boil and cook for 5 minutes. Add seasoning and cream or butter.

Cheese Sauce (4 people)

½ pint white sauce.   2 tablespoonsful grated
Made mustard to   cheese (either good
taste.   dry Cheddar and a
A little butter or   little Parmesan or all
margarine.   Parmesan).
    A shake of cayenne.

Make some white sauce but using only half the thickening, and stir in the grated cheese, mustard, butter and cayenne. Stir till the cheese is dissolved.

Cranberry Sauce (4 people)

⅓ pint water.   1 lb. cranberries.
4 oz. brown sugar.

Wash the cranberries and stew in the water till they become pulp, stirring them frequently. Add 4 oz. brown sugar at the end, stir till dissolved, then beat up well with a metal whisk.

Serve with turkey, roast pork, ragout of mutton, veal cutlets, or salmi of pheasant.

Cumberland Sauce

1 pint red-currant jelly.   2 lemons and
A few chopped sultanas.   2 oranges.
    1 tablespoonful of
    Worcester sauce.

Slowly dissolve the jelly, add the chopped sultanas and rind of lemons and oranges, and boil for 5 minutes. Then allow to cool. Add the juice of the oranges and lemons and stir in 1 tablespoonful of Worcester sauce. Let it stand from morning to evening, on ice if possible. If bottled and tied down it will keep for several days. *Do not strain.*

Curry Sauce (3-4 people)

½ pint vegetable stock.   1 tomato.
1 small onion.   1 tablespoonful curry
1 dessertspoonful flour.   powder.
Pepper and salt.   A few drops of lemon
1½ oz. dripping.   juice.

Heat the dripping and fry the sliced onion

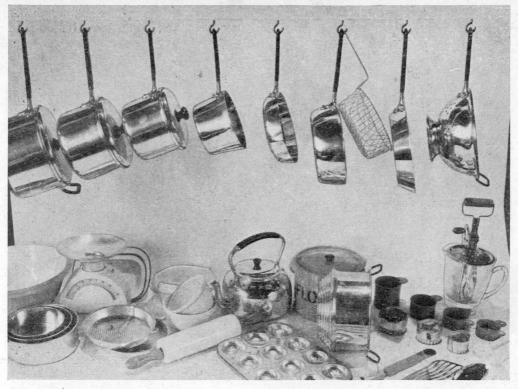

There is nothing that helps the amateur or experienced cook like an assortment of the right utensils and implements, with each one to hand, and kept in the same place, so that it is easy to find

lightly in it, then stir in the sieved flour and curry powder, with the lemon juice, and cook gently for a few minutes, stirring all the time. Add the stock slowly, then the sliced tomato, and seasoning to taste. Bring to the boil and simmer gently for about 10 minutes. Strain and re-heat.

Egg Sauce (4 people)

½ *pint white sauce.*   *2 hard-boiled eggs.*

Make ½ pint white sauce, and add the eggs chopped finely; or put eggs through a coarse sieve before adding.

Hollandaise Sauce (4 people)

½ *pint white sauce.*   *A little milk or white stock.*
2 yolks.   *2 oz. butter.*
Salt and pepper.   *Juice of half a lemon.*

Put the yolks of egg into the hot white sauce and beat with a metal whisk till cooked and thick, then add the milk or stock till it is the right consistency, beating well. Do not let it boil. Take off the fire and add the butter, seasoning and lemon juice.

Horseradish Sauce (3-4 people)

1 *tablespoonful grated*	1 *tablespoonful*
horseradish.	*vinegar.*
½ *teaspoonful granu-*	1 *gill white sauce.*
lated sugar.	1 *tablespoonful cream*
Pinch of salt and	*if desired.*
pepper.	*A very little made*
	mustard.

Put all the ingredients into a bowl and beat up well with a fork. This sauce keeps for some time if put into a corked bottle.

Lemon Sauce (3-4 people)

½ *pint white sauce.*   1 *lemon.*

Make the white sauce.

Peel the lemon, remove pips and pith, and cut it up into very small pieces. Add it to the sauce with a little grated lemon rind, and re-heat without boiling.

Melted Butter (4-5 people)

2 oz. butter.   *Squeeze of lemon juice.*

Melt the butter very slowly. It should never lose its creamy appearance. Add a squeeze of lemon juice if liked, or a few tiny flakes of parsley.

Mint Sauce (4-5 people)

2 tablespoonsful chopped mint.	A little boiling water.
2 teaspoonsful sugar (or to taste).	1 gill of vinegar, or half vinegar and half lemon juice.

Put finely chopped mint and the sugar into a sauce-boat and pour over a little boiling water, barely enough to cover. Let it stand till cold. Then add the vinegar, or half vinegar and half lemon juice.

Mushroom Sauce (3-4 people)

½ lb. mushrooms.	1 oz. butter.
Bacon bone or rinds.	Stock or cornflour as
A small piece of onion.	needed.
A little milk.	Pepper and salt.

Wash the mushrooms, put them in enough cold milk just to cover, with a small piece of onion, bacon bone or rinds and seasoning. Simmer till tender (about 10 minutes). Take out the bacon bone or rinds and the onion, and put the mushrooms through a sieve. Put the purée back into the saucepan and re-heat, but do not boil, adding a piece of butter right at the end.

If the sauce is too thick, add a little stock or milk; if too thin add a very little cornflour paste and simmer slowly till cooked.

Mustard Sauce (3-4 people)

1 gill white sauce.	1 teaspoonful raw mustard.
1 oz. butter.	Pinch of salt.
Pinch of sugar.	Tablespoonful vinegar.

Make a gill of white sauce, adding the mustard, butter and sugar while making it. When it has cooked sufficiently add the vinegar and a pinch of salt.

Onion Sauce (3-4 people)

2 or 3 onions.	½ pint white sauce.

Cook the onions in salted boiling water till tender, then drain them and chop finely. Add to the white sauce and re-heat.

Oyster Sauce (5-6 people)

¾ pint white sauce.	1 doz. oysters.
Pinch of cayenne.	Squeeze of lemon juice.

Beard the oysters and cut each up into 3 or 4 pieces, being careful to save the liquor in the shells. Blanch them in the liquor. Make the white sauce and add to it the oysters, the liquor, a pinch of cayenne and a squeeze of lemon juice. Re-heat the sauce but do not let it boil.

Parsley Sauce (4 people)

½ pint white sauce. 1 dessertspoonful chopped parsley.

Make some white sauce and when cooked and still boiling stir in the parsley.

Shrimp Sauce (3-4 people)

½ pint white sauce.	2 or 3 drops anchovy
A few drops of lemon juice.	essence.
	1 gill picked shrimps.

To make the white sauce, cook the shrimp shells in milk and water with a blade of mace and a bay-leaf and use the liquor for the sauce. Season well, then add the picked shrimps, anchovy essence and lemon juice, stir well and re-heat.

Tartar Sauce (4 people)

1 gill cold white sauce.	Chopped parsley.
1 gill of salad dressing or mayonnaise.	1 tablespoonful chopped capers.
1 tablespoonful chopped gherkins.	1 teaspoonful tarragon vinegar.

Mix all ingredients well together and serve cold.

Velouté Sauce (3-4 people)

½ pint chicken, veal or rabbit stock.	Squeeze of lemon juice.
1 tablespoonful flour.	Pepper and salt.
1 oz. butter.	A little cream.

Make the flour into a smooth paste with a little of the stock, heat the rest of the stock and pour in the paste, stirring well. Add pepper and salt. Let it simmer gently for 5 minutes.

Add a squeeze of lemon juice, the butter and a little cream right at the end. Do not let it boil.

If liked, a yolk of egg can also be added, when the sauce should be re-heated without being allowed to boil.

SWEET SAUCES

Brandy Sauce (or Rum or Sherry) (4 people)

1 dessertspoonful cornflour.	Yolk of 1 egg.
½ pint milk.	1 oz. butter.
Sugar to taste.	Brandy to taste.

Make the cornflour into a smooth paste with a little of the milk. Heat the rest of the milk with the sugar, and when boiling pour it over the cornflour. Put it back into the saucepan and bring to the boil, and cook for 5 minutes. Remove from the fire, and when it is no longer boiling add the beaten egg-yolk, butter and the brandy. Stir over a low heat until it thickens. Do not let it boil.

Rum or sherry can be used instead of brandy.

Chocolate Sauce (Plain) (4-5 people)

½ pint milk.
1 flat teaspoonful cornflour or custard powder.
3 teaspoonsful cocoa.
Vanilla essence.
A little butter.

Mix the cocoa and the cornflour, or custard powder, into a smooth paste with a little of the milk. Put the rest of the milk in a saucepan and bring to the boil, and then add the paste. Bring to the boil again, simmer for 5 minutes, add a few drops of vanilla essence, and lastly the butter.

Chocolate Sauce (Rich) (4-5 people)

½ pint milk.
¼ flat teaspoonful cornflour or custard powder.
A little cream or butter.
3 tablespoonsful granulated chocolate.
Vanilla essence.

Put the chocolate into a saucepan with 2 tablespoonfuls of the milk and stir until it boils. Add the rest of the milk (keeping back just enough to make the cornflour or custard powder into a paste), and let it boil. Add the paste, stirring carefully all the time and bring to the boil again. Cook for 5 minutes. Remove from the fire and add a drop or two of vanilla essence.

If desired a little cream or butter can be added to make it richer.

Coffee Sauce (4 people)

½ pint black coffee.
1 oz. Demerara sugar.
1 tablespoonful cream.
1 dessertspoonful arrowroot.
Pinch of salt.
Yolk of one egg.

Mix the arrowroot into a smooth paste with a very little water. Heat the coffee, sugar and salt to boiling-point, and pour on to the paste, stirring well. Put back into the saucepan, bring to the boil and cook for 3 minutes. Just before serving stir in the cream and beaten yolk. Serve hot, but do not let it boil after the egg is put in.

Custard Sauce (3-4 people)

1 egg.
½ pint of milk.
1 level teaspoonful cornflour.
1 oz. castor sugar.
Flavouring.

Put the milk and sugar on to boil, keeping back a tablespoonful of milk. Mix the cornflour to a smooth paste with this, and add the beaten egg. Pour the milk slowly on to the egg, stirring well. Put back in the saucepan and bring slowly almost to boiling-point. Add flavouring as desired.

Ginger Sauce (3-4 people).

½ small teaspoonful ground ginger.
½ pint water.
Lemon juice.
1 dessertspoonful cornflour.
1 tablespoonful golden syrup.
1 oz. butter.
Crystallised ginger, chopped.

Mix the cornflour and ground ginger together and make into a paste with a little of the water. Bring the rest of the water with the syrup to the boil and then stir in the paste. Cook for 5 minutes, adding the butter towards the end. Then add a squeeze of lemon juice just before serving.

A little chopped crystallised ginger greatly improves the flavour.

Jam Sauce (3-4 people)

3 tablespoonfuls of any jam.
½ pint water.
1 teaspoonful cornflour.
1 teaspoonful lemon juice.

Make the cornflour into a smooth paste with a little water. Boil the jam and the rest of the water and pour it on to the paste. Put it back into the saucepan and let it boil for 5 minutes. Then add the lemon juice and strain through a coarse sieve.

Lemon Sauce (3-4 people)

½ pint white sauce (unseasoned).
1 lemon.
4 oz. granulated sugar.

Make some white unseasoned sauce, putting the rind of the lemon in the milk to flavour, and 4 oz. white sugar. Bring to the boil, remove from the fire and after a minute or two add the lemon juice.

Orange sauce can be made in the same way.

Treacle Sauce (5-6 people)

1 gill water.
8 oz. syrup.
1 oz. butter.
1 level dessertspoonful arrowroot.
Lemon juice.

Get the fat really hot, dry the fish and dip it into the batter. When it is quite evenly coated, put it carefully into the fat

When the batter is crisp and brown, remove the fish from the fat and serve garnished with fresh, fried parsley

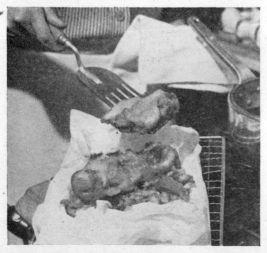

Mix the arrowroot into a paste with a little of the water. Put the rest of the water, the syrup and butter into a saucepan and bring to the boil. Add the paste and cook for 3 minutes. Add a squeeze of lemon juice just before serving.

Wine Foam Sauce (3-4 people)

1 *egg.*
1 *dessertspoonful sugar.*
$\frac{1}{4}$ *pint sherry or marsala.*
A strip of lemon peel.

Put all the ingredients into a basin, warming the sherry or marsala slightly first. Put the basin over a pan of hot water, whisk well for 10 minutes or until the sauce has a froth. Be careful not to get it too hot or it will curdle. Remove the lemon peel and serve at once.

Anchovy Butter

2 *oz. butter.*
Lemon juice.
Dessertspoonful anchovy essence.

Warm the butter till it is the consistency of thick cream, drop in the essence, beating all the time. A squeeze of lemon juice greatly improves the flavour.

Brandy Butter

2 *oz. butter.*
Brandy to taste.
1 *oz. castor sugar.*

Slightly warm the butter and beat it to a cream with the sugar. Add brandy to taste, and put in a cool place till required.

Maître d'Hôtel Butter

2 *oz. butter.*
A few drops of lemon juice.
Salt and pepper.
Dessertspoonful very finely chopped parsley.

Put the chopped parsley on a plate with the butter, lemon juice and seasoning to taste. Take a knife and work them thoroughly till they can be shaped into a pat. Tilt the plate to let the lemon juice run out. Put in a cool place till it is to be used. Then roll into pats. This may be served with fish, grills etc.

THE ART OF DEEP FRYING

While we are all familiar with simple shallow frying in the form of the ever-popular 'egg and bacon,' deep-fat frying is often neglected because it is considered either difficult and expensive or indigestible.

Perhaps it is a method of cooking a little more complicated than some others, but it is quick, and the finished dishes so attractive

It is worth mastering the art of crisp frying to be able to serve some of the very tasty food that you see pictured here

popular coatings are: (1) beaten egg and dry white crumbs; (2) batter; (3) pastry.

The temperature of the fat is important, it must be hot enough to seal the protective coating immediately and so trap all the juices and flavour of the food inside, and it varies for different foods and is between 320° and 400° F.

At these temperatures the fat has a faint blue smoke rising from the surface. It should be quite still, and if it splutters or 'splits' then water is present and must be driven off before the fat is hot enough to use.

A homely test can be made with a 1-in. cube of stale bread which will brown in one minute if the fat is ready for frying.

Fritters and Doughnuts	320°–360° F.
Fish, according to thickness	340°–380° F.
Meat	360°–380° F.
Whitebait and Potato Chips	400° F.

Heating

Care must be taken not to over-heat the fat, as it burns quickly. There is no such thing as 'boiling fat,' and if the contents of the pan are smoking too freely, a large crust of bread or a slice of raw potato should be added immediately to lower the heat.

Because such a high temperature is needed for deep frying, oil or fats with a high melting-point must be used and so butter and margarine cannot be used for this.

The following fats are most suitable for deep frying:

(1) Olive or vegetable oil. (2) Melted block suet and lard. (3) Lard. (4) Clarified dripping.

After use pour the fat through muslin or a

and appetising that everyone should learn to do it well; and *well*-fried food is not greasy and consequently indigestible, but crisp and delicious.

While a basket is very useful for lowering the food gently into the fat and removing it quickly, there is no need for an elaborate fryer; a strong saucepan will prove adequate providing it holds sufficient fat to cover or float the food to be cooked. Perfect results depend on the following:

1. Preparation of the food before cooking.
2. Temperature of the fat during cooking.
3. Draining of the food after cooking.

Preparation

Any article to be fried must have a coating, as this not only protects the food from the great heat of the fat, but also keeps the fat free from taste; and so foods of different kinds can be cooked in one fat bath. The most

fine strainer into a clean, dry enamel basin, and when cold cover and keep in a cool, dry place. In very hot weather heat the fat to 'haze' point every four to five weeks.

Fried food must be thoroughly drained. Do this first over the pan in the frying basket or on a flat whisk, and then on a wire rack or crumpled kitchen paper.

It should be served piping hot and if it has to be kept warm must never be covered or the crispness will be spoilt; for the same reason sauce should be served separately.

Garnishes

In frying, as indeed in all cooking, garnishing plays an important part. The garnish should attract the eye, improve the appearance of the dish, and be always edible.

For shallow-fried food the choice is fairly wide, and if parsley is used it is finely chopped, but for savoury food that is fried in deep fat, the parsley is fried in whole sprays. It is then all a garnish should be—delicious to eat and a perfect colour contrast to any fried food.

Economical Batter for Fish and Fritters

4 oz. plain flour.
A 'walnut' of yeast.
1½ gills warm water.
1 tablespoonful oil or melted lard.
1 teaspoonful sugar.

Cream the yeast with a teaspoonful of sugar and add the warm water. Sift the flour into a bowl with a pinch of salt and mix to a smooth batter with the liquid ingredients. Add the oil and stand in a warm place for half an hour before using.

Apple Fritters

Allow 2 cooking apples for 3 people.

Peel the apples, cut across into 1-in. slices and remove the core with a small cutter. Dip in batter and fry in deep fat until golden brown. Drain well, sprinkle with sugar and serve with a chocolate sauce. Sliced pineapple, halved bananas or apricots are good served in the same way. Tinned fruit may be used, but should be well drained first.

Vegetable Fritto Misto

Use any good selection of vegetables for this. Here are a few ideas:

Carrots. Trim these into even shapes, cutting in quarters if large, and cook carefully with a teaspoon of sugar and finely chopped mint in the water. Drain and leave to cool in a little french dressing. Dip in batter for frying.

Beetroot. Cooked beetroot is excellent if cut in thin slices, marinaded and coated in the same way as carrots.

Potatoes. Cook freshly and dry well. Sieve, beat in an egg yolk, seasoning and a grate of nutmeg. Shape into small balls on a floured board and coat with egg and crumbs for frying.

Parsnips. Cook until tender, cut into neat fingers, roll in seasoned flour and egg and crumbs.

Celeriac. When in season can be treated in the same way as parsnips.

Onion Rings. Soak raw in a little milk for ½ hour. Drain and dip in batter or slightly beaten egg-white before frying.

Cauliflower. Cook in boiling salted water until barely tender, drain and dip in batter for frying.

Mushrooms. Choose small button mushrooms, do not peel, but rub with salt and dry well. These are dipped in batter while still raw and fried until golden brown.

Drain all the vegetables thoroughly, arrange in a hot dish and garnish with plenty of parsley.

To Fry Parsley

Turn out the heat from under the fat bath and place the washed and well-dried parsley in the fat basket and lower this very gently into the fat. When the bubbling subsides somewhat remove the parsley and drain. It should be crisp and still bright green.

Doughnuts

½ lb. plain flour.
1 oz. butter.
¼ oz. yeast.
1½ oz. sugar.
1 egg.
¼ pint milk.

Warm the flour, sieve into a basin with a pinch of salt and rub in the butter. Cream the yeast with the sugar until liquid, add the beaten egg and the milk carefully warmed to blood-heat. Make a well in the centre of the flour, tip on the liquid ingredients and beat 5 minutes until quite smooth.

Cover the bowl with a cloth and set in a warm place for the dough to rise and double its bulk, about 45 minutes. Turn on to a floured board and knead well. Roll out ½ in. thick, cut into rings and place on a greased baking tin in a warm place to prove for 10 minutes.

Fry in deep fat until golden brown and when well drained roll in cinnamon-flavoured sugar.

NOTE. The fat should be showing only the faintest haze; if it is too hot the doughnuts will be hard.

FISH

Contrary to a popular belief, fish may not improve our brain-power, but it is light and easily digested (though here we must make an exception of lobster and crab) and can serve as the only source of protein for a meal. In fact, as far as nutritive value goes, food experts tell us that a pound of herrings is equal in food value to a pound of meat. Herrings rank highest among all fish in this important matter of food values.

With no other food is it more important that it should be absolutely fresh. The flesh of fresh fish is elastic, and the eyes and gills bright. Never buy fish that has sunken, dull-looking eyes, or the slightest sign of an unpleasant smell. Mackerel should be eaten only while the rainbow sheen still shows.

Fish out of season should usually be avoided, as it is usually poor and flabby.

Oysters, if thoroughly fresh, should be firmly shut, or if slightly open should shut at once if the blade of a knife is put between the shells. If the shells remain open they should be avoided.

All fish should be cooked as soon as possible after it is bought, with the exception of cod, which, *if the weather is cold*, improves by hanging for a day or two.

It is a mistake to be too conventional in one's choice of fish. The nutritive value of the lesser-known fish is often as high, if not higher, than the more expensive popular ones. Again, to insist on having the best cut often means that one pays a price out of all proportion to what one gets, as these cuts mean a lot of waste for the fishmonger, which has to be paid for.

Fish is usually cleaned and filleted by the fishmonger, but it is necessary to wipe it both inside and out with a clean damp cloth before cooking it. To remove the scales from salmon, etc., scrape with a *very* sharp knife.

In the case of sole, plaice, etc., which is to be cooked whole, cut off the head and fins. Always keep any trimmings to make stock, as a sauce served with fish is immensely improved by using fish stock.

Keep any left-over cooked fish, as there are many ways of using it up.

Baked Fish. Wash and wipe the fish with a clean cloth, and season well. A few drops of lemon juice should be squeezed over them. They should be put in a buttered baking tin, covered over with greased paper, and baked in a moderately hot oven. When cooked the skin will crack or the flesh come away from the bones easily if tested with a skewer. Some fish, fresh haddock, cod, sole, can be baked in a tin half full of milk and water.

Boiled Fish. Boiling is only to be advised when large fish or thick pieces of fish are to be cooked. A fish kettle is the best for this purpose, as the drainer makes it easy for the fish to be lifted out without breaking. If you have not a fish kettle use an ordinary saucepan, but tie up the fish in a pudding cloth.

The fish should be put into the water when it is hot, *but not actually boiling*, with a dessertspoonful of salt and one teaspoonful of vinegar, or lemon juice, to every quart of water. The water should just cover the fish, no more.

Exceptions to this are: (1) salmon, which on account of its tough skin should be put into gently boiling water; and (2) mackerel, which should be put into tepid water on account of its delicate skin. Allow about 6 minutes to each pound of fish and 6 minutes over. Thick cuts of fish such as salmon or cod need 10 minutes to the pound and 10 minutes over.

Fried Fish. Fish to be fried should be wiped over well with a clean cloth, and in the case of sole, whiting, etc., skinned. If shallow fat is used for frying, the fish should be dipped in seasoned flour (any superfluous flour being shaken off), or in a frying batter, or egg-and-breadcrumbed. For deep-fat frying the fish should first be floured before being egg-and-breadcrumbed; it should then be put into a frying basket and lowered into the smoking fat. If floured and dipped in batter it is best to dispense with the frying-basket, which leaves marks on the coating. Drain well on kitchen paper before serving. (Oil is very good for frying fish as it lessens the fear of burning.)

The time to be allowed varies according to what fish is used: steaks of fish, for example, naturally taking very much longer than thin fillets. For this reason large fish, or fish steaks, should be fried in a little fat, while fillets, or small fish like whitebait, should be fried in deep fat.

Grilled Fish. This method is particularly suitable for fillets or slices of fish, and is incidentally more digestible than frying. The fish should be wiped thoroughly with a clean cloth, and allowed to soak in a plate of olive oil, or brushed over with melted butter, before being put under the hot griller.

Steamed Fish. Steaming is to be preferred to boiling, though it takes almost twice as long, as more of the flavour of the fish is retained. Thin slices or fillets of fish should always be steamed, never boiled.

When steaming whole flat fish or fish cut in large pieces, rub them over well with a cut lemon to preserve the colour.

Wash and wipe the fish well, season, and squeeze a little lemon juice over, wrap in greased paper and put in a steamer over boiling water.

If liked, fish can be steamed by putting it between two greased plates, and placing them over a saucepan of boiling water, or in a moderate oven. The flavour of fish steamed in this way is more delicate than when steamed in the ordinary manner.

Generally speaking, the most successful ways of cooking fish are the simplest; such fish as salmon or turbot, for example, is far nicer cooked in the simplest possible way. Great care should, however, be taken in the preparation of the sauces which are served with fish, and fish stock should be used when possible in making them.

The range of sauces that can be served with fish is a wide one. Here are a few suggestions: anchovy, Béchamel, black butter, Dutch, egg, gooseberry, Hollandaise, lemon, maître d'hôtel butter and sauce, mustard, oyster, parsley, tartar, etc.

Buttered Lobster (or Crab)

Slice quite small and pull into flakes with a fork the flesh of lobster, and put into a saucepan with a few pieces of butter lightly rolled in flour. Heat slowly over a gentle heat. Then mix thoroughly with it a teaspoonful of made mustard (mixed with vinegar and cayenne) and a tablespoonful of cream.

When all is well heated serve in the shell; cover with fried breadcrumbs.

Cod's Roe

Take a whole fresh roe and put it in warm salted water for a little while, being very careful how you handle it. Then put it in a pudding cloth and fasten it securely. Place it in boiling salted water to cover with one tablespoonful of vinegar. Boil for 30 minutes, or longer, according to size. Take up and let it get cold.

Cut it into thick slices, egg-and-breadcrumb them, and fry till a rich brown.

Drain and serve with melted butter.

Cod Steaks, Stuffed, with Bacon (4 people)

4 *cod steaks.*	4 *rashers of bacon.*
4 *tomatoes.*	1 *tablespoonful chopped*
2 *tablespoonsful*	*parsley.*
browned bread-	1 *dessertspoonful milk.*
crumbs.	½ *teaspoonful mixed herbs.*

Mix together the breadcrumbs, parsley, herbs and milk. Put some of this mixture on to each steak, place a rasher of bacon on top and tie firmly in position with string. Bake in a greased fireproof dish in a moderate oven for about 25-30 minutes according to the thickness of the steaks. Remove the string and serve with the tomatoes, cut in half, and baked for 10-12 minutes.

Coquilles au Colin (3-4 people)

½ *lb. cooked boned fish.*	*About* 1½ *glasses*
2 *oz. mushrooms.*	*milk.*
2 *oz. butter.*	2 *dessertspoonsful*
Salt and pepper.	*grated Gruyère*
1 *large dessertspoonful*	*cheese.*
flour.	*A few shrimps.*

Make a white sauce with the butter and flour and the heated milk. Peel and cut up the mushrooms and add them with salt and pepper to the sauce. Cook for 10 minutes. (Be sparing with the salt because of the shrimps.)

Put the shelled shrimps into the sauce and add the grated cheese at the last moment.

Butter four shells, half fill them with fish, then pour over the sauce, and sprinkle a little grated cheese over each shell. Put a small piece of butter on each and put under a hot griller till brown.

Curried Fish (3-4 people)

½ *lb. cooked fish.*	*Squeeze of lemon*
1 *oz. butter.*	*juice.*
Curry powder to taste.	1 *teaspoonful chopped*
½ *oz. rice flour.*	*chutney.*
Boiled rice.	*Salt.*
1 *apple and* 1 *onion.*	½ *pint fish stock.*

Melt the butter and, when hot, fry the sliced apple and onion; then add the rice flour, curry powder and salt, stirring well.

Add the stock slowly; bring to the boil and simmer for 5 minutes.

Flake up the cooked fish and add it to the sauce, with the chopped chutney, and re-heat. Add a squeeze of lemon juice right at the end.

Serve with boiled rice.

Dressed Crab (4 people)

1 *cooked crab.*	1 *tablespoonful mayonnaise*
Chopped parsley.	*or French dressing.*
Salad.	*Pepper and salt*
	1 *oz. breadcrumbs.*

Remove the meat from the shell (be careful to discard the bag or sac near the head) and the flesh from the large claws. Mix the ingredients together, wipe the shell and fill with the mixture. Serve on a bed of salad garnished with parsley and the small claws.

Fish Pancakes and Spinach.

1 *small onion.*	2 *lb. spinach.*
$\frac{3}{4}$ *oz. margarine.*	$\frac{1}{2}$ *pint pancake*
$\frac{3}{4}$ *oz. flour.*	*batter.*
3-4 *tablespoonsful*	$\frac{1}{2}$ *pint Béchamel*
crayfish meat.	*sauce.*
Salt and pepper.	$\frac{1}{4}$ *pint milk.*
1 *teaspoonful lemon juice.*	*Mashed potatoes*
Garnish:	
1 *hard-boiled egg.*	8-10 *prawns.*

Fry chopped onion lightly in margarine. Add flour and cook for about three minutes, stirring continuously. Season to taste. Stir in milk gradually till mixture boils. Simmer for about three minutes. Mix in chopped egg, fish and lemon juice and heat through gently.

Make small pancakes with the batter, stuff each with filling and arrange on dish surrounded by a border of creamed spinach and mashed potatoes. Fill centre with Béchamel sauce and decorate with slices of hard-boiled egg and prawns.

Fish Mornay

1 *lb. cod, hake or*	1$\frac{1}{2}$ *lb. mashed potatoes.*
fresh haddock.	1 *dessertspoonful*
$\frac{1}{2}$ *pint cheese sauce.*	*grated cheese.*
Fish stock.	$\frac{1}{2}$ *oz. margarine.*

Poach the fish in buttered dish with a gill of fish stock. Flake the fish, removing all skin and bone. Mix in the cheese sauce. Pipe the mashed potato in a border on a fire-proof dish. Pour the fish mixture into the centre and sprinkle the grated cheese over the fish and potato. Dot with margarine. Brown under the grill or in a hot oven.

Fish and Potato Rolls

To each half-teacupful of cooked fish add the same quantity of mashed potato, a small piece of butter, pepper, salt, and just a flavouring of mace.

Work the mixture into a stiff paste with a beaten egg, and make into little rolls 3 in. long with flat ends. Flour well, egg-and-breadcrumb them, and fry in deep fat till a golden brown.

Serve with a garnish of parsley and lemon, and with melted butter.

Fish Custard

Cold cooked fish.	*Pepper and salt.*
Shallot.	*Milk and eggs for*
A few chopped capers.	*custard.*

Flake up the fish, removing any bones, and put some of it in a buttered pie-dish. Sprinkle pepper and salt over it, and then a little chopped caper, and a very little chopped shallot. Add some more fish and seasoning till all is used.

Make a custard, allowing 3 eggs to a pint of milk. Pour it carefully over the fish, and bake in a slow oven (standing the dish in a tin with a little water in it) till a delicate brown.

Fish Cutlets (3-4 people)

$\frac{1}{2}$ *lb. cooked fish.*	1 *yolk of egg.*
$\frac{1}{2}$ *oz. butter.*	*Teaspoonful chopped parsley.*
$\frac{1}{2}$ *oz. flour.*	*Teaspoonful anchovy essence.*
$\frac{1}{2}$ *gill milk or*	*Pepper and salt.*
fish stock.	*Egg and breadcrumbs.*

Remove the skin and any bones from the fish and flake it up finely. Add the parsley, anchovy essence, and pepper and salt.

Melt the butter in a saucepan, add the flour and mix it well. Then add the milk or fish stock and stir till the mixture thickens, and draws away from the side of the saucepan.

Take it off the fire and put in the fish, and the beaten yolk. Turn the mixture out on to a plate, and let it get cold. Then make it into neat cutlets, using a little flour if necessary. Egg-and-breadcrumb them and fry in deep fat till a golden brown.

Drain well and garnish with fried parsley and slices of lemon.

Fish Mousse (3-4 people)

1 *lb. cooked whiting or fresh haddock.*	*White sauce.*
	2 whites of egg.
1 *teaspoonful powdered gelatine.*	*1 tablespoonful cream.*
	Pepper and salt.

Make some white sauce—with fish stock if possible—and then dissolve the gelatine in it.

Pound up the fish and add it to the sauce, with seasoning to taste, the cream, and lastly the well-whisked whites of egg. Beat it lightly and put in a soufflé mould.

Serve cold with salad and cold tomato sauce.

Fish Omelette

Take about 2 oz. of cooked fish and flake it finely. Season it, add a little cream and work it into a paste. Heat it and put it aside in a warm place.

Make an omelette and add the fish to it just before dishing it up. Sardines can be added in the same way, boned and mashed.

Fish Patties

Make some patty cases.

For the filling use any cooked fish, flaked into small pieces and moistened with some good fish sauce. Season it well, add a squeeze of lemon juice or a little grated rind, a beaten yolk of egg, and if possible a little cream.

British Vacuum Flask Co., Ltd.

Everything tastes nicer if it is served in a decorative container. This pretty vacuum flask can hold a late, after-theatre warming drink or keep orange juice fresh for the morning

Heat the mixture, and then pile it into the patty cases. Put on the lids and put the patties into the oven for 2 or 3 minutes to heat them through.

If liked, a few shelled chopped shrimps may be added to the mixture.

Fish Pie (illustrated on page 411)

1½ *lb. cooked cold fish.*	*Salt and pepper.*
1 *large tomato.*	1½ *lb. mashed*
½ *pint prawns or shrimps.*	*potatoes.*
	½ *to* ¾ *pint anchovy*
Lemon juice.	*sauce.*

Garnish:

Prawns or shrimps.	*Sprigs of parsley.*
1 *hard-boiled egg.*	

Remove bones and skin from the fish. Mix fish into the anchovy sauce. Season with salt, pepper and lemon juice. Add sliced tomato, and half the prawns or shrimps. Turn into a fire-proof dish. Spread mashed potato over the fish and decorate the surface with a fork. Form the rest of the potato into small balls and arrange them on top of the pie. Brown in a hot oven or under the grill. Decorate with sprigs of parsley, sliced hard-boiled egg and the rest of the prawns or shrimps. Serve with lemon.

Fish Soufflé (3-4 people)

2 *oz. butter.*	*Pepper and salt.*
2 *oz. flour.*	*Yolks and whites of*
1 *teaspoonful anchovy essence.*	2 *or 3 eggs.*
	About a gill of milk.
5 *oz. white fish.*	1 *tablespoonful cream.*

Melt the butter, and add the flour, anchovy essence, and seasoning, stirring well. Then add the yolks of 2 or 3 eggs and about a gill of milk. Go on stirring over the fire till the mixture is just about to boil, then take it off. Stir in 5 oz. of finely pounded white fish, and a tablespoonful of cream.

When it is well blended stir in lightly the well-beaten whites of 2 eggs, pour it into a buttered soufflé dish and bake for about half an hour.

Fish Timbales (3-4 people)

1 *lb. cooked white fish.*	2 *whites of egg.*
White sauce.	*Pepper and salt.*

Make some white sauce, using fish stock if possible, and cornflour, not flour. Add seasoning and then put in the fish pounded up. Lastly fold in the well-beaten whites.

Butter some timbale moulds, fill almost full with the mixture, twist a piece of buttered paper over the top, steam for 20 minutes, then turn out carefully.

Fresh Haddock (Stuffed)

Wash and dry the haddock. Make sufficient veal stuffing to fill and then sew the fish together with a needle and thread. Put in a tin with some dripping or butter over it.

Put a piece of buttered paper over, cover with another tin, and bake for 30 minutes or according to size, basting well.

Serve with brown sauce.

NOTE. Cod or hake can also be stuffed and baked.

Halibut a la Suisse (3-4 people)

1 lb. halibut.	2 oz. mushrooms.
2 oz. butter.	2 tablespoonsful
½ teaspoonful beef	cream.
extract.	Pepper and salt.

Wipe the fish and put it in a buttered dish. Sprinkle pepper and salt over it. Put the butter in pieces on the top, and bake in a moderately hot oven for 10 minutes, basting well. Take out and put the chopped mushrooms over it and the cream, and let it cook for 10 minutes more. Finally, stir the beef extract into the liquor and finish in the oven, basting once or twice.

Halibut with Tomatoes (Baked) (3-4 people)

1 lb. halibut.	3 tomatoes.
1 oz. melted butter.	Very small onion.
2 tablespoonsful cream.	Pinch of castor sugar.
Pepper and salt.	Fat for frying.

Wipe the fish, and skin it. Then put it in a buttered dish and sprinkle pepper and salt over it. Pour the melted butter over it and let it cook in a moderately hot oven for about 20 minutes.

Meanwhile fry the onion (which should be sliced very finely) in a little fat till it is a golden brown, then take out the fish, put slices of tomato on top with a pinch of sugar, then the onion, and lastly the cream. Put it back in the oven for 10 minutes.

Herrings with Mustard Sauce

Wipe the fish with a clean cloth. Then split open and egg-and-breadcrumb them, or dip in coarse oatmeal. Fry in a little butter, cut side down first, for 7 to 8 minutes.

Serve with mustard sauce.

English Electric Co.

This oven is large enough to take an 18–20-lb. turkey, if you are lucky enough to have one. The roomy drawer holds kitchen utensils or dishes and will keep plates warm when dishing up a meal

Jombalayah (American) (3-4 people)

4 oz. Patna rice.	1 lettuce.
4 oz. cooked salmon.	Cayenne pepper and salt.

Wash the rice and put it into a large pan of quickly boiling salted water. Boil till tender, and dry well.

Flake up the salmon, season it, and add it to the rice when cold.

Serve on lettuce leaves as cold as possible.

Lobster au Gratin (4-5 people)

Good-sized lobster.	1 tablespoonful flour.
1 teaspoonful chopped	½ pint of milk.
shallot.	Cayenne pepper.
1 oz. butter.	Anchovy essence.
Chopped parsley.	1 yolk.
1 tablespoonful cream.	Butter.
Breadcrumbs.	

Cut the lobster in half, dividing the head from the body, and take out all the meat, saving the shells. Cut the meat into slices.

Take a teaspoonful of chopped shallot, put in a saucepan with the butter, and cook for a few minutes. Add the flour, mixing well, and then the milk. Stir it all the time, and let it boil gently for 5 minutes.

Then add the lobster seasoned with cayenne pepper, chopped parsley and anchovy essence. Put the saucepan back on the fire and stir till it boils. Then remove it from the fire, and stir in the yolk of 1 egg, and the cream.

Fill the shells with the mixture, sprinkle breadcrumbs over, putting pieces of butter on top, and bake in the oven for 20 minutes.

Mackerel with Apple or Gooseberry Sauce

Wash the fish, cut off the heads and wipe with a clean cloth. (Do not wash after the heads are cut off, as the flavour will be spoilt.)

Score them in two or three places and put small pieces of butter on the fish.

Put them under a hot griller and let them cook for 15 minutes, turning half-way.

If liked, they can be split open instead.

Serve with apple or gooseberry sauce or pats of maître d'hôtel butter.

Marinated Mackerel or Herrings (3-4 people)

3 or 4 *mackerel*.	12 *peppercorns*.
¼ *pint vinegar*.	*Bay-leaf*.
¼ *pint water*.	*Pepper and salt*.

Wash and clean the fish. Put them into a deep dish, head to tail, and pour over them the vinegar and water; then add the peppercorns, bay-leaf and seasoning. Put the dish into a slow oven and bake for about an hour. Then take out and allow to cool.

Serve cold.

Red Mullet au Gratin (2-3 people)

2 *red mullets*.	½ *teaspoonful chopped*
1 *tablespoonful sherry*.	*onion*.
1 *teaspoonful mush-*	*Grated rind of half*
room ketchup.	*a lemon*.
4 *button mushrooms*.	1 *tablespoonful*
1 *oz. butter*.	*browned bread-*
1 *teaspoonful chopped*	*crumbs*.
parsley.	*Pepper and salt*.

Wash the mullets, cut off the heads and fins, then dry with a clean cloth.

Grease a dish with some of the butter, then sprinkle over it half the onion, mushrooms, lemon rind and chopped parsley.

Score the fish across once or twice and put them on top. Season them and add the rest of the chopped ingredients.

Then add the sherry, ketchup, and lastly sprinkle over the breadcrumbs. Put the rest of the butter cut up in small pieces on the top and bake in a moderate oven for about 20 minutes.

Garnish with parsley and slices of lemon.

Plaice or Sole (Baked Fillets)

Fillets of plaice or sole.	1 *oz. margarine*.
Salt, pepper and lemon juice.	½ *oz. butter*.
Breadcrumbs.	

Wash the fillets and dry with a cloth. Season with salt, pepper and lemon juice and sprinkle with breadcrumbs. Heat enough margarine to cover the bottom of a fireproof dish. Put in the fillets, dot them with butter and bake until lightly brown. (About 10 to 15 minutes.)

Serve with hot tartar sauce, or maître d'hôtel butter.

Salmon Steaks (Grilled)

Scrape off the scales with a very sharp knife. Spread butter over both sides and grill in the usual way.

Garnish with lemon and serve with green peas, or cucumber and tartar sauce.

Salmon Steaks (Steamed)

Scrape off the scales with a very sharp knife. Put the steaks in a casserole with a tablespoonful of water, a pinch of salt, and a few lumps of butter. Put a piece of greased paper under the lid and cook in the oven till tender.

Sardines Fried in Batter

Drain the sardines well on paper to remove the oil; then skin them.

Make some fritter batter, dip the sardines in and fry in deep fat till brown.

Serve with lemon and bread and butter.

Sole Superbe

2 *Dover soles* (¾ *lb.*	2 *oz. margarine*.
each approx.).	¼ *pint white wine*.
½ *lb. grapes*.	2 *teaspoonsful orange*
Salt and pepper.	*juice*.
1 *lb. mashed potatoes*.	1 *orange*.

Fillet and skin fish. Shred 4 oz. of the grapes, skinned and seeded. Season fillets, spread with shredded grapes and fold in half. Fry fish lightly on both sides. Add wine and orange juice and continue cooking gently until done.

Put mashed potato on to a hot dish and arrange fillets on top. Add liquor from pan and decorate with remaining grapes and slices of orange.

Scalloped Scallops

Wash the scallops, wipe them, remove the beards and black part, then cut up into three or four pieces. Stew in a little milk with pepper and salt, and then take out. Thicken the liquor with flour. Then put in the scallops again and re-heat.

Butter the shells, scatter breadcrumbs over them and put in enough mixture just to cover. Scatter some more breadcrumbs over each, put a small piece of butter on top and brown them in the oven.

Scallops (2-3 people)

6 *scallops.*   *Flour.*
Pepper and salt.   *Egg and breadcrumbs.*
Fat for frying.

Scallops must be fresh to be wholesome. Open the shells and remove the beards and any black parts, leaving only the yellow and white part to be eaten. Wash them, dry and scatter seasoned flour over, then egg-and-breadcrumb them and fry in deep fat for 3-4 minutes. Drain well and serve garnished with parsley and cut lemon, or fried mushrooms or mushroom sauce.

Skate (3-4 people)

1 *lb. skate.*   1½ *oz. grated cheese.*
4 *oz. breadcrumbs.*   1 *gill white sauce.*

Boil the fish in salted water till it comes away easily from the bones, drain well and flake up. Put a layer of fish into a greased fireproof dish, cover with breadcrumbs and a good sprinkling of cheese. Continue these

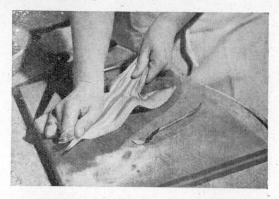

Sole Meunière. **Slit skin of your sole by the tail, then grasp the tail, and pull firmly**

Cut down the backbone with a very sharp knife, and slice the fillets. Use a floured board on which to work

Heat a frying-pan and drop in 1 oz. of butter. Wait till the butter froths, then put floured fillets into the pan

layers till all are used up, then pour over the well-seasoned sauce and bake in a fairly hot oven till brown on top—about 30 minutes.

Smelts (2 people)

6 *smelts.*   *Butter.*
Seasoning.   1 *dessertspoonful*
Egg and breadcrumbs.   *chopped parsley.*

Arrange the golden-brown fillets on a hot dish, arrange the bacon in between, and pour over the sauce made in the same pan

Wipe the fish, split them open, and season them. Then egg-and-breadcrumb them and fry them in a little butter till a golden brown. Sprinkle the chopped parsley over them. Serve with anchovy sauce, black butter, or melted butter.

Sole Meunière

One 1½-lb. sole (filleted).
5 thin rashers streaky bacon.
2 oz. butter.

1 teaspoonful chopped mixed herbs or parsley.
Juice of half a lemon.

Lightly flour and season the fillets. Heat a frying pan and drop in 1 oz. butter. When frothing, lay in the fillets and fry until golden brown, turning once only. Then put on a hot dish, arranging a rasher of bacon between each of the fillets of sole.

Pour the fat from the frying-pan, wipe, reheat the pan and drop in the remainder of the butter; when golden brown quickly add the lemon juice, herbs and seasoning, and pour over the dish. Serve at once. Sautéd artichokes, celeriac, mushrooms or tomatoes can replace the bacon.

Sole au Parmesan

Fillets of sole.
Pepper, salt and cayenne.

Cheese sauce.
Grated cheese.

Wipe the fillets, roll up and put in a well-buttered tin with a little pepper and salt and bake for 15 minutes.

Make some cheese sauce (if possible with some fish stock instead of milk), adding a little cayenne. Pour the sauce over the fish and sprinkle some grated cheese over the top. Finish either under a hot griller or in the oven.

NOTE. Fillets of any other white fish can be cooked in the same way.

Trout

This fish can be grilled or fried, or it can be baked. (Fresh-water fish after being cleaned must be well washed in salted water to remove any slime or muddy flavour.)

To bake trout, scale and remove the fins, cleanse in salted water, drain and dry. Grease a fireproof dish, put in the fish, sprinkle with pepper and salt, chopped parsley and shallot and pour a little melted butter over. Cover with greased paper and stand the dish in a tin of boiling water. Bake in a moderate oven for 20-25 minutes according to the size of the fish. Serve with black butter sauce.

MEAT, POULTRY AND GAME

How to Choose Meat

Tough meat may not *always* be the butcher's fault; wrong cooking can ruin the choicest cuts. However, it is equally true that the best cooking in the world will not help if the meat itself is at fault. For that reason it is essential that you should know something about how to choose meat.

Beef should be bright red in colour, quite firm to the touch, and well covered with fat. This should be firm and white. The actual food value of the less tender cuts is very much the same as the more expensive ones, though naturally they need longer cooking. There is more nourishment in beef than in mutton, but it is not so easily digested. It should be hung well before cooking.

Mutton should be a dull red, firm and fine in grain. The fat should be white and hard, and there should be a larger proportion of it in good mutton than in beef. It should also be hung well before it is cooked. It is more easily digested than beef.

Lamb is pink rather than red, and the bone at the joint in chops should be reddish. It is also more digestible than beef. It should not be hung long.

Veal should be pinkish-white and not so firm as beef. The fat should be slightly pink. It requires longer cooking than other meat, and is less easily digested.

Pork fat should be white. The lean varies in colour according to the age of the animal. In a young pig it is practically white, while in an older one it is pink. Pork, again, is not so digestible as beef or mutton.

Imported meat (if still frozen when it comes to you) should be very carefully thawed, preferably in a warm kitchen, during which time it will change colour. This is merely the result of defrosting it and does not mean that the meat is not good.

We next come to the different methods one can use in cooking meat, and below you will find directions for each.

Always wipe meat with a damp cloth before using.

Boiling. Fresh meat should be put into boiling water and simmered, salt meat into tepid water and brought to the boil, then simmered. It is a little difficult to generalise about the time needed for this process as it depends so much on what meat you are using, and what particular dish you have in view. An average of 20 minutes to each pound and 20 minutes over will act as a rough guide. Small joints do not lend themselves to boiling so well as larger ones, as they are very easily overcooked òr made tough. Never let the water in which the joint is cooking boil hard, as the meat will then not only be tough but probably tasteless. *Gentle simmering is all that is required.*

Braising is a delicious way of treating meat, and also an economical one as the less tender cuts can be used if desired. The meat is usually first browned and then cooked very slowly with vegetables. Small joints, kidneys, cutlets, fillets, sweetbreads, etc., are excellent braised.

Frying, in either deep fat or shallow, is a very tasty way of serving meat, though it is less digestible than grilling. Meat to be fried in deep fat is usually encased either in flour and then egg and breadcrumbs, in which case it is put into the basket and lowered into the hot fat; or in batter, when a frying-basket is not advisable as the batter may stick to the wire of the basket, the food being put straight into the pan. As it cooks it will rise to the top and so can be easily taken out. Drain well on kitchen paper, then keep hot till ready to be served. Be careful to heat up the fat again before putting in a second lot of cutlets or whatever it may be, and never cook many at a time or the temperature will be lowered too much.

In shallow frying, which should be used for all food which is not encased in batter, etc., whatever is to be fried should be put into the hot fat and browned on one side, then turned over for the other side to brown. It should then be drained on kitchen paper.

Of the two methods deep-fat frying, though it needs far more fat to begin with, is the more economical, since the same fat can be used again and again provided care is taken to keep it in good condition. After use and when it has cooled a little it should be run through a strainer into a jar.

To Clarify Fat. Fat that has become brown and discoloured can be clarified by putting it into a saucepan and covering it with water. Bring to the boil, stir in a pinch of bicarbonate of soda and then let it cool. When cold the fat will have risen and formed a cake on the top. Lift it off, scrape away any sediment on

Left-overs can always be curried, but it is not wise to give guests curry unless you are sure they like it

the underside, and, after wiping the fat, put aside for future use.

To run down fat. Any scraps of fat from beef, mutton, pork or veal can be used. Remove any skin, flesh or discoloured parts, then cut the fat into little pieces, put into a strong saucepan and cover with cold water. Allow a level dessertspoonful of salt to a pound of fat, bring slowly to the boil and skim. Simmer, uncovered, for several hours, stirring frequently, till the liquid left is a clear yellow. Let it cool and then strain through a cloth. When set it can be used for all frying purposes.

Grilling is undoubtedly one of the most delicious ways of serving meat, and it is also a very quick method. For this reason it is only suitable for the best thin cuts such as fillets of beef, steaks, or for kidneys, sausages, bacon, etc. First light your griller so that it will be red-hot when you want it. Next grease and warm the grid. Spread the food to be cooked with butter, on both sides, or let it stand in some olive-oil on a plate for a few minutes. Then season it, put it on the warm greased grid and let it sizzle gently till one side is cooked. Turn it with two knives, and cook the other side, basting it with the running fat. Do not use a fork for turning as the juices will then ooze out.

Roasting (or Baking). Put the joint on a

rack in a baking tin, with the fat side upwards. Stand this tin in another tin and put a little water in the lower one, filling it up when necessary. The steam from the water not only helps to keep the joint moist and prevent burning, but you will find the joint does not shrink so much as when it is put in dry. Cover the meat with greased paper; this prevents it from getting scorched and also helps to keep the oven cleaner.

If the joint is rather lean put some pieces of dripping on the top or any trimmings of fat. The oven should be very hot for the first 10 minutes; then the heat should be reduced until you have a moderate oven. Allow roughly 20 minutes for each pound of meat and 20 minutes over for beef and mutton; veal and pork require slightly longer, say 25 minutes for each pound and 25 minutes over. Baste frequently.

Remember that a joint cooked quickly, though it may save a little fuel, will not go as far as a slower-cooked joint, and is not really economical. When the meat shrinks away from the bone it is a sure sign that it has been overcooked.

Steaming is a lengthy process, especially where a big joint is concerned, but it is a very tasty one, and far more of the flavour of the meat is retained than when it is boiled.

Stewing is often the busy housewife's refuge when she has little time to spare, as once a stew is prepared it needs little attention beyond an occasional stir and an eye kept to see that it simmers and does not boil fast if cooked on the hot plate. It has the advantage, too, that it can be cooked in the oven if that happens to be convenient.

How to Make Gravy

Drain off the fat from the baking tin, leaving only the sediment, and put the tin over a low heat, add a little pepper and salt and some stock and stir well. Serve it clear with beef and mutton.

To thicken the gravy leave a tablespoonful of the liquid fat with the sediment, stir in a tablespoonful of flour and cook for 5 minutes till brown, stirring frequently, then add stock and seasoning, together with a little browning if liked.

How to Boil Rice for Curries

Wash the rice in fresh lots of water until as you drain the water off it is quite clear, then put into plenty of salted boiling water and cook till soft but not mushy. Stir frequently with a fork so that the grains are kept moving about. Drain into a colander (keeping the liquid for soups, sauces, etc.), pour tepid water over to separate the grains and spread them out on a sheet of kitchen paper. Put into a cool oven to dry off and re-heat. It is important to remember that rice increases to three times its weight when cooked.

BEEF

Beef Olives (4-5 people)

1 lb. lean beefsteak cut very thin in small slices.	1 oz. butter or dripping.
	Pepper and salt.
½ pint stock.	1 oz. flour.
1 dessertspoonful mushroom ketchup.	1 onion.
	Veal stuffing.

Make some veal stuffing. Put the slices of meat on a board and spread them with stuffing, keeping it well away from the edges. Roll them and put them four deep on a skewer or tie each up with cotton. Shake a little flour over them. Melt the butter and when hot fry the sliced onion till brown. Put the onion into a casserole and then fry the meat and add it to the onion.

Make some thick gravy in the frying-pan with the flour and the stock, season, and strain it over the olives. Put the casserole either in a moderate oven or over a slow flame for 1 hour or till the meat is tender. Add the mushroom ketchup just before serving.

Garnish with shredded cooked carrot and turnip in little heaps, sprinkling a little chopped parsley over them.

NOTE. Cold, underdone beef can also be made into olives, but in this case fry the onions only. Add the olives to the gravy and cook over a low heat or in the oven for 30 minutes. Then serve.

Beef Stew (4-5 people)

1 lb. shin of beef.	1 level tablespoonful flour.
Onion, carrot and turnip.	
¾ pint of water or brown stock.	Pinch of herbs if desired.
Fat for frying.	Seasoned flour.

Wipe the meat, cut it into small pieces, roll it in seasoned flour and fry quickly in a saucepan or casserole in just enough fat to prevent it burning. Then add the water or stock, the cut-up vegetables, bring it to the boil and simmer very gently for about 2 hours.

Make a smooth paste with the flour and a little water and add, stirring well, just before the stew is done. Let it simmer gently for 5 minutes.

If dumplings are served with it, give them 20 minutes' cooking and then remove them, putting them on a hot plate, while you stir in the flour. Then replace them if the stew is to be served in a casserole, or put them with the stew on a hot dish.

NOTE. Instead of shin of beef, oxtail, ox-cheek or thick flank can be used.

Boiled Beef and Dumplings

Silverside of beef. Carrots, turnips and onions.

Weigh the meat and rinse it well. Allow 20 minutes' for each pound and 20 minutes over. Put the meat into enough warm water to cover it and bring it slowly to the boil. Then skim. Simmer it very gently. The sliced vegetables should be added half an hour before the end. Suet dumplings should also be added, and these will take 20 minutes to cook.

Serve a little of the liquid in a sauceboat.

NOTE. Thick flank, round of beef, brisket or aitchbone can also be boiled in this way.

Braised Beef

2 lb. rib of beef (boned, rolled and skewered).	Onion, carrot, turnip, parsnip, celery, as
2 oz. butter or dripping.	desired.
About 1 gill water.	Pepper and salt.

Wipe the meat and tie it into shape. Melt the fat in a deep casserole or saucepan and put in the vegetables cut up, and the seasoning. When they are hot add the meat and the water. Put a piece of greased paper under the lid, and cook in a slow oven for at least 2 hours.

NOTE. Round of beef, lean and meaty shin of beef, thick flank, oxcheek or oxtail can be used instead.

Grilled Fillets of Beef (Tournedos) (or Steak)

Cut the meat into neat rounds $\frac{1}{2}$ in. thick, and grill for about 8 minutes, using plenty of butter or olive-oil and turning once.

The fillets can be served on a bed of mashed

Cut the meat into squares	*Colour quickly on both sides*	*Add stock or water, then beer*

Carbonnade of Beef

$1\frac{1}{2}$ lb. braising beef.	1 clove of garlic.
$\frac{1}{2}$ pint beer.	Dripping.
$\frac{1}{2}$ oz. flour.	6 oz. onions.
Bouquet garni—bayleaf, parsley, thyme.	

Cut the meat into large squares. Heat dripping in a heavy casserole or saucepan. Add the meat and colour quickly on both sides. Cut onions in thin slices, add to the pan and allow to brown well. Pour off a little of the fat, dust with the flour and add garlic creamed with a little salt. Add $\frac{1}{2}$ pint hot water and the beer to the beef, add the bouquet and season with salt, pepper, nutmeg, a little sugar and a dash of vinegar. Cover closely and cook gently in the oven for about $1\frac{1}{2}$ hours.

potatoes, or any green vegetable, and garnished with a little shredded horseradish on each fillet, or a pat of maître d'hôtel butter. Serve with a good gravy.

A more elaborate way to serve them is to fry some croûtes of bread just the size of the fillets, then put a slice of grilled tomato on the croûtes, next the fillets and finish off with a mushroom on top and a little butter. You can add a scrape of horseradish to this if you like.

Filet à Cheval is made by putting a poached egg on top of the fillet, and mashed potato around it.

When grilling chops or steak allow a little longer. Serve on a bed of vegetables or potatoes and garnish with grilled tomatoes.

The steak can be slashed across the top three or four times and a piece of butter put into each slash.

It is a good thing to beat steak with a rolling-pin or meat chopper before grilling.

Jugged Beef (7-8 people)

2 lb. thick lean beef-steak.	Rind of half a lemon.	Tied
2 rashers of fat bacon.	4 cloves.	up in a
1 large onion.	Bay-leaf.	muslin
1 pint stock or water.	Bunch of	bag.
2 oz. butter or dripping.	herbs.	
1 carrot.	1 tablespoonful red-	
Port, claret or marsala.	currant jelly.	
2 tablespoonsful flour.	Forcemeat balls.	

Cut up the meat into 1-in. cubes and flour; also cut up the bacon. Melt the butter or dripping in a frying-pan and when hot fry the sliced onion till brown. Put it into a deep casserole or saucepan. Then fry the meat and bacon till brown, and add them to the casserole with the stock, the carrot (cut in half), and the lemon rind, cloves, etc., tied up in a muslin bag.

Make some thick gravy in the frying-pan with a little stock or water and flour and strain it into the casserole. Simmer gently for 2 hours, or it can be put into a moderate oven.

Make some forcemeat balls, roll them in breadcrumbs and fry them till brown; then put them into the casserole 10 minutes before you are going to dish up.

Just before serving, remove the carrot and the herbs, and add the wine as desired and a tablespoonful of red-currant jelly.

Serve with red-currant jelly.

Sea Pie

Slices of either beef or mutton.	Salt and pepper. Suet crust.
Slices of carrots, turnips, onions.	Water to cover.

Well flour the meat and cut the vegetables into slices. Put into a saucepan with enough water just to cover, season and let it come slowly to the boil.

Make a suet crust not quite so big round as the saucepan, put it on top of the meat and steam for 2 hours.

When cooked take off the crust, arrange the meat and vegetables on a dish, put on the crust and decorate the top with a few slices of carrot.

Steak en Casserole (4-5 people)

1 lb. lean beefsteak.	1 tablespoonful flour.
Large onion.	¾ pint stock or water.
Carrot.	Seasoning.
Turnip.	1 oz. butter or
Small head of celery.	dripping.

Cut up the steak into fair-sized portions and dip it in the flour and seasoning. Heat the butter in a frying-pan, slice the onion and fry it quickly till brown. Remove and put it into a saucepan or casserole. Put the meat into the frying-pan and cook quickly till brown. Then place it on the top of the onion; slice the other vegetables and put them on the meat. Pour in the stock. Brown the flour in the remaining fat in the frying-pan, add enough water or stock to make it into a paste and cook till it thickens. Strain it into the saucepan or casserole and cook in a slow oven, or on the hot-plate for at least 1½ hours.

If water is used add a little Marmite or Oxo or Bovril to it.

Boiled macaroni cooked separately can be placed round the dish when serving.

A half teaspoonful of anchovy essence adds very much to the flavour of a stew, or a teaspoonful of paprika gives an appetising taste.

Vienna Steaks (3-4 people)

1 lb. lean beefsteak.	Very small pinch of spice.
1 rasher of bacon.	Pepper and salt.
Very small onion.	1 level tablespoonful
Egg or milk to bind.	flour.

Mince the beef, bacon and onion and mix with the spice, seasoning and enough egg or milk to bind. Make into small cakes about 1 in. thick, flour lightly and fry in a very little hot fat, browning quickly on both sides. Then cover over the pan and let it cook very slowly for a quarter of an hour.

Serve with thick brown gravy or tomato sauce, chip or cone potatoes, small tomatoes baked whole, and fried onions.

MUTTON, PORK AND VEAL

Boiled Mutton

Leg or middle neck can be boiled, and served with either caper or onion sauce.

Braised Shoulder of Mutton

Shoulder of mutton.   1 pint hot water.
Onion, carrot, parsnip,   Pepper and salt.
   turnip, celery.   Bunch of herbs.
1 tablespoonful flour.   2 oz. butter or dripping.

Have the bone removed from the meat. Wipe the meat and tie it into shape.

Melt the fat in a deep baking tin (or a very large casserole) and put in the cut-up vegetables, herbs, and pepper and salt. Cook for a few minutes. Put the mutton in a quick oven for 10 minutes and then place on the top of the vegetables, pour over the hot water and put a piece of greased paper over the meat. Cover over with another tin and let it cook in a slow oven for at least 3 hours, removing the lid for the last half-hour.

Take out the meat, strain off the gravy, and put the vegetables round the meat. Then thicken the gravy with the flour and serve separately.

Red-currant jelly should also be served with this dish, or cranberry sauce.

Haricot Mutton (4-5 people)

1 lb. best end of neck   1 onion.
   or middle neck.   1 small carrot.
1 oz. flour.   Pepper and salt.
1 oz. butter or dripping.   ¾ pint stock
2 oz. haricot beans.   (or water).

Put the beans (which should have been soaked overnight) into cold water and boil gently till soft. Keep them hot. Prepare the meat by cutting off the fat, and divide into small pieces. Melt the butter in a saucepan or casserole and fry the sliced onion till pale brown. Take it out and keep hot; then fry the meat and when brown remove. Put the flour in the pan, and brown it, then add the stock and seasoning and bring to the boil, skimming well. Put the meat and onion back, and the

sliced carrot, and let it simmer gently for 1½ hours.

To serve, put the meat on a hot dish, season the sauce and pour over it and add the beans either in small heaps or at either end. Sprinkle them with parsley. Garnish with any seasonable vegetables.

Hotpot (5-6 people)

1½ lb. best end or middle   2 sheep's kidneys.
   neck of mutton.   1 oz. flour.
1½ lb. potatoes. ·   Pepper and salt.
1 onion.   1 tablespoonful mush-
½ pint warm stock or   room ketchup.
   water.   1 oz. dripping.

Cut up the meat into neat pieces and brown in the hot dripping; then put them in a casserole, or any deep fireproof dish that has a lid, and sprinkle with pepper and salt. Brown the sliced onion in the dripping, add it to the casserole, and season. Next brown the cut-up kidneys and add them, seasoning them, and put half the potatoes cut into thick slices (the other half should be cut into quarters) on the top.

Make a thick gravy with the stock and flour in the frying-pan; add the ketchup and strain over the potatoes. Then add the potato quarters and put a few bits of dripping on top. Put on the lid and cook in a moderate oven for 2 hours, removing the lid for the last half-hour so that the potatoes may brown.

Serve in the dish in which it is cooked. Mushrooms may be added if desired.

Irish Stew (5-6 people)

1½ lb. middle neck or   1 lb. onions.
   scrag end of mutton.   About ½ pint water.
3 lb. potatoes.   Pepper and salt.

Wipe the meat and cut it up, and peel half the potatoes and the onions and cut up. Put first a layer of potatoes, then the meat, then the onions and lastly the rest of the potatoes, cut thick or left whole if small. Add the water and pepper and salt, and simmer very gently for 2 hours.

Goulash of Mutton

1-1½ lb. middle neck   1 oz. flour.
   of mutton.   A good ½ lb. onions.
1 level dessertspoonful   A bay-leaf.
   best paprika pepper.   Stock or potato
1 oz. dripping.   water.

Joint or cut up the meat, finely slice the onions. Heat a thick iron or aluminium casserole, put in the dripping, and when smoking add the meat and brown quickly.

Remove meat, add the onions and the paprika. Lower the heat and allow to soften a little for about 5 minutes. Draw aside, mix in the flour, add salt, the meat, bay-leaf and enough liquid to barely cover.

Shake pan gently until it comes to the boil. Cover and put into a slow oven, or keep on a very low top heat for about 1½-2 hours, according to the quality of the meat.

Just before serving, pour over 2 or 3 spoonfuls of sour cream, or Yoghourt, thinned with a very little top milk. Amount of paprika depends on taste. A teaspoonful of cayenne pepper can be added, too. If in a hurry, a tin of meat will make a quite tasty goulash.

Ragout of Mutton (5-6 people)

1½ lb. middle neck.	1 bay-leaf.
Onion, parsnip, turnip.	2 oz. dripping or butter.
1 pint water.	1 tablespoonful mush-
1 tablespoonful pearl	room ketchup or a
barley soaked over-	few mushrooms.
night.	Pepper and salt.

Wipe the meat and cut it up. Melt the dripping in a frying-pan and then brown the meat. Put it into a casserole. Cut the vegetables into dice and fry them. Put them in the casserole with the water, bay-leaf, pearl barley, pepper and salt, and ketchup or some mushrooms. Bring to simmering-point. Cover over with a well-fitting lid and cook in a slow oven for 2 hours, or on the hot-plate.

Mutton Boulangère

With a sharp knife make a few incisions near the bone of the joint of mutton and press a split clove of garlic into each. Finely slice four onions and eight potatoes. Prepare a *bouquet garni*. Butter a fireproof dish; arrange onions and potatoes, leaving a space in the middle. Put the meat in this with a few pieces of butter or dripping on top, moisten the potatoes with a little stock and roast in the oven, allowing 15-20 minutes per pound of meat. This dish should be baked in a steady, moderate oven. Remove the bouquet and serve with cauliflower polonaise. Cook the cauliflower, drain well, and arrange on a hot dish. Cook one tablespoonful breadcrumbs to a golden brown in 1 oz. of butter and spoon over the cauliflower. Garnish with chopped parsley.

Stuffed and Roasted Shoulder of Mutton

Take out the bone, wipe the meat well and season.

Make some veal stuffing and put it in the middle of the mutton. Then tie it into shape with a piece of string, or sew it up. Weigh the meat and roast in the usual way.

When about to serve, take off the string or remove stitches.

NOTE. Leg of mutton or breast can also be stuffed and roasted.

Boiled Ham

If very salt let it soak overnight. A lightly cured ham does not need quite so long. Then put it in a saucepan of warm water and bring it slowly to the boil, letting it simmer very gently till it is tender. Allow 25 minutes to the lb. and 25 minutes over. Test with a skewer or by seeing if the rind comes away easily. If overcooked the meat will shrink away from the bone.

If it is to be eaten hot, serve with amber or Cumberland sauce.

If it is to be eaten cold, leave it in the water in which it was cooked till cold. Then remove the rind. Breakfast crisps rolled with a rolling-pin and scattered over it can be used instead of the ordinary raspings.

Curried Sausage (4-5 people)

1 lb. sausages.	1 onion.
1 oz. butter.	Squeeze of lemon juice.
Curry powder to taste.	Salt.
½ oz. rice flour.	1 teaspoonful chopped
Breadcrumbs.	chutney.
Boiled rice.	1 pint stock.
1 apple.	

Skin the sausages and cut them in half, then roll them in breadcrumbs and fry till brown.

Melt the butter and when hot fry the onion and apple sliced; then add the rice flour, curry powder and salt, stirring well, and cook gently for 5 minutes. Add the stock slowly and bring to the boil. Put the sausages and chopped chutney in the sauce and re-heat, adding a squeeze of lemon juice right at the end.

Serve the sausages on a hot dish with the boiled rice round, and pour the sauce over them.

Mock Goose (3-4 people)

1 lb. sausages, skinned.	1 lb. mashed potatoes.
Onion.	Pepper and salt.
Sage.	

Put alternate layers of sausage and potatoes, seasoned with chopped onion, sage, pepper and salt. The sausages should be broken up with a fork and the potato smoothed down well. Finish with a layer of potatoes.

Bake in the oven till brown and serve with apple sauce.

Roast Pork (Stuffed)

Bone the pork. Make some sage-and-onion stuffing and place it on the meat. Roll the meat up and tie it firmly.

Serve with apple sauce.

Toad-in-the-Hole

Make an ordinary batter mixture and let it stand for at least half an hour.

Pour the batter in a greased baking tin and then put in the sausages. Bake in a moderate oven for 30 minutes.

Narrow slices of steak can be used instead of sausages.

Blanquette of Veal (3-4 people)

1 *lb. fillet of veal.*	1 *gill of stock.*
2 *oz. butter.*	2 *or 3 cloves.*
Pepper and salt.	*Button mushrooms*
1 *bay-leaf.*	*or small whole*
1 *tablespoonful flour.*	*tomatoes.*

Coat the fillet with flour. Melt the butter in a frying-pan and fry the veal till it is golden brown on both sides. Put the meat and the butter into a casserole, add the stock, cloves, bay-leaf and seasoning. Put on the lid and simmer for 1½ hours. Add the mushrooms or tomatoes a quarter of an hour before the end. Take out the meat and the mushrooms or tomatoes. Strain the liquor and pour it over the meat. If it is too thick add a little water and re-heat it.

Fricassée of Veal (3-4 people)

1 *lb. fillet of veal.*	*Pepper and salt.*
1 *onion sliced.*	1 *oz. butter.*
1 *yolk.*	1 *tablespoonful flour.*
6 *peppercorns.*	1 *gill milk.*
Pinch of dried herbs.	½ *pint water.*
Half a lemon.	

Cut the meat into neat pieces and put in a saucepan, with the warm water, and bring it to the boil. Add the herbs, onion, peppercorns, lemon peel and seasoning, and simmer very gently for about 1½ hours.

Appetising meat dishes served with cauliflower polonaise. Instead of serving the cooked cauliflower with a white sauce, cook one tablespoon of breadcrumbs to a golden brown in one ounce of butter and spoon over the cauliflower. Garnish with chopped parsley

Take up the veal, strain off the stock, and make it into a sauce with the butter and flour and a little milk. Bring it to the boil and let it cook for 5 minutes. Take it off the fire and stir in the beaten yolk and a teaspoonful of lemon juice.

Put the meat in the sauce and re-heat without boiling.

Garnish with rolls of bacon (grilled on a skewer) or grilled rashers, or with fried diamonds or crescents of bread.

Ragout of Veal (or Rabbit) (3-4 people)

1 *lb. lean meat (breast*	1 *oz. butter.*
or fillet) or a small	½ *pint stock.*
rabbit.	*Salt and pepper.*
1 *tablespoonful flour.*	1 *bay-leaf.*
Pinch of mixed spice.	*Thyme.*
1 *large onion.*	*Parsley.*
Garlic, if desired.	*Grate of nutmeg.*
4 *or 5 carrots.*	

Wipe the meat and cut it into neat pieces.

Melt the butter and fry the meat till it is a golden brown, being careful it does not burn.

Beef Duchesse. It is surprising how an attractive way of serving a dish gives it ' just that little extra the others haven't got.' This is as tasty as it looks, arranged with snippets of toast and surrounded by creamy mashed potatoes

Stuffed Breast of Veal

Boned breast of veal.
Lemon juice.
Veal stuffing.
Pepper and salt.

Put the meat flat on a board, the skin side underneath, and rub over with a little lemon juice. Then season. Put the stuffing over it, roll it up, skewer and tie it securely. Trim the ends if necessary. Put it in a baking tin and roast.

NOTE. Or use fillet of veal or loin, boned.

Veal Cutlets (3-4 people)

1 *lb. fillet of veal.*	*Mashed potato.*
1 *egg.*	½ *pint mushroom*
Breadcrumbs.	*sauce.*
A little lemon juice	2 *oz. dripping.*
and rind.	*Rolls of bacon.*
Chopped parsley.	*Pepper and salt.*

Cut the veal into neat rounds or ovals, and if necessary beat them till they are a good shape. Squeeze a little lemon juice over them.

Break the egg on a plate, beat it and add the chopped parsley, seasoning, lemon juice and rind. Dip the cutlets into this mixture and then roll them in the breadcrumbs, pressing them on well. Let the cutlets stand for a time till they are dry.

Meanwhile make the sauce and mash up some freshly cooked potatoes.

Put a few small rolls of thin slices of bacon on a skewer and cook them in the oven while the cutlets are frying.

Melt the dripping in a frying-pan. When hot fry the cutlets till they are brown on both sides. Cook them fairly slowly and give them between 10 to 12 minutes. Drain well.

To serve, pile them on a heap of mashed

Take it out of the saucepan and keep hot. Make a thick sauce with the flour and stock. Add salt, pepper, mixed spice, herbs, onion (whole), garlic, carrots cut in rounds, and a grate of nutmeg. Put the meat back in the saucepan and cook slowly for 1½ hours, keeping the lid on.

Take out the onion, put the meat on a hot dish with the carrots, and strain the sauce over it.

Stewed Knuckle of Veal (4-5 people)

2 *or* 3 *lb. knuckle of*	1 *turnip.*
veal.	*Hot water.*
¼ *lb. rice.*	1 *teaspoonful chopped*
2 *onions.*	*parsley.*
1 *carrot.*	*Pepper and salt.*
Squeeze of lemon juice.	*Small dumplings.*

Wipe the meat with a damp cloth. Put it into a saucepan with enough hot water to cover, bring it to the boil and skim. Put in the chopped onions, carrot and turnip, and seasoning, and simmer slowly for 1½ hours. Put in the rice (which should be well washed) for the last half-hour of the cooking.

Small dumplings should be added during the last 10 minutes.

Add a squeeze of lemon juice right at the end.

Put the meat on a hot dish, with the rice and vegetables round, and sprinkle with chopped parsley, or serve with parsley sauce.

potatoes, and garnish with slices of lemon, and the rolls of bacon. Serve the sauce separately.

If preferred, serve the cutlets on a bed of green peas or spinach, with a border of grilled half-tomatoes.

Veal in Tomato Sauce (Italian Recipe)
(3-4 people)

1 *lb. lean veal.*	2 *oz. sausage or*
1 *oz. butter or some*	*chopped ham.*
olive-oil.	*Salt and pepper.*
1 *onion.*	3 *tablespoonsful*
1 *small carrot.*	*tomato purée.*
Stick of celery.	*Flour.*

Put the butter or oil into a saucepan and add the meat (whole), the vegetables cut up, the sausage cut in small pieces, and the seasoning. Cook them till brown, being careful they do not burn.

Then pour in 3 tablespoonsful of tomato purée, and sprinkle in a little flour. Stir in some hot water now and again, and simmer the mixture gently till the veal is tender.

The veal should be served separately with potatoes or other vegetables, the sauce being served with macaroni and grated Parmesan cheese as a first course.

TASTY DISHES

Beef Duchesse

1 *lb. minced raw beef.*	1 *teacupful chopped*
2 *oz. margarine.*	*mushrooms.*
1 *lemon.*	*Toast 'corners.'*
1 *rounded tablespoon-*	1 *lb. cooked, mashed*
ful flour.	*potatoes.*
Pepper and salt.	1 *egg yolk.*
2 *teacupsful stock (or*	1 *tablespoonful top*
1 *teacupful stock and*	*milk cream.*
1 *teacupful tomato*	*Nutmeg.*
purée).	

Put meat into pan with melted margarine and stir with fork until all redness has disappeared. Stir in lemon juice and flour, mixing until smooth, add stock, etc., and cook for several minutes. Season well with pepper and salt and stir in chopped mushrooms. Transfer to casserole and cover. Bake in moderately slow oven for about an hour. Remove lid. Cream potatoes with yolk of egg and add top of milk cream with seasoning to taste. Add a little grated nutmeg, if liked, mixing well. Pipe potato mixture round contents of casserole. Slip under hot grill—or return to hot oven—

and brown lightly. Serve with corners of toast and garnish with watercress or parsley.

Calves' Liver (Fried)

Wash and dry the liver, and cut into slices. Remove the rinds from a few rashers of bacon and fry with the rashers. Keep the bacon hot while you fry the liver in the bacon fat for 10-15 minutes, according to the thickness of the slices. Put on a hot dish with the rashers on top. Brown a little flour in the fat, add water and cook for 5 minutes, then season well and pour round the liver. This can be served with fried onions.

Calves' Sweetbread (Baked)

Put in warm salted water for half an hour. Take out and drop into fast-boiling salted water for 2 minutes. Take them out and dry well. Dip them in egg and breadcrumbs, or flour them. Put some fat bacon on top, cover them with a piece of greased paper and bake them in a slow oven for 30 minutes, or according to size.

NOTE. Ox sweetbread can also be baked, and also lamb's, but lamb sweetbread takes less time to cook.

Calves' Sweetbread (Braised)

Clean the sweetbread as above. Slice an onion and a carrot and put them in a saucepan. Put the sweetbread on the onion and carrot, with a little pepper and salt, and a gill of milk. Put a piece of greased paper under the lid and simmer very slowly for 40 minutes. Take out the sweetbread and put on a warm dish.

Thicken the liquor with a little cornflour and let it simmer for 5 minutes, and put in some button mushrooms which have been cooked separately in a little stock. Take out the mushrooms and put them round the sweetbread. Remove the onion and carrot. At the last moment add a little cream and a beaten yolk to the sauce and stir well, and then a little chopped parsley. Pour the sauce over the sweetbread and serve.

Kidneys (Grilled)

Put the kidneys into very hot water for 2 or 3 minutes, then drop them into cold water to cool. This prevents them from curling up when being cooked. Remove the skin, almost cut them through and lay open. Brush them over with melted butter, season them and grill.

Serve each on a croûton of bread with a small pat of maître d'hôtel butter, closing the kidney on the butter. Sprinkle a little chopped parsley over them.

They can also be served with grilled tomatoes, bacon, or flat mushrooms on the bread, and the kidney on top.

Stuffed Heart (Sheep's or Lamb's)

Soak the heart in warm salted water till thoroughly clean. Then take away the pipes from the top and cut through the division in the middle. Stuff with veal stuffing. Tie a piece of greased paper over the stuffing, and bake in a very slow oven, either in a casserole with the lid on, or in a covered-over baking tin, for 1 to 1¼ hours. Put plenty of dripping over the heart and baste occasionally.

Serve with red-currant jelly.

NOTE. Ox heart can also be done in the same way, but takes 2 hours. It should be partly steamed first to get the best results.

Tripe and Onions (4-5 people)

1 *lb. dressed tripe.*	1 *tablespoonful flour.*
2 *onions.*	1 *pint milk (or milk*
1 *gill milk.*	*and water).*
Chopped parsley.	*Pepper and salt.*
1 *oz. butter.*	

Wash the tripe well. Put into cold water and bring to the boil, drain and cut into neat pieces. Put in a saucepan with the pint of milk and simmer for 1½ hours, adding the onions, sliced, for the last half hour. Take out the tripe and keep it hot. Make the flour into a paste with the gill of milk, and add it to the liquor, stirring it well. Bring it to the boil, add the seasoning and butter and cook for 5 minutes. Pour the sauce over the tripe, and sprinkle a little chopped parsley over before serving.

Tripe with Bacon (4-5 people)

1 *lb. cooked tripe.*	*Milk to cover.*
4 *rashers of bacon.*	*Grated rind of half a lemon.*
1 *onion chopped.*	1 *gill of milk.*
Chopped parsley.	1 *dessertspoonful cornflour.*
Pepper and salt.	*Mashed potato.*

Cut the tripe into strips, and put a piece of bacon, some chopped onion, parsley, lemon rind and seasoning on each. Roll up and tie them firmly. Put them in a saucepan with enough cold milk just to cover, bring to the boil and simmer gently for 20 minutes. Take out the tripe and keep it hot. Make a sauce with the liquor and the cornflour made into a paste with the milk. Let it simmer gently for five minutes.

Put the mashed potato on a dish, arrange the rolls on it and pour over the sauce. Sprinkle chopped parsley over and serve.

POULTRY AND GAME

It is very important when choosing poultry to be able to tell whether a bird is young or not, as the method of cooking which would be excellent for, say, a young chicken might be quite inadequate in the case of an older bird, whereas if it had been properly cooked it would have been quite satisfactory.

Fowls when young should have soft, rather moist feet, a smooth skin, and the cartilage at the end of the breastbone should be soft. When older their feet are hard and dry, and the end of the breastbone is stiff.

Ducks should be soft and white. When young they have yellow feet and bills, which tend to get darker as they grow older.

Goose should always be eaten young, as it is not suitable for table use when over a year old.

Turkeys should have white flesh, pliable cartilage at the end of the breastbone, and the wattles should be bright red. Hens are best for boiling, and cocks for roasting.

Pigeons. Tame pigeons are supposed to be tastier than wild ones. They should be cooked at once, whereas wood-pigeons can be hung for a day or two. The legs of young pigeons are pinkish.

Poultry should be eaten fresh.

Game birds are usually sold unplucked, and it is therefore not so easy to judge of their condition. They should have soft feet and smooth, pliable legs. If young, the feathers under the wing and on the breast should be soft and downy. The breast should feel hard and plump.

The time for which game should be hung varies according to individual fancy, what is high for some taste being not nearly enough so for others. The weather must, of course, be taken into consideration, muggy weather being bad for keeping. If the weather is cold and the birds are freshly shot, a night in a warm kitchen will bring them to a fit stage for cooking. They should always be hung unplucked and undrawn.

Hares and Rabbits. Hares should always be allowed to hang (not paunched) for at least

a week, or even longer if the weather is not too mild.

Tame rabbits have a more delicate flavour than wild ones, and take a shorter time to cook. Many people, however, prefer the stronger flavour of wild ones. The flesh should be quite stiff without any discoloration. If young, the teeth are small and white and the claws long and pointed. In an older rabbit the teeth are long and yellow and the claws round and rough. They should be used fresh.

Generally speaking, birds are sent prepared ready for table, or, if one should have a present of game, it is a simple matter to get one's fishmonger to prepare them for one for a very small charge.

Chicken en Casserole (5-6 people)

1 *chicken.*	1 *tablespoonful flour.*
2½ *pints of water.*	1 *or 2 hard-boiled eggs*
3 *rashers of bacon.*	*broken up.*
1 *lb. raw sausage*	*Pinch of dried thyme.*
meat.	*Boiled rice.*
Pepper and salt.	*Breadcrumbs.*
1 *oz. butter.*	1 *or 2 small onions.*

Joint a fowl and cook it in 2½ pints of water on a slow fire for about 2 hours, until it is quite tender and easily separated from the bone. Line a 3-pint casserole with well-boiled rice. Put in the joints of chicken cut into small pieces. Between these pieces put in the rashers of bacon cut up small and fried, the sausage meat in bits; 1 or 2 hard-boiled eggs cut up, and the onion, which can be omitted, to suit the taste.

Thicken the stock, which should measure 1 to 1½ pints, with the flour, season and add a tiny pinch of dried thyme. (2 teaspoonsful of paprika can be added if liked.) Strain into the casserole and bake for 1 hour.

Take off the lid of the casserole and put some browned breadcrumbs, and a few dabs of butter on the top, and return to the oven without the lid for 5 minutes or so. Then serve. Serve with herb or bacon dumplings. Add a little chopped bacon to the dumplings, if desired, and use fewer herbs.

Herb Dumplings

2 *oz. flour.*	*Seasoning.*
2 *oz. chopped suet or*	2 *oz. fresh bread-*
ham or melted bacon	*crumbs.*
fat.	*Fat.*

Mix altogether and add chopped herbs. Moisten with a little cold water and make a firm dough or, if you like the dumplings rich, beaten egg instead of water.

Make balls the size of a walnut and add to the pot. The herbs should be a mixture of a leaf or two of sorrel, ordinary wood sorrel, the same of spinach, a few young nettle tops, parsley—a good handful in all. Lemon thyme is a good substitute for sorrel.

Fricassee of Chicken (4-5 people)

A young chicken.	2 *oz. butter.*
1 *onion.*	1 *dessertspoonful corn-*
1 *yolk.*	*flour.*
6 *peppercorns* ⎫ *in a*	1 *pint white stock or*
Pinch of dried ⎬ *bag.*	*milk and water.*
herbs ⎭	*A squeeze of lemon*
Pepper and salt.	*juice.*

Cut the chicken up and remove as much of the skin as possible. Put it in a saucepan with the stock, onion, herbs and peppercorns, and seasoning, and let it simmer very gently for three-quarters of an hour. Remove the chicken and keep it hot, and strain off the liquor. Put the stock back into the pan, make a paste with the cornflour and a little milk, and add it to the stock, stirring all the time. Bring it to the boil and let it simmer for 5 minutes. Remove it from the fire and add the beaten yolk, butter and a squeeze of lemon juice. Re-heat without boiling.

Pour the sauce over the chicken, and serve with grilled rolls of bacon, or decorate with slices of lemon. If liked, fried bread cut into fancy shapes can be served with it.

NOTE. If cooked chicken is used, simmer the stock, onion, herbs and peppercorns, and seasoning together for about 20 minutes, then strain the liquor and make the sauce. Add the chicken and re-heat without letting it boil.

Chicken and Egg Cocottes (*illus. page 445*)

¼ *lb. mushrooms.*	*Salt and pepper.*
½ *oz. margarine.*	2 *hard-boiled eggs.*
6 *oz. cooked chicken.*	*Lemon juice.*
1 *small tin cream of*	*Chopped parsley.*
chicken soup.	

Fry half the peeled mushrooms gently in margarine, season with pepper and salt. Add chicken, cut in small pieces, and chopped mushrooms to the soup. Heat till simmering. Thin, if necessary, with a little milk, and season. Add 1½ quartered eggs. Simmer for about 10 minutes. Flavour to taste with lemon juice. Pour into small fireproof dishes. Top

Illustration: Easter Chicken, Sole Superbe, Fish and Spinach Pancakes.

with the rest of the cooked mushrooms, sliced egg and parsley.

Chicken and Egg Risotto (*illus. page 445*)

1 teacupful rice.
1 oz. butter.
1 chopped onion.
Pinch saffron.
6-8 oz. cooked chicken.

½ pint stock.
2 dessertspoonsful of tomato purée.
3 dessertspoonsful grated cheese.

Wash and drain rice. Melt butter in thick stewpan. Add chopped onion and brown slightly. Stir in rice and cook slowly for about 10 minutes till lightly coloured. Add salt, pepper, saffron and stock. Cover pan and simmer gently for about 10 minutes. Stir in tomato purée and chopped chicken and continue cooking until rice is tender. Stir in cheese just before serving. Add hot, quartered hard-boiled eggs. Arrange a border of rice on a hot dish or in small dishes and pile chicken mixture in the centre.

Easter Chicken à la Marie (*illus. page 446*)

2 spring chickens (1¼ lb. each approx.).
8 chicken quenelles.

¼ lb. mushrooms.
6 stuffed pimentos.

The Chickens. Cover the breasts of the chickens with margarine or lard and roast them slowly for about ¾ of an hour. Serve with the following:

Chicken Quenelles:

1 spring chicken.
¼ pint milk.
1 small onion.
A few mushroom stalks.
4 oz. margarine.
1 oz. flour.

1 egg.
A little top milk (1 tablespoonful).
1 teaspoonful lemon juice.
Salt and pepper.

Cut the chicken meat from the carcase. Mince meat finely. Simmer milk, onion and mushroom stalks for about 10 minutes. Strain. Melt 1 oz. of the margarine, add flour and cook slowly for 5 minutes. Add flavoured milk and stir until boiling. Simmer for about 3 minutes. Add minced chicken, slightly beaten egg, top milk, seasoning, lemon juice and mix together.

Heat the rest of the margarine in a thick frying-pan until a faint smoke is visible. Shape chicken-meat mixture into ovals, using 2 dessertspoonsful, and drop into the fat. Fry gently for about 3-4 minutes on each side until firm and lightly browned. Lift on to grease-proof paper and keep hot.

Mushrooms. Fry about ¼ lb. chopped mushrooms gently in a little margarine.

Stuffed Pimentos:

½-¾ lb. small pimentos.
2 oz. chopped onion.
½ lb. sausage meat.
Salt and pepper.

1 oz. mushrooms.
1½ gills chicken stock.

Scoop seed from centre of pimentos. Melt margarine in a thick frying-pan. Add finely chopped onion and brown slightly. Add sausage meat and chopped mushrooms and fry gently together. Stir in half chicken stock, add seasoning and cover the pan. Stuff the mixture into pimentos. Stand them upright, packed closely in a pie-dish or casserole. Add rest of the chicken stock to half cover. Cover the dish with a lid or double greaseproof paper. Bake until tender.

To serve. Arrange chicken, with a row of quenelles and mushrooms in between, and decorate with stuffed pimentos and parsley.

Salmi of Pheasant (or any Cold Game)

Cut up the pheasant into neat pieces. Make some thick brown sauce with trimmings of the bird and some vegetables. Put the pieces of pheasant into the sauce and re-heat it without letting it boil. A few stewed prunes and a tablespoonful of sherry or marsala add greatly to the flavour. Serve with red-currant jelly.

Wild duck can be used instead.

Jugged Hare (10-12 people)

A hare.
Bacon rinds or bone.
Large onion.
1½ pints of water.
2 oz. butter or dripping.
1 carrot.
Port, claret or marsala.
1 tablespoonful red-currant jelly.

A stick of celery.
2 tablespoonsful flour.
Rind of half a lemon.
4 cloves.
Bay-leaf.
Bunch of herbs.
Veal stuffing.

tied up in a muslin bag.

Wash the hare well, cut it up, and flour the pieces. Melt the butter in a frying-pan, and when hot fry the sliced onion till brown. Put it into a deep casserole or saucepan. Then fry the meat till brown, add to the casserole with the carrot cut in half, the celery cut up, and the lemon rind, cloves, etc., tied up in a muslin bag. Put the bacon rinds last and add the water. Make some thick gravy in the frying-pan with a little stock or water and flour, and strain it into the casserole. Simmer gently for

2 hours on the hot-plate, or bake in a moderate oven.

Make some forcemeat balls, roll them in breadcrumbs and fry them till brown; then put them into the casserole 10 minutes before you are going to dish up.

Just before serving, remove the carrot, celery, bacon rinds and the herbs, and add the wine as desired and a tablespoonful of red-currant jelly.

Serve with red-currant jelly.

Poulet à l'Americaine (*illus. page 445*)

1 *young roasting chicken.*	1 *egg or* ¾ *oz. flour.*
2 *tablespoonsful flour.*	1-2 *teaspoonsful*
Salt and pepper.	*lemon juice.*
1 *egg and* ¼ *pint milk.*	2 *lb. green peas.*
¼ *pint chicken stock.*	3 *or* 4 *thin rashers of*
Breadcrumbs.	*bacon.*

Cut chicken in neat pieces or have it done at the butcher's. Remove the skin, coat in flour and season with salt and pepper. Brush with beaten egg and milk, then coat evenly with crumbs. Fry till golden brown in deep smoking-hot fat. Remove chicken and keep hot. Add stock and milk to pan. Heat to boiling point, add beaten egg and stir over low heat, but do not boil till egg thickens. Boil for about 3 minutes, stirring continuously. Flavour with lemon juice and season with salt and pepper. Arrange chicken on a dish and cover it with the sauce. Serve with green peas and crisp grilled bacon rolls. Sauce Hollandaise can be served with this dish, if preferred.

MEAT DISHES WITH PASTRY OR SUET CRUST

Beef or Mutton Patties (5-6 people)

Filling for Beef Patties:

6 *oz. fresh meat* (*minced*)
A little chopped kidney
Pepper and salt } *to be mixed together.*
Stock to moisten

Filling for Mutton Patties:

6 *oz. fresh mutton* (*cut very small*)
Teaspoonful chopped onion
Teaspoonful chopped parsley
Pinch of mixed herbs } *to be mixed together.*
Pepper and salt
Chopped mushroom
Stock to moisten

Make some rough puff or puff pastry and grease some patty pans.

Roll out the pastry about a quarter of an inch thick, and let it rest for 5 minutes to allow for shrinking.

Then cut out rounds to fit the patty pans, allowing two rounds for each. Put one into the bottom of each pan, and fill with meat, etc. Moisten the edges and put on the tops, pressing them firmly together. Nick up the edges with the back of a fork and make a hole in the centre. Decorate with small pastry leaves.

Bake the patties for about 45 minutes, lowering the heat after the pastry has risen well. Brush them over with beaten egg 10 minutes before they are to come out. Test with a skewer before removing them from the oven.

Chicken or Veal Patties (4-5 people)

Filling for Chicken Patties:

4 *oz. cooked chicken cut very fine*
1 *oz. ham or bacon cut very fine* } *pounded together.*
Squeeze of lemon juice
A little cream to moisten

Filling for Veal Patties:

4 *oz. cooked veal cut into small dice*
1 *oz. ham or bacon cut into small dice*
A little grated lemon rind } *well mixed together.*
Hard-boiled egg, if liked (*chopped*)
Pepper and salt
White stock

Make or buy some patty cases. Mix together either the chicken or veal filling, heat it and then pile it into the patty cases. Put on the lids and put the patties into the oven for 2 or 3 minutes to heat them through.

Cornish Pasty (3-4 people)

6 *oz. short pastry.*	*Small onion.*
4 *oz. uncooked beef.*	*Pepper and salt.*
4 *small potatoes.*	

Cut up the meat, potatoes and onion into small pieces and season. Make some short crust, roll it out and cut it into rounds about ⅛ in. thick. Put some meat, potato and onion in the centre of each round, moisten the edges, fold over and press the edges well together. Nick up the edges. Put them into a hot oven for 10 minutes, then lower the heat and cook for about 50 minutes.

If desired, one large pasty can be made instead of small ones.

NOTE. If cooked meat and potatoes are used, half an hour should be enough to cook the pasty.

Pork Pie (4-5 people)

¾ lb. lean pork.	Pinch of sage.
Salt and pepper.	½ lb. flour
2 tablespoonsful hot stock or water.	½ gill milk
Hard-boiled egg.	½ gill water
Egg to coat.	2 oz. lard
	Pinch of salt

Hot-water crust.

Cut up the meat in small pieces and season it.

Make some hot-water crust as follows: put the sieved flour and salt into a basin. Boil the lard and water and milk together, and pour it into the middle of the flour. Mix well with a knife. Knead the dough till it is smooth, and line a tin with it, leaving enough for the top. Fill the tin with the pork and hard-boiled egg cut in slices, and sprinkle in the sage. Pour in 2 tablespoonsful of hot water or stock. Moisten the edge of the pie and put on the cover, making a hole in the centre. Decorate with pastry leaves. Brush over the pie with yolk of egg and bake in a hot oven for 1½ hours.

Add some good stock flavoured with onion (if there are any bones, put them in a stewpan and let them simmer for this) while the pie is cooling.

NOTE. The most suitable tin for making pork pies is a collar tin, the sides of which open on a hinge kept in place by a skewer, thus enabling one to take out the pie very easily. Failing this, use a cake tin with a movable bottom.

Sausage and Bacon Pudding (5-6 people)

1 lb. sausages.	1 dessertspoonful flour.
3 rashers lean bacon.	White stock or water.
1 onion and 1 apple.	Pepper and salt.
Pinch of dried herbs.	½ lb. suet crust.

Grease a pudding basin and get ready a pudding cloth.

Cut up the sausages into short pieces, and roll the bacon.

Make some suet crust and roll it till it is large enough to line the basin, leaving enough to cover the top. Put in the sausages, bacon, thinly-sliced onion and apple, and dried herbs in layers, sprinkling a little flour and seasoning in between each. Fill the basin three parts full with stock or water. Moisten the edge of the suet crust and put on the top, pressing the edges well together. Put a piece of greased paper over it, then the pudding cloth and steam it over boiling water for 2½ to 3 hours.

Steak and Kidney Pie (5-6 people)

1 lb. rump or beef steak.	Flour.
1 kidney (calves' or sheep).	Seasoning.
1 gill water or stock.	8 oz. rough puff or short crust.

Wipe the meat, skin the kidney and cut into small pieces; then dip them into the flour and seasoning. Put the pieces into a pie-dish with a pie-funnel in the middle and add a gill of water or stock.

Make some rough puff or short crust and roll it out to the size of the pie-dish (it should be about ½ in. thick). Cut a strip wide enough to fit the edge of the dish; wet the edge and put the strip on. Then moisten the strip and put on the top. Trim round the edge and decorate as desired. Cut a hole in the centre, so that steam can escape, and decorate round the hole. Put a piece of greased paper over the pie, bake in a very hot oven till the pastry has risen (about 20 minutes), then lower the heat and cook slowly for about 2 hours, reducing the heat gradually all the time.

If beefsteak is used it is advisable to cook the meat partly first, simmering it very slowly, and then allow it to cool before putting on the pastry. Add the kidney just before you put the crust on, and cook the pie for 1 hour.

Beat up an egg and paint the surface of the pie about 10 minutes before you take it out of the oven, turning up the gas so that the crust will brown.

Before serving, add a little hot stock or water through a paper funnel into the pie funnel.

If the pie is to be served cold, add a very little gelatine to the liquid before putting it through the funnel. A layer of slices of hard-boiled egg between layers of meat adds to the richness.

USING UP THE COLD MEAT

Beef Croquettes

Cold beef (or veal or cold roast mutton).	Flour and egg and breadcrumbs.
Equal quantity of cold mashed potatoes.	Milk, egg or gravy to bind.
1 or 2 onions.	Chopped parsley.
Pepper and salt.	Fat for frying.

RAISED MEAT PIE

1. To make the hot-water crust pastry, sieve the flour and salt together. Melt the fat in a pan with the water, then pour on to the flour and mix thoroughly. Turn on to a board and roll while still warm. Divide the dough in half

2. Cut rounds for bottom and lid of pie from one half and a long strip for sides from the other. Arrange bottom and side pieces in tin. Keep lid in warm place or it will harden. Cut leaves and rose from left-over pastry

3. Put filling into pie and press down firmly. If the meat is tough simmer gently for 20–30 minutes first. Cover with lid. Add decorations; a hole in centre of rose and lid allows steam to escape. Brush with egg or milk

4. Cook for 1¼–1½ hours in centre of moderately hot oven—425° F. (Reg. 6). Allow to cool slightly before removing from tin. Do not add the jelly until quite cold. Dissolve gelatine in stock and when it begins to thicken pour through hole in lid, using paper funnel

5. Now your pie, complete with garnish of parsley or watercress, is ready to eat!

To make this pie you will need: 12 oz. flour, 1 level teaspoonful salt, 4 oz. cooking fat, ¼ pint water, 1¼ lb. raw or cooked meat (or sausage meat and chopped herbs), egg or milk to glaze, 1 good teaspoonful powdered gelatine, ¼ pint well-flavoured stock

Mince up the meat and add it to the mashed potatoes. Cut the onions into slices and fry till brown. Then add them to the mixture with a little chopped parsley and pepper and salt, and use enough egg, milk or gravy to make them into a firm dough. Shape them into rounds, ovals or rolls and sprinkle them well with flour, then egg-and-breadcrumb them. Fry in deep fat till brown, and serve with brown sauce.

Corned Beef Hash (5-6 people)

1 lb. tin of corned beef.   Milk or cream.
1½ lb. cold boiled potatoes.   Pepper and salt.

Mix the beef and potatoes, chopped small, well together, then season. Put the mixture into a hot buttered frying-pan, moisten with milk or cream, stir it well, then spread it evenly over the pan and let it cook very slowly over low heat for 40 to 45 minutes. (It is safer

A little left-over meat minced or some sausage meat with minced onion can provide a variety of dishes. Tomatoes, onions, cabbage, marrow can all be stuffed and served with colourful garnishings, peas, tomato-halves, pimento, red pepper

A savoury thick sauce is a good addition to such dishes

to use an asbestos mat if the pan is on a direct flame.) Then turn it and fold it on a hot dish. Garnish with parsley.

Ham Mousse (4-5 people)

½ lb. lean ham.
About ½ pint savoury stock.
2 small teaspoonsful powdered gelatine.
1 gill cream (unsweetened condensed milk can be used).
Pinch of cayenne pepper.

Put the ham through the mincer twice. Melt the gelatine in a little stock. Strain the rest of the stock on to the minced ham and add the seasoning. Pour in the gelatine and cream and whip together till smooth and frothy. Put the purée into a plain soufflé mould and smooth it down *very* lightly.

Garnish with aspic jelly.

If the mousse is to be turned out of the mould, add another teaspoonful of powdered gelatine, and put some slices of hard-boiled egg at the bottom of the mould. When turned out garnish with aspic jelly.

Chicken, pheasant or veal mousse can be made in the same way, garnished with green peas or baby carrots, and mayonnaise sauce served as a dressing.

Jombalayah (Meat) (3-4 people)

4 oz. Patna rice.
4 oz. cooked ham.
1 lettuce.
Cayenne pepper and salt.

Wash the rice and put it into a large pan of quickly boiling salted water. Boil till tender,

and dry well. Shake pan to separate grains.

Chop the ham into small bits, season it, and add it to the rice when cold.

Serve on lettuce leaves as cold as possible.

Curried Left-overs

Cold cooked mutton.
1 oz. margarine.
1 large onion.
1 large apple.
1 tablespoonful curry powder.
1 tablespoonful flour.
½-¾ pint gravy or potato water.
3 tomatoes.
1 tablespoonful mango chutney.
1 oz. sultanas (optional).

Fry the sliced onion and apple in the margarine until golden brown. Add the curry powder and flour and cook for a few minutes. Tip on the stock, bring to the boil, add seasoning and the tomatoes skinned (cut in four and the pips removed), the chutney and the sultanas and simmer gently for 20-30 minutes.

Add the sliced mutton and leave in the hot sauce (but do not cook) up to 40 minutes.

Savoury Cake (3-4 people)

1½ lb. boiled potatoes.
½ lb. minced mutton.
1½ oz. butter.
1 teaspoonful mushroom ketchup.
Salt and pepper.
1 egg.
½ pint stock.
½ oz. flour.
1 tablespoonful brown breadcrumbs.

Put the potatoes through a sieve. Add ½ oz. melted butter, salt, and yolk of egg and mix well.

Butter the inside of a deep cake tin.

Put in the breadcrumbs and cover the sides and bottom with potato, pressing it well in.

Brush over the inside and edge of potato lining with beaten white of egg and bake till a nice brown.

Turn out, then carefully turn over on to a dish so that the opening faces upwards. Keep hot.

Melt the remainder of the butter in a pan; add the flour and brown well.

Add stock, seasoning and ketchup and bring to the boil.

Add meat and let it get hot through; then pour it into the potato cake. Serve with gravy.

Savoury Mince (5-6 people)

1½ lb. cold mutton.	Pepper and salt.
½ oz. gelatine.	2 or 3 tomatoes.
Teacupful of water.	2 lb. potatoes.
¾ pint brown stock.	1 egg.
A few button mush-	1 oz. butter.
rooms.	Flour.

Mince the meat. Dissolve the gelatine in the warm water.

Put a few button mushrooms into the stock and let them cook till they are tender.

Boil down two or three tomatoes to a pulp in another saucepan, sieve and add the juice and the pulp to the stock. Add the mince and the dissolved gelatine and season with pepper and salt. Keep the saucepan on the side of the fire where it may keep hot without boiling.

Boil the potatoes, drain them and mash them well with a fork; whisk in the butter, the beaten egg, and add a sprinkling of flour. Beat the mixture well and arrange it as a border round a dish, and bake in a moderate oven. When golden brown remove from the oven, pour in the mince and serve.

Stuffed Marrow

If young and tender, the marrow need not be cooked before being stuffed. If fairly well grown, however, the marrow may require boiling first in salted water for about five minutes or so to tenderise it partially.

Stuffing:

1 breakfastcupful minced cooked meat.	Chopped herbs— 3 sprigs parsley, 1 sprig thyme and 3 leaves sage.
1 parboiled onion.	Seasoning.
1 breakfastcupful brown bread- crumbs.	Grated outer rind of piece lemon.
1 egg.	

Prepare the marrow by peeling and cutting a slice from one end. Scoop out seeds. According to age, par-cook, or use marrow raw. Mix minced meat with chopped onion, chopped herbs and breadcrumbs. Season to taste, add grated lemon rind and bind with egg. Put mixture inside marrow and replace slice. Tie in position with piece of tape, or wedge stuffed marrow in well-greased baking tin. Spread a little dripping over the marrow and bake in moderate oven for about an hour, basting now and again. Serve with a thick brown gravy.

Norfolk Stuffing. This is a mixture of mashed potatoes, chopped par-boiled onions, well seasoned with pepper and salt, with sprinkling of mixed herbs. Fill marrow and then bake as above.

Stuffed Cabbage

1 firm-hearted cabbage.	1 breakfastcupful cooked rice.
½ lb. sausage meat.	
2 rashers bacon, minced.	Pepper and salt. A pinch of mace.

Remove tough outer leaves from cabbage. Wash well in salted water. Put cabbage into boiling salted water for about 5 minutes or so. Drain well. Mix stuffing ingredients and spread a portion between each limp cabbage leaf. Press leaves together again to restore shape, tying with tape. Cut wedge of stump from centre. Fit stuffed cabbage into well-greased pudding basin, cover and steam for about 1½-2 hours.

Alternative treatment: Break away the largest leaves after par-cooking the cabbage. Place a spoonful of stuffing on each and roll up. Wedge these rolls firmly in casserole with stock to cover. Put on lid. Cook in moderate oven for about 40 minutes after contents of casserole commence cooking.

Stuffed Onions

Par-boil some large onions. Cut slice from each and remove centres, but leaving firm shell. Finely chop slices and centres of onions and mix with equal amount of grated cheese and breadcrumbs. Flavour with a little made mustard or tomato ketchup. Put mixture into onion cases, topping them well up. Sprinkle with baked crumbs, a further sprinkling of grated cheese and a nut of margarine. Bake in moderate oven until onions are tender. Hot green peas can be used instead of cheese.

Stuffed Tomatoes

Cut slice from each and scoop out centres. (Use large tomatoes.)

Meat Stuffing. Mix some minced cooked meat with a little cooked rice (or brown bread-crumbs), and season well. Moisten with sieved pulp from tomatoes. Pack mixture into tomato shells and sprinkle baked crumbs on top, adding knob of dripping or margarine. Bake in moderate oven until piping hot throughout.

Cheese and Egg Stuffing. Make a filling of lightly scrambled egg and grated cheese, adding seasoning to taste. Divide between tomato shells and replace slice from top. Make very hot throughout, and serve each on round of buttered toast.

STUFFINGS

Chestnut Stuffing

2 *lb. chestnuts parboiled.*	2 *oz. butter.*
Liver of turkey parboiled.	*Pepper and salt.*
Minced rasher of bacon.	

To parboil the chestnuts cut a slit in the skins and put them in boiling water for 20 minutes. Then put them in the oven to crisp the skins, when the chestnuts should come out easily.

Mince the chestnuts, liver and bacon. Add the butter, warmed, and the seasoning and mix well together. (Sufficient for medium-sized turkey.)

Sage and Onion

4 *onions.*	1 *oz. butter.*
Dessertspoonful powdered	*Egg to bind.*
sage or 6 leaves of fresh	*Pepper and salt.*
sage.	*Stock or water.*
4 *oz. breadcrumbs.*	

Peel the onions, chop them finely and simmer them in a little water or stock till tender. Add the sage (chopped or powdered), bread-crumbs, butter, pepper and salt, and stir it well. Then add enough beaten egg to bind. (Sufficient for 2 ducks or a goose.)

If preferred, this can be served in a sauce-boat instead of as a stuffing, in which case omit the egg and add instead enough stock to make it into a purée.

Veal Stuffing

4 *oz. breadcrumbs.*	1 *dessertspoonful chopped*
1 *oz. suet chopped.*	*parsley.*
Grated rind of	*Milk or egg to bind.*
½ *lemon.*	*Pinch of dried herbs.*
Pepper and salt.	*Chopped ham as desired.*

Put all the dry ingredients in a basin, mix them well and then add enough milk or beaten egg to make it into a stiff paste which will bind together very firmly. (Sufficient for 2 chickens or rabbits, or a turkey.)

(For fish, meat and poultry.)

Aspic Jelly

1½ *pints water.*	*A few peppercorns.*
¼ *pint mixed vinegar*	*Rind and juice of half*
(Tarragon and French	*a lemon.*
wine).	2½ *oz. sheet gelatine.*
Small carrot, onion and	*White of egg and egg*
turnip.	*shell.*
Small piece of celery.	

Cut the vegetables into small pieces. Put all the ingredients into a stewpan excepting the egg, and stir until the gelatine is dissolved. Add the shell and the white of egg and whisk well till it forms a thick scum on the top. Let it boil well to the top and then draw it to the side for 20 minutes.

Pour gently through a jelly bag or cloth.

Aspic Jelly (Quick Method)

1 *teaspoonful Marmite.*	*Seasoning.*
½ *pint water.*	1 *teaspoonful lemon*
2 *level teaspoonsful*	*juice.*
powdered gelatine.	1 *dessertspoonful*
	Tarragon vinegar.

Heat the water, add the Marmite, seasoning and gelatine, and stir well till the gelatine is dissolved, and the mixture clear. Then remove from the fire, add the lemon juice and vinegar and stir well.

VEGETABLES

Few people cook vegetables properly, boiling them far too long and with insufficient salt (where necessary), as if their attitude is 'It's only a vegetable!' instead of part of a good meal. Food experts say that we should be more sensible if, instead of serving up the vegetables and throwing away the water, we were to keep the water and let the vegetables go. In olden days when tea was worth almost its weight in gold there was a woman who had never seen tea-leaves before. She was completely nonplussed what to do with them, and finally decided they were a vegetable. She boiled them hard and long, drained them and threw away the precious liquid. This, according to experts, is just what is happening with vegetables all over England today, although we still eat what is left when we have boiled all the goodness out!

Never overcook vegetables. If you boil them, put them in the minimum of water covered over and do not let it go off the boil. Do not use soda to preserve the colour. A pinch of sugar does just as well, and does not make vegetables indigestible as soda is said to do, nor does it destroy their vitamins.

The quickest way to cook vegetables is, of course, by boiling, and if given the treatment suggested above they lose little of their value. Just before serving drain them well and put them back in the saucepan with a little butter or margarine (or into a warmed casserole in which they can be served) and put back on the stove for a few minutes. This makes a great difference to their taste and takes very little time.

Remember to keep the water in which vegetables have been boiled, as it is a useful addition to many soups. As a drink, it is an excellent complexion-clearer.

Artichokes (Globe)

Allow one for each person. Cut off the stalks close to the leaves and take off outer leaves; trim the points if discoloured. Wash well and soak in cold water for at least half an hour. Drop into salted boiling water to which a little lemon juice or vinegar has been added. Allow from 40 to 45 minutes. When cooked the leaves should come away easily. Be careful not to overcook, as they will then lose their colour. Drain well and serve with melted butter separately.

Globe artichokes can also be served cold with cream salad dressing.

Stuffed Cabbage (*Another method*)

1 *white cabbage.*	2 *oz. margarine or dripping.*
1 *small onion.*	2 *teaspoonsful chopped parsley.*
3 *tablespoonsful fresh bread-crumbs.*	1 *egg.*
	Seasoning.

Wash and trim the cabbage, cut off the stalk and remove the outside leaves. Line a basin with a clean cloth and arrange the leaves inside.

Cut the cabbage in four, slice finely, place in a saucepan with the margarine and cook slowly for about half an hour, stirring frequently with a wooden spoon. When the cabbage is soft and golden, add the parsley, chopped onion, and seasoning. Continue cooking for 10 minutes.

Add 2 tablespoonfuls of the breadcrumbs and the egg and place the mixture in the cabbage leaves. Tie up the cloth and cook in a pan of boiling salted water for 1 hour.

To serve, take out the 'pudding,' undo the string, place the cabbage on a hot dish and sprinkle the top with the remaining crumbs fried golden brown in a little extra margarine. Pour round a good tomato sauce and garnish with small browned onions and sauté potatoes.

Artichokes (Jerusalem)

Wash and peel. Cook whole, or if large cut into halves. Put them for a few minutes into cold water to which a little lemon juice or a few drops of vinegar have been added. Then drain and put them into boiling salted water with a squeeze of lemon juice or a little vinegar. Cook for 30-35 minutes. Drain as soon as they are tender, and serve with white or parsley sauce.

Asparagus

Cut off the lower parts of the stalks, wash well, and re-tie into a bunch, getting the stalks as even as possible. Stand the bundle upright in salted boiling water and cook till tender (25-40 minutes according to size). A sprig of fresh mint boiled in the water greatly improves the flavour. Drain well and serve either with melted butter or with Hollandaise sauce.

Asparagus can also be served cold with cream salad dressing.

Broad Beans

Use young beans if possible; shell and put at once into enough salted boiling water to cover, with a lump of sugar. Boil till soft (15-30 minutes according to age). Drain well and serve with parsley sauce.

Black butter sauce is very good served with beans at a later stage when it is necessary to skin them.

Beans (Haricot)

Soak the beans for 12 hours in cold water. Put them into cold water with 2 or 3 bacon rinds or a bacon bone and bring to the boil; then cook gently for 2 hours. Melt a little butter or margarine in a stewpan and put in the beans. Cook for 2 minutes. Scatter chopped parsley over. Serve.

Beetroot (Young)

As well as sliced for salads, these can be used as a hot vegetable. Serve with white, cheese or Mousseline sauce.

Carrots

Cook in boiling water—fairly quickly when young. Drain carefully. Toss in melted margarine and finely chopped parsley.

Cauliflower

Take off the older leaves, cut off stalk, and put into cold water for half an hour. Then place head downwards in salted boiling water and cook until it is soft; it should take about 20 minutes if young. Drain well and serve with white sauce.

Celery (Braised)

Wash and scrape the sticks and cut into 3-in. pieces. Dry well. Cook the sticks slowly in butter till they are tender and a nice brown. Remove the celery and keep hot. Then add either a very little water or some stock to the liquid, season and pour over the celery. They can be served with a cheese sauce, and on toast, if desired.

Cucumber (Boiled)

Peel and cut lengthways, removing seeds. Cook in boiling salted water until soft (about 10 minutes). Add butter, pepper and salt, and mash together. Brown stock or chicken stock can be used instead of water, if desired.

Cucumber (Fried)

Peel and wipe; then cut into small slices. Dry in a cloth, season and dip in egg and breadcrumbs. Fry till brown and drain.

Kohlrabi

Wash, peel and cut into 1-in. cubes, then cook in a little salted boiling water till tender (about 30 minutes). Drain and serve with white sauce.

Leeks (Boiled)

Cut off the roots and take off the outer covering. Wash very thoroughly under running water, splitting if necessary to get them clean. Put into salted boiling water and cook till tender (30-35 minutes). Drain well. Pour a little melted butter over and season with salt and pepper.

Leeks (Cooked in Milk)

Proceed as above but take them out of the boiling water after a few minutes and cook them slowly in milk. Using the milk as a foundation, make a sauce with a little butter and flour, and pour over the leeks. An excellent dish is made with a slice of ham on toast, leeks or braised celery and a cheese sauce over the whole, then browned under the grill.

Marrows

Don't wait until marrows become enormous before you cook them. Their flavour is best when they are small. In addition to boiling marrow, try it fried in rings or baked with a variety of stuffings.

Mushrooms (Fried)

Remove stalks, scrape and cut into pieces if large. Melt a little butter in a frying-pan. Dredge mushrooms with flour, and cook for 5 minutes, or till tender, with a little salt and pepper. Serve on toast, with a squeeze of lemon and a little pepper, if liked.

Parsnips

Wash and scrape. Cut lengthways or in slices and cook, until soft, in enough salted boiling water to cover them (45-50 minutes). Put into a casserole with a little butter or margarine and seasoning, and sauté them a light brown. Sprinkle chopped parsley over.

Radishes

One difficulty with growing radishes is that they all tend to mature at once and cannot be entirely used in salads. If you don't like their rather 'hot' flavour, then cook them as you would small turnips. Serve with a white sauce and you lose some of the 'bite.'

Spring Onions

Fry in hot oil or dripping until pale golden brown and crisp. Delicious as an accompaniment to any green vegetable.

Sea Kale

Wash very carefully, separating the stalks. Tie into bundles or break into small pieces and place in sufficient salted boiling water, with a squeeze of lemon juice, just to cover. Boil gently till soft (30-40 minutes). Serve with white sauce.

Spinach

Wash carefully in several different waters. Put into a pan with the moisture that clings to it, cover with a lid, and cook till tender, stirring occasionally to prevent burning (20-30 minutes). Then drain well, using a wooden spoon to get rid of all the moisture. Put a small piece of butter or margarine into the saucepan, or into a warmed casserole, and add the spinach chopped finely. Season well.

Turnips, Swedes

Quite delicious when young. Peel thinly and either cut into slices or cook whole. Add salt, lemon juice and a small pinch of sugar. Strain and toss in melted margarine, or sprinkle with grated cheese and paprika pepper. As these vegetables become older, mash them when cooked, adding margarine and a pinch of nutmeg.

Potatoes, New

These contain a useful amount of Vitamin C, so cook them as quickly as possible in boiling salted water, in a covered pan. Don't forget the sprig of mint. When cooked, drain and toss in melted margarine, then add chopped parsley or paprika pepper. New potatoes are delicious in a salad. They can also be semi-cooked and then fried to serve with fish.

Potato Croquettes

Mash some hot potatoes. When cool, season; add the white of an egg well beaten and a very little flour, just enough to make it hold together. Then make the mixture into balls, roll them in flour, coat with egg and breadcrumbs and fry in deep fat till a light brown. Drain well and serve.

This mixture can also be made into cottage loaves or little rolls and baked in a quick oven. In this case pour a little oiled butter over them before putting them in to bake.

Potatoes (Puffed)

Cut the potatoes into slices $\frac{1}{8}$ in. thick. Put them into deep fat, but remove them just *before* they brown. When all are cooked put them back in the basket, boil up the fat and plunge the basket into it. Repeat this process twice. Drain well and serve.

Curried Vegetables

1 *apple*.	$\frac{1}{2}$ *oz. rice flour*.
1 *onion*.	*Curry powder to taste*.
Squeeze of lemon juice.	*Salt*.
1 *teaspoonful chopped chutney*.	*Cold potatoes, carrots, turnips, green peas,*
$\frac{1}{2}$ *pint vegetable stock*.	*parsnips, etc., cut up*
1 *oz. butter*.	*small if necessary*.

Fry the onion and the apple, sliced, in the hot butter till brown. Add the rice flour, curry powder and salt, stirring well, and cook for 5 minutes. Stir in the stock, and bring to the boil.

Put the cold vegetables in, and add the chopped chutney and re-heat. Remove from the fire and add a squeeze of lemon juice right at the end.

Note. If uncooked vegetables are used, cook them all together first, and use the vegetable stock to make the curry. Then add the vegetables as above.

Macédoine of Vegetables

Cold carrots, green peas, turnips, ½ *pint velouté parsnips cut into small pieces.   sauce.*

Make a thin velouté sauce and warm the vegetables in it, or serve cold in mayonnaise sauce.

VEGETARIAN DISHES

Vegetarian dishes are a help in solving the problem of what to eat, whether one is a vegetarian or not.

Buck Rarebit

Make some Welsh rarebit and put a poached egg on top.

Savoury Spaghetti with Mushrooms

¼ *lb. mushrooms.*	1 *teaspoonful*
½ *pint milk.*	*paprika pepper*
½ *oz. margarine.*	*(or mustard).*
½ *oz. flour.*	*Salt.*
4 *oz. grated cheese.*	4 *oz. spaghetti.*

Stew mushrooms in a little milk. Prepare sauce with margarine, flour, milk and 4 tablespoonful of stock from mushrooms, adding paprika (or mustard), salt with flour and 2 tablespoonsful cheese when sauce is cooked. Cook spaghetti till tender in 1¾ pints stock seasoned with salt. Drain. Arrange spaghetti mixed with ½ oz. cheese on fireproof dish, hollowing centre. Place mushrooms in centre. Pour sauce over and sprinkle with rest of cheese. Brown quickly under the grill. This dish can also be served with hard-boiled eggs.

Cheese Pudding (3-4 people)

1 *oz. butter.*	½ *pint milk.*
2 *oz. breadcrumbs.*	2 *oz. grated cheese.*
A pinch of mustard and salt.	1 *egg.*

Heat the milk and stir in the butter, breadcrumbs, mustard and salt, and add the cheese and the beaten yolk of egg. Whip the white to a stiff froth and fold in lightly. Pour the mixture into a well-greased pie-dish and bake for 15-20 minutes.

Cheese Soufflé (4-6 people)

1 *oz. butter.*	2 *eggs.*
1 *gill milk.*	2 *oz. Parmesan*
1 *dessertspoonful corn flour.*	*cheese.*
	Cayenne and salt.

Make a paste with the cornflour and a little of the milk; heat the rest of the milk and pour in the paste, stirring well. Add the butter and seasoning. Cool slightly.

Separate the whites and the yolks. Beat in the yolks and the cheese. Whip the whites till they are very stiff and fold into the sauce. Put into a prepared buttered soufflé dish and bake in a moderate oven from 20-25 minutes till it has risen and is a light brown. Serve at once.

Galette au Nouilles (3-4 people)

6 *oz. macaroni.*	2 *oz. grated Gruyère*
2 *eggs.*	*cheese.*
A little minced ham.	2 *oz. butter.*

Cook the macaroni in boiling salted water for about ¼ hour. Then drain well and put it in a basin.

Add half the butter to the macaroni while it is hot, mix well and then add the Gruyère and the minced ham. Beat the eggs in a basin and add them to the macaroni.

Melt the rest of the butter in a saucepan. Put the above mixture in the saucepan and brown the galette on one side. Turn it on to a plate for a moment, put a small piece of butter in the saucepan, replace the galette and brown it on the other side. The galette can be served alone or with tomato sauce.

Gnocchi of Semolina (4-5 people)

1 *pint milk.*	1½ *oz. grated Parmesan*
6 *oz. semolina.*	*cheese.*
1½ *oz. butter.*	2 *eggs.*
Salt.	

Cook the semolina in the milk, take it off the fire, and add seasoning, half of the butter, half the cheese, and then the eggs. Mix well. Spread about an inch thick on a plate. When firm cut into almond-shaped pieces.

Pile the gnocchi on a dish, sprinkling the layers with the rest of the cheese and the butter in tiny pieces, but not putting any on the top layer. Lastly brown it in the oven and serve hot, either alone or as an accompaniment to meat. Gnocchi can be made without the cheese, lightly fried and eaten with jam.

Lentil Cutlets (6-7 people)

8 *oz. red lentils.*	2 *oz. mashed potatoes.*
½ *onion.*	1 *egg or milk to bind.*
2 *slices carrot.*	*Pinch of dried herbs.*
Stick of celery.	*Pepper and salt.*
Fat for frying.	*Flour, egg and breadcrumbs.*

Soak the lentils overnight. Cook them until soft, with the half onion, slices of carrot, and cut-up celery in just enough water to cover. Then put them through a sieve. Add the purée to the potatoes, dried herbs and seasoning. Add enough egg or milk to bind. Allow the mixture to cool. Then form into cutlets, flour and egg-and-breadcrumb them and fry in deep fat till brown.

Serve with brown, onion or tomato sauce.

Macaroni Cheese (3-4 people)

4 oz. macaroni.	1 oz. butter.
4 oz. grated cheese.	Teacupful of milk.
Pepper and salt.	

Put the macaroni into boiling salted water and cook till tender. Then drain it well and put it in a fireproof dish with layers of grated cheese, seasoning each layer.

Add a teacupful of milk, and sprinkle grated cheese on top. Put a few lumps of butter on this.

Bake in the oven till slightly brown.

Potatoes Stuffed with Cheese

Potatoes.	Grated cheese.
Butter.	A little milk.
Pepper and salt.	

Wash the potatoes thoroughly, dry them, prick with a fork and bake in a hot oven till soft. Remove them and cut in half lengthways. Scoop out the middle. Add to it the butter, pepper and salt, a little milk, some grated cheese and mash together. Put the mixture back into the shells, sprinkle a little cheese on top, and put them in a hot oven for 5-10 minutes.

NOTE. Or proceed as above, but use hot green peas instead of the cheese, and put a little butter over them.

Or chop some onion very finely, fry it and add it to the potato. Use tomato purée instead of the milk.

Risotto (3-4 people)

1 medium-sized onion.	Pinch of saffron.
5 dessertspoonsful rice.	1 oz. butter.
2 dessertspoonsful of tomato purée.	1 dessertspoonful of oil.
½ pint of stock.	3 dessertspoonsful grated cheese.
Salt and pepper.	

Wash the rice and cook it in boiling salted water for 10 minutes, then drain. Put the butter and oil in a saucepan and when hot add the rice, and cook till it is golden brown, stirring all the time. Then add the sliced onion and stir for a few minutes. Add a little of the stock, the seasoning, tomato purée and a pinch of saffron. Cover over the saucepan and cook it over an even heat, adding a little hot stock from time to time to keep the rice grains separated.

Add the grated cheese at the last moment. Stir for 1 or 2 minutes till it is melted, and serve.

NOTE. Risotto can, if liked, be served with ham, chicken livers or with fish.

Savoury Pie (4-5 people)

Breakfastcupful brown breadcrumbs.	Pinch of salt.
2 potatoes (cooked).	½ lb. cooked rice.
Tomato (sliced).	2 oz. melted margarine.
Spanish onion parboiled and sliced finely.	1 tablespoonful soaked tapioca.
1 teaspoonful mixed herbs.	1 oz. ground nuts or grated cheese.
Teacupful vegetable stock.	Butter.

Grease a pie-dish and line it with half of the breadcrumbs, keeping the rest for the top.

Mix all the other dry ingredients together, and put into the pie-dish. Pour the stock over them and then sprinkle over the breadcrumbs. Put some butter in small pieces on the top and bake in the oven for ½ hour.

Savoury Rice

Cook some rice slowly in stock till very tender. Season to taste. Then put it into a shallow fireproof dish, and cover with a good layer of grated cooking cheese.

Bake till the top is a nice golden brown.

If liked, the rice can be flavoured all through with layers of cheese, finishing with a sprinkling of cheese on the top. It can also be served as an addition to meat.

Savoury Rice with Onion

Cook some rice in some good stock till tender.

Melt some butter, slice up a large onion and fry it till brown.

Put the rice and onion in layers in a greased fireproof dish, with a pinch of mixed herbs and a little pepper and salt.

Put lumps of butter or margarine on

top and bake in the oven till brown (about ½ hour).

Vegetable Pie (4-5 people)

1 lb. mashed potatoes. 1 lb. cooked turnips,
1 oz. butter. carrots, tomatoes,
½ pint gravy or stock. parsnips, onion and
Pepper and salt. peas.
¼ lb. mushroom stalks. 2 tomatoes.

Put the vegetables, cut up, in a greased fireproof dish in layers and pour over the gravy; then season. Add the potatoes and smooth down, decorating with a fork. Put the butter in small pieces on the top.

Bake in a hot oven for 30 minutes or until brown.

SAVOURIES

Savouries, coming, as they do, at the end of a meal, must be specially good to be appreciated. Two things are essential to their success: they must have a distinctive taste, so do not be too sparing with the seasoning, and they should be served really piping hot, if possible absolutely straight from the grill or oven. Of course this is not always possible, but savouries suffer more than other dishes from being kept hot, especially as they are served on croûtes (fingers or rounds of fried or toasted bread), which must not get sodden or hard.

Anchovy Toast

Fry some croûtes, spread with anchovy paste and garnish with a little chopped parsley or a round of hard-boiled egg.

Cheese Aigrettes (8-10 people)

1 gill water. 2 oz. flour.
1 oz. butter. 2 oz. cheese.
2 eggs. Pepper and salt.

Put the water and the butter in a saucepan and bring to the boil. Shake in the flour and stir all the time till the mixture comes away from the sides. Then stir in the cheese, still beating, till the mixture is smooth. Add a pinch of pepper and salt. Let it cool a little and then beat in the eggs one at a time and go on until it is smooth.

Break the mixture into little rocky lumps and drop into deep boiling fat; cook slowly at first, increasing the heat towards the end. Allow 10-15 minutes.

Drain well on paper and scatter a little grated cheese over before serving.

Cheese d'Artois (5-6 people)

Flaky or short pastry. 3 oz. grated cheese.
2 yolks of egg. Cayenne pepper.
1 white of egg. Salt and pepper.
1 oz. butter. A little made mustard.

Make some flaky or short pastry.

Put the cheese in a basin and add yolks and melted butter. Add seasoning and stir in the stiffly beaten white of egg.

Roll out the pastry thinly. Spread the mixture on half of the pastry. Moisten the edges with beaten egg and fold over the other half of the pastry. Mark across in squares or strips. Brush with beaten egg and sprinkle with cheese.

Bake in a hot oven from 10 to 15 minutes and cut where marked.

Cheese Straws (6-7 people)

2 oz. flour. Salt and cayenne.
2 oz. butter. A little water.
2 oz. grated Parmesan Yolk of egg.
cheese.

Sift the flour and seasoning together and rub in the butter. Then put in the grated cheese and mix well. Mix to a stiff paste with the yolk and a little water. Put the mixture on a floured board and roll out thinly. Cut into narrow strips.

Grease a piece of paper and put it on a tin, lay the straws on it, and bake till a light brown and firm to the touch.

If liked, two or three straws can be placed through a ring, which should be cut from the pastry and baked with the straws.

Chicken Liver on Toast

Uncooked chicken's liver. Pepper.
Rashers of fat bacon. Croûtes.
Fat for frying.

Get ready some fried croûtes and keep them hot.

Cut some uncooked chicken liver into neat pieces, and roll it in slices of fat bacon with a pinch of pepper. Roll up the bacon and skewer. (Cocktail sticks do very well for this.) Fry quickly on both sides in hot fat and serve on croûtes.

Cod's Roe

Smoked cod's roe. Butter.
Yolk of egg. Pepper.
A little milk. Fried croûtes.

Fry some croûtes, drain and keep them hot. Soak the roe in water for an hour to soften it, then dry and slice. Warm it in a little butter; add the beaten yolk, a little milk and pepper. Re-heat without boiling.

Serve on the croûtes and garnish with a few capers, or ½ slice of lemon.

Haddock Croûtes (3-4 people)

2 *tablespoonsful cold,*	*Chopped parsley.*
cooked, smoked	*Chopped gherkins.*
haddock, flaked.	1 *dessertspoonful cream.*
½ *oz. butter.*	*Yolk of egg.*
Cayenne.	*Croûtes.*

Prepare some fried croûtes and keep them hot.

Melt the butter and add the haddock, cream, cayenne and gherkins. Then stir in the yolk and heat, but do not let it boil.

Put in neat piles on the croûtes and scatter a little chopped parsley over them.

Scotch Woodcock

Croûtes.	*Pepper.*
Anchovy paste.	½ *oz. butter.*
Yolk of egg.	1 *tablespoonful milk or cream.*

Fry some bread, cut into croûtes and make a dent in the middle. Spread with anchovy paste. Keep hot.

Mix the yolk, butter, pepper, and milk or cream in a saucepan and stir till it is a smooth batter. Do not boil.

With a teaspoon fill the hollow in the croûtes with the mixture and scatter chopped parsley over, or put a curled anchovy on each.

Stuffed Mushrooms

Cup mushrooms.	*Chopped parsley.*
Chopped ham or liver.	*Butter.*
Breadcrumbs.	*Pepper and salt.*
A very little chopped	*A little milk or stock.*
onion.	*Croûtes.*

Wash the mushrooms and remove the skin and stalks.

Mix together the ham, breadcrumbs, onion, parsley, and seasoning and bind with a little milk or stock. Fill the mushrooms with the mixture, and put a small piece of butter on top of each.

Put the mushrooms on a buttered tin in a moderate oven and bake for 15-20 minutes. Prepare some fried croûtes and keep hot. Serve the mushrooms on the croûtes.

Venetian Toasts (3-4 people)

1 *yolk.*	*Butter.*
2 *tablespoonsful minced ham.*	*Pepper.*
Pinch of dried herbs.	*Croûtes.*

Mince the ham very finely and add a pinch of herbs, and pepper. Put it into a saucepan with a little butter and a yolk of egg and heat it. Pile it on croûtes and serve at once.

A little minced chicken liver can be added to the ham.

Welsh Rarebit (5-6 people)

4 *oz. grated cheese.*	1 *oz. melted butter.*
Made mustard to taste.	1 *tablespoonful milk.*
Cayenne and salt.	*Buttered toast.*

Make a large round of toast and cut into neat pieces. Butter them and keep hot.

Put the cheese, mustard, melted butter, milk and seasoning into a basin and mix well. Spread the mixture smoothly over the toast. Put it in a hot fireproof dish and place it under the griller till it is a light brown.

Thin slices of cheese can also be put on bread toasted one side, put under the grill to melt and brown, and serve with small pieces of bacon and tomatoes.

EGG DISHES

Anchovy Eggs

HARD-BOIL some eggs, shell them and cut them in half. Take out the yolk and mix it with some anchovy essence and cream, or oiled butter. Mash it together with a fork on a plate. Put the mixture back in the whites, and garnish with mustard and cress or watercress, and put a few capers on the top of each half.

Serve with brown bread and butter. The yolk can be mixed with mashed sardine instead.

Curried Eggs (3-4 people)

4 *hard-boiled eggs.*	*Squeeze of lemon*
1 *oz. butter.*	*juice.*
Curry powder to taste.	1 *teaspoonful*
½ *oz. rice flour.*	*chopped chutney.*
Boiled rice.	*Salt.*
1 *apple and 1 onion.*	½ *pint stock.*

Melt the butter and when hot fry the sliced apple and onion; then add the rice flour, curry powder and salt and cook for 5 minutes, stirring well. Stir in the stock and bring to the boil.

Cut the eggs in halves or quarters and add them to the sauce with the chopped chutney and re-heat. Add a squeeze of lemon juice right at the end.

Put the eggs on a dish with the rice round, and pour the sauce over.

Devilled Eggs (4-5 people)

6 *eggs.*	2 *tablespoonsful cream.*
Pinch of castor sugar.	1 *tablespoonful vinegar.*
A little mustard.	*Parsley and thyme.*
Cayenne and salt.	

Hard-boil some eggs, cut them in half, and take out the yolks. Pound them very fine and add to them the sugar, mustard, cayenne, salt, cream and vinegar. Mix well together with a little chopped parsley and thyme, and fill the whites.

Serve cold. Garnish with mustard and cress or watercress.

Eggs à la Béchamel

Poach some eggs in good white or brown stock and serve with Béchamel sauce poured over. Garnish with chopped gherkins, capers or parsley.

Eggs and Cheese

Make some cheese sauce. Chop up some hard-boiled eggs. Pour the sauce into a greased fireproof dish, put in the eggs and sprinkle some Parmesan cheese over them. Then put the dish under the griller or in the oven till brown on the top. Small pieces of celery can be added to this dish or mushrooms, tomatoes, and a few flakes of left-over chicken.

Eggs en Cocotte

Eggs.	*Pepper and salt.*
Butter.	*A little cream.*

Butter some small fire-proof cocotte dishes. Break the eggs into them, put a little cream on each egg and a sprinkle of pepper and salt. Bake in a moderate oven for from 6 to 8 minutes, according to taste.

A little grated cheese can be sprinkled over the top, or some chopped ham put at the bottom, or some tomato purée, or a few fried mushrooms.

Poached Eggs in Soup

1 *large tin of tomato*	3 *eggs.*
soup.	3 *tablespoonsful fried*
½ *teacupful of milk.*	*bread croûtons.*

Heat soup thinned with milk to boiling-point, break in eggs and poach slowly till set. Lift eggs into soup bowls, pour in soup and top with croûtons.

Egg Mayonnaise

Hard-boiled eggs.	*Ham, crab or lobster.*
Mayonnaise.	

Cut the eggs lengthwise. Take out the yolk and mash with a fork on a plate. Fill the whites with chopped ham, crab or lobster. Pour some mayonnaise sauce over them and sprinkle the yolk on the top.

Garnish with strips of cucumber cut very small, or beetroot or peas, and serve with mustard and cress around, and slices of tomato.

Eggs Stuffed with Cheese (3-4 people)

4 *hard-boiled eggs.*	*Salt and pepper.*
2 *tablespoonsful Parmesan*	*Melted butter.*
(*grated*).	*White sauce.*
1 *teaspoonful vinegar.*	*Tomatoes.*
A very little made mustard.	

Cut the eggs in half. Scoop out the yolk and add to it the cheese, vinegar, mustard, seasoning and enough melted butter to make a firm mixture. Roll it into balls to fit into the whites.

Serve either hot or cold with tomatoes, either baked (hot) or raw (cold). If served hot make some white sauce, place the eggs in it and re-heat in a casserole in the oven.

French Omelette (1-2 people)

2 *eggs.*	1 *dessertspoonful water.*
Pepper and salt.	½ *oz. butter.*

Slightly beat two eggs with a dessertspoonful of water and a pinch of pepper and salt. Well butter a pan and when very hot pour in the mixture. Stir quickly with a fork for about a minute. Put a knife round the edge and underneath so that the mixture does not stick, and tilt the pan to allow the still liquid part to run under and get evenly cooked. Continue until top of omelette is just moist. Quickness is essential to success. When just set, fold over quickly with a knife and slide on to a hot dish. *Serve at once.* It is said, *You may wait for an omelette, but an omelette must not wait for you.*

Omelettes with Different Flavours

Mixed Herbs. Add a pinch of mixed herbs and half a teaspoonful of very finely chopped onion to the mixture before pouring it into the pan.

Cheese. Add a tablespoonful of grated Parmesan cheese to the mixture before pouring it into the pan, or grate in some cheese just before folding over.

Ham. Add a tablespoonful of finely chopped ham to the mixture before pouring it into the pan.

Mushrooms. Add a tablespoonful of very finely chopped cooked mushrooms to the mixture before pouring it into the pan, and serve with a layer of mushrooms along the top of the omelette.

Kidney. Fry some minced kidney and add it to the omelette just before it is turned over.

Chicken. Mix a little chopped chicken in enough thin white sauce to hold it, and add to the omelette before it is turned over.

Fricasseed Eggs (3-4 people)

1 *tablespoonful chopped onion.*	*Fried bacon.*
1 *oz. butter.*	*Teacupful of milk.*
Pinch of ground ginger.	*A little flour.*
Squeeze of lemon juice.	*Pepper and salt.*
	4 *eggs.*

Fry the onion in the butter till a golden brown, then sprinkle in a little flour, pinch of ginger, pepper and salt, and cook for 3 minutes, stirring all the time. Add the milk slowly and bring to the boil. Add a squeeze of lemon juice after it is removed from the fire.

Hard-boil some eggs, cut them in slices, pour over the sauce and serve with a little fried bacon.

Scotch Eggs (5-6 people)

1 *lb. sausage meat.*	*Breadcrumbs and*
4 *hard-boiled eggs.*	*flour.*
Fat for frying.	1 *egg.*

Hard-boil 4 eggs, shell them and dry them. Sprinkle them with flour and cover with sausage meat. Roll them in egg and breadcrumbs and fry in deep fat till a golden brown. Drain well and serve brown gravy or tomato sauce with them. They can also be served cold with salad.

BREAKFAST DISHES
(or Brunch for Sundays)

Most people are inclined to be conservative about breakfasts; either they have a little toast and marmalade, or, if they indulge in a larger breakfast, then it consists of boiled eggs, scrambled eggs and bacon, or tomatoes. A little imagination, serving tomato juice, or grapefruit juice a quarter of an hour before the meal; trying out a few of the dishes usually used as savouries, or serving fish not usually labelled in the mind as 'breakfast fish,' all adds to the variety of life.

Baked or Fried Cod with Sauce (enough for 4 people)

4 *medium slices cod.*	$\frac{1}{4}$ *pint water.*
$\frac{1}{2}$ *lemon.*	$\frac{1}{2}$ *oz. margarine.*
Seasoning.	1 *tablespoonful*
$\frac{1}{4}$ *pint milk.*	*breadcrumbs.*

Sauce:

$\frac{1}{2}$ *oz. margarine.*	$\frac{1}{4}$ *pint milk.*
$\frac{1}{2}$ *oz. flour.*	1 *hard-boiled egg.*
Seasoning.	1 *oz. grated cheese.*

Rub both sides of the fish with the lemon, season well. Grease a shallow pie-dish which is large enough to hold the fish without putting one piece on top of the other. Put in the fish and cover with the milk and water. Bake for 12 minutes. In the meantime prepare the breadcrumbs and the sauce. Melt the margarine in a pan, and when hot sprinkle in the breadcrumbs, season and fry quickly until golden brown. For the sauce, melt the margarine in a pan, stir in the flour, season. Add the milk a little at a time, stirring well until the sauce is smooth. Chop up the egg, stir this and the cheese into the sauce. Take the fish out of the oven, and drain any milk left in the dish into the sauce. Sprinkle the fish with the golden breadcrumbs, then pour on the sauce. Serve immediately.

Bacon and Apple

Allow a moderate-sized apple to 2 rashers of bacon. Wipe and core the apples without peeling them, cut into slices $\frac{3}{4}$ in. thick. Cut the rinds from the bacon, then fry it. Remove from the pan and keep hot, then fry the sliced apple in the bacon fat. Put on to a hot dish, sprinkle lightly with sugar and add a scrape of nutmeg, then arrange the rashers on top.

Bacon and Kidney

Fry the bacon, take out of the pan and keep hot. Fry the kidneys, previously washed and cored, in the bacon fat, turning them over once; when the red gravy flows freely, arrange on the bacon. Brown a teaspoonful of sieved flour in the fat, stir in a very little stock and bring to the boil. Season well and pour over the kidneys. Serve at once.

Bacon and Macaroni (2-3 people)

2 *oz. macaroni.*	2 *oz. rashers.*
Pepper and salt.	$\frac{1}{2}$ *pint stock.*
Scrape of nutmeg.	$\frac{1}{2}$ *oz. butter.*

Break the macaroni into small pieces, put into quickly boiling salted water, and boil for 5 minutes, then drain. Put the macaroni into the boiling stock and simmer gently till tender. Cut the bacon into small pieces and fry, then add the drained macaroni, the butter, nutmeg and seasoning. Mix together over a gentle heat until the macaroni is brown, then turn on to a hot dish and serve.

Bacon and Liver Rolls (4 people)

4 *thin rashers bacon, each cut into 3 strips.*	*A little grated lemon rind (optional).*
4 *oz. cold minced liver.*	1 *teaspoonful tomato sauce.*
Seasoning.	
2 *tablespoonsful breadcrumbs.*	1 *egg.*
	4 *skewers.*

Cut the rinds off the bacon. Put the liver into a basin, season well, add the breadcrumbs, lemon rind and sauce. Lightly beat the egg and bind the liver mixture together with it. Spread a little of the mixture along the centre of each piece of bacon and roll it up carefully. Put three bacon rolls on to each skewer, or if more convenient tie up the rolls with thin string. They can be cooked equally well in the oven, under the grill or in the frying-pan. In the oven, allow 15-20 minutes, under the grill allow 5-10 minutes with medium heat, in the frying pan 7-10 minutes with medium heat. If you use the grill or the pan, turn the rolls over after half the time has gone. This dish is quite substantial when served alone, but for those who like a larger breakfast, try garnishing with grilled tomato or whole fried mushrooms and watercress.

Baked Finnan Haddock (4 people)

4 *tablespoonsful cooked finnan haddock.*	*Cayenne pepper.*
2 *eggs.*	$\frac{1}{2}$ *oz. margarine.*
4 *tablespoonsful milk.*	*Breadcrumbs.*
Salt.	1 *oz. grated cheese.*

When you are preparing the fish, make sure that you take off all the skin and remove the bones. Lightly beat the eggs with the milk and season (be careful with the salt, as this is usually quite salty). Melt the margarine in a frying-pan and pour in the egg mixture. Stir carefully until the mixture begins to thicken slightly, then remove the pan from the heat. Stir in the fish, put the pan back on the heat. Using a fork, stir the mixture until the fish is well heated, but *don't let it boil*. Grease a shallow pie-dish and pour the fish mixture into it. Sprinkle with breadcrumbs, then with grated cheese. Bake for 7 minutes.

Haddock à la Reine (4-5 people)

4 *oz. boiled rice.*	*Dried haddock (cooked).*
3 *hard-boiled eggs.*	1 *oz. butter.*
Seasoning.	*Fried bread.*

Fry half the well-drained dry rice in the hot butter. When thoroughly hot add the chopped whites of 2 eggs, seasoning and the flaked-up haddock, and stir until thoroughly heated through, then pile up on a hot dish, put the rest of the rice (heated) round, and garnish with the remaining hard-boiled egg cut in slices and the yolks of the 2 eggs sprinkled over the fish, etc. Arrange fried bread round and put the dish in the oven for a few minutes.

Kidney Special (4 people)

4 *sheep's kidneys.*	$\frac{1}{2}$ *teaspoonful flour.*
$\frac{3}{4}$ *oz. margarine or dripping.*	3 *tablespoonsful water.*
1 *teaspoonful finely chopped onion.*	1 *egg.*
Seasoning.	4 *rashers bacon.*
	4 *slices toast.*

Take the skin and any fat off the kidneys and cut them up into small pieces. Melt the fat in the frying-pan, add the onion and cook lightly for 1-2 minutes. Put in the kidneys and cook for 4 minutes, stirring carefully. Season well. Sprinkle with flour, then add the water. Cook for 1 minute. Lightly beat the egg and season it. Take the pan off the heat, quickly stir in the egg and mix well. The pan can be put back on to the heat for a few seconds if the egg is not cooked quite enough, but don't let the mixture boil. Lightly fry the bacon. Spread the toast with margarine, put $\frac{1}{4}$ of the kidney mixture on to the top of each slice. Decorate with the bacon and serve very hot.

Kedgeree (4-5 people)

6 *oz. cooked fish (any fish will do but haddock is perhaps the nicest for kedgeree).*	1 *egg.*
	2 *oz. butter or margarine.*
	2 *chillies (or a little cayenne).*
4 *oz. boiled rice.*	
2 *hard-boiled eggs.*	*Seasoning.*

Flake up the fish smoothly. Chop up the hard-boiled eggs and chillies. Melt the butter in a pan and when hot add the fish, rice, eggs and chillies and heat thoroughly. Beat the egg, stir it in, adding seasoning if necessary, re-heat and serve.

SALADS AND SALAD DRESSINGS

A CRISP, cool salad on a hot day is the most inviting dish. Preceded by a hot soup, and followed by a hot sweet, it is welcome in winter, too. A combination of various vegetables, meat and fish make a colourful and attractive meal, and are full of health-giving vitamins. To ensure a salad being at its best, several important things should be borne in mind.

Green vegetables, such as lettuce, watercress, endive, etc., should be very carefully handled. If they are inclined to be limp let them soak for half an hour in fresh cold water before using. After washing, they should be well dried, first by shaking them in a salad basket, a sieve, or colander, and then by tossing them very lightly in a cloth.

Mustard and cress should be well washed and the black seeds should be removed. It should then be well dried.

Watercress needs very special attention. It should be washed in several waters, with some common salt, any decayed leaves or fibrous matter being removed. It should be well dried.

Radishes should be washed in cold water, and dried with a cloth. The young ones can, if liked, be served with their green tops still on, as they look more attractive left as they are. Large ones are better sliced.

Spring onions should have their roots cut off, the outside skin removed, and a little of the green tops. They should be thoroughly washed and dried. They can either be used whole or cut into thin slices.

Celery should be carefully washed, and only the inner white part should be used for salads. (The tough outer leaves can be kept for soup.) Any discoloured part should be scraped away with a sharp knife. If it is to be served alone it should be put into a glass jar, but in a salad it should be cut into small pieces.

Any green vegetables, such as lettuce, watercress, etc., if not to be used at once should be put, unwashed, into a tightly covered receptacle, or in the refrigerator.

Cooked vegetables, such as carrots, turnips, or potatoes, are excellent for salads. They must be very firm in order that they can be cut up into small dice, or any fancy shape desired. It is best to boil potatoes for salad in their skins and peel them afterwards.

Cooked green peas are also useful, either as an ingredient of the salad or as a garnish. Cucumbers and beetroot should be sliced very thinly or cut into neat dice. The inner leaves of a young white cabbage (uncooked) are an excellent alternative to lettuce.

Serving. Salads can be served either in a big glass or china bowl or in small dishes, allowing one for each person. They can be served with hot chicken or steaks, as well as cold meat.

The arrangement of the ingredients is most important. They can either be arranged in layers or (as in the case of Russian salads, for example) mixed together; but in this case special care should be taken with the garnish, so that the mixture does not look just a shapeless mass.

An attractive scheme is to arrange the top in different-coloured quarters, of course taking care to blend only such colours as go well together. Hard-boiled whites and yolks of egg, chopped very fine, green peas, beetroot dice, sprigs of parsley, celery tops, diced cucumber, capers, scraped raw carrot, etc., can all be used in this way.

Radishes can be cut so as to resemble flowers, by cutting the skin away from the radish in the shape of petals. Do not cut it right off, of course, but cut nearly down to the green.

Curled celery is another attractive garnish. Take a stick of celery and with a sharp knife cut about five or six parallel cuts downwards, one-third of its length. Put the celery into water and leave for an hour or two, when the ends will all curl back. If liked, both ends may be curled.

Fruit and vegetable salads, with the addition sometimes of nuts, are becoming more popular in this country, and make a pleasant change from purely vegetable salads. Oranges, bananas, apples, dates, etc., can all be combined with ordinary salads.

Dressings. The dressing of a salad is an important part of its preparation. French dressing, or *vinaigrette*, is extremely simple to make (it can be made just a few minutes before it is wanted) and is served with green salads and the less elaborate mixed salads. Cream salad dressing can be used when something richer is required.

Mayonnaise is more suitable for salads such as lobster, salmon, chicken, etc., and is a much richer mixture than the *vinaigrette*.

The question of which dressing to serve with salads will always be very much a matter

MAIN COURSE SALADS

VINAIGRETTE FLAN. Cook broad beans, peas, young carrots, tomatoes, cucumber and beetroot separately, then drain and cool. Mix with french dressing, arrange in flan case with slices of cooked ham; coat with cream dressing

PEAR AND CHEESE SALAD. Cream a little Roquefort cheese with butter, peel some dessert pears, remove the cores and fill with cheese. Take a large spoonful of cheese for each pear, thin with a little milk and season carefully. Place each pear on a lettuce leaf, coat with cheese, dust with paprika. Serve very cold with a hot cheese biscuit

TOMATO CHARTREUSE. Add the rind of half a lemon to one pint of well-seasoned tomato juice and bring to the boil. Strain, add 1 table-spoonful of gelatine dissolved in the lemon juice. Cool, pour into a ring mould, leave to set. Turn on to serving dish, fill the centre with shredded chicken mixed with mayonnaise; surround with summer vegetables sprinkled with french dressing and chopped herbs.

STUFFED EGGS WITH RICE SALAD. Cut 5 hard-boiled eggs in two, pound the yolks with a nut of butter and enough cold Béchamel sauce to make a cream. Flavour one half of the mixture with anchovy essence, and the other with finely chopped cooked mushroom. Cook $\frac{1}{2}$ lb. rice till just soft, add diced cucumber, cooked carrot, peas, french beans, seasoning and dressing. Pipe alternate fillings into the egg whites, and lay on the rice. Place a tongue of tomato between each egg, garnish centre with watercress.

PRAWN AND RICE SALAD. Boil $\frac{1}{2}$ lb. of rice, season, mix with french dressing, and shredded tomatoes. Add diced cucumber, broad beans, peas. Mix 1 pint of prawns with mayonnaise and shredded tomato. Put on serving dish, spoon over prawns and mayonnaise; decorate with quarters of egg, lettuce and watercress.

of individual taste. Whichever is used, do not mix it with the salad long before it is to be eaten, and always use a wooden or horn spoon for mixing.

Apple, Cabbage and Celery Salad

Shred some white cabbage finely, using only the inside; cut up some celery, and peel and dice one or two apples. Make some cream salad dressing and pour over.

Banana and Walnut Salad

Skin some bananas and cut them in three. Then cut each piece in half lengthways and roll in chopped walnuts (any other nuts will do). Arrange the banana pieces on lettuce and pour over some French dressing.

Beetroot and Walnut Salad (*illus. page 463*)

2 *cooked beetroot.*	1 *oz. shelled walnuts.*
1 *lettuce.*	*Seasoning.*
1 *head celery.*	*Salad dressing.*
Cress.	

Peel the beetroot, cut into thin slices. Separate the lettuce leaves, wash and dry as described above. Wash the celery and chop up into small pieces. Keep a few whole walnuts to decorate the top of the salad, and chop up the rest. Line the bottom of your salad dish with lettuce leaves, then a layer of beetroot. Sprinkle some celery and nuts over the beetroot. Cover with a thin layer of cress. Shred the remaining lettuce, and put this on top of the cress. Add the beetroot, celery, walnuts and cress, as before. Make the top layer of beetroot, and decorate with the walnuts. Pour a good salad dressing over the top of the dish immediately before serving.

Celery, Cabbage and Nut Salad

Head of celery.	*Small cabbage or*
Chopped walnuts.	*lettuce.*

Clean the celery and dice it, and shred the lettuce or the cabbage finely, using only the inside. Mix together, sprinkle the chopped nuts over it and serve with cream salad dressing.

Celery and Potato Salad

4 *medium-sized potatoes cooked in their skins and cut in cubes.*	*Apple, peeled, cored and sliced.*
	Celery tips.
Stick of celery cut into small pieces.	*French dressing.*

Mix the potato, apple and celery together, and add the French dressing. Garnish with celery tips.

Cucumber Boats (*illustrated on page 463*)

These boats make a delicious meal and can be served equally well hot or cold. A large variety of fillings will make your boats both attractive and tasty. If you want to make a special dish for the nursery, shape the filling as shown in the photograph. The children will enjoy each having his own submarine. A simpler method for every day is to fill the boat, then either rough up the filling with a fork or smooth it with a knife. Here are some suggestions for hot and cold boats.

Hot, enough for 4 people:

2 *cucumbers.*	2 *tablespoonsful cooked*
4 *oz. cooked meat*	*rice.*
(*ham, beef, lamb,*	*Parsley.*
sausage).	1 *egg yolk.*
1 *small onion.*	1 *small tin tomato soup.*

Cut the cucumbers in half lengthwise, carefully scoop out the insides. Put the meat into a bowl. Chop up the onion and parsley and add these and the rice to the meat; mix together. Lightly beat the egg yolk, and bind the mixture with it. Season well. Fill the cucumbers with the stuffing. Place them in a greased casserole, pour the tomato soup round. Bake for 15-20 minutes at 375° F. (Regulo 4).

Cold, enough for 4 people:

2 *cucumbers.*	*Seasoning.*
4 *large potatoes.*	3 *oz. grated cheese.*
1 *tablespoonful milk*	1 *oz. chopped nuts.*
(*approx.*).	*Paprika.*
1 *oz. margarine.*	

Slice the cucumbers in half lengthwise. Scoop out the seeds along the centre. Peel and boil the potatoes, drain well. Add the milk, margarine, seasoning and cheese, mash thoroughly, making sure that no lumps are left. When the potato purée is cold, fill the cucumber with it, using a forcing sack and decorative nozzle, or else fill with a spoon and shape with a fork. Garnish with the nuts and a few shakes of paprika. Serve very cold.

Date Salad

Dates.	*Cream cheese.*
Chopped stoned raisins.	*Chopped almonds.*
Lettuce.	

Stone the dates, and stuff them with a mixture of raisins, cream cheese and chopped almonds.

Almost any cold vegetable will add to the collection of hors-d'oeuvre, if it is seasoned and combined with another. Garnishes are important to the general appetising effect

There are many gay pottery hors-d'oeuvre containers to be found, unless you prefer the plain glass dishes

Serve on lettuce or any green salad with French dressing.

Hors-d'Oeuvres

Brown Bean Salad. Cook and soak $\frac{1}{2}$ lb. beans until tender. When cold, mix with 1 cooked, sliced onion, 2 sliced tomatoes, chopped parsley, cream dressing.

Beetroot Salad. Cut beetroot paper-thin, dust with sugar and leave for 1 hour. Sprinkle with French dressing and scatter over a few dill or carraway seeds.

Cauliflower and Watercress Salad. Coat cooked sprigs of cauliflower with mayonnaise or cream dressing, dust with paprika and surround with 'bouquets' of watercress dipped in French dressing.

Sweet Corn and Onion Salad. Mix tinned or fresh sweet corn with cream dressing and lemon juice to taste. Garnish with small cocktail onions.

Mushroom Salad. Quarter mushrooms and sauté quickly in butter; add 2-3 tablespoonsful red wine, salt and freshly ground black pepper, and reduce. Marinade in French dressing mixed with a little finely chopped parsley, shallot, caper and gherkin.

Prawn and Leek Salad. Cook young leeks until tender, season with black pepper and lemon juice; coat with mayonnaise mixed with prawns previously soaked for half-hour in cold water.

Curried Potato Salad. Sprinkle small new potatoes with French dressing while hot; when cold, coat with mayonnaise lightly flavoured with curry paste.

Sardine Salad. Drain sardine and coat with a *vinaigrette* dressing as used for the mushrooms.

Vegetable Salad. Dice cooked potato, carrot and turnip; mix with French beans or peas in a cream dressing.

Tomato and Cream Cheese Salad. Skin small ripe tomatoes, and fill with cream cheese flavoured with chives. Scatter over browned, shredded almonds; just before serving, sprinkle with French dressing flavoured with finely chopped onion.

Potato Salad. Cut up some freshly cooked cold potatoes into cubes (they should be cooked in their skins), and squeeze a few drops of onion juice over them. Make some French or cream salad dressing and mix the potato cubes well in it. Serve with a little chopped parsley sprinkled over.

Russian Salad

2 *carrots.*	2 *gherkins.*
2 *medium-sized potatoes.*	1 *onion.*
1 *turnip.*	1 *teaspoonful capers.*
4 *sprigs cauliflower.*	*A few anchovies.*
1 *cooked beetroot.*	*Seasoning.*
1 *tablespoonful cooked*	*Mayonnaise.*
peas.	*Lettuce.*

Clean and dice the carrots, potatoes, turnip and cauliflower, cook until tender, and leave until quite cold. Peel and dice the beetroot. Slice the gherkins into wafers. Peel and finely chop up the onion. Prepare the lettuce. Mix all the vegetables together in a bowl with the mayonnaise, season lightly. The salad can be served in individual lettuce leaves, decorated with crossed anchovies as shown in the photograph, or here is an alternative way of serving it. Line a salad bowl or glass dish with the crisp lettuce leaves, then put the Russian salad in the centre and decorate with the anchovies. Coarsely grated Cheddar cheese and chopped parsley will also give your salad an attractive appearance as well as adding extra vitamins.

Orange Salad

Peel and quarter the oranges, removing the white pith and the pips. Season with salt, pepper and a little lemon juice mixed together with a little olive oil.

Garnish with watercress.

Serve with roast guinea fowl or duck.

Salmon Trout Salad (6 people)

Salmon trout between 3 and 4 lb.
3 hard-boiled eggs.
1½ tablespoonsful mayonnaise.
½ teaspoonful made mustard.
Seasoning.
6 radishes.
1 lemon.
1 teaspoonful cooked peas.
Parsley.
Watercress.
Prawns.

The trout is always cooked and served whole. Allow about 8 minutes per lb. weight when cooking, and 10 minutes over. If you have not got a fish kettle, use a pan which is large enough to hold the fish lying flat. Boil the water, adding 1 teaspoonful of salt to each pint. Gently lower in the trout, lightly wrapped in butter muslin or vegetable parchment to facilitate removal, leave to simmer for 35-45 minutes (approx.). Cover the fish with a warm folded cloth while it is cooling.

Shell the eggs, cut in half and scoop out the yolks. Put these in a small basin and mix to a smooth paste with mayonnaise, mustard and seasoning. Squeeze the paste back into the centre of the egg white, using a decorative nozzle, or else replace it with a teaspoon and decorate it with a fork. Wash the radishes, then slice diagonally, cutting only three-quarters of the way through each radish so that it remains whole. Cut the lemon into thin slices. When the salmon trout is abso-

Tomatoes stuffed with cream cheese; prawns mixed with leeks; sweet corn blends well with onions or small cocktail sausages. Sardines, potato salad, sliced onion rings. . . . Just a few of these tempting appetisers make a good luncheon snack as well as the start to a meal

lutely cold, lay it along the centre of your serving dish. Garnish the fish as shown in the photograph on page 463.

Salad Marguerite (illustrated on page 463)

1 small cauliflower.	Parsley.
½ lb. French beans.	Seasoning.
3 medium-sized potatoes.	Mayonnaise.
2 tomatoes.	1 hard-boiled egg.
Mint.	

Cook the vegetables. When they are cold, sprig the cauliflower, slice the beans, cut the potatoes into small pieces. Skin the tomatoes and slice them. Chop up the mint and parsley. Fill your dish with alternate layers of the vegetables, sprinkling a mixture of chopped mint, parsley and seasoning between each. Blanket the whole dish liberally with mayonnaise. Take the shell off the egg, cut the white into petals and decorate as shown.

Sprinkle with the mixed mint and parsley. Serve very cold.

Winter Salad

Beetroot.	Nuts.
Potato.	Chopped parsley.
Apple.	Watercress.
Celery.	

Dice the beetroot, potato and apple, cut up the celery into small pieces, chop the nuts and parsley and put on a bed of watercress.

Serve with French dressing or cream salad dressing.

Chicken Salad

Cooked chicken.	Beetroot.
Lettuce.	Capers.
Cress.	Mayonnaise.

Slice up the meat into strips and put them in the centre of the dish. Make some mayonnaise and cover the meat.

Then arrange the lettuce and cress round the chicken. Cut the beetroot into small dice and place in groups on top of the sauce, and garnish with capers in between.

Fish Salad

Any cooked fish.	Cress.
Cooked potatoes.	Cucumber.
Mayonnaise.	

Flake up the fish and put it in a dish with very thin slices of potato and cucumber.

Make some mayonnaise and pour it over and put the cress round. The fish can also be mixed with a little cooked rice.

Salmon Salad

Cooked salmon (fresh	Radishes.
or tinned).	Pepper and salt.
New potatoes.	French dressing.

Flake up some salmon, and season it. Then pile it in a dish and pour over it a little French dressing. Slice the potatoes thinly and pour dressing over them, and season.

Then arrange the potato slices round the salmon, with an outer ring of small radishes with a little of their green left on.

SALAD DRESSINGS

French Dressing

½ gill vinegar.	1 gill olive-oil.
Salt and pepper.	

Mix the vinegar, oil and salt and pepper together.

To vary French dressing:
  Use lemon juice instead of vinegar; or
  Add a little dry mustard; or
  A little finely chopped shallot.

French dressing is used for plain green salads, and can be made at the last moment and poured over.

Mayonnaise

The thought of making mayonnaise often rather frightens busy people on account of the idea still prevailing that it is such a slow process. Certainly the oil must be poured in in a very thin stream, but it is not necessary to put it in drop by drop after the first few minutes. The mixture should be stirred smoothly and quickly the whole time with a wooden spoon or a wire whisk. When sufficient oil has been added the sauce should be so stiff that it can only be stirred with difficulty. Vinegar is then added to thin it to the required consistency.

Mayonnaise Sauce

Yolks of 2 eggs.	Oil.
Salt and pepper.	Vinegar.
½ teaspoonful made	1 tablespoonful white
mustard.	sauce.

Put the yolks into a bowl with the mustard, and seasoning. Pour the oil in drop by drop at first, then in a very thin stream, stirring smoothly and quickly all the time. When the mixture is very stiff stir in the white sauce (this will do away with any chance of its curdling and improve the taste): although it can be dispensed with. Add sufficient vinegar to make the sauce of the required consistency.

A little cream adds greatly to the flavour, or it can be used instead of oil.

If desired, lemon juice can be added instead of vinegar.

Mayonnaise sauce keeps for a short time. It should be added to the meat or vegetables just before serving.

Salad Dressing

Pinch of salt and pepper.	*1½ tablespoonful melted butter.*
1 teaspoonful dry mustard.	*1 egg.*
1 tablespoonful flour.	*1 teacupful boiling milk.*
1½ tablespoonsful sugar.	*¼ teacupful vinegar.*

Mix the dry ingredients together, and then add the egg, slightly beaten. Next add the melted butter and then the hot milk. Stir well. Put over a saucepan of boiling water and stir till it thickens, being careful it does not boil. Take off and add the vinegar slowly.

When cold, put it into a well-corked jar, or one with a screw top. It will keep for weeks.

SWEET COURSE

A WIDE repertoire of sweet recipes is a great boon to all housewives.

In the recipes which follow ordinary flour is used, and the necessary amount of baking powder, or bicarbonate of soda, given. If self-raising flour is used, the baking powder must, of course, be omitted. Where bicarbonate of soda is to be used it is best to use ordinary flour.

Sultanas and currants should be thoroughly cleaned before being used. The quickest way to do this is to put them on a wire sieve, sprinkle them with flour, and rub them well over the sieve with the hand. Look them over carefully before you use them and remove any stalks that still remain.

Raisins (unless, of course, they are bought already prepared) should always be stoned before they are used.

Apple and Raisin Pudding (5-6 people)

8 oz. rice.	*Butter.*
1 pint water.	*1½ lb. apples.*
Pinch of salt.	*4 oz. raisins.*
Sugar.	

Boil the rice in the water; not too soft. Then add a pinch of salt and a small piece of butter whilst the rice is still hot, and stir it well.

Peel and core the apples and cut into thin slices; add the raisins.

Butter a pie-dish, put in a layer of rice, then one of apples and raisins sprinkled with sugar and so on, finishing with a layer of apples on the top.

Put the butter in small pieces on the top and bake in a moderate oven for ¾ hour.

Apple Charlotte (I) (4-6 people)

4 oz. breadcrumbs.	*Juice and rind of*
2 lb. cooking apples.	*1 lemon.*
2 oz. brown sugar.	*2 tablespoonsful syrup.*
Butter.	*1 tablespoonful water.*

Stew the apples, peeled, cored and sliced, gently in a little water with the sugar.

Grease a pie-dish and sprinkle some breadcrumbs over the bottom. Then add alternate layers of apples and breadcrumbs, finishing with breadcrumbs.

Put the lemon juice, syrup and water and lemon rind in a saucepan and heat. Then pour over the mixture.

Put a few pieces of butter on top and bake in a moderate oven for about half an hour.

Turn out on a dish and sprinkle with castor sugar.

Apple Charlotte (II) (4-6 people)

Slices of stale bread.	*3 oz. clarified butter.*
2 lb. cooking apples.	*1 oz. margarine.*
Juice and rind of half a lemon.	*2 oz. brown sugar.*

Stew the apples with the lemon juice, rind, sugar and margarine.

Take a soufflé tin and cut two rounds of bread to fit the top and bottom. Then cut fingers of bread to fit round the sides. Dip the bread into clarified butter and put it into the tin. (To clarify butter, melt it in a pan over a gentle heat. Remove any scum that rises, pour off the clear liquid, and throw away the sediment.)

Pour in the apple purée and put on the top. Put a piece of buttered paper over and bake in a moderate oven till the bread is crisp and brown (about 45 minutes). Put a plate on the top and weight it down while baking.

Turn out on a dish and sprinkle castor sugar over it.

Apple Dumplings with Suet Crust

Peel some good baking apples thinly, core them and fill the centres with castor sugar.

Make some suet crust and roll it out on a floured board. Cut into rounds large enough to cover the apples. Put an apple on each round, moisten the edges, then work the pastry round the apple till covered, pressing the edges well together. Turn over on to a greased tin and bake in a moderate oven for 30-40 minutes.

Apple Soufflé (4-5 people)

1½ *pints milk.*	1 *oz. butter.*
1 *oz. castor sugar.*	1 *lb. apples.*
1 *teacupful rice.*	2 *eggs.*

Boil the rice in the milk until cooked, then add the butter and the yolks of the eggs. Do not let it boil.

Stew the apples with sugar to taste and put in the bottom of a buttered pie-dish. Put the rice on the top. Bake in a cool oven till set.

Whip the whites of egg to a stiff froth, then fold in the sugar. Pile on to the soufflé and bake till golden brown.

This may be eaten hot or cold.

Baked Bread Pudding (3-4 people)

4 *oz. baked breadcrumbs.*	3 *oz. currants.*
1 *tablespoonful sugar.*	½ *oz. chopped lemon*
1 *tablespoonful golden*	*peel.*
syrup.	½ *teaspoonful mixed*
Pinch of salt.	*spice.*
1 *pint milk.*	1 *egg.*

Heat the milk and pour it over the breadcrumbs.

Add all the other ingredients, except the syrup, which must be mixed in last. Stir the mixture well.

Put into a greased pie-dish and bake in a hot oven for 1 hour.

Baked Custard (3-4 people)

1 *pint milk.*	2 *eggs.*
Sugar to taste.	*Flavouring.*

Beat up the eggs, milk and sugar together, and add flavouring as desired.

Pour the mixture into a pie-dish and stand it in a tin of water in a moderate oven. (This will prevent curdling.) Add a cupful of cold water to the tin about half-way through. Cook for 30 to 40 minutes.

Bakewell Pudding (6-7 people)

4 *oz. butter.*	*Good-sized lemon.*
4 *oz. castor sugar.*	*Jam.*
Short pastry.	2 *oz. ground almonds.*
4 *eggs.*	

Beat the eggs well. Beat the butter and sugar to a cream and add the eggs slowly. Then add the ground almonds, the juice and grated rind of the lemon, and beat well together.

Line a dish with short pastry and put first a layer of jam at the bottom; then pour over the mixture, and bake in rather a quick oven for 20 minutes.

Bread Pudding

Stale bread.	*Brown sugar.*
Suet or dripping.	*Pinch of spice.*
Sultanas.	*Chopped peel.*
Currants.	

Put some stale bread in a basin and pour boiling water over it. Let it stand for a few minutes, then squeeze dry.

Beat some dripping or suet into the bread, then add sultanas, currants, sugar, spice and peel to taste, and mix well.

Grease a pie-dish, sprinkle the sides and bottom with brown sugar, and put in the mixture. Bake in a moderate oven till brown (about 45 minutes). Then turn out on to a dish.

If liked, this pudding can be steamed instead, but in this case an egg should be added.

Cabinet Pudding (6-7 people)

5 *oz. sponge fingers*	2 *oz. glacé cherries.*
or cakes.	1 *pint milk.*
3 *oz. sugar.*	*Rum or Madeira.*
4 *oz. sultanas.*	3 *eggs.*

Put the sultanas and the cherries in a bowl with a little rum or Madeira and let them soak, stirring them well with a fork.

Butter a pudding basin and sugar it. Then line the bowl with sponge fingers cut up in pieces; arrange the remainder in alternate layers with the cherries and sultanas and sugar. Make a custard with the milk and eggs and pour in slowly, so that the fingers get well soaked.

Steam for an hour and serve with custard or any sweet sauce.

Caramel Custard (3-4 people)

2 *oz. loaf sugar.*	2 *whole eggs and 2 yolks.*
½ *gill cold water.*	½ *pint milk.*
Squeeze of lemon	*Flavouring.*
juice.	*Sugar.*

To make the caramel put the loaf sugar, water and lemon juice into a saucepan and cook until a golden brown, shaking the pan now and again. Pour it quickly into a dry hot soufflé tin and turn the tin to let the caramel run over the bottom and sides. Then leave it to cool.

For the custard, put the eggs with the sugar and beat well; then add the milk, warmed to blood heat, and flavouring to taste, and strain it into the soufflé tin. Cover with a double piece of greased paper and steam *very* slowly for about 50 minutes, or till the custard is set and firm; or bake in a moderate oven, putting the tin in another tin with water in it.

Turn it out on to a hot dish.

Caramel custard can also be served cold, in which case it should be left till cool and then turned out.

Chocolate Pudding (3-4 people)

2 *oz. chocolate powder.*	*Pinch of salt.*
	2 *eggs.*
½ *pint milk.*	2 *oz. butter.*
2 *oz. breadcrumbs.*	2 *oz. sugar.*
2 *oz. ground rice.*	*Vanilla essence.*

Beat the butter and sugar together till creamy. Separate the whites and yolks. Add the yolks, well beaten.

Then add the dry ingredients (sieved together) and stir the mixture lightly. Then add

the milk, and lastly the stiffly beaten whites and vanilla essence.

Put it into a greased mould, cover with a double piece of greased paper, and steam for 1½ hours.

Serve with custard.

Christmas Pudding (about 20 people)

2 *lb. raisins.*	2 *lb. chopped suet.*
2 *lb. currants.*	2 *oz. chopped almonds.*
2 *lb. sultanas.*	½ *teaspoonful salt.*
1 *lb. breadcrumbs.*	½ *gill sherry.*
1 *lb. flour.*	½ *gill brandy.*
¼ *lb. mixed peel.*	*A little milk.*
1 *lb. brown sugar.*	*Juice of 2 lemons.*
2 *teaspoonsful baking powder.*	*Grated nutmeg.*
	½ *teaspoonful ginger.*
6 *eggs.*	

It is comforting to have a good supply of Christmas puddings in the cupboard.... They *may* be eaten at times other than Christmas!

HOW TO TURN OUT A PUDDING

Wear your oven gloves and first make sure that the pudding is loosened from the sides of the basin. This can usually be done by tilting. Rest the pudding basin on one hand and invert the dish over it. Hold both firmly together and turn them over. Give the pudding a good shake, still holding it firmly against the dish. Lift the basin off slowly. This is the best way of turning out any pudding, and fails only when the bottom of the basin has not been thoroughly greased

Prepare all the ingredients, and mix all the dry ones together. Stir in the beaten eggs and the sherry, brandy and lemon juice. Add enough milk to make the mixture of the right consistency—that is, fairly stiff.

Put into greased basins, put a piece of greased paper on the top, and then a scalded pudding cloth. Steam for 8 hours, or according to size. Re-boil for several hours when the pudding is to be eaten.

NOTE. This quantity makes about 12 lb. The time required for cooking the puddings naturally depends on their size. Puddings of 1 to 2 lb. would not require as long as 8 hours.

Turn out your pudding on to a well-heated dish, and decorate the top with a sprig of holly. If liked, just as you are going to take the pudding into the dining-room, pour a wineglass of brandy round the bottom and set a light to it.

Alternative Sauces:

The sauce you serve with the pudding is also a matter of personal choice. Here are two as alternatives to custard.

(1)

2 oz. margarine (butter if possible).	2 *large teaspoonsful brandy, rum or sherry (optional); or brandy or rum flavouring.*
¼ *lb. castor sugar.*	*A few drops vanilla essence.*

Beat the margarine until light and creamy. Beat in the sugar a little at a time, add the brandy, if used, or the rum or brandy flavouring. Mix in the vanilla. Serve this sauce *very* cold, piled up in a glass dish or sauce boat.

(2)

1 *egg yolk.*	1 *tablespoonful*
¼ *pint milk.*	*brandy or a few*
1 *dessertspoonful sugar.*	*drops of brandy flavouring.*

Lightly beat the yolk in a basin, add the milk and sugar. Put the basin over a pan of boiling water, or a double boiler. Lightly whisk the mixture for 1 minute, add the brandy or flavouring. Whisk the mixture until it thickens.

Fig Pudding (4-6 people)

8 *oz. breadcrumbs.*	2 *eggs.*
8 *oz. figs.*	*Scrape of nutmeg.*
6 *oz. sugar.*	*Teacupful of milk.*
6 *oz. shredded suet.*	

Chop the figs very finely and mix with the breadcrumbs, sugar, suet and nutmeg. Add the beaten eggs and the milk.

Put the mixture into a greased basin, cover it with a double piece of greased paper, and steam it for 3 hours.

Serve with wine foam sauce.

Ginger Pudding (3-4 people)

2 *oz. flour.*	1 *teaspoonful ground*
4 *oz. breadcrumbs.*	*ginger (or more,*
3 *oz. shredded suet.*	*according to taste).*
Milk.	½ *teaspoonful baking*
2 *tablespoonsful golden syrup.*	*powder.*

Mix the dry ingredients in a basin, add the golden syrup, and lastly enough milk to make a fairly firm mixture.

Put it into a greased basin, cover with a double piece of greased paper and steam for 2-2½ hours.

NOTE. A little chopped ginger adds greatly to the flavour of this pudding.

Golden Lemon Pudding (3-4 people)

1 *gill boiling water.*	2 *oz. sugar.*
1 *oz. cornflour.*	1 *egg.*
1 *oz. butter.*	1 *lemon.*
Short pastry.	

Mix the cornflour with a little cold water and pour the boiling water on to it, then stir in the butter and sugar, the lemon juice and grated rind. Lastly beat the yolk of egg and stir in.

Line the edges of a pie-dish with short pastry, pour in the mixture and bake for ¼ hour.

Beat the white of egg stiffly, fold in a little castor sugar, pile on top and set in the oven.

Marmalade Pudding (3-4 people)

2 *oz. breadcrumbs.*	2 *oz. castor sugar.*
2 *oz. flour.*	1 *egg.*
2 *oz. shredded suet.*	¼ *teaspoonful baking*
Grated rind of a lemon.	*powder.*
2 *tablespoonsful marmalade.*	½ *gill milk.*
	Sauce.

Mix all the dry ingredients together, sieving the flour and baking powder. Add the marmalade, the egg and the milk. If the mixture is too stiff add a little more milk.

Put the mixture into a greased basin, put a double piece of greased paper over it, and steam for 2½ hours.

To make the Sauce. Peel a lemon very thinly and cut it into short strips. Boil these in water till soft, then add 2 tablespoonsful of sugar and 2 teaspoonsful of cornflour made into a paste with a little water. Stir well and let it simmer for about 3 minutes. Take it off the fire and add 2 teaspoonsful of lemon juice.

Cherry Delight. You will need stewed cherries; 6–8 slices of French or currant bread; 1 oz. butter or margarine; 1 tablespoonful of chopped walnuts. It is quick to make, delicious to taste

Stew cherries in very little water to get thick syrup. Dip slices of bread

Dish up the pudding and serve the sauce with it.

Milk Pudding (3-4 people)

2 oz. rice, sago or tapioca.
½ oz. butter.
1 pint milk.
1 tablespoonful sugar.
Pinch of salt.

Just cover the cereal with water and let it stand for 5 minutes. Strain off the water, and put the cereal in a greased pie-dish, with the sugar, butter, salt and milk. Let it soak for about 1 hour. Then stir it well and cook slowly in a cool oven for 2 hours, stirring well after half an hour.

The above recipe makes a pudding of medium thickness; more or less rice, etc., should be added according to taste.

An egg can be added if desired, in which case the cereal should be boiled in the milk first, and the egg added when cool. Then put it in the oven to bake for 20 minutes.

Fry slices in butter until golden brown

Oatmeal Pudding (3-4 people)

4 oz. coarse oatmeal.
2 oz. shredded suet.
½ pint milk.
Nutmeg.
2 oz. currants.
Sugar to taste.
Small egg.

Boil the milk and pour it on the oatmeal. Let it stand till the next day. Then add the other ingredients and bake in a slow oven for 2 hours.

Arrange the bread on the serving-dish, pile the cherries on top

Queen's Pudding (3-4 people)

½ pint milk.
2 oz. sugar.
2 oz. breadcrumbs.
1 oz. butter.
Rind of half a lemon.
3 tablespoonsful jam.
2 yolks.
Meringue:
2 oz. castor sugar and 2 whites of egg.

Heat the milk, to which the lemon rind has been added, remove the peel, and pour over the breadcrumbs. Add the sugar and the butter, and let it soak for about 30 minutes. Then add the beaten yolks.

Butter a pie-dish, pour in the mixture, and bake in a moderate oven for ½ hour, or till set.

(Continued on page 479)

Decorate with cream or yoghourt and a sprinkling of nuts. Serve ice-cold

PANCAKES

They are delicious as a sweet with lemon and sugar, jam, or syrup. They can also be used with a savoury filling to make a meal

You will need 4 oz. plain flour, 1 egg, half a pint of milk, a pinch of salt. Sieve flour and salt into a bowl. Batter is usually better if it stands for an hour, but may be used at once if liked

*   *   *

Break the egg into a well in the centre of the flour. Use a wooden spoon to mix in the egg gradually. Then stir in the milk a little at a time until the batter is of a smooth pouring consistency

*   *   *

Use an omelette pan if you have one. Otherwise make sure that it is clean and fresh. Heat lard, then pour batter quickly into one side of pan

*   *   *

Tip the pan quickly from side to side, spreading the batter very thinly. Cook for about one minute. Slide a knife around the outside edge of the pancake, then toss or turn pancake and cook on other side

*   *   *

When cooked, roll up each pancake and place on a hot dish. Before serving, sprinkle with sugar and decorate with lemon. Put syrup and jam on the table in case it is preferred

Take out the pudding, spread the top with jam, and pile on the stiffly beaten whites of egg into which 2 oz. sugar has been folded. Sprinkle the top with castor sugar and put the pudding back in the oven till the meringue is slightly brown.

NOTE. This pudding can also be made with any dry biscuit crumbs or stale cake.

Snowdon Pudding (5-6 people)

12 *oz. breadcrumbs.*	½ *pint water*
8 *oz. moist sugar.*	½ *lb. lump sugar*
Raisins.	*Rind and juice*
1½ *small lemons.*	*of* 1½ *lemons*
3 *eggs.*	

Sauce.

Put the breadcrumbs, sugar, juice and grated rind of the lemons in a basin and mix well together. Then add the well-beaten eggs and beat.

Line a greased basin with raisins and pour in the mixture. Let it steam for 2½ hours.

Make some sauce with the lemon rind cut into very thin strips and boiled in the water till soft; then add the lump sugar and boil till it is quite clear. Add the lemon juice and pour it over the pudding.

Soufflé a la Vanille (3-4 people)

4 *oz. sugar.*	5 *yolks of egg.*
1½ *oz. flour.*	4 *whites of egg.*
1½ *oz. butter.*	*Vanilla essence.*
½ *pint milk.*	

Put the milk, sugar, butter and a few drops of vanilla essence into a saucepan and heat. Make a smooth paste with the flour and a little milk and add it to the hot milk, stirring well. Cook for 2 minutes. Then let it cool.

Beat in the yolks and, when quite cool, fold in the stiffly beaten whites.

Pour the soufflé into a buttered, sugared dish which should not be more than three-quarters full.

Cook in a moderate oven for 20 to 25 minutes, and serve directly.

Soufflé Omelette (1-2 people)

2 *eggs.*	½ *oz. butter.*
Pinch of salt.	*Flavouring.*

Separate the yolks from the whites. Get ready a buttered pan. Whisk up the yolks and add any flavouring desired (vanilla, lemon, etc.). Then whisk up the whites very stiffly, adding a pinch of salt. Fold the whites into the yolks and pour the mixture into the hot, buttered pan, and let it cook for about 4 minutes over a moderate flame. Do not stir. Take it off and put it under the hot griller for 2 or 3 minutes until it is slightly firm.

Cut a slit almost across and put in your filling (hot jam, hot fruit purée, etc.); then fold over carefully and slide on to a hot dish. Sprinkle a little castor sugar over and serve *at once.*

This omelette can also be served unfilled, in which case make some chocolate, coffee, ginger or jam sauce to go with it.

Soufflé Omelette (Baked) (3-4 people)

5 *eggs.*	*Vanilla.*
2 or 3 *oz. sugar.*	

Separate the yolks from the whites. Beat the yolks with sugar for 20 minutes. Beat the whites separately for 10 minutes (just before serving). When the time to serve has arrived, stir the yolks and whites lightly together and put the mixture on to a flat dish and into a *very* hot oven for 3-5 minutes, when the soufflé should have risen at least 5 in. and be well browned.

Sprinkle with castor sugar and serve immediately.

NOTE. An ice can be put in the centre and the soufflé mixture poured over it to cover the ice well. The oven must be very hot to cook the soufflé before the ice melts.

Ten-minute Dumplings (4-5 people)

4 *oz. breadcrumbs.*	2 *eggs.*
4 *oz. shredded suet.*	*Salt and nutmeg.*
4 *oz. currants.*	*Milk* (*if required*).
2 *oz. sugar.*	

Mix the dry ingredients together, add the beaten eggs and a little milk (if required) and make into about 10 firm dumplings. Boil for 10 minutes, when they will be ready to serve.

Serve with lemon sauce.

Toffee Pudding (4-5 people)

12 *oz. bread, cut in*	*Milk.*
squares.	8 *oz. Demerara sugar.*
4 *oz. butter.*	8 *oz. golden syrup.*

Put the sugar, butter and syrup into a frying-pan and let the mixture boil until it is a golden brown.

Dip the squares of bread into some milk. When the liquid in the frying-pan is ready, put the squares into it and let them get really hot. Then pile them up on a hot dish. This can be served with whipped cream.

Victoria Pudding (4-5 people)

3 *yolks and* 2 *whites* 4 *oz. butter.*
  of egg.   4 *oz. powdered*
4 *oz. castor sugar.*   *biscuits.*

Beat the yolks, add the sugar and the melted butter, and about 4 oz. powdered biscuit. Mix well together. Then beat the whites very stiffly and fold them into the mixture.

Put some jam in the bottom of some small, buttered moulds and fill with the mixture.

Bake in a moderate oven for 30 minutes, then turn out carefully.

Yorkshire Pudding (4-6 people)

8 *oz. flour.*   1 *pint milk.*
2 *eggs.*   *Pinch of salt.*

Sieve the flour and the salt into a basin. Make a well in the centre and break the eggs into it; add a little of the milk and mix it in well. When half the milk is in beat well for 10 minutes and then add the rest, still beating.

The batter should stand for at least an hour before it is used.

Bake it in a moderate oven for 30 minutes, raising the heat just enough to brown it at the end. This can be served with roast beef, or as a sweet course, with jam.

Apple Snow (3-4 people)

1½ *lb. apples.*
2 *tablespoonsful castor*   2 *whites of egg.*
  sugar.   *Strip of lemon rind.*

Peel and core the apples, cut them up and put in a wetted saucepan with the lemon rind; let them steam till they are pulp. Then stand away to cool.

When cool beat in the sugar, and fold in the stiffly beaten whites.

Arrange in a dish and decorate with cream

Cherry and coconut sponge

and red-currant jelly. A few chopped pistachio nuts are an excellent addition.

Charlotte Russe (4-5 people)

Savoy finger	½ pint cream
biscuits.	1 gill milk
Cherries.	½ oz. powdered gelatine
Angelica.	½ gill water
Jelly.	Castor sugar to taste
	Vanilla essence

— Cream.

Line the sides of a soufflé mould closely with the finger biscuits, so that no spaces are left in between.

Pour in a thin layer of coloured jelly and let it almost set.

Then arrange some cherries and angelica in it.

Next make the vanilla cream as follows: Slightly whip the cream, and add the sugar, milk and vanilla. Then dissolve the gelatine in the water (warmed), and when cool add it to the mixture. Stir till it begins to set, then pour it into the mould.

Turn out carefully and serve with apricot jam sauce poured round the Russe.

Chestnut Surprise

Wash some chestnuts and put them on to boil, cutting a slit in the skin. Cook till they are soft enough to peel. If they are put in the oven for a minute or two the skin will come off much easier.

Flavour a small quantity of milk with vanilla and add a little sugar, and boil the chestnuts in it until they are perfectly soft. Then pass them through a sieve until they have the appearance of vermicelli.

Serve with custard round or over them, or whipped cream.

Cherry and Coconut Sponge

8 *oz. self-raising flour.*	2 *oz. glacé cherries*
3 *oz. castor sugar.*	*cut in halves.*
3 *oz. margarine.*	1 *heaped tablespoonful*
2 *eggs.*	*desiccated coconut.*
1 *gill milk, or there-*	*Some shredded coco-*
abouts.	*nut.*
Few drops vanilla	1 *teaspoonful apricot*
essence.	*jam.*

Sift flour. Cream margarine and sugar together very thoroughly. When soft and smooth stir in well-beaten eggs and vanilla essence. Add flour gradually, stirring in a little milk between each addition. When consistency is right the mixture should drop from spoon

STRAWBERRY AND MINT JELLY

Dissolve a one-pint lemon jelly tablet in boiling water with a bruised sprig of mint. When cold and showing signs of setting, spoon a teaspoonful of liquid jelly into the bottom of a lightly greased mould and set in this a few small even-sized leaves of mint, radiating from the centre. In the middle set a choice fresh strawberry. Stir some strawberries into remainder of jelly (removing sprig of mint) and fill up mould when design has set at the bottom. When firm, turn out jelly and decorate with fresh strawberries and sprigs of fresh mint as above. Serve with cream

with a slight shake. Then sprinkle in desiccated coconut. Have ready well-greased basin and press halves of cherries all round inside. Fill up basin with pudding mixture and cover over securely with greaseproof paper. Put basin into saucepan with water to reach well up sides, and steam steadily for about 2 hours. Turn pudding out carefully on to heated serving plate. Spread teaspoonful of jam over top of pudding, then scatter shredded coconut and top with glacé cherry.

Serve custard sauce with pudding.

Chocolate Mayonnaise (5-6 people)

4 *small sponge cakes.* 4 *eggs.*
½ *lb. chocolate.* *A little sherry.*

Flake up the chocolate into a basin and dissolve over hot water. Cut the sponge cakes in half across and put in the bottom of a soufflé dish. Pour a little sherry over them. When the chocolate has melted take out of the hot water and stir in the beaten yolks of egg. Whip the whites stiffly and fold them into the chocolate, then pour the mixture over the sponge cakes and leave to stand for 12 hours.

Coffee Cream (3-4 people)

½ *pint milk.* ¾ *oz. powdered*
2 *eggs.* *gelatine.*
½ *pint coffee (strained).* 2 *oz. sugar.*

Separate the whites from the yolks.

Put the milk, coffee, gelatine and sugar into a saucepan and let them soak for 15 minutes. Then heat slowly, being careful they do not boil. Stir till the gelatine is dissolved and then take off the fire.

When the mixture is a little cooler pour it gradually on to the yolks and beat well.

Beat the whites to a stiff froth and fold into the mixture. Then pour it into a soufflé dish and allow it to set.

Cream Cheese (Petit Gervais)

Stand a pint of milk in a temperature of about 70° for about 30 hours. Drain off through muslin for about 4 to 6 hours, and turn it into a dish.

This can be eaten as a sweet with fresh cream over it, and served with strawberries, or it can be eaten as cheese. Sour milk can be used up in the same way by being drained for a day through muslin.

Ginger Cream (3-4 people)

½ *oz. powdered gelatine.* ¾ *pint cream.*
1 *gill hot water.* 2 *oz. castor sugar.*
2 *tablespoonsful ginger* 3 *oz. preserved ginger.*
syrup.

Dissolve the gelatine in the hot water. Whip the cream and the sugar together till stiff, then add the gelatine and water (just warm), the ginger syrup and preserved ginger cut small. Stir the cream gently until it begins to set, then pour it into a mould. (It must be stirred till it is poured into the mould, or else the gelatine and sugar will sink to the bottom and spoil the appearance of the cream.)

Serve cold.

Gooseberry Fool (6-7 people)

2 *lb. gooseberries.*	½ *pint custard or cream.*
8 *oz. sugar.*	1 *gill water.*

Stew the gooseberries in the water, with the sugar. When cooked put through a fine sieve.

When cool add the custard or cream and beat together well.

Serve with cream, either in custard glasses or in a dish.

NOTE. Any fresh, soft fruit can be used.

Strawberry Cake

2 *eggs.*	2 *tablespoonsful red-*
3 *oz. castor sugar.*	*currant jelly.*
2 *oz. flour.*	*Whipped cream.*
½ *lb. strawberries.*	

Whisk the eggs and sugar together in a bowl over a saucepan of hot water. When thick, remove from the heat and continue whisking until the mixture is cold. Sift in the flour lightly and quickly, and turn at once into a greased and floured sandwich tin. Bake in a moderate oven 15-20 minutes. When cold, split the cake in two and sandwich with whipped sweetened cream and a few of the strawberries cut in thick slices.

Brush the top of the cake with the melted red-current jelly, arrange the remaining strawberries on the top, brush again with the jelly and decorate with a little cream.

Lemon Sponge (3-4 people)

½ *pint water.*	*Juice and rind of*
½ *oz. powdered gelatine.*	2 *lemons.*
2 *whites of egg.*	2 *oz. sugar.*

Put the lemon rind in the water and let it stand at boiling-point for 5 minutes. Then strain. Dissolve the gelatine in the water, and add the lemon juice and sugar. Let it stand till cold.

Whisk the mixture well and fold in the stiffly beaten whites of egg, whisking the mixture till it is firm enough for a spoon to stand upright in.

Pour into a glass dish.

Serve with custard.

Meringues

2 *whites of egg.*	*Cream.*
4 *oz. castor sugar.*	*Vanilla essence.*

Whip the whites very stiffly and stir in the sugar as lightly as possible.

Take two dessertspoons and with them form the mixture into egg shapes. Put them on a greased tin covered with greased paper. Sift a little castor sugar over each one and bake in a *very* slow oven, till a crust has formed on the outside. Take out the meringues, turn them upside down, and make a hole in the bottom of each with a skewer. Put them back in the oven and leave them until they are crisp inside as well as outside.

Keep them in an airtight tin till needed.

To serve, whip some cream, adding a little sugar and vanilla essence, and fill the meringue cases. Then put together in pairs.

Mocha Cream (4-5 people)

6 *small sponge cakes.*	4 *oz. butter.*
3 *yolks of egg.*	3 *oz. castor sugar.*
½ *teacupful strong coffee.*	

Cream the butter and sugar together, then add the coffee and the beaten yolks slowly. Line a plain mould with the sponge cakes cut in slices, pour in some of the mixture, then add more sponge cake. Continue till the mould is full. Put a saucer on top, with a heavy weight on it. Stand till next day, then turn out and serve with whipped cream.

Orange Jellies

Make some orange jelly.

Cut some oranges in half, scoop out the inside and keep for orangeade. Then fill the oranges with jelly.

Cover the jelly with whipped cream and decorate with thin slices of crystallised orange or with glacé cherries.

Make handles of thin strips of angelica.

Pudding à la Royal (4-5 people)

½ *pint whipped cream.*	3 *oz. brown bread-*
½ *pint milk.*	*crumbs.*
3 *eggs.*	*Sugar and vanilla to*
7 *sheets of gelatine.*	*taste.*

Make a custard with the milk, sugar, vanilla and eggs, and when cold add to the whipped cream. Add the dissolved gelatine and breadcrumbs. Stir lightly and pour into a wetted mould. When cold turn out and serve with whipped cream or custard and fruit.

Prune Caramel (3-4 people)

½ *lb. prunes.*	½ *cupful of milk or*
¼ *lb. brown sugar.*	*thin cream.*
Piece of stick	2 *eggs.*
cinnamon.	1 *pint cold water.*

Put the prunes (soaked overnight in the cold water), brown sugar and cinnamon into a saucepan and cook gently for 2 hours. Then put through a hair sieve, taking out the cinnamon.

Next add the eggs, well beaten, and the milk or cream, and pour the mixture into a mould which has been previously lined with burnt sugar.

Steam for half an hour.

When cold turn out and serve with whipped cream.

Prune Mould (3-4 people)

1 *lb. prunes.* 1 *pint water.*
Powdered gelatine. 2 *oz. brown sugar.*
Rind and juice of a lemon.

Wash the prunes and put to soak with the lemon rind in the water overnight. Then cook with the sugar till soft. Put through a sieve. Allow ½ oz. gelatine to a pint of prune purée. Dissolve the gelatine in a little water and add, together with the lemon juice, to the purée. Stir till it begins to thicken, then pour into a wetted mould. When set turn out and decorate with blanched almonds and whipped cream.

Raspberry Sponge (5-6 people)

1 *oz. powdered* 8 *oz. raspberry syrup* (*or jam*).
  gelatine. 1 *pint boiling water.*
½ *pint water.* *Juice of a lemon.*
8 *oz. sugar.* 2 *whites of egg.*

Sundaes can so easily be made with ice-cream, fruit, marshmallow, cream and nuts, and served up in pretty glasses

Put the gelatine into a saucepan with ½ pint of water and dissolve. Then add the pint of boiling water. Let it cool.

When cool add the sugar and raspberry syrup (or jam), the juice of the lemon and the beaten whites of 2 eggs. Whisk for half an hour. Then pour into a dish.

Serve cold with cream.

Left: Strawberry cake

Russian Cream (5-6 people)

2 oz. sugar.	Flavouring.
1 pint milk.	2 oz. ground rice.
½ pint whipped	½ oz. powdered gelatine.
cream.	Chopped glacé cherries.

Wet the ground rice with a little milk. Put the rest of the milk and the sugar on to boil, then stir in the ground rice gradually, and continue stirring for about 8 minutes. Then draw the saucepan to one side.

Dissolve the gelatine in a little warm milk and pour it into the rice, stirring well.

When sufficiently cool add the whipped cream, and mix lightly together. Flavour with vanilla or some liqueur and pour into a mould which has already been decorated with preserved cherries chopped small.

Let it set and serve cold.

NOTE. If liked, omit the cherries in the mould and colour the mixture with cochineal, and decorate with chopped pistachio nuts.

Strawberry or Raspberry Cream (5-6 people)

1 pint strawberries	½ oz. powdered gelatine.
(or raspberries).	½ pint double cream.
1 gill water.	3 oz. castor sugar.

Prepare the fruit and put it into a basin, sprinkle the sugar over it, and let it stand for a hour, then rub it through a sieve.

Dissolve the gelatine in the warm water, and add the fruit.

Whip the cream till it is quite stiff, and then add the fruit and gelatine to it, stirring well together.

Pour the mixture into a wetted mould to set.

Summer Pudding

This pudding can be made with any soft, fresh fruit, such as raspberries, black currants, etc., or with tinned or bottled fruit.

If fresh fruit is used, stew it with a little water and sugar to taste.

Take some stale bread and a pudding basin and cut first two rounds, to fit the top and bottom, and then pieces to overlap round the sides. Dip in the fruit juice and line the basin with the bread.

Pour in some hot fruit, then put in some bread, then more fruit, and so on, finishing with a round of bread. Put a plate on the top with a weight on it and let the pudding stand for the night.

Turn out and serve with custard or cream.

NOTE. This can also be made with sponge cakes.

Tapioca Cream (3-4 people)

¼ oz. gelatine.	1 tablespoonful tapioca
1 pint milk.	de groult.
1 tablespoonful sugar.	1 tablespoonful cream.

Dissolve the gelatine in a little milk.

Put a pint of milk in a saucepan and bring it to the boil. While boiling, stir in the tapioca. Boil from 5 to 10 minutes.

Add the sugar and cream. Then stir in the gelatine.

When nearly cold put into a wetted mould to set.

Trifle

Cut some sponge cakes in half lengthwise, and spread the lower halves with jam. Then put together again and arrange neatly in a glass dish. Put some ratafia biscuits on the top of the cakes and stick some blanched split almonds into the sponge cakes.

Pour about a wineglassful of fruit syrup, made either with fresh fruit stewed and strained, or with jam diluted with hot water and strained, over them and let them soak well.

Then pour over them a good cold custard and let the trifle stand overnight.

Before serving decorate with almonds, angelica, 'hundreds and thousands,' glacé cherries or crystallised fruit, according to taste, and small piles of whipped cream.

NOTE. Sherry poured over the cakes adds greatly to the flavour.

APPLES AND PEARS

Pear Victoire (illustrated on page 412)

A sponge sandwich.	1 pint-packet lemon jelly.
2 tablespoonsful	1 gill water.
sweet sherry.	¼ pint cream.
2 oz. sugar.	2 tablespoonsful pear
Lemon rind.	syrup.
4 cooking pears.	2 or 3 cloves.

Decorations:

4 tablespoonsful	6 tablespoonsful
sweetened whipped	chopped jelly.
cream.	Angelica.

Buy or prepare a flat sponge sandwich. When quite cold soak with sherry and pear syrup.

Heat sugar and water together in a large shallow pan. Add lemon rind, cloves and peeled, halved and cored pears. Cover pan and cook gently till fruit is tender. Allow pears to drain on a cake wire. Put a little of the cream prepared for decoration and fill into hollows of the pears. Invert each half pear on to cake, stalk end to centre. Place cake on an icing wire.

Whip cream till stiff. Stir in jelly melted with ½ pint water and cooled, sweeten to taste. Stir well till mixture is of a thick coating consistency, then pour quickly over the cake to coat top and sides evenly. Leave till firm. Decorate with piped cream, chopped jelly and angelica cut in leaf and stalk shapes. Serve any left-over cream jelly in a separate dish.

Pears Cardinal (*illustrated on page 412*)

6 oz. sugar.	½-1 teaspoonful
½ pint water.	vanilla essence.
4 pears.	2 oz. rice.
1 pint milk.	¼ pint whipped
2 teaspoonsful cornflour.	cream.
2 tablespoonsful straw-	3 tablespoonsful
berry jam.	port wine.

Decoration:

½ oz. blanched	4 tablespoonsful
shredded almonds.	whipped sweetened
	cream.

Melt 4 oz. sugar and jam in water and heat to boiling-point. Strain, add vanilla essence and heat again. Peel pears; leaving stalks on. Stand them upright in syrup, in a pan just large enough to take the four. Cover and stew slowly, keeping pears whole. Boil rice in milk till thick and soft. Add 1½ oz. sugar. Turn into bowl and cool. Whip cream till stiff, add remaining ½ oz. sugar and fold into cold rice. Spoon the mixture on to a dish and spread flat. Lift cooked pears on to a separate dish. Blend cornflour with a little cold water. Stir in the hot syrup, return mixture to pan, stir to boiling-point. Simmer for about 3 minutes. Cover pan and leave to cool. Flavour to taste with port wine. Coat pears evenly and arrange on rice. Stick each with shredded almonds. Decorate with whipped cream.

Apple and Blackberry Flan (*illus. page 412*)

6 oz. short pastry.	2 oz. sugar.
1 lb. cooking apples.	4 teaspoonsful orange
4 oz. blackberries.	juice.
Finely grated rind of	¼ oz. margarine.
½ orange.	Cream.

Line a flan case with the pastry. Arrange sliced apples in circles over the bottom with blackberries round edge and centre. Sprinkle each layer of apple with sugar, orange rind and juice. Top with sugar and dots of margarine. Bake for 30 to 40 minutes, till apple is tender and pastry crisp.

Apfel Strudel (*illustrated on page 412*)

Pastry:

3 oz. margarine.	2 dessertspoonsful
3 oz. lard.	milk or water.
Pinch of salt.	3 cupfuls flour.

Filling:

1 lb. apples.	1 teaspoonful grated
1 teaspoonful	nutmeg.
cinnamon.	4 tablespoonsful sugar.
2 tablespoonsful	2 tablespoonsful
currants.	sultanas.
1 dessertspoonful	Rind of ½ a lemon.
candied peel.	Icing sugar.
2 tablespoonsful	2½ oz. butter or
breadcrumbs.	margarine.

Rub margarine and lard into flour with pinch of salt. Mix to a stiff dough with milk or water for nearly 10 minutes. Let the dough stand in a cool place for half an hour. Sprinkle flour on clean cloth laid over the kitchen table. Roll dough out as thinly as possible, brush with melted margarine (or butter) and line with breadcrumbs.

Peel, core and shred apples. Mix in spices, sugar, dried fruit, peel and grated rind. Sprinkle with sugar. Lift corners of cloth and roll the paste into a long roll. Place on a greased baking tray very carefully. Score through with a knife at intervals to about the centre of the roll. Brush with melted margarine. Bake near top of the oven for 20 minutes at 440° F. (Regulo 7) and for 10 minutes at 390° F. (Regulo 5). Brush again twice with melted margarine while cooking. When cool dredge with icing sugar.

NOTE. If you have no Regulo, bake in oven till golden brown.

Apple, Grape and Nut Salad (*illus. page 412*)

4 eating apples.	2 tablespoonsful
2 oz. mixed chopped nuts.	cider.
½ lb. black or white	1 tablespoonful
grapes.	castor sugar.

Remove a slice from the top of each apple and scoop out pulp and core, leaving the apple shell ¼ in. thick. Slice pulp finely, mix with chopped nuts and 4 oz. of the shredded grapes. Add cider and sugar to taste. Serve in the apple shells surrounded with remaining grapes cut in halves.

FRUIT FLAN

A fruit flan is a useful sweet in that advantage can be taken of any fruit in season. This is the right way to make a flan, simply set out for you. When tinned fruit is used its own syrup can substitute for sugar

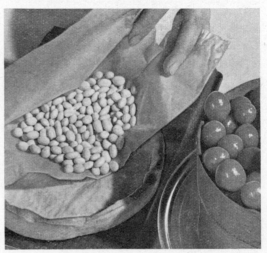

1. Make the pastry by creaming 3 oz. margarine with 1 oz. sugar. Work in 6 oz. sifted flour and bind with an egg-yolk or water. Knead *thoroughly* together. Roll pastry and line flan case or sandwich tin. Level top edge. Short-crust pastry may be used instead if you prefer it

2. Bake the pastry ' blind,' i.e. with beans or bread on greaseproof paper to prevent bottom rising, for 15 minutes—450° F. (Regulo 7). Remove paper and return to oven for further 5 minutes. Meanwhile, cook fruit in syrup made with sugar and water until soft but unbroken. Drain on sieve, then arrange in the flan case

3. Blend 1 teaspoonful cornflour or arrowroot with ¼ pint syrup. Boil until thick and clear, stirring well all the time. Pour glaze slowly and evenly over fruit. To keep pastry crisp, allow to cool before the fruit is put into the flan, and the glaze to cool before coating fruit. Decorate with small ' rosettes ' of cream

PASTRY

THE great secret of success in pastry-making is to use the hands as little as possible. When the fat is rubbed in, it should be done lightly with the tips of the fingers and thumb. What kneading is necessary should be done very lightly, and the dough should be just gathered together.

Another essential for making light pastry is to mix it in as cool a place as possible, use very cold water, and see that your flour and shortening are cool, too. A marble slab is ideal for rolling out pastry.

Never economise on the shortening; good dripping or lard is preferable to cheap butter. As a matter of fact, lard makes a more tender crust than butter, though of course it does not give the pastry the flavour butter does.

The amount of water required varies according to what flour is used. The lighter and finer the flour the more water it will take.

Flour the board, and the rolling-pin so that the pastry does not stick. Be very sparing with the flour you sprinkle over the pastry, as too much dry flour spoils its appearance.

The cooking of pastry is as important as the making. The oven must be hot enough to prevent the butter or lard melting and running out before the starch grains in the flour have had time to burst and absorb it.

Directly the pastry has come up and is a good brown, put a piece of greaseproof paper over it and lower the heat until the pie or tart, or whatever it may be, is cooked enough.

There are several different kinds of pastry, and below are the recipes for making them. Short pastry is the quickest and easiest and should be used at once.

Flaky pastry can be kept for several days provided the weather is cold. In any case it should be made at least an hour before you intend to use it.

Puff pastry requires more time in the making. It can be used the day that it is made, or, if the weather is cold or if put in a refrigerator, it will keep if wrapped in well-greased paper.

Rough puff pastry should be left for at least half an hour before it is used, or if wrapped in well-greased paper it will keep several days in cold weather.

Potato pastry is economical. It is excellent for jam puffs, tarts or pies.

Choux pastry is made in an entirely different way from the other kinds of pastry. It is used for making Continental pastries such as éclairs, cream buns, etc.

Choux Pastry

1 *gill water.*	2½ *oz. flour.*
3 *eggs.*	1¼ *oz. butter.*
Pinch of salt.	*Pinch of sugar.*

Put the butter and water, with a pinch of salt and sugar, on to boil. Then shoot in the flour and stir over the fire until the mixture leaves the bottom of the pan quite clean. Let it cool. Then mix in the eggs one by one and flavour as required.

Flaky Pastry

8 *oz. flour.*	4 *oz. lard.*
½ *teaspoonful salt.*	*Cold water.*

Put the flour and salt in a basin, and rub in one-third of the lard. Mix it into a stiff dough with water.

Roll out into a long piece on a floured board. Place half the remainder of the lard, cut into small pieces, on the top two-thirds of the paste. Flour well and fold the paste into three. Press the edges well together with the rolling-pin.

Turn the paste so that the sides become ends. Roll out again and add the rest of the lard in the same way as before. Flour, fold in three, turn, and roll out again.

Fold in three once more and, if possible, put away in a cool place in a covered basin for an hour, or overnight.

Roll out again before use and bake in a hot oven.

NOTE. When using up trimmings of this pastry always put them one above another and beat together with a rolling-pin before rolling out. This preserves the flaky effect.

Potato Pastry

9 *oz. flour.*	3 *oz. mashed potato.*
2 *oz. lard.*	*Cold water to mix.*
Pinch of salt.	

Sieve the flour and salt into a basin and rub in the lard finely, then work in the mashed potato. When smooth mix to a dough with a very little cold water. Roll out and bake in a hot oven.

Puff Pastry

Equal quantities of best-quality	*Cold water.*
flour, butter or marg.	*Pinch of salt.*

Sieve the flour and salt on to a board and make a well in the centre. Pour water into the well and mix in the flour gradually with the hand. Make the mixture of the same con-

BETTER HOME MAKING

sistency as the butter, soft if the butter is soft, and hard if it is hard.

Roll out the mixture and leave for 15 minutes.

Bang the butter on the slab to remove moisture. Put it in one piece in the middle of the pastry. Fold the pastry round the butter, beat slightly with the rolling-pin and leave for 15 minutes.

Roll the mixture out into a long, narrow piece, fold it in four, and leave for 15 minutes.

Repeat this four times, allowing the pastry to rest for 15 minutes between rolling.

Leave till next day, or roll out and use, as desired.

Rough Puff Pastry

8 oz. flour. 3 oz. butter.
½ teaspoonful salt. 3 oz. lard.
Cold water. (Use less fat in summer.)

Chop the lard and butter into the sieved flour, keeping it in fairly large pieces.

Add the salt and sufficient water to bind the mixture. Do not use the hand but mix the water in with a knife.

Turn the mixture on to a floured board and roll it out four times, folding it in three each time.

Put the pastry away in a cool place for at least half an hour. Then roll out and use as required.

NOTE. This pastry is the best to use for meat pies which have to be in the oven a long time.

Deal with trimmings in the same way as in flaky pastry.

Short Pastry

8 oz. flour. 4 oz. lard.
¼ teaspoonful salt. Cold water.

Add the salt to the sieved flour. Place the lard in the flour and chop into small pieces with a knife. Rub the lard lightly into the flour with the finger-tips. Then add sufficient water to make a dry dough, mixing it in with a small knife.

Roll out the pastry once on a floured board and use at once.

Almond Cheese Cakes (5-6 people)

Flaky pastry. Grated rind of quarter
2 oz. ground almonds. of lemon.
2 oz. butter. 1 drop of almond
2 oz. castor sugar. essence.
1 tablespoonful ground 1 drop of maraschino
rice. (or sherry or brandy).
1 egg and 1 yolk. Raspberry jam.

Make the pastry and line some patty pans with it. Put a drop of raspberry jam in the bottom of each tartlet.

Cream the butter and sugar, then add the egg and yolk unbeaten. Add the rest of the ingredients and beat well. Put a spoonful of the mixture into each tartlet.

Cook in a hot oven till risen and brown. Finish off in a cooler oven till the pastry is cooked through (about 25 minutes altogether).

Apple Dumplings (4-5 people)

8 oz. short pastry. 6 medium-sized apples.
(see above). Castor sugar.

Pare the apples and cut out the cores. Fill the centre of each apple with some castor sugar.

Roll out the pastry to about ⅛ in. in thickness and cut out six rounds large enough to cover the apples. Moisten the edges of the rounds, put an apple on each, and work the dough over the apple, pressing the edges together. Brush over with cold water and sprinkle some castor sugar over, or paint with a little milk.

Bake in a moderately hot oven till the apples are tender and the pastry crisp.

Apple Tart (Open) (3-4 people)

6 oz. short pastry. Raspberry jam.
Apples and brown sugar.

Grease a deep enamel plate and line it with pastry. Spread over it a thin layer of raspberry jam, then put a layer of thinly sliced apples, sprinkle with brown sugar and bake till the apples are cooked and the pastry brown.

Apple Turnover

Short pastry. Apples and brown sugar.

Roll out the pastry and cut it into fairly large rounds. Put some thinly sliced apple with a sprinkling of brown sugar in the centre of each; moisten half the round with water and double over, pressing the edges well together. Nick the edges with the back of a fork.

Brush them over with cold water and sprinkle with castor sugar.

Bake in a moderate oven till the pastry is nicely browned.

Cornish Treacle Tart

Make some short pastry and roll it out.

Grease an enamel plate and line it with pastry. Cut another round to go on the top.

488

Sprinkle some breadcrumbs over the pastry, then pour some golden syrup over it, and then add some more breadcrumbs and a little grated lemon rind.

Moisten the edges and put on the top, pressing it down gently. Nick up the edges with the back of a fork.

Bake in a moderately hot oven for about 40 minutes. Be careful that the tart is not too full, or the mixture will ooze out.

Custard Tarts (5-6 people)

8 oz. short pastry.   1 pint milk.
3 eggs.   Sugar to taste.
Grate of nutmeg.

Make some pastry and roll it out. Line some small fireproof dishes, prick the pastry at the bottom and bake lightly. Then take out of the oven.

Make a custard with the milk and eggs; add sugar to taste and fill the tarts. Grate a little nutmeg on each.

Put them back in the oven and bake slowly till the custard is set.

Eccles Cakes (6-7 people)

8 oz. flaky or rough   1 oz. castor sugar.
  puff pastry.   1 oz. butter.
4 oz. currants.   ½ oz. chopped peel.

Melt the butter in a pan and add the sugar, currants and peel.

Roll out the pastry and cut into rounds. Place a little mixture on each round. Wet the edges of the pastry and draw it all together round the mixture. Turn over and roll out each one until currants begin to show.

Bake in a hot oven till done.

Eclairs

Choux pastry.   Cream.
Icing.

Pipe out some choux pastry to the desired size into an éclair tin or on a baking tin, brush over with beaten egg, and bake in a moderate oven. Be very careful of draughts while they are cooking.

When cooked let them cool, then make an incision in the side near the bottom, take out the soft part in the centre, and fill with whipped cream, sweetened and flavoured with vanilla, if liked.

Spread some glacé icing over the top.

NOTE. For the piping, use either a forcing bag or a metal syringe. The éclairs before going into the oven should be about ¾ in. wide and 3 or 4 in. long.

Jalousie (Venetian Blind)

Puff pastry.   Chopped apples and sugar.

Roll out the pastry to the length of the baking tin. Cut it into two long strips, 3 or 4 in. wide. Place one strip on the tin. Paint all round the edge with beaten egg.

Put the apple and sugar down the middle of the pastry, piling it fairly high but keeping ½ in. away from the edges. Fold the other strip in half, sideways. Cut the folded side evenly with a knife, right through to within ½ in. of the other side; cuts should be about 1 in. apart. Unfold the strip of pastry, which will now resemble a Venetian blind.

Place this strip over the other strip on the tin, and press the sides down well together. Paint all over with egg. Decorate the edges by nicking with the blunt side of a knife.

Bake in a hot oven. When baked, scatter sugar all over it and return it to the oven for 1 minute to glaze.

Jam, Lemon Curd, or Treacle Tart

Short pastry.   Jam, golden syrup or lemon
                             curd.

Grease an enamel plate and line it with pastry. Fill the centre with lemon curd or jam; or golden syrup mixed with breadcrumbs. Decorate the tart with strips of pastry twisted and stretched across the tart. Nick the edge with the back of a fork.

Bake in a fairly hot oven for about 15 minutes, but be careful that the filling does not burn or get too dark.

Jam Puffs

Flaky pastry.   Raspberry jam.

Roll out the pastry and cut it into squares 4 or 5 in. across. Put a little jam in the centre of each square. Wet round the edges with beaten egg. Fold each square diagonally and press down the edges. Brush the tops with cold water and scatter sugar over them.

Bake in a hot oven till brown (about 20 minutes).

Jam Roly-poly

Make some short pastry, and roll into an oblong, making one end slightly wider than the other. Spread some jam evenly over it, leaving 1 in. all round, moisten the edges and roll up, starting at the narrower end. Press gently as you do so.

Put it in a baking tin and bake in a moderately hot oven for about 45 minutes.

Mille Feuilles (Gâteau)

Puff pastry.   *Glacé icing.*
Apricot jam.   *Browned almonds.*
Whipped cream.   *Pistachio nuts (chopped).*

Roll out the pastry fairly thin. Cut four large rounds 6 in. across. Leave for $\frac{1}{4}$ or $\frac{1}{2}$ hour. Prick very well all over with a fork.

Bake in tins in a hot oven. When cooked take out and allow to cool. When cold put the rounds on the top of one another. Trim the edges with a sharp knife so that they fit and are quite circular.

Chop up the trimmings and place them in a bowl. Add boiling apricot jam and stir together. Spread one round of pastry with this. Place another round on the top. Spread this round with whipped cream. Add another round and spread with jam. Place the fourth round on the top.

Chop the almonds. Spread the sides of the cake with hot apricot jam. Scatter chopped almonds all round.

Then ice the top of the cake and decorate the edge with pipings of cream and chopped pistachio nuts.

Mille Feuilles Biscuits

Make in the same way but line a tin with the pastry. This can be cut into strips and put together with jam and cream, then cut into fingers and iced on the top.

Mince-pies

Flaky or short pastry.   Mincemeat.

Roll out the pastry and cut it into rounds.

Grease some patty pans and line them with half the rounds of pastry. Put 2 teaspoonsful of mincemeat in each patty. Wet the edges all round with cold water. Put the other rounds of pastry on to the patties to form lids. Press down well together all round the edges.

Paint the tops of the mincepies with cold water or egg yolk beaten with a little milk, and scatter sugar all over. With a skewer prick a hole through the pastry in the centre of each mince-pie.

Bake in a hot oven (450° F., Regulo 7) for 20 minutes.

Pastry Fingers

Take any flaky or short pastry you may have over, roll it out, and spread jam over one half of it. Moisten the edges of this half, then fold over the other half. Brush over the top with cold water, and sprinkle castor sugar over it. Bake in a moderate oven. When cooked cut into squares or fingers. They can be eaten either hot or cold.

Mincemeat can be used instead of jam, if liked.

A little glacé icing spread over the top when cold is an improvement.

Patty Cases

Roll out some rough puff or puff pastry to a little more than $\frac{1}{4}$ in. in thickness. Let it stand in a cold place for a few minutes.

Then cut rounds with either a plain or crinkly cutter about $2\frac{1}{2}$ in. across. Take a small cutter ($1\frac{1}{2}$ in. across) and cut a round in the centre of half the large rounds. These are for the lids.

Damp the edges of the whole rounds with cold water or beaten egg, and put the rings on the top. Put the patties on a baking tin and prick the middles of them with a fork to prevent them rising. Brush them over with beaten egg and bake them for 20 to 25 minutes in a

Mince-pies are another standby, not only as Christmas fare. They make a nice snack for elevenses with a cup of tea or coffee

hot oven. Scoop out a little of the soft part from the centre when they are cooked.

The small rings, or lids, should be put on another tin, brushed over with egg and baked for 10 to 12 minutes.

If the patties are to be served hot, fill them with the warm filling, put on the lids, and then heat them in the oven for 2 or 3 minutes.

If they are to be served cold, let both the patties and the mixture get cold before putting in the filling.

FRUIT

THERE is an art in cooking fruit. Nothing can be more tasteless than watery stewed apples, for instance, yet, properly cooked they can be excellent.

For stewing fresh fruit such as apples, soft pears, raspberries, loganberries, blackberries, gooseberries, cherries, rhubarb, white and red currants, and for grapefruit or oranges it is a good plan first of all to make a syrup.

Allow 4 oz. of sugar (more or less according to the acidity of the fruit) and $\frac{1}{2}$ pint of water for every pound of fruit. Let it boil for 10 minutes, and then put in the prepared fruit and let it simmer gently till it is cooked. The time naturally varies according to what fruit you are using—rhubarb, for example, only takes a minute or two in the hot syrup.

Black currants, on account of their hard skins, should, however, be treated differently. They should be put into *cold* water with the sugar, and when they come to the boil they should be allowed to simmer very gently.

Hard stewing pears should also be put into cold water.

Dried fruit, such as apple rings, apricots, peaches, prunes, pears and nectarines, should be well washed and allowed to soak overnight. They should then be put on to cook in the water in which they were soaked, with the addition of sugar to taste, and brought to the boil. They need very gentle cooking after they have once come to the boil.

Apple Porcupines (3-4 people)

4 *apples.*	*Sugar.*
Jelly or jam.	*Water.*
Whipped cream.	*Almonds.*

Wipe, core and peel the apples. Boil together enough sugar and water (in the proportion of 4 oz. sugar to $\frac{1}{2}$ pint water) to cover the apples and a little over; let the syrup cook for 7 minutes. Then put in the whole apples and let them simmer until soft. Skim occasionally.

Take out the apples and let them cool. Then fill either with jelly or apricot jam, and stick with blanched split almonds.

Serve in the syrup and decorate with whipped cream.

Apple Salad (2-3 people)

1 *lb. ripe eating apples.*	4 *oz. of red-currant jelly.*
2 *oz. preserved ginger.*	*Whipped cream.*

Peel and core the apples and slice them finely. Then put them in a dish and put over them the preserved ginger, cut into very thin shavings.

Warm the red-currant jelly till it is sufficiently dissolved to run over the apples and ginger. Let it cool a little, and then pour over.

Just before serving, whip up some cream and decorate with it.

Baked Bananas (I) (4-5 people)

6 *bananas.*	2 *tablespoonsful melted butter.*
3 *oz. sugar.*	2 *tablespoonsful lemon juice.*

Peel the bananas, cut them in half lengthways, and put them in a fireproof dish.

Mix together the butter, sugar and lemon juice, and pour it over the bananas. Put them in the oven and cook slowly for about 20 minutes, basting with the mixture occasionally.

Baked Bananas (II) (4-5 people)

6 *bananas.*	3 *oz. sugar.*
Sherry to cover.	*Arrowroot.*

Peel the bananas and cut them in half lengthways. Let them soak in a little sherry for half an hour, then put them into a fireproof dish, sprinkle 2 oz. of sugar over them, add a little water and bake them in a moderately slow oven for about 20 minutes.

Put the sherry into a saucepan, add the rest of the sugar, and a little arrowroot mixed to a paste with cold water, and let it simmer till it thickens. Then pour over the bananas and serve.

Banana Creams (Quick Sweet)

A spoonful of jam.	*Grated chocolate.*
Slices of banana.	*Whipped cream.*

Fill champagne glasses with the following mixture: a spoonful of jam, then some whipped cream, next slices of banana covered with grated chocolate, then some whipped cream and then jam. Finish with cream, and decorate with cherries and angelica.

Banana Custard

Peel some bananas and cut them in half lengthways. Spread the halves with raspberry jam and put together again. Put them in a dish, and pour some custard over them.

Baked Apples

Core some good-sized apples, cut round the skin with a sharp knife (this prevents the contents bursting out) and fill in the centre with either butter, sugar and a pinch of cinnamon and scrape of nutmeg: or golden syrup, or sugar, sultanas and chopped nuts.

Put them in a fireproof dish, sprinkle them well with sugar, and pour in a little water.

Bake in a moderate oven till the apples are soft.

Compote of Apples (2-3 people)

1 *lb. apples.*   4 *oz. loaf sugar.*
½ *pint water.*   *Lemon juice.*

Put the sugar, water and a few drops of lemon juice into a casserole and boil quickly for 10 minutes.

Peel the apples, quarter them and remove the cores. Put the pieces into the boiling syrup and cook slowly in the oven till they are tender. Be careful they do not break up.

Take out the apple, boil the syrup a little longer to reduce it, and then pour it over the apples.

Serve with cream.

NOTE.—A little wine or kirsch is a great improvement to this compote. Cooking sherry will also serve.

Fruit Jelly

Make some lemon, orange or wine jelly, and pour into a mould into which have been put slices of banana, strawberries, raspberries, grapes, apricots, peaches, stoned raisins, etc., etc. Serve with evaporated milk, or cream.

FRUIT SALADS

All fruit used in the making of fruit salads should be ripe and absolutely sound. They should be very carefully prepared; for instance, oranges should have all the white pith removed and, of course, the pips. Plums should be well wiped, cut in half and stoned. If the skin is coarse they should be peeled. Other fruit such as bananas, apples, etc., should be peeled and cut in neat small pieces.

When tinned fruit is used the syrup from them can be used as a dressing. A little sherry, Madeira, brandy or liqueur can be added as desired.

To make a syrup allow 4 oz. sugar to ½ pint of water (this should be enough to cover a pound of fruit) and boil them together for 10 minutes. Let the syrup cool and then pour it over the salad and mix well.

Always let a salad stand for some hours, if possible, to allow the syrup to soak in well.

A few shredded almonds, chopped walnuts or shredded coconut can also be added.

Small meringue cases filled with cream are very good served with fruit salads, or a handful of ratafia biscuits put over the top just before serving is an excellent addition.

Party Fruit Salad

6 *oranges.*	*Chopped walnuts.*
1 *grapefruit.*	3 *bananas.*
1-*lb. tin peaches.*	½ *lb. grapes.*
1 *small bottle goose-*	2 *oz. golden syrup.*
berries.	½-*lb. tin pineapple.*

Simmer the finely cut rinds of 3 oranges in a very little water with the golden syrup for quite ½ hour.

Cut up all the fruit (except the grapes and gooseberries) into small pieces and pour the syrup over them, together with that from the tinned fruit.

Let the whole remain covered for 6 hours before serving.

Serve very cold with cream.

NOTE.—This is a most delicious salad and suitable for children's parties, etc. The above makes enough for 30 helpings.

Suggestions for other Fruit Salads

Oranges, bananas, pineapple cubes, maraschino cherries.

Oranges, stoned dates, stoned raisins and chopped nuts.

New Baked Apples

Apples.	*Brown sugar.*
Slices of bread,	*Marmalade.*
½ *in. thick.*	*Butter.*

Core the apples and cut round with a very sharp knife under the skin to allow them to expand. Do not peel them.

Next fill the apples with butter, marmalade and brown sugar. Spread the slices of bread with butter, marmalade and brown sugar, and put an apple on each slice.

Put them in a buttered fireproof dish not too near together and add lumps of butter and a few dessertspoonsful of marmalade. Pour in a little water and sprinkle the apples well with brown sugar.

Bake for half an hour or longer, basting them frequently.

Serve in the dish in which they are cooked.

Oranges with Coconut

Oranges.　　　　　　*Finely grated*
Sugar.　　　　　　　*coconut.*

Peel some oranges, taking away all the pith, and cut them into slices. Do this on a plate so that none of the juice is wasted. Put some of the slices in a deep bowl, and sprinkle finely grated coconut and sugar over them; next put another layer of orange and then coconut till the bowl is full, letting the top layer be coconut and sugar. Let it stand for an hour or two so that the orange and coconut get well blended.

Serve with cream if liked.

Stewed Pears

Hard stewing pears.　　*Strip of lemon peel.*
Water to cover.　　　　*2 or 3 cloves.*
Sugar to taste.

Peel, quarter and core the pears, and put them in a saucepan with enough cold water to cover them. Add the lemon, sugar and cloves. Then bring them to the boil, and let them simmer gently for at least 2 hours.

When they turn pink, boil more rapidly, as this will deepen the colour.

CAKE-MAKING

CAKE-MAKING is one of the pleasantest forms of cookery, and nothing gives a cook a greater feeling of satisfaction than a perfectly made and perfectly baked cake.

There are three main methods used in cake-mixing:

1. Beating the sugar and eggs together with an egg whisk till the mixture is thick and creamy, and then folding in the flour lightly. This method is used for sponge cakes.

2. Beating the sugar and butter (or other fat) together until the mixture is light in colour and creamy. The longer they are beaten the better the cake. Scrape the sides of the basin with a palette knife at intervals to ensure that all the mixture is well beaten.

In winter the basin may be stood in warm water for a minute or two to soften the butter, which, however, must never be allowed to get oily.

The eggs should be beaten and added separately, the mixture being beaten hard the whole time. Add them slowly or it will curdle. When many eggs are used, a little flour may be added towards the end to prevent this.

The main bulk of the flour and the baking powder are added last. In some recipes the whites of egg are kept till the end, whisked stiffly and folded in. This makes cakes very light.

This method is used for all rich cakes.

3. Rubbing the butter (or other fat) into the flour lightly with the tips of the fingers and thumb till the mixture is like fine breadcrumbs. In hot weather rinse the hands in cold water first. The eggs and any other liquid are added at the end.

This method is used for plain cakes.

Good margarine can be substituted for butter when necessary, with excellent results.

Preserved eggs can be used for all cakes except where the whites have to be beaten stiffly, when new-laid eggs must be used.

Castor sugar should be used for biscuits and sponges. Either granulated or castor can be used for other cakes. Soft brown sugar should be used for dark fruit cakes.

Flour should be ordered in fresh every week; the new should never be mixed with the old in the bin. It is best to use plain flour and add the necessary baking powder or soda. Always sieve flour and baking powder before use.

Here is a recipe for home-made baking powder:

Put equal parts of bicarbonate of soda, cream of tartar and ground rice through a sieve seven times to get them well mixed. Then put away in a tin. Stir well before using.

Currants and sultanas should be well cleaned before use. Put them on a sieve, sprinkle some flour over them, and rub them well. This will remove many of the stalks; the fruit should then be carefully looked over. Raisins should be stoned if necessary.

Sugar and fruit keep well if stored in a cool, dry place.

SWEET
SHORTCRUST

If you can make a really melt-in-the-mouth sweet shortcrust, you have the basis for many French pastries by using a little ingenuity with fillings

You'll need 4 oz. flour, 2 oz. margarine, 2 oz. castor sugar, 2 egg yolks. Sieve the flour on to a board and make a well in the centre

Put the sugar, margarine and egg yolks into the well in centre of flour, and work together with fingers till they are soft and creamy

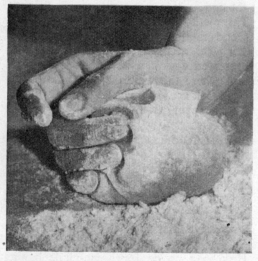

Combine all the ingredients into a smooth dough without using any liquid, then leave the paste in a cool place for half an hour before using

When about to make a cake:

Light the oven in good time so that it is hot enough when the cakes are ready to go in.

Get your cake tin ready first. To do this melt a little lard and paint the sides and bottom of the tin well (keep a pastry brush for the purpose); cut a strip of grease-proof paper for the sides and one for the bottom and press them down well. The cake will not be a good shape unless the paper fits well round the sides.

For rich fruit cakes, which have to be in the oven a long time, put a double lot of paper, greasing the first layer well.

Small crinkly paper cases can be used for little cakes if liked.

Next weigh out the ingredients. Break the eggs separately into a basin in case of a bad one.

Then make your cake. Be careful the mixture for fruit cake is not too moist, or the fruit will sink to the bottom.

Cake-baking

To the inexperienced cook this is the most difficult part of cake-making. If the oven is too hot a hard crust forms on the cake, and the inside cannot rise properly; if it is too slow the cake becomes dry and does not rise properly. For those who cannot judge the heat with the hand an oven thermometer is a great help. Here is a chart of the required heats:

Bread, scones and pastry	450°
Small cakes and Swiss roll	400°
Genoese, Madeira and sponges	370°
Small fruit cakes	340°
Large, rich fruit cakes	320°
Biscuits	330°

In the recipes for sandwiches, small cakes, etc., the time required for baking has been given. In the case of larger cakes, however, this varies so much according to the size of the tin used that it is not possible to give a definite time. Remember that the thicker through the cake the longer it will take to cook.

When the cake has risen and begun to set on the top the heat can be lowered a little, or the cake moved to a cooler shelf.

Some ovens are apt to burn cakes at the top or bottom even when the heat is correct. In this case put some kitchen salt or silver-sand on a baking sheet and put it under the cakes. Water in the bottom of a gas oven helps to prevent burning and prevents the cake getting too dry.

To test whether a cake is cooked, touch the top lightly with the tip of the finger. If the cake is done the surface should spring back once the finger is removed. If you hear a little crunch as you touch the cake it is not quite done. To test a large, rich fruit cake it is best to put a heated fine steel knitting needle right through the middle. Then draw it out carefully. If the cake is done the needle should be quite clean.

Sponge cakes are best left alone, but it does not hurt other cakes to open the oven door now and again just for a second to see how they are getting on. Be sure to shut the door gently.

When the cake is done lift it out of the tin by the paper, or turn it gently on to one's hand, and put it on a rack or sieve to cool. When cold put it in a tin till wanted.

Icing Cakes

The icing and decorating of cakes is a very fascinating occupation, as it gives free rein to the artistic fancy. Not only are there many different kinds of icing but the ways in which iced cakes can be decorated are legion, and it is great fun exercising one's ingenuity and thinking out original designs.

As the different icings call for different treatment you will find descriptions of how to use them under each recipe.

Much practice is needed to become expert at icing, but, of course, some icings are much easier to deal with than others. Butter icing is, perhaps, the easiest to begin on, as it is soft and does not set quickly. Glacé and meringue icing are the next easiest.

Royal icing is really in a class by itself, as it is only used for very special cakes, such as Christmas, Wedding, etc. This icing will set into any shape and therefore lends itself to elaborate designs. Considerable skill is required to get perfection in this, the most formal of icings, but one is amply repaid by the result. Truly, when one has iced a

Use a little imagination in choosing fillings for your shortcrust cases. Top with icing and decorate with cherries and angelica; add jam or use as a basis for little fruit tarts

wedding cake in different tiers, really beautifully, with an original and artistic design, one understands a little that feeling of achievement a sculptor must have as he puts the finishing touches to a work of art.

ICED CAKES

Chocolate Layer Cake

4 oz. butter.	4 oz. flour.
4 oz. sugar.	1 teaspoonful baking
2 eggs.	powder.
4 oz. Mexican chocolate.	2 tablespoonsful milk.

Melt the chocolate in the milk. Then cream the butter and sugar, add the chocolate, which must be quite smooth and not too hot, and then the beaten eggs gradually. Beat well. Finally, add the flour and baking powder.

Put the mixture in a prepared cake tin and bake in a fairly quick oven for about an hour.

When cold cut it across and put in a chocolate butter icing filling. Put together again and ice all over with chocolate glacé icing. Decorate with walnuts, cherries and angelica.

Chocolate Sandwich

4 oz. soft brown or castor sugar.	2 eggs.
	2 oz. chocolate powder.
4 oz. butter.	½ teaspoonful baking
5 oz. flour.	powder.

Cream the butter and sugar, add the beaten eggs, and lastly the flour, baking powder and chocolate powder sieved together.

Put the mixture into two greased sandwich tins and bake in a fairly quick oven for 20 minutes.

When cold put a vanilla butter icing filling between them, and ice the top with chocolate glacé icing. Decorate with blanched almonds, cherries and angelica.

Coffee Cake

2 oz. butter.	1 dessertspoonful
3 oz. brown sugar.	coffee essence.
6 oz. flour.	¼ pint milk
1¼ teaspoonsful baking powder.	3 oz. castor or granulated sugar } for the sauce.
1 egg and 1 yolk.	

Put the milk and white sugar in a pan and heat till the sugar is dissolved. Then allow to cool.

Cream the butter and brown sugar, then add the beaten eggs gradually, and beat in well. Fold in the flour and baking powder,

and add the sauce and, lastly, the coffee essence.

Bake in a fairly quick oven for about an hour.

Ice on the top with coffee glacé icing or coffee butter icing. Or cut open once or twice and fill with coffee butter, and ice all over with coffee glacé icing. Decorate with walnuts.

If coffee butter icing is used for the top, put a little in a forcing bag with a rose squeezer and pipe designs on the top.

Coffee Nougatine

Make a coffee cake as above, and when cold cut it open and fill with coffee butter icing. Spread butter icing all over the cake as smoothly as possible, and scatter chopped browned almonds over it.

Genoese Cake

4 oz. butter.	½ oz. ground rice.
4 oz. sugar.	¼ teaspoonful baking powder.
2 eggs.	4½ oz. flour.

Cream the butter and sugar. Then add the beaten eggs gradually and beat well. Put in the flour, ground rice and baking powder, and when it is well mixed turn into a prepared tin and bake in a fairly quick oven for about an hour.

When cold cut in half and put either a layer of apricot, raspberry or strawberry jam in the middle. Then ice the top with meringue icing, flavoured with a little sieved jam and coloured according to which jam is chosen.

Orange Cake

5 oz. butter.	½ teaspoonful baking powder.
6 oz. sugar.	3 eggs.
6 oz. flour.	1 orange.

Beat the sugar and butter to a cream and add the beaten eggs. Then add the grated orange rind. Fold in the flour and baking powder.

Put the mixture into a prepared cake tin and bake in a fairly quick oven for about an hour.

Ice with orange glacé icing. One or two fillings of orange curd can be put in if desired. Decorate with crystallised orange slices.

Orange Sandwich

2 eggs and their weight in butter, sugar and flour.	¼ teaspoonful baking powder.
	Grated rind of half an orange.

Beat the butter and sugar to a cream, and add the beaten eggs. Then add the grated rind and, lastly, the flour and baking powder.

Put the mixture into two greased sandwich tins and bake in a fairly quick oven for 20 minutes.

When cool, but not cold, spread orange glacé icing on both sides of the sandwich and put them together. When the sandwich is completely cold and the filling absolutely set, ice the top with orange glacé icing and decorate with crystallised orange slices and angelica.

CAKES EITHER ICED OR PLAIN

Cherry Cake

8 oz. flour.	A little milk.
4 oz. sugar.	1 teaspoonful baking powder.
4 oz. butter.	4 oz. cherries.
2 eggs.	1 oz. chopped almonds.

Cream the butter and sugar, and add the beaten eggs gradually.

Cut the cherries in half and add them with the almonds. Then put in the flour and baking powder, and, lastly, a little milk.

Put the mixture into a prepared tin and bake in a moderate oven for about 1¼ hours.

If desired, ice with white meringue icing and decorate with cherries and angelica.

Pineapple Cake

6 oz. flour.	1 oz. glacé pineapple cubes.
2 oz. butter.	½ teaspoonful baking powder.
3 oz. sugar.	A little milk.
1 egg.	

Cream the butter and sugar, and add the beaten egg. Then mix in the flour and baking powder, and add a little milk. Lastly, put in the cubes cut in small pieces.

Put the mixture into a prepared cake tin and bake in a fairly quick oven for about an hour.

If desired, ice with pineapple glacé icing and put in a pineapple filling.

Preserved Ginger Cake

6 oz. butter.	Rind of ½ lemon.
6 oz. sugar.	4 eggs.
10 oz. flour.	4 oz. preserved ginger.
1 teaspoonful	4 oz. mixed peel.
baking powder.	½ teaspoonful ground ginger.

Cream the butter and sugar, and add the beaten eggs gradually.

Sieve the flour and baking powder and add the peel and ginger chopped small, the grated lemon rind and the ground ginger. Then add all these to the mixture and mix them in well.

Put into a prepared cake tin and bake in a fairly quick oven for about 1¼ hours.

If desired, ice with white meringue icing and decorate with preserved ginger and angelica.

Coconut Cake

6 oz. flour.	3 oz. desiccated coconut.
3 oz. butter.	2 small eggs.
4 oz. castor sugar.	Small teaspoonful bak-
A little milk.	ing powder.

Cream the butter and sugar, and add the beaten eggs gradually. Then add the flour, baking powder and the coconut, and, lastly, a little milk.

Put the mixture into a prepared cake tin and bake in a moderate oven for about 1¼ hours.

To be able to make a really successful layer cake is a passport to popularity!

Cornflour Cake

4 oz. cornflour.	1 teaspoonful baking
1 oz. flour.	powder.
2 oz. castor sugar.	1 egg.
2 oz. butter.	A little milk.

Cream the butter and sugar, and add the egg beaten with a little milk. Then add the cornflour, flour and baking powder.

Put into a prepared cake tin and bake in a moderate oven for about an hour.

Honey Cake

8 oz. flour.	3 oz. butter.
4 oz. honey.	3 oz. sugar.
2 eggs.	1 teaspoonful baking powder.

Cream the butter and sugar, and add the beaten eggs gradually. Beat in the honey, and, lastly, add the flour and baking powder.

Put into a prepared shallow cake tin and bake in a moderate oven for about 45 minutes.

Jam Sponge

3 oz. castor sugar.	2 oz. ground rice.
3 eggs.	1 teaspoonful baking
2 oz. flour.	powder.

Beat the eggs and sugar together till thick. Then add the flour, rice and baking powder.

Pour the mixture into two buttered sandwich tins and bake in a fairly quick oven from 7 to 10 minutes.

Turn out on to a piece of paper sprinkled with castor sugar. When cold put together with jam.

NOTE.—If liked, a little grated lemon rind can be added to the mixture and lemon curd used as a filling instead of jam.

Lemon Madeira

8 oz. flour.	4 eggs.
5 oz. butter.	1 teaspoonful baking powder.
5 oz. sugar.	Grated rind of a lemon.

Cream the butter and sugar, and add the beaten eggs gradually. Then mix in the flour, baking powder and lemon rind.

Put in a prepared cake tin and bake in a moderate oven for about $1\frac{1}{4}$ hours.

Orange Madeira

Make in the same way as for lemon madeira, but substitute orange peel for lemon peel.

Sponge Cake

3 eggs.	$\frac{1}{2}$ teaspoonful baking powder.
4 oz. castor sugar.	4 oz. flour.

Prepare a tin by first brushing it over thoroughly with melted butter. Then mix together equal quantities of sieved flour and castor sugar; put it into the tin and shake the tin well till both sides and bottom are well coated. Then shake out any superfluous flour and sugar.

Beat the eggs and sugar together until the mixture is thick and creamy (quite half an hour). Then fold in the flour and baking powder very lightly with a steel spoon.

Put the mixture into the tin and bake *at once* in a hot oven for 20 minutes. Do not touch the mixture once it is in the tin.

Swiss Roll

3 eggs.	$3\frac{1}{2}$ oz. castor sugar.
$2\frac{1}{2}$ oz. flour.	Small pinch of baking powder.

Grease a Swiss-roll tin, line with greaseproof paper and then grease the paper well.

Beat the eggs and the sugar together till the mixture is thick and creamy; then fold in the flour and the baking powder lightly with a steel spoon.

Pour the mixture into the tin and bake in a hot oven for about 10 minutes.

While it is cooking get ready a piece of grease-proof paper a little larger than the tin, and sprinkle it well with icing sugar. Also heat some jam.

Turn out the cake on to the paper, trim the edges and spread with the hot jam rather thinly. Roll up quickly.

Victoria Sandwich

2 eggs, their weight in butter, sugar and flour	$\frac{1}{4}$ teaspoonful baking powder.

Cream the butter and sugar, add the beaten eggs gradually, and then the flour and baking powder.

Put the mixture into two greased sandwich tins and bake in a fairly quick oven for 20 minutes.

When cold spread with raspberry jam and put together.

Gingerbread

6 oz. flour.	2 oz. golden syrup.
1 dessertspoonful ground ginger.	2 oz. black treacle.
Pinch of salt.	1 tablespoonful marmalade.
2 oz. butter.	$\frac{1}{2}$ teaspoonful bicarbonate of soda.
2 oz. moist sugar.	A little milk.
1 egg.	

498

Sieve the flour, salt and ginger into a basin.

Put the butter, sugar, syrup, treacle and marmalade into a saucepan and stir over a gentle heat until liquid. Then pour into the flour, etc., and beat well.

Add the well-beaten egg. Then add the soda dissolved in a little hot milk. Beat well and pour into a greased, shallow cake-tin.

Bake for about 1 hour in a slow oven.

Walnut Layer Cake

6 oz. margarine.	3 eggs.
6 oz. castor sugar.	6 oz. S.R. flour.

Cream the margarine, add the sugar and continue creaming until soft and white. Beat in the eggs gradually and, lastly, fold in the sifted flour. Divide the mixture between three 7-in. sandwich-tins and bake in a moderate oven 10-15 minutes.

Frosting:

6 oz. castor sugar.	$\frac{1}{8}$ teaspoonful of
1 egg white.	cream of tartar.
2 tablespoonsful water.	Walnuts.

Place all the ingredients in a double saucepan, stir over gentle heat until the sugar dissolves. With the water in the bottom pan boiling gently the whole time, and using a rotary beater, whisk for 7 minutes or until the mixture will stand in peaks.

Turn the cakes if necessary and sandwich with one tablespoon of the frosting mixed with 2 oz. roughly chopped walnuts. Spread the top and sides of the cake with the remainder of the frosting and decorate with a few halved walnuts.

Lunch Cake

12 oz. flour.	2 oz. lard.
2 oz. butter.	2 oz. chopped peel.
3 eggs.	8 oz. currants.
1 teaspoonful ground ginger.	6 oz. sugar.
$\frac{1}{2}$ oz. caraway seeds.	2 teaspoonsful baking powder.
A little milk.	

Rub the butter and lard into the flour and baking powder. Add all the dry ingredients. Then add a little milk to the yolks and stir them into the mixture. Beat up the whites to a stiff froth and stir in lightly.

Put the mixture in a prepared cake tin and bake in a slow oven for about $1\frac{1}{2}$ hours.

FRUIT CAKES

Dundee

$4\frac{1}{2}$ oz. butter.	$\frac{1}{2}$ teaspoonful baking powder.
6 oz. brown sugar.	
6 oz. flour.	Pinch of salt.
6 oz. sultanas.	Pinch of spice.
3 oz. currants.	3 eggs.
3 oz. mixed peel (chopped).	Almonds for top.

Cream the butter and sugar, add the beaten eggs gradually, and then add the dry ingredients.

Put the mixture into a prepared cake tin, scatter the almonds on the top and bake in a moderate oven for about $1\frac{1}{4}$ hours.

Empire Cake

6 oz. flour.	2 oz chopped peel.
4 oz. butter.	3 eggs.
4 oz. sugar.	Small $\frac{1}{2}$ teaspoonful baking powder and mixed spice.
4 oz. sultanas.	
2 oz. currants.	
1 oz. chopped almonds.	Grated lemon rind.

Cream the butter and sugar together, and add the beaten eggs gradually. Then mix in all the other ingredients.

Put the mixture into a prepared cake tin and bake in a moderate oven for about $1\frac{1}{4}$ hours.

Family Cake (Inexpensive)

8 oz. flour.	1 oz. chopped lemon peel, if liked.
4 oz. soft brown sugar.	
4 oz. sultanas.	$\frac{1}{2}$ teaspoonful bicarbonate of soda.
4 oz. margarine.	
Half teaspoonful mixed spice or nutmeg.	1 teaspoonful vinegar.
	$\frac{1}{2}$ gill milk.

Rub the margarine into the flour, and add the sugar, fruit and spice or nutmeg.

Mix together the milk, soda and vinegar and stir it into the flour at once. Put into a prepared cake tin and bake in a quick oven to begin with, lowering the heat when the cake has risen (about $1\frac{1}{2}$ hours altogether).

Plum Cake

12 oz. flour.	4 oz. treacle.
6 oz. butter.	8 oz. raisins.
4 eggs.	8 oz. currants.
1 teaspoonful bicarbonate of soda.	4 oz. chopped mixed peel.
A little milk.	4 oz. brown sugar.

Cream the butter and sugar. Then add the treacle, next the beaten eggs gradually, and then the flour and fruit.

Dissolve the soda in a little warm milk and add to the mixture at once. Stir well.

Put the mixture into a prepared cake tin and bake in a moderate oven for 1½–1¾ hours.

Raisin Cake

8 oz. brown sugar.	1 teaspoonful mixed spice.
4 eggs.	8 oz. butter.
8 oz. currants.	1 lb. flour.
1 teaspoonful bicarbonate of soda.	8 oz. stoned raisins.
	½ teacupful milk.

Rub the butter into the flour and add the rest of the dry ingredients. Then add the beaten eggs and, lastly, the milk.

Bake in a moderate oven for about 1¾ hours.

Seed Cake

3 eggs.	4 oz. flour.
3 oz. butter.	4 oz. sugar.
2 teaspoonsful caraway seeds.	Small half-teaspoonful baking powder.

Beat the butter and sugar to a cream, then add the yolk of one egg and a third of the flour and baking powder sieved together. Then add another yolk and some more flour, and so on till all the flour is in. Lastly, add the caraway seeds.

Whisk up the whites to a stiff froth and fold them in at the end.

Put the mixture into a prepared cake-tin and bake in a moderate oven for about an hour.

Sultana Cake

6 oz. butter.	10 oz. flour.
6 oz. sugar.	12 oz. sultanas.
4 eggs.	Level teaspoonful
Grated lemon rind.	baking powder.

Cream the butter and sugar together; beat the eggs and add them gradually. Then add the flour, baking powder, lemon rind and sultanas and mix well.

Put the mixture into a prepared cake tin and bake in a moderate oven for about 1½ hours.

CAKES FOR SPECIAL OCCASIONS

Birthday Cake

10 oz. butter.	4 oz. currants.
10 oz. sugar.	4 oz. chopped peel.
10 oz. flour.	4 oz. ground almonds.
6 eggs.	1 eggcupful of rum.
8 oz. sultanas.	½ teaspoonful baking powder.

Beat the butter and sugar to a cream. Then add the beaten eggs one by one, beating well. Add a little flour with the last two or three eggs if the mixture shows any signs of curdling.

Put all the other dry ingredients together and add them to the mixture gradually; halfway through add the rum. Stir the mixture thoroughly so that everything is well blended.

Put the mixture into a cake tin, greased and doubly lined with greaseproof paper, and bake in a slow oven till thoroughly cooked through (about 2½ hours).

When cold, cover with almond paste and ice with either American icing and decorate at once, or with royal icing.

Decorate as desired, and when the icing is set, write: 'A Happy Birthday,' or whatever is liked, in coloured royal icing.

Sugar rose-holders in different colours and tiny candles to match can be bought from any good confectioner.

NOTE. Of course, birthday cakes need not necessarily be fruit cakes. It is entirely a matter of taste. A large chocolate or orange cake is popular with children, and in this case use chocolate or orange glacé icing.

Christening Cake

8 oz. butter.	½ gill brandy.
8 oz. castor sugar.	¼ teaspoonful almond essence.
12 oz. sultanas.	
12 oz. currants.	8 oz. chopped peel.
12 oz. flour.	½ teaspoonful baking powder.
5 eggs.	
2 oz. chopped almonds.	1 dessertspoonful black treacle.

Cream the butter and sugar. Beat the eggs and add them slowly, beating well. Add a little flour towards the end if the mixture shows any signs of curdling.

Mix all the dry ingredients together and add them to the mixture, putting in the almond essence, treacle and brandy alternately with the flour. Stir the mixture well so that all the ingredients are well blended.

Put the mixture into a well-greased double-lined cake tin and bake in a slow oven till thoroughly cooked (about 3 hours).

Christening cakes should be iced with royal icing and decorated with formal pipings.

A sugar cradle with a tiny doll inside, or a sugar stork holding a cradle, can be bought from any good confectioner, and should be placed in the centre of the cake.

Christmas Cake

8 oz. flour.	4 oz. orange peel
8 oz. butter.	(chopped fine).
8 oz. dark sugar.	4 oz. lemon peel
8 oz. currants.	(chopped fine).
8 oz. sultanas.	1 oz. ground almonds.
4 oz. cherries.	½ teaspoonful
A little rum or	cinnamon.
brandy.	¼ teaspoonful mixed
½ teaspoonful baking	spice.
powder.	4 eggs.

Cream the butter and sugar. Add the beaten eggs one at a time, beating well. Add a little flour with the last egg or two if the mixture shows any signs of curdling.

Put all the other dry ingredients together, and add them to the mixture. Put in the rum half-way through. Stir the mixture well so that all the ingredients are well blended.

Put the mixture into a well-greased double-lined cake tin and bake in a slow oven till thoroughly cooked (about 3 hours).

NOTE. This cake should be made at least three weeks before Christmas, as it improves with keeping.

A Christmas cake can be iced in several different ways.

First put on a layer of almond paste. Then ice with royal icing in one of the following ways:

1. Coat with royal icing and when set decorate with formal pipings and finish off with marzipan berries, silver balls, angelica leaves, etc., etc.; or with a Father Christmas, Esquimaux, Polar bears, etc.

2. Coat the top only and decorate in the same way as above. Put a paper frilling of whatever colour is desired round the sides: white and gold or white and silver look very attractive.

3. Beat up the royal icing extra stiff (double the ordinary amount will be required) and lay it thickly and roughly all over the cake. Do not smooth it down. Then take a fork and with it rough up the icing all over the cake till it resembles a wind-blown snowdrift. Make the points of icing all go in the same direction to look more realistic.

Put red marzipan berries unevenly between the points of icing and finish off with tiny diamond shapes of angelica, two to each berry.

This is a very attractive decoration and makes a change from the usual extremely formal icing.

Simnel (or Easter) Cake

8 oz. butter.	4 eggs.
8 oz. sugar.	½ teaspoonful baking
12 oz. flour.	powder.
6 oz. sultanas.	1 dessertspoonful
6 oz. currants.	black treacle.
6 oz. chopped peel.	Almond paste.

Beat the butter and sugar to a cream. Beat the eggs and add them gradually to the mixture, beating well.

Put all the dry ingredients together and add them to the mixture, stirring well. Add the treacle half-way through.

Cut a round of almond paste the size of the cake tin. Put half the mixture into the tin. Then put in the round of almond paste and press down well. Put in the rest of the mixture and bake in a moderate oven till thoroughly cooked (about 1¾ hours). (If a plainer cake is required omit the filling.)

When cold put another round of almond paste on the top, sticking it on with a little melted golden syrup. Cut a strip about an inch wide, or according to the size of the cake, and put it round the edge, first painting it with a little beaten yolk to make it stick. Mark the strip with a fork. Then paint the whole top lightly with yolk of egg and put the cake in a very hot oven till the almond paste is a golden brown. Take out of the oven and let it cool on a rack.

When quite cold place Easter decorations in the centre, small sugar eggs, fondant sweets, chickens, and so on.

Wedding Cake (Three-tiered)

1 lb. 3 oz. butter.	1 lb. 12½ oz. flour.
1 lb. 3 oz. castor sugar.	12 eggs.
2 lb. 6 oz. currants.	9½ oz. chopped almonds.
2 lb. 6 oz. sultanas.	1¾ gills rum.
9½ oz. cherries.	1 lb. 3 oz. chopped peel.
9½ oz. raisins.	1½ tablespoonsful black
½ teaspoonful almond	treacle.
essence.	½ teaspoonful mixed
2 teaspoonsful baking	spice.
powder.	½ teaspoonful cinnamon.

Cream the butter and sugar. Add the beaten eggs gradually, beating well, and adding flour towards the end if the mixture shows any signs of curdling.

Put all the dry ingredients together and add them slowly to the mixture, stirring well. Put in the almond essence, the treacle and the rum alternately with the flour. Mix well so that all the ingredients are well blended.

Put the mixture into well-greased double-lined cake tins (10-in., 8-in. and 6-in.) and bake in a slow oven till thoroughly cooked.

NOTE. Wedding cake should be made at least a month before it is needed, as it improves greatly with keeping.

To ice a wedding cake:

Wedding cakes are usually made in two or three tiers. First cover each cake thickly with almond paste. Then coat smoothly with royal icing, and put each cake on a thick silver board a little wider than the cake.

When the coating is absolutely hard, decorate with formal pipings rather more elaborately than for other cakes, and ornament with wedding favours, which can be bought from any good confectioner—sugar doves, little silver shoes, silver horse-shoes, small sprays of orange blossom, etc.—arranging them round the edge only of the tops of the cakes, and round the sides. Leave the centre of the cakes bare.

For a wedding cake in tiers it is necessary to have small sugar pillars, three or four, to support each tier. Put them towards the centre of the cake and then build it up. The small cake on the top should be finished off with a central ornament standing rather high. A small silver vase filled with sprays of orange blossom makes a good decoration for this purpose.

LITTLE CAKES

Basic Dough for Buns

1½ *lb. plain flour.*   1 *large egg (or 2 small*
1 *oz. yeast.*   *ones).*
3 *oz. castor sugar.*   3 *oz. dried fruit.*
½ *pint milk*   1 *oz. chopped candied peel.*
   (generous).   3 *oz. margarine.*

Sift ½ lb. of the flour into a warm bowl. Crumble yeast into a small bowl and mix with a teaspoonful sugar until liquid. Heat milk until lukewarm, then stir into yeast, mixing well. Add this liquid to flour gradually, mixing with wooden spoon until smooth. Cover bowl with clean teacloth and leave in warm place for about an hour. Meanwhile, sift remainder of flour and rub in fat. Sprinkle in remainder of sugar and cleaned, dried fruit and peel, mixing thoroughly.

Beat the eggs in readiness. When yeast mixture is 'sponged,' add second mixture, alternately with eggs, beating with the hand to mix well. If only one egg is used, add a little milk if necessary. Again, cover bowl and leave in warm place until double in bulk—about 1½ hours. Turn on to floured pastryboard and knead lightly but well. Divide into pieces and shape into buns. Arrange on floured baking trays, spaced apart, and leave for a further 15 minutes in warm place to recover their size. Then bake in hot oven for about 20 minutes. Meanwhile, make a little sugar syrup. When buns are cooked take from oven, brush with glaze, and leave on wire tray to cool.

Quicker Dough for Buns (or Small Loaves)

1½ *lb. plain flour.*   2 *tablespoonsful castor*
2 *oz. yeast*   *sugar.*
  (fresh).   ½ *teaspoonful mixed*
¾ *pint milk.*   *spice (optional).*
Good pinch salt.   1½ *oz. margarine.*

Cream yeast with a teaspoonful sugar until liquid. Heat milk until lukewarm and stir into yeast, mixing well. Sift flour and salt (with spice, if liked), add sugar and rub in margarine. Make well in middle and stir in yeast mixture gradually, mixing to a soft dough, using your hands. Turn on to floured board and knead lightly but well.

Then divide the dough into an equal number of pieces. To make small loaves, break a little of the dough from each piece. Knead larger pieces into rounds and flatten with palm of hand. Knead smaller pieces to rounds and place one on each of larger pieces. Flatten again, then push knob of knitting needle or skewer through top piece to make deep indent. Arrange on floured trays spaced apart and leave until well risen before baking as for buns in hot oven. If liked, glaze as for previous buns.

Nutty Twist Bread. Make one or other of above mixtures. Divide into pieces, shaping each into long finger rolls. Plait neatly, joining firmly at top and bottom. Leave to prove, then bake as above. Remove from oven, brush over with glaze and sprinkle with chopped roasted nuts, then put back into oven for a minute to candy.

Lemon Buns. Make one or other of above mixtures and divide into small portions as for buns. Flatten with rolling pin and shape into squares. Put a small blob of lemon curd on dough and spread thinly over surface. Fold corners to middle and press firmly to join. Bake as for buns. When cooked, glaze and

Dissolve the sugar in the water, without letting it boil, add the cream of tartar, then boil to 240° (or until a drop or two will make a soft ball when tested in cold water).

Beat the white of egg very stiffly and pour the syrup slowly into it, whisking hard all the time. Add the flavouring and beat until the icing will pile up without spreading. Then spread quickly on the cake.

This is a delicious icing for fruit cakes, but it is rather tricky to make, so follow the instructions carefully.

Butter Icing

6 oz. sieved icing sugar.   4 oz. butter.

Beat the butter and sugar together until thick and creamy.

For Chocolate Butter Icing. Grate some unsweetened couverture chocolate (about a tablespoonful) into a saucer and stand it in a warm place, but away from direct heat, until the chocolate is quite dissolved. Pour it into the butter icing and beat it in well.

For Coffee Butter Icing. Add a tablespoonful of Camp coffee to the butter icing and beat well.

For Vanilla Butter Icing. Flavour the butter icing with a little vanilla essence.

Butter icing should be spread as smoothly as possible over the cake with a small palette knife.

If used for decorating purposes, put some into a forcing bag or syringe, using whichever icing head you like (a rose squeezer is always effective) and pipe little roses or a border, or whatever you please.

Glacé Icing

1 lb. icing sugar. 3½ tablespoonsful warm water.

Put the warm water in a basin and add the icing sugar gradually, beating all the time. The basin should be placed over warm water, but the icing should not be allowed to get more than lukewarm. When ready for use it should be of the consistency of thick sauce.

This icing is inclined to be transparent, but a second coat can always be put on if necessary.

It should be spread evenly over the cake with a small palette knife as soon as it is made. The cake should then not be moved till the icing is quite set, or it will crack.

For Chocolate Glacé Icing. Warm the icing a little and add grated unsweetened couverture chocolate until the icing is well flavoured and a good colour. If too thick add a very little water.

For Coffee Glacé Icing. Use rather less water in mixing the icing and then add some Camp coffee until the icing is well flavoured and a good colour.

For Orange or Lemon Glacé Icing. Make the icing with orange or lemon juice instead of water and colour it with a few drops of orange or lemon vegetable colouring.

For Pineapple Glacé Icing. Take a small tin of crushed pineapple, strain off the juice and use it instead of water for making the icing. Use the pineapple pulp, mixed well with castor sugar, for the pineapple filling.

Meringue Icing

Slightly beat a white of egg and gradually add to it sieved icing sugar. When fairly stiff add a tablespoonful of water and put the basin over warm water. Beat the icing hard and add more icing sugar until it is the same consistency as thick sauce. Continue beating for about 10 minutes, when it should be thick and creamy. Never let it get more than lukewarm.

This is the best icing for doing a slab and then cutting it up into small iced cakes, as it sets slowly. It can be coloured or flavoured as desired.

Royal Icing

White of egg.   Lemon juice.
Icing sugar.

Take as many whites of egg as you require. (Roughly, two whites will be sufficient to coat or decorate a moderate-size cake.)

Sieve your icing sugar on to a piece of paper, using a hair sieve. Allow 7-8 oz. for each white of egg.

Slightly beat the whites with a whisk. Then take a spatula and gradually add the icing sugar, beating hard. If it is added too quickly the icing will be rough and sugary instead of smooth and creamy. Add a few drops of lemon juice and continue beating and adding sugar till the spoon will stand up when stuck in the icing. Now stop adding sugar, but continue to beat the icing hard until you can make a point of icing stand up on the end of the spoon without turning over. It is absolutely essential, especially for decorating, that the icing should be sufficiently stiff to stand up by itself, otherwise the decorations will lose their shape and effectiveness.

Royal icing sets harder and keeps better than any other, and is therefore the best to use for large, rich fruit cakes, such as Christmas, Birthday, Christening and Wedding cakes.

How to use Royal Icing:

1. *Coating.* Beat up the quantity of royal icing required.

Place the cake, covered with almond paste, on an upturned plate and spread the icing evenly all over the cake. Smooth it round the top and round and round the sides until it is quite even. A good way to get it smooth is to dip a palette knife in hot water, shake off the drops, and give a last sweep all over the icing with the hot, wet knife.

A turning board can be used to stand the cake on if desired.

Now leave the cake all night or until the icing is absolutely set and hard. (This takes longer in wet weather.) Before the icing hardens trim it round the bottom with a knife. It is a good plan to put the cake on a silver board, as it looks nice and is much easier to handle.

2. *Decorating.* Beat up some royal icing as stiffly as possible. Choose the icing head you wish to use (a rose squeezer is a very popular one and is most effective, or a shell squeezer is also attractive and not difficult to use). Put it in the end of an icing syringe or forcing bag and fill up the bag or syringe with icing.

Cover the basin of royal icing over with a damp cloth while you are not using it.

Now squeeze any patterns you choose all over the cake in any design you fancy. It is best for a beginner to practise on the back of a plate until even patterns can be produced.

If desired, the icing can be coloured. Pink piping on a white-coated cake is very effective. By using a head with a small plain hole at the end, anything desired can be written on the top of the cake.

The pipings must be ornamented before they set. Silver balls are always an attractive addition.

If the cake is on a silver board, squeeze a pattern of icing all round the bottom of the cake where it joins the board, to finish it off.

DELICIOUS FILLINGS

The addition of a good filling to a plain sponge or a Genoese cake is an excellent way of making such a cake even nicer. The butter icing recipe given above can be used equally well for a filling, but here are some other suggestions.

Apple Filling

2 good-sized eating apples.
1 *lemon.*
8 oz. granulated sugar.
Sherry (optional).

Wash, peel and core the apples and grate them into a saucepan, add the strained lemon juice and grated rind, and then the sugar. Bring slowly to the boil, stirring well, then cook gently for 5 minutes, stirring all the time. Add a very little sherry if liked. Leave the mixture to get cold, then spread on one half of the cake and press the other half on top.

Banana Filling

2 or 3 bananas.
Cream.
2 tablespoonsful apricot jam.

Put the bananas through a hair sieve and mix the apricot jam with the purée. Whip up a little cream and fold into the mixture. Spread on one half of the cake and put the other half on top, pressing together well.

Coffee Candy Filling

Make half the quantity of butter icing given above and flavour with coffee essence. Spread on half the cake, then sprinkle crushed sugar candy on top. Spread the other half of the cake very lightly with coffee icing and put the halves together, pressing well.

Confectioners' Cream

½ teacupful cold milk.
1 dessertspoonful cornflour.
1 teaspoonful lemon juice.
Yolk of an egg.
3 oz. castor sugar.

Make the cornflour into a smooth paste with the milk and add the sugar. Put into a saucepan and stir over a gentle heat till it thickens. Allow to cool, then add the beaten yolk and, lastly, the strained lemon juice. Stir well and put aside to get quite cold. Then spread on one half of the cake and press the other half on top.

Prune and Almond Filling

4 oz. prunes.
8 oz. granulated sugar.
2-3 oz. chopped almonds.
½ gill prune liquid.
2 whites of egg.
1 tablespoonful sherry.

Wash the prunes and put to soak overnight in cold water, then cook in the same water till

MILK ROLLS

How to Make Them

1. Sieve the flour and salt into a bowl. Make a well in the flour

2. Add the creamed yeast, egg and sugar, beat well, cover and leave to rise

3. When the dough has risen, knead well, roll until ¾ in. thick, then cut out rolls

4. Leave to prove. Bake in a quick oven and when almost done brush with milk

tender. Take ½ gill of the juice and put into a saucepan with the sugar, heating slowly while the sugar dissolves. Then boil to 245° F. (or till a drop or two tested in cold water forms a soft ball between the finger and thumb). Have ready the whites of egg beaten to a stiff froth and slowly add the boiling syrup to them, beating all the time. Lastly, add the stoned chopped prunes and the chopped almonds, together with the sherry. Spread on each half of the cake and press lightly together.

Raspberry Filling

Whip some cream and spread each half of the cake with it. Crush some fresh raspberries in a basin with a little castor sugar and spread

over one half, put the other half on top and press gently together.

BREAD, FANCY BREAD AND SCONES

One sometimes hears people complain that bread-making at home takes too long and that kneading is such hard work. But it is really no more tiring than beating a batch of cakes, and while the dough is rising one can get on with other work. Only one day a week need be given up to it, as good home-made bread will keep a week.

Yeast Bread. Compressed yeast can be bought from any baker and should be ordered as required. If kept moist and at blood-heat its cells multiply and let off gases which give bread its light, porous consistency. Too much

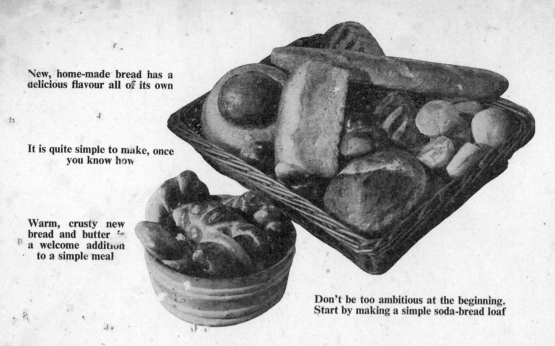

New, home-made bread has a delicious flavour all of its own

It is quite simple to make, once you know how

Warm, crusty new bread and butter is a welcome addition to a simple meal

Don't be too ambitious at the beginning. Start by making a simple soda-bread loaf

heat kills the yeast, while too little prevents its action. It should be kept in a cool place till needed, and then creamed with a little sugar to start it working before the warmed liquid is added to it.

The basins used for mixing bread, the flour and the milk or water should always be warmed to blood-heat. While the dough is rising it should be covered with a cloth and put in a warm place (but away from direct heat) either in front of or over the oven. It should be left till it has risen to double its original size.

The kneading is extremely important, as it distributes the yeast and its gases evenly through the bread.

Soda Bread, etc. Soda bread or scones make a change from yeast bread, and are very quick to make, as they can be baked at once. Scones should be eaten fresh, but if any are left over they can be toasted and served hot the next day.

Bridge Rolls

1 *lb. flour.*	1 *egg.*
2 *oz. lard.*	*Salt.*
½ *oz. yeast.*	1 *teaspoonful sugar.*
½ *pint water.*	

Rub the fat into the flour. Make a well in the middle. Cream the yeast with the sugar and pour the lukewarm water over it. Then add the mixture to the flour. Set to rise for 30 minutes in a warm place.

Then add the egg and a little salt and mix well. Stand to rise again for 1½ hours.

Put on a saucepan of water to boil.

Knead the dough and cut it in half. Cut up and form into oval rolls. Put them on a baking sheet and stand them over the steam from the boiling water for ½ hour.

Bake them in a very hot oven from 10 to 15 minutes.

NOTE. Be careful of draughts while the rolls are rising.

Lardy Cake (Buckinghamshire Recipe)

1 *lb. dough (which has just finished rising).*	Pinch of spice.
	3 *oz. sugar.*
3 *oz. currants.*	6 *oz. lard.*

Knead the dough and flatten it out with a rolling-pin. Then spread it with lard, sprinkle the currants and sugar over it and a pinch of spice.

Then roll the dough up, flatten it out again and slash it on the top with a knife.

Put in a greased tin and let it stand in a warm place for 10 minutes. Then bake in a fairly quick oven, lowering the heat well towards the end.

NOTE. Lardy Cake should be eaten the day it is made.

Spiced Loaf

1 *lb. flour.* 6 *oz. sultanas.*
3 *oz. lard.* *A little chopped peel, if liked.*
3 *oz. sugar.* ½ *teaspoonful mixed spice.*
½ *oz. yeast.* *Not quite ½ pint of milk.*

Dissolve the fat in the milk. Heat to blood-heat.

Cream the yeast with a little sugar, and add it to the milk. Pour this mixture into the warmed flour, sugar, sultanas, chopped peel and spice. Mix well. It should be a very soft dough.

Set it in a warm place for 1½ hours and then knead well, keeping the hands dry with a little flour. Put into a bread tin and set it in a warm place again until it is well risen.

Bake in a moderate oven for 40 minutes.

Mix together a dessertspoonful of milk and a teaspoonful of castor sugar, take out the loaf, brush it over with this mixture and put it back in the oven for a few minutes.

Tea Cakes

8 *oz. flour.* 1 *oz. lard or butter.*
½ *teaspoonful salt.* *About a gill of milk or*
1 *teaspoonful sugar.* *milk and water.*
½ *oz. yeast.*

Rub the lard into the flour and warm slightly. Then add the sugar.

Cream the yeast with a little extra sugar and pour some of the warm milk into it. Then pour this mixture into the centre of the flour. Add the salt round the edge away from the yeast. Scatter flour over the yeast lightly.

Let it stand in a warm place for 10 minutes.

Then add the rest of the milk. Mix to a light dough and knead well. Put in a warm place to rise, covering the bowl over with a cloth. Leave till risen to double its size.

Knead again, divide into three, roll and shape into round tea cakes. Prick each one with a fork.

Put them on a warmed, greased tin and stand in a warm place to rise covered over with a cloth for 10 minutes. Then bake in a quick oven for about 12 minutes.

Brush with butter and put back in the oven for 1 minute.

NOTE. To test if they are done tap them. If cooked, this should make a hollow sound.

Tea Cakes (with Currants)

Make in the same way as tea cakes (see above). When the dough has risen to double its size knead in

1 *oz. currants.* ½ *oz. sugar.*

and work in well. Allow to rise again.

Then cut into three and roll into rounds. Stand the rounds on a warm tin covered with a cloth to rise (about 20 minutes). Then bake in a quick oven for about 12 minutes.

Brush with butter and put back in the oven for 1 minute.

White Bread

3½ *lb. flour.* 3 *oz. lard.*
2 *teaspoonful salt.* 1½ *pints milk and*
1 *tablespoonful sugar.* *water (half and*
1 *oz. yeast.* *half).*

Rub the lard into the flour. Cream the yeast with the sugar and add to it the milk and water heated to blood-heat.

Make a hole in the centre of the warmed flour and pour in the milk and yeast. Scatter a little flour over the top and sprinkle the salt round the edge away from the yeast and milk.

Stand to rise in a warm place for 20 minutes.

Mix the flour with the hand to a dough till there is no dry flour left. Clean the hand with flour and knead for 5 minutes.

Stand to rise in a warm place covered with a cloth for 1½ to 2 hours.

Knead for 15 minutes.

Then form into loaves and put in warm bread tins, or make into any shape liked and put on a warm baking tin. (For a Coburg loaf mark the top with a cross just before baking.)

Put in a warm place for 10 minutes.

Bake in a hot oven which gradually cools down till the bread is done (about 1 hour).

NOTE. Brown bread can be made in exactly the same way, using 2 lb. of wholemeal flour and 1½ lb. of white flour instead of all white flour.

Drop Scones

4 *oz. flour.* ½ *teaspoonful cream of*
Half an egg. *tartar.*
1 *dessertspoonful* ½ *teaspoonful bicar-*
 golden syrup. *bonate of soda.*
Milk to mix. *Pinch of salt.*

Sieve together the flour, cream of tartar, soda and salt. Make a hole in the middle, drop in the beaten egg and the golden syrup. Mix to a stiff batter with milk, adding the milk gradually.

Grease and heat a girdle. Drop the mixture on it in tablespoonsful. Brown on one side, then turn over with a palette knife and cook on the other side.

Allow to stand between a soft cloth. Then butter and serve hot.

Plain Scones

8 oz. flour.	½ teaspoonful bicarbonate of
1½ oz. butter.	soda.
1 teaspoonful	½ teaspoonful cream of tartar.
castor sugar.	Buttermilk or sour milk to
Pinch of salt.	mix.

Sieve the dry ingredients and rub in the butter. Add enough buttermilk to make a soft spongy dough. Turn on to a floured board, knead lightly and roll out. Cut in rounds and put them on a hot girdle. Bake steadily till well risen and a very pale brown. Then turn over and bake the other side.

NOTE. These scones may be put on a floured tray and baked in a quick oven for 10 to 15 minutes.

Potato Scones

Boil some potatoes and when cooked drain off the water and put the potatoes through a masher on to a floured board. Add a pinch of salt, and work in as much sifted flour as will make the mixture into a stiff dough. Roll out, sprinkle with flour and cut into rounds or triangles.

Grease and heat a girdle and put the rounds on it. Brown on one side, then turn over with a palette knife and brown the other side.

Serve hot.

Soda Bread, Brown (I)

8 oz. flour.	Flat teaspoonful bicar-
8 oz. wholemeal flour.	bonate of soda.
Good teaspoonful salt.	About ½ pint of sour
2 teaspoonsful sugar.	milk or buttermilk.

Sieve all the dry ingredients together, and mix with milk or buttermilk. Knead to a dough and then roll out and cut into two cakes or four smaller ones.

Put on a floured baking sheet and bake in a very hot oven for about 20 minutes.

Soda Bread, Brown (II)

Use the same quantities as for Soda Bread (Brown) (I). Rub 3 oz. butter, lard or dripping into the flour, then sieve in the other dry ingredients and mix with buttermilk or milk. Instead of rolling out the dough make it moister by adding a little more sour milk or

buttermilk, put it in a greased cake or bread tin and bake in a very hot oven.

Soda Bread (White)

Make in the same way as Brown Soda Bread (I) or (II) (see above), but use all white flour.

MAKE YOUR OWN ICES

Ices are so useful, either alone or as part of a more ambitious sweet. These recipes can be made with any type of freezer. If you are using a refrigerator, set the dial at 'maximum' or 'quick freeze' about an hour before you make your mixture.

Beat cream ices with a little evaporated milk when taking them from the trays to give them a smooth consistency.

Water Ices

Water ices need a syrup made of sugar and water as a foundation. To this syrup either fruit purée or fruit juice can be added. A little wine or liqueur added to a water ice is a great improvement

Syrup for Water Ices:

1 pint water.	Juice of half a lemon.
½ lb. sugar.	

Put the water and sugar into a saucepan and bring to the boil. Then let it boil for 10 minutes, skimming when necessary.

Add the lemon juice and strain it through a jelly bag.

Lemon or Orange Water Ice

½ pint syrup (as above).	1 white of egg.
½ pint of lemon or orange juice.	

Make some syrup and pour it while still hot over the thinly peeled rinds of two lemons (or oranges).

Let it get cold and then add the lemon or orange juice. Strain it through a jelly bag.

When half frozen whip in the stiffly beaten white of egg, and freeze until ready for the table.

Raspberry Water Ice

1 pint raspberries.	1 gill water.
4 oz. sugar.	Lemon juice.

Sprinkle the sugar over the raspberries and let them stand for 2 hours. Mash the raspberries, squeeze through muslin, add the water and a squeeze of lemon juice, and then freeze.

NOTE. Strawberry ice can be prepared in the same way.

Ice Creams

Though they are generally known as ice *creams*, cream need not form part of the foundation. Custard made with custard powder, or with eggs, is generally used. If a richer ice is desired a little extra cream can be added, or if a very rich ice is wanted, half cream and half custard makes a delicious mixture. Remember that if cream is used the same proportion of sugar must be used, as if only custard were employed, i.e. 3 oz. to 1 pint. Evaporated milk can be used in place of cream.

To make the custard (with eggs), put 1 pint of milk and 3 oz. of sugar into a saucepan and bring it almost to the boil. Then beat 4 yolks of egg well and add them to the milk, stirring all the time. Put the mixture over hot water and stir until it thickens.

Chocolate Ice Cream

1 *pint custard.*   3 *oz. grated chocolate.*
Vanilla essence.   *A little water.*
1 *gill cream (if liked).*

Make a custard and let it cool. Dissolve the chocolate in a little water, and add it to the custard. Then add a few drops of vanilla essence, and mix well.

Add the cream, which should be lightly whipped, and freeze till required.

Coffee Ice Cream

Make a custard as directed above, but use equal parts of milk and strong coffee.

Cream can be added, if desired.

Raspberry Ice Cream (or Strawberry)

½ *pint raspberry (or*   10-12 *oz. sugar.*
strawberry) pulp.   ½ *pint cream.*
1 *pint milk.*   *Juice of a lemon.*
1 *white of egg.*

Boil the milk, add the sugar, and let it get nearly cold. Then add the fruit pulp, the lemon juice, and lastly the stiffly whipped cream.

Partially freeze the mixture and then add the stiffly whipped white of egg, and continue to freeze till required.

NOTE. Any other fresh fruit can be used instead.

If tinned fruit is used, put it through a sieve and use a little of the syrup—of course, adding less sugar.

Walnut and Raisin Ice Cream

Make some vanilla ice-cream mixture and add some chopped raisins and walnuts. A little coffee flavouring is also delicious with this.

Chocolate Ice Cream

Boil together 1 gill of evaporated milk, 1 gill of water and 4 oz. castor sugar. Put 1½ dessertspoonsful of powdered gelatine to soak in 1 tablespoonful of cold water. Then dissolve it in the hot syrup. Stir in 4 oz. grated chocolate till dissolved. When cool add ½ teaspoonful of vanilla essence, 1 gill of chilled evaporated milk and the same quantity whipped enough to hold its shape, and stir thoroughly. Freeze till of the right consistency, stirring now and again in the trays.

Vanilla Ice Cream

3 *gills milk.*   1 *egg and 2 yolks.*
1 *gill cream or*   1 *tablespoonful sherry*
evaporated milk.   *(optional).*
½ *teaspoonful vanilla*   2 *oz. castor sugar.*
essence.

Heat the milk and sugar without boiling. Beat the egg and yolks, stir in the milk, mix well and put back in the saucepan. Then cook over a gentle heat till the mixture thickens without letting it boil. Stir all the time. Pour into a basin and leave till cool. When cold put into the trays with the control switch at hard freeze and when half frozen turn into a chilled basin, and add the sherry, vanilla and cream or evaporated milk whipped just enough to hold its shape. Beat well, return to the trays and continue freezing till ready, then turn the control back to normal.

Decorate with crystallised cherries, angelica or serve with hot chocolate sauce, or a little maple syrup and walnuts.

JELLY-MAKING

When making jelly it is essential to have a good jelly bag. Various kinds can be bought, but it is quite easy to make one's own. Use strong butter muslin, and make the bag wide at the top and taper to a point. Sew on loops. A broom-handle threaded through them can be balanced on two tables over the basin.

Always scald jelly bags before using them. Here are a few points you should bear in mind when making jelly:

(Continued on page 513)

STORE AWAY SOME JAM

JAM-MAKING can be exciting. But so often a disappointment, too—when you are faced with a runny, syrupy mess! The whole secret of jam-making lies in the amount of pectin in the fruit. This is a natural gum-like substance and is found only in small quantities in strawberries, cherries and vegetable marrow, but is plentiful in black currants, red currants and gooseberries. When using fruit with a low pectin content it is advisable to use one of the following ingredients to be certain your jam will set . . . the acid juice of gooseberries, apples or red currants . . . commercially prepared pectin . . . tartaric or citric acid added either in powder form dissolved in a little water, or the latter in the form of lemon juice.

Fruit	Water	Sugar	Method
Gooseberries —3 lb. of fruit make 7 lb. of jam	1 pt. to every 3 lb. of fruit	1 lb. to each lb. of fruit and 1 lb. to each pt. of water	Stew fruit with water until soft. Add sugar, dissolve and boil until set. Cooking time—15-20 minutes
Strawberries —4 lb. of fruit make 7 lb. of jam	None	To 4 lb. fruit allow 4½ lb. sugar and juice of 2 lemons or ½ pt. of red-currant or goose-berry juice	Heat strawberries and juice until soft. Add sugar and cook 20-25 minutes
Raspberries —4 lb. of fruit make 7-8 lb. of jam	None	1 lb. to every lb. of fruit	Heat fruit until juice flows. Add sugar. Boil 3 minutes for freshly picked fruit and 10-12 minutes for shop fruit
Plums —5 lb. of fruit make 9 lb. of jam	½ pt. to every 5-6 lb. of fruit	1 lb. to each lb. of fruit and 1 lb. to each pt. of water	Stone fruit, tie half in muslin and remove kernel from rest. Cook fruit in water until soft. Add sugar, stones, etc. Cook 25 minutes. Add kernels before potting.
Blackberry and Apple —4 lb. fruit make 6¾ lb. of jam	To 3 lb. black-berries and 1 lb. apples use ¾ pt. of water	1 lb. to every lb. of fruit	Stew fruit with water until tender, adding apple peel and pips tied in muslin bag. Add sugar; cook for 15-20 minutes

1. Use dry, barely ripe fruit and either loaf or granulated sugar, as this helps the colour and keeping-power of the preserve.

2. Wash or wipe the fruit according to the kind and pick it over, removing blemished fruit. Allow the correct amount of sugar and water to each pound of fruit.

3. Warm the sugar before adding, as this prevents lowering the temperature of the boiling fruit too much, and consequent over-cooking, which is disastrous.

4. When the sugar is completely dissolved, but not before, boil briskly, stirring gently and slowly until the jam sets on trial. To test the jam put a little on a plate and cool it quickly.

5. Skim the jam, if necessary, towards the end of cooking only, as continuous skimming is unnecessary and wasteful.

6. Have the jam jars perfectly clean, dry and warm before filling, and fill quite full. To avoid fruit rising, leave to stand 20-30 minutes, stir, and pour into jam jars.

7. Wipe the jars with cloth rung out from very hot water. Tie down, label and date and place in a cool, dry store cupboard.

Jelly Making—*continued*

1. The fruit should be put in the preserving pan with water and simmered till tender.

2. The whole contents of the pan should then be put into the jelly bag. Let it drip all night into a basin. *Never* squeeze the bag nor try to hurry up the dripping process. If you do the jelly will be cloudy instead of clear.

3. The next day measure the juice and add the sugar. Let the sugar dissolve; then boil rapidly till the jelly will set, stirring all the time. Skim towards the end if necessary.

4. Test as for jam, but the drops should keep their shape, as well as crinkling on the surface.

5. Pour jelly into the jars as soon as it is done. Do not stir after it leaves the fire, or it will be full of bubbles.

Apple Jelly

Cut the apples in quarters and cut off all the bad places. Put the quarters in the preserving pan with enough water to float them, and boil till they are soft but not pulpy. Put the mixture into a jelly bag and leave it to drip through all night.

Measure the juice and allow 1 lb. of sugar to every pint. Put the juice and sugar into the pan and let the sugar dissolve before the mixture boils. Stir all the time. Then boil till it will set when tested, skimming if necessary. Pour into warm, dry jars and tie down.

Black- or Red-currant Jelly

6 *lb. black currants.*   2 *pints water.*
Sugar.

Put the fruit and water in a pan (the fruit need not be stalked) and simmer until the fruit is tender. Mash it up well and pour it into a jelly bag. Leave it to drip all night and then measure the juice and add 1 lb. sugar to every pint of juice. Put the sugar and juice in a preserving pan and heat slowly till the sugar is dissolved, stirring all the time. Then bring it to the boil and continue boiling till the jelly will set when tested, skimming if necessary. Pour into warm, dry jars and tie down.

Bramble Jelly

6 *lb. blackberries.*   1 *pint water.*
Sugar.

Pick the blackberries on a fine day. Remove the stalks and put the blackberries and the water into the preserving pan and boil gently for about 20 minutes, until the fruit is tender. Mash it up well. Then pour the pulp into a jelly bag and leave it to drip all night.

Measure the juice and add 1 lb. of sugar to every pint of juice. Put the sugar and juice into the preserving pan and let the sugar dissolve before it boils. Stir all the time. Boil quickly till it will set in a good jelly, skimming if necessary. Pour into warm, dry jars and cover at once.

NOTE. Blackberries gathered early in the season make the best jelly.

Crab Apple Jelly

Make in the same way as apple jelly but do not cut up the apples, put them in the preserving pan whole just as they are. Do not on any account let them get mashed or the jelly will be too acid.

Gooseberry Jelly

Wash the gooseberries but do not top and tail them. Place them in a preserving pan with just enough water to cover the fruit. Simmer until the fruit is a pulp. Pour the mixture into a jelly bag and let it drip all night. Remove the pulp, place it in the preserving pan, cover it with water and simmer for about 1 hour, stirring occasionally. Strain it again through the jelly bag and mix both lots of juice. Weigh the juice and allow 1 lb. of sugar to every pint of juice. Let the sugar dissolve slowly, then bring the mixture to the boil and boil briskly till it sets. Skim if necessary. Pour into warm, dry jars and cover at once.

Loganberry Jelly

6 *lb. loganberries.*   *Sugar.*
1½ *pints water.*

Make in exactly the same way as blackcurrant jelly.

MARMALADE-MAKING

Home-made marmalade has a fresh, fruity taste of its own. Seville oranges can always be bought from the beginning of January till the beginning of March. February is the best month in which to make marmalade, as the fruit is then at its best and cheapest.

For those who find the cutting up by hand too laborious, a special cutter can be bought.

Grapefruit Marmalade

3 *grapefruit.*   6 *lb. sugar.*
3 *lemons.*   6½ *pints water.*
1 *sweet orange.*

Boil the grapefruit for 2 hours in 6 pints of water. Then take out and allow to cool.

Cut the lemons and orange in half and scoop out the insides. Break them up well and put them to soak in the water the grapefruit was boiled in.

Put the pips to soak in ½ pint of water.

Peel the grapefruit and slice the peel very finely. Break up the insides and put in a separate basin from the other fruit, keeping out the pips. They should be added to the lemon and orange pips.

The next day add the grapefruit and the water the pips were soaked in to the other fruit and water. Bring it to the boil and boil sharply for 10 minutes. Then add the sugar, heat it gently till the sugar is dissolved, stirring all the time, and then boil quickly till the juice will set in a jelly when tested. Skim if necessary, pour into warm, dry jars and tie down at once.

Orange Marmalade (I)

Slice some Seville oranges very thinly, only taking out the pips. To each lb. of sliced fruit add 3 pints of cold water, and let this stand for 24 hours.

Then boil till the peel is quite tender, and allow to stand till the next day. Then weigh, and to every lb. of fruit add 1½ lb. of sugar. Boil the whole until it is clear, skimming if necessary.

Let it stand for a little while before pouring it into warm, dry jars. Tie down at once.

Orange Marmalade (II) (Another Method)

12 *Seville oranges.*   12 *pints cold water.*
2 *lemons.*   12 *lb. sugar.*

Peel the oranges and lemons; break up the insides into a large basin, taking out the pips and putting them into a small basin. Slice the peel as finely as possible and add to the large basin.

Next add the water, keeping back ½ pint, which should be poured over the pips. Let all stand for 24 hours.

Strain the water from the pips through muslin and add it to the fruit. Boil the fruit for about 2½ hours until the peel is quite tender. Then add the sugar and let it dissolve, stirring all the time. Boil quickly until the juice is clear and will set into a good jelly. Skim if necessary. Pour into warm, dry jars and tie down at once.

BOTTLING
FRUIT AND VEGETABLES
FOR THE WINTER

A GOOD supply of home-bottled fruit is a real help to winter catering, so it's well worth while to take advantage of summer supplies. Bottling need not be the rather dreary task it sounds, if you go about it in a businesslike way—and, of course, with a pressure cooker it takes no time at all. If you tackle it in small quantities, it should not upset your normal household routine.

You can do your bottling any of the following ways. There are others, but it is wise to use a really reliable method to be sure of good results.

(1) *Sterilising Under Water.* For this method you will not need any special apparatus. A deep pan, bucket or even the wash boiler is suitable, but the bottles must not be put directly on the bottom of the receptacle. Use a wire tray, or some slatted wood, or even thick folded brown paper, as a base. Having filled your jars with fruit, pour on *cold* water or syrup, then put on the rings and tops firmly. Put the bottles carefully into the container, with sufficient *cold* water to cover them if possible, but at least to the neck of the bottle. Heat the water very slowly indeed until it reaches 165° F., keeping it at this temperature for 10-20 minutes, depending on the type of fruit you are bottling. Almost all fruits need 10 minutes, except currants which require 15 minutes, and pears 20 minutes.

Tomatoes are the exception. Raise the temperature to 190° F., and keep it there for 30 minutes. They will always need extra time, by whichever method they are bottled.

Take the bottles out of the water carefully, and put them on a wooden table or several layers of paper. Screw up very tightly and leave until cold. Next day, test the bottles as shown in the photograph to make sure that they have sealed properly, before storing them away in a cold place.

(2) *Sterilisation in the Oven.* Fill your bottles in the ordinary way with the fruit, but do not add liquid. Cover, but don't put on the rubber rings or seal. Have your oven at 250° F. (Regulo ½) and put in the bottles. Maintain this temperature for ¾-1½ hours, depending on

FRUIT BOTTLING WITH
A PRESSURE COOKER

Make sure that your bottles are sterilised and dry. Press the fruit down lightly with a wooden spoon, fill to the top

Pour on the hot syrup or water, leaving half an inch of space at the top, then place the rubber ring in position on the jar and screw the cap on firmly

Above: Put 1 pint of hot water into the cooker, and stand bottles on the inverted rack. Use the 5-lb. pressure for fruit and 10-lb. for vegetables

Right: Test to see that your bottles are properly sealed by removing the metal ring, and holding the bottle in the air by the glass top as shown in the photograph

which fruit you are bottling. If, after allowing the minimum time, juice has begun to run, the fruit is ready. By this time it will have shrunk in the jars, so it is wise to fill up the bottles from one of them, unless you want to have a lot of juice with the fruit. Boil up the water or syrup while the fruit is in the oven, so that it is ready at the same time as the fruit. Take the bottles out of the oven *one at a time* as you need them, and fill to the brim with *boiling* water or syrup. Put on the rubber rings and screw down tightly. Be sure to have the liquid literally boiling when you pour it over the fruit. An important point, also, is to make sure that the rim of the bottle and the rubber rings are absolutely dry. Don't move your bottled fruit until the next day, but tighten the top an hour after sealing. Next day, test to see if the bottles are properly sealed, as shown in the photograph.

(3) *Sterilisation in a Pressure Cooker*. This is by far the easiest and the quickest method. Fruit preserved by this method will take from 3–7 *minutes*, depending on the type of fruit. Fill the bottles in the ordinary way, then cover with hot water or syrup to within $\frac{1}{2}$ in. of the top of the bottle. Slide the blade of a knife down the inside of the jar, to let the air bubbles out. Put on the rubber rings and screw on the top. Pour 1 pint of hot water into the cooker. Invert the rack, and put the bottles on this, but don't let them touch. Using the 5-lb. weight, bring to pressure and keep there for 3–7 minutes according to the type of fruit. Let the pressure reduce slowly to normal. Take out the bottles and make sure that they are tightly sealed.

If you are doing your bottling in a pressure cooker, take great care to follow the makers' instructions, as the timing is very important. An extra minute can make a great difference.

Selection of the Fruit. Choose firm, dry, ripe fruit. Don't attempt to use over-ripe or damaged fruit, as it will ferment and spoil the whole bottle. Wash all the fruit carefully but lightly. If you want to preserve your plums whole, prick the skins to prevent them bursting. Top and tail gooseberries and currants. Hull raspberries and similar fruits. Scald tomatoes in boiling water for $\frac{1}{2}$ minute, then put them quickly into cold water to loosen the skin. Peel and preserve in brine. Certain fruits like apples, pears and peaches will go brown if they are left exposed to air, once they have been peeled. So immediately you have cut them to the right size, drop them into a weak brine solution.

Preparation of Syrup. Dissolve $\frac{1}{2}$ lb. sugar with 2 pints water, then boil for 3 minutes. Syrup is not essential to the success or to the keeping qualities of your bottled fruit, but it gives it a better flavour and colour. Golden syrup can be used instead of sugar, if this is more convenient. Allow 4 tablespoonsful to each pint of water.

Brine. Allow 1 oz. salt to 2 quarts of water.

Preparation of Bottles. Inspect each bottle carefully, making sure that there are no cracks or chips, especially round the rim. Faulty bottles will not allow the vacuum to form and the fruit won't keep. Use wide-necked bottles for all large fruits.

Rubber Rings. New rings must be used each time to be sure of success, as faulty ones will allow the air to get into the bottle and ruin the fruit. Boil your rings for 5 minutes before using them.

Bottling Tomatoes

Tomatoes can be bottled most successfully in the same way as fruit except that to get the full flavour no liquid at all should be added. If liked, the tomatoes can first be skinned, after being well washed. (Plunging them into boiling water for a minute will loosen the skins.) They should be packed as tightly as possible into the bottles, large or medium tomatoes being cut into halves or quarters so as not to waste space. Sprinkle in $\frac{1}{4}$ oz. salt to each 2 lb. tomatoes between the layers, and if liked a teaspoonful of sugar. Press the tomatoes down well with the handle of a wooden spoon, then put on the rubber bands, etc., and proceed as for the previous method. Bring the water round the bottles up to 195° F. in $1\frac{1}{2}$ hours and keep at this temperature for 30 minutes.

It is always a good plan to inspect your bottled fruit from time to time, especially within a week or two of sterilising, just to make certain all is well. The only really harmful condition that can appear is if fermentation sets in, as this is a sign that some form of bacteria is active. The signs of this are discoloration of the fruit, small bubbles all over it and a distinct taste rather like vinegar; the liquid will probably have begun to ooze from the bottle. The reason for this fermentation is insufficient sterilising. so make a point never to try to hasten the process. It is advisable not

Pressure cookery represents a saving of time and a retention of
taste and vitamins

to eat fermented fruit even if the vinegary taste is only very slight.

If you should find traces of mould on the top of bottled fruit it is an indication that spores from the air have somehow found their way in while the fruit was cooling. To prevent this make a point of tightening screw caps the moment the bottles are removed from the water in the hot-plate method, or seeing that the bottles are sealed quickly after oven bottling. Usually the mould can be removed easily and the contents are not affected provided one detects the trouble in its early stages.

Vegetable Bottling

The bottling of vegetables is a more difficult process than that of fruit on account of the difference in their chemical composition. The acid contained in fruit actually helps the sterilising process, while in vegetables there is little or no acid present. Also, vegetables contain soil bacteria which are very resistant to heat, so that even if heated to boiling-point and maintained at that temperature for 2 hours the spores may not be killed and, if the vegetables are stored for some time, may cause decomposition. For this reason it may be safer not to bottle vegetables at home unless you have a pressure cooker, where such a high temperature is obtained that the bacteria are destroyed without any doubt.

PRESSURE COOKERY

PRESSURE cookery does help to retain the natural taste of food, but, apart from that, where does it differ from ordinary methods and what are the advantages of it?

Everyone knows the tremendous power generated by steam. In pressure cooking the steam given off by water heated beyond boiling-point to what is called pressure-point is kept hermetically sealed inside the cooker, thus producing far greater heat than when it is allowed to escape into the air, and so cooking whatever is in the cooker far more quickly. So great in some cases is the reduction in time when food is cooked in this way that the novice tends to disbelieve that anything could cook so quickly, and allows just a few minutes longer than the time specified, with the result that, say, the bones in an Irish stew would be quite porous and could be scrunched up like sugar. Meat on the bones would also be overcooked. You will see, therefore, that it is important to follow the instructions as to the time to be allowed *exactly*.

This tremendous saving of time is one advantage of pressure cookery of particular interest to the housewife of to-day, always on the lookout for ways of saving that precious commodity.

Yet another big consideration is the amount of fuel saved. Many most wholesome dishes —oxtail is one which comes at once to one's mind—need such long cooking if treated in the normal way that the thrifty housewife sometimes wonders if it is really worth such an expense in fuel. A pressure cooker will do the job for you in 25 minutes!

Another advantage is that one can cook different kinds of food together in the cooker without the least chance of the strong taste of, say, onion mingling with and spoiling that of stewed fruit. Each will retain its own distinctive flavour and character. This is because the high pressure in the cooker seals *in* the flavours and juices, thus preventing one spoiling another. In addition, no water actually touches the food to act as a carrier of its taste.

The idea of pressure cookery is by no means a modern idea. In fact, John Evelyn in his famous Diary, writing in 1682, recounts a wonderful supper he ate cooked in what he calls 'Monsieur Papin's digestors,' and from what he says it looks as though these are ancestors of our present-day pressure cookers.

There are various different makes and sizes of pressure cooker on the market, but generally speaking the working principle is the same. If you decide to buy one, your best plan is to go to some big store, which is certain to have the latest models, and inspect them for yourself. What size you choose must, of course, be largely governed by the number of people for whom you cook. The smaller types of cooker are known as pressure saucepans or casseroles, and are designed to give a pressure of 15 lb. a square inch, or about 250° F. Many of these are so designed that they can be taken straight to table once pressure has been reduced. In some types a spare lid is supplied for this purpose. The large cookers, suitable for very large numbers, or for bottling fruit and vegetables, have a pressure gauge which registers pressure from 5 to 40 lb.

Important points to remember whatever model you choose are:

1. You are enlisting the aid of a powerful force which should be treated with respect and intelligence, but every cooker is fitted with a safety device which operates automatically if too much pressure is building up, and releases it. In the pressure saucepans these small safety-plugs are quite easy to replace oneself.

2. Never fill your cooker more than two-thirds full of food. In the case of liquids, such as soups, not more than half full. Allow for swelling in the case of such foods as rice, or pulse vegetables. On no account should food ever be allowed to touch the lid of the pressure cooker.

3. Sometimes it is advisable to use the rack supplied with your cooker, as, for instance, when you are cooking green vegetables by themselves; when making stews, on the other hand, you do not need to use it.

4. The amount of liquid necessary for pressure cookery depends on the length of the cooking time, not on the actual quantity of food to be cooked. The amount given may seem very inadequate to the beginner, but it is essential that the exact quantity given in any recipe should be used. The small amount needed is due to the fact that in pressure cookery there is no evaporation.

5. Be sparing with seasoning. The speed of pressure cookery means that the natural mineral content of the food is retained and less seasoning is therefore needed than in normal cooking. It is advisable for this reason, generally speaking, to add seasoning after cooking is finished.

6. When gravy or stock is to be thickened, as for example when braising meat, the flour, mixed to a smooth paste with water or stock, should be added at the end of the pressure cooking and cooked till the liquid thickens. The reason for this is that a liquid thickened beforehand might, during the rapid cooking process, stick to the bottom of the pan.

7. Fix your lid firmly in position and bring to pressure as directed. Then lower the heat and cook for the prescribed time. Don't worry about the very definite whistle or hiss you will hear coming from the cooker. It merely indicates that pressure is present in the pan. Exact timing is essential for good results, so keep an eye on the clock once the cooking has started.

8. When the food cooking has had the required time, take the pan off the heat, and follow the directions for reducing pressure. Cooking will continue until all pressure is gone, when you can safely remove the lid. Should you have any difficulty in doing this it is an indication that some pressure still remains. In this case continue reducing pressure as before.

Don't, by the way, expect your pressure cooker to do the impossible. Your cooker will not actually bake, nor crisp fry, nor roast meat in oven fashion, but it will make the toughest cuts of meat deliciously tender, and in a surprisingly short time, too.

If you do not want to have your oven on for cake-baking there are certain types of cakes, such as 'boiled' fruit cake and gingerbread, which can be steamed in your cooker. It is advisable to put the cake, once you've taken it out of the cooker, under a fairly hot grill for a few minutes so as to dry off the top. Never fill your cake-tin more than two-thirds full, and cover the top of the tin over with a double piece of greaseproof.

The speed of pressury cookery makes it well worth while to make stock with quite a small quantity of bones. Here is a recipe using 2 lb.

Bone Stock

2 *lb. bones—marrow* 1 *turnip.*
  if possible. 1 *small stick of celery.*
2 *onions.* 1 *or 2 cloves.*
1 *carrot.* *Seasoning.*
1 *quart of water.*

Wash the bones and break up if large. Put into the cooker with the rest of the ingredients and bring slowly to the boil. Skim, then put on the lid and bring to pressure. Reduce the heat and pressure cook for 45 minutes. Reduce pressure to normal before removing the lid. When cold lift off any fat on the top.

Meat Cooking

Tough meat responds to pressure cookery in an amazing way, so that you can use the cheaper cuts of meat with some confidence that they will be tender to eat. You can either pot roast, stew or braise meat.

Oxtail

1 *oxtail.* 1 *oz. dripping.*
1 *onion.* ¾ *pint water.*
1 *carrot.* 1 *small stick of celery.*
1 *oz. flour.* *Seasoning.*
2 *or 3 cloves.* *Lemon juice if liked.*

Wash the oxtail and cut into neat joints. Heat the dripping in the pan and fry the oxtail on both sides till brown. Add the vegetables cut into thick pieces, the water and cloves. Put on the lid, bring to pressure, then lower the heat and pressure cook for 20-25 minutes (allow 20 minutes per pound of tail). Reduce pressure, remove the lid and stir in the flour mixed to a paste with a little cold water or stock. Bring the mixture to the boil and cook until it thickens. Add seasoning and, if liked, a little lemon juice just before serving.

Vegetables

To get the best out of vegetables one should either eat them raw, or cook them as quickly as possible in as little water as possible. Vege-tables cooked by pressure are done in so short a space of time that they can be left until the last moment, before being pooped into the cooker. They should be cooked on the rack, and if broken into sprigs, as in the case of cauliflowers, or sliced, as with carrots, the pieces should be as much of a size as possible, to ensure even cooking. Cauliflower broken into sprigs needs 2-3 minutes only at 15 lb. pressure; if left whole, 4-5 minutes according to size.

Young carrots need only 3 minutes; old carrots, sliced, will also take 3 minutes. Large carrots, left whole, about 8 minutes.

Small potatoes, or large ones cut in half, will need about 8 minutes' cooking; large ones left whole, 15 minutes. Large potatoes cut in quarters will take only 5 minutes.

The amount of water to be added for the different kinds of vegetables varies, but is seldom more than ¼ pint, frequently less.

Puddings

Ordinary recipes for steamed puddings can be used when cooking puddings in your pressure cooker, but it is generally advisable when using the smaller cookers to steam the mixture in the normal way for at least 20 minutes of the whole cooking time. This can be done quite simply, because until the lid is fixed in position and the pan sealed you can treat it just like an ordinary saucepan. This preliminary cooking means that the pudding rises well before it is subjected to pressure. Fill your basin not more than three-quarters full, and cover with a piece of greased paper and a pudding-cloth. Stand in the cooker on the rack and pour in sufficient *boiling* water to come half-way up the basin, put on the lid and steam normally for 20 minutes, then bring to pressure and cook for the necessary length of time—the time needed for the whole process is one-third of what you would allow if steaming the pudding in the normal way.

Jam and Marmalade Making

If you are making jam with dried fruit, such as apricots, or marmalade, you will find your pressure cooker a wonderful time-saver in softening the skins of the apricots or the orange peel. Dried apricots will be quite tender after 10 minutes' pressure cooking, instead of taking 45 minutes or longer. Orange peel will require only 15 minutes' pressure cooking instead of the lengthy simmering required in a preserving pan.

LET'S HAVE A PICNIC!

A PICNIC can be great fun, especially as the open air makes everyone hungry; take rather too much food than too little. There is no reason why packed meals should not be every bit as nourishing and appetising as the Sunday roast is at home.

Try to make your sandwiches exciting as well as filling; the variety you can achieve is almost unlimited. See that they are really fresh! They will dry up very quickly in the sun, so keep them well covered and in the shade.

It is advisable to keep your food simple for picnics; don't try to take things with a lot of jam or cream. Lettuce, tomatoes, fresh fruit, etc., are always popular, and not difficult to pack.

Drinks are important, as the warm weather makes everyone thirsty. Bottles of mineral water (don't forget the opener!), milk or tea, are all good stand-bys. When you are making tea for a flask, there are one or two minor points to keep in mind if you want your tea to taste good. Rinse the inside of the flask well with water, then heat it before the tea is poured in. Soak the cork in boiling water for 10 minutes, then allow it to get cold, before wrapping it in greaseproof paper and putting it in the flask. Make your tea in the ordinary way in the teapot and, when it has infused, strain into the heated flask. *Never* put the milk into the flask with the tea—it will ruin the taste. Take it in a separate bottle. Hot soup is appetising on blowy days, and can be easily taken in a flask. Home-made lemonade is a delicious cool drink, and economical.

An Eye to Comfort

A word of warning! *Don't sit on the damp grass or sand*. Take a rug or groundsheet with you. Take a cushion or two for comfort. An umbrella will be a protection from too much sun or rain.

Practical and decorative grease-proof containers for food, in all sizes, can be bought in the shops. These are most useful for picnics, as there is no danger of broken china and food being wasted. They are also ideal for fruit jellies, etc.

Here are some suggestions which will make the contents of your picnic basket a treat to which the family look forward, whether it is lunch high in the hills or tea on the beach.

Sandwiches

Use fresh bread and have a really sharp knife. Don't cut your bread too thick; leave on the crusts. Always thinly spread the insides of *both* pieces, with softened margarine. For a little extra flavour with it add a dash of mustard, chopped mint, mayonnaise, any piquant sauce or anchovy sauce, but only use a little in proportion to the amount of margarine. A thin coating of peanut butter makes another tasty base. Any of the following fillings are suitable with brown or white bread, bridge or luncheon rolls.

Fillings

It is a good idea to consult individual tastes before making these. Some people don't like

British Vacuum Flask Co., Ltd.

This half-gallon giant vacuum flask keeps food or fluid hot or cold. It is ideal for keeping picnic fare fresh, and has a stout handle by which it can be carried. There are two screw-on serving bowls, one at each end

A picnic repast that is set out properly is more appetising than one eaten out of paper bags !

cheese; children very rarely care for highly seasoned things. Plain meat and lettuce appeal more to some appetites.

Sweet. A mixture of chopped apple and date with a few drops of lemon juice, and a dash of nutmeg. Mashed banana mixed with a little raspberry jam.

Cheese. Grated cheese with chopped cress, a little mayonnaise and paprika. Grated cheese with lettuce, a few chopped nuts and sweet pickles.

Meat. Chopped ham, mixed with a piquant sauce and thinly sliced cucumber. Minced or sliced beef with chopped celery and tomato sauce.

Egg. Hard-boiled egg with chopped beet-root and watercress. Scrambled egg with mayonnaise and chopped fried bacon.

Chocolate Swiss Roll

3 eggs.
3 oz. sugar.
4 oz. plain flour.
½ teaspoonful baking powder.

1 tablespoonful cocoa.
¾ tablespoonful hot water.

Filling:
2 oz. margarine.   Vanilla essence.
3 oz. icing sugar.   ½ oz. chopped nuts.

Whisk the eggs and the sugar together until thick. Sieve the dry ingredients together. Fold these, one-third at a time, into the egg mixture, using a metal spoon. Lastly add the hot water. *Pour* the mixture into a Swiss-roll tin which has been well greased and lightly floured. Allow the mixture to cover the bottom of the tin completely before putting it in the oven. Bake for 7-10 minutes at 450° F. (Regulo 7). Turn out on to a sugared paper and roll up till cold. Then un-roll, spread with the butter icing, and roll up again.

Filling. Cream the margarine, mix in the icing sugar gradually, add a few drops of vanilla essence, then the nuts. Or fill with whipped cream flavoured with vanilla and a little castor sugar.

Parkin Biscuits

2 oz. porridge oats.
2 oz. plain flour.
2 oz. sugar.
½ teaspoonful bicarbonate of soda.

½ teaspoonful of cinnamon and ginger mixed.
1 tablespoonful syrup.
1 oz. margarine.
1 egg.

Put all the dry ingredients into a basin. Warm the syrup and melt the margarine in it.

Lightly beat the egg, and carefully stir it into the syrup. Pour the liquid mixture into the bowl with the dry ingredients and mix well together. Roll into little balls and put them on to a well-greased baking sheet, spaced sufficiently apart to allow for spreading. Bake for 10 minutes at 425° F. (Regulo 6).

Individual Egg Pies (4 people)

3 oz. short crust pastry.
1 oz. bacon.

1 oz. mushrooms.
4 eggs.
Seasoning.

Roll out the pastry and line 4 deep patty tins with it. Cut tops for each tin, and put aside until required. Chop up the bacon and mushrooms, fry lightly together. Break each egg into a small dish, then gently slide it into the patty tin. Sprinkle with salt and pepper. Put a quarter of the mixed bacon and mushroom lightly on top of each egg. Cover with the pastry top, making a decorative edge as you seal the pie. Make a small hole in the centre of the lid, but make sure that you don't burst the yolk of the egg while you are doing it. Bake for 15-20 minutes at 450° F. (Regulo 7). Leave the pies to become absolutely cold before taking them on a picnic.

Cold Sausage Rissoles (4 people)

½ lb. sausages.
1 small onion.
½ oz. fat.
3 oz. rice.
1 pint water.

1 egg.
Seasoning.
Breadcrumbs.
Deep fat for frying.

This picnic case is also a table; it can be set up when everything has been taken out, by unfolding the legs from inside. In the home, it makes a useful little bed-table. It contains 2 flasks, 4 cups, milk bottle, 3 containers to keep food, a combined salt and pepper sprinkler, and 4 plates. The table is 10 in. high

British Vacuum Flask Co., Ltd.

Prick the sausages well, then fry them slowly until light golden brown, but be careful not to burst the skins. In the meantime, chop up the onion and fry it lightly in a pan with the melted fat and rice. Season well. Pour on the boiling water, and allow to boil for 15 minutes. Drain into a colander and allow to cool. When the sausages are cooked, let them drain on a piece of brown paper. Beat up the egg lightly and season, put a little aside to dip the rissoles in later. Stir the rest of the egg into the rice with a fork, mixing well. Coat the sausages with this mixture, pressing it firmly on. Roll each rissole lightly in the remaining egg (a few drops of milk can be added to the egg, if necessary) and then coat with bread-crumbs. Fry in deep, very hot fat for several minutes until golden brown. Drain on brown paper till cold.

Individual Cheese Creams (4 people)

1 oz. cornflour.	4 oz. grated cheese.
1 teaspoonful made mustard.	Seasoning.
	½ oz. margarine.
¾ pint milk.	1 hard-boiled egg.
4 tablespoonsful freshly made breadcrumbs.	Paprika.

Mix the cornflour, mustard and milk to a smooth paste in a pan. Stir in the bread-crumbs and cheese. Season. Stir over the heat until boiling, add the margarine and continue to boil for ½ minute. Allow to cool slightly before filling the containers. Slice the egg into four pieces. Line the dish with the cheese mixture, then lay a piece of egg in the centre. Add a few shakes of paprika, and fill the dish with cheese mixture, finishing with another shake of paprika. This cream is attractive decorated with shrimps or prawns, etc.

Cold Chicken Soufflé (4 people)

½ oz. gelatine.	4 oz. finely minced or chopped cooked chicken.
½ pint water.	
Seasoning.	½ small grated onion.
2 egg whites.	Paprika.

Dissolve the gelatine in the water over a low heat. Season well with salt and pepper, then allow to cool. Put the egg whites into a large cold basin, strain on the liquid and whisk until very stiff. Mix the chicken with the onion and season well, then stir it into the stiff whites. Drop the mixture into a large dish, or 4 small ones. Shake on the paprika. Leave for an hour to 'firm up' if possible. If liked, make overnight and leave in a cool place.

HOME-MADE SWEETS

SWEET-MAKING is an attractive hobby and can very easily be done at home. Such sweets bear the personal touch, and in an attractive box make charming presents. If it is to be done at all seriously it is as well to buy a sweet thermometer, a set of steel bars, and a marble slab.

These are particularly useful for toffee, fudge and caramel. The thermometer can be put into the mixture while boiling and the degrees registered will show you when the right consistency is reached. Fudge should boil to 240°, caramel to 255° and toffee to 300°.

The steel bars are for setting the candy. They should be arranged on the slab to en-close a square or an oblong of the size re-quired. The inner side of the bars and the en-closed part of the slab should be well greased with olive oil; a pastry brush is best for the purpose. When ready the hot candy should be poured between the bars. When cool the bars can be removed and the candy cut up.

If, however, sweets are to be made only occasionally, the following test can be used. Drop a little of the candy into some cold water and then roll it between the fingers: fudge should boil until a soft ball is formed, caramel till a hard ball is formed, and toffee till it will crack when tested.

Instead of steel bars, well-oiled tins or dishes can be used.

Everything used for sweet-making must be scrupulously clean, and it is a good plan to keep a special aluminium saucepan for the purpose. Enamel should not be used, as it is inclined to chip.

An upturned enamel tray or an enamel slab can be used instead of the marble slab.

Boiling sweets should be stirred occasion-ally to prevent them sticking to the bottom of the pan and burning, but the stirring must be as gentle as possible or the mixture will go sugary.

Caramel

1 lb. castor sugar.	4 tablespoonsful glucose.
½ pint cream.	
½ pint milk.	4 oz. unsweetened couverture chocolate.
2 oz. butter.	

Grate the chocolate. Put the butter, sugar, cream, milk and glucose in a saucepan, heat and stir until the sugar is dissolved. Then let the mixture simmer gently for 10 minutes.

Add the grated chocolate and let the mixture boil quite hard, stirring gently all the time, until the temperature is 255° (or till the caramel will form a hard ball when tested in cold water). Take it off the fire and, when the bubbles have settled, pour it at once into an oiled tin (or on to an oiled slab between bars).

As soon as it is cold, cut it into neat squares with a sharp knife.

Coconut Ice

1 lb. granulated sugar. ½ gill cold water and
6 oz. desiccated coconut. milk mixed.

Dissolve the sugar in the milk and water, and then boil to 240° (or until the mixture will form a soft ball when tested in cold water). Take it off the fire and add the coconut. Stir until the mixture is thick.

Pour half into an oiled tin (or on an oiled slab between bars). Colour the remainder pink and pour it on top of the white ice. When cool cut into fingers.

Fudge (Chocolate)

1 gill milk. 1 lb. granulated sugar.
1 gill cream or top milk. ½ gill grated, unsweet-
2 oz. butter. ened chocolate.

Put the milk, cream, butter and sugar into a pan, and bring to the boil. Add the chocolate and boil for 15 to 20 minutes until it is 240° (or will form a soft ball when tested in cold water). Stir gently at intervals to prevent it burning.

Take it off the fire and let the bubbles settle. Beat against the sides with a spatula until the mixture granulates. Then pour it quickly into an oiled tin (or on an oiled slab between bars). When cold cut into squares.

Fudge (Coffee)

1 lb. granulated sugar. 1 gill milk.
1 dessertspoonful coffee essence. 1½ oz. butter.

Make in exactly the same way as chocolate fudge, adding the coffee essence after taking the mixture off the fire and before beating it.

It will need rather more beating to make it granulate than chocolate fudge, owing to the extra liquid.

Fudge (Walnut)

2 lb. granulated sugar. ½ pint milk.
2 oz. butter. ½ pint chopped walnuts.
3 oz. grated unsweet- Pinch of cream of tartar.
ened chocolate. 1 teaspoonful vanilla
essence.

Make in exactly the same way as chocolate fudge, adding the walnuts, cream of tartar and vanilla after taking the mixture off the fire and before beating it.

Lemon Creams

1 white of egg. Icing sugar.
1 lemon. Yellow vegetable
A little crystallised colouring.
lemon peel.

Sieve a good lot of icing sugar on to a piece of paper. Slightly beat the white of egg in a basin and gradually stir in the icing sugar. When thick and creamy add the lemon juice and grated lemon rind, and continue stirring in icing sugar until the mixture forms a dough. (Just before this add the colouring till the mixture is pale lemon colour.)

Roll out the dough on a sugared board and cut into rounds with a small cutter. Line a rack with greaseproof paper, scatter some sieved icing sugar on it, and put the creams on the rack. Press down a small square of crystallised lemon peel on the top of each and leave them to set.

Marzipan

1 lb. loaf sugar. 3 oz. icing sugar.
1 gill water. 2 whites of egg.
12 oz. ground almonds.

Dissolve the loaf sugar in the water and boil to 240° (or until it forms a soft ball when tested in cold water). Draw the pan aside and when slightly cooled add the ground almonds and whites of egg. Stir by the side of the fire for a few minutes. Then turn on to a sugared slab and add the icing sugar, working it in with a spatula until the mixture is cool enough to handle. Knead till quite smooth.

When cold, wrap up the marzipan in greaseproof paper and store in a tin till required.

NOTE. Marzipan can be coloured or flavoured, as desired, by dabbing it with vegetable colouring or essence and kneading it on a board sprinkled with icing sugar. (Little oranges, apples or lemons can be made in this way.)

Marzipan Potatoes

Model some marzipan into shapes like new potatoes. Prick them with a skewer to resemble eyes and roll them in fine chocolate powder.

Mint Cake

1 lb. granulated sugar.
1 gill milk.
2 teaspoonsful peppermint essence (or a few drops oil of peppermint).

Boil the sugar and milk until 240° (or until a soft ball is formed when tested in cold water). Take off the fire and add the peppermint. Beat hard until the mixture thickens. Pour into an oiled tin (or on an oiled slab between bars). When cold, cut into squares with a sharp knife.

For brown mint cake use Demerara sugar.

Nougat

9 oz. granulated sugar.
1½ oz. glucose.
½ gill water.
½ teaspoonful vanilla essence.
½ teaspoonful brandy or rum.
½ oz. angelica (cut up small).
1 white of egg.
1 oz. chopped walnuts.
1 oz. chopped cherries.
1 oz. chopped, blanched almonds.
½ teaspoonful lemon juice.
Rice paper.

Line a tin, or bars and slab, with rice paper. Dissolve the sugar and glucose in the water in a pan, and then boil to 240° (or until the mixture forms a soft ball when tested in cold water). Meantime, beat the white of egg very stiff in a basin. Pour half the syrup gradually on to it, whisking all the time.

Boil the rest of the syrup to 270° (or to a very hard ball) and then add to it the beaten mixture and all the other ingredients. Stir for a few minutes until the mixture is firm and white, and then put it in the prepared tin. Put a piece of rice paper on the top and press down till it sticks to the nougat all over.

When cold, cut the nougat into bars with a sharp knife and wrap them in wax paper.

Peppermint Creams

2 whites of egg.
1 teaspoonful water.
Icing sugar.
Oil of peppermint (or peppermint essence).

Sieve plenty of icing sugar. Slightly beat the whites of egg and gradually add the icing sugar, beating hard. When fairly thick add the water and a few drops of oil of peppermint (or two teaspoonsful of essence). Continue adding sugar until the mixture will knead.

Put it on a sugared board and knead to a dough. Then roll out and cut into rounds with a small cutter. Place on sugared paper to set.

Toffee (Plain)

1 lb. granulated sugar.
4 oz. butter or margarine.
1 gill water.
1 large dessertspoonful glucose.

Put the sugar, water and glucose into a pan and heat till completely dissolved. Boil for about 10 minutes. Add the butter and boil to 300° (or until it will crack when tested in cold water). Let the bubbles settle. Then pour out at once into an oiled tin (or on to an oiled slab between bars). As soon as it is cold, cut it into squares with a sharp knife.

Store it in an airtight tin or a glass jar with a lid.

Treacle Toffee

12 oz. Demerara sugar.
4 oz. butter or margarine.
8 oz. black treacle.
Pinch of cream of tartar.
¾ gill water.

Dissolve the sugar, butter and treacle in the water and then bring them to the boil. Add the cream of tartar and boil to 260° (or until a hard ball is formed when tested in cold water). Pour into an oiled tin (or on to an oiled slab between bars) and cut up as soon as it is cool.

Put it at once in an airtight tin or glass jar with a lid, as it soon goes sticky if exposed to the air.

Turkish Delight

1 lb. loaf sugar.
1 oz. gelatine.
Icing sugar.
2 oz. almonds.
1½ gills water.

Put the gelatine to soak in ½ gill of cold water. Blanch the almonds and chop them rather coarsely. Dissolve the sugar in 1 gill of water and then boil to 240° (or until it will make a soft ball when tested in cold water). Meantime, bring the gelatine to the boil and add it to the mixture as soon as it is ready. Add the nuts and pour the mixture into an oiled tin.

When cold and set, cut into squares and roll in sieved icing sugar.

Timely Tips

String or cord should be wound around handles of kettles and saucepans which are liable to get too hot to hold.

If you burn your finger and have no proper medicament to hand, plunge it into flour to keep it dry.

Make some extra-strong peppermints—one taken before medicine disguises the taste.

PASTA

PASTA, the staple food of the Italians, can be made into an endless variety of main dishes by the addition of different sauces prepared from vegetables, meat, poultry, fish or cheese.

Pasta	Boiled in Water or Stock	Baked	In Soup	Croquettes	Sauces
Tagliatelle	3 minutes		Pre-cooked then 2 minutes		
Macaroni	8-10 minutes	Boiled in milk, then 20-30 minutes	15-20 minutes	3-4 minutes	Tomato Cheese Kidney Liver Mushroom
Spaghetti	5-6 minutes	Boiled in milk, then 20-30 minutes	10-12 minutes	3-4 minutes	Pimento Spinach Chicken
Vermicelli	3-4 minutes		6-8 minutes		
Ravioli	10-12 minutes	Boiled in water, then 10-15 minutes, in sauce		**Stuffings** Minced beef Chicken liver Minced chicken Rabbit Spinach	Tomato Cheese Meat Mushroom

Serve with:

Cheese Sauce

When using spaghetti or tagliatelle, pour the sauce over the cooked pasta, sprinkle with remaining cheese and serve. For Macaroni Cheese add 2-3 oz. cooked macaroni. Pour into a fireproof dish, sprinkle with cheese and brown under grill.

Italian Tomato Sauce

> 1 tablespoonful olive oil; 1 shallot; 1 level teaspoonful mixed herbs or fresh herbs to taste; 1¼ pints sliced tomatoes or bottled tomato purée; salt and pepper.

Heat oil slightly. Add sliced shallot and herbs. Fry gently until the shallot is slightly browned. Strain. Return oil to pan. Add tomato and a little salt and pepper. Cook gently with a lid, until reduced to a fairly thick pulp. Strain, reheat and pour over the cooked pasta.

Kidney Sauce

> 1 teaspoonful chopped fresh herbs (parsley, marjoram, thyme); ½ oz. dripping; ½ oz. onion; 4 oz. kidney; 1 oz. flour; 2 tomatoes; ¼ pint stock; 1 small blade mace; salt and pepper.

Sauté herbs for 2 minutes in the dripping. Strain and return dripping to pan. Add chopped onion and finely sliced kidney and sauté until onion is lightly browned. Add flour and continue cooking for 5 minutes until flour is lightly browned. Stir in sliced tomato, stock, mace and seasoning. Stir until boiling. Simmer for an hour. Pour over the cooked pasta.

A Children's Party

A GOOD idea, when you are giving a party for the little ones, is to tie the edges of the cloth underneath the table with tapes, or pin around top of table with safety-pins, so that cloth cannot be dragged to one side by excited children.

The next most important thing to remember about a children's party is that though the food should be as plain and wholesome as possible it must be made to look pretty.

This is best done by cooking plain cakes in fancy and amusing shapes, by the liberal use of coloured icing, and by adding attractive-looking decorations to everything. There are countless tiny figures and other objects sold for this purpose, and the children can be allowed to take them home with them.

Many modern children seem to prefer sandwiches with a definite taste to the most fascinating cakes. Tiny flags showing what the different sandwiches contain give a festive and grown-up air.

Be sure to serve lemonade or orangeade as well as weak tea and hot milk, and, since many a child's enjoyment of a party would not be complete without, include some pure ice cream (chocolate or strawberry ices are usually popular) in your menu, if possible, between wafer biscuits.

Children love jellies, so make some:

Sailing Ships (6 people)

1 *pint greengage or lemon*   *Mock cream.*
  jelly (*with a few drops*   *3 ripe pears.*
  green colouring added).   *3 ice-cream wafers.*

Make the jelly and put into six shallow glass dishes or deep saucers. When quite set, place a little mock cream in a paper forcing bag, or an icing syringe, with a plain pipe. Draw uneven lines on the jelly to look like waves of the sea. Cut the pears in halves lengthways; remove core and peel. Cut the wafers into triangular shapes to look like sails; you will need very sharp scissors. Just before serving put the pears on to the dishes with a little mock cream in the centre of each. Arrange the 'sails' in position.

Assorted Biscuits (enough for about 20)

4 *oz. margarine.*   *Few drops vanilla.*
2 *oz. sugar.*   8 *oz. flour* (*preferably*
1 *good tablespoonful*   *plain*).
  golden syrup.   *Egg or milk to mix.*

(NOTE. A biscuit dough can be handled very roughly without ill effect, so is a safe thing for rather energetic cooks to try.)

Cream the margarine, sugar and golden syrup in a large bowl until very soft and white. Add a few drops of vanilla essence. Add the flour, and work in with a wooden spoon. Next, gradually stir in the beaten egg or milk until you have a dough firm enough to roll into a ball and leave the mixing bowl clean. This is your basic mixture.

Fancy-shaped Biscuits. Take one-third of the basic mixture. Using attractive cutters, roll the dough out until about ¼ in. thick, and cut firmly into shapes. Put shapes on to an ungreased baking tin, and bake for about 10 minutes near the top of a moderate oven at 400° F. (Regulo 5). When the biscuits are golden brown take out of the oven, let them cool on the baking tin. Cover, when quite cold, with water icing or sieved icing sugar.

Almond Rings. Roll out the second third of the dough to ¼-in. thickness. Use two cutters and make ring shapes about 2 in. in diameter. Put the rings on to ungreased baking tins. Mix 1 tablespoonful sugar with 1 tablespoonful milk and brush the rings with this mixture. Sprinkle chopped almonds over the top. Bake for 10 minutes near the top of a moderate oven at 400° F. (Regulo 5). Cool on the baking tin.

Cherry Slices. Make two equal-shaped oblongs with the rest of the dough. Cover with chopped cherries, then use a sharp knife to cut into fingers. Bake for about 12 minutes just above the middle of a moderate oven at 400° F. (Regulo 5). Cool on the baking tin. When quite cold, dust with icing sugar.

'Crinoline Lady' Cake

For the 'Crinoline Lady' cake shown in our picture, bake whatever cake mixture you wish to use—sponge, fruit, or a Madeira type of cake—in a pudding basin instead of a cake tin. Grease and flour the basin well and fill about two-thirds full with the mixture. As the cake will be so deep, allow approximately half as long again as usual to bake. Turn out, and leave until it has been quite cold for several hours. In the meantime, buy a small pretty china head, similar to that shown in our cake, and make up the following water icing. Mix together 8 oz. sieved icing sugar with a few drops lemon juice and enough water to make a very soft consistency. First put a good spoonful of the icing on top of the cake, then spread the rest over the sides, smoothing with a palette knife dipped in hot water. Press the head firmly but carefully on the top and leave to set.

Next make up approximately 1 lb. royal icing. (You could manage with a little less for a smaller cake, but the cake used in the photograph was baked in a 2-pint basin.) Beat the whites of two eggs lightly, add a dessertspoonful lemon juice and work in 1 lb. icing sugar. Beat the icing until it is very white and stands up in peaks in the basin. Decide what colours you wish to use for the decoration, then divide the icing into the required quantities and basins. We used well over half as pale pink, and coloured part of the remainder apple-green.

Keep the pink and white icing soft by placing basins in a bowl of water and covering with a damp cloth, and spread the green icing down the front of the lady, smoothing on with a palette knife dipped in hot water. Leave for about 30 minutes, so that the edges begin to harden. Next cover the rest of the cake with the pink icing, smoothing in the same way. Allow this to become quite firm. Put the white icing into either a cloth or paper bag, or an icing syringe with a very small icing rose. Make the design of rose buds round the bottom of the dress and down the part where the green and pink icings join. Put a narrow band of ribbon round the pretty lady's waist.

Orange Fluff (4 people)

2 *eggs.*	1 *level teaspoonful powder*
2 *oz. sugar.*	*gelatine.*
1 *pint milk.*	1 *tablespoonful orange*
½ *teaspoonful*	*juice.*
finely graded	*Small pieces of orange and*
orange rind.	*cherries to decorate.*

This makes an easy but attractive alternative to an egg custard.

Separate the egg yolks from the whites. Beat the yolks lightly with just under half the sugar, then add the hot milk and grated orange rind. Cook gently—in a basin over hot water or a double-saucepan—until the custard thickens slightly. Soften the gelatine in the orange juice, then pour on the hot, but not boiling, custard. Continue to stir until you are sure the gelatine has dissolved. Pour into a rinsed mould and allow to set. Turn out on to a flat dish. Beat the egg whites until stiff, then fold in the sugar. Pile over the mould and decorate with cherries and orange sections.

Vita-Weat Sandwiches

Butter two pieces of Vita-Weat and chop up some stoned raisins and dates and put between.

This makes a most excellent sandwich.

A Tip About Milk

If you find it hard to get your children to drink and enjoy milk, then you may find some of the following suggestions helpful.

For small children it often works wonders if you slightly flavour or colour the milk. Use chocolate, Marmite, a few drops of cochineal. Add a few cherries or other fruit, and let them drink through straws.

Remember, when making gravies for stews, that you can thicken with flour and *milk* rather than water or stock.

Be sure that milk puddings are interesting in colour, and attractively decorated. Sprinkle hundreds and thousands over the top.

Make jellies and junket for tea. You will find many different junket powders on the market with a variety of flavours.

Milk Jelly
(Enough for 4 people)

1-*pint packet of flavoured jelly.*
½ *gill water.*   3½ *gills milk.*

Method.—Dissolve the jelly in the boiling water. If this proves difficult with such a small amount of water, then stand the basin over a saucepan of boiling water. Let the mixture cool slightly, then whisk in the cold milk. Pour into a rinsed mould to set.

English Electric Co.

This delightful and decorative plate-warmer will keep food hot until all late-comers have arrived. It is made of bonded glass in a polished metal frame, with handles for carrying. Perfect for parties, an informal meal by the fire, or a buffet supper

Children love lemon-curd, and the older ones like mincemeat. Both are useful fillings for tarts the year round.

Lemon Curd

6 *lemons*.	6 *oz. butter*.
6 *eggs*.	18 *oz. castor sugar*.

Place the butter in a 7-lb. stone jam jar and stand it on the fire in a saucepan ¼ full of water. Let the water boil.

Sieve the sugar on to a piece of paper. Grate the yellow part of the lemon rind on to a plate. Squeeze the lemon juice into a small basin. Beat the eggs together in another basin.

When the butter is melted add the sugar, then the lemon juice and rind, and finally the eggs. Stir over the boiling water without stopping till the mixture becomes thick (20 minutes to ½ hour). Pour it into the jars and tie down as soon as it is cold.

Mincemeat

1 *lb. suet*.	4 *oz. candied peel*.
1 *lb. raisins*.	1 *lemon*.
1 *lb. sultanas*.	1 *teaspoonful salt*.
1 *lb. currants*.	*Cinnamon*.
1 *lb. apples (peeled and cored)*.	*Nutmeg*.
1 *lb. castor or Demerara sugar*.	1 *gill rum, brandy, sherry or cider*.

Chop up the suet very finely and put it in a basin. Stone the raisins and chop them up finely with the apples, sultanas, currants and peel, and add them, with the sugar, to the suet. Add the grated lemon rind and strain in half the juice. Lastly add the brandy, salt and spices and stir the whole mixture thoroughly.

Tie a piece of greaseproof paper over the basin and put it away for a few days. Then give it another good stir and put it into jam jars, tie down the covers and store the mincemeat in a cool, dry place. Halve the quantities if less is needed.

* * *

FINGERS BEFORE FORKS

In case you want to know—

Olives are eaten in the fingers. The stone is put on the edge of the plate you are using.

Potato crisps, even when served with a hot meal, may be picked up with the fingers, if difficult to negotiate with your fork.

Asparagus is sometimes served as a separate course, and is also eaten with the fingers. Very few people have asparagus tongs. The green ends are dipped into the sauce and then sucked. When served as a vegetable with meat, use knife and fork.

When corn is served on the cob, spread on some butter, sprinkle pepper and salt, and eat from the end of the cob, holding it in the fingers.

If globe artichokes are served whole, you detach each leaf one by one, dipping the tip into the sauce, and discarding the rest on the edge of the plate.

Peel and eat seagull's eggs, using your fingers. Grapes and cherries also need no ' implement.'

HOME HINTS

Scorch Marks

Here are some suggestions for scorch marks. Mix a little oatmeal to a paste with vinegar and with the finger gently rub this paste into the scorch. Leave material to dry for a few hours. Brush off the dried oatmeal and the mark should have disappeared.

Scorch marks can be removed from linen by making a thin paste of magnesia and water and spreading it over the mark. When dry, the powder will brush off and should take the scorch with it.

To remove scorch marks from a white article, cover with a piece of muslin which has been soaked in peroxide, and iron.

Rub scorch with a slice of freshly-cut lemon.

Stains. For furniture stains, oil and salt left overnight on stained part of table should remove stain. Rubbing with Friar's Balsam sometimes helps. Salt and paraffin paste for grimy baths.

Iron Stains. Hold over steaming water, sprinkle salts of lemon to cover, then wash.

Perspiration Stain. Moisten stain, cover with borax, pour hot water through, squeeze stained part in borax solution, rinse, dry and press.

Leather Shoes. To remove stains, rub with a piece of rag dampened with methylated spirits. Polish in the usual way. Pure glycerine removes marks on suède.

Ink. Melt end of wax candle over; when removed after several hours, stain will have disappeared.

How to Give a Party

Almost any special gathering can be a 'party' and a good one, if it is approached in the right way. Here are also suggestions for refreshments for cocktail parties; menus for lunch and dinner; games for an evening get-together.

ALMOST anything can be a party if you bring the right frame of mind to it. An anniversary dinner with the table beautifully laid, you in your prettiest frock and your husband there, with no guests, a few little surprise presents . . . its success lies in the way things are done.

Some folk are inveterate party-givers; if they can't afford the refreshment, they'll tell friends to come and bring their own. Nearly everyone, at some time or other in their lives, has a party. The constant party-givers have worked out their own technique and need no help. But the occasional hostess is apt to get rather flustered and nervous and may begin to spoil the whole thing through a wrong mental attitude.

One. If there are any mishaps (short of anything serious, which is unlikely), laugh them off. Don't let them worry you. Tell yourself that you are giving a party to make your friends happy, and you can't do more. Relax. *But do try to make them happy.* There are hostesses who let the party revolve around themselves, leaving their guests high and dry with no introductions, not even bothering to look after them where refreshment is concerned. There are others who introduce people, and then snatch them away from one another before they've had an opportunity to say 'How d'you do?' Nevertheless, the latter is rather better, for the hostess *is* trying, even if overdoing it a trifle. DO INTRODUCE EVERYBODY. Keep an unobtrusive ear on surrounding conversations unless they are fast and furious, but if they are halting and embarrassed, then change the partners.

You can easily say something like, 'Captain Cloggs, you don't mind if I steal Miss Primly away for a moment, do you?' Then take the shy Miss Primly to someone talkative who'll put her at ease, and try to pair off Captain Cloggs with another guest of similar tastes. Once you have got everyone introduced, they will inevitably gravitate to the person or people they want to speak to. But if you *don't* introduce them, they will stand, frozen, petrified and miserable, clutching a glass as though it were a life-line. Mostly at sherry or cocktail parties, there are not enough introductions. Say names clearly, too. You may have a busy time but it will be worth it when everyone tells you later what a wonderful time they had. You will probably be surprised to find that the people you thought would *not* get on together are the ones who become lifelong friends, so do not make up your mind too firmly on affinities!

Cocktail Party

People rarely stay all the time at a cocktail party, but come and go between the hours of 5.30 and 7.30. Unless they are having a specially good time, when there will be some hardy spirits who will stay on till midnight for eggs and bacon. This, however exhausting it may be, is a sign of success and popularity, so don't take it too amiss!

Group Your Chairs

Most people stand about, but seats are very welcome to others. Arrange a few chairs in groups, two here, three there, a settee with a couple of chairs around a small table; a window seat, a pouffe, a stool . . . anything, but keep the centre of the room clear so that people can circulate. Borrow seats or glasses from neighbours or friends if you haven't enough. It certainly does not matter in this day and age if they match or not.

If you can have two adjoining rooms in use, so much the better, for it creates a feeling of change and space. Luckily, this type of party can be prepared for beforehand. However much work you do in the morning, lie down and relax after lunch, *whatever there is still to be done.* Twenty minutes will recharge you with energy, and will make no difference to your preparations except that they will be done more easily when you are refreshed.

Lemon pies are luscious and good to serve at a party

A Table for Savouries

Prepare a table with drinks on, or make them in the kitchen and get a friend or two to help carry them in on trays. The table should be laid with cocktail savouries and, if you wish, sandwiches. Either make the sandwiches yourself, wrap them in damp napkins, put them in cellophane and in the refrigerator if you have one; or get a catering firm to deliver them on the day.

The Beverage Question

When buying supplies of alcohol ask if the firm takes back unopened and unused bottles, for some of them do. Or a bottle or two over may come in for your own cocktail cabinet; or, if you don't usually drink much, for a birthday or some celebration.

When mixing cocktails, if you add a bottle of white wine to every two of gin (pouring them together into a large receptacle), you will find that you still have an excellent cocktail, and save a certain amount of expense. *Always have tomato juice, soft drinks, or iced coffee for those who do not drink.*

Keeping to simplicity, there need only be sherry, and a few chipolata sausages speared with toothpicks; potato crisps, very small sausage rolls; biscuits spread with cream cheese and a slice of pickled cucumber or a walnut; slices of hard-boiled egg and anchovy. This is sufficient if you have 'asked a few people in for drinks' just because you want someone to meet someone else. For a real party, it is better to have more of a display.

You can make a refreshing fruit cup, served from a large bowl. A quart of cider (these are basic quantities which can be diminished or increased); a bottle of orange squash; two liqueur glasses of brandy; the juice of a lemon, a sprig of bruised mint; a small bottle of tonic water; some slices of apple (which need not be peeled), some stoned grapes, a banana sliced, and, if liked, a few drops of angostura. Ice-cubes help.

Here are a few suggestions for extra cocktail savouries:

Potato Sticks

3 oz. freshly cooked sieved potato; 3 oz. margarine; 3 oz. flour; dill, caraway or poppy seeds.

Work the potato, margarine and flour to a dough, adding plenty of salt and pepper. Leave for about 1 hour to firm. Roll out to a rectangle, brush with beaten egg and sprinkle with the seeds. Cut into sticks and bake in a moderate oven 10-15 minutes.

Stuffed Celery

2 oz. Roquefort, Stilton or Danish Blue cheese; ½ oz. margarine; crisp celery; pimento; brown bread and butter.

Cream the cheese and margarine together. Dry the celery well and fill each stalk with the cheese mixture. Reshape into a stick, wrap in paper and leave in a cool place to firm. Cut small rounds from the bread and tiny rounds from the pimento. Slice the celery across into rounds and lay one on each round of bread. Decorate with the pimento.

Prawns with Mayonnaise

Choose a large rosy apple and spike with cocktail sticks, each holding a large prawn. At the side of this serve a bowl of ice-cold mayonnaise into which the guests can dip their prawns before eating.

Pancake Crisps

Cook very thin pancakes and when cool cut into strips. Fry until crisp in deep fat and drain thoroughly. Dust with grated Parmesan cheese and cayenne.

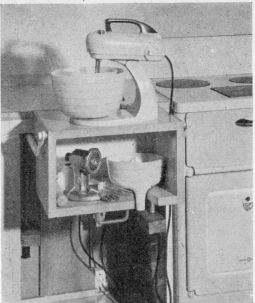

English Electric Co.

Your food mixer can be tucked away in a cupboard, and swung up on two ratchet arms when needed, clipping into place at counter level

Egg Nogg is a delicious drink to serve on special occasions. With a food mixer, it can be made in twelve minutes. See recipe on page 536

It is always a good plan to have a selection of more substantial snacks ready, as a really good cocktail party so often over-runs its appointed time, and guests then begin to get really hungry! The following recipe for a Danish open sandwich is excellent for this and is also good for later and after-theatre parties.

Buckling Sandwich

A slice of French bread, spread with butter

creamed with lemon juice and a point of cayenne. Arrange on this fillets of buckling, slices of pickled cucumber and decorate with sieved hard-boiled egg yolk and chopped white.

DINNER PARTY

The less help you have, the simpler should be the meal. It is best to choose dishes that can be prepared beforehand, and also ones with which you are familiar. To try something very ambitious that you have not cooked before is rather tempting Fate!

It is not a bad idea to have the names of a few favourite dishes written down so that you can compose a suitable menu to be carried out without difficulty.

An electric hot-plate in the dining-room is very useful when one is single-handed. The first course can be put on the table before the guests come into the room, the second on the hot-plate. Then, if the sweet is a cold one, the hostess need only put each course as it is finished on a trolley, which can be wheeled away when the meal is finished.

Earthenware and fireproof dishes, in which the food can be served as well as cooked, are a great help when one has to do most of the work oneself, besides being very attractive.

Table decorations should be simple: shining glass, well-polished silver, and a bowl of fresh flowers (low enough to allow the guests to see each other's faces) are all that is required to create a welcoming effect.

A Simple Luncheon or Dinner

Here is a suggestion for a menu:

Hors-d'oeuvres, soup, melon, grapefruit or prawn cocktail.
Sole meunière. (Sole, whiting, trout or slices of almost any white fish will serve.)
Maryland chicken.
Peas, potatoes, runner beans.
Pineapple en surprise. (Or melon.)

Sole Meunière (*Another method on page 433*)

Melt enough clarified butter in an earthenware dish (in which the fish can be served) to half cover the fish. Make small cuts on each side of the fish, dip into seasoned flour, and brown well on one side before turning it over on to the other.

Just before serving add a very little finely chopped parsley and a squeeze of lemon juice.

Maryland Chicken

Cut a young bird into joints, brush each piece over with melted butter, season and roll in flour and breadcrumbs. Put into a well-buttered dish and bake in the oven for about ½ hour, basting frequently with butter. Serve with a sauce made from the giblets.

Fried bananas go excellently with this dish.

By Greatrex

Do not forget to put plenty of mats all over the place for your guests, unless you want stained tables. These are non-skid, of leather

Pineapple (or Melon) en Surprise

Take a ripe pineapple, cut a slice off the bottom so that it stands firmly on a dish, then cut off the head low enough to enable the contents to be removed with a sharp knife. Put aside the head with the leaves intact.

Cut out the inside (keeping the juice carefully), chop it into neat pieces and mix with it any fresh fruit in season, as you would do for a fruit salad. Add the juice and put the mixture back into the pineapple. Just before serving add plenty of fresh cream. Replace the top.

A Cantaloup melon is equally good served in this way. Pineapple or melon-flavoured ice cream can be used instead of ordinary cream.

Do not forget to provide some form of 'slimming' bread, as well as ordinary bread.

Remember, too, that fresh fruit is not only always appreciated inwardly but is a delight to the eye, too.

EVENING PARTY

If you are giving an evening party at which you have a cold buffet . . . sandwiches, cold ham and/or chicken; salad; fruit salad; fish with mayonnaise; fruit flan . . . then you will need some games to keep the party going. Here are some that refuse to be played too sedately and result in a good deal of fun. Small prizes need cost very little and do add so much to the general enjoyment. A small powder-puff; a handkerchief; a posy; a packet of pins; a tube of shoe-cream; a duster; a tiny sweet-dish; a slab of chocolate and so on.

Treasure Hunt is a good first game for breaking the ice when many guests are unacquainted with each other. Give each player a pencil and a piece of paper on which twelve hidden things are listed. Actually they are usually camouflaged rather than concealed. For example, hang a short piece of string up against a cream net curtain, or describe a postage stamp on the list as 'Portrait of the Queen.' Each guest, on discovering a treasure, looks as unconcerned as possible, in order to give no clues to others and writes down the position of the find. The first to complete the list correctly gets a small prize.

Ring on a String. Thread a finger ring or small curtain ring on to a long string, then knot the ends of the string together. The players stand around in a circle, their hands gripping the string, except for one inside the circle. They make continual passing movements of their fingers on the string, whether the ring is in their hands or not; and the inside player must try to find the position of the ring. He can touch any suspected hand, which must then leave the string and be outstretched towards him. If it contains the ring or the ring is left exposed by the hand being lifted, the owner of it takes the centre place and tries in turn to find the ring.

Who Am I? Identities again, but with a difference! This is specially a game for keen

Liver Paté is useful either at parties, as an after-theatre snack, or a beginning to lunch. The recipe is given on page 537

English Electric Co.

A mincer, with a wooden food press, is an addition to the electric mixer. It switches on to do all the mixing, blending, whipping, creaming, mincing and juicing at the flick of a switch

film fans. Each player in turn pretends to be a favourite film star and has three minutes in which to describe himself, talking all the time but trying not to give away too many revealing facts. The first person to identify correctly the star being impersonated provides the next description for guessing. The same star may not be picked twice.

Mime It! Guests not clever at pencil-and-paper games often score high in this. On separate slips of paper write out beforehand various actions, such as: dog wagging tail, baby crying, woman rolling out pastry, man digging, postman delivering letters, etc. Fold the slips with the writing concealed, place in a hat or box and let each player draw out one. That player must then mime the action on his slip till it is guessed by the others. The

miming, whether well or badly done, can be most amusing and the guesses often very wide of the mark!

In Touch. Have ready a firmly fastened pillow slip which contains twenty objects, some of which are very much alike to the touch; for example, a lemon and an orange, a penny and a button, a saucer and a shallow ashtray. Some objects should be too small to be easily felt in the mixture, as a teaspoon, a safety-pin or a luggage label. Each guest feels the pillowship for two minutes, trying by touch only to identify its contents. Then the collection passes to the next player, while the first writes down all he or she can remember. The winner is the one with the largest list of *correct* 'touches.'

Yes and No. Many games can be copied from the radio. To play this, one guest is elected as Question-master, and the rest become 'victims' in turn. The victim must not answer 'Yes' or 'No' to any question. Fifteen questions are asked, very quickly and naturally, and it is not the easiest thing in the world not to slip up. For instance, the first girl may be asked, 'Do you wash your own hair?' and she may unthinkingly reply 'Yes' or 'No,' whereas the answer should be 'Of course I do,' or 'I couldn't be bothered,' or something similar. 'You're a good dancer, aren't you?' might draw 'I've been told so' or 'I wouldn't know' rather than 'No, I don't think so.' The speed at which the questions are asked is likely to trip the victim. If 'Yes' or 'No' is answered within 15 questions, there is a forfeit . . . to imitate an animal, do a war-dance, sing a song, recite a poem in an old man's voice or a childish way, or pick up a handkerchief from the floor kneeling with arms folded behind the back.

Memory Test. While you are, perhaps, replenishing the buffet, try putting 15-20 small articles on a tray, leave them on show to your guests for about a minute, and then leave them to write down a list of the various articles from memory. The one with the largest score receives a prize. This could be in the form of a joke—such as a small parcel wrapped up and labelled 'Something to keep you warm in the winter' and containing a couple of pieces of coal.

Telegrams. Call upon each player in turn for a letter; these are written one under the other by the other players on a piece of paper. Each player then writes the most humorous telegram he can think of using these letters as initials for the separate words. Allow four to five minutes for each attempt and then get each player to read out his immediate partner's telegram.

Passing the Matchbox. This is for younger people and can become quite hilarious. Divide guests into two sides, standing in lines opposite each other. Take two matchbox covers and wedge each firmly on the nose of each side's No. 1. Without touching it with his hands he must transfer it to the nose of the guest next to him, and so on right down the line. If the cover is dropped that side is penalised by going back one player before continuing. The side finishing first is the winner.

TO MAKE WITH YOUR FOOD-MIXER

ONE of the kitchen delights that Grandma had to do without is a food-mixer. It saves an enormous amount of time for all the chores of whipping and mixing, and invites you to try your hand at all sorts of dishes usually left to the professional.

Here are three recipes you may like to try. For Christmas, New Year or special anniversaries, here is an Egg Nogg which will be enjoyed by every member of the family.

EGG NOGG

What you will need:

3 eggs.	½ pint milk (chilled).
¼ lb. castor sugar.	½ pint brandy, whisky
½ pint cream	or rum.
(chilled).	Grated nutmeg.

With the food mixer control dial set at No. 16, whip the egg whites until stiff but not dry. Reduce the speed and add sugar. Beat again at No. 16 to recover the stiffness. Again reduce the speed, drop in the egg yolks and beat a minute at setting No. 16. Reduce the control to No. 4 and gradually pour in the chilled cream and milk and finally the liquor or a mixture of two of the liquors. Turn into a punch bowl. Serve in small glasses with a sprinkling of nutmeg on top of each.

Preparation time. Egg whites 4 minutes, add sugar, beat 2-3 minutes, yolks 1 minute, cream, milk, liquor 1-2 minutes. Snap-in type beaters release easily for cleaning and large ridged glass bowl is quickly rinsed in warm water. Maximum total time of preparation 12 minutes.

LEMON MERINGUE PIE

Everyone loves this attractive sweet, which is easy to prepare, with or without a mixer.

You will need sufficient short pastry to line a shallow pie-dish. Use your food mixer at setting No. 1 throughout for the pastry.

What you will need:

Filling

4 oz. sugar.	Walnut of butter.
2 oz. plain flour.	2-3 egg yolks.
Pinch of salt.	Juice and grated rind
½ pint boiling water.	1 large lemon.

Meringue

2-3 egg whites.	3-4 oz. icing
¼ teaspoonful lemon juice.	sugar.

The Filling. Place the sugar, flour and salt in a smallish saucepan or double boiler and pour the boiling water on to them, stirring all the time. Simmer gently for 10-15 minutes to cook the flour thoroughly. Add the butter. Beat the egg yolks, lemon juice and rind together—this may be done at setting No. 1, having taken the mixer head from the stand—then gradually stir the flour sauce into them, a little at first so as not to cook the eggs too quickly. Fill the pie shell with this mixture.

The Meringue. Place the egg whites and lemon juice in the small mixer bowl. Set the control at No. 16 and beat until the mixture is stiff (1½-2 minutes). Turn the control to No. 1, slowly add the sugar and beat until the mixture is well blended and will hold its shape. Spread and pile in blobs on the filling or pipe in fancy shapes with a large rose pipe. Bake for 15-20 minutes at 300-325° F.

Preparation time. Total beating time for short pastry 6-8 oz. is 5 minutes. Cooking and preparation time for filling, 15 minutes. Preparation time for meringue using three egg whites, 7 minutes.

LIVER PATÉ

A dish which can be prepared when the housewife has time to spare, and kept in the refrigerator for a few days until required, is Liver Paté. Liver Paté is delicious as hors-d'oeuvres or may be served with freshly made toast as a lunch or after-theatre snack. For this dish the mincer attachment combines with the mixer to give a smooth texture, ready in the shortest possible time for baking.

What you will need:

½ lb. liver.	1 clove garlic.
¼ lb. fat salt pork.	1-1½ oz. flour.
4 anchovy fillets.	¼ pint of milk.
½ apple.	1 small egg.
1 small onion.	Pepper, salt and
1½ oz. butter.	1 small bay leaf.

Soak liver in water with a few drops of vinegar in it. Drain and put through the smallest cutter of the mincer attachment of the mixer four times, together with pork, anchovy fillets, apple and onion. Mix together in a bowl. Melt the butter and sliced garlic together, then remove garlic. Add the flour and cook for 1-2 minutes without browning. Away from the heat, stir in the milk, bring to boil and simmer gently until the flour is cooked. Cool and turn into the large mixer bowl. Add the liver mixture and the egg. Set control to No. 8 and beat until thoroughly mixed. Add seasoning. Press the mixture into a greased small round casserole with bay leaf on top. Stand the dish in a pan of water and bake for 1½ hours at 250-300° F. After half an hour place butter paper on top and finish baking. Remove from oven and cool with weighted plate on top. Pour some melted butter on top of paté and when cold store in humidrawer of refrigerator or on low shelf covered with plastic or greaseproof paper.

HOUSEHOLD HINTS

A small piece of soda when boiling **split peas** will soften them.

Place soft **tomatoes** in a dish of salt and water for an hour or even overnight and in the morning they will have firmed considerably.

Potatoes—New. Use a pot scourer to scrape them, not a knife.

Bread—New. Dip bread knife in boiling water before cutting.

Bacon. Try sprinkling small pieces of bacon with flour to stop curling while being fried.

Add the juice of a lemon if **a jelly** will not set.

If, when making **jam**, it froths on top, put on a small piece of butter.

* * *

Before **making tea,** spread the portion of tea on paper and place in warm oven for a few minutes. It brings out the full flavour and goes further.

When preparing **rhubarb** for cooking, to cut it into short lengths with scissors instead of a knife is quicker and cleaner.

Boric acid powder is a stand-by in hot weather. A saltspoonful stirred into a pint of milk keeps it sweet and fresh for 24 hours. A little sprinkled over raw meat has the same effect. A dessertspoonful added to the water when washing pantry shelves helps to keep away flies.

A squeeze of blue when **rinsing glass** gives a brilliant shine. Add a few drops of turpentine to your washing water and glassware will look as new.

Wash **windows and mirrors** with a little vinegar in the water, both to give a sparkle and to keep flies and blue-bottles away, especially during hot weather.

* * *

Bacon kept in a glass jam jar keeps moist, and does not get hard. Boil the rashers for a minute or so before frying, if slightly hard.

Milk or cream that is on the verge of becoming sour, may be sweetened with the aid of a pinch of carbonate of soda.

To prevent milk from **souring,** dissolve half a teaspoonful of california borax in a drop of hot water. Mix this with the milk and it will keep sweet.

Will You

Have a Little Wine?

MANY hospitable folk are rather alarmed at the idea of serving wine with a meal, because of ignorance in choosing or serving. This is a mistake for, after all, the only criterion, in the last resort, is enjoyment. But there are a few tried and true maxims governing their choice, although these days such rules are much less rigid. It is rare now to serve a different wine with each course. An apéritif, perhaps sherry, with the soup, and a wine with the main dish are all that is expected. It is only natural that someone who is not a wine-drinker should not have a very comprehensive knowledge, but a little wine does transform a meal—making it more of an 'occasion.' Here, therefore, are a few helpful suggestions:

WINES BEFORE MEALS, AS APÉRITIFS
(served cold)

Sherry, dry or medium

Spanish sherries—Fino (dry) and Amontillado (medium dry) — are favourites. Landdrost, a medium-dry Cape Sherry, is also good. Sherry is the only wine whose taste is not impaired by cigarette smoke!

Champagne

Usually drunk throughout a meal, but admirable as an apéritif. All champagne is blended: if a year is marked on the label, it means that wines of only that year made up the blend and that it is a Vintage Champagne. Champagne ranges from absolutely dry to sweet, thus: *Brut, Extra Sec, Sec, Demi Sec* and *Doux.*
Other wines, champagne type: Sparkling Muscatel; Sparkling Saumur; Sparkling Burgundy, Hocks, Moselles.

Vermouth

Wine strengthened with spirit and flavoured with aromatic herbs. French vermouth is pale and dry. Best known is Noilly Prat. Italian vermouth is usually dark and sweet. Cinzano is very popular served with a piece of lemon-peel on the rim of the glass. Vermouths can be served mixed, alone, or with soda or gin.

Cocktails

Mixtures of wines and/or spirits with fruit juices, bitter wines and vermouth. Here are recipes for three popular cocktails. Shake the ingredients together in a shaker, with ice, and strain into glasses.
GOLDEN LADY: Third orange gin, third brandy, sixth lemon juice, sixth grapefruit juice.
MANHATTAN: Half whisky, quarter French vermouth, quarter Italian vermouth.
CHAMPAGNE: Soak one lump of sugar in Angostura bitters, add juice of 2 or 3 pieces of lemon peel, fill up with champagne.
QUARTER DECK: Two-thirds rum, one-third sherry, teaspoonful lime juice.
There are also many popular proprietary brands of apéritif such as Dubonnet, Pernod, Pimm's No. 1, etc.

The Reason Why

Certain wines enhance the flavour of certain foods and vice versa. For instance, whereas a dry white wine actually improves one's enjoyment of fish, a red wine often makes it taste sour. *A useful general rule for the occasional hostess to remember is that dry white wines go well with fish and white meat,*

If you would like to serve a little wine and are not quite sure which would be suitable, this will be a guide.

red wines with red meat and game, and sweet white wines and port with dessert. Sherry, champagne, hock, or moselle go well with any course. However, here is a little more detail which may be of interest for special occasions:

WINES WITH SOUP

Medium Dry Sherry

Amontillado.

Madeira

'Sercial' and 'Verdelho' are medium-dry types, Verdelho being the sweeter of the two.

WINES WITH HORS D'OEUVRES AND FISH (served chilled but not iced)

Dry and Semi-dry White Wine

Famous dry white wine from Bordeaux is Graves. Many others are sold as *Bordeaux Blanc* or *Côtes de Bordeaux*. *Entre deux Mers* is another, reasonably priced, somewhat sweeter white wine. They are all usually best while young. The leading white Burgundies are Montrachet, Meursault, Pouilly-Fuissé, Chablis. Chablis is driest and a favourite with oysters and shellfish; Pouilly the least dry. Best vintage years: 1947, 1949, 1945, 1950.

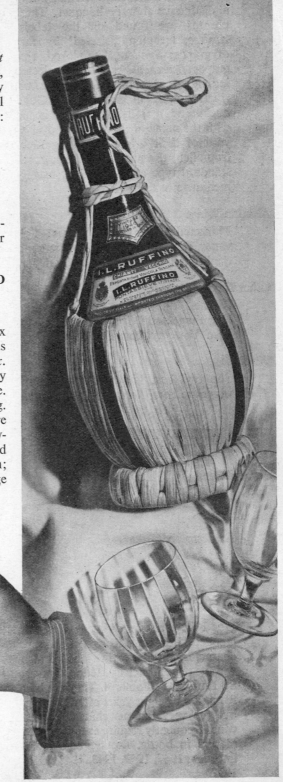

Even just two people can have 'a party,' and a little wine adds to the occasion

Hocks and Moselles`

These white wines from Germany have a distinctive flowery bouquet. These phrases are found on the labels: *Auslese*, meaning 'selected' bunches of grapes; *Spatlese*, late-picked, ripe grapes; *Beerenauslese*, specially selected individual grapes; *Goldbeerenauslese*, ripest grapes on each bunch. Good hocks and moselles are also labelled with the name of the village and vineyard of their origin, excepting Liebfraumilch, the name given to a good, standard type of Rhine wine, usually medium sweet.

Alsatian Wines

Marketed under grape names: Sylvaner, Riesling and Traminer are good quality, all white and generally dry.

Other Dry White Wines

Rhône Valley wines, notably white Hermitage and Côtes du Rhone blanc. Also Vouvray from the Loire valley.

Vin Rosé

The two best known of these pink wines are *Tavel Rosé* and *Rosé d'Anjou.*

WINES WITH WHITE MEAT AND POULTRY

Dry and Semi-dry White Wine

As described.

Vin Rosé

As described.

Champagne

As described.

Claret (dry)

Good inexpensive ordinary claret is labelled 'Bordeaux Rouge.' For more character, choose a wine labelled also with its region, such as Médoc, Graves, St. Emilion or Pomerol. They are best from five to eight years after bottling, but the very famous château-bottled wines frequently require even longer to mature in bottle. Best vintage years, in order: 1947, 1949, 1943, 1948, 1950, 1937.

Beaujolais

See under Red Burgundy.

Empire Dry Red

These are of claret and burgundy character, and come from Australia and South Africa.

WINES WITH RED MEAT AND GAME

Red Burgundy (dry)

Usually fuller, stronger and heavier than claret. For a good burgundy, see the name of the vineyard as well as the district, e.g. from the Côte du Nuits and the Côte de Beaune come the big, perfumed wines such as Chambertin, Romanée Conti, Clos de Vougeot, Richebourg and Corton. However, excellent and cheaper wines are sold under village names, as Beaune, Pommard, Nuits-Saint-Georges, Volnay. Wines from more than one village in Burgundy of the cheaper quality are blended together, and labelled 'Bourgogne Rouge.'
Lighter, red wines come from the famous Mâconnaise, Côte Chalonnaise and Beaujolais districts farther south; these are best drunk young. Burgundies are best with strong-tasting meats and dishes like curry, eggs, and strong cheese, as these all incline to override claret. Best vintage years in order: 1949, 1947, 1945, 1937, 1943.

Algerian Red

Reasonably priced, full, round wines.

Empire Dry Red

Châteauneuf-du-Pape

A full-bodied Rhône wine, excellent with game or cheese.

WINE WITH BISCUITS OR DESSERT

Natural Sweet Wines

Sauternes, most famous of which is the Château Yquem. Other notable names: Barsac, St. Croix-du-Mont and Loupiac: Cérons. Monbazillac.

Champagne

See foregoing.

Port

Ruby and Tawny Port are blended, but there are also vintage ports.

Rich Sherry

Sweet sherry, such as Oloroso or brown, is usually dark in colour.

Marsala

An Italian wine resembling sweeter sherries.

Madeira

Richer and sweeter types, like Bual and Malmsey.

Liqueurs

Including brandy, are served with coffee.

It is usual to serve dry wines before sweet wines, and light wines before heavier ones. Nevertheless, feminine taste often inclines to sweet wines where dry are generally recommended, but naturally there is no *law* against indulging one's own preference!

Notes to Remember

Wines must be kept on their sides so that the wine touches the cork and keeps it moist. Store them somewhere dark and fairly free from vibration and extremes of temperature, smell or dampness (about 55° preferably). A dark cupboard is often suitable.

Handle all wines carefully, especially older red ones, which have grown a sediment during maturation. Before opening a red wine which has 'thrown a crust,' stand it up for about 24 hours to allow the sediment to fall. Open it a good hour before use to let it 'breathe' and take the temperature of the room. Whilst white wines are always served chilled, red wines should be served at room temperature. Open them with a corkscrew having a flat, broad spiral, and wrap the neck of the bottle in a napkin.

All wines may be decanted, and those which have thrown a crust should be. Wipe the lip and inside the bottle neck with a cloth, then rinse the decanter with a drop of the wine. Holding the bottle in your right hand with the light behind it, and the decanter in your left, pour gently, leaving crust undisturbed and sediment in bottle. You can use this later for cooking.

Never mix beer with wine. Follow beer with whisky, wine with liqueur or brandy.

There are five chief traditional shapes for glasses, but one which is excellent for all wines. It is tulip shaped and should be filled about two-thirds full. It narrows at the top in order to collect and give back the bouquet of the wine; it is colourless so that the colour of the wine can be appreciated. Nevertheless, coloured wine-glasses do add to the attractiveness of a table decorative scheme.

When you are about to serve your wine, first taste a little in your own glass to make sure that you do not pour your guests wine which is off temperature, musty or tainted by a bad cork, or sprinkled with scraps of cork or wax!

HOME-MADE WINES

In case you would like to try the old-fashioned pastime of making your own wine, here are some recipes.

Damson Wine

4½ *lb. damsons.*   4 *lb. sugar*
1 *gallon of boiling water.*

Put the damsons in a pan and pour 1 gallon of boiling water over them. Let them stand for 10 days, stirring every day. Then take the crust off the top, strain through muslin and squeeze the fruit.

Put the liquid into a pan with the sugar, and stir. When dissolved, bottle (cork loosely) and allow it to work. When it has finished working put in the cork lightly.

Dandelion Wine

1 *gallon of flowers.*   3½ *lb. sugar.*
5 *quarts of boiling water.* 1 *orange and* 1 *lemon.*

Pick the flowers on a sunny day. Put them, with the orange and lemon cut into slices, in a bowl and cover with the boiling water. Leave for 9 days, then take off the mould. Strain the flowers and liquid through muslin and add the sugar. Stir until dissolved.

Put in bottles or jars to ferment. Keep the bottles filled to the top while fermenting.

Loganberry Wine

4 *lb. loganberries.*   4 *quarts water.*
4 *lb. sugar.*

Boil the water. Put the berries into a clean, dry earthenware pan and pour the water over them. Let them stand for 10 days. Then strain the liquor, but do not squeeze the fruit.

Add the sugar and let it stand until the next day. Then put it in a gallon jar and cork loosely until it has done working (about 3 weeks). Then put in the cork lightly.

The wine is ready to drink in 3 months, but it improves with keeping.

Orange Wine

13 *oranges.*   9 *pints boiling water.*
3 *lb. sugar.*

Wipe the oranges with a warm, wet cloth and then cut them in slices and remove all pips. Put the slices in a large bowl and pour over them the boiling water. Cover with a clean cloth and leave for 7 days, but stir well each day.

Strain through muslin and add the sugar. Let the sugar dissolve, and pour into a cask or wine jar to ferment. When fermentation ceases, seal up. Bottle in 4 months.

Parsnip Wine

4½ *lb. parsnips.*   1 *gallon cold water.*
2 *lemons.*   4 *lb. sugar.*
Cloves to taste.

Scrub the parsnips thoroughly and put them in the sun to dry. Cut up the lemons and boil them with the parsnips in a gallon of cold water until tender, taking care the parsnips do not break. Strain and, when, blood-heat, add the sugar and cloves to taste. When the sugar dissolves, put in a stone jar or bottles and allow to work. When it has finished working, lightly cork.

Rhubarb Wine

5 *lb. rhubarb.*   2 *lemons.*
4 *lb. sugar.*   1 *gallon water.*
2 *or 3 pieces bruised ginger.*

Cut the rhubarb into small pieces and pound well.

Slice the lemons and add them with the ginger. Cover with a gallon of boiling water and leave to stand for 10 days, stirring daily.

Then strain and add the sugar; when dissolved, bottle and allow to work. When it has worked, cork lightly.

BOUQUET GARNI

You will often find the expression ' bouquet garni ' in cookery recipes to be added to soups and stews.

This is parsley, thyme, shrive, sage, marjoram, etc., put into a muslin bag and added to the pot for seasoning.

MORE HOME HINTS

Cracked Eggs. If you want to boil a cracked egg, wrap it in a small bag, tightly twisted at one end, or a piece of greaseproof paper twisted at each end.

Hot-weather Tip. If you have no refrigerator, immediately the milk arrives pour it into a vacuum flask which has been previously rinsed out with cold water. Keep corked until needed. There is then no need to boil it.

*   *   *

Turn your milk pan upside down immediately after use. The steam will cause the skin to loosen, thus saving time and trouble when washing up. If burnt, turn it over a flame to loosen blackening.

To rinse baby's bottle, put in a little washing soda with some hot water; it cleans it like new.

*   *   *

If a screw-topped bottle will not open and your hand slips when trying to turn it, grasp the top with a piece of emery paper, after having held it under hot tap for a while.

When mixing mustard, use milk instead of water. This will prevent it from going dry.

*   *   *

Lettuce. Soak limp lettuce in very cold water to which a teaspoonful of sugar or a piece of coal has been added, for 20 minutes.

Carrot. Grate large carrot, squeeze pulp through butter muslin. Drink first thing in morning. Excellent for complexion, head-aches, rheumatism, etc.

*   *   *

To open Cans. 1. Stand tin in cold water 10 minutes. 2. Open one end, put hole in the other end and blow through.

If the sink plug does not fit tightly and the water gradually disappears, wind a piece of adhesive tape round the plug until you get it firmly placed.

*   *   *

An ordinary tin funnel makes an excellent string holder. Draw the end through the funnel and hang the latter on a nail or hook in the kitchen.

Stained Decanter. Light piece of brown paper, put inside, hold hand over until filled with smoke. When rinsed, it should be clean.

JUST *for* FUN

LIFE may be real and earnest, as the poet says, but there are times when we like to relax, and imagine the future may hold all the most exciting things for us. You will always be a popular hostess or guest if you can read the teacups, and this does not demand anything very drastic in the way of special talent. Once you have learnt to associate various images in the cup with their meanings, you will find it simple to link these together. For instance, you see that the leaves form what looks like a dog, there is an initial 'B' next to it, and a low row of dots. . . . You would say, 'There is a good friend of yours whose name begins with B, coming on a journey.' If there is a rose also there, you could add that there is a happy outing with this friend. Do not predict anything bad. You could be wrong, and thus might affect a suggestible person disagreeably for no reason. Teacup fortunes are for gay sociability—and whether it is the law of averages at work, or the instinct of the reader—*sometimes they come true!*

Acorn. Success crowning some effort, which has been slow in showing results.

Aeroplane. Hasty news.

Anchor. Security is at hand. Good luck.

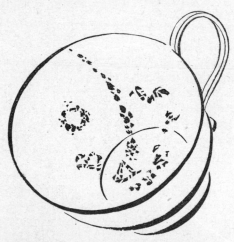

Look steadily into a cup and the leaves form pictures. Here is a ring, the initial B, a journey (long dotted line), money (triangle), news (bird on the wing)

Angel. You are protected and will swerve out of the way of some danger.

Arab. News from a hot country. All signs such as palm trees, camels, mountains, relate to the countries they indicate.

Arch. An opportunity to start something new and unexpectedly good.

Arrow. You will be shown the way to take.

Axe. Broken friendship. Knife or sword is the same.

Baby. Teacup signs are not always symbols but mean just what they show. So this would be news of a birth, or of a baby.

Bat. News by night, perhaps not too pleasant.

Bear. Lucky. Travel.

Beehive, bees. Money from your own efforts. Success.

Beetle. Passing annoyances. All insects are the same.

Bell. News of a wedding.

Bellows. Possibility of a new home. A happy hearth.

Bird. News, possibly of a domestic kind. Two birds together on a bough, happiness in love.

Boat. If a large one, an arrival from afar. If small, a short but pleasant holiday.

Book. A book may suggest an idea that helps you.

Boot. An old boot, a small legacy or other money luck. A high-heeled shoe, a new feminine friend.

Bouquet. Present of flowers.

Bowl. Increased income.

Bracelet. Gift of jewellery.

Bridge. At last you will find the way to your heart's desire.

Bugle. An appeal for help. Do not disregard it.

Building. These will have some influence on the life of the enquirer—describe how they appear, bungalows, tall buildings, skyscrapers.

Buoy. A way out of some problem. A sign to relax.

Butterflies. Gaiety, pleasant outings. Flowers mean the same thing when seen as a single bloom.

Cage. A proposal you should think twice about.

Car. Unexpected and pleasant outing.

Cat. Lucky omen.

Chair. Someone calls on you as a surprise.

Church. News of a death.

Circle. This is the same as a ring, and indicates marriage or news of an engagement.

Clouds. Light clouds, happiness in the summertime, blue skies ahead. Dark ones, watch your step, trouble brewing.

Comet. A wish granted . . . the one that comes into your head.

Crown. An honour bestowed upon you. Also governmental news.

Devil. Temptation—beware!

Dog. True friend. A horse is the same.

Dots. Many dots in clouds, a shower of small sums of money. A long dotted line, a journey.

Duck. Domestic happiness.

Ear. Be careful what you say. You may be overheard.

Elephant. An expensive present.

Faces. These are often seen with the characteristics that they really bear. Describe them.

Frog. A successful change.

Fruit. Prosperity. Fruit trees, good health.

Hand. Offer of friendship, lasting a long time.

Heart. A happy love-affair. If one side broken, the enquirer is possibly even now unhappy about a love-affair.

Horseshoe. Lucky, as always.

Initials. These can be the initials of friends, new acquaintances or places. A letter near the initial F might mean news from France, and so on.

Key. Some new study opens the door to a better position.

Ladder. You'll rise in the world with a little effort.

Numbers. These indicate the date or number of days before something happens, or could be an amount of money.

Pipe. The enquirer may marry an old friend.

Ring. Same as circle, marriage. An oval ring, luck in the home.

Snake. Deceit around. Sometimes a death.

Star. Success, maybe fame.

Triangle. Large, individual sums of money. Maybe a good sale.

Vulture. Don't lend money to someone you doubt.

MORE HOME HINTS

Glove Hints

(1) If you have not got a glove-dryer, to keep wash-leather gloves a good shape after washing and prevent shrinking, push clothes pegs down each finger while they are still damp, and allow to dry.

(2) Kid gloves, white or light coloured, can be cleaned with ordinary toilet eau-de-cologne. Just apply with a piece of cotton-wool and rub marks or stains.

(3) Cover your hands with talc powder or flour before drawing on your rubber gloves. After use, peel off, thus turning them inside out. Repeat every time in use, this prevents tears and gives them a much longer life.

From an old pair of gloves cut the first finger and thumb together, slip these on when peeling vegetable to prevent staining the hands.

From the least-worn part of an old towel make a pair of gloves shaped like baby's mitts; **after a shampoo**, massage head vigorously to dry hair quickly and to give it a shine.

* * *

Washing. Use a teaspoonful of sugar in rinsing water for satins.

If you add a tablespoonful of paraffin to an ordinary-sized tin of **floor polish** and work it well in with an old knife, a much better and more lasting polish will be obtained, also the polish in the tin will not harden quickly.

For polishing old cork lino that has not been polished before, rub well all over with a good polish, then wash lightly and quickly with very hot water. The next polishing will be much easier.

* * *

If you have a Victorian range, after a **black-lead session**, put on a coating of wax polish, then it will be a long time before it needs doing again.

Just for Fun—*continued*

Method

The method is to take the cup with a little tea left in, in the left hand, twirl it three times anti-clockwise, then empty it. Leave to drain a moment or two. Tea still in the cup indicates passing tears, or with good signs, sometimes drinking and conviviality. A cup is supposed to represent three weeks; near the handle is almost immediate; at the bottom of the cup, further away and so on.

Keep Some Stores in Reserve

Stores should be checked every two weeks, so that some necessary commodity is not lacked at a crucial moment. Type or write out a list of stores in hand, and drawing-pin it on the inside of the cupboard door, crossing off items as they are used

THE store cupboard should be dry, adequately ventilated and well lit. It should have plenty of narrow shelves, and, if used for perishable food as well as dry stores, there must be a marble slab or tiled shelf near the window. Fine gauze should be fixed across the window frame to keep out insects.

Choose jars to hold 1-4 lb. of dry stores, or 4 oz. at the most of spices, herbs, etc. Jars that fit closely together are ideal. For food in daily use, jars need not be airtight, but air should be excluded from most reserve stocks. If reserves and daily stocks are kept together, it is wise to use two different types of jar, to avoid confusion.

Glass or clear plastic jars are easy to clean, need no labelling, and allow easy examination of food. Pottery makes most satisfactory and attractive containers, but labelling is essential. Aluminium also must be labelled.

As a general rule, buy small quantities of all foods, remembering that although dry foods keep for a long time they will not store indefinitely. Have a small stock of all items used regularly and a reserve stock kept separately on a different shelf. When stock is finished replace with the reserve, and add the item to the week's order. This simplifies housekeeping and ensures against running short of essentials.

Although there are certain things that must be included in every store cupboard, there are many that are a matter of taste. Keep the stores limited to a small variety at the start, and increase it gradually as the need arises. The suggested list includes most items that are likely to be required, but essentials are marked with a star.

The quantities mentioned in this list are given as a guide to the minimum stores needed for two people. They are not intended to allow for entertaining and must, of course, be adjusted according to personal needs.

Seasonings. *Cooking salt, 1 packet or 1 block. *Table salt, 1 small drum. *Mustard, 4 or 8 oz. tin. *White pepper, 1 oz. Cayenne, 1¼ oz. Paprika, 1¼ oz. Black pepper, 1 oz.

Whole Spices. Cloves, 1 oz. Mace, 1 oz. Nutmeg, 2 oz.

Ground Spices. Cinnamon, 2 oz. Curry powder, 3-4 oz. tin. Ginger, 2-4 oz. Mace, 1 oz. Mixed spice, 2 oz. Nutmeg, 2 oz.

Dried Herbs. Basil, 1 oz. Bay leaves. Mixed herbs, 2 oz. Parsley, 1 oz. Sage, 2 oz.

Flavouring Essences. *Almond, 1 fluid oz. Coffee, 1 fluid oz. Lemon, 1 fluid oz. *Vanilla, 1 fluid oz. Rennet, 3 fluid oz.

Colouring Essences. Saffron, 1 fluid oz. Sap green, 1 fluid oz. Strawberry, 1 fluid oz. Gravy browning, 3½ fluid oz.

Pickles and Vinegars. Capers, 2-4 oz. jar. Chutney, 1 jar. Gherkins, one 6 oz. jar. *Malt vinegar, 1 pint. White vinegar, 1 pint.

Sauces. Mushroom ketchup, 6 fluid oz. Tomato ketchup, 8½ fluid oz. Worcester sauce, 10 fluid oz. *Salad dressing, 8 oz. bottle. Anchovy sauce, 6 fluid oz.

Jellies. Aspic jelly, 2 oz. Gelatine, 4 oz. packet. Packet jellies, 2-4.

Preserves. Honey, 1 lb. Jam, 2 lb. Marmalade, 2 lb. Black treacle, 1 lb. Syrup, 2 lb.

Cereals and Pulses. Breakfast cereal, 1 packet. All-Bran, 1 packet. Porridge oats, 1 packet. *Rice, 1-2 lb. *Pearl barley, ½ lb. Haricot beans, ½-1 lb. Butter beans, ½-1 lb. *Lentils, 1 lb. Split peas, ½-1 lb.

Ground Grains. Arrowroot, ¼-½ lb. Cornflour, 1 lb. Custard powder, 12 oz. tin. Ground rice, ½ lb. Oatmeal, ½ lb. (fine or medium). *Plain flour, 1-3 lb. *Self-raising flour, 1-3 lb. Blancmange powders, 2-4 packets.

Pastes. Macaroni, ½ lb. Spaghetti, 1 lb. Vermicelli, ½ lb.

Raising Agents. *Baking powder, 4 oz. *Bicarbonate of soda, 2 oz. Cream of tartar, 1 oz. Tartaric acid, 1 oz.

Beverages. Coffee, ¼-½ lb. ground. Coffee, ½ lb. vacuum tin. Tea 1 lb. Cocoa, ½ lb. tin. Commercial preparations for making milk beverages. Drinking chocolate powder, ½ lb. tin. Meat and vegetable extracts, 2-4 oz. jars.

Dried Fruit. Angelica, 2 oz. Currants, 1 lb. Glacé cherries, 4 oz. Mixed peel, ½ lb. Prunes, 1 lb. Raisins, 1 lb. Sultanas, 1 lb.

Tinned Food. Condensed milk, 2 tins. Evaporated milk, 2 tins. Fruit, 12 tins or bottles. Herrings or pilchards, 4 tins. Meat, 4 tins. Salmon, 1-3 tins. Sardines, 4 tins. Soups, 6-12 different varieties (tins or packets). Vegetables, 6 tins.

Two Tips

Dresses will not slip from your **coat hangers** if you wrap several rubber bands around the end of each hanger, or a length of rough string.

Old white shoes. Clean off all dirt, then when dry give them a coat of white Chinese lacquer paint. They will need a damp cloth only to clean.

EARN A LITTLE
EXTRA MONEY

DO you want to earn a little extra money, even if it is only enough to buy yourself an occasional new suit, an ornament for the house or to ease the economic shoe if it pinches? Then really try to find some demand which you can supply. Everyone has some talent that is of use, if they will only think about it. Here are a few suggestions. If none of them appeals to or suits you, then look around for a part-time niche which you can fill.

Neighbourhood Children

For instance, many mothers would like to send their children to a kindergarten from 9.30 till 12.30, and know that the babies (about 3-5 years of age) were being taught, as well as kept out of mischief. You would need just a little capital to set up in this since a small blackboard, books, tiny tables and chairs all cost money. You might be able to buy the goodwill of an existing kindergarten from someone else. In some districts you can charge as much as 30s. a week; in others, people would be hard put to it to find 5s. You may just take in, say, half a dozen children at a sum that would not be too much strain on the mothers, and make it worthwhile to yourself.

Are you clever with your fingers? Some people fashion necklaces and ear-rings that are original and manage to sell them to the big shops or by post. Don't be discouraged if you fail at first, but remember amateur work will not do. If you have a good idea, persist in it till your work has a professional finish.

Can You Type?

Home typing for authors (or anyone else who needs it). Advertise in your local paper, or a writers' journal, or any other that seems suitable to you. But this, too, has to be top-class and well checked.

How is your artistic sense? Can you make rugs? Design simple patterns? Match colours well? Many people would like a handmade rug at not too great a cost to blend with their own decorative scheme. Advertise in a suit-

These suggestions are to start your own thoughts working. Write down everything you like to do, and at which you excel. Choose to explore the possibilities of a line in which the demand is most and the supply least!

able journal that you make rugs to match any patterns sent. Clients should write for details, and you can quote prices according to the work done. Lampshades can be made in the same way.

Are you good at talking to people in a friendly way? Social surveying may be your market. Big firms commission surveys of public preferences, and people are needed to contact others with a view to finding out just how they react to certain products, cosmetics, foods and matters of public interest.

The Artistic Type?

You can learn to make all sorts of things at handcraft or pottery classes, and if your wares are sufficiently enticing, can slowly build up a clientele who will tell others about you.

Women's Institutes can take jam, fruit, vegetables or flowers, although this is not necessarily profit-making. However, others—friends or local shops—may buy your wares. Cakes, too. You can start with a connection among friends who are not gifted that way. Cook for children's parties.

If you speak good English (by which is meant correct English) and have a working knowledge of grammar, you may be able to give lessons to visitors from abroad who are here for some time, at anything from 3s. 6d. to 10s. a lesson. You may be able to get work at a language school, or translations to do.

Baby-sitting is much better paid than it used to be, and if you are conscientious, like children and have books you want to read or sewing to do, this provides an evening's occupation.

How is Your Needlework?

If you are good with your needle but do not wish to be a whole-time dressmaker, then do alterations, or renovations. Many women would be only too glad to know of someone who sewed who did not consider themselves 'above' alterations. After all, they can make the success of a garment.

Some corset-firms employ local fitters. This may appeal to you. Or home helps for the sick or busy are always urgently needed, and you

have the satisfaction of being of use as well as being paid!

If you live in a district famed for something, such as a Wishing Well, or being near a lighthouse, you may find some way of embroidering handkerchiefs, making small brooches, or little pictures to sell to visitors, perhaps through the local shop.

Can you cook? Perhaps you can help with school meals (apply to your local Council) or look after children while at table. Any boarding-schools in the vicinity may be able to employ an assistant, part-time matron. Put an advertisement in the local paper that you will cook and serve meals for special dinner-parties. You can gradually work out a suitable fee to charge and one that is worth while both to the hostess and yourself.

Mending for bachelors. Put an advertisement in the local paper.

Be a Reminder!

Remind busy business-men of anniversaries, birthdays and so on. They give you all the dates they need to remember. You remind them and send a list of suggested presents and/or flowers, with approximate price in time for that day. Charge so much a year for this service. If you get enough people you need not charge too much. Have some letters roneoed setting out details of your service and send to the heads of large firms, or at first, send a few nicely typed personal letters. An advertisement in the 'Personal' column of a newspaper could help, either the local paper or one read by busy men—say, a financial or evening paper.

If you are good at flower decorations, then make wreaths, wedding bouquets or arrange flowers for festivals, parties and so on.

Big stores, especially the cheap-price ones, are often glad to be offered novelties, such as weather-houses, original tea-cosies, miniature gardens. If they sell you may find yourself employing staff, and making in bulk.

If your husband is away, there may be part-time work available as visitor's guide (the Holiday Travellers' Association keep a register), or demonstrating products in shops or exhibitions.

EVERYDAY ETIQUETTE

These days there are very few ' cast-iron ' rules of behaviour, but it gives confidence to know the right thing to do on various occasions

IT is a great help to know a few recognised rules of etiquette which you can put into use without hesitation. Keep in mind, however, that a sympathetic consideration for others is the basis of good manners. Then, even if you are not sure of the exact procedure, you will never go badly astray.

Introductions

There is a simple, set formula for these which saves much trouble and doubt. This is: present the less important of the two people to the more important one. Socially speaking, a woman is more important than a man, a married woman than an unmarried one, an older person than a younger one of the same sex. Following this rule, you say, 'Miss Brown, may I present Mr. Green? Mr. Green—Miss Brown.' Or, 'Mrs. White, I'd like to introduce Miss Black to you. Miss Black—Mrs. White.' When introducing two people of about the same social importance and age, it does not matter which name you mention first.

Whenever possible, start the newly-introduced pair off easily by telling them of something they have in common, such as, 'I know you're both keen on tennis,' or 'Miss Black comes from your home town, Mrs. White.'

When you yourself are introduced, listen carefully to the other person's name, so that you will remember it. You *both* say, 'How do you do?' (a set opening remark when introduced and, of course, *not* a question requiring an answer) and then start talking together on the common interest your mutual friend has mentioned, the weather or any other topic that comes handy. Should you shake hands or not when introduced? There is no set rule. Some people merely bow. But shaking hands is really friendlier, and if the other person offers a hand it should always be taken. Continentals nearly always shake hands on every possible occasion and it is as well to remember this when abroad.

Casual Meeting

When you are out with someone and meet a friend whom your companion does not know, it is often a moot point, if you stop to exchange a few words, whether you should introduce them or not. If it *is* only a word or two, it is not necessary to do so. But if you stop to talk several minutes with the friend who is passing, it is considerate, and therefore good manners, not to leave your companion hovering about and looking lost, but to perform an introduction. If you are talking to several friends and a stranger is drawn into the party, see that the conversation is not kept too much to personal issues, otherwise there is nothing for the stranger to talk about. Make the conversation more general, and draw in the newcomer.

Tipping

The broad rule to remember here is: tip 10 per cent., or a trifle over, of the bill, if this is 5s. or more. Thus for a 5s. meal in a restaurant you would tip 6d. But on a smaller total the tip must be higher in proportion. It should still be 6d. if the bill is 3s. 6d. and, say, 3d. on a bill of 1s.

At an hotel or on shipboard, where there are several people to be remembered, take 10 per cent. of the total bill (or the cruise charge) and split this up among those who have served you. The lion's share of the 10 per cent. should be divided between the waiter (or waitress) and the chambermaid in an hotel; and between the table and cabin stewards on board ship. Smaller sums go to the liftman, bath stewardess (in a ship) and so on. When anyone has rendered you special service (such as the chambermaid or stewardess if you have had meals in bed) give her something extra outside her share of the 10 per cent. People who can afford it sometimes like to tip more liberally to create goodwill, but this is quite optional.

Taximen for some unknown reason get

When laying a table, the silver is always placed exactly in the order in which it is to be used, from the outside in, with forks to the left of the plate and knives and spoons to the right. A fork for sea-food or shellfish cocktail is, however, placed on the outside right. Water tumblers are put in front of the dinner knife, and sherry or wine glasses to the right of the water glass. Napkins can be placed to the left of the forks or on a bread-plate when used. Linen mats shown here are very pale primrose against the dark polished table, and candles a deep vivid blue

more than 10 per cent., usually about 25 per cent. (a quarter) on a small fare, and 15 or 20 per cent. on a larger one.

Abroad, when a service charge is added to a hotel or restaurant bill, tipping in addition is often expected. Although the 10 or 15 per cent. is supposed to be divided among the staff, there are small hotels where you may be told say, by a chambermaid, 'But *we* do not get the 10 per cent., Madame.' To give an additional tip or not is a matter of principle. There are some people who never tip above the percentage on the bill, and others who always give a small extra sum of money.

Motor-coach Tours

It is usual at the end of the tour for all the passengers to combine in giving a joint money present to the guide (courier) and driver. Generally a sum is fixed (say 10s. per passenger for a ten- or fourteen-day trip, or about 2s. for a day trip), so that all will give the same. One of the men passengers makes a little speech thanking the two men for all they have done to make the holiday enjoyable. The money, in an envelope, is then handed to the courier, who will privately divide it up in an agreed proportion with the driver. It is as well to keep back enough for your share of this present before spending all your holiday allowance.

Air Travel

The air company's staff who take your luggage from you when you reach the airport terminal, produce it for Customs examination and return it to you on arrival, do *not* expect tips. But any taximen you employ at the beginning and end of your journey will, of course, look for the usual addition to the fare.

What's In a Name?

Remember that a waiter in a ship or on a train is always called ' steward.'

WEDDING ETIQUETTE

IF you are uncertain about procedure for a wedding, then do not be afraid to ask your minister any questions. You can also hold a rehearsal in your own home to give you confidence on 'The Day.'

A special licence may be granted by the Archbishop of Canterbury, if the circumstances are sufficient reason. The fee is £25.

If the bride and groom live in different parishes, banns must be called in each parish. On the wedding day the bridegroom must take to the church the certificate proving that banns have been called in the other parish, or the ceremony cannot be performed. You can be married without banns if you have a common licence, which can be obtained by the one who has lived at least 15 days in the district where the wedding is to take place. This costs £2 and is valid for three months. Personal application must be made for a wedding at a Register Office. A divorced person must show a certified copy of the Decree Absolute.

Wedding etiquette, with all it implies of large trousseaux, huge wedding breakfast, and who shall pay for various expenses, is not nearly so strictly observed in these more informal days. But for those who wish to know just what the convention is in this respect, here are some details:—

The Bridegroom is responsible for the bride's bouquet, bridesmaids' bouquets and presents, all fees and expenses at the church.

The Bride's Parents pay for the reception, trousseau, flowers at the church, organist and choir, and cars to take the bride, family and guests to and from the church. The bridesmaids are chosen by the bride.

The Best Man's duty is to look after the groom. He can help in many of the preliminary details, and at the wedding takes charge of the ring (to keep it on his little finger is a good plan) and the clergyman's fee; also arranges transport for himself and groom to church, seeing that they arrive about twenty minutes before the bride.

The Bride's Father (or whoever is giving her away in the absence of a male parent) stands beside her until the clergyman asks, "Who giveth this woman to be married to this man?" He says, "I do," and then sits in the front pew on the left-hand side of the aisle.

At the Reception one of the bride's

OTHER HOME HINTS

For Burns. Take a large lump of household washing soda, damp it and smooth on the burn till stinging stops, then leave it to dry. A white powder will form over the skin and prevent blisters or burn marks. If the burn is severe, crush a lump of soda into a powder, put on a bandage large enough to wrap around the injured part, and keep it damped till the pain is soothed.

For a burn from scalding water or a stove, if you have no medicament in the house, try smearing the burn lightly with jam. It will remove stinging.

To be economical, buy a small piece of **chamois leather** instead of a large one. Sew it on to the centre of a duster and use for polishing. Most of the sides are usually gathered up in the hand and therefore are not actually used when rubbing.

Save all the ash from your log fires; it is an excellent fertiliser for the garden.

If the handle of **your suitcase** is broken, thread a dog collar through the loops and fasten at the required length.

If you have no glue, next time you have an accident with your **glass or china ornaments,** use clear nail varnish. It is quick and suitable for minor repairs.

To stop water running down your arms when washing windows or high woodwork, it is a good idea to tie a piece of old towelling around your wrists.

Wedding Etiquette—*continued*

parents welcomes the guests as they arrive. Some form of buffet is provided—sandwiches, cakes, little savouries, or cold meat and salads. Champagne or wine, beer and soft drinks are served. If there is a table at which to sit (although many wedding parties today use one as a buffet and stand around), then the bride and groom occupy the head of the table, with parents next, and then bridesmaids. The best man is at the groom's right hand, and it is he who reads the telegrams aloud. Either the best man or an old friend of the family proposes toasts, including a toast for the health of the bride and groom. The bridegroom gives a short speech of thanks.

The best man sees that the car is at the door and the guests assemble to wave them on a happy honeymoon.

JUMPER   CARDIGAN

Knit it in gay candy-stripe or plain, to suit your own taste

The wardrobe can hold no more useful garment

THERE is no garment more useful than a jumper cardigan, worn buttoned and with a blending scarf for chic; over a blouse for attractive warmth. This can be knitted all in one shade, of course; or in one colour, with contrasting edging, cuffs and basque.

Materials.—8 oz. Wakefield Greenwoods' W.G. 'Springtime' Super Botany Fingering, 4-ply in a dark colour; 5 oz. 4-ply wool in a light colour; 2 No. 11 and 2 No. 13 knitting needles; 6 buttons.

Measurements.—To fit a 34-in. bust. Length from shoulder, 19½ in. Sleeve seam, 18 in.

Tension.—7 sts. to 1 in.

Abbreviations.—K., knit; p., purl; sts.,

stitches; tog., together; inc., increase; ptn., pattern; cont., continue; rep., repeat; fin., finishing; folls., follows; rem., remain or remaining; in., inches; sl., slip; p.s.s.o., pass slipped st. over; dk., dark; lt., light.

Please Note. The main part of the garment is knitted in stocking-stitch in two colours, the first 2 rows in dark, then the next 2 rows in light. These will not be referred to in the pattern. The front-band and cuffs are worked in rib in dark wool.

The Right Front

Using dk. wool and No. 13 needles, cast on 58 sts., and work in k. 1, p. 1 rib for 3½ in.

Change to No. 11 needles.

1st Row—K.

2nd Row—P. twice into first st., p. 2, p. 2 tog., turn. Change and work in stripe ptn.

3rd and Every Alternate Row—K.

4th Row—P. twice into first st., p. 5, p. 2 tog., turn.

6th Row—P. twice into first st., p. 8, p. 2 tog., turn.

8th Row—P. twice into first st., p. 13, turn (inc. of 1 st.).

10th Row—P. twice into first st., p. 15, p. 2 tog., turn.

12th Row—P. twice into first st., p. 20, turn.

14th Row—P. twice into first st., p. 22, p. 2 tog., turn.

16th Row—P. twice into first st., p. 27, turn.

18th Row—P. twice into first st., p. 29, p. 2 tog., turn.

20th Row—P. twice into first st., p. 34, turn.

22nd Row—P. twice into first st., p. 36, p. 2 tog., turn.

24th Row—P. twice into first st., p. 41, turn.

26th Row—P. twice into first st., p. 43, p. 2 tog., turn.

28th Row—P. twice into first st., p. 48, turn.

30th Row—P. twice into first st., p. 50, p. 2 tog., turn.

32nd Row—P. twice into first st., p. 55, turn.

34th Row—P. twice into first st., p. 57, p. 2 tog., turn.

36th Row—P. twice into first st., p. 62, turn.

38th Row—P. twice into first st., p. until 2 sts. rem., p. 2 tog.

39th Row—K.

40th Row—P. twice into first st., p. to end.

41st Row—K.

Rep. last 4 rows twice more (69 sts.). Then cont. thus:

50th Row—P. twice into first st., p. until 2 sts. rem., p. 2 tog.

51st Row—K.

Rep. last 2 rows until long edge measures 11½ in. fin. after a k. row.

Shape Armholes. 1st Row—Cast off 4 sts., p. to end.

2nd Row—K.

3rd Row—P. until 2 sts. rem., p. 2 tog. (64 sts.).

4th Row—K. until 2 sts. rem., k. 2 tog. (63 sts.).

Rep. last 2 rows until 55 sts. rem., then cont. in ptn. as 50th and 51st row, until *short* edge measures 10 in. from beg., fin. at short edge, work thus:

1st Row—K.

2nd Row—P. until 2 sts. rem., p. 2 tog.

3rd Row—K.

4th Row—P. twice into first st., p. until 2 sts. rem., p. 2 tog., rep. last 4 rows until 42 sts. rem., then cont. in ptn. as 50th and 51st rows, until long edge measures 19 in. from beg., fin. at long edge.

Shape Top. 1st Row—Cast off 2 sts., p. until 2 sts. rem., p. 2 tog.

2nd Row—K.

Rep. last 2 rows until 3 sts. rem. Cast off.

The Left Front

Using dk. wool, and No. 13 needles, cast on 58 sts., and work in k. 1, p. 1 rib for 3½ in.

Change to No. 11 needles.

1st Row—K. twice into first st., k. 2, k. 2 tog., turn.

2nd Row—P.

3rd Row—Change to stripe ptn., k. twice into first st., k. 5, k. 2 tog., turn.

4th and Every Alternate Row—P.

5th Row—K. twice into first st., k. 8, k. 2 tog., turn.

7th Row—K. twice into first st., k. 13, turn (inc. of 1 st.).

9th Row—K. twice into first st., k. 15, k. 2 tog., turn.

11th Row—K. twice into first st., k. 20, turn.

13th Row—K. twice into first st., k. 22, k. 2 tog., turn.

15TH ROW—K. twice into first st., k. 27, turn.

17TH ROW—K. twice into first st., k. 29, k. 2 tog., turn.

19TH ROW—K. twice into first st., k. 34, turn.

21ST ROW—K. twice into first st., k. 36, k. 2 tog., turn.

23RD ROW—K. twice into first st., k. 41, turn.

25TH ROW—K. twice into first st., k. 43, k. 2 tog., turn.

27TH ROW—K. twice into first st., k. 48, turn.

29TH ROW—K. twice into first st., k. 50, k. 2 tog., turn.

31ST ROW—K. twice into first st., k. 55, turn.

33RD ROW—K. twice into first st., k. 57, k. 2 tog., turn.

35TH ROW—K. twice into first st., k. 62, turn.

37TH ROW—K. twice into first st., k. until 2 sts. rem., k. 2 tog.

38TH ROW—P.

39TH ROW—K. twice into first st., k. to end.

40TH ROW—P.

Rep. last 4 rows twice more (69 sts.).

49TH ROW—K. twice into first st., k. until 2 sts. rem., k. 2 tog.

50TH ROW—P. Now work to match right front, substituting p. rows for k. and k. rows for p.

The Back

Using dk. wool and No. 13 needles, cast on 116 sts. and work in k. 1, p. 1 rib for 3½ in.

Change to No. 11 needles.

1ST ROW—K. twice into first st., k. 2, k. 2 tog., turn.

Now work as for **Left Front,** until the 36th row (a p. row) has been worked.

37TH ROW—K. twice into first st., k. 63, k. 2 tog. (leave these sts. for the present), then still using dk. wool k. across other 58 sts. and now work as for **Right Front** from the 2nd row, until the 37th row (a k. row) has been knitted.

NEXT ROW—P. twice into first st., p. 63, p. 2 tog., p. across other sts.

Change to the foll. ptn.:

1ST ROW—K. twice into first st., k. to centre 4 sts., sl. 1, k. 1, p.s.s.o., k. 2 tog., k. until 1 st. rem., k. twice into st.

2ND ROW—P.

3RD ROW—K. twice into first st., k. to last st., k. twice in st.

4TH ROW—P.

Rep. these 4 rows twice more (138 sts.). Now cont. thus:

1ST ROW—K. twice into first st., k. to centre 4 sts., sl. 1, k. 1, p.s.s.o., k. 2 tog., k. until 1 st. rem., k. twice into st.

2ND ROW—P.

These 2 rows form the ptn. Rep. them until outside edge measures 11½ in. from beg., fin. after a p. row.

Shape Armholes. 1ST ROW—Cast off 3, k. to centre 4 sts., sl. 1, k. 1, p.s.s.o., k. 2 tog., k. until 1 st. rems., k. twice into st.

2ND ROW—Cast off 4, p. to end.

3RD ROW—K. to centre 4 sts., sl. 1. k. 1, p.s.s.o., k. 2 tog., k. to end.

4TH ROW—P.

Rep. last 2 rows until 110 sts. rem., then cont. in ptn. until long edge measures 19 in., fin. after a p. row.

Shape Top. 1ST ROW—Cast off 2 sts., k. to centre 4 sts., sl. 1, k. 1, p.s.s.o., k. 2 tog., k. to end.

2ND ROW—Cast off 2 sts., p. to end. Rep. last 2 rows until 26 sts. rem. Cast off.

The Sleeves

Using dk. wool, and No. 13 needles, cast on 70 sts., and work in k. 1, p. 1 rib for 2½ in.

Change to No. 11 needles.

1ST ROW—K. twice into first st., k. 2, k. 2 tog., turn.

2ND ROW—P. Change to stripe ptn.

3RD ROW—K. twice into first st., k. 5, k. 2 tog., turn.

4TH AND EVERY ALTERNATE ROW—P.

5TH ROW—K. twice into first st., k. 8, k. 2 tog., turn.

7TH ROW—K. twice into first st., k. 13, turn.

9TH ROW—K. twice into first st., k. 15, k. 2 tog., turn.

11TH ROW—K. twice into first st., k. 18, k. 2 tog., turn.

13TH ROW—K. twice into first st., k. 23, turn.

15TH ROW—K. twice into first st., k. 25, k. 2 tog., turn.

17TH ROW—K. twice into first st., k. 28, k. 2 tog., turn.

19TH ROW—K. twice into first st., k. 33, turn.

21st Row—K. twice into first st., k. 35, k. 2 tog., then k. across the other 35 sts., making this the first row for second side.

2nd Row—P. twice into first st., p. 2, p. 2 tog., turn.

Change to stripe ptn., weaving the wool along 3 extra sts. each time.

3rd Row—K.

4th Row—P. twice into first st., p. 5, p. 2 tog., turn.

5th and Every Alternate Row—K.

6th Row—P. twice into first st., p. 8, p. 2 tog., turn.

8th Row—P. twice into first st., p. 13, turn.

10th Row—P. twice into first st., p. 15, p. 2 tog., turn.

12th Row—P. twice into first st., p. 18, p. 2 tog., turn.

14th Row—P. twice into first st., p. 23, turn.

16th Row—P. twice into first st., p. 25, p. 2 tog., turn.

18th Row—P. twice into first st., p. 28, p. 2 tog., turn.

20th Row—P. twice into first st., p. 33, turn, break off lt. wool.

22nd Row—P. twice into first st., p. 35, p. 2 tog., p. across other sts. Work as follows:

1st Row—K. twice into first st., k. to centre 4 sts., sl. 1, k. 1, p.s.s.o., k. 2 tog., k. until 1 st. remains, k. twice into st.

2nd Row—P.

3rd Row—K. twice into first st., k. until 1 st. rem., k. twice into st.

4th Row—P.

5th Row—As 1st row.

6th Row—P.

Rep. these 6 rows until there are 110 sts. on needle, then cont. in ptn. as 1st and 2nd rows, until outside edge measures 18 in. from beg., fin. after a p. row.

Shape Top. 1st Row—K. to centre 4 sts., sl. 1, k. 1, p.s.s.o., k. 2 tog., k. to end.

2nd Row—P.

Rep. these 2 rows until 30 sts. rem., fin. right side row.

Next Row—Cast off 4, p. to end.

Next Row—Cast off 4, k. to centre 4 sts., sl. 1, k. 1, p.s.s.o., k. 2 tog., k. to end. Rep. last 2 rows once more. Cast off.

The Band

Using dk. wool and No. 13 needles, cast on 16 sts., and work in k. 1, p. 1, rib for ¼ in.

Next Row—Rib 6, cast off 4, rib to end. In next row cast on 4 sts. in place of those cast off. Cont. in rib, making 2 more buttonholes at intervals of 1½ in., then 3 more buttonholes at 3-in. intervals. When the 6th buttonhole is completed, cont. straight in rib until the band is long enough to go round back and fronts. Cast off.

Press. Sew up all seams.

Sew on band and buttons.

Before sewing up the various pieces of any finished article, they should be pressed separately. Lay a clean damp cloth on the wrong side of the work, and press gently but firmly with a moderate iron.

When sewing or knitting, many women do not like a 'shut-in' feeling, and prefer a chair without arms. Big upholstered arms can also screen from the warmth of a fire. These chairs are planned to suit either taste. They have walnut frames and foam rubber cushions over cable-sprung seats

Courtesy of
Minty of Oxford

CLASSIFIED KEY

FURNISHING

LINEN AND CHINA

A GARDEN INDOORS (Flower Arrangement)

SOFT FURNISHINGS

START AN AQUARIUM

ON BEING BEAUTIFUL

HANDYMAN ABOUT THE HOUSE

HEALTH IN THE HOME

HEALTH IN THE HOME—*continued*

YOUR CHILDREN

MODERN LAUNDERING

DO A LITTLE EMBROIDERY

HOME COOKERY

ENTERTAINING

MISCELLANEOUS